The Development of the Economies of Continental Europe

1850–1914

The Development of the Economies of Continental Europe 1850–1914

BY
ALAN S. MILWARD
AND S. B. SAUL

LONDON GEORGE ALLEN & UNWIN LTD
RUSKIN HOUSE   MUSEUM STREET

First published in 1977

© George Allen & Unwin (Publishers) Ltd, 1977

ISBN 0 04 330277 7 Hardback
     0 04 330278 5 Paperback

Printed in Great Britain
in 10 on 11 pt Times New Roman
at the Alden Press, Oxford

Preface

This book sets out to analyse in some detail the work that has been done on the modern economic history of continental Europe. Our intention has been to study the economic development of the continent in order to provide British and American students with a truer view. We have provided note references only where they are essential to make sense and our suggestions for reading are mainly in the English language. We give some indication of the value of work published in other languages but we hope that the book itself is the best indication of that.

In a previous work, *The Economic Development of Continental Europe 1780–1870*, we analysed the economic development of France and Germany up to 1870 and we have therefore in this volume begun our study of those two countries at that date. Because we had earlier studied Scandinavian development up to 1914 we have omitted it here. The reader is reminded that the studies on population and technology in the earlier book also cover the period of this volume and to restrict the size of this book we have made only fleeting references to these subjects. We have in fact followed the plan proposed in our previous work with one exception. We felt that the history of the south-eastern European countries, because of the different problems it presented and because of the revealing light it shed on the problems of development in the other states, merited some analysis. To that extent we have written more than we promised.

This volume is even more a joint effort than the earlier one. So little is still known about some of the areas into which we ventured that without the constant encouragement and help each author in turn gave to the other the book would surely have been abandoned. Originally the basic materials and exposition of Chapters 1, 2, 4, 5 and 8 were the work of Milward and Chapters 3, 6, 7 and 9 of Saul. But each chapter soon became a joint project; the authors would now be incapable of sorting out their own contribution and those trying to do it for them are likely to have a fruitless search. In particular the last chapter is in every sense a joint undertaking and its conclusions are those of both authors. The comprehensiveness of the work inevitably means there must be mistakes and errors of interpretation. If we provoke discussion of these that is all to the good since our intention has always been to stimulate more research in the subject and to show where it most needs to be done.

All measurements are metric. Except where in everyday usage there is an English name for a foreign town or region we use the contemporary name and if the modern name is different we note it, on the first occasion in each chapter, in parentheses. Our reason for deciding to use the contemporary rather than the modern name is simply that so many states and provinces have no exact modern equivalent and it is easier to be consistent in using the historical names. Our decision is purely practical, has no other significance for us, and we hope will cause a minimum of offence to the linguistic and political sentiments of others.

The number of people whose ideas and comments contribute to a work of this kind is very large and where they recognise them we hope they will take that as an acknowledgement. But for the actual making of the book we would particularly like to thank people who took time to answer troublesome queries or to read or discuss particular aspects of the work. Our joint thanks for this are now extended to Professor I. Berend, Dr D. Berindei, Professor L. Berov, Ian Blanchard, Professor L. Boicu, Professor M. de Cecco, Dr P. Cernovodeanu, Professor I. Corfus, Professor G. Dobre, Professor A. Duţu, Professor S. M. Eddie, Professor G. Fuà, Professor V. Georgesco, Richard Griffiths, Joe Harrison, Dr C. Murgescu, Henry Palairet, Professor G. Ránki, Professor T. C. Smout, Dr Helena Statelova, Dr Svetama Todorowa, and Dr A. Zub. The British Council enabled one of the authors to visit both Bulgaria and Romania, which made the book in its present form possible, and we would here like to acknowledge most gratefully their help and support. We would also like to acknowledge the help we received from a number of institutions, The British Library of Economics and Political Science, Edinburgh University Library, Harvard University Library, The Karl Marx Institute of History and Archaeology of the University of Iasi, The National Library of Bulgaria, and the Nicolae Iorga Institute of History. The complicated task of getting the manuscript ready for press would never have been achieved without the great efforts of Christiane Angold, Christine Clarke, Moira McIntyre and our wives, Claudine Milward and Sheila Saul. The maps were again drawn by Barbara Morris. The patience of all in face of our working methods deserves our warmest thanks. So also does the tolerance and patience of our publishers, who have supported us throughout this task. For the authors themselves it has been a task which they do not regret and they hope that a synthesis at this level, whatever its faults, can lay claim to sufficient originality as well as comprehensiveness to put teaching and research in their subject in a new and better position.

Contents

9

Maps

Table of Measurements

hectare	2·471 acres
metric ton	2204 lb
kilometre	0·621 miles
kilogram	2·204 lb
hectolitre	22·0 imperial gallons (liquid measure)
	2·75 imperial bushels (cereal measure)
arshin	28 inches
pood	36 lb
dessiatine	2·7 acres
joch (hold)	1·421 acres

Ton is used throughout to mean metric ton. 1 quintal = 100 kg

ha	=	hectare
hl	=	hectolitre
kg	=	kilogram
km	=	kilometre
m	=	metre
m.	=	million
t	=	ton

Exchange Rates against Sterling, 1913

The following is a list of the exchange rates applying in 1913. In Sweden, Denmark, the Netherlands, Germany, Belgium and France these rates had been stable for the previous forty years. The other rates had varied from time to time.

Germany Mark		20
France ⎱		
Belgium ⎰ Franc		25
Switzerland		
Italy Lira		25
Spain Peseta		25
Bulgaria Lev		25
Serbia Dinar		25
Romania Leu		25
Greece Drachma		25
Norway Krone ⎱		
Denmark Krone ⎰		18
Sweden Krona		
Russia Rouble		9·55
Netherlands Guilder		12
Austria Kroner ⎱		24
Hungary Korona ⎰		
United States Dollar		4·87

Chapter 1

The Economic Development of Germany, 1870–1914

THE DIMENSIONS OF THE PROBLEM

Intro

The economic history of continental Europe after 1870 was dominated by the persistent growth and development of the German economy, so that by 1914 Germany had displaced France as the most powerful of the continental economies and had attained a level of per capita income probably slightly higher than the French. To contemporaries this seemed the most outstanding fact of the period and viewed in retrospect it is still a phenomenon that should command the respect of the historian. The changes in central Europe which laid the foundation of this remarkable development were described in our previous work.[1] That a disunited collection of agricultural territories in 1830 could by 1913 have become the symbol of what seemed a new form of European society in the making is the strongest evidence of the daunting capacity of economic change to alter rapidly the course of history and of human society. It would be too

17

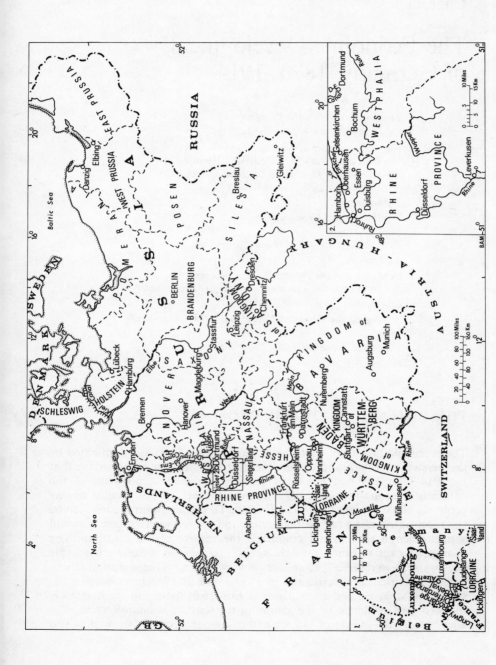

bold to pretend to offer complete explanations. There is still much research to be done on questions of vital importance and without this explanations of the phenomenon will remain in several respects incomplete.

The dimensions of the phenomenon give some indication of how complex the explanations will be. The mean annual rate of growth of net domestic product between 1850 and 1913 was 2·6 per cent. As we shall see there were marked short- and medium-term fluctuations in this rate of growth. After 1873 there was a period of comparative stagnation, whereas in the European industrialisation boom after 1896 net domestic product increased at an annual average rate of 3·1 per cent a year until 1913. But the picture is still one of much more persistent growth than in France or Britain. The contribution of the different sectors to that growth was also more even. The output of the industrial sector increased by 3·8 per cent

Table 1   Structure of net domestic product in Germany, 1870–1913 (at 1913 prices)

Period	Agriculture, forestry and fisheries (%)	Industry, handicrafts and mines (%)	Transport and services (%)
1870–4	37·9	31·7	30·5
1880–4	36·2	32·5	31·3
1890–4	32·2	36·8	31·0
1900–4	29·0	39·8	31·2
1910–13	23·4	44·6	32·0

Source: W. G. Hoffmann, Das Wachstum der deutschen Wirtschaft seit der Mitte des 19. Jahrhunderts (Berlin, 1965), p. 33.

annually over the period 1850–1914, of commerce, banking and insurance by 3·2 per cent, and of agriculture by 1·6 per cent. The share of industry and services in the composition of net domestic product grew and that of agriculture fell until by 1913 the agricultural sector was contributing less than one-quarter (see Table 1).

One consequence was that the physical volume of output in many important areas surpassed that in France and Britain although those countries had begun much earlier on the path of rapid industrialisation. With an annual average production of steel in 1910–13 of 16·2 million tons Germany was making at least two-thirds of all Europe's output. With an output of electric power in 1913 of 8,000 million kilowatt hours she was producing 20 per cent more electrical energy than Britain, France and Italy combined. In certain modern industries, engineering and organic chemicals in particular, the value of her output and the level of her technology were higher than in other European economies. Between 1910 and 1913, when the annual average quantity of coal and lignite mined was 247·5 million tons, she was mining well over half the quantity mined on the continent. The second consequence was a noticeable increase in real incomes for the population as a whole in spite of a rapid growth in numbers. Real wages in industrial employment doubled after 1871. The real wages of those employed in the agricultural sector did not increase so rapidly, but with the shift towards industrial employment there was still a large increase in spendable consumer incomes. This was reflected in the growth of the textile and other consumer industries whose role in the initial stages of economic transformation had been less significant than in the countries further west. There were 11·2 million cotton spindles in 1913, the biggest cotton industry on the continent, and the annual raw cotton consumption of 435,000 tons was almost twice as high as in France.

Table 2   *Proportion of employed persons in different sectors of the German economy, 1878–1913*

Period	Agriculture, fisheries and forestry (%)	Industry, handicrafts and mines (%)	Transport, trade and public services (%)
1878–9	49·1	29·1	14·1
1890–4	42·6	34·2	16·5
1900–4	38·0	36·8	19·4
1910–13	35·1	37·9	21·8

Source: W. G. Hoffmann, *Das Wachstum der deutschen Wirtschaft seit der Mitte des 19. Jahrhunderts* (Berlin, 1965), p. 35. The figures for domestic service are omitted.

To some extent the physical size of output reflected the greater availability of factors of production. The labour force grew much more rapidly, for example, than in France. In spite of the high rate of emigration the population increased by 24·1 million between 1871 and 1911 so that by the First World War Germany was by a great margin the second most populous country in Europe. But the labour force is estimated only to have doubled between 1850 and 1913. The productivity of labour increased over the same period at an annual average rate of 1·5 per cent so that much of the growth in output and incomes was also accounted for by changes in production methods. Therein lies a considerable part of the explanation of what happened and the figures for size of physical output are given only to show how the balance of economic power in Europe was transformed.

As everywhere, the main aspect of this sustained improvement in the productivity of labour was the increase in the share of the labour force working in industry and services. The extent of this movement is shown in Table 2. But it will also appear later that there were smaller but

substantial improvements in the productivity of the labour that remained
in the agricultural sector of the economy and these also contributed more
to the growth of the economy than in the other large continental economies.
Compared to Britain both the absolute numbers and the proportion of
people working in agriculture by 1913 were still high and by most conventional measurements of the level of economic development Germany
could be considered less advanced than some of the smaller European
economies. Even in some industrial fields it could be argued that Germany
remained more backward than France. In trying to explain the growth of
productivity and the growth of the economy in a more detailed and
comprehensible way we shall, however, be concentrating on those aspects
in which the German economy was technologically more advanced. This is
not misleading for many of the explanations of the phenomenon we are
faced with are to be found in the interrelationships of technology and
industry. It will often be necessary to pay as much attention to smaller
industries where these interrelationships were most present as to the large
cotton industry, for example, whose growth was more easily understandable
in terms of the rise of consumer incomes generated by changes elsewhere
in the economy.

SHORT-TERM GROWTH FLUCTUATIONS

The creation of the German Empire was a period of remarkable prosperity.
A boom beginning in 1869 triggered by railway investment was only briefly
interrupted by the heavy doubts cast by the war against France in 1870. In
that year itself the net domestic product did not grow. But the triumphant
conclusion of the war quickly restored the climate of confidence. The war
indemnity paid by France, one-third of German national income in 1870,
stimulated a burst of intra-European trade and a spate of company
foundations on the German stock exchanges. In spite of the stagnation of
1870, net domestic product (at 1913 prices) grew in the quinquennium
1870–4 at an annual average rate of 4·6 per cent. These were the so-called
Gründerjahre, the foundation years, of the Empire. The investments of
1869 bore fruit in 1870 when 1,500 kilometres of railway were completed,
the biggest annual rate of increase to the system yet achieved, and one
which brought about a response in the iron and coal industries even before
the wave of business confidence which followed the victories in France.
In 1871 207 joint stock companies were floated compared to the 295
floated over the whole period 1851–70 and in 1872 the number of new
floatations rose to 479. The consumption of pig iron rose from 1·8 million
tons in 1871 to 2·95 million tons in 1873 and hard coal output over the
same period from 29·4 million tons to 36·4 million tons. The textile
industries had less of a share in this burst of prosperity, which mainly

affected, as it had in the investment boom of the 1850s, the railway, iron, coal and engineering industries.

By mid-1873 the boom had turned into a structure of risky financial speculations on the Berlin stock exchange as business conditions in the United States and Britain worsened. The financial crash in Vienna[2] spread to Berlin producing a spate of bankruptcies and by the end of the year the great boom had turned into the *Gründerkrise*, the foundation crisis. No year in the century has had to bear such a colossal load of vague economic and social interpretation as 1873. In Britain it was for long regarded as the start of the mythical 'Great Depression'. In Germany it has been interpreted as the year in which the liberal hopes which accompanied the foundation of the Empire were snuffed out by a long period of hard times; as the grand climacteric of the century leading to a protectionist, illiberal, highly cartelised, bureaucratised, internally uncompetitive and externally aggressive economy and society. In fact almost every way in which the evolution of the German economy and society differed from the 'western' model has been blamed at some time or other on the economic events of 1873. What actually happened?

The fall in production was quite small. Pig iron production fell from 2·2 million tons in 1873 to 1·9 million tons in 1874 and coal output from 36·4 million tons to 35·9 million tons. The very imperfect indicators we have for cotton cloth suggest that output may have fallen by less than 5 per cent. Railway construction continued unchecked at the high levels it had reached in 1870; in fact 1874 set another record for the total length added to the system and in 1875 this was eclipsed again by the 2,436 kilometres added in that year. Domestic demand for iron and coal therefore did not continue to sink after 1874. But foreign demand was very low and this prevented any complete recovery. The consumer goods industries were less buoyant and output of textiles continued to fall after 1874. Mottek's recalculation of Spiethoff's earlier figures suggests that a rough hypothetical index of industrial production based on 1872–3 as 100 would show a figure of 95 for 1874–5.[3] The dismayed clamour from contemporaries was mainly attributable, as in Britain, to the fact that 1873 ushered in a long period of falling prices.

But if the actual depth of the slump has been exaggerated its length has not and it was this which really made it the greatest crisis of the German economy in this period. The few reliable figures available suggest that only in 1880 did industrial production again achieve its levels of 1872–3. This was the first severe check to the rapid industrialisation of the economy since the boom of 1852. Over the period 1875–80 net domestic product did not grow. The psychological effects of this prolonged stagnation were certainly profound, but almost all the social and economic consequences attributed to these events can be more accurately explained in other ways. The 1880s in Germany were sharply distinguished from the same decade in France and Britain by being a period of growth and prosperity, particularly after 1886. There is no way in which the term 'Great Depression' can have any meaning when applied to Germany after 1880. The overall growth rate of domestic product in the decade was 2·5 per cent and it was in this very decade that the die was cast decisively for the future shape of the European economy. Investment flowed into new industries and technologies in Germany while investors in Britain, France and Austria-Hungary followed a more cautious path. Whereas in the period 1870–5 only 10·6 per cent of total net investment flowed into industry, in the decade of the 1880s 41·4 per cent did so. In fact the decade marks a decisive break in the long-run pattern of investment. From the start of the railway boom in 1851 railway investment had on average accounted for almost one-fifth of total investment and in the 1870s, when it had sustained the economy in bad times, had reached higher proportions. From 1880 it seldom reached even one-tenth of total investment and was usually much less. It can be seen from Table 1 that this was the decade in which industry became for the first time more important than agriculture in the economy and that the rapid trend towards industrialisation, once recommenced, continued unbroken by any major setbacks until 1913. The main weight of investment after 1880 was always in industry, about 42 per cent of the total over the whole period.

The recovery from the stagnation was led by the demand for export orders for rail and railway equipment from the United States in 1879. In two years German exports to the USA rose from $31·8 million to $53·5 million and the effect was, once again, felt firstly in the metallurgical and coal industries. But the growth of consumer goods industries seems this time to have been more buoyant and exports of consumer goods also rose and this, together with growing domestic demand, did much to remedy the imbalance between capital and consumer goods which had prevailed since the onset of industrialisation. At the same time the rates of interest took a long-term downward step and this may have been due to increases in the supply of money and credit which then became more easily available to industrial investors. But a more detailed examination of individual industries shows that there were also powerful non-monetary forces making for greater investment and growth. Of these the greatest, and most fortuitous, was the patenting of the Gilchrist–Thomas steelmaking process which enabled Germany to utilise her own low-grade phosphoric iron ore resources to make basic steel and thereby turned the high-cost German iron and steel industry, increasingly uncompetitive on international markets, into a low-cost industry waging fierce and successful competition with its rivals. The burst of investment in the steel industry was occasioned even in the midst of prolonged stagnation by the indisputable economic advantages for Germany of the new technology.

The stagnation of the 1870s had led to a sharp rise in the productivity of labour, especially in the textile industries where there had been an unqualified slump. Output of yarn per worker in the major Augsburg spinning mills had been almost static in the period 1870–5, whereas it increased by 23 per cent between 1875 and 1880. The number of hand looms in Chemnitz (Karl Marx Stadt), which had increased until 1873, fell by more than a quarter by 1876 and everywhere handworkers found themselves replaced much more rapidly in these depressed circumstances by the newer machines. Elsewhere in the economy also the effect was to encourage the use of less labour and to concentrate production in the more efficient units. The number of blast furnaces dropped from 456 in 1873 to 210 in 1879, although iron production was virtually the same in the two years. The annual output of pig iron per worker increased at the same time from 80 tons to 126 tons and the average output of coal per worker seems to have increased by about one-fifth. The ultimate consequences of this process, given the high rate of addition to the population of working age, could only have been to pile up once more a surplus of underemployed people in the agricultural sector but it also had the immediate consequence of making industry more competitive after 1880 and able to seize a set of opportunities which were either not available to, or missed by, manufacturing industry elsewhere in Europe.

Steel production doubled between 1879 and 1882 and iron production increased by about 50 per cent. After 1882 building and construction also began to recover. The economy faltered again in 1886 but the following year recovery was restored by orders from the United States, and the domestic forces making for growth were now so strong that the consumer goods industries grew as vigorously as those making capital goods. The period 1887–90 saw another burst of company foundation when 948 joint stock companies were founded. After 1891 the growth of the economy was remarkably consistent. There were two severe but very short crises, 1901–2, and the 1906 crash which affected almost all other developed economies but had only the mildest effect on the German economy slowing down the growth rate to 2·5 per cent for two years. Otherwise from 1892 to 1913 the average annual rate of growth of net domestic product was 3·3 per cent and only in five years did it fall below that level.

Distinctions can still be made between the behaviour of various industries in this period. The slowing down in 1905–6 was mainly a slowing down in the older-established industries and it may have been better overcome in Germany than elsewhere because the newer technologies which were more established there did not suffer so badly. Sales of electrical machinery, for example, continued to increase throughout those two years. It was newer industries of this kind eager for expansion which created the greatest stock market boom of the period in 1896–9 when 1,129 new joint stock companies were created. This was also the period when the proportion of net investment going to industry reached its peak. But 1896 was not otherwise a turning point in the overall growth pattern. Nor were the newer industries expanded at that time alone responsible for making the fluctuations in growth less severe in Germany than elsewhere. The increased productivity of agriculture was closely associated with the greater deployment of machines and in the years of weaker trade the old-established makers of agricultural machinery remained as unaffected by the general trend of falling sales as the newer electrical industries. Furthermore the last burst of growth after 1909 had as one important component the expansion of the output of traditional raw materials, especially coal, to meet the needs of industries both in Germany and abroad. The worst years, 1900 and 1901, were in fact ushered in by a stock exchange crash which was the result of the attempts by the electrical industry to expand into new lines of production, such as larger dynamos and heavier machinery, for which demand in the event proved faltering for a time.

The situation was therefore complex and the growth can be attributed to the continued vigorous expansion of the older industries as much as to the newer technologies, which remained, in a quantitative sense, less significant. But in most periods of bad trade some of the older or the newer industries managed to avoid the worst effects of depression. In general the greater buoyancy of the German economy can be attributed to the greater complexity of the industrial sector. There was always something which sold well; sales of organic chemical products, for example, increased from 1874 to 1878. But this in turn was the result of other powerful and more precise forces making for growth which created this great variety of industrial output, and these forces we have still to analyse.

THE DEVELOPMENT OF GERMAN INDUSTRY

The industries which had played the leading role in the early industrialisation of the country were still capable of a rate of growth of output between 1870 and 1913 well above the average rate of growth of total industrial output. Metal producing industries grew at an annual average rate of 5·7 per cent between 1870 and 1913, and pig iron production at 5·9 per cent. On the other hand, as Table 3 indicates, the rate of growth of the two major consumer industries, textiles and foodstuffs, was relatively slow. The fastest rates of growth were naturally shown by the newer industries, but it is clear that the metallurgical and engineering industries at least were still able to make important improvements in productivity associated with technological innovation, and because their contribution to total industrial output was much larger this was crucial to the processes of economic growth and development.

– Iron and Steel

In annexing part of Lorraine from France in 1871 Germany acquired extensive deposits of low-grade phosphoric iron ore. But these deposits did little at first to ease the difficulty of German iron and steel producers arising from an inadequate domestic supply of ore, particularly of non-phosphoric ores for use in the Bessemer process. Steelmakers were increasingly dependent on ores brought at some distance from older German orefields and from Spain and Elba. The Hörder Verein, which installed its first Bessemer converters in 1863, at first used low-phosphorous ores from the Siegerland and Nassau but was increasingly driven to high-cost Spanish ore imports. The Dortmunder Union invested in Swedish ore mines which proved virtually unexploitable and had to import ore from Britain throughout the seventies. In spite of the ample supply of suitable coals this pushed

Table 3 *Annual average rate of growth of output and of labour productivity in German industry, 1870–1913*

Industrial sector	% growth rate of output 1870–1913	% growth rate of labour productivity 1875–1913
Stones and earth	3·7[1]	1·2
Metal producing	5·7	2·4
Iron manufacture	5·9	n.a.
Steel manufacture	6·3	n.a.
Metal working	5·3	2·2
Chemicals	6·2[1]	2·3
Textiles	2·7	2·1
Clothing and leather working	2·5	1·6
Foodstuffs and drinks	2·7	0·9
Gas, water and electricity	9·7[2]	3·6[3]
Average for all industry and handwork	3·7	1·6

[1] 1872–1913   [2] 1868–1913   [3] 1882–1913

Source: W. G. Hoffmann, *Das Wachstum der deutschen Wirtschaft seit der Mitte des 19. Jahrhunderts* (Berlin, 1965), pp. 63, 69.

the cost of steel well above the level in Britain and Belgium and because the Bessemer process was the main and cheapest process for making steel rail allowed these competitors to take a valuable share of the domestic market for rail during the vigorous expansion of the railway system after 1869. The tariff reductions of 1873 furthered this process although many German steel producers benefited from the lowering of the import duty on imported British pig iron. When Eberhard Hoesch founded his new steel works in Dortmund in 1871 it was designed to use British pig. German pig iron production in the seventies was only about 75 per cent of the total consumption. The great confidence which had prevailed in the industry in the 1850s was now replaced by careful specialisation in those markets safer from foreign competition.

The patenting of the Gilchrist–Thomas process in 1879, which permitted the use of phosphoric ores in the Bessemer converter, and the contemporary adaptation of the Siemens–Martin open-hearth to the use of the same ores changed the situation utterly. From having an inadequate and worsening resource base Germany now found herself richly endowed as far as the manufacture of basic (phosphoric) steel was concerned. Two firms, the Hörder Verein and the Rheinische Stahlwerke at Ruhrort, bought the rights of the Gilchrist–Thomas process instantly and within six months had each produced Thomas steel on an experimental basis. The Hörder Verein had a new plant operating the process commercially in 1881; the Dortmunder Union, Hoesch, Phönix and the Gutehoffnungshütte at Oberhausen followed suit. Even the Ilseder Hütte, built on the local Hanoverian ores, had converted to producing Thomas steel by the end of 1882. It was there that Hayermann built the first plant to process the basic slag left over from the process into fertiliser, reducing the overall production costs still further. The cost advantages were huge, and as the average charge of the converter was increased about sevenfold during the 1880s they were widening. From 1887 onwards basic slag was widely sold to farmers as fertiliser. International price comparisons are difficult to make but the evidence suggests that these cost reductions eventually led to a point between 1887 and 1890 where German basic steel became decisively cheaper than the same product elsewhere and the major part of the German steel industry came to specialise in its manufacture. The number of pure Bessemer converters dropped from 46 in 1880 to 26 in 1900 when there were 91 Thomas converters in use. The financial returns to those switching to the new process were as handsome as those which accrued to the builders of the first coke smelting blast furnaces in the 1850s and brought the industry out of the doldrums in which it had been drifting. The Aachener Verein, which used the nearby phosphoric ores of Lorraine and the Saarland, only once paid a dividend of less than 20 per cent between 1882 and 1898. About 85 per cent of the 7·8 million tons of steel manufactured in 1903 was basic steel. Without the Gilchrist–Thomas process it is difficult to conceive any way in which the industry could have reached such heights of production.

The minette ores of Lorraine and Luxembourg, although they were one hundred miles from the site of the Ruhr coalfields on which most of the iron works had originally been built, accounted by 1909 for almost 80 per cent of the iron ore mined in Germany. Domestic output of ore rose from an annual average of 5·5 million tons in the period 1871–80 to 22·5 million tons in 1901–10 and in the final raw materials boom after 1911 reached 33·3 million tons. But with the successful opening up of the northern Swedish mines after 1890 the Rhineland works found it technically more satisfactory to use Swedish ores. These ores were twice as rich in iron content and this, combined with the availability of water transport on the

Rhine, almost eliminated the cost differences caused by distance. With the major investments in new plant which began in the mid-nineties some companies built alongside the river so that Swedish ore could be directly unshipped into the blast furnaces. The quantity of foreign ore imported was still only 2·6 million tons annually in 1891–1900, and an important part of this was Spanish ore for making non-basic steel, but in the next decade it averaged 6·9 million tons. The cost advantages of using Lorraine ore on site, however, also developed. Stumm built his new iron works at Uckingen (Uckange) in 1890 and Karl Röchling built the Carlshütte in 1898. In 1912 August Thyssen built a new steel works at Hagendingen (Hagondange) to rival his recently built Ruhr plant. Some of the Lorraine works confined themselves to the production of pig iron which was finished in the Rhineland and by 1913 a third of total pig iron production originated there and a further 7 per cent in the Saarland. But increasingly the comparative costs dictated the production of the cheaper steels there also, and about 12 per cent of national steel production took place in Lorraine by 1913, 2·06 million tons compared to the 2·3 million tons made by French firms in French Lorraine and the 1·18 million tons by Luxembourg firms in the same region. Indeed the growth of the Lorraine iron industry tended even before 1914 to make the national frontiers absurd. The former French manufacturer de Wendel had works on each side of the new frontier connected by an international passage and the family played a prominent part in the politics of both countries. There was a substantial export trade in iron ore from Germany to immediately neighbouring firms.

The first decade of the Gilchrist–Thomas process was one of fierce competition for markets but after 1894 the industry was organised into a series of tightly controlled cartels. Within one year of their formation the average price of pig iron on the domestic market jumped well above the British price once more. The comparison of production costs is very complicated. Labour was cheaper in Germany and the size of the new works and the nature of the technology brought many economies of scale which offset the cost of importing ore. Protection ensured a lack of foreign competition in comparable products on the home market and maintaining a high price there by cartels permitted exports at lower prices. Across the whole range of Rhineland steel products in 1903 export prices varied between 7 and 19 per cent lower than prices for the domestic market. This reflected the growing importance of export markets during the 1890s. Iron and steel exports were notoriously subject to huge fluctuations but in the period 1898–1903 German iron and steel exports doubled and reached almost the same level as those of Britain. The massive investments needed to increase steel output almost threefold between 1900 and 1913 needed a high level of exports to justify them. In some years as much as one-quarter of the total output of finished iron and steel was for foreign markets. But the interesting thing is the extent to which these foreign markets narrowed, for the majority of the output went to other major iron and steel producers, and particularly to Britain. With increasing specialisation of production and with the growth of international cartel arrangements the iron and steel exports of the developed countries became increasingly interdependent.

The age of the entrepreneur who was himself a technician and supervised the shop floor, like Alfred Krupp or Jacob Meyer, founder of the Bochumer Verein which led the way in high-quality large steel castings, was passed, although Krupp still tried to convey this romantic image to his workers by erecting in the middle of his works a fake copy of the humble cottage where he had not in fact been born. With the growing use of Swedish ores the huge capital investments demanded great economies of scale and these in turn demanded larger plant. What was to become the largest German steelworks, that of Thyssen at Hamborn, was begun in 1890. Krupp built a new works west of the Rhine in 1896. The Meiderich steelworks at Ruhrort was begun in 1901. By 1902 the annual average output of steel per works in Germany was 75,000 tons compared to the average in Britain of 40,000 tons. Economies of scale also demanded vertical integration and these large companies acquired their own orefields, coal mines and coking plants at one end of the process, and foundries and machine shops at the other. The Krupp concern, which remained primarily an armaments and cast steel works, dominated the large town of Essen with its steel plant, machine shops and coal mines. It owned extensive tracts of housing, 6,000 dwellings in 1906, and provided savings banks and a variety of other social services for well-behaved employees. It also owned ore concessions in Lorraine and Spain and additional blast furnaces at Duisburg and in the Siegerland. The financial interests of Friedrich Grillo who had created the Schalker iron works at Gelsenkirchen in 1872 dominated the life of that town in the same way, embracing several other steel works and big coal mines in the area. Thyssen owned one coal mine which employed 3,600 workers and produced about 1·2 million tons of coal annually, as well as having an important capital stake in the new iron industry in Normandy. The Hörder Verein employed 7,700 people by 1903, the year when it also began to build its own housing estates.

Price and market sharing agreements were the protection for these investments and the major banks and financial trusts encouraged the process. The market was always volatile; there were heavy losses and a short steep drop in production in the economic downturn of 1906. But in retrospect the astonishing thing was the expansion of the domestic market for steel. Machine building and engineering accounted for a more important share of industrial output than in other European economies. One steel using industry, shipbuilding, was expanding more rapidly than elsewhere and in addition the government spent 2,700 million marks after 1898 on the construction of a modern heavily armoured navy. But, important though the building of warships was, after 1900 the expansion was sustained because of the extra demand arising from new industries, particularly the electrical industry, and from the construction of large buildings and tramway systems in the numerous rapidly growing cities. The process of urbanisation was an underlying cause of the sustained growth of many of the German industries and though it will be examined later it is worth noting its effects here because steel became the essential basic constructional material of the modern industrialised economy and the growth in its output was to some extent a function of the growth of all industrial output.

– Coal

The annual output of coal and lignite did not pass the 100 million ton mark until after 1894 but the subsequent growth of output was as rapid as in the iron and steel industry, increasing by 7 million tons a year after 1900. About one-fifth of the output continued to come from the Upper Silesian coalfields and about one-sixth from all the other scattered coalfields including Saxony and Lorraine. The main force in the growth of output was the extension of mining operations northwards from the Ruhr valley towards the north German plain. A substantial proportion of the mines were therefore new ones and because the coalfield dipped downwards they were deeper and more costly to sink, but the height of the seams and the richness of the coals obtained offset these costs, providing the newer mines were on a large scale. Only 16 per cent of the pits by 1900 produced less than 100,000 tons of coal a year and pits mining over 350,000 tons were common. The increase in the number of working collieries between 1850 and 1900 was very small but the average output of a colliery over the same time went up almost forty times. The demand was mainly from the home market, but after 1900 net exports were about 10 per cent of output. The cost of water carriage meant that Ruhr coals could often be more cheaply sold in western Europe than in Berlin and north-eastern Germany. Any attempt artificially to reduce their price in Berlin by subsidised freight rates would have damaged the interests of the Silesian mines for which Berlin was an important market. The consequence was that in Berlin and northern Germany British coal was still widely used and Germany continued to import coal on a growing scale until 1913.

The capital for this extension of mining activity often came from the iron and steel industry and many of the larger collieries were owned or otherwise associated with metallurgical concerns. These links had developed very early. The Gutehoffnungshütte bought its own mines in 1854. It is estimated that by 1900 about one-fifth of total output was controlled by iron and steel companies. The collieries owned by Thyssen employed 17,000 in 1912, those owned by Krupp 13,000. Their interest was in the coke and from the 1860s larger collieries increasingly had coking plant attached to them. After Coppée invented the recovery oven in 1867, which saved the gas, coking plant of this modern kind increased and the coal companies were selling not only gas but also coal tar which served as the basic raw material for the new dyestuffs industry. Some collieries were coking between 40 and 60 per cent of the total amount of coal mined.

It does not necessarily follow, however, that these apparent economies of scale were matched by improvements in labour productivity. The surge of output after 1900 was achieved by employing more men with picks, and in some large collieries for which we have records output per man declined after the mid-1890s. Everything depended of course on the location of the pit. On the advancing northern frontier of mining pits were more productive and paid higher wages than in the older areas where the best seams were worn out. There was a constant migration of younger workers northwards across the area which produced sharply different patterns of population behaviour between the now neglected Ruhr valley and the booming new industrial towns in the Emscher and Lippe valleys. These were exaggerated by the tendency of industry also to migrate northwards to where the coal was cheaper at the pit head.

– Textiles

As Table 3 shows, the textile industries did not grow as rapidly as all industries combined although there were important differences of behaviour between the different textiles. Their contribution to the improvement in labour productivity was greater than that of most industries, but the main aspect of this was the gradual elimination of the older handicraft methods of production. In spite of the size of output their history is not very interesting to our analysis. The pattern of change in textile production in the period is considered in more detail below in the context of the French economy where it is of more analytical value.[4]

The growth figures for textile output are misleading in one respect: the output of cotton goods grew much more rapidly. As everywhere cotton replaced the older fabrics, especially linen, and with the annexation of Alsace Germany acquired the most modern and the most highly specialised part of the French cotton industry. With this acquisition the number of cotton spindles was increased by 56 per cent and the number of mechanical cotton looms by almost 90 per cent. In spite of French tariff concessions in their favour the Alsatian entrepreneurs were soon locked in fierce competition with the more recent south German cotton industry, a competition which was in fact in the long run to be to their disadvantage. The German domestic and export markets were geared more towards the lower counts of yarn and towards coarser fabrics than the export markets on which Alsace had depended and the German tariff did not offer the same degree of protection as the French to the finer fabrics. The Alsatian industry now had to continue its rivalry with the other finer-grade producers on less favourable terms and was no longer able to compensate for higher fuel, raw material and machinery costs. Retreating into competition on the domestic German market it had to sacrifice one of its great advantages, quality, and produce coarser yarns at lower prices.

The growth of cotton cloth output in the country as a whole reflected the increase in spendable incomes. Table 13 shows how astonishingly consistent was the increase in cotton consumption compared to the other developed economies.[5] Between 1871–5 and 1896–1900, when the population increased by about 30 per cent, the consumption of woven cotton goods increased by 133 per cent. Much of this was catered for by imports but conversely German textile exports grew at roughly the same rate as imports. At all counts of yarn above 45 imports were two-thirds or more of the yarn used, but below those counts German yarn exports were highly competitive and there evolved a complex trade in semi-manufactured textiles involving primarily once again the most developed and industrialised economies although the markets for woven goods were by now found throughout Europe and America.

The growing quantities of raw cotton consumed, which increasingly came from the United States, eventually turned Bremen into a cotton exchange as important as Liverpool and Le Havre. The technical innovations in the factories also followed closely on the French and British pattern, on which indeed they were often dependent, for much textile machinery was still imported. Power looms were introduced rapidly after 1874 and their speed of action increased by one-third by 1910. The speed of a spindle in Alsace increased from 7,000 revolutions a minute in 1876 to 9,000 in 1910 and the annual output of yarn from each spindle increased by 60 per cent over the same period.

The history of the other textiles was more chequered. The woollen industry lost its earlier dynamism as an exporter. Most of the growth was now in the worsted sector based on the import of combed wool and worsted yarn from Britain and Belgium. At the same time a large export trade to the south and east of Europe in semi-manufactured and finished woollens and worsteds developed. By 1913 woollen exports were less important than those of coal and coke. They remained, however, on net balance much more important than cotton exports. The mechanisation of the silk industry was effected more quickly and comprehensively than in France. By 1905 in Krefeld power looms were 60 per cent of all looms and this was reflected in the relative increase of German silk exports compared to those of France. In some years after 1900 they were 80 per cent of the French level. As for the oldest of the German textile industries, the linen industry, its history after 1870 was simply the prolongation of the decline begun before that date. Its mechanisation came later than elsewhere and was nipped in the bud by already established competition so that the industry sank into insignificance.

– Chemicals

The structure of the German chemical industry was quite different from that of France and Britain. It was only in the decade between 1860 and 1870 that the industrial application of chemical processes on a large scale developed in Germany. In retrospect this can be seen as one of the few advantages of late industrialisation. There had been little investment in the old-established Leblanc process of soda manufacture, the basis of many other inorganic chemical processes, and when tariff barriers were erected against soda imports from Britain the German industry began straightaway with the newly discovered and far more efficient Solvay process. The comparative success of German manufacturers in this area is mainly to be attributed to the fact that they were not saddled with heavy investment in an outmoded technology dating from an earlier period of industrialisation and could select the best technology available. But it is on the more modern aspects of the chemical industry, the industrial application of organic chemistry and the synthesis of new materials, that the interest of historians has been most directly focused. For before 1914 Germany enjoyed a remarkable world monopoly in most areas of synthetic production and it has always been tempting to suppose that in the explanation of this difference between German industry and industry elsewhere in Europe could be found an explanation for the success of the German economy in these years.

The first industrial applications of organic chemistry did in fact lead to a long chain of production techniques which, because of the German monopoly, were all initially established in Germany. The basic scientific processes were at first concerned with the commercial production of synthetic dyestuffs but from this developed the manufacture of medicinal drugs, photographic materials, artificial fibres, the first plastics and new forms of explosives. Many of these manufactures were still in their infancy before 1914 and some of the new substances, such as bakelite and celluloid, had severe limitations. Organic chemistry had nevertheless begun a new stage in the history of manufacturing. By creating wholly new materials through processes of chemical synthesis it had removed many of the constraints which the availability of raw material resources placed on the process of industrial manufacture. That this important step to a further and more advanced stage of manufacturing should have been confined to Germany is certainly a very interesting comment on the evolution of German technology. But once explained it still forms only a small part of any full explanation of the sustained development of the economy over these years.

The organic branch of the chemical industry, insignificant elsewhere except in Switzerland, accounted for more than half the capital investment and employment in the industry by 1914. The inorganic branches also grew rapidly, partly because of the high demand for fertiliser from German agriculture and partly because a larger quantity of their production was being consumed by the chemical industry itself as intermediate products. The annual rate of growth of output after 1872 was clearly exceeded only by the electrical industry. But neither in numbers employed nor in value of production did the chemical industry match the size of the older industries. Its total workforce of 290,000 in 1913 may be compared with the 728,000 employed in coalmining, the 443,000 in metal production or the

1·1 million in textile manufacture. Although this new technology contributed to the high rate of growth of the industry, the industry's own contribution to the growth of the total economy was limited.

Germany was well endowed with resources for the chemical industry. The potash deposits at Stassfurt were the richest and most easily mined on the continent, other raw materials were present and coal tar, the basic raw material of the dyestuffs industry, was a by-product of the coking process. But since the essence of the organic chemicals branch was to substitute one material for another it can hardly be argued that these advantages in resources were important. Indeed until the 1880s a high proportion of the coal tar was still imported from British gasworks. In one other sense the industry was fortunately placed. The large quantities of heavy materials handled required water transport to reduce costs and this the Rhine and its tributaries provided – providing also a dumping ground at other people's expense for the large amounts of unpleasant or indeed poisonous waste materials which the industry needed to get rid of. Until the development of electro-chemical industries most of the works were situated on these rivers.

Such advantages, however, were not uncommon. The unique advantage which the German industry enjoyed was its supply of highly trained scientific personnel. Much more than earlier industries the synthetic dyestuffs industry depended on a steady stream of theoretical scientific research bringing speedier and better manufacturing processes and theoretical principles by which new products might be brought into being. In this sense it was the herald of much twentieth-century industry, depending for innovation no longer on the technician and inspired amateur mechanic but on the systematic research of a more rigorously trained scientific staff whose primary concern was discovery. This was recognised by German patent law which protected the process of production and not the product itself, thereby leaving the field open for the development of better manufacturing processes of identical products.

The number of scientists required was not large. The biggest of the dyestuff firms in 1900, Badische Anilin und Soda Fabrik (BASF), employed 6,300 workmen and only 233 'experts and chemists'; Meister, Lucius und Brüning, which later became Farbwerke Hoechst, employed 3,500 workmen and 165 'experts'. In the early stages the number of chemists needed was very small because most of the early research was done in Britain and France and acquired through the purchase of patents. Meister, Lucius und Brüning, for example, bought the patent for alizarin in 1869; they employed only 12 chemists in 1875 and 25 in 1880. Only when they began to make pharmaceutical goods in 1883 was the need for a large volume of research by the company itself fully accepted. Once this point had been reached by several firms, however, the supply of such trained personnel ran short. Even so the situation was not as acute in Germany as elsewhere for a modern education in chemistry, and one of better quality, was more available in universities there. In the 1880s as the demand for research personnel mounted German chemists returned home to the German industry and other countries found themselves unable at the crucial moment to provide adequately trained chemists in sufficient numbers. Within a brief period the German chemical firms, from being dependent on outside knowledge, had themselves established a monopoly of knowledge. This monopoly was then almost impossible to break and the continuing input of knowledge proved the crucial factor in the growth of the industry until 1914.

Typical of this process was the laboratory which Carl Duisberg organised for BASF. Its research into methods of producing indigo led also to a new process for making liquid chlorine, to new bleaches, to a new process for making concentrated sulphuric acid and to discoveries with catalysts later applied in the synthesis of ammonia. This last process opened the way to the Haber-Bosch process of fixing nitrogen, first operated at Oppau in 1913, and thus to different methods of explosive and fertiliser manufacture and ultimately to the manufacture of synthetic petrol. The importance of scientific personnel can be seen in the fact that Duisberg became one of the leading directors of BASF within thirteen years and it was he who was the driving force behind the building of the vast new works at Leverkusen.

Ultimately, therefore, Germany's advantage was a social rather than an economic one – the availability of appropriate education. At the lower level this was provided by the *Hochschulen* where the rudiments of technical and scientific training were provided more methodically and to larger numbers than in France or Britain. They had about 14,600 students in 1903. But for the precise purposes of the chemical industry the men needed were trained in university laboratories. Here the tradition of an individual rational training at the laboratory bench in scientific principles, rather than in applied science or technology, had been started by chemists such as Bunsen. As a result, a scientific chemical education was available in many German universities, and cheaply available, to the young man of talent whereas in Britain and France it was expensive, difficult to find and almost non-existent within the universities. This was one of the latest benefits of the enlightenment in Germany. The emancipation of the rational enquiring mind from ties of routine and tradition, which the great eighteenth-century educational reformer Pestalozzi had spent his life advocating, bore some of its finest fruit in the bold educational ideas and individual scientific enquiry of the small group of German chemists who followed the intellectual path of Liebig and Bunsen.

– The Electrical Industry

This was the branch of industrial production whose output grew the fastest after 1870. The total numbers employed were much fewer than in the chemical industry but to some extent the statistic is misleading because in many directions the electrical industry as it grew more complex shaded indistinguishably into engineering and other industrial sectors. Here it is not merely the rapid rate of growth that is interesting but, as in the chemical industry, the dominant position of Germany in an industry which was developing and employing essentially new forms of technology. By 1913 two huge financial combines, the Allgemeine Electricitäts-Gesellschaft (AEG) and Siemens-Schuckert, produced electrical equipment in much wider variety and on a much greater scale than any European rivals and held an impregnable position on world export markets. Exports of electrical equipment were about three times bigger than those of the United States, the only comparable producer.

The early history of the electrical industry is closely associated with one of the most remarkable families and firms of the nineteenth century, that of Siemens, founded in Berlin by Werner von Siemens, a former Prussian army officer, as a cable and telegraph company, and run by him with his brothers who managed the firm's other branches in London and St Petersburg (Leningrad). The cable business was by its nature the most international of industries and in 1872 two-thirds of the employees were employed outside Germany and less than 600 at Berlin. The firm is justly famous for its discoveries and for the important lead it gave Germany in the practical industrial application of electrical energy: it was here that the first dynamos were made. The later growth of the electrical industry was not based on international communications, however, but on the production, distribution and use of current for industrial and domestic consumption and this had to await the discoveries and patents of Edison and others.[6] Siemens at first stood aloof from these and they were taken up by another entrepreneur, Emil Rathenau, who was to dominate the later history of the industry as Siemens had dominated the earlier. Visionary and politician, Rathenau was to become the grandiloquent prophet of a more massive industrial organisation which, he thought, would resolve the social tensions caused by economic development and eventually create newer and larger forms of political society; these in turn, like business and industry, would come to accept the inherent logic of economic development that national markets and frontiers were losing all economic validity. He was of Jewish descent and the opposition to his own outlook was cruelly demonstrated when his son, who became Minister for Foreign Affairs after the First World War, was shot by German nationalists.

The company he built up, Allgemeine Electricitäts-Gesellschaft (AEG), was already the biggest of the electrical firms by 1890. Its success was based on its dominance in the techniques of power distribution and for some time it relied heavily on patents from the American firms Edison and General Electric. By 1903 it employed 17,000 people, whereas Siemens in 1902 had less than 4,000, and in its structure and the huge scale of its operations more than any other company exemplified forms of company organisation and methods of capital combination which developed in the late nineteenth century as the size and capacity of markets grew. But it also has to be said that the market for electric power had its own peculiarities. The number of local authorities and semi-public bodies involved, the necessity to standard-ise methods and equipment for distributing and using current in towns and in transport systems, the heavy initial investments needed, the amount of work and profit involved in each single contract for supply, which might be to a whole city, were all inherent forces tending towards the rapid concentration of the industry into an extremely small number of firms. Siemens merged in 1903 with a firm on the current-distribution side of the industry, Schuckert, and became a company on the same scale as, and with similar interests to, AEG. By 1913 Siemens-Schuckert employed 57,000 people in Germany and 24,000 abroad and had built its own quarter of Berlin, Siemensstadt.

The growth of the market for electric power was a function of the rapid growth of cities and urban life in Germany, itself of course a reflection of the sustained growth and industrialisation of the whole economy. In a later section we consider the advantages of this urbanisation for continued growth throughout the economy but we may note here its particular impact on the electrical industries in Germany. That they were bigger than in other developed European economies and that they grew so rapidly may be explained by the fact that nowhere else in the same period except in the mid-west of the United States did so many large cities grow so quickly to such a size.

This growth provided the two largest early markets: municipal lighting systems and municipal transport systems. Estimates suggest that by 1902 about half the length of electric tramways in Europe was in Germany. When these markets became saturated new markets were opened up, inter-urban electric transport systems, municipal electric railways such as the Berlin underground, and large-scale central power stations for distribut-ing power over wide areas of the country; of these power stations 110 had been built by 1911. Most of these markets involved joint operations with municipalities or other powerful organisations. Towns would often demand a sufficient degree of capital participation in the distribution or production of current to bring about a close mingling of private and public investment, and the electrical companies would sometimes sell their systems by lending part of the capital to the town to cover the heavy initial investment. Many of the power stations were also built in association with large colliery companies and some in Prussia and Bavaria in association with the state. Concentration of capital by the electrical companies not only enabled them to match this scale of operations but also allowed them to force the sales of machinery manufactured by themselves on their partners.

The links of the electrical industry to other industries were numerous and this provided another series of important industrial markets. Electric motors made the factory floor tidier and more efficient and were usually cheaper than steam engines. In Berlin in 1907 48 per cent of the engineering firms used electric power but the percentage for the whole of Germany was much lower because many machine builders had settled in areas where coal was cheap. Electro-metallurgy, beginning with the electric furnace invented by Wilhelm Siemens in 1878,[7] and electro-chemistry, beginning in the late 1880s, added new categories of machinery. It was electrical machinery which particularly dominated the industry's exports and gave Germany almost as big a share of this growing international market as she had with dyestuffs.

– Engineering

The engineering industry is difficult to define and it was not always accurately defined in employment statistics. But even allowing for these inaccuracies it was, in terms of employment, one of the largest, if not the largest, of the German industries. Its size was a function of the size and diversity of industrial production because it was also the capstone of the other industries, making the machines which produced their output. In its own diversity of production and the size of its total output, it was superior to all European rivals. But so general a statement needs considerable qualification.

The most rapid growth of the industry came after 1890 and with it came radical changes in production. Until that date most machines were built to order because they were too costly to be stored for sale. It behoved engineering firms not to specialise too closely and the variety of products turned out by most factories of whatever size is bewildering. Certain types of machine making were linked together. For many big firms such as Hannoversche Maschinenbau (Hanomag), formerly Egestorff, and Maschinenbau Nürnberg (MAN), steam engines remained an important item and with this went the manufacture of boilers and pumps. Another related activity was the manufacture of all kinds of textile machinery, but even Elsässische Maschinenbau in Mühlhausen (Mulhouse), in the heart of the main cotton spinning area, devoted only 42 per cent of its total output to textile machinery in 1912–13. Even shipbuilders were diversified. Schickau in Elbing (Elblag) and Danzig (Gdansk), which specialised in important navy contracts, turned out its two thousandth railway locomotive in 1914. Typical was Maschinenfabrik Augsburg, later part of MAN, which in 1884–5 made steam engines, boilers, turbines, electrical transmission equipment, ice making machines, and presses, all in significant numbers. In part this was attributable to the workshop origins of the industry which died only slowly; almost half of the workforce in 1882 was in firms employing less than fifty people. But it was also attributable to the nature of the market, diverse, difficult, demanding new specifications, and, above all, not large enough for any one commodity to permit standardisation of production techniques and specialisation of output.

This was a fundamental difference between the German industry and the only other engineering industry of comparable size, that in the USA. American engineering, because of the size and standardisation of the market, was more geared to mass-production methods by single-purpose machine tools, interchangeable components and a narrower range of specifications for final products. German firms were well aware of the advantages to be obtained in this way, but for them 'americanisation' of the methods of manufacture always stopped well short of the ideal. Reasonable specialisation to meet the demands of the market required a different policy. Locomotive builders such as Borsig were able to standardise the number of types on offer to the domestic market. But as the locomotive business slackened off in Germany the export markets created by railway building elsewhere, especially in Russia, produced a resurgence of locomotive construction to meet a wide range of different foreign needs. Until 1894 the overwhelming majority of the locomotives built by Hanomag were for the domestic market. After that date, of the total number made 79 per cent were exported. The rising demand from the export market led Schwartzkopff, later Berliner Maschinenbau, to build a new locomotive works manufacturing new types. Even with goods like sewing machines and small arms the market did not justify complete specialisation and the only firm which achieved American levels of standardisation before the mid-1890s was the plough manufacturers, Rudolph Sak of Leipzig. Even they had twenty-six different combinations of their 'universal plough' in 1880, because they exported throughout eastern Europe, especially to Russia and Romania, and had to cater for a wide variety of farming conditions.

In the 1890s there came abrupt changes in the composition of the industry's total output. In 1882 the largest number of people were still employed in the building of steam engines and locomotives, with shipbuilding second. The great increase in size of the German navy after 1900 brought shipbuilding to the forefront. By 1907 shipbuilding was the biggest sector of employment but employment in steam engine and locomotive manufacture had increased only slightly and now employed fewer people than the manufacture of textile machinery and constructional materials. The manufacture of motor vehicles, not worth listing in 1882, employed 14,500 by 1907 and that of petrol and gas engines, likewise not listed, 4,500, while employment in the making of sewing machines and their parts rose from 8,600 to 20,000. Some of these activities lent themselves more readily to standardisation and all of them greatly increased the demand for machine tools. So did the making of 250,000 bicycles a year by the mid-1890s and the start of typewriter and office machine manufacture about 1900.

It was on the basis of these new lines of output that most engineering firms first developed into major concerns. The technological impact this had, however, was still limited. J. E. Reinecker in Chemnitz, the first German firm to make only machine tools, made lathes which were acknowledged as the equal of the best American product (although this was not true of their other tools), but even in 1888 the firm employed only 175 people. By 1899 the floorspace had increased by a factor of twenty-four and there were 1,150 employees. The basis of this expansion was special-purpose machine tools for the new bicycle and car industries, but interestingly Reinecker was almost unique in confining its activities in this way. The biggest and oldest of the machine tool firms, Ludwig Loewe, remained far behind the quality of American production and the degree of standardisation of production methods, while the first firm to try to standardise the production of machine tools, J. Zimmermann, later the Chemnitzer Werkzeugmaschinenfabrik, still made steam engines to order by 1913. The demand for machine tools for the newer engineering industries would not have been met without a spate of American imports. Technological copying of the imports was rapid and one German–American firm, Deutscher Niles, founded in Berlin in 1898, was intended to produce the same machine tools in Germany. But only in certain areas was German competition successful, in heavy machine tools and in sheet metal working machines for example. Automatic lathes, revolving lathes, and most of the smaller precision instruments were still imported. Although exports of agricultural machinery from Germany grew very rapidly after 1900 and after 1907 first surpassed the value of imported agricultural machinery, reaping machines were still imported in large quantities from America; so too were office machines, typewriters and cash registers. Although all these items were produced in Germany after 1900 the American product was often better and, because of the standardisation of manufacturing methods, cheaper.

The insufficient size even of a market as large as that of Germany was a persistent obstacle throughout the period to the advance of engineering technology. The two early typewriter firms, the Wanderer Werke and Adler, also made cars. The leading sewing machine firm, Frister and Rossmann, also made typewriters and cars until 1914. Opel had made 15,000 bicycles at Rüsselsheim by 1900 but still clung to sewing machines until 1911.

The difficulties of an insufficient market, and of a market where incomes were still marginally lower than in Britain or France, are best seen in the car industry. Most of the early development of the internal combustion engine and the car occurred in Germany. The number of internal combustion engines in use in 1907, 552,000, was more than four times the number in France one year earlier. Gottlieb Daimler and Wilhelm Maybach made the first car in 1886 in a shed in Cannstatt and were soon followed by Karl Benz. Both these enterprises started commercial manufacture very early and in 1896–7 Benz, which made 500 cars at Mannheim, had probably the biggest output in Europe. But the subsequent growth of car production was slower than in France and the United States, in both of which countries, as in Britain, the market for cars was more buoyant. There were still only 27,000 motor vehicles in Germany in 1907 and only 70,000 in 1912. In 1901 925 cars were made by 12 producers, in 1911 16,370 by 58 producers. None of the firms produced on the scale of the French firms Peugeot or Renault; the biggest was probably Opel with a production of 3,000 vehicles in 1912.

In many ways, therefore, the engineering industry, in spite of its great size, showed a technological pattern which is an instructive contrast to the electrical and chemical industries. Like those industries it dominated European markets in the area in which it specialised but this had much less effect on the structure of the firms and the specialisations were narrower. Technical education in Germany provided a large supply of well-trained engineers. There were 5,000 pupils in the technical continuation schools in Chemnitz in 1909 and firms like Borsig and MAN began their own apprentice schools in the 1890s. In 1912 60 per cent of the 5,200 workers in the MAN factories at Nuremberg were trained in a skill. But in this case technological education and ingenuity do not seem to have overcome the pressure of those market forces which determined the structure of the industry, and in some areas, textile machinery and cars for example, it continued to play second fiddle to its international rivals.

– *Conclusion*

The overall pattern of German industry was determined by so extreme a diversity of forces as to show the futility of ascribing its growth to any one particular factor. Whereas the successes of the chemical industry could be attributed to educational advantages, themselves part of a fortunate historical legacy, the same social and educational advantages could do little to overcome weaknesses elsewhere. The deficiencies of the engineering industry, for example, were the unavoidable result of market forces which for most of the period restricted the market for many of its more standardised products. Later industrialisation was an advantage in the chemical industry where it permitted the adoption of the best available technology for soda manufacture because there had been so little investment in earlier technologies. But in most industrial sectors there was already considerable investment in older technologies and this, for example, worked against the development of the steel industry in the 1870s. There the earlier technologies put Germany at a disadvantage because her resource base was poor, until the Gilchrist–Thomas process reversed the position and, aided by the political accident of the annexation of Lorraine, gave Germany certain cost advantages. The size of Germany's raw material resources and their appropriateness for late nineteenth-century industry has usually been understated. They were not a cause of industrial growth but they did permit the growth of output in certain areas such as coal, steel and chemicals to very high levels without raising acute trading problems. But the most powerful force at work was the self-reinforcing nature of industrial development once it had reached a certain level. The growth of the steel, coal and engineering industries was a function of the growth of all industries and that in turn promoted more rapid urbanisation which promoted further growth in the same industries and was the prime force in the growth of the electrical industry. That industry in its turn gave an additional stimulus to coal mining and to engineering, and the increase in incomes resulting from these developments provided the stimulus for the continued expansion of the consumer goods industries. The complexity of these interconnections meant that the range of markets for each industry was growing and after 1880 this became apparent in the limited effect which bad trading years had on the total level of industrial production, even though their impact on certain sectors was still severe.

TRANSPORT

Most of the main railway lines were completed by the end of 1876, the year in which railway investment reached its peak. After 1880 it dropped steeply and was at its lowest level in the period 1884–94. It then began to climb once more to high levels with the duplicating of tracks, improving of layout and, above all, the growth of local and suburban services into towns and the extension of capacity necessary to cope with this commuter traffic. By this later period, however, investment in industry so far exceeded railway investment that the latter no longer constituted an important proportion of total investment. But the length of track added to the system averaged little under 10,000 kilometres for each decade before 1913 leaving Germany with a total system about 50 per cent as large again as that of France or Britain. Once again the importance of rapid urbanisation is evident, sustaining the market for railway equipment until 1913 at a high level after the uncertainty of the mid-1880s.

The ownership and administration of the railways was only partly centralised, some of the states retaining their own systems. But the tendency towards a resumption of public control was as strong in Germany as elsewhere. In Europe it was only in the United Kingdom that railway building was undertaken almost entirely by private enterprise, although even there the state laid down complicated legal guidelines. Elsewhere it was seen as a matter of public policy too important for the state not to be closely involved, and, equally important, the capital requirements, once the major profit-making lines had been built, were such that some element of government financial support was always necessary. In the last quarter of the nineteenth century, when most of the lines being built were branch lines, there was a decisive swing everywhere, even in the richer countries, towards public investment and regulation of national railway systems, from which again only the United Kingdom remained immune. In 1879 the Prussian government purchased 5,000 kilometres of private railway and a consistent pursuit of this policy meant that there were less than 3,000 kilometres of private track left in Prussia by 1909. Bavaria followed the same policy so that the railways became the biggest single sector of public employment in Germany, providing employment in 1912 for an army of 697,000 people.

Until the 1880s one source of the increase in railway traffic continued to be former traffic from the inland waterways and from coastal shipping. But this process came to a halt after that date, perhaps because of the increasing use by industry of raw materials with a high unit cost of carriage, such as coal and iron ore, and investment again began to flow towards internal waterways. The Dortmund–Ems canal was built after 1890 and after 1900 carried an increasing traffic in imported iron ore and grain from Emden. The Kiel canal, built primarily for naval purposes, provided a through route from Lübeck to the North Sea avoiding the Sound. The total length of canals and canalised rivers increased from 3,400 kilometres in 1873 to 6,600 by 1914. Along with these developments went the widening and deepening of navigations so that the weight of cargo which could be carried in one ship up the Rhine to Mannheim or up the Elbe to Magdeburg more than doubled between 1877 and 1905. But as regards the increase of traffic as a whole the primacy of the Rhine was indisputable. By the end of the century it was more thickly covered with vessels than it had been before the railways, becoming the chief waterway into and through the greatest industrial region of the continent, a river of unique economic importance. Growing cities and new factories crowded the 600 miles of its navigable course upwards from Rotterdam and 40 per cent of the total tonnage per kilometre carried on the German waterways was carried on it alone. If the volume carried on the Rhine canals were added the proportion would be even greater. The weight of traffic handled by the river and canal port of Ruhrort increased more than threefold between 1880 and 1900, most of it coal and iron ore. The tonnage handled in Mannheim rose from 750,000 in 1870 to 6·5 million in 1911.

The growth in trade, both internal and external, meant also a rapid growth in shipping. The total tonnage of steamships rose from 82,000 net registered tons in 1871 to 1·6 million in 1903 and to 4·1 million in 1912. It was the growth of foreign trade after 1900 which produced this last surge of shipbuilding, the developing transatlantic trade demanding the building of bigger and more modern steamships. Of the total tonnage in 1912 3·4 million was registered in Hamburg and Bremen, dominated respectively by the huge transatlantic fleets of the Hamburg–Amerika line and North German Lloyd, both companies helped by the fact that they were seen as instruments of national policy to oust British shipping. The Hamburg–Amerika line took the lead in the modernisation of the German fleet, being the first to convert to compound steam engines and later to oil firing. Since by 1905, with its 150 ocean-going vessels, it was the largest shipping company in the world, its forward-looking policy was of no small importance. It was in fact the compound steam engine which finally gave a decisive advantage in productivity to the ocean-going steamship over the sailing ship between 1875 and 1880. Sailing ships fell from 43 per cent of all clearings in German ports in 1873 to 21 per cent in 1887, and a high proportion of the latter figure was now accounted for by coastal traffic.

POPULATION AND URBANISATION

Industrialisation on such a scale and at such a speed could only be achieved by a great uprooting and displacement of the population. This had already begun in the 1830s with emigration to the United States, and in the 1850s this emigration affected also the agricultural north-eastern provinces where it was prompted by poor conditions there.[8] Migration overseas had essentially the same causes as internal migration and as the demand for labour in Westphalia, the Rhineland, Berlin and the other main industrial areas rose it was met first of all by the high surplus of births over deaths, secondly by the wholesale emigration of the population of the north-eastern provinces, and thirdly, on a much smaller scale and only after 1890, by the immigration of foreigners, mostly Poles. A rising demand for labour in the western industrial areas would reduce the proportion of external migration to the United States from the more agricultural areas and increase the proportion of long-range internal migration. For most of the period this made Germany different from France and Britain where internal migration tended to take place over shorter distances. The beginnings of emigration to the United States and elsewhere as an escape from the problems of impoverishment in an underdeveloped country where the population was increasing rapidly had already accustomed the inhabitants of the eastern provinces to the idea of labour mobility when the very rapid industrialisation sharply increased the domestic demand for labour.

In Prussia in every decade after 1851 the surplus of births over deaths was always over 10 per cent and between 1891 and 1910 it was 15 per cent. Furthermore the birth rate in the industrial areas remained higher than in the agricultural areas because the population was younger and because the demand for labour was greater. The Rhineland had a higher birth surplus than Berlin which meant that after 1880 Berlin became a bigger target for internal migration than the Rhineland and Westphalia. As an indication of the redistribution of population which took place, Silesia, which contained 14·7 per cent of the Prussian population in 1880, had only 13 per cent in 1910, and yet it was by no means an unindustrialised province, whereas Westphalia's share rose over the same period from 7·5 per cent to 10·3 per cent. In that period the Rhineland population grew by 3 million and that of Westphalia by 2·1 million. Table 4 shows the extent of the gains and losses of population in the provinces of the state of Prussia and shows how dependent the industrialisation process was on internal migration. It also shows that it was only the four provinces with the biggest proportion of their population employed in industry and services that actually gained in population through migration. The provinces with the highest proportion of their population in agriculture lost most, but industrialised areas such as Saxony and Hanover still saw a drift of population towards areas where the market for non-agricultural labour was expanding more rapidly.

These longer-range movements were only part of a general movement of the population from the countryside to the towns. There were eight towns with 100,000 people or over in 1871; in 1910 there were forty-eight.

Table 4   *Migration of population in the provinces of Prussia, 1881–1910*

Province	Gain (+) or loss (–) on natural rate of increase	As % of surplus of births over deaths	% of population in industry, trade, transport and services 1882	1907
Brandenburg	+841,749	85·5	69·6	73·8
Berlin	+479,910	102·3	99·2	99·6
Rhineland	+434,792	16·6	68·2	81·0
Westphalia	+376,482	22·1	74·9	80·8
Posen	−631,625	61·4	34·5	42·1
East Prussia	−629,649	82·9	34·5	41·8
West Prussia	−492,240	62·3	38·5	46·0
Silesia	−492,148	28·8	54·0	67·0
Pomerania	−468,975	72·6	44·5	51·5
Saxony	−328,717	29·7	61·9	70·9
Hannover	−147,039	15·2	49·3	61·2
Schleswig-Holstein	−57,060	10·4	56·0	68·5
Hesse-Nassau	−6,586	1·0	58·3	61·3

Source: W. Köllmann, 'Demographische "Konsequenzen" der Industrialisierung in Preussen', in Centre National de la Recherche Scientifique, *L'Industrialisation en Europe au XIXe siècle* (Paris, 1971), pp. 273, 275.

These towns had less than 5 per cent of the population of the country in 1871; in 1910 they had 21·3 per cent. The increase in population went almost entirely to the larger urban areas of the country. This was the most extensive and rapid process of urbanisation yet seen in Europe, creating large new industrial cities alike out of mere villages such as Gelsenkirchen and Bochum and smaller ancient trading centres like Mannheim, Düsseldorf and Essen. Essen had about 10,000 inhabitants in 1850; in 1900 it had about 200,000 and one-fifth of those in employment worked for Krupp. To take a smaller example the population of Hamborn increased from 5,300 in 1885 to 103,000 in 1910. Only in the most thriving parts of the United States was there anything to compare with this increase in new urban households. In 1900 31 per cent of the male inhabitants of Berlin were aged between 16 and 30; the percentage in this age group for the whole of Prussia was only 24·4 per cent and in the area providing the most migrants, Posen, the proportion was only 21·3 per cent. Between 1870 and 1910 investment in non-agricultural dwellings was 29·5 per cent of all net investment at 1913 prices. The building of these endless miles of late nineteenth-century stucco dwellings was in itself a perpetual reinforcement of the process of industrialisation which created them, providing a demand for building materials, glass, gas, water works, electricity and the vast apparatus of trade and transport which alone enabled them to function.

It can be seen from Table 4 that the Prussian province which provided the most migrants was Posen. A large proportion of these were Polish-speaking and after 1890 they were joined by immigrants from Russian Poland. This was the start of the influx of foreign workers to do the least attractive jobs which was to become such a feature of the German economy in the next similarly prolonged periods of growth of industrial output. They came mainly as coal miners and agricultural labourers. Even in the early 1920s there were quarters of some Ruhr mining towns which were still Polish-speaking. Polish agricultural labourers were attracted mainly to sugar beet farming where the methods of cultivation were labour intensive and where they filled the gap left by the westward migration of German agricultural workers to other sources of employment. Many of them were seasonal workers and their migration added to the seasonal migration of German farm workers which still took place in the east. It is estimated that there were about one million Polish immigrant agricultural workers in 1913 of whom three-quarters were seasonal migrants. From being one of Europe's major emigrant countries Germany had now become an immigrant country, with the flow of emigrants to the USA after 1890 diminishing to a trickle.

CAPITAL MANAGEMENT

– Banking

The important role which the investment banks had played in the development of the iron industry in the 1850s has led to much theorising about their subsequent importance to the economy. With the formation of the Dresdner Bank in 1872 the four institutions which were to remain the biggest investment banks until 1913, the Deutsche Bank, the Dresdner Bank, the Diskontogesellschaft and the Darmstädter Bank, were already in existence. They have been variously held to have been dynamic forces for industrial expansion and a cautious influence holding back the growth of industry, to have held the controlling influence over the whole economy and to have been merely the subservient tools of industrialists and states-men. The early close connections between banks and joint stock com-panies were not broken and on the supervisory board of directors of the company (*Aufsichtsrat*) bank representatives still sat and were able to exercise direct influence on company policy. How much and what sort of influence remains to be determined.

The circumstances in which firms raised capital loans through the medium of the investment banks did not change, assistance being required either for a heavy initial investment in capital equipment or a sudden large expansion. When firms were small and operating in limited markets they tended to avoid any possibility of bank control. Before 1880, for example, the chemical firms had little recourse to external financing. Like textile firms in an earlier period they ploughed their profits back into the firm and expanded in small but frequent stages. When larger capital investments were needed the bank was necessary but even then local banks seem to have been chosen to handle share issues on the stock exchange in preference to the bigger institutions, and it is difficult to find any connections between the major banks and the capital raising activities of the chemical firms. Most engineering firms were even smaller and the banks themselves fought shy of businesses with such varied markets. Their attitude was often reciprocated by the owners of the firms who were anxious to keep control in the family. Even at the end of the 1890s the Duisburger Maschinenbau raised extra share capital without the intermediation either of banks or of the stock exchange. When driven to use the banks engineering firms, like chemical manufacturers, frequently had recourse to the private banking houses which still played a big role, such as Mendelssohn or Wiener, Levy. It was a group of local Stuttgart private financiers which provided the capital for Daimler to begin manufacturing cars on an industrial scale in 1890.

But for bigger ventures with a seemingly guaranteed market the major banks were quite ready to provide industrial finance, often by acting in consortium. The expansion of the Deutz gas engine works in 1911 was jointly undertaken by the Deutsche Bank, the Dresdner Bank and the Schaafhausenscher Bankverein. When Deutscher Niles was founded in 1898 the capital of 6 million marks was jointly provided by the Niles company in the United States, the Loewe machine tool works in Berlin, the Diskontogesellschaft, the Dresdner Bank, the Berliner Handelsgesell-schaft, a small private bank, Born and Busse, and the AEG. In an industry like the electrical industry, ventures requiring this amount of initial capital were more usual and the rapid concentration of production in a few firms made the banks' role indispensable. Much the same was true of the big steel firms; the Diskontogesellschaft was particularly associated with the Dortmunder Union and the Deutsche Bank with the foreign interests of the Mannesmann tube works.

The capital of a few of the bigger joint stock companies was by 1912 almost as great as that of the major investment banks. This was the case with Krupp, with the AEG and with the Gelsenkirchener Bergwerks-gesellschaft. In such circumstances it is difficult to be sure who was influencing whom. The bank representatives never had a sufficient know-ledge of the detailed operations of the firm to dictate its policy and to some extent they became its prisoners. In issuing share capital the bank would itself provide the sum required and often retain for some time a substantial proportion of the new shares issued. The bank's interest was to unload these as soon as circumstances were propitious. But there were many occasions when the bank was forced to retain part of the capital issue and the natural tendency of bank policy in such circumstances was to urge caution on the firm. The existence of so many banking houses and the relative ease with which investment capital could be obtained in industry therefore acted as a dynamic force in so far as it facilitated company foundation and expansion in Germany. But at the same time the way in which this was done sometimes tended to make the companies subsequently more cautious and less competitive in their behaviour. The influence of the banks seems to have been to reduce competition in order to minimise the risks, and they entered willingly into the cartel agreements and other agreements in restraint of competition which characterised German industry after 1880. They advocated the type of semi-competitive oligo-poly which came so quickly into existence in the electrical industry; in no sense could the major joint stock banks be regarded as promoting economic efficiency. Their increasing power on the capital market weakened the free operation of that market and may have reduced its efficiency, while furthering the development of some firms such as the large electrical companies and steelworks.

There was, however, another means by which the banks encouraged industrial development apart from presiding over such major incidents as the birth or sudden expansion of the firm. By extending current account facilities to firms for their fixed and working capital they provided an easier source of constant credit to industry. After 1896 the use of this credit device was practised more widely and was particularly important in the period of high growth rates of national income between 1896 and 1906. The share of the banks in all industrial finance, which grew only slightly from 1885 to 1895, grew more strongly from that date onwards. It was from the readier offer of this sort of facility that the connections between banks and industry in general became much closer. In 1912 only one big bank had more than 3 per cent of its assets in industrial stocks and shares, but the interest of the banks in industry can be judged from the fact that the Deutsche Bank was represented on the boards of 159 firms. The joint stock banks were the locus of important business decisions in a way that was not true of French or British banks. Ultimately this was probably due to the fact that a higher proportion of German industry throughout the period demanded heavy capital investment over short periods which could not be met by self-financing out of company profits.

Control of the banking system was exercised by the Reichsbank, a central bank of issue. It differed in one important respect from the central banks of the other developed economies, being obliged to have branches throughout the country; there were over 4,100 of these by 1900. The big joint stock banks confined their activities to the more important centres of business and industry and outside those left a network of small local banks only some of which were under their control. The Reichsbank was obliged to offer facilities for transferring money to any part of the country to all citizens, a system which avoided the need for cheques. It filled in this way a gap in the banking services which was often unfilled elsewhere – in France for example – until the creation of post office savings banks and similar institutions. At the same time by its monetary policy it controlled interest rates and bank policy nationally and had particular obligations to co-operative and savings banks.

The efficiency of the German banking system did not depend on the joint stock banks. They were never responsible for more than one-quarter of all bank credit. Mortgage banks, land credit banks, village co-operative banks and savings banks all had a long history, some of the mortgage and savings banks dating from the eighteenth century, and all received help and encouragement from the state. Raiffeisen founded the first rural credit co-operatives in 1849 and Schulze-Delitsch the first industrial credit co-operatives in 1850. The principles which they popularised, especially those of Raiffeisen, were before 1914 to effect the first radical change for many centuries in the provision of rural credit in several European countries. This network of credit institutions throughout the economy which lowered interest rates to peasant farmers and small businesses had as great an impact as the major joint stock banks and merits a share of the scholarly attention that is still devoted to the latter.

– The 'New Capitalism'

The size of many of the German firms, their involvement with the banks, their paternalistic interest in their workers' existence beyond the factory gates, and above all the prevalence of agreements between firms restricting competition, usually at the expense of the consumer, all transformed the nature of the capitalist enterprise and its role in society. Whereas Rathenau saw these developments as the first steps towards a wholly new form of social organisation in which the management of capital for the benefit of mankind would henceforward be easier, socialist theoreticians saw them as a stage in the senility of the capitalist enterprise, 'late capitalism'. To them the union of joint stock bank and steelworks to create capital equipment on such a scale was more like two drowning swimmers clinging to each other in ever stormier seas. It was natural enough that living in so violently changing a society contemporaries of all persuasions should have evolved cataclysmic theories to explain it. But the reality was very complex, a mixture of the influence of the past, still attaching itself powerfully to many aspects of German society, and a struggle to come to terms with problems of economic and social organisation which had not yet been met with elsewhere in Europe.

To many of these new problems solutions from the pre-industrial period were still applied. The paternalism of many firms drew on the older tradition of the guilds and closed corporations. The engineering firm of Haniel und Lueg in Düsseldorf ran a general library of 3,000 books for its workers. When BASF built its new works at Leverkusen it provided, for 3,000 workers only, a co-operative store, bachelors' quarters, a canteen, a carpentry school, a school for training employees' daughters as house-keepers, insurance against unemployment and sickness, and a savings bank. Provision of this kind was not made because such facilities were lacking in the world outside the firm, as in Russia. Compulsory national social insurance against unemployment, sickness and old age began in the 1880s in Germany, almost twenty years before it was copied in other societies. Bismarck, who lent to such legislation his wholehearted support, saw social insurance as a curb on the unrestrained activities of capitalist society, as a method of mitigating the socially disintegrative effects of capitalist development and restoring the organic and harmonious society of man which his rural aristocratic upbringing led him to suppose had existed before industrialisation. This boldest of all attempts to solve the problems of mass unemployment and the disintegration of the family unit – compulsory insurance against the unavoidable disasters of the new society – was motivated by romantic misinterpretations of the past combined with a practical determination to come to terms with an ill understood present.

When, in a less practical way, leading economists such as Schmoller and Schaeffle welcomed the combinations of firms in cartels and trusts as a step towards limiting socially disruptive competition, they were still expressing, in a more sophisticated manner, the opposition to industrial society voiced by the artisan revolutionaries of 1848. When Siemens was forced to drop the informal organisation appropriate to a family concern and to produce and sell on the same scale as AEG, the only available model of organisation which could be copied was that of the pre-industrial state bureaucracy with its promotion procedures based on seniority and its rigorously formal administrative methods. If the 3,000 office workers at Siemensstadt seemed to outsiders to represent a new stage in the organisation of the capitalist firm they were in fact living out their working lives on a social pattern established in Germany well before the advent of industrial society. The idea that there was some inherently good quality in competition, or that it was a defence of the public interest, was often weaker in Germany than the contrary view which survived from older traditions. At the height of the legal actions to break up financial and industrial trusts in the United States a decision of the Imperial Supreme Court made agreements by firms in Germany to restrict competition legally enforceable. The attitudes of statesmen, judges, intellectuals and even entrepreneurs were quite different from those in France or Britain and this was mainly the consequence of a different history.

How much the evolution of 'new' forms of capitalism was in fact determined by these attitudes is a harder question to answer. Most of the differences in the behaviour of firms and banks in Germany were the result of differences in economic conditions, particularly in size and speed of growth of the market. It was this fundamentally which determined the concentration of capital in bigger units of production and which forced these units of production into agreements of all kinds with each other. Since such conditions would eventually apply to the other developed European economies and already applied in the United States the evolution of the capitalist enterprise in Germany did point the way into the future, however old the intellectual ideas it took with it, and for that reason it is a subject of great interest still worthy of study. But to investigate the matter here would divert us from the main question, and the one which has been most ignored by the many works on this issue. Did the concentration of capital and the apparent diminution of competition further the development of the economy in these years?

The forces which could lead firms into associations were diverse and so also were the kinds of associations which were formed. Although such associations were widespread in Germany they are easier to discover there and the contrast with France and Britain may be less striking than most writers suggest. The most typical early arrangements were cartels to equalise prices for raw materials or semi-finished products such as yarn and chemicals. Price control of raw materials usually implied restraints on production. In the 1870s associations of collieries in the Ruhr already co-operated to control production and prices, and by 1887 larger groupings were establishing central selling agencies with regulatory powers over the individual producers. The Rhenish-Westphalian Coal Syndicate established in 1893 made the cartel's control almost universal over the area where Ruhr coal was sold. Similar arrangements existed among the companies mining potash and they were enforced by national legislation in 1910 when the mines with a higher productivity tried to break the agreements. In this case the association existed to keep up the export prices of a raw material where a high proportion of the quantity entering international trade came from Germany.

A different form of association was the vertical integration of firms with their raw material supply. Such integrations were directly provoked by the attempts of raw material producers to raise prices, which constituted one of the main incentives for steelworks to acquire their own coal and iron ore mines. Even an engineering works like Borsig bought a colliery to keep down the price of its coal and coke. It was difficult to maintain raw material cartels in the face of such actions but the steel manufacturers themselves soon formed similar agreements. The German Steelworks Association, formed in 1904, regulated prices and output for a wide range of steel products in four large steelworks. In 1903 the Ruhr coal syndicate managed to incorporate, by a complicated differential pricing policy, the collieries which had become associated with metallurgical companies. But such an arrangement was bound to be shaky, and by 1914 it had broken down completely because the interest of the vertically integrated concerns was usually in the lowest possible raw material price and the highest possible price for finished steel.

Quite different again, and a response to different conditions, was the mesh of financial trusts which began to link the organic chemical firms in 1904, the year in which Hoechst and Casella and later BASF and Bayer formed associations. By pooling profits, agreeing to pay the same level of dividends and allocating part of the capital to a common holding company these pairs of firms were trying to cope with the high level of costs imposed on them by the research necessary to find new products. It could be several years before such programmes of research brought any financial return in sales. The firms were minimising the risks in such development and financing it independently of bank capital. The sharing of patents and licences to manufacture soon extended these arrangements into market sharing and price fixing.

There was a close association between the reduction in competition on the internal market and protective tariffs. Protective tariffs, by excluding foreign competition, made market sharing agreements and vertical integration of the firm easier and as integration proceeded the objections to protective tariffs diminished in force. Once steel firms owned their own sources of iron ore they stopped objecting to the tariff on imported pig iron. All such associations ignored the consumer where his interests clashed with theirs. They were one way of ensuring the domestic price levels which the tariff only theoretically guaranteed although they began before high tariffs. In fact many protected industries such as textiles remained fiercely competitive, but these were cases where the market was too complicated and diverse to permit such controls. For goods such as coal, steel, paper, glass and cement the market was more homogenous. As it kept on growing firms were forced into greater capital investments to supply it and the underlying motive of cartels and trusts was most frequently to protect these huge investments from risk. The increasing size of the firm and the associations between firms were both responses to the same situation.

It is still impossible to say with any certainty how far this process was responsible for the greater evenness of economic growth in Germany after 1880. In the worst depressions sales fell less and unemployment was less severe than in the other developed economies and it is often claimed that this was because the domestic market was better regulated and the annual fluctuations in production smoothed out. The only industries where effective control of the levels of production was higher than three-quarters of the total output, however, were paper making and mining, and later dyestuffs and organic chemicals. In coal mining there is clear evidence that the control of markets and production still left the industry open to fluctuations of trade coming from the outside. In some years, such as 1906, coal had to be imported in larger quantities from Britain because output had been kept too low, whereas in others, 1901 and 1908, there was over-production leading to price cutting by the few independent collieries and to attempts to break the cartel. It is somewhat fanciful to suppose that the effects of such associations in smoothing out the rate of growth of output could achieve what comprehensive economic planning could not. Although the effects of these agreements and of the concentration of capital in fewer enterprises in certain industries were, in the short run, often a brake on the dynamism of the economy, in the long run they could function as a further stimulus to economic development by sustaining the level of profit or by facilitating further technological innovation. The financial trusts which bound together the organic chemical industry had the promotion of research into new products as one of their main reasons for existence and the purpose of market sharing, whether at home or abroad, could often be, as in the case of the steel industry, to provide a safe background for investment in a further stage of technology. How far this was at the expense of the less developed economies is an issue to be discussed later in the context of those economies themselves.

AGRICULTURE

With all the attention of contemporaries and historians focused on the growth of industry and trade it is easy to forget that in 1913 35 per cent of the employed population, over 10 million people, officially still worked in agriculture. The total labour force in agriculture temporarily ceased to show an upward trend after 1883 when it stood at 9·7 million, but it did not fall permanently and after 1907 the official figures show it rising again. This is probably an error for most circumstantial evidence suggests that the agricultural labour force remained static until the war. The greater natural increase of population meant, however, that the number of workers in agriculture did not begin to decrease significantly before 1914 as it did in France; but this mattered less since agriculture made a real contribution to the growth of the economy. This was one of the decisive differences in the history of Germany and France in this period for in the eighties the agri-cultural sector in France was making no such contribution. Even using the official employment figures the increase in agricultural production during the century in Germany was more than threefold whereas the population increased by a factor of 2·3. Over the same period non-agricultural produc-tion increased by a factor of twenty-six, but this disparity was inherent in the process of nineteenth-century development and the much slower increases of output and productivity in agriculture still served to raise, even if only slightly, the incomes of a large number, to restrain the need for food imports to feed the growing urban population, and to provide some food exports. The average productivity of an agricultural worker, as far as it can be calculated, increased between 60 and 90 per cent in the period 1851–5 to 1896–1900, which compares quite favourably with the 123 per cent increase in industry and mining. This was not the only cause of rising output. The average weight of most animals doubled over the period. The average milk yield of a cow increased between two and a half and three times between 1842 and 1892. The result of these improvements in productivity was a steady increase in output of the principal crops, although the total land area in agricultural use dropped by 1·9 million hectares after 1878.

There was virtually no reduction in the area of arable land and this reflected the influence of protective tariffs which encouraged the continued concentration on bread grain production. Table 5 shows that wheat and rye production did not decrease with the arrival of cheaper foreign supplies

Table 5 *Annual average output of certain crops in Germany, 1871–1913 (000 tons)*

	Potatoes	Wheat	Rye	Barley	Oats	Sugar beet
1875–84	24,840	2,552	6,673	2,632	4,823	5,810
1885–94	30,460	3,045	7,237	2,666	5,587	9,510
1895–1904	39,100	3,491	8,831	2,959	6,979	13,380
1905–14	45,790	3,956	10,665	3,244	8,382	16,090

Source: W. G. Hoffmann, *Das Wachstum der deutschen Wirtschaft seit der Mitte des 19. Jahrhunderts* (Berlin, 1965), pp. 292–3.

and that after the high agricultural tariff of 1902 the output of rye in particular increased steeply. This was in part achieved at the expense of fodder grain production, especially barley which was imported by 1913 in large quantities at high prices through the tariff. Bread grain farmers, although they could no longer produce their crops at prices which were competitive, were sheltered from the fall in international prices. The strong political influence of the larger estate owners – organised in a pressure group, the Bund der Landwirte – especially after 1893, peasant attitudes which supported this influence, political uneasiness that too many food imports would leave the country in a strategically dangerous situation, and a romantically conservative feeling that the country should not become an 'Industriestaat', all combined to introduce and then strengthen agricultural protection. The levels of the food tariffs themselves, first introduced in 1879 and increased in 1885, 1887 and 1902, were only bargaining points. When modified by tariff conventions they were less protective than those of France and Austria-Hungary. But as world grain prices continued to fall in the 1880s German prices stabilised and thereafter remained well above the prices in the free-trade London market.

One weakness of the tariff was that the demand for animal foodstuffs grew with rising incomes. The number of cattle rose from 15·7 million in 1873 to 20·9 million in 1913, and of pigs from 12·1 million in 1892 to 25·6 million in 1913. As elsewhere in Europe this was partly achieved by a sharp decrease in the number of sheep kept. In spite of the tariff, imports of Russian barley into the north-western ports for pig feed increased rapidly after the 1890s. The compensation for these imports was a re-surgence of rye exports after 1902. But in foreign markets the price of rye relative to other grains was falling constantly. There was in fact, if strategic arguments are discounted, little economic justification for the tariff. It preserved, as did contemporary agricultural tariffs in France, a set of structural problems in agriculture of which the European Economic Community is even now the unlucky inheritor, and the increases in productivity which took place would certainly have been greater without it.

But its basic causes were not economic. Like agricultural protection in most other European countries they lay deep in the social and political structure of the country. The tariff was the instrument which Bismarck used to bind together in an uneasy harmony those groups who controlled the political destiny of the new Empire. Once introduced in 1879, it served as a quasi-constitution, a set of half-expressed guarantees to certain social groups about the political future of the country, which could not be renounced without shaking to its foundations a ramshackle political structure. The agitation for protective tariffs came first from the iron industry which was suffering from the lower production costs of its foreign competitors. There was no support from farmers because Germany was still a grain exporter to the London market. With the appearance of cheap American grains at the end of the decade, however, agitation for protective tariffs from German grain producers began. The major wheat and rye producers in Germany were not peasant farmers but the large estate farmers of the north-east whose political influence was still very strong. The protective tariff of 1879 reconciled the two political interests which had divided the country: the Junker landlords who had controlled the political destiny of Prussia and the more liberal business and entrepreneurial classes who had been their main opponents in the hard-fought constitutional struggles after 1848. Their reconciliation only laid up worse problems for the future, but the frail balance of power survived until 1914 and with it the large estates and the landlord class of north-eastern Germany. And this alliance was confirmed by the federal government's reliance on the external tariff which became an important source of income in a period of low taxation and few other sources of revenue. Fundamentally, therefore, the tariff has to be seen as a set of political alliances and to criticise its economic rationale is to attack it on a superficial level, the more so as the federal structure of the German Empire was so loose that the political alliances built on the tariff were holding the Empire together. In general it was true everywhere in the last quarter of the century that in the return to protection the political influences far outweighed the economic.

After 1894 all grain exporters could claim certificates, equivalent to the value of the export duty, which they could then sell to any grain importer permitting him to avoid payment of that amount in import dues. The original purpose was merely to facilitate the re-export of Russian grains from Danzig and Königsberg (Kaliningrad). After 1902, however, types of grain were interchangeable in this system so that the certificates, for which there was an active market, served as a premium to rye exporters from the eastern estates. This was the cause of the extraordinary increase in rye production between 1901 and 1912 which appears in Table 5. The area devoted to rye cultivation increased by 459,000 hectares between 1900 and 1913 although elsewhere in Europe its cultivation was tending to decrease. By 1913 the net exports of rye were 582,000 tons. Ironically, it served as a fodder grain to produce the cheap animal foodstuffs in Denmark which kept down the cost of living to British workmen.

Protected and subsidised in this way, however, the big estates still improved their productivity. The yields per hectare of rye and wheat showed their biggest improvement of the period between 1900 and 1913, though it must be remembered that this was also the greatest period for improvements in the productivity of peasant farms. It may well be that if better figures become available the increase in productivity on German farms will appear as a less evenly spread process over time and to be concentrated, as in France, more in the period after 1894.

As Table 6 shows, the divide between large estate and peasant farming remained essentially an east–west one with the river Elbe still an important dividing line. West of the river the pattern was typical of most of western Europe, peasant proprietors cultivating small land units. Technical progress, however, was more marked on German peasant farms than on those of France or Belgium. One reason was the more rapid conversion to dairy farming which became, in spite of the persistence of grain growing in the east, the most valuable branch of agricultural production. The number of co-operative dairies increased from 28 in 1880 to 2,000 in 1900. After the the mid-1890s this was associated with the greater availability of cheap machinery. The number of reapers grew from 35,000 in 1895 to 301,100 in 1907 and the number of threshers doubled in the same time. In the early 1890s were developed the first electrical motors for driving threshers, milk separators and butter churns. Improvements in crop breeding began to benefit peasant farms as well as the big estates. Square-head wheat arrived in Germany from Denmark in 1874. The plant breeder Wilhelm Rimpau combined it with American winter wheat to produce after 1889 'Rimpau's early bastard'. Petkus rye was developed after 1880 and these two breeds so increased the productivity of bread grain cultivation that they long remained the commonest strains of grain. Improvements in sugar beet were an important factor in the increases in output. The total area devoted to its cultivation doubled between 1881 and 1901, while the increase in out-

Table 6   Regional pattern of landholding in Germany in 1907

Size of farm (ha)	% of agricultural area covered by such farms in East and West Prussia, Brandenburg, Pomerania, Mecklenburg, Posen and Silesia	% of agricultural area covered by such farms in rest of Germany	% of area covered by such farms in whole of Germany	Total land area covered by such farms in whole of Germany (m. ha)
0–5	8·7	21·0	16·2	6·57
5–20	21·3	41·0	33·4	13·77
20–100	29·5	29·9	29·8	12·62
100+	40·5	8·1	20·6	9·92

Source: M. Sering, *Deutsche Agrarpolitik auf geschichtlicher und landeskundlicher Grundlage* (Leipzig, 1934), p. 27; *Agricultural Co-operation and Rural Credit in Europe*, Information and Evidence Secured by the American Commission, Senate Document No. 214, 63rd Congress, 1913.

put in the same period shown in Table 5 was much greater. Sugar was an export of major importance in the 1890s. But the most important crop was the potato; well over half Europe's total production was grown in Germany.

The peasant farmer was able to keep pace with these changes in productivity because of the spread of agricultural credit and co-operation to the poorer sections of rural society. Land mortgage institutions, the Landschaften, which provided mortgage credit on a co-operative basis within each region, had existed in Prussia since 1770. But their success came from confining their activities to the larger estates for which, indeed, they were intended. The Prussian Central Land Credit Company, a joint stock corporation set up by the Diskontogesellschaft, Rothschild, Bleichröder and Oppenheim in 1870, extended the functions of the Landschaften by opening to them the main Berlin credit institutions and also partly centralising their activities. By 1912 over 90 per cent of its loans were to smaller landowners. Most of its business was still confined to the eastern provinces of Prussia, however, and although the total value of the bonds it issued increased threefold between 1870 and 1900, after that date it no longer increased, probably because easier mortgage credit facilities were by then becoming available throughout the country.

The growth of rural co-operation throughout Europe depended on the work of two German pioneers. Hermann Schulze-Delitzsch developed the concept of a small co-operative group with unlimited liability whose members would act as creditors and guarantors to each other. He intended these small co-operative banks to be urban institutions but their usefulness as rural credit banks was unmistakable. They grew at first in the Prussian province of Saxony and by 1874 there were already 174 of them. But the crash of 1873 dealt them a bad blow; even with small funds unlimited liability was still dangerous and only after 1899 were they allowed to convert, if they wished, to limited liability. Their growth, however, seems to have taken place vigorously from 1890 onwards. The other and nobler figure is Friedrich Wilhelm Raiffeisen, mayor of a group of Rhineland villages in 1846, one of the worthiest and least celebrated heroes of nineteenth-century economic development. His career as a social reformer began with the acute rural distress of that year and after numerous experiments in self-help institutions for village communities he began to popularise after 1862 the concept of single-village co-operatives on similar financial lines to those of Schulze-Delitzsch. The social implications of Raiffeisen's work were altogether more profound for his institutions did not stop at the mere provision of cheaper credit. Each Raiffeisen co-operative bank, confined to one village, was seen as an instrument for the social regeneration of village life. The co-operative itself was run, not by a central organisation, but by the peasants themselves and on their joint initiative depended the elimination of private moneylenders, the acquisition of agricultural knowledge so that loans for improvement purposes could be properly assessed, and the coherence of the whole village as a social and economic community. Such banks became collective purchasers of ferti-liser and fodder and managers of wholesale warehouses, the centre of the village's economic existence. The Schulze-Delitzsch co-operatives remained largely financial institutions, not managed by the peasants themselves.

Both concepts were of enormous importance subsequently for the con-tinent as a whole, but Raiffeisen's basic principles began a more funda-mental reform in European rural society because they altered the peasant's ways of thinking. By 1913 there were 16,000 co-operative credit associa-tions of all kinds in Germany. The most numerous type was the co-opera-tive association of dairy farmers, using dairying machinery in common, but similar associations existed for almost every agricultural purpose. The Raiffeisen co-operatives were given financial backing in 1876 by the Agri-cultural Central Loan Bank created by Raiffeisen himself; by 1907 it had 5,000 village branches under its care.

Associated with these enormous improvements in the fabric of rural economic life was the development of agricultural education. Rural con-tinuation schools (Landliche Fortbildungsschulen) were started in the Rhineland in 1856 and by 1913 there were 3,500 of them established throughout the whole country providing an education in agricultural studies and in business methods. They were supplemented by 300 agricul-tural 'winter schools', in the slack season for agricultural employment, teaching adolescents between the ages of 15 and 20, and by the 50 Acker-bauschulen ('agricultural schools') for sons of peasant farmers who could study there for up to two years after leaving elementary school. Only in Denmark was so much education available to rural society. Indeed the differences in this respect across Europe in the late nineteenth century were flagrant and the consequences no less so. It was necessary, if agricultural productivity was to be improved, to improve the whole social framework of the peasant's existence. Here again the heritage of the eighteenth-century Enlightenment stood Germany in good stead, even though the education provided was only an emasculated version of what the eigh-teenth-century educational reformers would have wished. The influence of the Enlightenment was overlaid by a heavy romantic sentiment favouring the supposed virtues of a rural life which was fast being displaced. This yearning for the past, itself a result of the alarming rapidity with which German society changed, was in part responsible for the fact that between 1850 and 1870 the seeds of rural regeneration were being sown throughout Germany. That regeneration took the form of more responsible manage-ment of the agricultural enterprise, cheaper credit, and greater technical knowledge, to all of which the Raiffeisen banks made an immediate con-tribution.

Rural regeneration, however, stopped short of rationalising the pattern of landholding left over from the open field system. Although agriculture played an important role in the development of the German economy by comparison with others, if yields in Germany are compared to those in the Netherlands or Denmark the structural limitations to the further progress of agriculture become clear. Tariff policy exaggerated these problems by maintaining the great eastern estates through an export trade which was not only conducted at the expense of the rest of the community but offered no long-term future. Junker and peasant alike adapted to the changes brought about by rising urban incomes and better transport but in each case it was only an adaptation and by 1914 had exhausted all possibilities of improvement. What remained were still on the one hand large uncompetitive grain farms and on the other small, badly laid out peasant farms. Systematic rearrangement of the strips in the open fields to make contiguous land areas began in Prussia in 1872 but proceeded very slowly. Two-thirds of the farms in the Prussian Rhine province occupied only 26 per cent of the cultivated area; only 4 per cent of the farmers had more than 20 hectares of land. Holdings were frequently dispersed into ten or twenty separate strips of land. The cadastral maps could only be redrawn if a majority of the community requested it and before 1914 only a beginning to this enormous task had been made. The task still proceeds.

Further improvements in productivity on both estates and peasant farms would hardly have been possible as long as so many people were employed in agriculture. There, too, the tariff was an obstacle, narrowing the gap between agricultural incomes and industrial wages. Once the complicated social balance which the tariff was designed to preserve was destroyed after 1914 there began an avalanche of labour from the land and a spate of land sales. The problems shelved before 1914 were to have the gravest repercussions on the economy, and on political society, in the inter-war period.

GERMANY AND THE INTERNATIONAL ECONOMY

– International Trade

The increasing volume of industrial output resulted in the eruption of German exports into world markets. This arrival of a major new exporter only began to disturb the balance of these markets in the 1890s. In 1890 the total value of German exports was about 10 per cent higher than those of France; by 1911 it was over 60 per cent higher. At the same time the gap between the total value of German and of British exports began to narrow. Although sugar and coal were at different periods important exports, the increase in total exports was particularly due to the export of manufactured goods. Furthermore Germany's share in total world exports of manufactured goods rose between 1899 and 1913 faster than her share in the total world output of such goods. Between these two dates Germany not only overtook Britain's share in world production of manufactured goods but her ratio of exports to production rose while that of Britain and of France fell. Between 1891–2 and 1911–12 exports grew at an annual average rate of growth of 5·5 per cent, whereas in the two previous decades they had grown only at about 2·5 per cent. In the export boom of 1908–13 exports grew in value by 60 per cent; over half of their total was now manufactured goods.

It has been argued that Germany had the advantage of trading with areas where demand was growing more rapidly. The bulk of German trade remained with Europe, and the industrialisation of Austria-Hungary, Russia and Italy did stimulate a greater demand for German goods. More than three-quarters of all exports went to Europe but after 1900 the area to which exports seem to have been growing the fastest was South America. It has also been argued, with more plausibility, that the composition of German exports was better suited for growth in this period because they consisted of those goods for which world demand was growing fastest. If the growth of manufactured exports between 1889 and 1911 is considered, exports of textiles from Germany (the most valuable group in 1889) increased by only 35 per cent whereas exports of metal products and machines increased by 332 per cent and of chemicals by 181 per cent. These were the categories of goods in demand by industrialising economies. By 1913 over one-half of Germany's manufactured exports consisted of capital goods, a much higher proportion than in Britain.

Even here caution is necessary because although the economy followed the long-run pattern of all industrialising economies – with exports consisting increasingly of manufactures and imports of raw materials, whereas in 1870 manufactured goods and raw materials had been exported and imported in roughly equal proportions – the composition of exports and imports varied considerably over short periods. Foodstuffs were 28 per cent of exports in 1870–3 and only 9·8 per cent in 1910–13. But in the 1890s sugar was the leading export, over 6 per cent of the value of all exports. With the withdrawal of the export bounty under international agreements it fell to sixth place in the next decade. One traditional staple export, woollens, held its place consistently, still bringing in a greater return than machines in 1903. And if the real growth came from metal products and chemicals it came also from one raw material, coal, 2·8 per cent of all exports in 1878 and 4·3 per cent in 1903. Raw materials in fact did not shrink as a proportion of exports until after 1893 and were still 15·7 per cent of exports in 1910–13 compared to 19·7 per cent in 1870–3.

The implications of Germany's development on the international economy are considered later,[9] but the effect on the German economy itself was an important one. Since the setting up of the Zollverein German development had been seen as a problem of central Europe and of Germany's relations with neighbouring states. A different perspective was now opened up. The late acquisition of an overseas empire made almost no difference economically. But the spread of German business over the world and the great growth in shipping brought Germany into a series of direct confrontations with the older imperial powers, many of which, like those in Morocco and China, had important economic implications. If the export trade remained largely European, imports of raw materials came increasingly from outside Europe. German traders abroad were given active help by consular officials and, more importantly, by German banks abroad which usually extended much longer credit terms to purchasers than their British and French competitors. The German-Asiatic Bank was started in 1889, the German-South American Bank in 1906 and the Deutsche Orientbank in the same year, indications of the way in which the economic horizons of the country were widening.

– Foreign Investment

It is not yet possible to analyse German capital investment abroad in any detail, but it was in any case smaller than French foreign investment. An active demand for investment capital at home kept interest rates higher than in Paris for most of the period. French capital and investors were intricately involved in the development of the whole continent but the German role was restrained. Nonetheless foreign governments and entrepreneurs raised loans on the German stock exchanges; German firms attempted to beat tariffs by opening subsidiaries in other countries, and the search for raw materials led German capital into mines all over the world.

How much was involved we do not know. There is one estimate of doubtful reliability for 1884 which puts the value of foreign shares handled on the Berlin stock exchange alone up to that date at 11·4 million marks. Of this total 3·6 million marks is estimated to have been in railway shares (2·4 million in Austria-Hungary and just under one million in Russia). After the Franco-Russian alliance German capital flowed less to Russia but German banks continued to play a part in the syndicates which arranged the Russian loans. The director of the Berliner Handelsgesellschaft, Carl Fürstenberg, continued to pass as the leading financial authority on Russia, and many Russian bankers were of German descent. As investment in Russia was replaced by French investment in the nineties, the same process of German investment was repeated in Italy.

Compared to France, however, whose total foreign investment was much greater, a high proportion of German investment seems to have been in industry or direct investment by firms rather than participation in state loans. Again it is hard to be certain because the main area for investment was Austria-Hungary and the pattern of German investment there has been little explored. In Russia when the financing of railway building passed from German hands investment still flowed into industry. Hoechst opened the first dyestuffs factory in Moscow in 1885, to beat the tariff, and by 1890 there were four such works, mostly importing semi-manufactured products from Germany to be finished and sold in Russia. The Warsaw Steelworks Company was partly created by the Rheinische Stahlwerke and imported its pig iron from Germany. The Sosnowiec steelworks in

Siedlce in Russian Poland was founded by two German Silesian steel companies and imported its pig iron from Silesia. The Diskontogesellschaft and the Berliner Handelsgesellschaft financed the operations of the Swedish entrepreneur Alfred Nobel in the Caucasus. Chemical and electrical firms particularly drew on the support of German banks for their foreign ventures. In this case banks were eager to sustain the virtual monopolies in dyestuffs and certain kinds of electrical machinery which these firms had established and which had already induced the banks to provide finance so readily. In Austria-Hungary and Italy the electrical industries and the provision of current were particularly dependent on German capital. Almost all dyestuffs factories everywhere except in Switzerland were branches of German firms. Hoechst opened the first of these branches in Paris in 1881, soon followed by BASF near Lyons. The French branch of Bayer was founded in 1893. The best-known example of investment in raw material resources was the laborious and finally successful attempt by German steelworks to exploit the ore deposits of Arctic Sweden. But equally striking was the opening up of the Normandy orefields by Thyssen after 1907, and the development of Romanian oilfields by the Deutsche Bank.[10]

The total value of foreign investment held in Germany has been estimated to have reached 14,000 million marks in 1899, 16,000 million by 1905, and perhaps 30,000 million by 1913, of which about 20,000 million was in securities and about 10,000 in direct investment. It was smaller than the sum of French foreign investment even allowing for a large margin of error in these calculations in both countries. There is much work still to be done, however, before exact figures can be offered.

CONCLUSIONS

On the basis of Hoffmann's calculations net social product per capita in 1913 was about 818 marks.[11] This would make it slightly above gross national product per capita in France, which was about 760 marks. It was, however, distributed very unequally between the regions, as Table 7 shows. The main agricultural provinces of Prussia had the lowest per capita incomes, and per capita income in Posen and in East and West Prussia was more than 40 per cent lower than in the most industrialised areas, Brandenburg, the Rhineland and Westphalia, or than in the Kingdom of Saxony which had industrialised early. Orsagh shows that if a regional, rather than a provincial, analysis is made regional per capita income in the main agricultural region in 1913, the north-east, was only 59 per cent of the national average.[12] The north-west had a regional per capita income 117 per cent of the national average and the south-central region, including the developed areas of the Kingdom of Saxony, 142 per cent.

Unfortunately there are no directly comparable regional figures for France. But if the disparities in testamentary bequests later discussed[13] are considered it will be seen that they are of roughly the same dimensions as the differences in regional per capita income in Germany. Their origins are obviously also the same, lying in the failure of the process of national economic development to make substantial improvements in income in regions which remained essentially agricultural. How far these differences

Table 7 *Per capita income by provinces and states in Germany, 1913*

	Income per capita (marks)	% of labour force in agriculture (1907)
Prussia	747	30·8
East Prussia	486	58·2
West Prussia	480	54·0
Pomerania	576	48·5
Posen	465	57·9
Silesia	603	33·0
Berlin	1,254	0·4
Brandenburg	962	26·2
Saxony	700	29·1
Schleswig-Holstein	763	31·5
Hanover	697	38·8
Westphalia	735	19·2
Hesse-Nassau	899	28·7
Rhineprovince-Hohenzollern	832	19·0[1]
Kingdom of Saxony	897	n.a.
Württemberg	672	n.a.
Baden	710	n.a.
Bavaria	629	n.a.
Hamburg	1,313	n.a.

[1] Rhineprovince only

Source: K. Borchardt, 'Regionale Wachstumsdifferenzierung in Deutschland im 19 Jahrhundert unter besonderer Berücksichtigungen des West-Ost-Gefälles', in *Wirtschaft, Geschichte und Wirtschaftsgeschichte, Festschrift zum 65 Geburtstag von Friedrich Lütge* (Stuttgart, 1966).

were of long standing and how far they were the result of, or were exaggerated by, the local nature of nineteenth-century industrialisation is an unanswered question, but one of vital historical importance. The German evidence suggests, but certainly does not prove, that the disparities in regional per capita income were lessening after 1882 as the effects of development spread to the south and east of the country. Nevertheless these differences were still so great, and so perhaps were those in France, as to suggest that examples of extreme regional inequality which have been much studied in the twentieth century, such as the problem of southern Italy, were normal rather than exceptional in the nineteenth century and may even have been produced by the pattern of economic change in that century.

But this is too gloomy a note on which to conclude a study of fortunate and successful economic development. Wage rates were much lower in the east than in the west and this difference was reflected in real wages also. But the improvement in national real wages was unmistakable. The main cause of their improvement was the improvement in industrial productivity. The tariffs on food meant that these gains in productivity were less reflected in real wage improvements. But against this must be weighed the greater security of income throughout working life provided by the national system of social insurance. German money wages were lower than those in France and Britain and this, together with higher food prices than in Britain, was reflected in what seems to be a rather lower standard of consumption. Social insurance raised the cost of labour to the employer from the 1880s but even with these extra costs labour was probably still cheaper in Germany and this may have constituted a permanent advantage in the whole period. But it is impossible to contemplate the period after 1895 without being struck by the general national increase in welfare, to which only the improvements in Sweden are comparable.[14]

Seen in perspective the successful development of the German economy was the decisive phase in the development of the continent. By its geographical situation, by its close economic connections with the neighbouring economies, by the relative unimportance until the last two decades of its extra-European connections, Germany was the most European of the major economies. The centre of the continent had now achieved the same level of development as the western periphery. What was more, by its size and power the German economy now dominated intra-European exchanges. The view was already widely held by liberal economists in Germany that the European economy would have to be dominated by the national German economy if the German economy was to find its own domestic equilibrium and that this would mean that a new European economic structure would have to evolve. Conservative and nationalist circles took the view that this 'new economic order' guaranteeing Germany's economic and social equilibrium would have to be created by force. Few believed that the future nature of the German economy could now be determined without determining the nature of the economy of the whole continent. In our century this has proved to be so.

It was not, however, only the fact that the development of the German economy demanded fundamental political and economic adjustments by the other European powers which commanded the interest of contemporaries and still commands the interest of historians and economists. It was also that the events in Germany seemed to indicate more clearly than those elsewhere what the future nature of European capitalist society would be. Whereas in the early nineteenth century economists, statesmen and social reformers in the less developed countries in Europe sought for clues to the future of their own society by analysing that of Britain and France, by the end of the nineteenth century this interest had rightly become focused on Germany, for the development of the German economy was so rapid and sustained that it was now pointing out the future to both Britain and France. The locus of economic power and interest in Europe had shifted as decisively as it had during the sixteenth century.

A NOTE ON THE ECONOMIC DEVELOPMENT OF LUXEMBOURG

It might not at first seem worth commenting here on the transformation of one of Europe's smallest countries. In its general outlines it exemplifies once more the way in which a high level of demand in neighbouring countries and a fortunate raw material endowment could alter the whole course of history for smaller western European states. But the way in which the Luxembourg government seized its advantages provides an interesting contrast to the attitudes of governments in Spain at the same time. Furthermore, the important economic consequences flowing from the development of the minette iron ore field can only be fully understood in the context of Luxembourg's role in that development.

An infertile upland area of the Ardennes, Luxembourg was already a substantial iron producer in the Napoleonic period, supplying the arms manufacturers of Liège with their iron. But although pig iron production was between 13,000 and 14,000 tons annually in the first decade of the nineteenth century this did not sustain the population and a high proportion of Luxembourgers were migrant workers in Belgium and Germany. The break up of the Napoleonic empire and the imposition of the national tariffs which divided the area after 1816 produced the same acute problems as in Belgium.[15] The Zollverein tariffs were the lowest and this began a flow of trade from Luxembourg to Germany which was to be a dominant factor until 1914. In 1842 Luxembourg acceded to the Zollverein although it did not join the German Empire in 1871. Incorporation in the German market provided the basis for the later exploitation of the minette orefield in the Esch region, but it was not until the invention of the Gilchrist–Thomas process that this tiny country, still with only 260,000 inhabitants in 1910, could respond to the industrialisation of its neighbours. Until that time an old-fashioned iron industry smelting non-phosphoric ores with inadequate techniques struggled not very successfully against its Belgian and German competitors. The first use of the hot blast did not come until 1847 and coke smelting was not introduced until 1858. There were no railways until 1859. In the 1850s in fact Luxembourg had taken on the attributes of one of western Europe's most backward regions.

The railway brought a great improvement, reducing the price of transport at a time when the Rhineland iron makers were becoming alarmed at their rapidly diminishing supply of domestic iron ore. The Borbach works bought an iron ore mine in Luxembourg in the early 1860s. The major Luxembourg manufacturer, Société August Metz, which had introduced the coke smelting process there, could also now get cheaper coke from Germany. But it was the response of the Luxembourg government to this situation which set the pattern for the future and which is most interesting to note. A grand-ducal decree laid down that licences for the exploitation of iron ore mines could only be conceded to entrepreneurs who would manufacture the ore into pig iron in the country. The Borbach company was in fact forced to construct its own blast furnaces near Esch or sell out. By 1875 there were already 24 blast furnaces in the country. After the Gilchrist–Thomas patents, which gave Luxembourg's major reserves of minette ore a new European importance, the Council of State refused to alter these earlier laws. They laid down the policy in public in 1881:

'While ironmasters process ore into pig iron within the country itself and thus multiply in enormous proportions the amount of national employment and the sources of public wealth the merchants by contrast only exploit our mines with the simple aim of speculation on raw materials, intending them primarily for export. Evidently the former therefore deserve more protection and encouragement than the others and a very marked distinction between them is justified from the point of view of the country's own interest.'[16]

Such a policy must have required considerable determination in the 1880s and 1890s when the early avid interest in the technological possibilities of the Gilchrist–Thomas process was followed only sluggishly everywhere by the construction of iron and steel works on the minette orefield itself. What may have been the first Gilchrist–Thomas licence on the continent was taken up in 1879 by a Luxembourg firm, Forges d'Eich-Luxembourg. The first firm to make Thomas steel there, however, the Dudelange blast furnaces and forges, did not manufacture until 1886 and for a long time it was the sole example. Most production was of pig iron which was exported to steel manufacturers in the Rhineland and the Saarland. Total pig iron production in 1900, when there was still only one steelworks with an output of 185,000 tons, was only 970,000 tons. After 1900 things changed rapidly. The Differdange steelworks opened in that year, Rodange in 1908 and Belval in 1912. The consumption of minette ore rose from 368,000 tons in 1870 to 8·65 million tons in 1913. The output of Thomas steel on the orefield itself by 1913 was over half the output attained on the orefield by France and Germany respectively, as Table 8 indicates. There were additional quantities of steel made in the older metallurgical region away from the minette ore, so that by 1913 the per capita production of steel in Luxembourg was about sixteen times greater than in the nearest European rival, Belgium.

What this meant in real terms was that the country was virtually built on one raw material and one industry. It was only after 1895 that the population began to grow consistently and at the rates prevailing elsewhere in western Europe. In 1913 42 per cent of the total labour force in industry was employed in the metallurgical sector alone. The government did not alter its attitude to development. All the steel companies were required after 1898 to offer a fixed proportion of the basic slag which they produced at a low price to the government as an aid to agriculture. The total consumption of fertiliser in such a small country was of course very low, about one-twelfth of output, and there was plenty left over for the companies to export. It is only the different legal requirements which prevent us from

Table 8 *Output of Thomas steel on the minette orefield (000 tons)*

	France	Germany	Luxembourg
1895	248·8	190·7	134·5
1900	581·2	498·5	184·7
1905	1114·6	960·0	397·9
1910	1688·5	1160·9	598·3
1913	2298·7	2060·0	1182·2

Source: C. Prêcheur, *La Lorraine sidérurgique* (Paris, 1959), passim.

regarding Luxembourg merely as a region of the German economy, but these laws were of vital importance in determining what happened. The only western European government to take a similar stance was that of Norway. Where eastern European governments tried, their economic position was often too weak for them to succeed.

Yet the outcome in Luxembourg was inevitably to show that in spite of increasing production domestic demand in so small a state became ever more insignificant compared to the international influences. Over the period 1898–1913 about 70 per cent of all metallurgical production was exported to Germany and over 90 per cent of all pig iron production. In 1913 3·2 million tons of coke were imported, of which 2·95 million came from Germany. The capital which built up the industry came almost entirely from France, Belgium and Germany, the technical expertise from France and Germany. But most remarkable of all, 60 per cent of the labour force in mines and metallurgical industries was also foreign in 1913, about one-quarter being Italian and about 20 per cent German! In 1907 there were more Italians employed in these two sectors than Luxembourgers. It was perhaps hardly surprising that in spite of its legislation Luxembourg should have been a driving force in the movement towards European economic integration.

SUGGESTED READING

There is little published work on German economic history in English and not all of it can be recommended. Of general works there are only three which are reliable: the first-rate K. BORCHARDT, 'The Industrial Revolution in Germany 1700–1914', in *The Fontana Economic History of Europe*, vol. 4 (London, 1972), part I; D. S. LANDES, *The Unbound Prometheus* (Cambridge, 1969), a study of technological development; and P. HOHENBERG, *Chemicals in Western Europe 1850–1914* (Chicago, 1967). Among the more specialised studies the student is on safer, but less exciting, ground. J. RIESSER, *The Great German Banks and their Concentration in Connection with the Economic Development of Germany*, National Monetary Commission (Washington, DC, 1911), is a translation of the third edition of *Die deutschen Grossbanken und ihre Konzentration im Zusammenhang mit der Entwicklung der Gesamtwirtschaft in Deutschland* (Jena, 1910); it is out-of-date. I. LAMBI, *Free Trade and Protection in Germany, 1868–79*, Beiheft 44 of the *Vierteljahrschrift für Sozial- und Wirtschaftsgeschichte* (Wiesbaden, 1963), is fastidious but dull. N. J. G. POUNDS, *The Ruhr: A Study in Rural and Economic Geography* (London, 1952) is useful but slight; so is J. J. BEER, *The Emergence of the German Dye Industry*, Illinois Studies in the Social Sciences, vol. 44 (Urbana, 1959). There remain only statistical works: G. BRY, *Wages in Germany, 1871–1945* (Princeton, 1960); A. V. DESAI, *Real Wages in Germany 1871–1913* (Oxford, 1968); and E. H. PHELPS-BROWN, *A Century of Pay* (London, 1968). These refer back to a long history of interest in social questions in Germany exemplified by W. J. ASHLEY, *The Progress of the German Working Classes in the Last Quarter of a Century* (London, 1904).

For fuller interest it is often necessary to read more in what is usually called in Britain 'social history', for economic history has never really succeeded in emancipating itself in Germany from consideration within a diffuse social context. This often means that 'social history' is altogether more rigorously theoretical than in Britain but that the basic economic knowledge of the past on which it should be based is still lacking. As an example of a good and interesting contribution of this kind may be cited J. KOCKA, 'Family and Bureaucracy in German Industrial Management, 1850–1914: Siemens in Comparative Perspective', in *Business Historical Review*, vol. 45, 1971. This is a brief glimpse into the same author's *Unternehmensverwaltung und Angestelltenschaft am Beispiel Siemens, 1847 bis 1914. Zum Verhältnis von Kapitalismus und Bürokratie in der deutschen Industrialisierung* (Stuttgart, 1969). Unfortunately, other works of this kind often serve only as fashionable and inadequate substitutes for economic history.

There is, in fact, very little good economic history of Germany in this period even in German. And yet the basic statistical foundations have been better laid there than elsewhere by the indispensable W. G. HOFFMANN et al., *Das Wachstum der deutschen Wirtschaft seit der Mitte des 19. Jahrhunderts* (Berlin, 1965) and A. SPIETHOFF, *Die wirtschaftlichen Wechsellagen; Aufschwung, Krise, Stockung*, 2 vols (Tübingen, 1955). There are a number of general economic histories of which only two are worth considering: J. KUCZYNSKI, *Die Geschichte der Lage der Arbeiter unter dem Kapitalismus*, vols I–IV and VIII–XIV (Berlin, 1960–71), and F. W. HENNING, *Die Industrialisierung in Deutschland, 1800–1914* (Paderborn, 1973). The best guide to the literature is H. VON AUBIN and W. ZOM (eds), *Handbuch der deutschen Wirtschafts und Sozialgeschichte, Bd. 2, Das 19 und 20 Jahrhundert* (Stuttgart, 1976). On the few occasions where economic history has emancipated itself it has produced work of high quality and the student might read W. KÖLLMANN, 'Industrialisierung, Binnenwanderung und "Soziale Frage": zur Entstehungsgeschichte der deutschen Industriegrossstadt', in *Vierteljahrschrift für Sozial- und Wirtschaftsgeschichte*, vol. 49, 1959, or H. MOTTEK, 'Die Gründerkrise', in *Jahrbuch für Wirtschaftsgeschichte*, vol. 2 (1966). There are few modern studies of particular industries, extraordinarily enough in view of their interest not merely for Germany but for the world. One useful exception is E. BARTH, *Entwicklungslinien der deutschen Maschinenbauindustrie von 1870 bis 1914* (Berlin, 1973). The best works on agriculture are H. HAUSHOFER, *Die deutsche Landwirtschaft im technischen Zeitalter* (Stuttgart, 1972), and H. W. Graf FINCK VON FINCKENSTEIN, *Die Entwicklung der Landwirtschaft in Preussen und Deutschland 1800–1930* (München, 1960).

There is great scope for important and original research throughout the whole period. Current research and reviews of recent publications appear in *Jahrbücher für Nationalökonomie und Statistik, Jahrbuch für Wirtschaftsgeschichte* (published in the DDR), *Kyklos, Tradition, Vierteljahrschrift für Sozial- und Wirtschaftsgeschichte, Zeitschrift für die gesamte Staatswissenschaft* and *Zeitschrift für Wirtschafts- und Sozialwissenschaften* (formerly *Schmollers Jahrbuch*).

NOTES

1 A. S. Milward and S. B. Saul, *The Economic Development of Continental Europe 1780–1870* (London, 1973), pp. 365–431.
2 See below, pp. 320–1.
3 H. Mottek, 'Die Gründerkrise', in *Jahrbuch für Wirtschaftsgeschichte*, vol. 2, 1966; A. Spiethoff, *Die wirtschaftlichen Wechsellagen*, 2 vols (Tübingen, 1955).
4 See below, pp. 80–6.
5 See below, p. 83.
6 A. S. Milward and S. B. Saul, op. cit., p. 214.
7 He was knighted in Britain as Sir William Siemens.
8 A. S. Milward and S. B. Saul, op. cit., pp. 148–9.
9 See Chapter 9, passim.
10 German foreign investment is further discussed on pp. 492–503.
11 W. G. Hoffmann, *Das Wachstum der deutschen Wirtschaft seit der Mitte des 19. Jahrhunderts* (Berlin, 1965).
12 T. Orsagh, 'The Probable Geographical Distribution of German Income 1882–1963', in *Zeitschrift für die gesamte Staatswissenschaft*, vol. 124, 1968.
13 See below, pp. 130–2.
14 A. S. Milward and S. B. Saul, op. cit., pp. 499–502.
15 ibid., pp. 437–48.
16 C. Hemmer, *L'Economie du Grand-Duché de Luxembourg*, vol. 2 (Luxembourg, 1953), p. 37.

Chapter 2

The Economic Development
of France, 1870–1914

THE OVERALL PATTERN

Superficially the French economy in this period appears to have followed
the same pattern of growth as it had experienced in the years prior to 1870.
The national product increased, the shares of industry and agriculture in
that product continued to shift in favour of industry, and the proportion
of the active labour force employed in agriculture and forestry fell from
about 53 per cent in 1870 to 37·4 per cent in 1913. The productivity of
labour continued to rise but rose more slowly in agriculture. This increase
in productivity when combined with falling food prices after 1873 produced a rise in real wages which was only retarded by a reversal of the
downward trend in food prices after 1896. Probably because the improvements in productivity were greater in manufacturing industry than agriculture the rise in real wages was greater in the industrial sector and this laid

the basis for a growing migration of the rural population to the towns. With the overall growth in the economy went also an increase in trade. The per capita value of exports and imports more than doubled over the period. This continuation of the process of economic development was accompanied by a growth in the volume of French capital invested outside France, fed by the continuing process of capital accumulation and the high rate of saving in France. The Paris money market continued to be the main source of foreign capital for the rest of the continent. Not only the economic but also the cultural influence of France over the continent remained strong. Furthermore France acquired a huge world empire and laid the foundations of a similar economic and cultural predominance over large parts of Africa.

But in reality the path of economic growth in France after 1870 was very different from what might have been forecast on the basis of the previous two decades' experience. In the light of what we now know about the capacity even of developed economies to sustain a high rate of economic growth over a long period of time and when compared to the growth and development of other major economies in the same period, the growth of the French economy after 1870 seems a faltering process; so faltering, in fact, that it is sometimes discussed simply in terms of the question: 'What went wrong?' Such a question is not really appropriate because there is certainly no more basis for assuming a 'normal' path of development for economies which have already passed the first stages of development than there is for assuming a set of norms for the beginnings of economic development. But in the period 1870–1913 France was overtaken as a producer by both Germany and the United States and the process of closing the gap between French and British output and income levels which had begun between 1850 and 1870 was arrested, so that by 1913 the relative economic position of the two countries was little altered.

To a certain extent France's relative position was bound to be affected by the fact that both Germany and the United States were better provided with labour and raw materials, for both were larger and more populous countries. And this difference was exaggerated by the fact that in France the net increase of population in this period was insignificant when compared to population growth in other states. Although German output of pig iron, which in 1870 was roughly comparable to that of France, was well over twice the French output by 1890, and although by 1896 even the consumption of raw cotton in Germany had not only passed but doubled the consumption of France, when these figures are expressed on a per capita basis the comparison is much less disadvantageous to France. After 1871 the value of German foreign trade surpassed that of France and so after 1878 did that of the United States, but the per capita value of French exports kept pace with that of all the other major trading powers. To some extent, therefore, what seems a relative decline in France's position may partly have been the result of the constant stream of labour and raw material inputs into the German and United States economies. The net increase in population in France between 1871 and 1911 was only 3·5 million, an increase of less than 10 per cent, whereas the German population in the same period increased by more than 50 per cent. The average annual rate of growth of total output per capita in France after 1870 was very close to the combined average of that of all the other developed European economies.

An examination of the short-term changes in the rate of growth of national income in France after 1870 shows in fact no correlation with the demographic movements over the period. The gross product of industry more than doubled between 1870 and 1914. The increase in gross agricultural product was much less, and over the whole period the annual rate of growth of the combined gross product of agriculture and industry was lower than in the period 1815–70. Until the later part of the period we know little about movements in the service sector of the economy. Between 1870 and 1896 the growth rate of industrial production did not exceed an average of 1·6 per cent per year, which was a marked slowing down compared to the high growth rates after 1830. Moreover, the value of agricultural output in the seventies and eighties remained virtually unchanged; indeed the statistical evidence available suggests that in the 1880s the French economy may not actually have been growing at all. In the mid-1890s there was a decisive upward movement in industrial production and the annual average rate of growth of industrial product between 1896 and 1913 rose to 2·4 per cent. The rate of growth of agricultural product was still much slower but it also showed a distinct improvement, growing now at an average rate of over one per cent annually. Gross national product over the same period grew at 1·8 per cent annually.

The picture, therefore, is one of an economy in which the process of growth was retarded after 1870 and only recommenced after 1896 with the same vigour as in the earlier period. One major influence in arresting the process of growth was the two decades of stagnation in the agricultural sector. Such a stagnation had a powerful effect in an economy where even in 1896 43·4 per cent of the active labour force was still employed in this sector. This was by no means just a problem of growth rates; it was a problem of economic development in the fullest sense, and the relationship of agriculture to the rest of the economy raised urgent questions of general significance about the nature of continuing economic development in a developed economy, questions which were not confined to the French economy alone but were common to all continental Europe. Only in Britain, among the major developed economies, did the agricultural sector diminish in importance in this period to the point where it became relatively insignificant in the performance of the economy as a whole. Elsewhere industrialisation, and the more rapid growth of productivity in industry than agriculture, created acute social and institutional problems, and the lower rate of growth in the agricultural sector became both cause and symptom of a deep-seated economic and political malaise.

But it would be wrong to ascribe these fluctuations in the rate of growth of the national product solely to the behaviour of the agricultural sector. It is clear also that there were important differences in the behaviour of the industrial sector over the whole period which were independent of what was happening in agriculture. It would not be unfair to characterise French industry between 1870 and the mid-1890s as falling behind those of other developed economies not merely in terms of total output but, more significantly, in terms of productivity and techniques. After 1890 the picture is different and in some of the more modern industries, especially in the manufacture of cars, France became a technological leader and a powerful exporter on world markets. The revival of the economy in the last two decades of the period was an industrial revival not to be explained by the better performance of agriculture. On the other hand the earlier stagnation of the agricultural sector had a powerful influence on slowing down the rate of growth of industrial output. All general explanations of the comparative 'slowness' of growth have therefore to be looked at sceptically, not only because no criterion can be derived from history to say how fast an economy should grow but also because the short-term fluctuations in the growth rates of industry and agriculture were so marked as to suggest that particular explanations more limited in time and scope must be an important part of the true explanation. General arguments that the French economy was short of labour or capital or entrepreneurial talent cannot make much sense for the whole period. Within the overall pattern of growth of the economy throughout the period a variety of special circumstances, some of them deriving from the new international framework of economic development, had their particular impact on France and created a unique pattern of growth and development. Many of the explanations are still unclear and are still the subject of detailed research, some of which indeed may soon modify the conclusions set out here. This is particularly the case where research may change the statistical basis of some of the calculations, such as those on the volume of foreign investment, which we have been obliged to use. It is unlikely, however, that the picture of significant fluctuations in the rate of growth in this period will be modified. Rather is it likely that the industrial recovery in France after 1896 will come to be seen as one important aspect of a simultaneous spurt of industrialisation over the continent as a whole comparable in scope and importance to that which occurred in the 1850s.

One other important event may well have been underestimated in its effects on the overall pattern of development: the invasion and defeat of France by the German forces in 1870 and the peace treaty which followed. The financial indemnity which France had to pay proved no great penalty; indeed the mechanism of international payments through which it was paid stimulated exports. But the annexation of Alsace and part of Lorraine by Germany proved a heavy blow. Not only did it effect an important transfer of raw materials, especially iron ore, from France to Germany; it also transferred to Germany the most advanced sector of the French cotton industry and one of the most modern and developed provinces of the country. More than this, the symbolism of the German capture of Paris could hardly be missed; it marked, with an extraordinary timing and emphasis, the arrival of another great European power. For France it proved a psychologically shattering interruption of the course of history the effects of which cast a deep and gloomy shadow over the beginning of the period after 1870. The rapid development of the German economy and the bitterly suspicious political relations between the two countries after that date did nothing to dispel this shadow.

THE DEVELOPMENT OF INDUSTRY

A detailed examination of the growth rates and relative importance of the different industries reveals something more of the nature of development in this period. In terms of output the textile and clothing industries and the metal producing and processing industries continued to dominate the industrial sector until 1914 and their fortunes still directly affected its general development. But they were no longer quite as predominant as in the period before 1870. The early revolution in the modes of industrial production had particularly affected the textile and metal industries. But one aspect of industrialisation in the later nineteenth century was the growing complexity of the industrial structure and of the interrelationship between industries. Another was the extent to which the greater demand resulting from increasing wealth shifted services and industries which had hitherto changed little on to a much higher level of organisation and production. A striking example of this is the transformation in the scope of postal services. The number of letters handled by the letter post in France increased from 64 million (an average of about two letters per inhabitant) in 1830 to 358 million (about nine per inhabitant) in 1869 and to 1,541 million (about 38·5 per inhabitant) in 1910. The average annual number of passengers carried by rail was 101 million between 1865 and 1874; between 1905 and 1913 it was 479 million. In a similar and related fashion the growth of output of a small industry, already well-established in the eighteenth century, paper manufacturing, reflected the same trends. The average annual consumption of paper between 1803 and 1812 was 14,000 tons, in 1855–64 110,000 tons and in 1905–13 650,000 tons. After 1875 an increasing part of this consumption had to be met by imports but the average annual domestic output in the period 1905–13 reached 245,000 tons.

The continuing process of industrialisation could not take place without a continuing shift from a circumscribed market of high-income consumers to something approaching a mass market. This was the path of transition which the cotton industry had begun to travel in the late eighteenth century and along which it was followed by other consumer goods industries in the nineteenth century. The important changes in the mode of production therefore spread, although in the case of some industries only gradually, throughout the industrial economy to enable producers to cope with these higher levels of output. The changes were less noticeable than they had been earlier in the cotton industry, but by 1913 many consumer goods industries were making a substantial contribution to gross industrial product. This is true, for example, of the leather industry about whose history little is yet known. The net annual domestic consumption of treated hides rose from about 25,500 tons in 1820 to about 77,000 tons in 1871, reaching about 140,000 tons in 1913. As in the case of the paper industry, an industry already well-established in the eighteenth century was transformed in scope and size and its traditional organisation gradually altered. Foodstuff and drink industries changed in the same way. Such industries were particularly susceptible to marginal improvements in purchasing power. The annual output of beer doubled from about 7 million hectolitres in 1871 to over 14 million hectolitres in 1913, whereas the size of the population drinking it increased by only one-fourteenth.

In several of the industries involved in these great increases of output the essential organisational changes had in fact taken place before 1870, but it will be readily seen that the diffusion of mass-productive methods after 1870 was a vital aspect of the development of the economy. As this diffusion continued it is less easy to single out a particular field such as cotton or railways as of primary importance for the behaviour of the

Table 9 *Average annual rate of growth of output of certain industries in France* (%)

Period	Iron and Steel	Coal	Cotton[1]
1830–60	4·26	4·94	4·63
1860–92	2·58	3·24	1·52
1892–1913	4·01	2·04	1·92

[1] Based on consumption of raw cotton

Source: T. J. Markovitch, 'L'industrie française de 1789 à 1964. Conclusions générales', in *Cahiers de l'Institut de Science Economique Appliquée*, série AF, 7, no. 179, 1966, p. 139.

economy as a whole. The complexity is increased by the fact that industries became much more interdependent. The increased output of the paper industry depended on changes in wood processing industries both in France and elsewhere and on developments in the chemical industry, and like all industries involved in production on such a scale it also depended on developments in the engineering industry.

The average annual growth rate of production of those industries which had been most significant in the industrial revolution seems to indicate that they did not maintain their dynamism after 1870, although the iron and steel industry saw a revival in the period following 1892 (see Table 9). If the span of measurement is reduced still further the period 1875–84 to 1885–94 appears as the only one when the metal processing industries did not make the most significant contribution to the growth of gross industrial product. Other industries had markedly higher rates of growth of product which were sometimes sustained, as in the case of the rubber industry, for periods of up to twenty years but the value of their production was very much smaller. Such cases were usually new industries based on techno-logical innovation where the early period of growth was very rapid. In fact the increased rate of economic growth in the last two decades was partly attributable to the establishment of new and dynamic industries of this type. Such industries had an importance greater than their statistical weight in the national product because of their technological characteristics and their significance for the future. The product of the electrical industry grew between 1895–1904 and 1905–13 at an annual average rate of 14·5 per cent. In the same period the growth rate of the metal processing industries was sustained by what was virtually a new industry with great economic implications, the manufacture of cars. In the period before 1914

Table 10   *Movement in annual indices of French industrial production, 1873–1913 (1913 = 100)*

	1873	1881	1889	1895	1906
Mining	38·9	45·0	58·4	65·0	78·6
Primary metallurgy	28·6	38·3	33·2	36·2	63·4
Metal working	30·1	41·6	37·5	46·2	70·8
Chemicals	22·0	23·0	28·0	38·0	80·0
Food industries (including tobacco and matches)	50·3	57·4	78·7	73·2	94·2
Textile industries	57·1	72·3	75·3	75·6	87·1
Mechanical industries[1]	18·0	26·3	24·0	30·7	40·3

[1] The entry for mechanical industries is based on employment not on output

Source: F. Crouzet, 'Un indice de la production industrielle française au dix-neuvième siècle', in *Annales*, vol. XXV, 1970.

France was the largest manufacturer of cars outside the United States. Nevertheless, the continued growth of industry in the whole period was fundamentally and mainly dependent on the continued growth of those industries already established before 1870.

Annual indices of French industrial production reveal very clearly the turning point in the 1890s. Table 10 shows in almost every case a marked upward movement after 1895 amounting in some cases to an increase in production of almost 200 per cent between that date and 1913. The picture of the 1880s which emerges is more complicated, some industries showing stagnation and others, such as the food processing industries, showing a notable progress of output. The textile industries after continuing their expansion in the 1870s entered a long period of stagnation which must also have played a part in the general failure of the economy to grow in that period.

A further characteristic of the increase in industrial growth after 1895 is the way in which this was based on capital goods industries. This can be seen from Table 11. Investment in capital equipment and machinery, which was normally about 30 per cent of total capital formation, rose to 45 per cent between 1896 and 1900. This increase in production of capital goods led in its turn to an increase in exports. Exports grew at an average rate of 3 per cent annually after 1896 while production grew at only 2 per cent. After 1907 a continual increase in armaments expenditure also stimulated the output of capital goods, but it did not sustain the growth rate of the previous decade.

The development of hydro-electric power and the internal combustion engine contributed to a sharp increase after 1890 in the use of mechanical power, in which an increased use of steam engines also played its part. The

Table 11 *Average annual rate of growth per decade of output of consumer goods and capital goods industries, 1865–74 to 1905–13*

Period	% growth rate in consumer goods industries	% growth rate in capital goods industries
1865–74	2·0	0·9
1875–84	1·6	1·6
1885–94	1·8	1·2
1895–1904	1·2	3·0
1905–13	1·9	2·0

Source: T. J. Markovitch, 'L'industrie française de 1789 à 1964. Conclusions générales', in *Cahiers de l'Institut de Science Economique Appliquée*, série AF, 7, no. 179, 1966, p. 284.

total horse-power of steam engines in use in industry rose from 863,000 in 1890 to 1,441,000 in 1898. In spite of a series of innovations in hydro-electricity the development of better methods of electric power transmission stimulated the use of steam engines to make the power. By 1913 the generation of electrical current had become the biggest user of steam power. Even in industries such as textiles where the use of mechanical power had been long established the increase in the utilisation of power was conspicuous after 1890. In the textile and clothing industry total installed steam power rose from about 173,000 horse-power in 1890 to 408,000 horse-power by 1900. The total steam engine capacity in all industry grew at an annual average rate of 8·7 per cent in the period 1896–1901, at 4 per cent in 1901–6 and at 6·3 per cent in 1906–13. The main industries using electrical power were those branches of the metallurgical and chemical industries which developed rapidly after 1890 and where electrical current was often an integral part of the manufacturing process.

This increase in the use of machinery and power was also conducive to improvements in the productivity of labour which helped in the continued growth of the economy. The average annual growth rate of output per person employed in the industrial sector of the economy was 1·7 per cent between 1896 and 1913. In certain industries whose contribution to the national product was large, such as leather and woodworking, labour productivity improved at a much slower rate. In the textile industry, which had earlier been in the forefront of such improvements, labour productivity now improved only at about the national average rate. Table 12 shows that the total increase in labour productivity was very strongly influenced by a few industries, such as electricity, chemicals, engineering and metallurgy. All these were industries in which there were major technological innovations, many of which originated in France itself.

Table 12 *Increase in production per man-hour in certain sectors of French industry, 1896–1913 (1896 = 100)*

Sector	1913
Constructional materials	141
Solid mineral fuels, gas	107
Metallurgical industries	182
Mechanical and electrical industries	164
Chemicals	175
Textiles, clothing and leather	132
All industry	140

Source: J. J. Carré, P. Dubois and E. Malinvaud, *La Croissance française* (Paris, 1972), p. 134.

– Textile Industries

The textile industries, which had been the leading sector of French industry and a dynamic force in the economy before 1870, had a chequered experience after that date. This was the more serious in that the textile and clothing industries were still the biggest employers of labour in 1913. There is a lack of good studies on this important subject which might permit more exact comparisons to be made, but evidence points to the conclusion that the most important branch, the cotton industry, was particularly affected by two things. One was the loss of Alsace to Germany which weakened the industry's ability to compete internationally; the other was the stagnation of the economy in the 1880s which slowed down the sale of products on the domestic market to which it was now more confined. After 1873 the silk industry was adversely affected by its inability to reduce the costs of its products and did not begin to recover until the 1880s. Consumer goods sales were most susceptible to a general reduction of demand throughout the economy. Marczewski's calculations suggest that total demand fell between 1875 and 1894 whereas it grew by 19 per cent between 1905 and 1913.[1] Such a calculation remains only hypothetical and of course the fall in agricultural incomes due to lower food prices after 1873 meant more money available for clothing in other sectors of the population. Nor does the timing of these hypothetical shifts in demand coincide exactly with the pattern of developments throughout the industry. The silk industry experienced an investment boom in the 1880s when the other textile industries and the economy in general were depressed. But generally the weakness of the textile industries before the mid-1890s was related to the unsatisfactory conditions of slow growth in the economy as a whole. The deviations from this pattern were closely related to sudden shifts in fashion and occasionally to technological innovations which reduced costs.

Cotton remained by far the most important sector. In 1906 there were 7·5 million cotton spindles, 2·7 million wool spindles and 577,000 linen spindles, but developments in manufacturing mixed fabrics make such figures of less value than for the earlier period. The calculations for woollen spindles do not include doubling spindles, and if these are added the total would amount to 3 million spindles of which about 2 million were primarily engaged in spinning worsted. An index of per capita textile consumption in which consumption in 1801 is expressed as 100 shows the consumption of linen and hempen cloth in 1901 still at 100. Cottons by contrast are at 1,400, woollens at 316 and silks at 266.

Consumption of raw cotton was 146,000 tons in 1890 and 346,000 tons in 1912, of which 80 per cent came from the United States. After 1870 the other textile industries also became increasingly dependent on imports. The growth of the woollen industry was based on imports of raw wool from Australia, Argentina and Uruguay and the stock of sheep in France diminished throughout the period. The culture of flax in France practically died out and the linen industry depended on supply from Russia. A similar shift was made by the silk industry. In the earlier period Lyons had been the centre for the distribution of Mediterranean silk and Lombardy and Venetia had maintained a steady trade in raw and floss silk with French manufacturers. At the same time the domestic harvest of silk cocoons had grown steadily until in 1853 it reached a record level of 26,000 tons, about half of domestic consumption. Silkworm cultivation had spread throughout south-eastern France in response to rising demand, and the quality of the raw material produced now equalled that of Italy. But the process was brought to an abrupt halt by the silkworm disease, *pébrine*. By 1865 the cocoon harvest was only 4,000 tons. The onset of *pébrine* coincided with the opening of Japan to western trade and the increase in Europe's trade with China. Competition from both these countries proved so effective that the restoration of the French silkworm stock by eggs imported from Japan and the success of Pasteur in identifying and eliminating *pébrine* did not restore the French harvest to its former size. It seldom surpassed 10,000 tons while the output of cloth continued to grow. After 1885 Asian raw material was in fact more appropriate to consumers' demand than the more expensive and better quality European product and this helped distant imports to overcome the protective measures that were imposed. After 1900 the growth of silk spinning in Japan made that country the major supplier of both raw and floss silk.

These high levels of raw material imports sustained an equally high level of textile exports which maintained their relative importance in French trade. Silks remained the most valuable export because of their high cost, and cottons the biggest export by weight. About three-quarters of cotton exports, however, were to French colonial markets, especially Algeria, under the protection of French import duties. This major and growing French export was unable to gain a foothold in competitive markets whereas before 1870 it had been able to hold its own. Woollens and silks by contrast continued to be sold in highly competitive markets, silks to the United Kingdom and the United States and woollens to the United Kingdom, Germany, Belgium and the United States. The greater part of the French cotton industry had never succeeded in following the lead of Alsace in producing the higher-quality fabrics which would liberate it from the threat of British international competition, and after 1871 the Alsatian cotton industry was lost. Woollen manufacturers retained the markets in which they had established themselves before 1850. Silk manufacturers had more wavering fortunes to which they were particularly susceptible because of their high dependence on exports. The development of a silk industry in the United States in the late 1880s cut into one of the two largest markets for French silks: by 1898 almost three-quarters of American silk consumption was domestically produced, with the result that the proportion of French production consumed on the domestic market reached its highest level in the nineteenth century, 50 per cent. The growth of output to 1914 depended on searching out new markets in Europe, often through re-exports by way of Britain, a process helped by the change of fashion back to silken cloth so that by the end of our period the proportion of exports to total output had again risen to two-thirds.

The 1906 industrial census shows the textile industry as still the largest industrial employer other than the clothing industry, which was still heavily dependent on domestic labour. The growing use of steam power localised this employment increasingly on the coalfields, especially in the department of Nord. Cotton spinning employed 47,700, of whom 18,600 were in Nord, and weaving, which was more widespread, employed 118,000. Of the 21,400 employed in linen spinning 19,500 were in Nord and of the 66,000 in linen weaving 34,000 were in that one department. The most remarkable example of this localisation was the growth of the town of Roubaix after 1852 and the heavy concentration of the woollen industry there. Three-quarters of the 10,600 employed in wool combing were in the Nord, most of them in Roubaix itself, and so were half of the 30,300 in

Table 13 Increase in apparent raw cotton consumption in certain countries, 1870–1914[1]
(% increase over previous quinquennium)

	France	Germany	Britain	Belgium	Austria-Hungary	Russia	Italy
1870–4	–9·4	26·1	32·9	38·7	45·8	37·7	180·6
1875–9	18·6	55·0	1·6	–2·9	19·0	49·5	8·5
1880–4	13·7	23·8	19·3	25·7	33·0	39·0	129·9
1885–9	7·1	23·7	1·1	–24·4	9·7	18·0	32·9
1890–4	35·2	26·7	7·9	63·5	30·5	10·1	32·0
1895–1900	7·8	20·2	6·8	6·4	16·2	38·4	18·2
1900–4	13·6	21·1	–4·9	23·9	13·0	22·6	18·0
1905–9	21·8	24·6	16·8	35·3	26·6	–12·7	35·0

[1] The figures for France, Germany and Austria-Hungary are net imports, for Belgium and Italy special imports (i.e. imports intended for domestic consumption), and for Britain actual consumption

Source: Derived from B. Mitchell, European Historical Statistics, 1750–1970 (London, 1975).

wool spinning and the 121,000 in wool weaving. The silk industry, however, did not conform to this pattern. It burst the bounds of the old city of Lyons and the process of mechanisation of weaving took the industry to rural areas in the valleys of the Rhône, Loire and Saône. In this case the use of electric power impelled the weaving sector of the industry to find new sites. The peace treaty of 1871 also encouraged a geographical shift. Some Alsatian manufacturers did not willingly accept the situation and transferred their operations to the western flanks of the Vosges. Two towns, Epinal and St Dié, became the main targets of their immigration: both were already weaving and printing centres and served as an attraction for new spinning enterprises. The population of Epinal grew more than three-fold between 1870 and 1900.

But in spite of this migration Normandy had now more than half the total cotton spindles. It also had a higher proportion of hand looms to mechanical looms than Alsace and wove from its own coarser yarns. The most-favoured-nation clauses of the trading treaties permitted British and Belgian cottons to enter at low tariffs and it was the better quality goods which did so. Shorn of Alsace the French industry became confined to coarser goods and this confined exports to protected colonial markets.

The number of spindles did not reach its level of 1867 again until after 1900. The net consumption of cotton, however, increased more rapidly. If a comparison between France and other major cotton cloth producers is made in Table 13 several interesting points emerge, although the table must be used with care. The industries of the less developed economies were still very small in 1870–4, those of France and Britain very large, and this accounts for the generally lower average level of percentage increase of raw cotton consumption in the more developed economies. There is also no necessary strict correlation between net cotton imports, which is what the table mainly indicates, and cotton consumption; cotton could be and was stored for long periods. But the erratic course of the cotton industries in France, Britain and Belgium is in striking contrast to the consistency with which the German industry grew. In this respect the greatest difference between the French and German industries can be seen in the 1870s immediately after the German annexation of Alsace. In fact the catastrophic impact of this event on the French cotton industry appears even more starkly from the table. The high percentage increases in cotton consumption in the table for all countries except France arise from the fact that the previous period had been that of the 'cotton famine' caused by the American Civil War. France was deprived of the opportunity to recover from that event: there alone cotton consumption continued to fall. The period 1875–9 saw the beginnings of a genuine recovery, but it was stopped short by the sluggish growth of the 1880s. And in spite of the spurt of growth in 1890–4 the industry never regained the ground it had lost.

But the fact that consumption of cotton rose much faster than the number of spindles, which in 1892 was almost the same as in 1877, suggests a considerable degree of technical progress in this period. It is again difficult to know how technical progress was apportioned in the periods before and after 1896. The average speed of a cotton spindle in France increased from 7,000 revolutions a minute in 1876 to 9,000 in 1910 and this coincided with an increase in the number of spindles tended by each worker. Average output per spindle seems to have increased more in the period after 1896 than before. On the weaving side of the industry the speed of operation of mechanical looms also increased by about 30 per cent between 1872 and 1910. Here the major improvements certainly came after 1900 with the introduction on a larger scale of Northrop automatic looms which completely changed the ratio between workers and looms: one worker instead of tending between two and three looms might now tend fifty.

Another type of improvement in efficiency came from integration of the different processes in textile manufacture within single large firms and this was particularly evident in the woollen industry. Concentration of capital was evident on the spinning side of the cotton industry where the number of separate firms declined by 50 per cent. But the larger woollen firms took this process much further and covered the whole range of economic activity from importing the raw material to organising the retail sales of the final product. This type of integration was easier because most textile firms continued to be financed through close family networks which functioned also as regional business hierarchies. Even where firms were not legally integrated they were often joined by complicated networks of local family marriages because the textile industries were so concentrated regionally.

There are no figures for the growth of the woollen industry before 1885. After that date it grew slowly to 1899 but then stagnated until 1914. When the demand for silks in the 1870s was sluggish, especially after the disappearance of the crinoline, fashion had favoured the woollen industry, especially the higher quality woollen fabrics. The development of wool and cotton mixtures and the rapid growth of the worsted industry in Roubaix both belong to this period. But the heavy woollen industry suffered by comparison and the older woollen towns of Elbeuf, Evreux and Sedan declined in importance; there were few power looms in Elbeuf before the 1880s. They suffered also from the new competition of southern woollen towns like Mazamet which took up the manufacture of shoddy. In the later part of the period fashion swung in favour of mixtures of silk and other fabrics and the stagnation of the woollen industry contrasted with the recovery of the silk industry. This recovery was delayed by the fact that the making of mixed fabrics met with sterner resistance than in the wool industry. The long international pre-eminence of the French silk industry had been based on excellent workmanship and a product of the highest quality. Previous changes of fashion had not altered these fundamentals. But the underlying reason for the crisis of the 1870s was that the high price of silks was preventing expansion into the mass markets reached by cotton and wool, and was restricting the industry's growth. One cause of the high price was that the silk industry had remained much more dependent on artisanal skills than the other textile industries and this had caused it to remain organised in small-scale units. In order to reach a mass market the industry needed both a new technology and a cheaper product.

Mechanical looms for silk were first successfully developed in Switzerland in the 1870s. Before 1878 French manufacturers showed little interest but in that year began so rapid a transformation that by its end there were already 10,000 such looms at work in France. The speed and scope of this change were much faster than that experienced in the other textile industries. Silk now had to copy the pattern of large weaving sheds established by the other industries and this meant the abandonment of the Lyons garrets. Of the 33,400 mechanical looms in 1899 only 2,380 were in the city of Lyons. The change to mechanical weaving furthered the adoption of new cloths because the new looms themselves permitted cheaper types of silken cloth to be made. Raw silk could now be used as a warp without further treatment and this encouraged manufacturers to weave with yarn that was already dyed and to cut their prices accordingly in an attempt to broaden their market. After 1875 there was also a great increase in the use of silk yarn made from those discontinuous threads from the cocoon which could not be turned into the long continuous thread of floss silk. This former semi-waste material, *filés de schappe*, needed more initial capital to spin than floss silk because it also needed carding and combing and its use led to the establishment of much larger enterprises. The material itself, however, was cheaper. By 1894 *filés de schappe* accounted for about a fifth of the total yarn used in spinning. The use of such waste materials foreshadowed the development after 1884 of 'artificial' silk. The basic raw material of this was cellulose; but production was still very small in 1913. These changes in the manufacturing process all led to a higher output of cheaper products. But that part of the market which was concerned with high-quality goods was not lost. In the making of higher price goods the hand loom could still effectively compete by turning out a unique product and this accounts for the survival of 17,000 hand looms in 1914. Nevertheless there were already twice as many mechanical looms at work in the silk industry in France in 1900 as in the United States, the second largest producer.

– Iron and Steel

The first two mass-productive methods of steel manufacture, the Bessemer converter and the Siemens–Martin furnace, had early been adopted in France. The Gilchrist–Thomas process, by permitting the use of phosphoric ores, then made most of France's ample iron ore reserves available after 1878 for the cheapest methods of steel production. Cheap iron ore compensated for dear coal. But it was some time before these advantages were fully seized. After 1884 the demand for steel dropped, perhaps because of the sudden contraction in one of the main markets, rail, and it was another decade before the industry regained its rhythm of growth of the 1870s.

The arrival of the railway as a dynamic force in the economy in the 1840s had initiated a great expansion in the iron industry and the connection remained close and important. Railways were a source of regular, high-quality orders and provided a stimulus for economies of scale, in themselves a force for innovation. Throughout the century railway orders were always more than 10 per cent of total output in metal industries, reaching their peak of importance between 1855 and 1864. Until 1868 the trend of investment in railways had been constantly upwards; after 1870 the trend, although less marked, was downwards with occasional short upward movements as in the rapid expansion of 1880–5. But the downward turn in investment after 1868 did not affect orders to the iron and steel industry because the new steelmaking processes encouraged the replacement of iron rail by steel rail. The average annual production of rail between 1854 and 1872 was 177,000 tons, between 1873 and 1885 316,000 tons: this level of output in 1884 was not again achieved for twenty years. Railway construction was increased between 1880 and 1884 by the so-called Freycinet Plan, and the lack of profitability of much of the investment under this plan's auspices subsequently deterred investors and entrepreneurs. Another cause was the much greater durability of steel rail which drastically reduced the rate at which track needed to be replaced. After 1884, therefore, iron and steel manufacturers had to find new markets, in their case a particularly serious problem as the technological developments in steel manufacture all necessitated increases in the size of plant and in the cost of equipment.

These new markets were eventually found in constructional engineering, in armour-plate and armaments and in car parts, but the transition was a painful and lengthy one; the market for car parts was very small before 1900. It was made more painful by the relatively small size of French rail exports, notwithstanding that so much foreign investment went ultimately to finance railway construction. The quantities were determined by the international rail cartel and the French industry was too small for its export quotas to be improved. Before 1902 the annual quantity of rail exports never exceeded 20,000 tons; after 1902 the annual average weight of exports was 64,000 tons. Even this was significantly less than the quantity of rail exported from Belgium and far smaller than German rail exports. Whereas between 1872 and 1885 rail accounted for 69 per cent of the total weight of finished steel products, after 1895 it accounted for only 20 per cent.

The new steelmaking processes altered the balance of raw material costs in the industry. Some of the larger, older iron works, whose product was more costly because of the transport involved either of ore or coke, were unable to cope economically with the higher levels of input which Bessemer converters demanded. Production at Alès and Decazeville was run down after 1870. By contrast favourably situated works were able to convert successfully. The iron works in the Loire valley had the most suitable site and it was there that the Bessemer and Siemens–Martin processes became the foundation of steelmaking. The Fourchambault works installed two Bessemer plants in 1862 and 1868 and Commentry went over to Bessemer production in 1870. The Firminy works installed Siemens–Martin hearths in 1869. At Le Creusot the Bessemer process was installed in 1864, but it required some of the ore to be imported from Algeria.

But the greatest reserves of iron ore in France still remained virtually untapped in 1870. Starting on the west bank of the Moselle south of Nancy and reappearing at intervals along the course of the river and broadening westwards, the minette orefield stretched as far as the frontiers of Luxembourg and beyond, and after the peace treaty of 1871 beyond the new frontier of Germany. The iron content of the ore was low, between 30 and 40 per cent, but it was cheap to mine. It required only the removal of a shallow subsoil and in some areas, where river valleys had cut into the plateau, it could even be quarried. It was also cheap to use, requiring only a low fuel consumption in the smelting process and often being self-fluxing. Lorraine developed what was in effect a new steel industry in France, more akin to that in Germany, specialising in basic steel made by the Gilchrist–Thomas process.

For products other than rail steel was at first accepted only reluctantly, and this held back the development of the new process. Only in 1894 did steel output exceed that of puddled iron, later than in Britain or Germany. Pig iron output had risen to 1·7 million tons by 1880; by 1890 it was only 1·9 million tons, and thereafter it rose again reaching 4 million tons in 1910. The increase in steel manufacture in the 1880s was even slighter. Steel output, which had reached 1·3 million tons in 1880, was only 1·4 million tons in 1890. By 1910 it was 2·8 million tons and in the years 1910–13 it averaged 4·0 million tons. By that time only a third of the steel made was open-hearth steel; the bulk of the industry was accounted for by cheaper basic steel made in converters.

One of the biggest French companies, de Wendel, which found itself on the German side of the frontier after 1871, acquired the rights of the Gilchrist–Thomas process almost immediately on its invention and for what seems to have been an extraordinary low price. This act of enterprise gave a new impetus to the firm. Not only did de Wendel become one of the first firms to develop the new technique in Germany, but in 1879 they founded a related company to share the process in France with Henri Schneider, owner of the Le Creusot works. The two firms participated in a new steel works at Longwy, built virtually on the border of Luxembourg. The firms who had made the initial change to steel manufacture but who were ill-placed for minette ore specialised increasingly in higher-grade steels. The Le Creusot works specialised in one buoyant market for steel, armour-plate. For this they needed admixtures of other steels and a wide variety of engineering subsidiaries. They became, together with Krupp, one of a small and select band of western European firms whose main business was the private manufacture of armaments on an immense scale, for anyone who would buy them. By the end of the century they had their own gun factories at Le Havre and their own shipbuilding yards. The Holzer works at St Etienne specialised in car parts and high tensile steel.

The hold of the de Wendel companies over the Gilchrist–Thomas patents kept the process out of public domain until 1895; it became generally available as demand for basic steel increased. After 1895 France shared fully with Germany and Luxembourg in the remarkable expansion of steel manufacture on the minette orefield itself and the close association of all the firms involved, together with the fact that the new frontier was not regarded in France as permanent, had important consequences for the future of the European steel industry; it was the first step towards the formation of the European Coal and Steel Community. From 1895 French output of Thomas steel on the minette orefield rose from 249,000 tons to 2·3 million tons in 1913. Cheap ore still left French ironmasters with the problem of dear coal. Increasingly they sought control over reserves of coking coal elsewhere, particularly in the still expanding Ruhr coalfield. The Friedrich Heinrich AG, for example, was almost entirely financed by French capital and its purpose was to open new mining concessions in the Ruhr to supply French steelworks at Micheville and Pont-à-Mousson. The Longwy steelworks ceded half its rights in its iron ore sources to the German steel manufacturer, Röchling, in return for a smaller stake in a German coal company. Right up to 1914 pig iron was still transported from Lorraine to the Nord to be processed where coal was cheaper. On the whole the price of French steel seems to have been higher than German and this militated against French exports. These came mainly from the older works in the Loire area which produced the more highly specialised products. Only in armaments and in special alloys could France compete on world markets, and the increase in Thomas steel production in Germany was much greater, because costs were lower and exports higher.

– *Mining*

In spite of the increasing volume of industrial production French industry remained until 1914 heavily dependent on imported coal. This situation, unique among the larger developed economies, has always posed the question how far this particular deficiency in raw material supply slowed down the growth of industrial production. The question has never received an entirely convincing answer. The output of French coal rose from 17 million tons in 1875 to 28 million in 1895 and to 40·8 million by 1913. It received a strong impulse from the north-westward expansion of mining activities on the northern coalfield into the department of Pas de Calais, but it never sufficed to keep pace with consumption. Throughout the period imports were always between a quarter and a third of total consumption. When the expansion of mining in Pas de Calais was at its most vigorous between 1885 and 1890 the proportion of imports in total coal consumption was at its lowest. But with the increase in industrial output after 1895 the proportion of imports once again assumed its previous level.

The only accurate information on national coal prices comes after the formation of the cartel in 1901 covering most producers on the northern coalfield. It does suggest, however, that the price of coal was on average much lower in the departments where the northern and central coalfields were situated than elsewhere. Since the cartel's policy was to raise prices there in order to lower them in other areas where there was greater foreign competition there can be little doubt that many areas of France, in spite of the wide availability of imported coal, were at a disadvantage because most technological developments, including those in electrical power, depended on coal for energy until 1914. But this was common to all developing European economies and it does not necessarily mean that the development of the national economy was held back by the higher cost of fuel in certain regions. It is interesting that when coal mining was extended into Pas de Calais the new coalfield did not become a focus for other industries in the way that the older areas of the coalfield in Nord had for textiles and metallurgy. It remained for a long time an area dominated by modern coal mines in an agricultural setting with little other employment. Although a higher national average price of coal between 1870 and 1914 may have exercised at times a discouraging effect on French economic development compared to that of Germany it is hard to see it as a fundamental cause of the differences in the economic history of the two countries and it was clearly not an insurmountable obstacle.

Coal imports from Belgium no longer showed an upward trend after 1866, and after 1883, when they stood at 5·7 million tons, began to decline: from 60 per cent of total imports in 1866 they fell to only 20 per cent in 1913. One reason was the opening up of the Pas de Calais mines. Belgian imports had always been chiefly to the north where the zonal tariffs had favoured them, and as Belgian mines got older and deeper they could not compete with new and more productive French mines. Furthermore Belgium was itself becoming a coal-importing country. As imports from Belgium ceased to rise imports from Britain increased. Seaborne coal from Britain sold throughout western and north-western France and even at some points in the Mediterranean. Between 1866 and 1870 imports from Britain were 26 per cent of total imports and 9 per cent of total consumption; by 1911–13 when they stood at 12 million tons, they were 49 per cent of all imports and 18 per cent of consumption. At the end of the century imports from Germany began to compete in areas near to the German border, especially in the rapidly developing metallurgical areas of Lorraine. After 1901 they increased more rapidly than imports from Britain: France imported 2 million tons from Germany in 1900 and 6·8 million tons in 1913, more than a quarter of all imports.

The most rapid increase in output in the Pas de Calais coalfield came between 1885 and 1897. Its origins were a feverish burst of prospecting started by the high price of coal between 1871 and 1873. Later a more systematic exploitation by local financial groups built on these discoveries and the rise in output after 1885 was so marked that by 1890 output was greater than in the older parts of the coalfield in Nord. The result was a growing preponderance of the northern coalfield in total French coal output; though responsible for only 39 per cent of national output in 1875, between 1885 and 1890 it reached 50 per cent and by 1910 accounted for two-thirds of all the coal mined in France. There were no comparable discoveries on the older central coalfields. Only in the last decade did explorations begin on the deep western extension of the Saar coalfield into French Lorraine.

The productivity of the mines was dominated by geological conditions. Most coal was won by hard manual labour and expansion of mining required a large labour force. It may well have been the demand by the coal mines for labour that discouraged firms from clustering around the pit-head in Pas de Calais as they had done in an earlier period in Nord. Output per worker per day in Nord reached its peak in 1889; thereafter the increase in coal output was achieved only by greater inputs of less productive labour and by 1910 output per worker was more than 20 per cent below its level of 1890. In Pas de Calais labour productivity improved until 1899 but after that date it too shared in the common European decline. It remained, however, more than 10 per cent above the national average.

The important developments in the steel and electrical industries after the mid-1890s provided new and growing markets for coal. This for the first time brought significant changes in the financial structure of the mining companies. The opening up of the Pas de Calais coalfield had been the work of regional capital and local banks and there remained few connections between the coal companies and other firms. Between 1899 and 1904 the iron and steel producers began an active exploration of the coalfield in the hope of extending it further; at the same time they began to form financial links with the coal companies. Their motive was to reduce the price of their fuel supply: the increased demand had produced a sharp rise in coal prices and the mining companies had cashed in on this by the formation of a regional cartel, L'Entente des Houillères du Nord et du Pas de Calais, in 1901. The agreed policy was to raise coal prices in the mining regions in order to reduce them to the level of import prices in the border areas where imported coal undercut French coal. No doubt the attempts by the metallurgical companies to integrate their raw material supply were also a response to the cartel. At the same time mining companies began to invest in local electricity companies in order to create secure markets for their output. Associated with these developments was the raising of capital from the major Paris banks and on the Paris stock exchange and growing interconnections between banks, coal mines, metallurgical companies and companies supplying electric current.[2]

In Lorraine, the growth of the Thomas steel industry in Europe promoted a remarkable iron ore mining boom after 1900. Before that date there were two main areas for the mining of minette ores in France, around Nancy and in the Longwy area. The Longwy field was developed more rapidly but its development, which was closely tied to domestic steel production, was hesitant. The increased demand in France and Europe after 1900 led to the opening up of a new area of mining, around Briey, where an average of almost 5 million tons a year was mined between 1901 and 1914. Using a high proportion of immigrant labour from Belgium, Italy and Poland the companies exploited the low cost of mining to the utmost. Rhineland steelmakers began to use ores from French Lorraine in 1897 and by 1912 they represented 15 per cent of Rhineland consumption; between 1908 and 1913 ore exports to Germany increased threefold. Of the total French iron ore output of 22 million tons in 1913, 10 million were exported. The biggest part of the export traffic was that from Briey to Germany but the older regions of Nancy and Longwy also exported in growing quantities to Germany and Belgium. Even as late as 1900 in a rich economy which had been developing for so long it was still possible for a mining boom reminiscent of the gold rush to occur; western Europe's raw material resources were far from exhausted.

– The Chemical Industry

It was in Germany that the more sophisticated aspects of organic chemistry came to transform the industry; in France the industry retained a more traditional aspect. Nevertheless in some ways it too became a new industry after 1870 and a much more important one. Its importance is not to be judged by its relatively small contribution to the national product nor by the low level of employment it provided but rather by the significance of the techniques and knowledge which it represented for many other areas of the industrial economy. In all techniques except those of synthesis the French chemical industry appears to have kept pace with those of its rivals. By 1908 it was also responsible for 2·4 per cent of exports. In the traditional products of soda and sulphuric acid and the products associated with them in the new Solvay process the industry made a steady quantitative advance. The first Solvay plant was set up in 1873 on the salt deposits at Dombasle in Meurthe-et-Moselle. The installation of the Dombasle plant was in fact delayed until the state salt duty which had survived with little modification from the eighteenth century had been waived. The amount of soda produced by the Leblanc process did not increase after 1873 and after 1880 fell rapidly so that by 1883 output by the Solvay process was already one-half the total. In the 1890s, however, the fall was less rapid, although by this time over 80 per cent of total soda output was made by the Solvay process. The total output of soda grew from 73,000 tons in 1878 to 519,000 tons in 1913 and after 1900 it was growing faster than world production. Sulphuric acid production increased from 200,000 tons in 1878 to 850,000 tons in 1913. The basis of sulphuric acid production after 1880 was the metal ore, pyrites. Faced with increasing difficulties in obtaining sulphur from Sicily the St Gobain works developed this new process based on its own pyrites mines. Domestic mining of pyrites increased until 1897 but then stagnated as imported pyrites became cheaper. One of the main uses of sulphuric acid came to be the manufacture of superphosphate. There was a large domestic market for artificial fertilizers and substantial reserves of phosphates in France but the quantity mined reached its peak in 1900 and by 1910 was far smaller than imports from North Africa. Throughout the period the production of sulphuric acid became increasingly tied to this one market of overwhelming importance: about 2 million tons of superphosphate were made in 1913. The same market was responsible for the introduction of other chemical fertilizers; ammonium sulphate production using coal gas was established on the northern coalfield before 1900, although output remained small, and the manufacture of cyanamide began in two separate places in 1907.

In these cases the French chemical industry was reasonably well supplied with its own domestic raw material resources. But it is the very nature of the chemical industry to overcome deficiencies of resources and the problems of the substitution of one material for another were those with which its technology grappled in this period. In this respect the French industry was less successful than its competitors and French firms sometimes seem to have shunned the technical effort involved in translating scientific knowledge into practical production. They were unable to match the sustained mixture of research and production for a new market which drove the German chemical industry into new types of production. The basis of these new types of production was the synthesis of artificial dyestuffs from which eventually evolved a range of new products. In themselves these goods were less valuable than the industry's traditional output, but their significance for economic development was more weighty. By 1914 only about 11 per cent of the synthetic dyestuffs consumed in France were produced there, the rest were imported from Germany or Switzerland; and of the synthetic dyestuff factories only one, the Compagnie des Matières Colorantes de St Denis, was French, the rest were German-owned works set up to add the final stages to production inside France so that the foreign parent company's exports had to pay only the lower tariff on semi-manufactured goods.

This could certainly not be explained by a poor domestic market. Indeed a country like France with many high-quality textile exports had a very favourable market and the natural dyestuffs industry in France was a thriving one. In the early stages of research into synthetic dyes the Lyons manufacturers had been very active and in 1863 had founded a company, La Fuchsine, to exploit one of the first discoveries. While the company spent its time trying to defend its rights in the process German companies improved on their technology, discovered other processes and, even more importantly, began to manufacture their discoveries. The assets of the company were eventually bought by Poirrier and Dalsace who founded the St Denis company and it was they alone who pursued the same path as the German firms, devoting large amounts of time and money to research. Poirrier invented the dye known as Paris violet and manufactured it; the French chemist Roussin discovered the first colour derivatives of naphthaline in 1875, and Vidal produced the first colours from sulphur in 1896. The St Denis firm also competed for the latest German patents; it invested heavily in 1881 in the most commercially successful of all the dyes, alizarin. On the other hand the dyes known as *oranges Poirrier*, originally made at St Denis from Roussin's discoveries, were manufactured after 1890 in Germany on a larger scale and exported to France more cheaply than the French product.

The weakness of the French chemical industry in this field was its inability to turn a stream of invention and initiative into the regular large-scale production of a commodity in great demand. What was needed was not the ability to make single innovative discoveries but an adequate supply of trained research workers and engineers who could be integrated into the structure of the firm, and a determination by the firm to make the technical effort to manufacture a risky product. For the first time continuous research into production processes became an integral part of that process itself and thus of the structure of the firm. The French educational system may have failed to produce at the right moment sufficient numbers of properly trained research chemists to sustain such an industry in a competitive position: the teaching of chemistry as a separate research science with its own scholarly discipline was less well established in France than in Germany. The first attempt at the regular laboratory training of chemists was not made until 1882 when the School of Physics and Industrial Chemistry was opened by the City of Paris, and the first attempt in a university was only made at, understandably enough, Lyons, in 1883.

But the experience of the St Denis company hardly suggests that there was a deficiency of innovation and research in France. The problems were more on the production side and may have been due more to the small and undercapitalised nature of French chemical firms. The total nominal capital of the forty biggest chemical firms amounted to less than 600 million francs. The biggest, St Gobain, had only 60 million francs, and Péchiney 17 million. Chemical synthesis demanded a long period of research before success and in Germany, where the firms were much more capitalised, this required complicated trust and cartel arrangements between the firms and their financial backers. In France the chemical firms rarely sought the help of bankers for new ventures. Why the firms should have remained smaller is not so easy to see. The older dyestuffs technology was of course better established in France than Germany and there was a reluctance at first to see artificial dyes as anything more than a temporary invention. This hesitancy might have combined with a reluctance of the firms to involve themselves in a new process requiring big investment. This in its turn might have kept the French industry at a disadvantage in most of the modern developments which followed hard on the initial dyestuffs discoveries.

– *Electricity and Electro-metallurgy*

The electrical engineering, electro-metallurgical and electro-chemical industries were still very small in 1913. There were only about 25,000 workers in electrical industries and the total capital invested was scarcely more than 300 million francs. But the use of electric current changed the possibilities of many industries, laid the basis of new industries and had a powerful industrialising impact on one region in particular.

Although the problems of short-distance transmission of current were solved by 1882 and the telephone system had begun in Paris three years previously, electro-technical industries did not begin on any scale until 1888. Before that the main business was generation and transmission and the engineering market was restricted. The Société Alsacienne de Constructions Mécaniques, a Belfort firm, was the pioneer in dynamos and motors, often manufacturing under licence from the German firm Siemens. Several American companies also manufactured in France and one of them, Thomson-Houston, employed over 1,250 people in 1907. But French firms also moved into the new market. Bréguet, founded as a machine tool firm in 1883, passed through the stage of manufacturing telephone and telegraph equipment to making large electrical machinery in a new works at Douai. Of the total output of electrical engineering works in 1914 55 per cent was represented by dynamos, lighting equipment and lamps. The market had now become lighting and urban transport. The first electric tramways came in 1893 and the electrification of the suburban railways in Paris began in 1903. A valuable subsidiary market was lighting on ships and cars; about 4,000 were employed in 1913 in the manufacture of accumulators and batteries.

These developments mainly relied on steam to generate the power. The development of hydro-electric power was of greater economic importance for France because it changed certain fundamental economic circumstances. The high price of coal over most of the country and the consequent high cost of power had been a constant factor in nineteenth-century French history. But with hydro-electricity the situation was reversed; in the Alpine and Pyrenean valleys water power was relatively cheap. After Hérault had patented the electrolytic process for aluminium manufacture in 1888 a range of further processes based on electrolysis were developed. All used huge quantities of electric current and the chief determinant of the commercial feasibility of the process and also of its location was the cheapness of water power to manufacture the current. Only one-third of the installed hydro-electric capacity in 1910 was used for lighting and power, 44 per cent was used in metallurgical works and 13 per cent in chemical works. In the early stages these works were situated at the foot of high mountain waterfalls; later they moved further down the valleys. The consequence was a sudden industrialisation of some of the remotest parts of Alpine France. In Savoy the railway route from Paris to Turin up the valleys of the Arc and the Maurienne was a preferred site; so were the valleys of the Durance and the Isère. The firms making the industrial plant concentrated after 1902 on the town of Grenoble which gave access to these upland areas.

Hérault's invention did not give France any significant advantage in aluminium production for a similar process was patented in the same year in the United States. But in this as in many of the other electro-metallurgical processes French industry was a technological leader. To some extent France was favoured in aluminium production by its rich deposits of the raw material, bauxite. By 1913, when 300,000 tons were mined, France was the world's biggest ore producer and exporter; exports in fact accounted for about half the total output. The mines were quite independent of the industry and indeed were in some cases financed by foreign capital. After 1908, when the French producers left the international cartel, output of aluminium passed that of Germany and by 1913 was 22 per cent of world output. Only the United States was a bigger producer. It seems that French producers could produce at a lower price, and the high and rapidly growing productivity enabled them continually to reduce that price.

Chlorine and sodium as well as chlorates and perchlorates were made by electrolysis in Savoy before 1894. Ballier began to make acetylene commercially in 1894 and followed this by making cyanamide and ammonia. The manufacture of hydrogen and oxygen by electrolysis began at Clavaux in Isère in 1907 and it was a scientist from the same factory who made the Castner sodium patents into a commercial process in France. Hérault himself added a different process, but one equally dependent on a cheap source of electric power, when he devised the electric arc furnace for steel manufacture in 1900. The constant improvement of the plant in the first works at La Praz in Savoy not only improved productivity but made France also the main exporter of electric arc equipment. It needed 1,670 kilowatts of current per hour to produce a ton of electro-steel at La Praz in 1902; in 1908 under the same conditions it needed only 800. Of the 160 electric arc furnaces installed in the world by 1914 83 had been manufactured in the French Alps.

Some part of this success has to be ascribed to France's natural advantages, but there was in addition a strong current of enthusiasm and enterprise. In this sector French industrialists displayed the resolution required to master the technical difficulties of production which was so conspicuously lacking in the chemical industry. They were faced with daunting obstacles in the locations of their works, which were often built away from all facilities, even roads: the Girod electro-steel works at Ugine had to build 168 apartments for its workforce between 1903 and 1914, a situation like that of some late eighteenth-century firms. The workforce had to be drawn from everywhere to these inhospitable spots; all the factories had a high proportion of Swiss, German and British technicians. The entrepreneurs in the early period were the inventors themselves. Capital from the Paris financial institutions was unavailable and what was raised came usually from Lyons or Switzerland when it was not local in origin. Even the inventors were reminiscent of the practical technicians of the industrial revolution; very few had had a formal technical education.

– Engineering and Motor Cars

The increase in activity of the engineering industries after 1892, which was certainly one of the most important aspects of the faster growth of the economy after that date, can only be partly explained by the development of electrical power. The growing complexity of the industrial structure and the trend towards larger and more standardised production were all responsible for a far greater diversity of activity in the engineering industry and it was on this industry above all others that the development of other industries after 1870 depended. To trace all these developments would be tedious and the main tendencies have already been analysed for Germany.[3] But it is noteworthy that in this case the French industrial economy had no difficulties in shifting to a more complex and demanding stage of industrial production.

The salient features of this development can be shown by the history of one important type of production, the manufacture of the motor car. The development of the automobile was the culmination of several separate technical developments in engineering and its early history is associated with a large number of inventors and entrepreneurs in many countries. Otto and Benz, the two German engineers usually credited with its invention, each had close connections with French engineering firms such as Panhard and Peugeot which were to be associated with the early development of the car in France. In spite of the many different sources of invention and development in Europe the French car manufacturing industry established an early predominance which it had not relinquished by 1914 when French car output, about 45,000 vehicles, was the largest in Europe including Britain. Indeed it was only after 1900 that the massive American car output, associated particularly with the production innovations of Ford, began to surpass that of France. The success of this industry in France can be explained by a variety of separate advantages which the French economy possessed.

In the first place was the long tradition of practical engineering. The car was pre-eminently an engineer's product in its early stages when it was undergoing numerous and often radical improvements and changes, and for this form of inspired tinkering previous French industrial history had made good provision.[4] It was in this early period that the French industry assumed its technological lead over its competitors. Panhard and Levassor, the most important of the pioneering firms, were tool makers and Peugeot, the largest manufacturers, were bicycle makers; Darracq, the first firm to rationalise production on standardised models, was also a bicycle manufacturing company. Panhard had been one of the earliest firms to take a licence to manufacture the Deutz gas engine in 1875 and ten years later the manufacture of cars was undertaken in the same way: in 1902 the firm made 1,000 cars. A high proportion of the machine tools needed was imported from the United States, amounting to about three-quarters of those in the Panhard and Levassor factory in 1908, but otherwise the car made demands which could be met domestically. At the outset most manufacturers were assemblers of parts and buyers of engines. A large manufacturer like Peugeot made his own engines and even ball-bearings by 1895 but this was unusual. Forges which could take up car body production were essential; for some firms, like Lemoine at Ivry, this soon became the main focus of activity in spite of the relatively small annual output of cars. There was also a need from the start for firms to make the numerous vital small components: the Zénith firm in Lyons quickly came to dominate the European market for carburettors. This tradition of engineering kept France for some time the centre of technological innovation even when American output became much greater. The development of modern lighting and steering systems both took place in France after 1900. But the most important technical advance of the French car industry was the increase in the number of cylinders: the first V8 engine was produced in 1907 by the firm of De Dion Bouton.

In the second place France benefited from its excellent road system. It is interesting to note that social overhead capital of this kind could still be of fundamental importance for development even in the late nineteenth century, although completely disregarded during the railway boom of the mid-nineteenth century. Not only was the road network extensive but the rural roads were better surfaced than elsewhere. In most countries cars were for a long time confined for all practical purposes to the vicinity of towns, but long country journeys were possible in France from the start; they were indeed a potent way of advertising and selling the car. It is in this light that the third French advantage, the nature of the market, should be considered. Even by 1914 most cars were still luxury products. Although Peugeot produced a relatively high proportion of small two-seater vehicles, their price before 1914 never fell below 4,250 francs, which would have made big inroads into a substantial middle-class income. The number of people likely to buy a car was therefore still very restricted and studies have shown that there were two main markets. The first was the world of wealth and fashion. Paris was still the European centre of that world, and the centre for the retail trade in luxury products. In that sense the car fitted well into the structure of French exports which had always tended to be of high-value products. Throughout the period the world of wealth came to Paris to buy its cars, so that even by 1900 the car had beccme an important French export. In the period 1902–5 about one-third of French cars were exported to Britain. The second market was the rural middle class who needed cars for leisure or professional purposes and could manage to afford one. Doctors and country gentlemen were important purchasers of the smaller models; in Germany this group of consumers still found the horse cheaper.

Finally, the car fitted very easily into the structure of French business and manufacturing. Firms with few exceptions were small and there was no tendency to concentration before 1914; most producers grew through ploughing back their profits, often very large, into the firm. There were exceptions like Peugeot whose rapid growth was based on raising new capital almost every other year. About 10 per cent of the cars were made by firms in which foreign capital held a majority interest and in 1913 the Ford company began to assemble cars in Bordeaux. But in these early days of the industry it was dominated by inventors and entrepreneurs, and shifting combinations of small firms, which could operate more or less anywhere and sought to exploit small technical and commercial improvements. Even a large firm like Peugeot grew to size well away from the main markets. One reason for their comparative freedom from outside capital was that with the demand for early cars it was customary for the purchaser on ordering one to leave one-third of the final price with the manufacturer. Between them the small firms retained a very large share of the market. The only other producer on Peugeot's scale was Louis Renault, a latecomer to the scene who began business in one shed in Billancourt in 1898. In the period from June 1910 to June 1914 Renault's production averaged 4,811 cars a year, which would have represented 12·6 per cent of the market in 1910 and 10·7 per cent in 1913. Peugeot had only a slightly larger share.

Too much cannot be made of the home market, however. By 1901 exports of cars were already one-third the value of production. The most important market was Britain, where by 1914 a greater number of cars were registered than in France; but all the surrounding countries except Belgium, which had a well-developed car industry of its own, were big importers of French cars. In 1912 the value of car exports was 3 per cent of total French exports. The French industry was shielded by the high transport cost of American cars, and when Ford began to produce their simplified models in Europe French exports began to feel the pinch. French car firms followed their example and established branches abroad to circumvent tariffs. The Darracq works, opened in Milan in 1906, were the origin of the subsequent Alfa-Romeo works. Lorraine-Dietrich went virtually bankrupt in 1908 through manufacturing in Britain and Italy. Renault began to build and equip two factories in Russia in 1913. Foreign demand for French cars came from a higher income group than domestic demand and played a significant part in preventing the standardisation of models, by encouraging French producers to make higher-cost cars which had of necessity to be produced in smaller numbers by workshop methods. Renault made a brief attempt to circumvent this by specialising in taxi production: about half the motor taxis in London in 1913 had been made by Renault. But after 1908 the number of models manufactured by Renault increased again and in spite of much interest in work-study and 'Taylorism' his factories at Billancourt still looked in 1914 more like a series of gigantic workshops than like Henry Ford's assembly lines. This was equally true of Peugeot whose total output in 1913 was about 5,000 cars, although the 80,000 bicycles made by the same firm in 1914 were standardised products turned out on assembly lines.

The multiplier effect of car manufacture before 1914 was much less than that of the railway earlier because the initial investment was much smaller, but its effects in stimulating technological change were still strong. In particular it offered a market to the new rubber and aluminium industries. The development of a serviceable pneumatic tire by the Michelin company at Clermont-Ferrand created one of the biggest French manufacturing concerns from very small beginnings in less than a decade: in 1913 rubber exports, of which three-quarters were tires, had reached half the value of car exports. The car meant only a marginal increase in the market for steel producers, for whom armour-plate was more important in those years. But in the production of special high-quality steels and alloys the car was an important stimulus. One firm, Jacob Holzer of St Etienne, found what was almost its sole market in the constantly rising demand for such products. Furthermore the techniques developed in the car industry gave birth to the aircraft industry and the advantages of being a technological leader in a new industry emerged very clearly in this case. By 1913 France had also become the biggest producer and exporter of aircraft, manufacturing in that year 2,240 engines and 1,148 airframes.

– Domestic Industries

The emphasis on increases in production and productivity and the suitability of the factory for achieving these increases did not mean that the trend towards factory production inherent in the development of the economy was an unbroken process that had completely triumphed by 1913. On the contrary, by the close of the period domestic production was still a major source of employment. Although, for example, production which could fairly be described as factory production existed in most branches of the clothing industry by mid-century, it still employed one million domestic workers in 1896, 789,000 of them in the fashion and tailoring branches and 220,000 in shoe manufacture. Many economic factors favoured domestic production in industries of this kind. The domestic worker could compete because of far lower overhead costs, a factor which also stimulated the entrepreneur to use such labour. In addition domestic labour was usually not organised in unions and not subject to factory legislation. The Factory Act of 1900 which established a factory inspectorate caused a perceptible movement away from factory production towards domestic production. Where an industry was susceptible to sudden and violent fluctuations of demand, such as the dictates of fashion produced in the clothing industry, changes in output could more easily be managed by shifting the burden on to domestic labour; in factory production the capital costs of the plant would have to be borne in any overproduction crisis. Many firms combined factory and domestic production precisely for this reason.

It should be added also that technological innovation, although its general tendency was towards greater division of labour and factory production, did not always discourage domestic labour. The sewing machine could be used to exploit cheap labour in the home. In the knitwear industry also, although the hosiery looms of the 1860s encouraged factory development, the most popular, the Paget loom, could still be used domestically, if only in single units. The introduction of the Cotton loom in 1880, a much faster machine, might have swayed the issue decisively to factory production, but its invention coincided with the development of the knitting machine. The knitting machine was as cheap as the sewing machine and easily used by a housewife. In these circumstances the factors favouring domestic production still operated strongly, and domestic knitting developed as a 'sweated' industry with very low reward for the workers throughout entire quarters of Paris. The capital for the machine was provided by the retailers of the finished product, or in some cases the machine was lent free of charge, and the raw materials, as in the eighteenth-century rural textile industries, were provided and distributed by the entrepreneur. Only after 1890 with the introduction of the Consolidated loom did the shift towards factory production take a decisive turn.

In this example and in the case of the sewing machine – the basic implement of the 141,000 domestic workers making lingerie in 1896 – the fact that technological innovation might occasionally favour decentralisation of production, did not override the long-run factors favouring the factory. Of these the division of labour was the obvious one. But one which is often overlooked is the demand of the market for uniformity of product and quality. This demand made itself felt in the middle-price ranges of a product. In men's clothing for example it was middle-price goods that were made in factories. Uniformity of quality was not important in the cheapest goods and hand sewing was actually required for the more expensive articles. An increase of output in the middle range needed certain constant labour skills which were soon exhausted in the available domestic labour force. The factory also had the advantage of a closer supervision of labour, and it also produced cleaner goods. At some stage in production in most branches of the clothing industry in this period the gains in labour productivity achieved in the factory overcame the higher initial costs and the higher capital and labour costs involved, although in making the decision for factory production the entrepreneur was frequently influenced by combinations of the secondary factors involved. The lateness with which this decision was made, however, meant that domestic industry was still an important employer of labour in 1914.

– Conclusion

Although closer study of French industries tends to confirm the macro-economic evidence of a great spurt of industrialisation in the 1890s, some industries experienced their most significant technological developments in the 1880s. This was the case in steel, in the alkali section of the chemical industry and in the silk industry. The steel industry subsequently grew only slowly until the renewed expansion of the whole economy but the silk industry grew most rapidly in the period of stagnation in the 1880s when the cotton industry remained in the doldrums.

What accounted for the uneven pattern of growth? The answer is not simple. The expansion of the 1890s was associated with the introduction of new techniques, hydro-electricity, electro-metallurgy and the car, all of which were developed with particular success in France; but it was also associated with a strong expansion in the older industries. In both cases the utilisation of new resources, Alpine waterfalls, a new coalfield, large iron ore fields, was important. The silk industry was able to adopt new techniques in the 1880s because it was partly replacing other consumer goods on the market; otherwise consumer goods demand was very sluggish in the period when the agricultural sector was not growing. The period of more rapid industrial growth coincided with the introduction of higher agricultural and industrial tariffs; higher agricultural prices, at first due to the tariff and later to rising world food prices, raised incomes in the sector of the economy which had the most consumers and this stimulated demand for textiles, particularly cottons, in the 1890s. But many of the new industries did not depend on protection, nor were they entirely geared to the home market: in some years one-third of the output of cars was exported. Protection moreover did nothing to defend the French dyestuffs industry against German and Swiss competition, for the competitors established factories inside the French tariff. The new industries of this period in France, although small, were in some cases, like aluminium and cars, giant concerns by comparison with all European rivals. The association of aluminium manufacturers in fact renounced the protection which the international cartel offered them and set out to break it up. A good study of the effects of the tariffs across French industry is lacking but the industrial revival can only in part be attributed to the change of commercial policy. We are left, therefore, with a unique combination of factors affecting each single industry and with the likelihood that more of these equations worked favourably for French industries after 1896 than they had done after 1880. In the most favourable cases, as in the electrical industries, a combination of ample resources, a long tradition of engineering, a ready supply of skilled workers, an upward movement of incomes in a high-income market, the more rapid pace of urbanisation, and residual qualities of education and enterprise acquired in a long history of industrialisation, could still produce very high rates of growth of output.

THE DEVELOPMENT OF AGRICULTURE

Our initial discussion of French economic development and economic growth indicated that one explanation for the poor rate of growth in the 1880s lay in the depressing effects of the agricultural sector. There are several ways in which the agricultural sector can retard growth or develop-ment and each one has frequently been attributed to French agriculture in this period. As far as growth is concerned it has been argued that the low level of productivity in agriculture prevented a more rapid increase of agricultural, and thus of national, product. Alternatively it has been argued that the low level of productivity meant that labour which could have been released to other sectors was maintained in agriculture to sustain the level of output. The low level of incomes in the agricultural sector is sometimes blamed for not providing a sufficient market to stimulate output in the rest of the economy. The more pervasively inhibiting effects on development of the character of the large agricultural sector are also often stressed. Among them have been variously listed adherence to tradition, backward-ness, the desire to restrict population, ignorance, illiteracy and lack of labour mobility.

But the French peasantry have also had their defenders, and until recently there have always been powerful voices in France advocating the retention of a large agricultural sector. Sometimes the argument has been couched in moral terms, as though there were an inherent virtue in rural life. At other times it has taken a more commercial aspect and a large agricultural sector has been seen as helping to preserve a healthy balance of payments, as essential to national defence or even as sustaining a neces-sary internal market for the developing industrial sector. All these argu-ments raged with particular vehemence in France after 1870. In Britain the die had already been cast against the preservation of a large agricultural sector in the 1840s, but in France the political forces representing agriculture were still powerful after 1870. When food prices fell they launched a cam-paign for the introduction of tariffs against food imports, which they regarded as an essential step in maintaining agricultural incomes and the size of the agricultural sector at a time of falling world food prices. The rapid diminution of the agricultural sector in Britain was partly the result of free trade. In France and in Germany the correct social and economic balance of the developed economy was a widely debated issue and the general assumption of the agricultural interest was that the question should not be left to the free play of economic forces to decide as it had been in Britain. Opponents of this view argued that it was the tariff which held back the growth of productivity in agriculture and was responsible for maintaining so large an unproductive sector. The precise effects of the agricultural tariffs tended to be neglected in these political discussions. The tariff was a political act and many of the relationships between agriculture and industry were only marginally affected by it. The tariff increases which began in 1881 were only incidents in the complex history of French agriculture in this period and not always dominating influences.

Compared to most of the economies considered in this volume the agricultural sector of the French economy was neither remarkably backward nor unproductive; indeed it would stand as a fair model for agriculture in most of Europe. Small farm units, but by no means small in comparison with Belgium or Norway, dominated the picture statistically, but there was also a substantial number of larger farms on which most advances took place. Most farms were owner-occupied, but there was a complicated structure of tenancy and sharecropping and a farm owner could also be a labourer and a tenant. There were immense differences in methods and outlook according to region, so that it is impossible to speak with any exactitude of 'French agriculture' except in the broadest sense. Radical changes in farming practice coexisted with unchanging acceptance of very old methods. The same could be said of most areas of Europe. To say that French agriculture was inefficient means only that it was inefficient for so developed an economy and that by the side of the industrial sector it was under-capitalised, unmodernised and, as a consequence, growing more slowly and falling further behind in terms of productivity. In the long run, therefore, protection could not really function properly because the forces of economic change inside the country were still operating to the disadvantage of agriculture. It was, for example, no use trying to keep people on the land by means of higher food prices if the gap in productivity between industry and agriculture continued to widen, because industrial employers would be able to offer increasingly higher wages than agricultural employers. This did in fact happen and in spite of the tariff the migration from the land became much larger than in the previous period. As in the industrial sector, the rate of growth of total product was higher after 1895: Toutain calculates it at an annual average of 1·07 per cent between then and 1914 whereas in the earlier period 1875–94 it was stationary.[5] The tariff did mark the beginning of an economic recovery in French agriculture, but one which was too sluggish to realise all the hopes of its advocates.

The proportion of the active labour force employed in the agricultural sector continued to fall. The numbers involved are difficult to establish accurately. There is no clear evidence for the 1880s and the total number of people employed may have continued to increase until the 1890s. But the number of males employed did not increase; it remained steady at about

5·5 million. Between 1896 and 1913 the total number employed, both male and female, fell from 8·35 million to 7·45 million. The period when agricultural output was growing, therefore, was also the period when the labour force in agriculture was shrinking most rapidly. Evidence on wages indicates that money wages in agriculture were only about 75 per cent of those in industry in 1882 and only 61 per cent in 1910. But this apparently wide and growing wage-gap did not effect as substantial a transfer of labour out of agriculture as the figures might indicate. Only about 30 per cent of the male workers in agriculture were wage labourers, and of these about half also had land of their own.

But industry made bigger inroads into those rural dwellers who, although dependent on agricultural incomes for their living, were not actually employed in agriculture. The rural population declined from about 24·5 million to about 22 million from 1870 to 1913. One influence at work was the low rate of natural replacement. In industrial towns by contrast the population grew through high fertility levels, especially in mining areas such as Pas de Calais. The main factor determining these different fertility levels was the different age structure of the populations. It was the young who migrated to the town and left an older population behind them in the countryside. The way of life which supporters of the tariff sought to protect was becoming by 1914 an empty shell. The process of emigration from the countryside involved those outside agricultural employment because it was their incomes which were more threatened by the development of the economy. Those employed in agriculture continued to benefit to some degree from rising demand and the villages with the highest proportion of cultivators best retained their population. Those with a greater diversification of activity, more shops, more carriers, workshops for agricultural machinery and other goods, lost their population. The centralisation of services and industry in the larger towns eliminated these activities in villages, and many potential towns of the mid-nineteenth century remained small communities by 1914. It is possible to speak in this context of a 'ruralisation' of the countryside; the industrialisation of the countryside through the diversification of economic activity in the eighteenth century was now decisively reversed. Those villages in the weakest position were those where diversification had spread so far that the village's ancient lands were partly farmed by inhabitants of other villages. The migrants seldom went directly into industrial employment but into services and construction and in so doing liberated other labour for industrial employment. The proportion of people living in a department in which they were not born increased from 15 per cent in 1872 to 21 per cent in 1911.

The advocates of tariff protection were particularly concerned with the fall in world grain prices because they saw arable farming as the backbone of the French agricultural community. The growth rate for agriculture over the period, however, rose mainly because of the growth of output of animal products. Immediately after the introduction of the highest tariffs, in the decade 1895–1904, the output of vegetable products stopped declining and began to grow faster than animal products. But after 1905 it was once again animal products whose total output grew much more rapidly. This reflected fundamental changes in the composition of farming in France, as in the rest of Europe, caused by the much greater advantages which farmers in other continents had in the production of certain commodities, particularly wheat. The tariff was unable to set up any effective barrier against these forces, except to spin out their effects over a longer time.

– The Tariff Campaign

The beginnings of the tariff campaign lay in the bad harvest of 1879 and the large entry of foreign grain that year which prevented prices rising to their habitual height in bad harvest years. But it was only in the 1880s that it became clear that world economic circumstances had radically changed and with them the situation for French agriculture. The first increase in agricultural tariffs was in the duties on livestock in 1881. Only in 1885 did the campaign for protection by the agricultural interest, which had begun in 1880, succeed in winning an increase in the duties on grain; this was followed by a further increase in 1887. But the main political pressure from the agricultural sector was for legislation which would prevent the government from opening too wide a breach in the tariff by subsequent trade treaties. For both agriculture and industry it was the expiration in 1892 of the network of trade treaties begun in 1860 that marked the decisive date. The general election of 1889 saw the campaign carried throughout France by Jules Méline who was subsequently to give his name to the new tariff. Méline's own views were conservative, romantic and nationalistic, not really to be distinguished from the ineffective 'back-to-the-land' movement which became a fashionable intellectual idea in the last decades of the nineteenth century. But his campaign roused the French peasantry from the political apathy in which it had slumbered since the Revolution and gave it once again a positive political cause.

Under the terms of the 1892 law which followed his campaign only those agricultural products which were classified as industrial raw materials, such as wool, cotton and flax, were left duty-free. The duties on grain and livestock products were raised to very high levels. Imports of live cattle were banned, supposedly for health reasons, and the ban was not lifted until 1903 when duties on cattle were increased. Duties on wheat were further increased in 1894; by 1911–13 wheat prices were about 45 per cent higher than in a free-trade country like Britain and prices for oats between 10 and 30 per cent higher. In 1913 the average tariff on imports of foodstuffs into France remained higher than in any other European country except Austria-Hungary.

– Changes in Farming

It remained true, however, that in 1913 French agriculture was still fundamentally a grain-growing agriculture devoted to producing wheat, the
staple of human consumption, and oats for animal fodder. This continued
wheat production in face of the greater advantages of other areas of the
world is certainly to be attributed to the effects of the tariff in keeping
French wheat prices so far above international prices: in the decade before
the Méline tariff the average price of wheat in France had fallen by 18 per

Table 14   *Output of French agriculture, 1870–1914*

	1865–74	1875–84	1885–94	1895–1904	1905–14
Cereals[1]	14·1	14·3	14·7	15·4	15·5
Potatoes[1]	8·0	9·3	11·8	10·6	11·8
Wine[2]	60·4	46·0	30·7	45·0	52·8
Grass[1]	36·0	40·8	41·8	45·8	60·4
Fodder roots[1]	9·0	12·8	14·3	25·0	37·0
Meat[1]	1,091	1,251	1,374	1,464	1,535
Wool[1]	47·3	45·7	52·3	40·1	34·4
Silk[1]	11·8	7·7	8·4	7·9	6·6
Milk[2]	74	74	87	81	109
Butter[1]	200	200	132	150	170
Cheese[1]			137	154	174
Eggs[3]	2,562	2,697	2,885	3,416	3,989
Oil seeds[4]	227	164	89	62	52
Flax and hemp (yarn)[4]	103	91	61	39	33
Sugar beet[1]	7·7	7·8	6·4	7·5	7·7

[1] Million tons   [2] million hectolitres   [3] millions   [4] thousand tons

Source: J. C. Toutain, 'Le produit de l'agriculture française de 1700 à 1958: II, La
Croissance', in *Cahiers de l'Institut de Science Economique Appliquée*, série AF, no. 2,
pp. 13–15.

cent. Conversely the continuing decline in wool production can be attributed to the lack of import duties. As the raw material of an important
industry, wool was freely imported from other continents; the consequence
was a continued decline in the number of sheep in France. Table 14 shows
the other main movements in output. Wine production was halved between
1870 and 1890 and by 1914 had returned to something approaching its
former figure; in this case the fluctuations were largely independent of
tariff policy and due to a disease, phylloxera, which attacked the vine
stocks. The basic cause behind the increase in output of meat and milk was

the variation and improvement in diet over the old staple foods which came with rising incomes. The increase in fodder was due not to an increase in cattle but to the improved methods of breeding and feeding them: natural grass was about 46 per cent of total animal feed in 1870 and only 25 per cent in 1905–14. Wool was not the only product to show a noticeable decline; other industrial crops such as oil seeds and flax were abandoned as cheaper supplies appeared from outside France. Even the apparent stability of a crop like sugar beet is misleading in so far as there were sharp changes of government policy whose effect is obscured by the ten-year averages of Table 14.

One defect of Table 14 is that it does not break down the cereal crop into its various components. Improving incomes led to a decisive shift from inferior bread grains to wheat and, with the domestic market secured,

Table 15 *Production of and trade in wheat in France, 1861–5 to 1901–5*

Period	Average annual output of wheat (000 t)	Net imports (000 t)	Area devoted to wheat farming (000 ha)
1861–5	7,594	212	6,986
1871–5	7,586	90	6,801
1881–5	8,541	1,086	6,991
1891–5	8,101	1,339	6,762
1901–5	8,906	257	6,575

Source: M. Tracy, *Agriculture in Western Europe* (London, 1964), p. 76.

French farmers concentrated heavily on the production of this crop. The area devoted to wheat farming no longer increased after 1885 but output, after wavering in the early 1890s, again rose after 1900 due to better yields (see Table 15). Apart from Russia no other European country approached France as a wheat producer. Even large-scale producers such as Italy or Hungary seldom recorded a wheat harvest half the size of that of France.

The demand for this harvest came almost entirely from the domestic market. The per capita consumption of wheat in France over the whole period was much higher than anywhere else in the world, about 50 per cent above the level of the United States or Britain, and about 150 per cent above that in Germany. Wheaten bread was the basic diet of some 40 million consumers and the country was covered with a network of small grain markets, mills and bakers whose economic existence was bound up with this habit of consumption. To allow the sort of complete change in food production which took place in Britain or Denmark in the same period would certainly have been a more drastic social change and have encountered severer obstacles. The economies of scale practised on prairie farms, the opening of the American transcontinental railroads, the improvement in freighting and shipping techniques, all combined to make it possible for foreign farmers to sell wheat on French markets at prices lower than those of domestic grain. But the basis of this trade, which began at the same time in other European countries, was the high and sustained demand for wheat in France. In some European economies, in the face of these economic facts, the farming community did make a decisive shift to meat and dairy farming where lower input costs, rising incomes and nearness to markets gave them a comparative advantage. In Denmark, for example, the structure of agriculture was transformed along these lines.[6] But since the early nineteenth century the industrialisation of the French economy had created marketing structures in France which tied the food producer very closely to the domestic food consumer. Whereas in Denmark a system of agricultural credit existed to further an extensive trade in agricultural produce, the ambitions of French grain farmers seldom strayed beyond the nearest market town. Furthermore the capital needed to convert farms in Denmark was provided from the network of agricultural co-operatives, very poorly developed in France. In every part of France towns offered the farmer a limited market, limited credit possibilities, some legal facilities and provided for his physical needs. The intense regionalism of French farming methods is also in part explained by the prevalence of these small marketing centres. The wheat was sold to a multitude of local millers and bakers whose business was to provide the staple food of the country.

It is not in the least surprising that rather than effect so massive and radical a change French grain producers demanded protective duties, nor that their demands should have been successful. Where would they have obtained the capital to attempt so thoroughgoing an operation? And, given the fixity of domestic consumers' preferences over so long a period, what other possibility was open than an extremely rapid fall in agricultural incomes and a sharp reduction in the relative importance of agriculture in the economy, too sharp a reduction to have been politically feasible? The social and political realities of late nineteenth-century France could not be conjured away. It was necessary to compromise with them and the compromise meant a considerable loss to the economy. It is worth remembering that in the 1880s 16 per cent of males and 25 per cent of females in France could not sign their name to their marriage contract; they were almost entirely rural dwellers. Ignorance, illiteracy, reluctance to accept any change, and great intellectual isolation remained the characteristics of a substantial part of the French population, and the lack of change in French farming has also to be explained in terms of this.

Where new methods and crops could be fitted into the social pattern the tariff did not discourage this. One of the most striking increases in output in Table 14 is the increase in potato cultivation. The prices of potatoes and of sugar beet in France were low and competitive; these were labour-intensive crops admirably suited to the unit of farm production in France. Similarly, where the possibility of marketing early vegetables existed, on the coasts of Brittany and Normandy for example, whence they were shipped to Britain, or in the area around Paris, peasant farmers changed readily to market gardening. Even the larger farms around Paris by 1914 employed a labour force over twice as great as in 1850, many of them consisting of foreign immigrants. Sometimes grain farming would be abandoned for dairy farming if there was a strong enough market to overcome the structural obstacles to such a conversion. Dairy farmers in Normandy supplied butter to the London market. But where no market existed, as in the Auvergne, transhumance over thirty miles was still practised and half-starved cows were carried out to the fields in spring.

The clearest example of the readiness to make structural changes when the market existed was in the production and marketing of wine. Until railway building wine was produced everywhere in France for local markets. When the railways reached Languedoc entrepreneurs there seized the opportunity of rising wine consumption and the natural production advantages of their own area to market their wines in Paris and other northern areas. The area under vines in the department of Hérault increased from 114,000 hectares in 1850 to 220,000 hectares in 1874. Wine consumption in France increased from 51 litres per capita in 1858 to 77 litres in 1872. This was no small-scale agricultural change but the veritable disindustrialisation of a whole region of the country; an area with a long-established industrial basis became a sea of vines. The textile industries of towns like Carcassonne and Montpellier which had struggled on in the early nineteenth century with limited government markets and outdated equipment were replaced by wine as a profitable investment, and the vineyards dealt them the death-blow prepared by the advance of the textile industries of northern France and the stagnation of the traditional Mediterranean markets. This was a return to the soil of a scope that romantic agricultural reformers like Méline could scarcely have hoped for. In 1864 the iron forges in Alès were unable to compete for labour against the higher wages being offered by the surrounding vineyards.

The process of commercialisation was furthered by the attacks of a drastic vine disease, phylloxera. The cure was expensive, involving the grafting of native vines on to unaffected Californian rootstocks of European origin. In spite of government help many peasant holdings could not survive; indeed in the worst period of the phylloxera many Languedoc villages lost between 10 and 25 per cent of their population, some of whom left to lay out the new vineyards of Algeria. Reconstitution required capital and thus took place at first in the lower areas of Languedoc nearer to the towns on vineyards owned by the urban bourgeoisie. Furthermore, for the first ten years the new rootstocks would not grow successfully on the hillsides. This expensive cure for the phylloxera placed the cheaper end of the wine market more firmly in the hands of mass-producing companies involved in large-scale marketing. It will be seen from Table 14 that at the height of the phylloxera French wine production was only half the level it reached in the first flush of expansion into Languedoc between 1865 and 1874. However, in the last decade output once again passed 50 million hectolitres a year. In the areas of Languedoc where cheap table wines were grown the pattern of monoculture was not permanently disturbed by the phylloxera. Regional specialisation and even disindustrialisation of this type was not an uncommon phenomenon in European countries where the agricultural sector in one region could concentrate on a product which was highly susceptible to marginal increases in per capita incomes.

Throughout the whole range of products French wines remained highly competitive on international markets. In the production of higher-quality wines a small vineyard cultivated in the traditional way was still a rational and successful enterprise. Vines, for instance, did not suffer from the continued practice of strip-farming. Even in the 1880s at the lowest point of French wine production the quantity of high-grade wines exported was only slightly below the level of the 1860s. Until 1914 French wine exports fluctuated between two and three million hectolitres, but the rising demand in France together with the drastic fall in output between 1870 and 1890 led to an enormous increase in imports. From an insignificant level in the 1860s they rose to an annual average of 9·7 million hectolitres between 1881 and 1890, so that France, while remaining an exporter of more expensive wine on a large scale, also became for the first time a net importer of cheaper wine on an even larger scale. The assimilation of Algeria into the French tariff structure led to the migration of French capital and labour to open large vineyards purely for the French table in that devoutly muslim country. With the recovery of French domestic output the lower quality end of the market continued to be supplied from abroad, increasingly from Algeria. Imports fell to an annual average of 5·9 million hectolitres between 1901 and 1910 but rising consumption in France determined that France remained, at least in quantity, a net importer. But no other producer could break the control of French exporters over the better quality market. Wine production in France was based upon centuries of accumulated knowledge and skill and these were often decisive factors in quality production. In other labour-intensive crops they were far less important. Germany and Austria-Hungary both developed large sugar industries based on beet cultivation but developments in France were less successful. During the Second Empire domestic sugar production grew more quickly than imports. As Table 14 shows, this growth was not sustained after 1870. In an attempt to remedy this the government instituted in 1884 subsidies for producers and exporters of domestically produced sugar. The subsidy contained a built-in incentive towards efficiency because it was only applicable to those manufacturers whose sugar output was above a certain level for a given weight of beet. The idea was to induce farmers to produce a beet with as high a sugar content as the better German beet. However, the scheme was wrecked by international opposition from the larger exporting countries. At the Brussels conference of 1902 all countries agreed to refrain from the policy of export subsidisation and after that date French sugar exports ceased to develop.

– The Standard of Farming

It would be false to give the impression that French farming did not improve in this period and that the Méline tariff led to a stagnation of techniques. Indeed it was only after the tariff that agricultural output grew while inputs of land and labour both fell. Labour productivity per employed person increased at about 1·5 per cent a year between 1896 and 1913, which is not far short of the rate in industry. The main cause seems to have been an increase in mechanisation, but it is also possible to discern the first signs of a reawakening of pride and self-respect among the poorer members of the rural community. The first effective agricultural co-operatives and the first effective peasant credit institutions also belong to those years. There was no suggestion in the Méline tariff that it would be used to shelter French agriculture while it was brought up to the level of its competitors. It was an entirely defensive mechanism, in which the import duty would compensate for the difference in production costs between France and other countries. It brought a definite improvement in income only to those farmers who sold livestock or grain in bulk. For any farmer whose unit of land was less than 10 hectares the increase in wheat and feed-grain prices probably meant an increase in expenditure. But the tariff campaign had given the agricultural interest a new sense of being part of the body politic, and after the almost total emphasis on industrialisation under the Second Empire this in itself brought an increase in confidence, however ill-justified economically, about the future.

Immediately after 1870 larger farmers showed considerable interest in American reaping machinery and later in binders. This was expressed in a small surge of imports of agricultural machinery, usually manufactured in Britain. But the economics of using mechanical reapers were such that they were unlikely to find a large market in a country where small farms predominated. And for some time the binder was regarded with deep suspicion as being unsuitable for the more humid conditions of western Europe; it would have been more suitable for the climatic conditions of southern France but the pattern of French agriculture, firmly established in the late eighteenth century, in which innovations and improvements began in the north and were diffused southwards, did not change and in general agricultural conditions in the south remained more primitive. Mowing, reaping and threshing machinery was most used in the northern and north-eastern departments, particularly in Marne where it better suited the structure of landholding and the type of agricultural activity. After 1878 the weight of imports of agricultural machinery fell and did not again reach the total of that year until after 1896. The agricultural enquiry of 1892 showed that, apart from a plough, the 3·5 million farms in France had only the most rudimentary equipment. There were only 262,000 horse hoes and 234,000 threshing machines in use and only 39,000 mechanical reapers. After that date the picture began to change with an increasing volume of imports of agricultural machinery from the United States and Canada. The total weight of imports of agricultural machinery in 1913 had increased more than tenfold over its level in 1890. To that extent the loss of labour and of land was compensated for by the increased use of capital equipment.

Although it is true that small farms were predominant, the structure of landholding, which remained very stable in the nineteenth century, was such that a considerable area of land was in fact held in large farms. Peasant holdings were still growing at the expense of larger farms until the 1880s. But Table 16 shows that at that date the relatively small number of farms over 40 hectares in area in fact accounted for about half the total farm land. It was in the 1880s that the number of farms in France reached its peak and afterwards a tendency began for the amount of farming land constituted in the smallest holdings to decrease. As the number of farms began to decline, small and medium-sized farms grew at the expense of the largest farms, and to a lesser degree at the expense of the smallest plots of land; this is the usual pattern and agrees with what we know, although the accuracy and comparability of the figures in Table 16 can certainly be disputed. Peasant farmers acquired the plots of land belonging to those who had been forced to leave the countryside because their holding was too small to sustain them by itself. Subdivision of land into uneconomic holdings was slowed down by the process of migration and this may have furthered the increase in mechanisation. The decline in total area covered by holdings over 40 hectares between 1882 and 1908 must surely be a statistical confusion caused by the methods of making the enquiry which unfortunately related it to taxation. In any case the decline in the area covered by the biggest farms would not slow down the improvements in productivity since the medium-sized units, whose number was growing, were still big enough to incorporate all improvements.

It was only after 1890 that there was any real change in the institutions of French rural society. The law of 1884 which permitted the formation of *syndicats*, associations of employers or workers in particular professions or occupations (and hence of trade unions), had little effect in freeing the peasant from the individualist isolation sanctified by the Revolution. Co-operative organisation for bulk purchasing or sales or for dairy or wine farming developed very slowly before 1914 in France and where it existed it was often under the influence of the large landowners of the neighbourhood, the church or political parties. The initiative towards common organisation came from above, not below. By 1914 the anti-republican Union Centrale des Agriculteurs de France had 10,000 local *syndicats* and the various pro-republican co-operative associations probably about the same number. The *syndicats* never accepted the range of activities nor the

Table 16 *Number and size of farms in France in 1882 and 1908*

Size of farm (ha)	Number of farms 1882	Number of farms 1908	Area covered 1882	Area covered 1908
1–5	1,866,000 ⎱ 2,635,000	2,524,000	5,600,000 ⎱ 11,400,000	11,559,000
5–10	769,000 ⎰		5,800,000 ⎰	
10–20	431,000 ⎱		6,500,000 ⎱	
20–30	198,000 ⎰ 727,000	746,000	5,000,000 ⎰ 14,900,000	14,825,000
30–40	98,000 ⎰		3,400,000 ⎰	
over 40	142,000	148,000	22,300,000	16,271,000

Source: M. Tracy, *Agriculture in Western Europe* (London, 1964), p. 62; E. Golob, *The Méline Tariff: French Agriculture and Nationalist Economic Policy* (New York, 1944), p. 218.

social implications of agricultural co-operatives in other economies like Germany or Denmark; only in Brittany did the concept of 'peasant emancipation' take hold thanks to the proselytising activities of Félix Trochu.

A much more important result of these first stirrings of intellectual change in the countryside was the organisation of cheaper agricultural credit. The newly formed *syndicats* became the basis of a government policy of making short-term capital loans available on easy terms to smaller cultivators. The first step was taken with the formation of the *caisses* Durand. These were based on the peasant credit institutions which had been founded throughout Germany in accordance with the ideas of the social reformer Raiffeisen. The *caisses* were self-supporting banks, providing small short-term loans from the interest received on their collected subscriptions. Many *syndicats* formed such banks in the 1890s, but the possibilities of local and limited credit were of course small. The decisive step was taken when the charter of the Bank of France expired in 1896; it was renewed only on the condition that the Bank provided a regular sum, not less than one-eighth of its current circulation of cash, to subsidise rural credit banks. In 1899 nine regional credit banks were set up as an umbrella organisation for the local credit institutions, and bills endorsed by a *syndicat*, a local bank and one of the regional banks were henceforth discountable at the Bank of France. In 1912 the 4,000 local institutions had 250,000 members; between 1900 and 1909 they lent at least 160 million francs and in so doing transformed the credit possibilities of small cultivators. The one serious weakness in the system was the short-term nature of the credits provided. This weakness was remedied in 1906 when the law required the regional banks to make long-term loans to the co-operative associations so that they themselves might extend credits of up to twenty-five years. The maximum interest rate permitted was 4 per cent and the only serious restriction was that the sums extended in these larger credits should be limited to one-third of the total advances from the Bank of France. The connection of the central bank with village credit institutions was an astonishingly far-reaching policy in the light of the previous neglect of agriculture by the government. By turning the financial side of the *syndicats'* operations into a secure banking system it did more to change the economic attitudes of the small cultivators than any other event of the century.

In spite of these changes, the standard of farming in France in 1913, even allowing for the great regional variations, was still low. The average yield of the principal crop, wheat, was about 13·2 quintals per hectare, only about two-thirds the yield in Germany. The low yield was partly attributable to the fact that so large an area of the country was still devoted to wheat production and partly to the very slow improvement in production methods. Secure in the possession of a large and growing domestic market French grain producers did not have the necessary incentive to improve their methods. Wheat cultivation was by no means confined to the larger and more capitalised farms: strip cultivation persisted to 1914, between two rows of vines or sometimes on ridges piled up in the fields by the wooden ploughs which were sometimes still used. The field plan suitable for eighteenth-century farming was retained in quite different economic and social conditions and discouraged the adoption of many innovations. The consumption of fertiliser in France was lower than in any other area of north-western Europe, although there were considerable regional differences in this respect. The price was high, usually more than 30 per cent above its cost in Belgium where it was so heavily used; this was the more serious as organic manure in France was harder to obtain than in neighbouring lands because the ratio of livestock to land area was lower. Even the yield of a typical peasant crop like the potato was significantly lower than in most other areas of western Europe.

– Conclusion

The pattern of growth in the agricultural sector so closely coincided with that of the economy as a whole as to suggest that it influenced it very strongly. The effects of the stagnation of an entire sector of the economy in the 1880s must have seriously retarded developments in the industrial sector; to this must be added the effects of low productivity, reluctance to change, conservatism and ignorance throughout the whole period which may have shown itself in many less identifiable ways. The inherent social conservatism of the violent changes of 1789–93 had not much affected the economy before 1870 because the rapid changes in other sectors, and even in the non-peasant parts of the agricultural sector, had been able to take place independently of the 3 million peasant farmers. But it lay in wait throughout the nineteenth century and after 1870 the forces of change collided with an immense and real obstacle which they had chosen to ignore and with which they began to come to terms only after 1890.

THE EVOLUTION OF BANKING AND CREDIT

The growing popularity of share and bond capital testified to the success of the nationwide banking institutions which had followed the example of the Société Générale in channelling their clients' funds into railways and joint stock companies. It also testified to the growing activity and popularity of the Paris stock exchange. Yet it is sometimes argued that French banks did not channel sufficient funds into industrial investment and that they themselves were responsible for what is considered the relative slowness of French economic growth in this period. Since capital was so cheap in France, rarely above 3 per cent on public markets, and since there seems no evidence that French entrepreneurs were unable to find the capital they required, this opinion has little force. From the beginnings of large-scale railway building and the development of coke smelting iron works the banks played a vital role in investment in French industry.

The opinion is based on the shift of policy by the major deposit banks from their close initial involvement with such industrial enterprises to a more cautious policy with their depositors' funds. The most typical representative of this policy was the Crédit Lyonnais. Originally established by Lyons industrialists in an attempt to emancipate themselves from the Paris capital market, the bank was heavily committed to supporting an abortive dyestuffs company, La Fuchsine. This chastening experience produced a long period of great caution in industrial investment. The bank moved to Paris and led the way in what has come to be called 'deposit banking'. The basis of this business was a multiplicity of small low-profit transactions at a very large number of branches. Such activities naturally induced restraint in investment and gave the bank, and the institutions that copied it, a very different outlook on economic affairs from that of the Crédit Mobilier. The French Société Générale was at first heavily involved in loans to steel companies re-equipping themselves to meet the constant challenge of technological innovation, but as the profitability and safety of 'deposit banking' became evident it followed the safer path. None of this, however, excluded dealings in government paper. The initial loans to repay the war indemnity to Germany in 1871 were handled by the private banks, still dominated by the Rothschilds, but within one year the new banks had forced their way in. The management of most public loans still remained in the hands of the private bankers, although at first the loans to back the Freycinet plan were offered directly to the public; but after 1872 the joint stock banks always had to be given their share of such profitable operations. When foreign governments raised loans in Paris they occasionally dealt with the larger banks rather than with the Rothschilds or other private bankers. This was the case with the huge loans which the Russian government began to raise in 1889. What evidence we have does suggest that after 1870 the connections between banks and industry in France diminished rather than grew. Bankers and industrialists maintained a mutual suspicion which was only broken by the arrival of completely new industries some of which sought the large banks for their heavy initial investment in plant. Several banks, however, refused to become involved with Hérault's early operations in the industrial production of aluminium. After 1890 the connections between the big steel companies like de Wendel and Schneider, which dominated the iron and steel cartel, the Comité des Forges, and the big banks also became much closer. Yet it was still true that bankers showed a preference for government paper rather than industrial shares.

The preference of bankers for government rather than industrial bonds stemmed partly from the historical tradition of the *rentes*, and partly from the greater caution with which the banks undertook investment. This was both justified and increased by the rise and fall of the Union Générale. This bank was founded in 1879 by the financier Eugène Bontoux who had been closely involved with various attempts to drive a railway through the Balkans. Its foundation coincided with the Freycinet plan and a revival of interest in railway building in France and its first two years were years of amazingly rapid growth. The collapse of its Balkan projects in 1882 and the failure of the bank which followed provoked a wave of withdrawals from other banks which the Crédit Lyonnais, for one, was only narrowly able to survive. The attitude of the French public towards banks naturally remained very cautious thereafter: cheques were little used before 1914 in France except among the rich. But the basic reason why French banking institutions remained more independent of industrial investment than German banks was that there was less demand from industry for long-term bank capital, as a result of the structure of the industrial sector: textile manufacturers, for example, remained firmly independent throughout the period. But the deposit banks which did have national networks of branches were in fact mobilising the accumulated savings of a rich country in the way the Péreires had dreamed of. What they did with those savings still requires further investigation, but no complete answer can be provided without first considering the large volume of foreign investment made by France in this period.

TRANSPORT

– Railways

The continued importance of railway building for the metallurgical industries in this period has already emerged. Its importance for the engineering industry was no less, in stimulating technological innovations in cast steel, die stamping, methods of bridge construction and machine assembly and in electrical propulsion. Indeed, the railway network more than doubled in length between 1870 and 1913 and the many linkages between railways and the industrial economy remained important throughout. Nevertheless railways gradually ceased to dominate investment as they had done since 1840. Their role in stimulating economic change and promoting industrial development became less important, their role as a transport network more important. Passenger receipts continued to increase as did the number of journeys made. One factor in the increase was the rapid development of suburban commuter traffic into Paris; after 1900 the track capacity of the main lines out of the Paris termini was greatly increased to handle this traffic. More people arrived in Paris daily by each of the principal commuter lines in 1904 than had arrived in total in 1869. Freight traffic grew less regularly but equally persistently, increasing threefold between 1875 and 1913.

As a focus for investment, however, the railways played a less dynamic role. The rate of annual increase to the network never reached the level of the period between 1852 and 1867. There was one exception: the short period between 1880 and 1885 when an annual average of 1,128 kilometres was added. This peak of investment was the result of the railway construction programme advocated by General Freycinet, as a step to national revival after the defeat by Prussia. Before that there were two forces sustaining the rate of railway construction. After the realignment of the eastern frontier there was extensive local railway construction in French Lorraine to realign the system; at the same time there was a strong demand for lines of local interest all over the country, a demand which the companies leasing and operating the trunk routes were not always so eager to satisfy on the terms laid down by the earlier conventions. In 1865 the law had been changed so that concessions for local lines could be granted by the prefect of the department. Under the aegis of this law local lines were financed by the notabilities of the region and in one case a whole network in the Vendée was built and operated by the biggest locomotive and rolling stock builders, the Société des Batignolles. The new lines could not survive profitably in isolation and entrepreneurs such as Philippart and Delahante attempted to combine them into ramshackle through-routes rivalling the earlier main trunk lines. After 1876 many of these smaller companies were on the verge of bankruptcy. The Philippart group, which had tried to put together 4,000 kilometres of track in a through-route from Boulogne-sur-Mer to the Mediterranean, was refused operating rights by the government and went bankrupt in 1877.

It was Freycinet's ambition to take all this secondary building under the wing of the state and place it on a sounder financial and strategically more rational basis, while reordering and simplifying the relationship between the private companies and the government. This last of the great railway visionaries of France was able to persuade the chamber that the local networks were not just the low-profit minor investments of the big railway companies but a powerful instrument of rural and national regeneration. The state itself had already been actively engaged in railway construction since 1871 because the terms demanded by the companies had proved unacceptable. In 1878 the government repurchased a small network in the south-west, the beginning of the state railway system, and under the terms of the Freycinet plan itself directly undertook the construction cost and operation of some further sections. The total length of line to be added under the terms of the plan was 17,000 kilometres, which would have made the system longer than the network of national roads. An 'extraordinary' budget in 1879 allocated 3,500 million francs to railway building and 1,500 million for improving canals, rivers and ports over a twelve-year period. It also provided funds for the direct purchase and completion of part of the railway system by the state. Steelmakers hoped this plan would reverse the trend of falling prices since 1873 and other industries supported the plan in the hope that it would maintain competitiveness by reducing transport costs. Over the period 1879–84 there was a steep upward movement in rail production which reached record levels in the last year, but the introduction of the Gilchrist–Thomas process preserved the trend of falling rail prices. By the time of the stock market crash of 1882 the plan had already failed to meet the hopes of the steel industry while the railways built under its auspices were relatively unprofitable rural lines of local interest only. The cancellation of orders which followed the waning of enthusiasm brought rail production down sharply after 1884 and it was to be much less important for the rest of the period.

The 'extraordinary' budget continued until 1891, an interesting early example of increased public expenditure to overcome what was considered a depression. Although the burden of construction was handed back again to private companies in 1883 the expectation was that the treasury would be reimbursed from the revenue on the lines it had already constructed. What happened was the opposite; the sharpest contraction in traffic of the whole period came between 1884 and 1888, so severe that it threw a cloud of doubt over railway investment which remained until the improvement in receipts after 1906.

The subsequent period was dominated more by technical improvements designed to increase the productivity of the existing equipment. The greater weight of locomotives and rolling stock, improvements to layout and signalling, increases to station capacity, quicker turn-round of equipment, all resulted in a rate of growth of productivity of both labour and capital much higher than in the period 1860–83. The first successful experiments in electric traction were made in 1886 and the first regular electric run was made in 1900 between Paris and Versailles, the same year in which the Metropolitan railway was opened in Paris. Railway building continued actively until the end of the period, in spite of the declining return on investment. The total length of track added between 1900 and 1910 was twice that added to the smaller network in Italy, when that country was in the throes of rapid industrialisation.

– Inland Waterways

The Freycinet plan did not confine itself solely to rail; it involved also a scheme for the reclassification, standardisation, improvement and construction of navigable waterways. The 2,000 kilometres of canal which it was intended to construct proved as over-ambitious a target as the railway plan, but the great improvement in productivity resulting from the standardisation of dimensions and lock measurements on all the canals designated as first-class was the direct, if rather prolonged, consequence of the plan. The total length of canals increased by only 400 kilometres and included only one important new canal, the Canal de l'Est, joining the Saône to the Meuse. But the total tonnage transported increased by almost 60 per cent between 1885–94 and 1905–13. Three-quarters of it was made up of coal, stone, cement and bricks; the volume of manufactured goods transported had dwindled to insignificance. Canals remained a valuable part of the transport network where their regional density was greatest. Where there was a dense interconnecting system of navigable routes, as on the northern coalfield or in the basin of the Seine and its tributaries, traffic was still heavy. But the isolated canals elsewhere showed falling traffic in spite of heavy subsidisation. After 1905 the great increase in freight carriage generally went almost unnoticed by the inland waterways system.

– Roads

The road system fared worse than the inland waterways against competition from rail. The network of national roads scarcely increased at all in length for most of the period. The development of the car came too late to affect this. By 1856 the railways were already making a greater contribution to passenger transport than the roads. In the subsequent increase in passenger traffic neither road nor canal had any noticeable share; it was the monopoly of the rail system. As far as goods traffic was concerned the share of the road system measured in tons per kilometre fell from 24 per cent in 1865–74 to 9 per cent in 1905–13: over the same period the share of the rail system increased from 53 per cent to 67 per cent. The absolute volume of tons per kilometre carried by road moreover showed no increase. In most categories of goods and for all passengers railways brought about great cost reductions beyond the reach of the road or the canal system.

– Shipping

French shipping thrived on protected markets and particularly dominated the trade between France and her colonies. The total registered tonnage of the merchant navy in 1890 was only about one million tons. Between 1870 and 1890 there was little increase in size and even in the trade boom of 1871–3 French shipping did not fully share in the expansion of European shipping. However, the total tonnage of steamships in 1890, about half a million tons, was the same as in Germany. With the expansion of the economy after 1890, the merchant navy modernised less rapidly and expanded less than that of Germany, and only in the last decade before the war did tonnage increase at the same rate as in other major trading countries.

Furthermore, the replacement of sail by steam became a slower process than in the other major developed economies. The subsidisation of ships of French flag introduced in 1893 slowed down replacement because the subsidies protected the less efficient sailing vessels. The highly profitable

Bordeaux shipping company, A-D Bordes, which monopolised the nitrate trade to South America, operated almost entirely with sailing ships until 1900, exploiting their capital stock and their labour force to the last possible degree. The company actually took the decision to specialise in sailing vessels in the year the Suez canal was opened. After 1903 government subsidies were redesigned to encourage steamships and motor vessels; the statistical evidence is confused but it seems that only after that date did steam tonnage surpass sail tonnage.

THE FRENCH ECONOMY IN A WIDER WORLD

– Empire

The growing involvement of the French economy with the world beyond the frontiers of France is clearly seen in the international ramifications of French banking and in the role the banking system played in placing the accumulated savings of France in investments all over the world. The economic relationships of France with the underdeveloped world rested ultimately on superior strength and force and the readiness to use them. This was particularly evident in the extension of the French Empire. Before the formation of the Third Republic, France already governed Algeria, many islands in Oceania, Senegal, New Caledonia and Cochin-China. After 1870 French forces pushed southwards from Algeria to the oases on the northern edge of the Sahara and took control over Tunisia. The sub-Saharan African empire embraced the Senegal, Niger and Gabon basins, large areas of central Africa and the northern part of the Congo basin. Gradually the ancient kingdoms of Laos and Cambodia and the rest of Indo-China were 'pacified' as was the island of Madagascar. But foreign investment did not coincide closely with this control over huge areas of the world; Russia was the main target for French financial interests over the period as a whole. Nor did control always coincide with trading domination; in some Balkan countries, such as Bulgaria, although an important part of business was controlled by French investors the main trading partner was Germany.

Although the economic importance of the colonies was less when set against the worldwide network of financial and commercial operations it was in the colonies that economic domination was seen in its cruder and simpler forms. Both in Algeria and Tunisia the muslim land law was westernised to introduce a system of land registration and fixity of tenure whose main purpose was to guarantee sales of land to settlers. In 1884 alone in Tunisia 40,000 hectares of land were bought by French agents mainly for the production of wine, a crop offensive to the religious and social customs of the inhabitants. By 1900 there were 665,000 European settlers in Algeria. In both countries forests belonged to the state and could be easily exploited under French direction. In West Africa trade and commercial activity were controlled by powerful quasi-monopolistic companies with special privileges, the Société Commerciale de l'Ouest Africain and the Compagnie Française de l'Afrique Occidentale. They excluded foreign shipping and commerce from their areas and were typical of a general pattern of protection and exclusiveness in French colonial trade. They were also highly profitable; the latter firm recorded net profits of 40 per cent in certain years before 1914.

But it will be seen from Table 17 how limited a proportion of total investment was accounted for by colonial investment, although between 1900 and 1914 it was one of the two most rapidly growing sectors of foreign investment and between 1890 and 1914 probably second in importance only to Russia. Trade between the colonies and France also played only a limited part in French foreign trade. Indeed the benefits of this protected trade to the French economy were very dubious, for although it did guarantee control over certain raw materials it also preserved a soft market for the less enterprising French industries. In a strict accounting calculation the French Empire was probably not 'profitable' before 1914, but it is meaningless to see it as a separate aspect of history from France's economic connections with other areas not under French control and it is to these wider horizons we must turn to understand the nature of imperialism.

– Foreign Trade

The complexity of France's foreign trade is only fully comprehended in its international setting and for this reason it has been considered in a later chapter.[7] But it must first be seen as a problem for the national economy. In its outlines the problem was simple. The continued increase in production demanded a growing volume of raw materials which increasingly came from outside France, while foreign markets continued to play an important role in absorbing French industrial production. In the period of rapid industrialisation before 1870 these processes had worked well. After 1852 foreign trade had become once again as important to the economy as in the late eighteenth century and this had been acknowledged by the network of low-tariff trade agreements in Europe which the French government had played a big part in initiating after 1860. Between 1830 and 1860 France had had a growing share of world trade and by 1860 her exports were about 19 per cent of all European exports. Between 1850 and 1875 French exports of manufactured goods increased at an average rate of 5·3 per cent a year and took second place behind British exports of manufactured goods. The situation was made simpler for France by the fact that the main market for her high-value exports was Britain, giving France a trade surplus with the major exporting country.

All this was fundamentally changed by the industrialisation of Germany.

The German share in the exports of manufactured goods from all European countries passed that of France between 1881 and 1885, and by 1911–13 was almost twice as high. Exports from all European countries except Britain went principally to other European countries and the growth of German exports inevitably meant an increase in their appearance on French markets. They rose from 7·5 per cent of total French imports in 1898 to 13 per cent in 1913. Between 1875 and 1895 German exports grew much more quickly than French exports and displaced French goods from their position in many European markets. Britain suffered from the same competition but to her it was less important because her exports were so firmly established in non-European markets. After 1895 French exports began again to increase at an annual rate of 4·3 per cent which was not far below the level of the 1850s, but this increase was now less directed towards European markets where German goods had become so firmly established. In some European countries French imports were negligible. Such was the case in Russia and Scandinavia; French ships were a rare sight in Copenhagen or St Petersburg (Leningrad). The markets to which French exports were now going were in fact less competitive ones. Whereas between 1890 and 1900 only 9 per cent of French exports went to French colonies, between 1906 and 1912 the proportion rose to 15 per cent. Of all European countries France had the highest proportion of exports to Africa: in 1910 12·3 per cent. Where colonial preferences and other protective arrangements did not exist, as in Latin America or most of Asia, French exports, unlike those of Germany, made little headway against the long-established British domination.

For particular industries, however, the general pattern did not hold good. In those industrial sectors which were in the vanguard of the European export boom in the last two decades, chemical products and vehicles, French exports were competitive, increasingly important in the total exports of such goods by the industrialised economies. In the case of vehicles and chemical products exports were almost entirely to European markets and the proportion of such goods in total exports grew at a rate comparable to that of the most industrialised countries, in spite of the German domination of the dyestuffs industry. But the overall composition of French exports was still dominated by older industries and it was exports of clothing, textiles and semi-manufactured textiles which were increasingly driven on to the protected colonial markets. In most of these older manufactures, textiles, leather goods, woollen goods and processed foods, France's share of the exports of the major exporting countries was declining, whereas in vehicles it was growing and in chemicals and steel at least holding its own in a world of mounting competition. The revival of the 1890s augured well for the future and beneath the rather stagnant surface of the older industries important structural changes were taking place which would be responsible for the industrial prosperity of the 1920s.

In retrospect the defensive protectionist movement seems to have been too fearful a political reaction to the gloomy years after 1880. At the root of this anxiety lay the development of the larger and richer German economy. The origins of the tariff changes can be traced to the aftermath of defeat by Prussia in 1870–1 when Thiers, under the guise of raising revenue to pay off the war indemnity, tried to introduce a tariff increase. The basic idea behind Thiers's proposal was to extend the domestic market for French goods and thus lower prices through economies of scale. Subsequent events were no advertisment for his ideas for it was the resilience of French trade within the existing system which enabled the indemnity to be repaid so quickly. It was paid essentially out of the proceeds of the exports of French goods to other economies whose capacity to receive these goods often depended on their ability to export to Germany, an ability increased by the French indemnity payments to Germany. This might have persuaded opinion in France of the value of low tariffs, the more so as the slump of 1873 in Germany was felt less acutely in France. But the fall in food prices lent force to the previously weak agitation for protection which certain industries had been advocating since the treaty of 1860 with Britain.

The weight of attack of the protection movement was directed against the concept of trade treaties by which the tariffs agreed by the legislature could be breached and against the most-favoured-nation clauses which these treaties had always included and which had become the principal instrument of international tariff reduction. The Chamber had refused to ratify the November 1872 trade treaty with Britain which contained such a clause. In 1878 Méline persuaded the Chamber to reject a similar treaty with Italy and its action provoked the first of several short but vicious tariff wars before 1914. The two that occurred between France and Italy severely damaged France's trading position in that country. The agricultural interests forced the government to accept certain restrictions on its policy before the round of trade treaties could be renewed in 1881 and 1882, compelling it to increase conventional tariffs and exclude grain and cattle from the agreements. Only the United Kingdom refused these terms but the two states continued to grant each other most-favoured-nation status. The increased duties on agricultural produce introduced in the 1880s were followed by the electoral victory of the protectionist party which made it certain that the trade treaties, which were due for renewal in 1892, would be substantially altered. In fact the government had largely ignored the increase on duties on which the Chamber had insisted when the treaties had been renegotiated in 1881 and 1882. The Méline tariff when it emerged was a dual tariff, the lower set of duties being intended for use in bilateral agreements. In fact the new system was not so different from the old; a series of trade treaties were signed on the basis of the lower duties and under the threat of the higher ones so that a conventional tariff still applied to most of the important western European trading countries. Switzerland refused until 1895 in another crippling tariff war and Italy until 1899. After that date the higher range of duties applied only to

Latin America and British colonial countries among the significant trading partners.

Protectionist policies also returned to fashion in colonial affairs. The 'colonial party' in French politics was created out of the tariff agitation of the 1880s. The West Indian colonies were induced to renounce the tariff autonomy which they had gained in 1861 and to create tariffs favourable to French exports. Algeria was assimilated into the French tariff structure in 1884 and three years later Indo-China was also assimilated. With the final construction of the Méline tariff the colonies were divided into those considered too underdeveloped for the tariff to be applied and those which could be instantly assimilated, Martinique, Guadeloupe, Indo-China, Gabon and Réunion. The gradual assimilation of the others was to incorporate them also into this protective and exclusive organisation. The great increase in French exports to the colonies is therefore partly explicable simply on the grounds of this legislation.

One effect of the Méline tariff was to reduce the proportion of foodstuffs in French imports. But there was no slowing down in the import of semi-manufactures and manufactures. The rise in the imports of both between 1890 and 1913 kept pace with the rise of exports of manufactured goods. In so far as the protectionists had dreamed of a self-sufficient national economy tied to a large empire their dream came no nearer to reality and the French economy became increasingly dependent on a complicated network of foreign trade, multilateral payments and international investment.

– *Income, Investment and Foreign Lending*

Given the ease of international movements of factors of production in this period it was inevitable that the long process of capital accumulation in France should lead to the export of French capital to other European countries. The scale on which this took place, even if it has been exaggerated by previous scholars, and the simplicity of the mechanisms by which the capital was borrowed, seem astonishing in the present-day world. As France herself became increasingly integrated into the international economy French capital played a decisive part in bringing other economies into the same framework. The only greater lender was Britain and British capital flowed mostly to countries outside Europe. As far as the continent was concerned the Paris money market was the main source of funds.

Even in the late eighteenth century the pattern of French trade had attracted to Paris Swiss bankers interested in international operations because of the surplus of valuable foreign currencies there. In the early nineteenth century the involvement of private banking houses in the political and economic struggles of Spain and Greece had given them powerful positions in placing the state loans of those countries and also of some

Italian states on the Paris money market. In the liberal economic atmosphere of the boom years after 1852 French financiers and entrepreneurs provided major railway routes in Spain, Italy, Switzerland and Austria and also invested in mining and metallurgical companies in Germany. The joint stock banks which developed in those years sought avidly for a share in the placing of public loans of foreign governments and the more adventurous, such as the Crédit Mobilier, had a significant part of their investments abroad. It was in these years that the pattern of foreign investment was created in France. For some countries, Spain, Italy and Germany for example, the sums borrowed from France were larger in this period than after 1870. By 1870 the returns on these foreign investments were making themselves felt in the French balance of payments and were also of course available for reinvestment abroad.

The most usual assumption is that this stream of foreign investment grew in volume and flowed into more and more channels, irrigating as it did so the process of economic development throughout Europe and many other parts of the world. In addition, the argument is frequently made that the slow rate of growth of the French economy was partly caused by the preferences of French investors for investing their capital outside France. There is practically no evidence to support this argument and the assumption that there was a steady growth in the volume of foreign investment after 1870 is in itself highly questionable. There was virtually no control on the movement of capital, and foreign investment, although increasingly directed and channelled through banking institutions, remained essentially a private and often secret activity. Bank archives themselves are still only rarely open to historians; the only adequate approach to measuring even the total volume of foreign investment, therefore, is by means of the balance of payments, and there is no satisfactorily established balance of payments for France in this period. Most information in the circumstances has to come from the receiving countries and by its nature provides neither a detailed nor a comprehensive picture for France itself. But it is surely unrealistic to suppose that the export of capital from France was as regular as many studies imply. France did not always cover her deficits on commodity trade by means of invisible earnings. In two periods at least, 1870–3 and 1879–83, she seems to have done so by exporting bullion. In the first case of course the war indemnity to Germany was being paid but it is also perhaps significant that the French merchant marine did not share in the general growth of shipping in the post-war boom after 1870. The sketchy balance of payments figures which exist suggest that the main period of capital export came after 1895, that the outflow of capital may have been greater in the 1850s than in any decade before the 1890s, and that in the period 1910–13 it turned into a veritable flood. Possibly about as much as one-fifth of all foreign investment after 1881 occurred in these last four years. Thus the general tendency in France was for foreign investment to be at its peak when the domestic economy was also booming, and the two periods of most rapid economic growth in France, 1852–65

Table 17 *Geographical distribution of French long-term foreign investment: cumulative totals (million current francs)*

Area	Type of investment	1890	Date 1900	1914
Russia	Public loans	2,665	6,161	10,123
	Direct investment	244	921	2,245
	TOTAL INVESTMENT	2,912	7,081	12,368
Spain	TOTAL INVESTMENT		2,974[2]	
Austria-Hungary	State loans			1,545.1[3]
	Transport shares			955.5[3]
	Total investment for Hungary alone			950.0
	TOTAL INVESTMENT			3,338.2[3]
Latin America	TOTAL INVESTMENT	1,785.7[4]		8,150.9[5]
Italy[†]	TOTAL INVESTMENT		1,400	1,300
Egypt[†] and South Africa	TOTAL INVESTMENT		3,000	3,300
Colonies[†]	TOTAL INVESTMENT		1,500	4,000
Switzerland, Belgium[†] and the Netherlands	TOTAL INVESTMENT		1,000	1,500
Asia[†]	TOTAL INVESTMENT		800	2,200
Sweden	State debt			506.5[5]
	Mortgages			299.2[5]
	Municipal loans			98.6[5]
	TOTAL INVESTMENT			904.3[5]

Table 17 (cont.)

	1881–95	1896–1903	1904–9	1910–14	1914
Morocco					
State loans			7.5[2]		234.0
Direct investment			6.0[2]		150.0
TOTAL INVESTMENT			13.5[2]		384.0
Canada					
TOTAL INVESTMENT			155.0		500.0
USA†					
TOTAL INVESTMENT			645.0		1,500.0
Turkey					
State loans	283.0	122.1	374.4	651.6	2,209.0
Direct investment	203.3	140.7	79.3	78.8	587.1
TOTAL INVESTMENT	486.3	262.8	453.7	730.4	2,796.1

	1900	1914
Approximate overall totals	25,500	42,000

[1] Real, not nominal, sums   [2] 1902   [3] 1912   [4] 1880   [5] 1913

Source: The table which has served as a basis for all such calculations since it was published is in H. Feis, Europe, the World's Banker 1870–1914 (New Haven, 1930), and appears on p. 51 of the latest edition (New York, W. W. Norton & Co., 1965). Where the information presented here is the same as that in Feis this is indicated by the symbol †. In other cases the estimates are revisions and more detailed breakdowns of Feis's figures taken from the following sources: R. Girault, Emprunts russes et investissements français en Russie, 1887–1914 (Paris, 1973); P. Guillen, Les emprunts marocains de 1902–1904 (Paris, 1972); I. Berend and G. Ránki, 'Nationaleinkommen und Kapitalakkumulation in Ungarn, 1867–1914', in Studia Historica, 1965; J. Viner, Canada's Balance of International Indebtedness, 1900–1913 (Cambridge, Mass., 1924); J. Marseille, 'L'investissement français dans l'Empire coloniale: l'enquête du gouvernement de Vichy', in Revue historique, vol. 252, 1974; and papers presented by A. Broder, F. Mauro, B. Michel, I. Sundbom and J. Thobie to the second conference of French economic historians, Centre National de la Recherche Scientifique, 1973.

and 1895–1913, were almost certainly the years in which most capital left the country. In any case when the rate of interest was sometimes as low as 3 per cent it cannot make much sense to argue that capital was so scarce in France as to retard development.

The fluctuations in timing and direction of foreign investment were also strongly influenced by events abroad. French investment in Latin America was much higher in the periods 1880–90 and 1900–14 than in 1890–1900. The first period represented a wave of interest in industrial and commercial share capital in a developing continent; these were the years of the French Panama Canal Company. The second period represented a cautious withdrawal by investors after bad experiences. After 1900 another surge of interest was provoked by the large-scale building of railways on the South American continent and by the development of Mexico. Similarly, between 1892 and 1905 French investors were deterred from investing in Spain by the low level of the peseta on the foreign exchanges. Fluctuations of this kind were as important as the general trends throughout the period.

The best available evidence on the size and direction of French foreign investment is shown in Table 17. The primary importance of capital movements to Russia emerges, as well as the great significance of a much less developed economy, Turkey. It was economies where new capital investments on a large scale were taking place, such as railway building or deep-mining operations, which had recourse to the French capital market. The initial link in the chain was a demand for capital which could not be met in the underdeveloped economy. But this was only the initial link and it had often been forged in the railway boom of the 1850s. After that the process of borrowing became internationalised and a considerable part of the loans were to service earlier loans. But where there was little initial demand for large-scale capital investment the flow of capital could not build up and thus it was that Russia or Turkey were more important as recipients of French capital than the French Empire.

The figures in Table 17, however, seem very high even for a country with a high ratio of saving and it may well be that the statistical problems involved, and the fact that many of the contemporary estimates were the work of propagandists for foreign investment, have led historians to overestimate the totals. What is known about the size and composition of personal wealth in France tends also to confirm this. Above the poorest levels of the population the size of testamentary bequests on death was recorded by the fiscal authorities and this gives some indication of personal wealth. The proportion too poor to interest the fiscal authorities was very large, about 70 per cent in bigger cities, so that the figures certainly give too flattering a picture of income levels. The average private wealth recorded in 1908 was just over 5,000 francs. Of the sixteen departments where the average was higher than this fifteen were in the northern half of the country, the only exception, the department of Rhône, containing the city of Lyons. The average sum of wealth left in Paris was over three times the national average; in several departments of the Massif Central,

Ariège, Lozère, Corrèze, it was only one-fifth. In Corsica it was less than one-twentieth. The accumulation of wealth was therefore strikingly correlated with the geographical pattern of economic development. Furthermore the evidence indicates that economic growth had done nothing to alter the flagrant economic and social inequalities. The gap between the highest and lowest recorded holdings of wealth was virtually unaltered between 1815 and 1913, although at the top and bottom of the scale, which of course excludes the large part of the population who were very poor, the stock of wealth increased. The average recorded fortune in Paris in 1911 was 35,600 francs; the average for a skilled workman was 900 francs. Five per cent of the fortunes recorded in 1905 accounted for 72 per cent of the total. Economic growth had created extensive holdings of wealth in a small number of hands in a restricted area of the country. They were not, however, the same hands as in 1780; of the fortunes recorded above one million francs in Paris in 1911, only 10 per cent belonged to noble families.

The composition of private fortunes is revealing of investors' habits: after 1870 the proportion represented by investment in land and building declined as the proportion held in more readily liquifiable investments such as government bonds and industrial shares rose. The proportion of private wealth holdings represented by fixed assets such as land and buildings declined from 70 per cent in 1852 to 43·8 per cent; that represented by share capital and government bonds rose from 7 per cent to 39 per cent. In the early nineteenth century the bigger the fortune, the bigger the share of it held in property. By 1913 this was by no means true. One obvious reason was the gradually diminishing importance of agriculture in the economy and the consequent decline in investment in landed estate relative to other forms of investment; but this was partly compensated for by the enormous building boom in Paris and its suburbs. The other main reason was the growing attraction, not just of liquifiable investments, but specifically of share capital which, certainly after 1892, displaced the old *rentes* as the favourite form of paper for private investors. But the constitution of private fortunes varied from one area of the country to another as much as did the size of those fortunes. The amount held in share capital in Paris, Lyons and the department of Nord was far higher than elsewhere. In the remoter and less developed rural departments practically no wealth at all was held in share capital; this was the case, for example, in Lozère, Gers and Ariège. The proportion held in cash, although everywhere low, was highest in the remotest areas such as Corsica, the Pyrenees and the Alps; in Paris it was negligible.

Part of this increase in shares and bonds consisted of an increase in foreign bonds. Only now is the world again becoming familiar with the situation, frequent before 1914, when private individuals died leaving a part of their wealth in obligations on exotic companies in remote lands and on foreign governments of whose true nature they had been quite ignorant. Holdings of foreign share capital, as a proportion of all share capital bequeathed, rose from one-quarter between 1890 and 1895 to one-third between 1910 and 1914. These holdings were again unequally distributed in the country as a whole. The average share of foreign investments in the private fortunes studied by Cornut was 13·3 per cent.[8] In Paris the average proportion was 22 per cent, which as a total sum of money was six times the average value of foreign paper held in any other department. In large areas of France foreign capital was well under one per cent of private wealth. The public interested in foreign investment was the urban and commercial middle class in those parts of France most affected by economic development. Far from being a national phenomenon, foreign investment was a localised one interesting for the most part only a particular section of the population.

This group chose to invest mainly in government loans giving a fixed rate of interest. Only in South America did they show a preference for more speculative industrial shares. Most of the fixed interest loans were raised by foreign governments and thus bore a superficial resemblance to the long-established French *rentes*. But the purposes to which they were put were very different. They were frequently used to provide the basic social overhead capital of developing countries, especially railways and ports. In this case the borrowing government was giving a guarantee, sometimes dubious, to enable railway constructors to get hold of the capital which in France itself had often been raised on the stock exchange without government intervention. The apogee of this type of activity was the policy of the Russian government when de Witte was finance minister.[9] An alternative purpose, and one which began to play an ever larger role in the last two decades, was the purchase of military equipment. The enormous increase in the volume and complexity of armaments meant that smaller European countries were left practically defenceless without borrowing. But the sad and ironical fact is that often the main purpose to which these government loans were put was that of paying the interest on earlier loans. The full implications of foreign investment for the international economy and for the receiving countries are discussed later.[10]

Where French investors placed their funds in purely business ventures the framework was different. Even there, however, the companies in which they invested were most frequently French or other foreign companies. As public borrowing became more controlled and institutionalised so did French-owned banks install themselves in borrowing countries. One example of the importance of this type of lending will suffice. When the vast phosphoric iron ore deposits of northern Sweden began to be mined after the invention of the Gilchrist–Thomas process the mining operations, in themselves difficult, took place in a hostile terrain and in a region completely unprovided with transport or other forms of social overhead capital. The costs of expansion were very high and Swedish entrepreneurs met them by recourse to French banking syndicates who then placed the shares of the Swedish mining companies with their clients in France. Underdeveloped countries had no effective banking systems of their own and it was easy for French and other foreign bankers to fill this gap. Where such French banks obtained extremely powerful positions, as did the Imperial Ottoman Bank in Turkey, they began to direct the placing of private as well as public investment and to blur the distinction between the two. From controlling the Turkish public debt the Imperial Ottoman Bank passed after 1890 to placing French capital in direct investments in Turkey and by 1913 it held a controlling interest in about two-thirds of the French companies in Constantinople (Istanbul) and Asia Minor.

Nevertheless there was a valid distinction between public and private foreign investment for most of the period. The two most typical targets for French private investment were mines and insurance companies. The avid search for new sources of raw material could make certain mining ventures extremely profitable; one of the most profitable of the Rothschild investments was the Almadén mercury mines in Spain. French insurance companies did not find it difficult to use their long experience to advantage elsewhere. In Bulgaria the insurance market was dominated by French companies and in Italy they were also particularly active. A further target was the supply of public utilities in the growing cities of Europe: a Franco-Belgian company began to provide electric lighting and electric trams in Sofia in 1898, and in Naples at the same time the water company and 40 per cent of the gas and electricity supply were French-controlled. On the whole these types of investment were comparatively unimportant from the French point of view, although as far as the borrowing country was concerned it could mean that a significant part of a very small industrial sector was controlled by foreigners. French investors dominated four of the six most important metal companies in the Russian metal cartel Produmet by 1914; through the same companies they were controlling about half the coal mining in the Donets basin. It is estimated that over the whole period French investment was about 20 per cent of all investment in Bulgarian industry, although as far as France was concerned the sums, totalling approximately 20 million francs, were insignificant.

There were other ways in which French capital was deployed abroad and two were important. One was the opening of branch companies, often to exploit a new process or to reduce the effect of a protective tariff: Renault opened two car factories in Russia on the eve of the war and the Michelin tire company had a subsidiary in Frankfurt-on-Main. France itself was also the recipient of similar branch companies founded by United States, British and German firms; fourteen American companies had manufacturing facilities in France in 1914 and total United States investment there increased threefold between 1900 and 1914. The other, whose exact importance is difficult to measure, was the short-term use of French capital by financial institutions elsewhere. This was an important aspect of Franco-German economic relations in the period. Political tensions deterred most long-term investments in this case but the relations between major French and German banks presented many opportunities for profitable co-operation. Between 1898 and 1911 short-term capital move-ments from France played an important role in the German economy. The preoccupation of the London money market in 1898 with the Boer War meant that when German banks were unable to meet the heavy demand for funds they turned to the Paris market. There were many ways in which the Paris bankers could co-operate without involving their government: they could, for example, buy foreign exchange at three months payment on Berlin and thus make disguised loans. Such operations were safer because they implied no commitment. In each political crisis they were broken off but the withdrawal of French funds after the major political incidents at Tangier and Algeciras in both cases created difficulties in Germany. These movements were finally terminated by the Agadir crisis in 1911. Short-term lending of this kind was mainly to Germany, but on the eve of the war in 1914 there existed short-term loans from French banks to Russian banks and firms amounting to some 500 million francs.

French capital did not flow without political influence and the degree of political involvement in these capital movements grew after 1900. Where loans concerned armaments the French foreign ministry could not help but be closely concerned and on occasions it applied its own pressures on borrowing countries. When German companies tried to raise capital directly on the Paris stock exchange the French foreign office intervened to demand concessions in return. The military alliances also heavily influenced the direction of French investment. French capital had already begun to flow in large quantities to Russia before the Franco-Russian military alliance in 1894. But that alliance gave a semblance of security to this huge new field for investment, and the opening of a credit of 1,250 million francs in April 1906 was a political act undertaken to save the Tsarist government from impending bankruptcy. Over the period 1880–1913 the proportion of Italian industrial shares held abroad owned in France varied between 45 and 90 per cent and this wide variation was dictated mainly by political considerations. The lowest point, in 1895–6, was at the end of the worst period of political tension between the two countries.

The essential intermediary in these political manoeuvrings were the large investment banks, especially if there were French-owned banks in the country, which might act as a clearing house for public investment and also have their own private interests. By no means all French banks operating abroad had this importance. Some were quite small affairs and others soon passed out of French hands. Among the earliest were the French banks founded in Spain in the 1850s. Only one survived into the later period, the Crédito Mobiliario Español. It participated in the European enterprises of its French founder as well as financing specific enterprises in Spain. It very seldom provided credits for Spanish businesses and remained very much the representative of French and other foreign businesses in Spain until it was incorporated in 1902 into the Banco Español de Crédito. The Länder-bank, which Bontoux's Union Générale had briefly used as the instrument of its railway schemes in Austria, passed under Austrian control in the crash of the Union Générale, although French investors continued to draw interest on their share of the capital. Banks performing the same functions as the Crédit Mobilier sprang up in Argentina during the land and railway boom there, the Banque Française de Rio de la Plata in 1886, the Crédit Foncier et Agricole de Santa Fé in 1887, and the Banque Hypothécaire Franco-Argentine in 1905. Half the capital of the national Bank of Brazil in 1898 was owned by the Banque de Paris et des Pays Bas. Two-thirds of the capital in the Russo-Asiatic Bank came from French institutions. The older banks were not necessarily eclipsed in this competition; the French Rothschilds retained their virtual control of the placing of Italian public debt in France, which dated from their early financial connections with the Italian states. They also handled payments to Dutch and Belgian investors. But the importance of newer banks, the Imperial Ottoman Bank in Turkey and the Banque de Paris et des Pays Bas in Morocco, was such as to make them the equivalent of major organs of the state administration there.

It was in Turkey that this process reached its height. There the great powers agreed, as they did in Egypt, on a scheme of international co-operation to sustain debt payments. Turkey was not allowed to modify existing taxes nor impose tariffs without the consent of foreign powers, and after 1881 her budget and debt payments were supervised by an international body under French and British direction. This organisation, the Administration of the Ottoman Public Debt, was granted control over the former government monopolies of salt, alcohol, wood and tobacco and was itself responsible for the terms of many of the state loans. These loans were then negotiated and handled through the Imperial Ottoman Bank. In effect French administrators were raising loans to pay French investors in an unbroken circle of operations and the monopolies they controlled were only one instrument of an agreed political control over Turkey. In Greece the French government also had rights of control over the budget. The logical end of such policies was the division of Turkey into 'zones of influence' in which the great powers would not compete with each other.

The laws and customs of France came eventually to be imposed on many traditional societies in North Africa and eastern Europe, and this was accompanied by the cultural domination of France over the small middle class of the borrowing country so that it became easy enough for French statesmen and institutions to suppose that all Romanians or Egyptians were as francophile as those they dealt with. Backed by his own laws and customs, supported by international agreements, and ultimately depending on the massive military power of his own country it is no wonder the French investor felt his investment to be secure. Only revolt from below or the collapse of all agreement between the major powers could threaten it. Both of these things happened of course after 1914, but before then not even the Russian revolution of 1905 was any more than a temporary deterrent.

The institutional channels through which the capital flowed were all designed to play down the element of risk involved. The borrowing governments were able to maintain for the most part a decent façade of financial accountability and governmental respectability; the intermediary agency of a French bank gave the final stamp of soundness to the transaction. Large deposit banks actively sought such investments and used their offices to encourage the public to place its funds abroad. The relative ease with which they did so was frankly admitted by the leading officials of the Crédit Lyonnais in their evidence to the United States National Monetary Commission in 1910.

'What is very important in our way of floating a loan is that the sales are made in small quantities; the transaction is completed in a very few days, and each of our customers buys only the number of bonds corresponding to their investment requirement.

Question: As a matter of fact, anything you recommend they will buy?

Answer: Yes, and even with a very large issue.'[11]

A large financial press surveyed, canvassed and recommended all opportunities: in 1881 there were 228 separate financial journals published in France and 95 other papers carried financial bulletins. The first concern of any banker recommending a foreign loan was to bribe the press; under de Witte the Russian government had several Paris journals in its pay. An apparently secure situation was actually full of ambiguities. Spain refused Cuban debts after Cuban independence; Honduras staged a national bankruptcy and renounced its debts. In Mexico French investors had a clear forewarning of what was to come in Russia. Under the dictator Porfirio Diaz foreign capital was encouraged by terms more favourable than in any other country, so favourable that even French investors preferred private to public investment there. But during and after the Mexican revolution much of this capital, especially that in railways, ceased to pay any dividend.

It is clear that security was not the only motive. Although some foreign investments were unprofitable, on average they were more profitable than investments in France and on occasions they provided immense profits, encouraging further risks. The dividends paid by oil companies in Russia in which French investors were concerned never fell below 8 per cent between 1904 and 1913 and rose to 20 per cent in some years. Over the same period metallurgical firms paid dividends between 3·4 per cent and 10 per cent. The rate of return on Turkish state loans usually varied between 4·5 per cent and 5·5 per cent, a higher rate than on the French *rentes*. The highest profits were recorded by direct investments, often in fortunate mining ventures. Between 1900 and 1912 the Bolco company of Baja California, owned by the French Rothschilds, paid between 25 per cent and 200 per cent profit annually. Schneider's investments in Rosario were among their most profitable. The two factors that foreign state loans paid more than the French public debt, and that particular acts of direct investment were on occasions profitable beyond all expectations, combined to keep French capital flowing abroad until the First World War brought down in ruins the international economy which was both cause and result of these movements.

CONCLUSIONS

The potential for continued economic growth in an already developed economy proved to be large; indeed the greater variety of economic activity which came with economic development brought with it the possibility of drawing on a wider range of potential forces for growth. The growth that did occur in France was the combined result of all these different forces operating to a different degree in different sectors of the economy. The overall pattern of development of the economy over the whole period suggests that in spite of the growing influence of the international economy the pattern of development of the French economy was still principally determined by national factors. The stagnation of the years after 1880 had no such serious equivalent in other developed economies. And although the preponderance of an industry which was no longer particularly dynamic nor competitive on world markets, the cotton industry, presents certain analogies with the British economy in the same period and suggests that after 1870 there were certain penalties to be paid for early industrialisation, these analogies are only superficial. Both in Germany and Britain the cotton industry continued to expand in the 1880s. The industrial boom of the last two decades was also an experience very different from that of Britain. It owed much to the ready acceptance of new industrial technologies and to the first large-scale migrations of labour from the agricultural sector, something which had happened long before in Britain. Nor is a comparison made with an economy more similar in structure, Germany, any more revealing. The 1871–3 boom and the 1873 crash were both more marked there; and in the 1880s the continued growth and industrialisation of the German economy gives few points of comparison with France, in spite of the similar international setting. In the development of the new technologies in the 1890s, France, although noticeably lagging behind Germany in most sectors of the chemical industry and many of the electrical industry, developed in car manufacture and in the use of hydro-electricity industries which made a significant contribution to the economy as a whole and which in Germany were smaller and more derivative.

The central problem is to explain the pattern of stagnation and revival. One important aspect was the low level of efficiency and incomes in agriculture which gradually slowed down development and then brought it to a standstill. The protective tariffs, although they did nothing to improve efficiency, after 1892 marginally raised incomes in agriculture from the low and falling level caused by the arrival of foreign foodstuffs after 1873 and in so doing enabled the consumer goods industries to recover. It was probably fortunate that the Méline tariff was such a clumsy instrument because it did not raise incomes sufficiently to prevent the departure of large numbers of people from the agricultural sector once the industrial recovery had begun. After that recovery had begun it was strengthened by the fact that some of the new technologies were able to use hitherto unexploited resources in areas of the country which had been previously almost untouched by the industrial revolution. The industrialisation of Lorraine was based on the previously useless iron ore resources and on the raw materials which attracted the chemical industry; similarly the Alpine regions were industrialised on the basis of cheap electric current from water power. It is often forgotten how important developed European economies still were as exporters of raw materials in the late nineteenth century and it was precisely in those years that French exports of iron ore and bauxite developed, both also resources relatively unexploited earlier.

The structure of French exports was in an intermediate position between that of Britain and that of Germany. What had become the less competitive exports, textiles and foodstuffs, still dominated in 1914 as they did in Britain, but more competitive goods were rapidly gaining ground after 1890, more rapidly than in Britain, so that by 1912 for example cars already formed 3 per cent of total exports. Germany was less handicapped by the older export trades and the structure of her exports enabled her to benefit more from the growth of international trade between developed economies, especially between 1870 and 1890. But these are only partial explanations of what occurred. It is very likely that in this period the level of per capita income in Germany surpassed that in France and yet after 1890 the industrial revival in France, although it did produce a surge of exports, was at first dependent on the domestic market. The revival of industrial production cannot be entirely explained by the tendency of the tariff to increase incomes; the burst of investment which initiated that revival may well not have been motivated by economic factors alone. After all the Freycinet plan, deliberately conceived to bring about a similar revival ten years earlier, had fizzled out, whereas the unplanned revival after 1890 continued strongly, surviving all cyclical shocks to the end of the period. Many important changes of the 1890s, the financial arrangements which permitted effective agricultural co-operation to take but one example, could just as easily and appropriately have come two decades earlier. There is certainly more to be discovered about the strictly economic aspects of this apparent change in confidence.

Existing national income calculations put per capita income in France in 1913 at about the same level as in Germany or Scandinavia, although still substantially below the level in Britain. Our survey of the historical evidence suggests that these calculations may well exaggerate the level of French per capita income, and these exaggerations have perhaps been encouraged by exaggerations of the volume of foreign investment. German industrial wages had climbed above those in France by 1913 and the fact that there were more workers in German industry suggests that for French per capita income to be at the same level, per capita incomes in the agricultural sector would have had to be substantially higher in France than in Germany: this seems unlikely.

With the rapid industrial development of the last two decades the international framework in which the national economy functioned became a permanent and unavoidable influence. These years were a watershed not only for France but for the other western European economies also. The growth of international trade and foreign investment was such that domestic factors became of relatively less importance in determining the pattern of growth and development. The background to the protectionist movement was thus highly paradoxical. France did not merely participate in the European industrialisation boom of the 1890s, she was one of its progenitors, as she had been in the earlier continental industrialisation boom after 1852. But the forty years interval had shown how shallow the foundations of that first boom had been, especially in the agricultural sector. The European economy which France played so great a part in building after 1890 was now devoid of the unrealistic aspirations of Chevalier, the free-trade movement, or the Péreires. But it was also devoid of their nobler ideals; it existed amidst intense national rivalries which soon brought it to temporary ruin. Nevertheless for France and the developed western economies an irrevocable step had been taken; their national economic destinies had become permanently and inextricably bound together.

SUGGESTED READING

The literature in English on French economic development in this period falls into two types, brief general discussions of the period as a whole and detailed analyses of single issues. In the first category may be placed two works which, while not being economic histories of the period, serve as readable introductions to it. They are T. KEMP, *Economic Forces in French History* (London, 1971) and the lively C. P. KINDLEBERGER, *Economic Growth in France and Britain 1851–1950* (Cambridge, Mass., 1964). Two older works are still of some value: J. H. CLAPHAM, *The Economic Development of France and Germany, 1815–1914* (Cambridge, 1921) and S. B. CLOUGH, *France: A Study in National Economics* (New York, 1931).

On the more detailed aspects we may note first the singular absence of any good work in English on French industry in this period. There is an excellent article by F. CARON, 'French Railroad Investment, 1850–1914', in R. CAMERON (ed.), *Essays in French Economic History* (Homewood, Ill., 1970). Agriculture is much better served: E. GOLOB, *The Méline Tariff: French Agriculture and Nationalist Economic Policy* (New York, 1944) is a good work showing how searching history can be. M. TRACY, *Agriculture in Western Europe* (London, 1964) is a simpler book which students will find readable, and the early chapters of G.

WRIGHT, *Rural Revolution in France* (Palo Alto, 1964) are relevant and interesting. There is a sound review of the present state of research in P. HOHENBERG, 'Change in Rural France in the Period of Industrialisation, 1830–1914', in *Journal of Economic History*, vol. 32, no. 1, 1972. The only other area which can be studied in English is that of overseas trade and foreign investment. F. A. HAIGHT, *A History of French Commercial Policies* (New York, 1941) is exactly what its title describes. The effect of these policies is discussed in S. WEILLER, 'Long-run Tendencies in Foreign Trade: with a Statistical Study of French Foreign Trade Structure, 1871–1939', in *Journal of Economic History*, vol. 21, no. 4, 1971. H. D. WHITE, *The French International Accounts 1880–1913*, Harvard Economic Studies, vol. 40 (Cambridge, Mass., 1933) is a lucid study of foreign trade and the balance of payments, but its conclusions on the use of income from foreign investment and some of its many figures are no longer accurate. Beneath the more picturesque surface of D. S. LANDES, *Bankers and Pashas* (Cambridge, Mass., 1958) lies a subtle study of the mechanisms of French foreign investment and imperialism in Egypt. More information about banks may be found in B. GILLE, 'Banking and Industrialisation in Europe 1730–1914', in *The Fontana Economic History of Europe*, vol. 4.

For all further study it is necessary to read in French. The best bibliography, now out of date, is in *The Cambridge Economic History of Europe*, vol. 6. The general economic surveys in French are worse than those in English, but a small sample of the more specialised works will show how much there is. The statistical situation is being gradually transformed by the publication in sections of the *Histoire quantitative de l'économie française* by the Institut de Science Economique Appliquée; their work is hidden away in no logical sequence in the periodical *Cahiers de l'Institut de Science Economique Appliquée* and it would be useful to have it collected in more accessible form. For the period after 1890 there is a rare example of a good and unpretentious work on economic growth, J. J. CARRÉ, P. DUBOIS and E. MALINVAUD, *La Croissance française* (Paris, 1972). On particular industries the situation is almost as blank as in English and this must be one of the most important unexplored areas of research in economic history. Exceptions are P. FRIDENSON, *L'Histoire des usines Renault*, vol. 1, *Naissance de la grande entreprise, 1898–1939* (Paris, 1972); and M. GILLET, *Les Charbonnages du nord de la France au XIXᵉ siècle* (Paris, 1973). On agriculture the only general account is the rather vague M. AUGÉ-LARIBÉ, *La Révolution agricole* (Paris, 1955). But the tradition of local history, and the more modern nature of geographical studies in France, have produced some sound regional studies of which R. DUGRAND, *Villes et campagnes en Bas-Languedoc* (Paris, 1963) is an example.

In one field, that of the distribution and employment of capital, French economic historians have given a lead, so far not followed, to others. The most convenient summary of this research is in C. A. MICHELET, *Les Placements des épargnants français de 1815 à nos jours* (Paris, 1968). To this should be added A. DAUMARD, *Les Bourgeois de Paris au XIXᵉ siècle* (Paris, 1970) and P. CORNUT, *Répartition de la fortune privée en France par département et nature de biens au cours de la première moitié du vingtième siècle* (Paris, 1963). On banking there is J. BOUVIER, *Le Crédit Lyonnais: les années de formation d'une banque* (Paris, 1968). On the most important sector of foreign investment R. GIRAULT, *Emprunts russes et investissements français en Russie 1887–1914* (Paris, 1973), may be consulted.

Current research and reviews of the latest publications are published in the same periodicals as those listed in the appendix to Chapter 5 of our previous work: *Annales, Revue d'histoire économique et sociale, Revue d'histoire moderne et contemporaine, Revue internationale d'histoire de la banque, Revue du Nord,* and in English in *The Journal of European Economic History.* Some works are occasionally reviewed in *Economic History Review,* but only haphazardly.

NOTES

1 J. Marczewski, 'Le produit physique de l'économie française de 1789 à 1913', in *Cahiers de l'Institut de Science Economique Appliquée,* série AF, 4, no. 163, 1965, p. lxxiv.
2 The more prominent developments of this kind in Germany are discussed on pp. 35–8.
3 See A. S. Milward and S. B. Saul, *The Economic Development of Continental Europe 1780–1870* (London, 1973), ch. 3.
4 The famous early aviator Louis Blériot financed his aircraft building by making improved car headlights.
5 J. C. Toutain, 'Le produit de l'agriculture française de 1700 à 1958: II, La Croissance', in *Cahiers de l'Institut de Science Economique Appliquée,* série AF, no. 2, p. 129.
6 A. S. Milward and S. B. Saul, op. cit., pp. 502 ff.
7 See Chapter 9.
8 P. Cornut, *Répartition de la fortune privée en France par département et nature de biens au cours de la première moitié du vingtième siècle* (Paris, 1963).
9 See below, pp. 386–94.
10 See below, pp. 492–501.
11 Evidence of the Crédit Lyonnais before the United States National Monetary Commission, 1910. United States, Senate Document no. 405.

Chapter 3

The Economic Development of Belgium and the Netherlands, 1850–1914

We have discussed the two largest developed continental European economies as separate national entities in order to show the differences in their experience over this period. But the consequences for other economies of the continued development of Germany and France were increasingly important and their interactions with them closer. For this reason we concluded our discussion of development in France with an analysis of the economic relationships between France and the outside world. The influence of events in France and Germany was particularly strong in the much smaller national economies on their frontiers. In a general sense it is true that the economic development of two of them, Belgium and the Netherlands, can only be fully understood in the context of events in

France, Germany and Britain. Nevertheless, a proper understanding of the development of both Belgium and the Netherlands and of the general problem of the development of smaller economies requires that they both be discussed as national entities. Small states though they both were they each had many important distinctive economic characteristics and to ignore those would be to oversimplify the issues involved in European economic development.

In our earlier work we discussed the economic problems facing the Low Countries during the years from 1815 to 1830, when they were brought together as a joint monarchy, and the immediate consequences of the split in 1830.[1] Here we follow them further in their individual courses – Belgium already by 1830 in the throes of industrialisation, the Netherlands still suffering from the loss of her old financial and trading supremacy, a decline which had started in the eighteenth century and had been intensified by the disruption of the Napoleonic period. Although small, both were densely populated countries; in 1910 there were 5,900,000 people living in the Netherlands and 7,400,000 in Belgium. This gave Belgium the densest population in Europe, with 259 inhabitants per square kilometre compared with 239 in England and Wales. Following them came the Netherlands with 171 per square kilometre which was extremely dense for a country which was less industrially orientated. By the first decade of the twentieth century moreover the rate of population growth in the Netherlands was one of the highest in Europe: the excess of births over deaths was 15·3 per thousand, the result mainly of a very low death rate. In Belgium the rate of growth was 9·7 per thousand, one of the lowest in Europe; the death rate was somewhat higher and the birth rate much lower. With an extremely low rate of emigration from both countries, the pressure of population was therefore mounting very rapidly in the Netherlands; in Belgium, where the pressure was already acute, a low birth rate was helping to prevent it from worsening. As we shall see, though this density of population did not prevent rapid economic development, it had important consequences for land prices and for the nature of exploitation of the land. Above all, through its effects on wage levels it was a determining influence on the economic development of the two countries.

I. Economic Development in Belgium

AGRICULTURE

Though the authorities differ considerably in their estimates for the earlier years, one recent study suggests that in 1846 about one-third of the working population of Belgium was engaged in agriculture and that the proportion remained much the same for the next twenty years (Table 18).[2] Thereafter the share began to fall off sharply. The absolute numbers engaged in agriculture, however, appear to have fallen only slowly until 1895 and thereafter rather more quickly. The rural population, containing many who commuted to work in industry, continued to expand.

The geography of Belgian agriculture consisted first of an area of dunes to the north where there were very small farms, some engaged in market gardening but mainly concentrating on cultivating potatoes and rye by the end of the century, with few animals being raised. To the south were the clay polders, rich treeless plains but with a soil difficult to work, an area of big isolated farms where animals were very important. In the northeast, in Anvers[3] and Limburg, lay the Campine (Kempen), a land of poor soils brought into cultivation by the use of artificial manures and town waste: rye, oats and potatoes were grown but dairying was the main activity. The sandy region of Flanders, running from Dixmude to Ghent, was also basically poor soil but had been improved by centuries of intensive care: it was the region with the greatest concentration of very small farms. South of this was the sandy loam area running across the country from Courtrai to Liège, and from Louvain to Namur, high farming plains for cereals and sugar beet where some of the biggest farms of 200–300 hectares were to be found. East of this was the country between Liège and Eupen, a region of intensive small farms under grass. The land south of the Meuse between Namur and Liège was the most important cattle rearing area. Lastly came the poor soils of the Ardennes, where progress had been made only with the help of artificial fertilisers; pasture and forest were found side by side with fields of oats and potatoes but by and large the farms were too big for the capital available. In general the arable area was lowest on the polders and highest on the sandy soils of Brabant and the Campine.

Table 18 *Agricultural workers as a proportion of the working population in Belgium*

	1846	1866	1890	1910
Flanders	31·7	36·6	30·9	22·9
Hainaut–Liège	23·4	22·8	14·2	10·8
Brabant	31·7	35·3	21·9	13·0
Anvers	40·8	36·8	24·9	13·3
Belgium	32·0	32·4	23·7	17·0

Source: B. Verhaegen, *Contribution à l'histoire économique des Flandres* (Louvain, 1961), vol, 1, p. 330.

In 1895 72 per cent of all holdings were farmed by tenants and they covered two-thirds of the cultivated area. The United Kingdom provided the extreme example of tenant farming in the nineteenth century with 88 per cent of the area so cultivated in 1906, but Belgium ranked next. In France and the Netherlands the proportion was about 50 per cent; Germany (14 per cent in 1895) and Denmark (12 per cent in 1892) were at the other extreme. There were few landless farm labourers in Belgium, and most of these were found on the central plains, but considerable numbers of men worked as seasonal labourers away from their own tiny holdings. Tenancy was highest in the extreme west and lowest in the Ardennes and the Campine; tenants in the west worked farms of considerable size with rich meadows and high rents but such farms were too large for their tenants to buy even if the owners were willing to sell. The price of land was low in the Ardennes and the Campine due to low population density, poor soil and distance from markets. In 1895 rents in

Flanders and Brabant, where population pressure and subdivision were serious, stood at over 1,500 francs per acre compared with about 800 francs in the Ardennes. Very high rents were paid around Waremone, north-west of Liège; population was not dense there but the land was ideally suited for sugar beet, as it was also in the polder land to the extreme west of Flanders. In general, Rowntree suggested that in 1900 the rent of agricultural land was about 80 per cent higher than in England and Wales and the price twice as high as a result of pressure of demand rather than higher fertility.[4]

In 1846 89 per cent of holdings in Belgium over one hectare consisted of farms of less than 15 hectares. Only here and there was there any significant departure from this pattern, though in West Flanders a fifth of the holdings were above 15 hectares because of the larger farms of the polder region. More significantly, holdings of less than one hectare accounted for 55 per cent of all holdings in Belgium; in West Flanders and Hainaut they accounted for 65 per cent and in Liège for 60 per cent. These high figures for the industrial provinces probably reflect the large number of market gardens farmed part-time by industrial workers. In Flanders on the polders the big farmers rented small parcels of land to their workers but the main explanation for the number of very small holdings lies in the density of the agricultural population in certain regions.[5]

Already in the 1840s Flanders was a densely populated province with 230 people per square kilometre, compared with Brabant which had only 211, even though the number there was swelled by the inclusion of the city of Brussels. The population of Flanders had been exceptionally high in the period before industrialisation and this had been accompanied by an advanced level of cultivation, particularly through the heavy application of town wastes and other types of natural fertiliser. The most naturally fertile region of Flanders, the maritime area, was less densely populated. From 1846 to 1866 the rural population in Flanders rose quite sharply, though in part this was a result of domestic workers in linen devoting more and more of their time to farming. But the rise of farm prices during these years was a major factor also. From 1866 to 1880 agricultural wages were gaining by comparison with those in industry, though the rate varied from one region to another and was to some extent modified by the coming of mechanical threshing. However, there was a steady growth in migration, both seasonal and permanent. Table 19 gives the pattern of permanent migration for Belgium as a whole. The contrast between the rural and urban regions is obvious; in Flanders a loss was recorded every decade after 1840 while Liège and Brabant gained in every decade. Table 18 shows how sharply the proportion of agricultural workers fell in those two provinces between 1866 and 1890. Permanent emigration, especially to northern France, was a feature of all difficult periods, in 1830, in 1845–8, in the 1860s during the cotton famine and again from 1880 to 1900 at the time of the general crisis throughout European agriculture. In the area of Lille in 1900 Belgians comprised one-fifth of the working population; in Roubaix there were 35,600 Belgian workers and 88,800 French. But the numbers actually leaving Flanders were small in relation to the total, and failed to resolve the enormous problems of the area. Seasonal migration from that region developed rapidly after 1870 and around 1900 perhaps 15,000 workers crossed into France each day, not counting those going for a week. It is difficult to determine the factors behind the mobility of different groups; it has been suggested that there was a marked difference between the Flemish population, uncommunicative, timid and fearful, deeply attached to their native soil and families, and the Walloons who were expansive by nature, more willing to move and more easily accommodated to new circumstances. An important element might well have been education, for about 15 per cent of Belgian children did not go to school and in 1900 19 per cent of the population over 8 years of age could neither read nor write; significantly the proportion was highest in Flanders and lowest in the Walloon provinces. Internal migration was much encouraged by the practice of providing cheap season

Table 19   *Balance of permanent migration in Belgium by provinces, 1832–1910*

Anvers	+101,336	West Flanders	−163,853
Brabant	+253,835	East Flanders	−189,038
Hainaut	+22,184	Limburg	−48,221
Liège	+97,503	Luxembourg	−76,617
		Namur	−66,868

Source: B. Verhaegen, *Contribution à l'histoire économique des Flandres* (Louvain, 1961), vol. 1, p. 76.

tickets on the railways: the fares were at most half those charged in Britain, for example. In 1872 the number of journeys made annually under these tickets was 863,000; in 1882 it was 6·3 million, in 1900 48 million and in 1912 85 million. In 1910, of all industrial workers in Hainaut, Liège and Brabant, 45 per cent were migrating, that is not living in the same commune as their work. The family remained in a rural area, usually with a small holding, and the father commuted, often considerable distances, to the factory.

With permanent migration so limited, the pressure of population brought with it an intensification of *morcellement*, the break up of holdings into smaller size. Entail was illegal in Belgium but hereditary laws are at best only a partial explanation of changes in the size of holdings, for differences between various parts of Flanders must also be explained. It is possible to argue that the break up derived in part from the passing of land into the hands of the bourgeoisie; since small parcels sold for more per hectare than the larger, *morcellement* would be encouraged. Ultimately, however, it was a function of the whole pattern of population pressure, rural poverty and farming techniques.

Small-scale farming had its advocates, mainly on emotional grounds, but many were aware of the consequences of inefficiency, shortage of capital, poverty and ignorance. It is misleading to look at the high returns per hectare in regions like Flanders and to ignore the poor returns per capita. Small farms needed an amount of labour disproportionately large in relation to the returns from the farm; little machinery was used because it could not easily be adapted to such small farms and because of shortage of capital. As for the farmer, he found rents rising under population pressure. In the face of limited opportunities for technical improvement he had to cut costs and press his family into agricultural or supplementary industrial work. Any surplus, however, still tended to be absorbed by

Table 20   *Domestic workers in Belgium in 1910*

	Number	Change over 1896
West Flanders	55,960	+14,135
East Flanders	47,771	+11,344
Brabant	14,616	+2,406
Anvers	9,732	+2,923
Liège	8,820	−3,854
Hainaut	5,842	+105
Belgium	144,709	+26,089

Source: B. Verhaegen, *Contribution à l'histoire économique des Flandres* (Louvain, 1961), vol. 1, p. 311.

yet higher rents. Only the actual disappearance of the small farmer would bring an end to *morcellement*, but in Belgium they were slow to go in spite of the difficulties of living by the land. The lingering popularity of small plots is a singular aspect of the Belgian economy and hard to explain. It was perhaps linked with ease of marketing; it was also part of a long history of adaptability and the tradition of heavy feeding of the land. Furthermore, a substantial part of the family income on such holdings came from those who worked in industry. Perhaps above all it was the result of frugality. Frugality itself might be beneficial but carried to extremes it was a barrier to all progress, for it allowed people to survive on the land who would far better have left it.

The crisis of the late years of the nineteenth century brought a reduction in small holdings throughout Belgium. In Flanders the number of farm operators fell from 258,000 in 1890 to 192,000 in 1910, the decline partly due to an increase in seasonal migration and partly to a tendency for industrial capital to buy into agriculture. There was also some growth of industry in rural areas after 1880, especially in Flanders. Cotton works, for example, were moved to rural areas and to small towns of some 5,000–15,000 people to avoid trade union influences, and there was also a marked increase of domestic workers as Table 20 shows, mostly in Flanders but also in Brabant and Anvers.[6] The number of domestic lace workers rose, partly as a result of a big rise in American demand. Others were engaged in gun making near Liège, cutlery manufacture around Gembloux, hat making in the valley of the Geer, the manufacture of wooden shoes in the Ardennes. Elsewhere in the country nailing, basket weaving, tanning, rope making, weaving, embroidery and glove making all existed on a considerable scale. By and large domestic industries were most common where poverty was worst but most successful where they fitted into a more developed industrial pattern, like the cotton weavers near Ghent and the glove makers in the east, or responded to special demands, like the lace makers. Tradition and the inability to get other jobs helped keep

Table 21   *Cost pattern of Belgian agriculture in percentage shares*

	Rents	Wages	Fertilisers	Feeding stuffs	Seed and plants	Interest	Other
1846	20·9	55·2	0·8	1·4	8·1	3·6	10·0
1866	23·7	47·3	2·8	4·8	7·5	3·8	10·1
1880	17·6	50·4	2·3	10·5	6·1	3·2	9·9
1895	17·4	43·8	5·7	14·2	4·5	3·7	10·7
1910	17·5	37·6	7·0	16·3	4·7	4·8	12·1

Source: G. Bublot, *La Production agricole belge 1846–1955* (Louvain, 1957), p. 33.

workers in domestic industries. In 1896, for example, 12·7 per cent of males and 2·6 per cent of females in all industry were aged over 50 but in domestic industry 23 per cent of males and 14 per cent of females were of that age.

Despite the problem of high rents and rural poverty found above all in Flanders but in other provinces as well, it appears that although rents became more important in the overall cost structure of agriculture during the period of high prices of the 1850s and 1860s, they fell back sharply in relative terms during the 1870s. At that time, as Table 21 shows, there was a big rise in expenditure on feeding stuffs as the pattern of farming altered. Over the following thirty years this development continued, allied with a big increase in the use of fertilisers and in interest payments on machinery as techniques changed. The number of threshers, for example, rose from 6,900 in 1880 to 20,500 in 1910, harvesters from 1,000 to 6,600 and mowers from 420 to 12,650, mostly for use on the rich central plains. It is a striking fact that rents held their importance after 1880 and there was a marked decline in the role of wages as a result of mechanisation and the shift to less labour-intensive work. Mechanisation of arable farming accentuated the cost advantage of the larger-scale farms. The small man found his solution in animal husbandry, where costs did not fall so much in relation to the volume of activity. There was less opportunity for rationalisation and use of machinery; it was an industry operating close to constant returns. The major technical change benefiting the dairy farmer was the coming of the cream separator but Belgian farmers took advantage of the innovation only gradually. Ley farming and the production of forage crops advanced slowly too. In 1887 the first co-operative dairy was founded in Anvers but many of those set up later were very small, using hand machines. In Hainaut and Flanders they tended to be larger and to draw milk from wider sources of supply. In 1895 there were 63 co-operative dairies with 3,500 members and in 1910 there were 560 with 58,000 members. But the quality of the herds was low and Belgian farmers got prices for milk well below those in Britain, Denmark and the Netherlands.

Arable farming gained considerably from the introduction of machinery, even if tardily, and yet more from the application of fertilisers. The seed drill was first used in the mid-1840s; around 1840 ploughs with iron moulding boards appeared, though not seen on the smaller farms for another twenty years. About 1840, too, threshing machines arrived and twenty years later firms could be found doing threshing by contract and using steam locomobiles. Between 1848 and 1853 the government set up stations in Anvers and Liège where lime was made available at low prices, and from 1858 to 1865 lime subsidies were paid. The consumption of guano rose steadily to 1880 but farmers felt that they were often cheated over quality and when Chilean nitrates became available there was a quick changeover, for the price fell steadily and the product was quicker acting and more reliable. Consumption rose from 12 million kilograms, in 1876–80 to 74 million kilograms in 1891–5. Superphosphates were manufactured on a big scale and a considerable export was built up. Fertilisers made possible reduction of the fallow and encouraged the clearing of waste land: fallow stood at 81,000 hectares in 1846 and 8,500 in 1910; uncultivated land at 324,000 hectares in 1846 and 108,000 in 1910. There had been little fallow in Flanders anyway, but on the heavy lands of Namur, Hainaut and Brabant it was now considerably reduced, though the practice continued in regions of extensive cultivation such as the Campine and the Ardennes.

A particularly controversial development was the drive to expropriate uncultivated communal village land, begun in earnest with the law of 1847, though there had been some earlier attempts in the previous century which had met with little success. Such efforts had been seen as attacks on the privilege of grazing animals on common land, a vital right for small tenant farmers and the landless, at a time when technology was not capable of rendering these lands fertile. The extent of the problem varied from place to place. In the Campine it was desirable to fertilise and irrigate the land and create pasture to help a population hit hard by the linen crisis, as well as to settle immigrants from Flanders; but in the Ardennes the communal holdings were a valuable means of adding to the meagre incomes of small tenants. The government ignored such distinctions; under threat of expropriation communes were forced to put up the land for sale. Much of it was sold to big proprietors and speculators, sometimes working in syndicates, and the operation helped no more than the earlier state land sales to relieve rural land shortages.[7] Very little was sold initially to local individuals but much was subsequently resold in small parcels at high profits. After 1880 the communes put most of the land into productive use themselves, especially through afforestation, with the help of local and state funds. The most striking reduction of communal land came in the Belgian province of Luxembourg where it fell from 129,000 hectares in 1846 to 18,200 in 1910. In the Campine, in Limburg and Anvers the area fell from 125,600 to 67,100 hectares.

Certain technical features of agriculture were peculiar to Belgium. Flemish agriculture had long depended on heavy use of natural manure, forcing out two harvests a year. On fields cleared of rye, roots were sown and harvested the same season, providing food for the animals and plenty of dung. These practices spread during the nineteenth century to other parts of Belgium, to the plains of Hainaut and Brabant above all where the farmers improved on the Flemish techniques. It was there too, and especially in Hesbaye, that the cultivation of sugar beet spread most rapidly. After a short boom during the Napoleonic period it had died out again, especially as beet now had to compete on equal terms with cane from the Amsterdam refineries. It returned in the 1830s and by 1910 Belgium was a significant producer of beet sugar, exporting some 60 per cent of her output to England. The average size of factory, however, suggests that her industry was technically one of the least progressive in Europe.

Despite the fact that only oats were given even modest protection, in 1905 42 per cent of the cultivated area was still devoted to cereals, a proportion very similar to that in France and Germany where there were substantial tariffs on grain imports. In England and Wales, where grain was allowed in free, the proportion was 20 per cent, and it was 24 per cent in the Netherlands where the same policy was followed. Output of wheat in Belgium fell from 415,000 tons in 1880 to 350,000 in 1906 while that of rye rose from 388,000 to 525,000 and oats from 396,000 to 605,000. Two-thirds of the cereals and one-third of the potatoes were fed to animals, the straw making excellent litter too. This was similar to the Danish pattern where about 40 per cent of the cultivated land was also under cereals, without tariff protection. Like Denmark, too, Belgium was heavily dependent on cereal imports, the total rising from 303,000 tons in 1870 to 1·63 million in 1890 and 3·22 million in 1910. Her farmers could meet foreign competition, however, because yields of grains were so high. The share of cereals in agricultural output fell only gradually from 46 per cent in 1867 to 34 per cent in 1910. Taking the average for 1900–4, yields per hectare were higher in Belgium for wheat, rye, oats, sugar beet and potatoes than they were in France and Germany.[8] The area under grass rose but in 1914 it was still proportionately one of the lowest in Europe. This was offset by heavy feeding of home grains to animals, by the use of imported animal feeding stuffs and the important role of roots in the cereal rotations, a practice facilitated by the cheap labour available. The number of cattle and pigs was higher than in Denmark, for example, but no export trade had been built up. Cattle were as important for meat as for milk and their manure was highly prized. Yet the quality was low. Belgians liked to eat veal but their beef requirements were not met by a specialised beef cattle industry, for most of the beef eaten was cow or heifer beef. Pig rearing was poorly carried out for the most part and little attempt was made to link it with the use of cream separators and the feeding of skimmed milk as in Denmark and Germany. More often the animals were left to forage for acorns and beech nuts.

It could hardly be argued that agriculture was one of the most distinguished features of Belgian economic life. There were areas of high-quality farming but high yields were all too often bought at the price of extreme exploitation of labour. No advantage was taken of the opportunities for the export of animal products that her geographical situation seemed to offer. In fact animal husbandry was poorly carried out, particularly in Flanders. There was a notable absence of food processing industries also, again perhaps because of the poor quality of agriculture. The movement of workers between the land and the factory may have saved them from the darkness of the great factory towns but it failed to improve the quality of rural life, while at the same time overpopulation in the rural areas encouraged the payment of lower industrial wages. Wages in most industries were below those in neighbouring countries. This indeed was probably the major contribution of Belgian agriculture to industrial expansion; otherwise the frugality and immobility of Belgian agriculture had much to answer for, not least that they contributed little to the expansion of internal demand for industrial goods. Some indication of the backwardness in this respect can be seen from the fact that in 1910 agriculture produced 8·9 per cent of the gross domestic product but used 23·2 per cent of the labour force; the relative product of the agricultural workers was therefore only 38 per cent of the national average. This is the lowest proportion Kuznets found for any country, though in part such a figure reflects a relatively high productivity in industry.[9] In Germany the figure was 53 per cent, in France 84, the Netherlands 57, Sweden 53 and Italy 76 per cent. The rate of growth of agricultural output between 1846 and 1910 was only 0·6 per cent annually compared with an industrial growth rate in excess of 3 per cent. The rates of growth for French and German agriculture over comparable periods appear to have been noticeably higher. Between 1848 and 1867 output rose one per cent per annum and from 1888 to 1910 0·9 per cent, but for the two decades in between there was a regression of something like 0·12 per cent. Over the whole period about a quarter of the increase of output was due to an increase in the area cultivated, the rest due to higher productivity.

INDUSTRIAL GROWTH

Recent work has suggested that the Belgian economy as a whole grew by some 2·3 per cent annually between 1840 and 1858, 6 per cent from 1858 to 1873, 0·5 per cent per annum from 1873 to 1893 and 4 per cent from 1893 to 1913.[10] No details of the calculations are given but the results concur with Madison's suggestion of a 2·7 per cent growth rate for 1870–1913[11] and the figures for the last period come close to the rate of growth indicated by the older national income calculations of Baudhuin, who suggested 3,280 million francs (510 francs per head) in 1895 and 6,488 million francs (850 francs per head) in 1913.[12] Carbonelle, however, gives a rate of growth of real product (that is allowing for price changes) between 1900–4 and 1910–13 slightly below 2 per cent per annum, which is out of line with all other estimates.[13] Figures for national income per head are extremely unreliable but there is some evidence that towards the end of the nineteenth century average income was higher in Belgium than in most other continental European countries and Baudhuin's figure suggests that in 1913 it was as high as in France, slightly lower than in Germany, and higher than in the Netherlands.[14] In part this must be attributed to the low proportion of the labour force engaged in agriculture, although due also of course to the high rates of growth achieved by certain industries.

The general pattern of industrial growth, therefore, was one of limited expansion during the 1830s and 1840s, followed by a period of rapid growth for about a quarter of a century led by the iron and coal industries. There was also a spurt of growth after 1895 in Belgium in common with most other European countries but from 1873 to 1895 the country endured a long period of relative stagnation. As in France this was partly a consequence of the crisis in agriculture which both lowered the overall rate of growth directly and had a dampening effect on growth in other sectors. In some measure, however, the contrasts before and after 1870 are misleading because the dramatic but short-lived expansion before 1873 boosted the rate of growth up to that date and intensified in statistical terms the reaction after it. From 1886 the rate of industrial growth was more comparable to that for the last two decades before the First World War.[15]

Clearly Belgium benefited considerably from the early and rapid development of her industry, which unlike Britain she was able to maintain right up to 1913. We shall examine how this came about, first by studying the growth of particular industries and then by assessing some of the factors contributing to it.

– Iron and Steel

After 1815, as we pointed out in our earlier work, textiles gradually ceased to be the leading sector in the Belgian economy and the role was taken over by the iron and metallurgical industries.[16] This growth was founded on the local supplies of ore and coal, the adoption of English techniques and the increased demand arising mainly from the construction of railways and from the export of pig iron to the Zollverein. Leading the way were the great metallurgical works of John Cockerill at Seraing, employing 2,500 men in 1830; his works at Liège were also employing 700 men making textile machinery and steam engines. His was the first large industrial empire on the continent in the nineteenth century, fully integrated from coal mines through to the final metal product: in the mid-1830s Cockerill had interests in sixty different establishments. He still continued with the manufacture of textiles in Belgium; he owned woollen mills in Berlin and elsewhere in Germany; a cloth factory in Poland, a cotton mill in Barcelona, a sugar factory in Surinam, a zinc mine near Aachen were among his other activities. In 1837, with the suspension of the Banque de Belgique in which he was heavily involved, Cockerill was unable to meet his obligations. Typically, to retrieve his fortunes, he went to Russia to persuade the Tsar to build a network of railways. He met with no success and on the return journey died of fever in Warsaw at the age of 50 on 19 June 1840. Most of his assets were sold off but the Seraing works were reorganised as a joint stock company with half the shares held by the state and it was soon to regain its position as a driving force in Belgian industry. After 1848 they began to turn out artillery and later became specialists in the production of armour-plate which was used in the building of the great Belgian forts. They also made the pneumatic compressors used for driving the Mont Cenis tunnel and between 1855 and 1875 sales trebled from 8 million to 24 million francs.

The growth of the iron industry is indicated in Table 22. It will be seen that even during the difficult 1830s and 1840s growth was appreciable, under the impetus of railway building, although certainly the initial level of output had been low. It was also distorted by some years of depression after independence and again around 1840. In 1830, when the first four coke furnaces were in blast, there were something like 90 charcoal furnaces producing just under 90 per cent of the output of pig iron of 90,000 tons. Other firms joined Cockerill in the Liège region during the 1830s, but there was a parallel growth around Charleroi and nine coke furnaces were in operation there in 1831 with others under construction. By 1845 when the coke furnaces (33) now exceeded the charcoal (23), coke pig output was 121,000 tons compared with 14,000 for charcoal. By 1867 there was only one charcoal furnace left. The ready availability of coal and the big demand for iron rails had brought a much more rapid change of technology than in France. Furthermore the wood for charcoal had to come over greater distances, the price rose rapidly and the old industry located in Namur disappeared. French capital had played little part in the early development of the industry but between 1845 and 1847 and again during 1852–3 there was a great surge of French investment. A third of the joint stock companies founded in the metal industry during 1835–60 had at least one French director on the board. Table 23 shows that nearly half of the growth in pig output during the 1840s and 1850s went to exports, a large part of them going to the Zollverein. After 1865, however, Belgium became a net importer of pig iron and an exporter of finished products. In the early years the industry concentrated on feeding

Table 22 *Average annual growth of Belgian pig iron output (per cent)*

1831–49	3·1
1849–73	5·9
1873–86	3·2
1886–1913	4·2

Source: C. Reuss, E. Koutny and L. Tychan, *Le Progrès économique en sidérurgie* (Louvain, 1960), p. 14.

the local markets for wrought iron in Britain, France and the Zollverein but by the early 1870s it had greatly expanded the area of trade and was sending iron to over twenty-five countries. In 1863 Belgium also became a net importer of iron ore but the use of imported materials and the tapping of wider markets provided no locational difficulties, for Hainaut and Liège had excellent canal links with Antwerp.

The rapid maturing of the Belgian industry is further demonstrated by the average size of blast furnace which by 1870 was the largest in Europe, although the best in Belgium were probably not on a par with those in Middlesbrough. This growth in size of furnace was accompanied by the concentration of the industry into fewer plants, so that although from 1851 to 1875 the output of finished iron rose more than six times, the number of works fell from 102 to 54 and blast furnaces only rose from 30 to 41; on the other hand, the horse-power of steam engines employed rose from 1,743 to 16,604. Puddling furnaces, which were much less open to increases in size, rose from 201 to 676.

The Cockerill firm built the first Bessemer steel furnace on the continent in 1862 although they had difficulties with the supply of the right kind of iron ore. In 1874 the works were reconstructed to use molten pig made from non-phosphoric Spanish ore and the supply of that ore was ensured when in 1876 the same firm established the Société Franco-Belge des

Table 23 *Foreign trade in pig iron as percentage of Belgian output*

Net exports		Net imports	
1831	2·05	1873	3·0
1839	2·68	1878	43·4
1843	41·5	1889	29·0
1853	43·9	1900	29.2
1864	3·7	1911	30·5

Source: A. Wibail, 'L'évolution économique de la sidérurgie belge de 1830 à 1913', in *Bulletin de l'Institut des Sciences Economiques*, 1933, p. 44.

Table 24 *Average output per blast furnace in tons, 1870–1905*

	1870	1890	1905
Belgium	12,000	22,000	32,755
Britain	9,150	19,500	26,000
Germany	7,000	21,000	40,000
France	4,430	16,500	25,000

Source: C. Reuss, E. Koutny and L. Tychan, *Le Progrès économique en sidérurgie* (Louvain, 1960), p. 58.

Mines de Somorrostro in conjunction with two French companies. The ore was taken in Cockerill's own ships to their quay at Antwerp and thence by canal barge to Seraing.

In general progress in steelmaking was slow during the 1870s for it was costly for those without the special resources of the Cockerill firm to import foreign pig and reheat it. Technical problems were not the only issues; after the boom in 1873, demand for steel throughout Europe was stagnant for the remainder of the decade. But the basic process was to be as crucial to the steel industry in Belgium as it was in Germany. The Angleur works adopted the Thomas process first in 1879, buying the rights for a mere 1,250 francs. It was a new plant with no blast furnaces, relying till then on foreign haematite pig, and so the new process had more to offer there than to most steelmakers. However, this was the only major development until the Thomas patents ran out in the early 1890s.

The great swing to basic steel manufacture came after 1894, especially in Hainaut where the old ironmakers were less committed to acid steelmaking. Cockerill, like Krupp, retained the acid Bessemer process longer than the others in view of their ore supplies, but they too changed to the Thomas process in 1907. Even so, the change in the balance of the industry was striking; in 1905 the Charleroi group of firms in Hainaut produced 504,000 tons of pig iron compared with 627,000 in Liège but by 1913 the comparative figures were 1·36 million tons and 966,000 respectively. Some new companies were formed but in general expansion came from existing firms. During these years the 'steel triangle' of north-west Europe was formed and Belgian industry took a full part in this internationalisation of the steel industry by investment in Lorraine mines, in Luxembourg and Saar steel companies, by cross-border integration of firms and by interchange of output. The importance of the French basic ores to Belgium is shown by the fact that of total imports of 1·2 million tons in 1890, 71 per cent came from Luxembourg and 12 per cent from France, whilst in 1913 67 per cent of a total of 4·75 million tons came from France and 22·5 per cent from Luxembourg.

Belgian raw steel output grew at over 10 per cent per annum from 1892 to 1913, though there was a considerable decline in the production of wrought iron. This rate of growth was faster than that of western Europe as a whole, for whereas in 1880 Belgium provided 5·1 per cent of the steel output of the area, in 1913 it was 7·1 per cent, the gain being made almost entirely at Britain's expense. The industry was dominated by a group of highly integrated concerns, controlling steel furnaces, coke ovens, coal mines, rolling mills and finishing processes. In 1913 19 companies with 54 blast furnaces produced all the pig iron and 85 per cent of the crude steel: in 1887 there had been 17 companies with 32 furnaces. In certain technical respects they led the world, in coke oven technique and the use of gas engines. Figures given in Table 24 show that her blast furnace practice compared well with that elsewhere, even though the size of furnace was deliberately kept down since an industry so heavily dependent on exports needed a high level of flexibility in production and this was hard to achieve with a small number of giant furnaces. Nevertheless it is interesting to note that in the difficult years of consolidation from 1873 to 1886 when the number of both companies and furnaces was sharply reduced, physical output per worker rose by 6·5 per cent per annum compared with only 1·9 per cent in the expansionary years after 1886. The fall and subsequent rise of steel prices is reflected in the value of this per capita output which rose annually by 0·8 per cent from 1873 to 1886 and by 3·4 per cent thereafter. Located near the French and Luxembourg ores and only lightly committed to the acid process before 1878, the industry concentrated on the Thomas process almost exclusively and this proved eventually to be the most promising line for steelmakers everywhere.

By 1914 exports accounted for well over half of Belgium's steel output. It was the country's largest single export, in 1911 totalling 239 million francs compared with 144 million for transport equipment, 103 million for linens, 88 million for glassware, 79 million for cottons and 74 million for machinery in general. On the other hand there were substantial imports of ore and pig iron as well as scrap and some semi-finished iron and steel, so that net exports were probably no more than a quarter of the gross level; against that must be set the steel content of the 218 million francs derived from exports of machinery and transport equipment. Table 25 shows that the rate of growth of Belgian exports outpaced those from Britain over the whole period and grew as fast as those of Germany after 1900. In part, as we shall see later, the industry's success in expanding

Table 25   *Annual average iron and steel exports (000 tons)*

	1880–4	1885–9	1890–4	1895–9	1900–4	1905–9	1910–13
Britain	3,643	3,704	2,966	3,252	3,260	4,304	4,638
Germany	913	1,026	1,146	1,467	2,614	3,546	5,524
Belgium	391	447	458	554	596	1,007	1,341

Source: D. Burn, *Economic History of Steelmaking* (Cambridge, 1940), vol. 1, pp. 78, 81, 84, 93, 330.

exports was a result of close links with investment banks who frequently tied their loans to exports of Belgian capital goods. Nevertheless, Belgium's exports grew most quickly in markets where this was not the case, most of all in the British market itself and some of the markets of the British Empire which were difficult to penetrate such as India, Australia and South Africa. On the other hand investment links were particularly helpful in encouraging the rapid growth of trade in South America. The trends are shown in Table 26 where it is apparent that exports to continental Europe lost some of their relative importance after 1900.

The industry also benefited from inflows of capital, from Germany principally. One of the largest steel works, Sambre et Moselle, established in the 1890s at Montignies in Hainaut, was German controlled, and the Ougrée works, with an equally large output, also had German interests; the output of these two together exceeded that of Cockerill. Sambre et Moselle also controlled the main arms manufacturers in Belgium. Altogether in 1914 German holdings provided about 17 per cent of the capitalisation of Belgian steel.

Table 26 *Belgian exports of iron and
steel (million francs)*

Destination	1900	1911
Britain	20·9	51·1
Continental Europe	67·2	79·5
South America	10·2	53·4
India, Australia, South Africa, Canada	9·5	39·0

Source: *Tableaux généraux du commerce de la
Belgique avec les pays étrangers.*

Iron and steel, therefore, remained a key industry throughout the
century, created on the basis of home materials and of deliberately stimulated home demand, fostered always by investment banks, remaining
technologically to the fore in Europe, but becoming more and more reliant
on imported materials and foreign markets. Pig iron output per head of
the total population in 1910 was still very large, standing at 250 kilograms compared with 200 in Germany, 110 in Sweden and 100 in France.

– Coal

As in Britain, the coal industry was one of the main forces in early
industrialisation. In 1836 Belgium produced 2·5 million tons of coal,
rather over 0·5 million near Liège and the rest at Mons and Charleroi
in Hainaut; of this total some 700,000 tons were exported to France. By
1846 output had risen to 5·5 million tons and there were 46,000 men employed in coal mining compared with 12,600 in cotton and 10,000 in iron.
Consumption of coal rose by 4 per cent per annum between 1840 and 1870
and direct exports, mostly to France, grew to over 4 million tons. It is
hardly surprising that between 1835 and 1870 there was considerable
French investment in the industry, especially in the mines of the Borinage
in the region between the Sambre and Meuse rivers. Between those years
Frenchmen were to be found on the boards of directors of twenty-six
coal companies and in eighteen of those they held a majority of the issued
shares. The rate of growth of consumption of coal slackened to approximately 2·5 per cent per annum between 1875 and 1893 as a result of the
slower growth of the economy as a whole. Output grew more slowly still,
for in 1897 exports had risen to only a little over 6 million tons, and imports, which had begun around 1870, now stood at almost 2·5 million
tons. Low prices between 1873 and 1886 may have discouraged investment
but it was the physical problems of mining the coal that plagued the industry and made it difficult to achieve an effective response to higher prices
after 1886. The average thickness of seam was low and an exceptional

amount of preparatory work was required underground, while in 1902 hewers formed only a quarter of all underground workers. The risk of fire damp was great, although the precautions taken kept the accident record on a par with those of safer coalfields, and mines had to be sunk to great depths. So the Belgian industry experienced a stagnation in labour productivity, output per man reaching a peak of 186 tons per worker in 1888 (80 tons in 1831, 126 in 1851 and 146 in 1871) and falling to 171 tons in 1911. But the fall in productivity was not the result of tapping ever poorer seams to achieve a rapid growth of output; output grew very slowly. From 1897 to 1913 consumption of coal rose from 17·8 million tons to 27·6 million or 2·9 per cent per annum, but production rose only by 3 million tons or 0·9 per cent per annum. In 1910 imports exceeded exports for the first time and by 1913 amounted to 10·75 million tons compared with 7 million tons for exports. The absolute level of productivity was the lowest of the major producers in Europe; in 1896 116,000 workers were employed, far more than in any other Belgian industry; iron and steel took 23,600, machinery 26,200, glass 21,700 and all the textile industries 56,000.

So while coal output in France after 1900 was growing at over 2 per cent per annum and in Germany by about 4 per cent, in Belgium the industry had ceased to be a significant expansionary force. This was a general feature of Belgian growth, for local supplies of zinc and iron ore also proved inadequate for the needs of their fast growing industries. Raw material supplies encouraged industrialisation in its formative stages but had no powerful long-term impact.

Belgian coal was not easy to coke and from the start special ovens were devised to replace the simpler method of burning coal in covered heaps after the manner of the charcoal burning process. By-product recovery from coke ovens was pioneered by the Germans but from the 1890s onwards Belgian firms such as Coppée and Semet-Solvay built up a worldwide reputation for the construction of such ovens. Before 1860 coking was chiefly an activity of the ironmasters, for production by coal mine owners did not even cover the needs of the railways. Increasingly thereafter specialist non-consuming coke producers, *charbonniers*, emerged among the coal men, soon coming to dominate the industry and beginning to export on a considerable scale. In 1890 the output of coke was 2·2 million tons and exports totalled just over one million tons. But the position was quickly undermined by developments in the steel industry, for after 1896 the demand for pig iron began to rise rapidly and this encouraged the coke producer-consumers to develop production on their own account outside the cartel, using more and more imported coal. Although coal was relatively abundant in the Borinage and sufficient in the centre it was already running short at Liège and had been exhausted at Charleroi. Such was the growth of demand from industry that not only was coal imported for coking but by 1913 direct imports of coke had come slightly to exceed exports.

– *Textiles*

Coal and iron were the leading sectors of the industrial revolution but if textiles did not dominate the economy as in Britain and to an even greater degree in Switzerland, their very size made them still important for Belgium. In 1910 some 15 per cent of the working population (including domestic workers) were still to be found in textiles as well as another 11 per cent in the clothing trades. Taking into account only factory production, the evolution of the industry is shown in Table 27.

We discussed in our previous work the catastrophe that befell the quarter of a million or so domestic workers employed in both parts of Flanders during the 1840s.[17] Migration was one solution. From 1845 to 1850 alone some 10,700 workers left West Flanders for other parts of

Table 27 *Factory employment in Belgian textiles, 1846–1910*

	1846	1896	1910
Cottons	12,631	15,482	34,028
Wool textiles	16,543	22,456	23,547
Linens	9,471	22,859	23,311

Source: J. Lewinski, *L'Evolution industrielle de la Belgique* (Brussels, 1911), p. 320 and F. X. van Houtte, *L'Evolution de l'industrie textile* (Louvain, 1949), pp. 102, 108, 113.

Belgium, mainly Hainaut, and in 1851 there were 80,000 foreigners in the Nord region of France out of a population of 1·16 million, most of them from Flanders. The Belgian cotton industry attracted a certain amount of this labour. At the same time some new and quasi-domestic industries came into Flanders. Chicory making started at Roulers around 1854 and brush making a little earlier. Shoe making, the manufacture of matches at Grammont and tiles near Courtrai were all alternative occupations. As for the linen industry itself, there was a rapid shift to mechanical spinning in an urban setting after the crisis. In 1846 Belgium had 96,835 such spindles, half of them in Ghent, and by 1855 there were over 150,000. By 1896 this had risen to 292,000, of which 195,000 were in Ghent; thereafter their number declined. For some time after 1846 mechanically spun yarn was actually in short supply and some 20 per cent above the cost of British yarn. The British used cheaper Russian flax but Belgian weavers liked British yarn and when in 1851 import duties on yarn were relaxed, the domestic weaving industry advanced rapidly in West Flanders. Mechanical weaving came to Roulers in 1852 but it spread very slowly and in 1864 there were only 300 such looms there. In contrast the number in Scotland, for example, rose from 3,670 in 1850 to 15,762 in 1862. Over the next half century there was a steady rise in exports of yarn and at 103 million francs in 1911 it was the largest export of the whole textile industry, though French and British exports rose much more quickly.

In general the Belgian industry failed to adapt itself quickly enough to the new competitive situation. It limited itself for too long to what should have been a transitional stage, weaving by hand mechanically spun yarn. Possibly the industry suffered because the assistance it received from tariffs, and for a time subsidies, was removed too quickly after 1850. The cotton crisis during the American Civil War found the Flemish factories ill-equipped to respond to the surge of demand for linen. Flanders was poorly supplied with capital also and so the period of mechanisation saw the Belgian linen industry in large measure replaced by that of France, which had more capital and more enterprise. The old hand industry produced 4·5 million kilograms of cloth in 1835; in 1899 the reconstructed industry produced 2·7 million kilograms when 30 million kilograms of mechanically woven cloth was being turned out at Armentières. Now the specialisation of Flanders was restricted to the retting of flax on the river Lys, the legendary 'Golden River' to which the whole world sent its flax.

In 1846 exports of wool textiles provided about 9 per cent of all Belgian exports, much the same proportion as exports of linen, jute and hemp together. In 1913 wool provided about 3 per cent and linens 4 per cent; neither industry played a major role in Belgian industrialisation. The consumption of wool, stable between 1835 and 1854, rose sharply to 1873 with the adoption of new technologies and the boost given by the cotton famine. It only began to rise again, however, around 1903. Almost all the cloth produced was for the home market and imports were rising quickly just before 1914. About as much combed yarn for worsteds was imported as was spun within the country but the industry's speciality was the spinning of carded wool at Verviers. Inevitably any advanced Belgian industry exported a large proportion of its output and this was no exception, about two-thirds of the carded yarn being exported, mostly to Britain. The speciality of the whole textile industry was the production of semi-manufactures. Wool and linen yarn were the prime examples, but even the smaller silk industry did likewise and exported half as much yarn as the wool industry, 24 million francs compared with 50 million in 1911. The weaving of silk cloth was much less important. The lace industry met hard times after 1850 with competition from mechanically made lace; in 1875 there were 150,000 domestic workers and in 1896 only 48,400 were left. But then a surprisingly buoyant demand for hand lace developed from the United States and in 1910 there were some 80,000 workers active. Here as in all other sectors of the textile industry, real success could only be achieved in the export market.

The cotton industry's share of Belgian exports was always smaller; it was around 3·5 per cent in 1846 and still much the same in 1913, but even to achieve this level a rising proportion of cloth output had to be devoted to exports – in 1860 32 per cent and in 1913 as much as 71 per cent. Imports of cloth in 1913 were about a quarter of the level of home production. Table 28 shows that the expansion of exports was brought about primarily through sales to Britain mostly of cheap white and dyed cloths, whereas trade with the Netherlands fell away as the Dutch industry grew and Belgian printing declined. Yarn exports were less significant and were generally exceeded in value, if not in volume, by imports. Between 1830 and 1914 the production of yarn and cloth grew at an annual rate of about 3 per cent, only a little below that of industry as a whole. Cloth output expanded by two-thirds between 1840 and 1860, then by about one-half in the following twenty years. From 1880 to 1913 it rose by 170 per cent,

Table 28   *Belgian exports of cotton cloth, 1860–1913 (tons)*

			Destination			
	Britain	Netherlands	France	Argentina	Brazil	Congo
1860	283	1,123	636	98	93	nil
1890	1,618	1,293	554	468	230	666
1913	2,792	598	48	216	68	748

Source: F. X. van Houtte, *L'Evolution de l'industrie textile* (Louvain, 1949), p. 173.

nine-tenths of the increase going to exports. The growth was encouraged by a marked improvement in technology throughout the industry and in considerable measure this was brought about by a gradual movement of the industry into the countryside where labour was prepared to use new methods at low wages. In 1911 there were 950,000 spindles in Ghent, the biggest mill having 190,000 spindles, not a big establishment by inter-national standards. But there were now some 640,000 spindles outside the main centre. The total number of cotton spindles was more than that of the Scandinavian countries and the Netherlands together, a fact that indicates the traditional importance of textiles in Belgium and the con-tinued growth which was achieved on the basis of export demand.

Though unadventurous technologically and with a diminishing share in industrial employment and exports over the period, the Belgian textile industries like all others were big employers of labour and its exports were still significant in the overall pattern of Belgian exports, which were not dominated by particular commodities in the way Britain's exports, for example, were dominated by cottons and coal.

– Engineering

In Belgium as in Switzerland the machine building industry received its first boost in the nineteenth century from the demands of the traditional textile industry. From this it was only a short step to the manufacture of steam engines and machine tools. The industry expanded rapidly and in the census of 1896, with over 26,000 workers, it was the largest in Belgium after coal mining. Some sectors, particularly those making transport equipment, benefited greatly from overseas orders which were linked with Belgian foreign loans. The railway wagon industry had 7,000 workers in 1911 and was an important exporter to South America in particular. The largest locomotive works, with an annual output of 200 engines, and the most consistent exporter was the Société des Ateliers de la Meuse at Liège, founded in 1835. Cockerill turned out 100 locomotives a year before 1914 but the firm had a varied output, employing 11,000 men altogether; besides 250,000 tons of steel, they made steam engines, gas engines, pumps, turbines, machine tools and artillery. In the early years of the twentieth century visitors tended to find the works antiquated, and too diversified to be outstanding in any one field. Another of the fourteen locomotive makers was Carel, established at Ghent in 1839 and turning out a modest sixty or seventy engines a year for the state railways. The works were more famous for the manufacture of some of the finest steam engines in Europe and for active development of the diesel engine from its earliest days.

But like the British industry, Belgian engineering was slow to move into newer sectors, having such a powerful advantage in the older steam traditions. Moreover, its tradition of machine tool making, except for some very heavy machines, was never distinguished. Since that industry is almost always a fertile source of new ideas and techniques in engineering its absence was probably a serious source of weakness. Electrical engineering, for example, grew very slowly. A boost came in the late 1890s from two sources: the need to provide equipment for electric tramways being built overseas with Belgian capital and the rapid rise in the demand for electricity at home. Consumption rose 3·5 per cent annually from 1881 to 1898 but over the next fifteen years grew at more like 15 per cent, heavy industry particularly turning quickly to the use of electric power. Half of the 7,000 workers in the electrical industry in 1913 were employed in one large works, the Société des Ateliers de Constructions Electriques at Charleroi. The works had been established under a different name in the 1870s to make hydraulic presses powered by Gramme dynamos. Reorganised and renamed in 1904 partly at the suggestion of Leopold II, more capital was provided by the German AEG company and employment jumped from 715 to 3,500 in a decade. The industry was nonetheless a very modest one, and even to grow as it did a high proportion of exports was essential; they were worth 10·4 million francs in 1911 from an output of 24·3 million. Given the range of Belgian engineering it was not surprising that many individuals began to manufacture motor cars, again with a striking reliance on exports; they were in the region of two-thirds of output in 1911 and three times the absolute level of electrical exports. So although output was small compared with France, Britain and Germany and the largest firm, Minerva of Antwerp, responsible for half the exports, had only 900 workers, these exports were significant in the European context. It was home demand that was low.

Another modern industry was the manufacture of cream separators, which was dominated by one firm, Melotte. In 1890 it was a small business with twenty-five workers making a dozen machines a year by traditional methods. At about this time Melotte himself visited the huge arms factory at Herstal where a great deal of modern American machinery was in use. Applying the same techniques, he was making 25,500 separators a year by 1910, employing 450 workers and building up a worldwide reputation; around 21,000 of those machines were exported. But this was an exception. The modern agricultural machinery industry dated from the 1880s with the founding of firms like Melotte (1888), Delmotte (1885) and Persoons (1888), and the number of workers in the industry rose from 346 in 1890 to 1,630 in 1910. This was still very small and at least five firms in Britain were individually larger than the whole Belgian industry. Faced by a poor, reluctant market at home and fierce outside competition from Britain, Germany and North America, they had to concentrate for the most part on the low cost machines that most Belgian farmers, but hardly anyone else, liked.

The Fabrique Nationale d'Armes de Guerre de Herstal (Liège), where cycles and cars were made as well as guns, was established by a syndicate of gunmakers in 1889 on the basis of a government order for 200,000 Mauser rifles. At that date there were still some 6,000 domestic workers in the industry but now, rather belatedly, it was brought up to date. Some two-fifths of the capital came from Germany and by the outbreak of war they had captured possibly two-thirds of world exports of small arms, with big sales in Africa and other colonial countries but also dominating exports to the USA with a very cheap product. All the more advanced countries, of course, supplied their own demands for small arms.

Thus in 1913, despite the existence of a few outstanding modern factories, the major sectors of the Belgian engineering industry still remained rooted in the past. In modern development they were surpassed by the Swiss and to a lesser extent the Swedish industry; the inadequate technical development of the textile industries left that sector of machine making well behind the Swiss too. As in Britain, the early start had mixed blessings in the long run.

– Zinc

There were two industries where Belgium held a special place; one was zinc and the other, much more important, glass. The zinc industry was never a large employer of labour, involving 5,556 workers in twenty-four works in 1896, but it represented a small preserve successfully exploited. It required high-quality installations, expert labour, ample coal and good outlets for the by-product, sulphuric acid; with these at hand, the early exhaustion of the original mineral supplies was not significant.

Until production began in the Liège area in 1833, zinc had been made almost entirely in Germany. The Vieille Montagne company was formed in 1837 but expanded only slowly at the start. Output accelerated from the middle of the century onwards and during the 1880s the industry began to develop in the north of the Campine, though by this time most of the mineral treated was imported and the Vieille Montagne had investments for mining and smelting in Sweden, Spain, Sardinia, North Africa, Silesia and Russia. Until well after 1850 Belgium and Germany held a

Table 29   *Output of zinc: percentage of world total, 1849–1913*

	1849	1869	1894	1913
Germany	66	55	37·2	28·1
Belgium	34	37·3	25·4	20·4
France	nil	nil	6·3	6·4
Britain	nil	3·5	7·9	5·9

Source: F. Bézy, 'Les Evolutions longues de l'industrie du zinc dans l'ouest européen, 1840–1938', in *Bulletin de l'Institut de Recherches Economiques et Sociales*, vol. XVI, 1950, p. 13.

near monopoly of world supply. Diffusion was slow because zinc was not as essential as iron and other countries were long content to import, so throughout the period to 1914 Belgium maintained a leading position as Table 29 shows. Production of pure zinc was 10,000 tons in 1845; by 1900 it had passed 100,000 and in 1913 stood at 200,000 tons. Some 70 per cent of this zinc was exported, mostly to neighbouring countries, and of 50,000 tons of zinc sheet produced, two-thirds was exported, Britain and the Netherlands offering the best markets. It was not a spectacular industry but one that followed a typically Belgian pattern: a small niche was carved out, the advantage was maintained once the raw material base had disappeared, fuel was important, exports vital, and the industry enjoyed a relatively high growth of productivity. Output per man rose 3·5 per cent per annum from 1849 to 1869, 2 per cent from 1885 to 1913, while output per furnace rose yet faster. Output grew 5·5 per cent annually in the first period and 3·5 per cent from 1872 to 1913.

The by-product, sulphuric acid, was widely manufactured in Belgium as well. Of 300,000 tons produced in 1911, some 89,000 tons were exported to Germany; in fact Belgium was the only country in the world exporting acid in large amounts. Of the remainder, two-thirds was used to manufacture superphosphates, using the chemical deposits at Mons and Liège. Output rose from 230,000 tons in 1903 to 540,000 in 1910 and about half was exported, mostly to France, Spain, Germany and the Netherlands. Many chemical plants were to be found in the valley of the Scheldt in the west at Courtrai, Ghent, Antwerp and in the south-east along the Meuse at Namur, Liège and Charleroi. The network of canals provided the low cost transport which this kind of bulk industry needed. The soaring world demand for fertilisers was also met by exports of basic slag from the Thomas steel furnaces; in 1910 521,000 tons were exported, 60 per cent of it to Germany, and home consumption absorbed a fifth of that amount. Belgium also used her raw material supplies to export 700,000 tons of cement, 90 per cent of the output. These details are given to show how well Belgium fitted herself into the pattern of world demand making use of the local, if not particularly cheap, fuel supplies. Each example was small in itself but in total exports of chemicals were as large as those of cottons and only slightly below those of glass. It is a curious fact that the major innovation achieved by a Belgian in chemicals, Ernst Solvay's process for the manufacture of soda, could not be developed to any extent within Belgium because of material shortages. However, the Solvay company was soon enjoying a huge income from the profits of its many plants overseas.[18]

– *Glass*

Glass was the Belgian speciality *par excellence* and with the industry continuing to find almost all its materials at home, the import content of exports was negligible. Window glass manufacture developed in Belgium in the fifteenth and sixteenth centuries as the use of glass spread among the richer classes and, under the influence of Italian immigrants, the industry grew up in the valley of the Sambre as well as in Brabant. New techniques involving the use of coke led the industry to concentrate in the region of Charleroi in the eighteenth century. After 1815 there was a period of rapid growth which helped the economy through the traumatic years of independence. In 1823 10 factories produced 8,096 boxes of glass; in 1834 37 factories produced 35,500 boxes. Technological change doubled the output capacity of the blowers between 1825 and 1845 but reorganisation and standardisation of work were yet more important than individual inventions. Prices fell by one-third from 1823 to 1833 but costs fell yet more and the large profits brought about further expansion. Freights fell too; between 1822 and 1850 the rate for a ton of glass from Antwerp to New York dropped from 78 to 22 francs. By 1855 the price of window glass stabilised at about one-quarter that of the early 1820s and stayed at that level to 1914. Expansion now came to depend on exploiting an ever widening foreign market as world population and incomes rose. From 1840 to 1873 exports rose in volume by 9 per cent per annum and Belgium enjoyed a powerful, almost monopolistic, position in world trade. It has been suggested that in 1836 exports were eight times home consumption and a similar proportion seems to have persisted for most of the century. Technological skill and experience within the industry must have been the key factors.

After 1870 the industry changed significantly. The price of coal turned minds to saving fuel costs. The Siemens regenerative furnace of 1873 was succeeded in the 1880s by the tank furnace, the outstanding single technical improvement of the century. Invented in the 1860s, it was not developed commercially until pressure to save costs built up during the deflationary climate of the early 1880s. It reduced fuel consumption but above all dispensed with the potters, whose skill in making pots for the old type of furnace had been critically important. It also led to concentration of the industry and to an increase in size of plant: the tank furnace cost perhaps 250,000 francs in 1890 and this was beyond the means of small men. So whereas in 1880 there were 41 window glass works with 4,447 workers, in 1910 19 works employed 9,453 men. The new technology, the emigration of some Belgian workers and the growth of demand brought a sharp rise in production elsewhere but Belgium still retained a virtual monopoly of world exports. Exports to producing countries such as the United States decreased but the Belgian industry turned more to the markets of non-producers, though a quarter of her exports in 1907–11 still went to Britain. The low weight/value ratio of the product and the absence of substitutes for glass helped to keep exports rising at 2·25 per cent per annum between 1884 and 1913. The reduction of fuel consumption and a fall in the price of sodium sulphate kept prices down but still the manufacturing process remained predominantly manual: in 1911 the whole window glass industry used only 875 horse-power. From 1841 to 1897–9 the physical output per man rose only 13 per cent, whereas in zinc it rose three and a half times, in steel by a factor of 4·85, in cotton spinning by 5·4, and in weaving by 6·4. Glass blowers were the aristocracy of Belgian workers; of 391 workers shown in the 1896 census to be earning over 13 francs a day, 313 were glass blowers. Other wages in the industry ranged from 7·5 francs to 3 francs a day whereas in all industry the average was 2·8 francs. Already in the United States only a half of the glass was being made by hand methods in 1911 but this development had not yet affected the Belgian industry.

Plate glass had for long been a monopoly of the St Gobain works in France. Production in Belgium began in 1822. The first large factory was established in 1836 but rapid growth was not seen until after 1860. By 1880 the industry was controlled by a syndicate which also operated two of the three French factories outside the St Gobain empire. Plate glass was made in bigger sheets and was freer from faults than window glass but the latter was much cheaper and the quality was improving all the time. Nevertheless, the gap in the prices narrowed considerably. A piece of window glass one metre square cost 1·45 francs in 1847 compared with 60·3 francs for the same size of plate glass; in 1900 prices were 1·34 and 13·2 francs respectively. Larger pieces of plate glass fell more sharply still in price: a piece four metres square was 1,245 francs in 1835, 277 in 1884 and 76 francs in 1910. Demand for plate glass, a luxury product, was more elastic than that for window glass and this encouraged technological innovation. Belgian window glass makers might avoid competition by switching to the lower income non-producer markets but not the plate glass makers, for such markets were very limited. So competition had to be met by constant improvements in furnace efficiency and by the mechanisation of annealing and polishing. In 1765 it had taken 113 man

Table 30 *Production of glass in Belgium, 1841–1900 (000 square metres)*

	Window	Plate
1841	1,280	7·9
1870	13,170	166
1900	23,470	1,274

Source: Y. Douxchamps, 'L'Evolution séculaire du verre à vitres et de la glacerie en Belgique de 1823 à 1913', in *Bulletin de l'Institut de Recherches Economiques et Sociales*, vol. XVII, 1951, p. 512.

hours to polish one square metre of plate glass; in 1910 50–60 square metres were polished in 6·5 man hours. The plate glass industry in Belgium in 1911 was using over 20,600 horse-power compared with the trivial amount used in the larger window glass section. Plate glass exports, again a high proportion of output, went to the more developed countries such as Britain, the United States, Netherlands, Switzerland, France, Canada and Australia where Belgian technology was fully able to compete: in 1913 her exports were $5·7 million compared with $3·1 million for Germany and $1·9 million for Britain. Although, as Table 30 shows, the physical output of the industry was much smaller than that of the window glass sector, output of plate glass, with its much higher unit value, stood in 1913 at approximately 31 million francs, compared with something like 53 million francs for window glass.

In the industry as a whole in 1912 there were 76 works employing 32,000 people. The output of the whole industry in 1913 was in the region of 115–20 million francs and exports in that year came to 105 million francs,

32 million going to Britain alone. But the pressure of competition had brought a strong movement for international control. After a series of bitter strikes by Belgian glass workers, in 1904 Belgian, German, French, Dutch, Austrian and Italian producers agreed to restrict the numbers of their workers and the hours worked and to fix prices, although the price of a square metre of plate was set at 10·45 francs in Belgium, 16·78 in France and 18·51 in Germany. The cartel covered half of world production and of that total Belgium alone was given one-half. In 1912 the Union Continentale des Glaceries was formed, grouping into one syndicate several factories in Belgium, two glass works in France, other works in Germany, Austria and the Netherlands, and centralising orders and sales. The group also owned the Glaces du Midi de la Russie which produced a quarter of Russian output in 1913.

– Cartels

The glass industry was by no means unique in its interest in cartelisation. On the contrary, most Belgian industries had made some attempt to set up formal organisations to control their activities in the half century before 1914. One of the earliest industrial syndicates in Belgium was the Comité Houiller du Centre, established in 1841 to try to stabilise coal prices. Coke producers tried to fix prices for the railways as early as 1849 but generally at this time all that existed were selling agreements of a temporary nature to cover some unusual development such as a tariff change or a pay rise. Then came more permanent pools, mostly concerned with fixing prices at periodic meetings, found most commonly in the coal industry and also in bricks and glass. From the 1880s onwards syndicates of a more or less permanent nature began to appear, arrangements whereby those concerned would submit to conditions regulating a whole range of industrial activities. These were very common in the coal industry, where regional groups were linked to national and sometimes international syndicates. Syndicates in the steel industry were less significant but one of the more important was the steel rail syndicate, formed in 1880 by Cockerill and Angleur, then the only makers in Belgium. They joined the international cartel four years later. This lapsed in 1890 but was reconstituted in 1904 when Belgium was given 18 per cent of the output compared with 7 per cent under the earlier arrangement. Sugar refiners established cartels in the 1890s to control their purchases from the farmers, and this led to the Union Sucrière of 1901. Belgian industry was also deeply involved in international cartels. An arms syndicate covering Belgium, France, Germany, Italy and Austria divided out markets, leaving the British and Empire markets free for competition. The international zinc syndicate, of which Belgium, with a quarter of the world's output, was a very important component, was founded in 1886 and embraced all Europe except Britain and was run by the Vieille Montagne.

It lapsed in 1894 but was re-formed in 1909. The Belgian cement syndicate had agreements with the German industry over sharing the Dutch market and with Norwegian and Danish cement works over the Scandinavian market.

It was not surprising that Belgian industry should follow a course resembling so closely that of Germany. National frontiers could not alter the fact that for geographical reasons her fortunes were closely linked with those of the Ruhr and the industrial region of north-east France. It was inevitable that her industrialists should follow similar industrial policies and engage in cross-border arrangements. As in Germany, the powerful influence of the banks in Belgian industry encouraged rationalisation and limitation of competition between industrial units enjoying the same backers, and international investment connections had the same effect on a wider plane. The important role of Belgium in certain industries – zinc, glass and arms, for example – meant that no international cartel concerning these was complete without her. Basic aims of course varied from cartel to cartel. The glass industry demonstrated a desire to control competition in the face of technological change; the coke cartel was a straightforward attempt to form a monopoly against a particular consumer. What contribution the cartels made to industrial growth, if any, is difficult to determine since historians have been more concerned with detailing the pattern of institutions than in analysing their effects. There is, however, little evidence that they caused technological practice in Belgian industry to fall significantly behind that of her neighbours, though it may be that greater competition would have brought earlier mechanisation of the glass industry. It might be argued, too, that given the small internal market combined with a concentration on heavy capital-intensive industry, unusual in small countries, Belgian industry had a greater incentive than most to restrain the pressure of competition.

TRANSPORT

We pointed out in our earlier work the vital role of the railway plan of 1834 in allowing Belgium to break free from the economic crisis created by the revolution of 1830.[19] The plan was carried out in its entirety and by the end of 1843 559 kilometres of state lines were in use, about half of them double track. Such was the enthusiasm for the new medium that the Banque de Belgique concluded an agreement with the French government to finance a line from Paris to the Belgian frontier, but the French Chamber eventually refused to approve it. Roads and canals were not neglected either. The road system was already extensive in Flanders, Brabant and Hainaut, but elsewhere, and especially in the Campine and the Ardennes, it was very poor. Between 1830 and 1850 the total mileage under state and provincial responsibility was almost doubled. Up to 1845 railways were built simply to provide links with other countries and although in 1845 English financiers were given the right to start construction of an internally orientated network, little was done until Belgian finance took over the task in 1852. So for twenty years the roads had a vital internal role; thereafter their mileage grew more slowly, by a third from 1850 to 1880 and for the next thirty years hardly at all. Canal construction was concentrated on the Campine canal (1844–59) with the object of linking the Scheldt and the Meuse without going through the Netherlands. At the end of the century efforts were made to make internal cities accessible to ocean vessels and so new or enlarged canals were built to Brussels, Ghent and Bruges.

The second stage of railway construction was dominated by private builders and by 1870 these companies, fifty in number, had opened 2,267 kilometres of track compared with the 869 kilometres of state lines. However, while in 1862 97 per cent of state lines had double track, only 15 per cent of private lines were so constructed. There were in effect two quite different systems; and although the second was not planned like the first, attempts by German and French capitalists to obtain control of lines were invariably thwarted by official action. After 1870 the state began to take a more positive attitude towards investment and started to buy back the concessions. By 1875 it controlled 2,024 kilometres of line compared with 1,475 kilometres in the private sector, and in 1900 4,031 kilometres compared with 531 kilometres of private lines. After 1870, too, it was the state that assumed the responsibility for major improvements of ports and waterways and also established the telephone system, although allowing some local private concessions here.

The rate of railway construction reached its peak around 1867 but stayed high until about 1880 while the state was extending lines into areas with poorer traffic prospects. By 1885 the main system could be considered complete. From 1835 to 1852 an average of 54 kilometres a year were constructed, during 1852–70 109 kilometres on average, and between 1870 and 1885 an average of 94·5 kilometres. In 1884 the Société Nationale des Chemins de Fer Vicinaux was established with capital from the state, provinces and communes to build local lines, many of narrow gauge. By 1913 there were over 4,000 kilometres of track, about one-tenth electrified. Between 1858 and 1870 the freight carried by the railways grew at 12·5 per cent per annum, as this form of transport established itself over all others. Thereafter the growth rate followed much the same course as internal consumption of coal and industrial growth, averaging 2·6 per cent from 1870 to 1892 and 3·4 per cent from 1892 to 1913.

Belgian historians have not yet made a detailed analysis of the economic impact of railways, comparing costs and benefits with those of other forms of transport. However, there seems little doubt about their great importance in the years immediately after 1835 both in extending links with neighbouring countries and in stimulating the economy, since virtually all the rails, rolling stock and constructional materials were produced within Belgium. The railway network was dense and played an important part in giving mobility to Belgian labour, especially the local lines which permitted rural–urban commuting. They were also important in underpinning the export trade that was built up in railway material. Belgium benefited enormously, too, from the transit trade which was boosted by growth in the Rhine basin and north-east France. In competition between Rotterdam and Antwerp for this traffic, the former concentrated on supplying bulk goods to Germany, being connected by an excellent series of waterways. Antwerp, however, whose access depended essentially on the railways, traded more in general cargoes better suited to that form of transport.

The transit trade brought in a mere 24 million francs in the 1830s. After independence the Netherlands placed heavy tolls on the Scheldt until in 1863 Belgium and other interested nations paid her 17 million florins as the capitalised value of the tolls. The transit trade rose to 117 million francs in the 1840s, 623 million in the 1860s and 1,365 million francs in the 1880s. It then stagnated for some years as trade generally grew more slowly and countries began to encourage use of their own ports, but by the eve of the First World War the general expansion of trade had raised its value to 2,460 million francs. Yet Belgium had only a small mercantile marine and an unimportant shipbuilding industry – a fact attributed by most historians to the lack of any seafaring tradition among Belgians. However that might be, in 1913 the shipping fleet consisted of only 124 vessels of 236,000 tons and the major shipping line, the Red Star, was Anglo-American in control and operation. As we shall see in the next section, transit trade income was an important element in the Belgian balance of payments, though it must have been offset to some extent by freight payments to foreign carriers of Belgian seaborne trade.

COMMERCIAL POLICY

After 1830 Belgium continued to apply a highly protective tariff. Attempts to arrange customs unions with France and with the Zollverein were vetoed in turn by Britain and by France. The market problem, which seemed so serious in 1830, was intensified by the treaty of 1839 when Belgium lost a further 400,000 of its population in Limburg and Luxembourg to the Netherlands. It was King Leopold's idea to look overseas and try to widen frontiers that way. There were many plans, most of them hopeless from the start. There was talk of establishing a protectorate over Haiti; discussions were held with Spain over taking possession of the Philippines; an officer was sent to reconnoitre a possible trading centre in

Ethiopia. There was an air of panic about it all; indeed, but for railway building the economy would in all probability have been at a standstill. In 1843 a company was sanctioned to send emigrants to Guatemala and the next year 871 unfortunates made the journey. In eighteen months 211 died, most of the rest returned and by 1859 only forty were left. A similar venture in Brazil suffered the same fate. There was serious thought of establishing a colony in West Africa and a treaty was agreed with certain local chiefs, but the government hesitated over the costs and possible diplomatic complications and the opportunity, if such it was, slipped away. In fact, the unwillingness of Belgians to emigrate far beyond the frontiers of northern France left few areas overseas where local cultural patterns and loyalties might encourage the purchase of Belgian goods. In the late 1840s some 50,000 emigrated to other parts of Europe and the government set aside 500,000 francs to encourage emigration to the American continent but the disasters in Guatemala were a strong deterrent to further movement. In reality the Belgians had an invincible repugnance for expatriation, though later in the century at harvest time hordes of seasonal workers – 'franschmannen' as they were known – went searching for work in Beauce, Normandy, Picardy, Champagne and the Ile de France. As for the home market, protection was gradually advanced until by 1848 duties reached their peak with 30–60 per cent on cotton, woollen and linen yarn, 85 per cent on iron and glass and a sliding scale to keep up wheat prices.

Slowly relations with neighbouring countries improved. The treaty of 1844 with the Zollverein was the inevitable consequence of the completion of the Verviers–Aachen railway, which made Antwerp the best outlet for the Rhineland. There was a series of agreements with the Netherlands, and, between 1830 and 1860, eight treaties with France. The electoral reform following the crisis of 1848 extended the voting power of urban over rural regions and turned the tide against the protectionists. The young finance minister, Frère Orban, was an ardent free-trader and so Belgium began to adopt the policies which were finding support throughout western Europe. Such a trend, which owed nothing to Belgian initiative, was of great benefit to a small nation dependent on exports.

Already the harvest crisis of 1846 had led to decrees for the free entry of cereals and by 1850 only a small revenue duty was in force. All transit dues and city tolls were removed. Some differential duties went in 1856 and in 1859 the government announced that it would lower duties generally through reciprocal treaties. The first of these was signed with France in 1861, another with Britain the next year and a third with the Zollverein in 1863. The 1865 tariff embodied all these reductions and added more. In 1873 free entry of cereals, meat and live animals was agreed and two years later all duties on linen and jute yarn disappeared. Some modest duties remained, on iron for example, but Belgium had abandoned most restrictions by the time the cry for agricultural protection went up in the mid-1880s as it did almost everywhere in Europe. The Catholic party was now in power and with most of its support coming from the country-side, looked kindly on the demands. Even so action was modest. In 1887 duties were placed on live animals and meat and in 1895 they were extended to cover oats, flour, butter and margarine, malt and preserves; some duties on pig iron and semi-manufactured steel, however, were actually lowered. So the policy emerged as one giving limited protection to certain sectors of agriculture, without attempting in any way seriously to combat the inflow of cheap grain, and imposing modest industrial tariffs which were little changed after 1865. The treaty of 1892 with Germany actually brought about small mutual reductions of tariffs. As an exporter *par excellence* Belgium put her weight into preserving open markets. Her home industries in many cases found their protection through the medium of international cartels. Some industries such as linen would probably have benefited from protection during the difficult period of transition from hand to mechanical operation but no other general policy would have made economic sense. Nevertheless, the effects of tariff policies on Belgian expansion must have been small compared with the consequences of the widening of markets brought about indirectly by growth elsewhere and, in some instances, by Belgian investment overseas.

Free trade and the growth of world trade to some degree moderated the earlier drive for territorial expansion, but one powerful influence was always pressing in that direction. Already in 1853 Prince Leopold had addressed the Senate on the need to pursue the search for markets overseas and went himself on four study voyages, mainly in the east, on the lookout for export outlets. It was as Leopold II that in 1876 he brought to Brussels an international geographical conference devoted to the opening up of central Africa and set Belgium on the road to becoming a colonial power. Then again in 1898 when Li Hung Tchang made his tour of Europe, although Belgium was not originally on the itinerary, the King persuaded the Chinese Minister to change his plans and convinced him that a neutral, inoffensive country was an ideal helper in railway construction. It was Leopold, too, who sent the financier Edouard Empain into Egypt, but the main effort was eventually to be made in the Congo. There Leopold acted not as King but as a private individual, because no government at the time would follow his actions, and it was the company he originally established that was recognised as ruler of the Congo Free State in 1884. Up to 1905 the region was mainly a source of ivory and rubber; thereafter investment moved into minerals around Katanga, gold in the north-east, and diamonds in the Kasai. By 1913 3,500 Belgians were living in the Congo but the effect on the home economy so far had been slight.

In 1901 the value of Belgian special trade (exports of Belgian goods plus imports for home consumption) per capita was the highest in Europe at 595·5 francs, fractionally above that of Switzerland. Exports grew most rapidly between 1850 and 1880 and again after 1900, following the general pattern of growth of the economy as a whole. Little is known about the

Belgian balance of payments in our period but it is clear that there was a surplus for extensive overseas investment which in its turn had a substantial impact on Belgian exports.

FINANCE AND INVESTMENT

We have already described the way in which the Société Générale and the Banque de Belgique helped to finance the expansion of the economy after 1830 by extensive direct investment in industry.[20] Both survived the crisis of 1838 only with difficulty and the relatively slow growth of the economy during most of the 1840s can in part be attributed to the more cautious attitude that both banks adopted. Even so, by 1848 the Société Générale alone held 38 per cent of the capital of the coal companies in the Mons basin, 46 per cent in the Charleroi area, 14 per cent in the Liège basin. It had taken a big part in the formation of three iron making concerns – Marcinelle et Couillet, Sclessin and Chateaulineau – had made loans to Cockerill, was active in canal investment, with government aid helped to establish a company to stimulate the export of cottons, and invested in many smaller concerns. Its holdings of industrial shares rose from 3·5 million francs to nearly 30 million francs between 1835 and 1847 and loans and advances to industry rose from 7 million francs to 58 million francs. However, the immobility of resources implied by this kind of industrial investment left both banks ill-placed to survive the serious crisis of 1848. Both were forced to suspend payments and there was a run on the Société Générale's savings bank, the Caisse d'Epargne. However, prompt and liberal action by the government headed off the serious repercussions that might have followed. Both banks and their associates, the Bank of Liège and the Bank of Flanders, were enabled to resume payments again but the price to be paid was the surrender of their official functions. The Banque Nationale was founded in May 1850 to perform services required by the Treasury as well as ordinary commercial business, the two big commercial banks jointly subscribing all its capital. It soon had a virtual monopoly of the note issue. Prior to 1848 note circulation had been low because of public distrust and the unwillingness of the two big banks to accept each other's notes. In the second half of the century the issue grew rapidly with notes of small denomination available, and in fact notes soon became the main form of circulation, for the use of the cheque remained very limited even on the part of large industrial concerns.

After 1850 the Société Générale began to devote itself more single-mindedly to industrial investment, preferring now direct participation over loans. In 1847 half of the bank's assets were in long-term loans and shares in industry; a decade later the proportion approached 70 per cent and most of its short-term operations were directed towards financing working capital for the firms it patronised. By 1860 the bank estimated that one-fifth of the capital in Belgian joint stock companies represented firms under its aegis. It began to invest heavily in railways too, partly to help its own metal manufacturing concerns, and with the same idea in mind turned to overseas lending. The bank's role in leading the way to foreign investment both for the benefit of its own industrial properties and as an outlet for its funds outside Belgium is most important since in other respects it could be said that Belgium was a nation of limited horizons. The Société Générale, however, was no longer acting as a local bank but was joining the international activities of the body of European investment bankers. In 1858 it joined with the Crédit Mobilier to form the Société Anonyme des Chemins de Fer du Nord de l'Espagne, all the railway material being supplied by French and Belgian manufacturers. Both of these banks took part in the construction of local French railways and of lines in Italy, central and south-eastern Europe and Turkey. In 1865 the Société Belge des Chemins de Fer was established as an intermediary through which the parent could direct its railway investment and in the late seventies its activities grew rapidly with new lines in Germany, Italy, Austria and elsewhere. In 1876 Belgian industrialists founded the Compagnie Internationale des Wagons Lits et des Grands Express Européens though the capital came from several different countries. In contrast, from 1866 the Société Générale began to solicit deposits from the public, offering interest for the first time, becoming in effect a 'mixed bank', doing ordinary commercial as well as industrial banking.

The Banque de Belgique was much weaker. At first it was content to liquidate some of its loans and increase its short-term lending but soon the bank began to play a major role in placing railway shares on the Belgian market, activities which became more and more imprudent. It lost heavily in the seventies as a result of this speculation and the dishonesty of an employee, was reorganised in 1876 but finally liquidated in 1885. In 1870 there were four other banks of the mixed type including the Banque Liégeoise, whose operations, though small, were distinguished by a high reputation for prudence. More were founded in the early seventies, though most of these soon found themselves in difficulties during the slump after 1873, but during the boom years after 1895 a mass of financial institutions was founded, 58 from 1895 to 1900 alone, many very short-lived. Belgium was a land rich in capital and in financial enterprise and its company laws made it a good base for foreign capital too, but the financial system tended to be highly unstable in difficult times. Nevertheless it might be argued that the kind of heady expansion enjoyed by Belgian industry in not altogether easy circumstances could not be won without risks, and given a stable core by the Société Générale, the gains from growth outweighed the temporary setbacks. The Banque de Bruxelles did not at this time have the importance it was to assume after the First World War, although it was active in some industrial investment and prior to 1914 began to develop rapidly through its interest in the growing Coppée–Warocque industrial group.

With this growth of credit institutions went an increase in the number of Belgian joint stock companies. In 1852 there were 191 with a capital of 880 million francs; in 1873, 314 with a capital of 2,000 million francs. Between 1873 and 1892 another 1,610 were created, with a capital of 1,990 million francs, though only 667 with a capital of 915 million francs prospered; the remainder disappeared or reduced their capital. In 1873 the government had relaxed the law which gave it the right to have representatives on the directorate of any such company and for the next forty years Belgian company law was one of the most liberal in Europe and undoubtedly encouraged a considerable inflow of German and French capital.[21] In 1910 joint stock companies employed 404,000 workers, an average of 175 each, and private firms 438,000 or three each, excluding the owners and members of their families. The public companies were most important in coal, steel, glass and chemicals, the private in clothing, building, joinery, cotton textiles, shoes and confectionery.

After 1870 direct overseas investment became more important. Belgian industrialists and financiers were quick to seize the opportunities offered by local tramways, for example. In 1874 Tramways Bruxellois was founded as a grouping of the lines in the city but lines were soon being financed in Frankfurt, Cologne, Warsaw, Turin, Florence, Naples, Trieste, Munich, Lvov, Barmen, Prague and many other cities, including several in Russia, where in 1911 there were thirty-three Belgian tramway companies operating. It became a Belgian speciality and led to heavy exports of equipment.

The banks created a number of holding companies for tramways as well as railways. In 1880 the Société Générale des Chemins de Fer Economiques was formed by the Banque de Bruxelles, the Banque de Paris et des Pays Bas and several private bankers, a typical consortium of the time. It played a major role in Belgian investment in Egypt, Spain and Italy. The same group in 1895 founded the Société Générale Belge d'Entreprises Electriques, and the next year the Société Financière des Transports et d'Entreprises Industrielles (SOFINA) was founded by the Banque Liégeoise and a German group. These three companies, with a combined capital of 100 million francs, controlled companies with a capitalisation seven times as great in the tramway and electricity fields. In 1905 the Société Générale itself set up the Société Belge des Chemins de Fer de Mexique and the same bank participated heavily in the financing of the Peking to Hankow railway, some 1,300 kilometres in length, begun in 1898. One of the more spectacular figures in these overseas activities was Edouard Empain who began promoting the electrification of railways in the Lille area in 1893 and then those of Cairo. In 1896 he created the Compagnie Russo-Française de Chemins de Fer et de Tramways which not only undertook large investments in Russia but also built the Metropolitan subway line in Paris, opened in 1900. Six years later came perhaps his most grandiose venture, the creation of a new city, Heliopolis, some ten kilometres from Cairo. The Société Générale invested heavily in the Congo too, first through railways and then in providing much of the money for mining investment. It shared the capital of Union Minière, for example, equally with a British company, Tanganyika Concessions.

But the most remarkable area of Belgian investment was without doubt Russia. The interest began in a small way when in 1864 Cockerills built a small shipyard at St Petersburg (Leningrad) to assemble naval craft built from Belgian iron, though the yard was sold after the contract had been fulfilled. It was the heavy Russian tariff of 1877, hitting Belgian exports of iron very badly, that stimulated thoughts of more extensive investment there. Cockerills made a study of the iron resources near Krivoi Rog and eventually decided to build a steel works there and a shipyard at Nikolaiev, on the Black Sea. To forestall possible local opposition they took in the Warsaw Steel Company as partners and together set up the Société Métallurgique Dniéprovienne du Midi de la Russie in 1886. The Polish company brought capital and orders from the rail producers' syndicate, Cockerills more money and above all the expertise. They also provided a great deal of the machinery needed in setting up the plant; in later years the specialised Belgian machinery producers like Coppée were to benefit greatly from orders of this kind. The Cockerill venture was extremely successful; in 1894 they established another company to mine coal and make coke mainly for the Dnieper works. It too was highly profitable initially but was hit badly by the depression of 1900 and was sold three years later, paying the penalty of over-investment near the top of the trade cycle. In addition to street railways, electric power stations were erected at Saratov, Yaroslavl and Rostov, a Solvay chemical plant in 1887 in the Donetz, glassworks there and in Moscow. But the very success of Cockerills encouraged all manner of wild investment in the late nineties. Belgian capital in corporations operating in Russia rose from 17 million roubles in 1890 to 220 million in 1900, making it greater than French or German involvement to that date. However, the depression burned fingers so badly that by 1914 Belgian investment was still at much the same level, whereas investment by Germany, France and Britain now far outstripped it. There had been new investment of course, since possibly one-half of the 1900 capital was lost or sold, but nothing comparable to that of the other countries. The main areas of Belgian investment were 61 million roubles in steel, 32 million in electric lighting, 31 million in machinery, 25 million in tramways, 18 million in coal, 10 million in cement and glass. Belgian investors played almost no part in the heavy investment in oil, banks and chemicals.

According to one estimate total Belgian overseas investment in 1913 amounted to some 7,000 million francs.[22] The question is how Belgium managed to create a balance of payments surplus making possible this investment overseas. No modern calculations have been made but contemporary statistics give Belgium regular deficits on visible trade throughout the nineteenth century, averaging 145 million francs annually in the 1860s, 265 million in the 1890s and 1,300 million in 1913. Some commentators suggest that exports were undervalued but presumably the main source of invisible income providing the necessary surplus was the interest on former investments, which must have amounted to 350 million francs in 1913, as well as the profit made on the transit trade, for Belgium must have had a deficit on shipping freights and no large income from emigrants' remittances. It must also be remembered that there was considerable foreign investment in Belgium, mostly in the coal and metal industries and, above all, in Belgian companies operating outside the country. To this extent the required balance of payments surpluses would be reduced.

We have devoted considerable space to the discussion of banking partly because Belgium led the way in a development that was to spread throughout Europe after 1850 but above all because it was so important to Belgium herself. The close links between banks and home industry and between investment and exports gave a powerful impetus to industrial expansion. As in Germany it was not simply a matter of money and goods but of active grouping and rationalisation of firms, not simply a financing operation but a positive drive to develop Belgian industry. International investment banking on this scale meant too that Belgian industry could play the part in the economy of north-western Europe that its geographical position justified but that its political boundaries might inhibit. For a small country such deliberate stimulation of the internal and above all the external market was of unusual significance, and in such a country the influence of one outstanding institution such as the Société Générale could be unusually large. In Belgium too there was no difficulty in finding others to follow the lead. There were bad moments it is true, in 1838 and 1848 and again in the mid-seventies and eighties, but with a sympathetic government standing by the crises were never insurmountable.

ECONOMIC GROWTH

It is difficult to generalise effectively about Belgian economic growth because the basic statistical data on which such analyses are now made is simply not available. We have given indications of the overall growth rate but we know nothing, for example, about the proportions of national income devoted to investment at any time, nor the extent to which these proportions changed over time. However, such calculations as are available suggest that the per capita rate of growth between 1870 and 1913 was as high as that of the other major continental industrial countries, France and Germany. To this we must add the fact that Belgium began her period of rapid industrial growth earlier than those two countries and achieved a total rate of growth in excess of 4 per cent for the three decades before 1870. The overall rate of growth from 1814 to 1914, therefore, was probably above that of France and Germany and certainly higher than that of the

Netherlands. Belgium, to some degree, followed the British pattern with a very low proportion of her labour force engaged in agriculture, the lowest on the continent, and this in part accounts for the rapid overall growth. One should not take this comparison too far, however, for the contraction of the agricultural sector in Britain is a phenomenon unique in the nineteenth century. The rate of industrial growth would suggest that the heavy investment overseas did not starve home industry of capital, nor does it seem likely that investment moved overseas because capitalists at home were unwilling to borrow. All this is conjecture as the necessary research has still to be undertaken but our study of industry and the banking system makes it a tenable argument. It is true that Belgian industry was not leading in the new lines of industry emerging at the turn of the century but this was probably due more to the existing emphasis on heavy industry and the predilections of the investment banks than to any shortage of money at home. Furthermore the evidence is that in the heavy industries Belgium was maintaining a high technological reputation. It is possible that the poor education system was a disadvantage when it came to developing the more scientifically based industries; that, however, remains a debatable question.

Yet the meagre evidence available suggests also that per capita income in Belgium was much the same as in Germany and the other more advanced continental countries in 1913. This can only be explained in terms of a very low income level in 1830, a reasonable supposition in view of the fact that the high labour productivity of farming per unit of land was already being achieved by intensive techniques which gave a low level of productivity per capita. There is some evidence that prices in Belgium were lower than those of her neighbours so that Belgian real incomes were somewhat higher than comparisons according to normal exchange rates might suggest but, equally, contemporaries gave the impression that the standard of living of the Belgian worker was low. In part this may have reflected the continued high employment in some domestic industries and the particularly poor living conditions found in a densely populated country with so many industrial workers living in meagre rural housing. Nevertheless it suggests too that the distribution of income was decidedly unequal by European standards. The slight evidence on wage levels does show a marked difference between Belgian and other workers in the major industries and it is hard to find any other explanation.[23] The development of the Belgian economy may well fit the combination of high growth rate and highly unequal income distribution found in Lewis's model of growth with unlimited supplies of labour.

We have noted the overpopulation of certain parts of the country, most of all in Flanders, and seen that Belgian workers were willing to commute great distances rather than emigrate. This suggests that labour was in general available at a low price, and that profits would be high. It would also mean that the level of home demand for certain types of goods might be deficient. It is not possible to prove this, but the fact that Belgian industrialisation was based on capital goods from its outset is consistent with such an argument. The high proportion of output going to exports even in consumer goods industries such as cotton weaving, which were not important Belgian specialities, makes it even more plausible. Belgian development certainly does not fit into the mould of those models of growth that envisage a gradual transition from consumer to capital goods production. The sudden and spectacular expansion after 1840 under the impetus of railway building is more consistent with Rostow's 'take-off' analysis whereby, after a period of slower development, an economy moves into a stage of much more rapid expansion under the stimulus of an event of that kind. We must remember, though, the role of the state, indeed of the crown, in encouraging investment and in being willing to support the major banks in times of crisis during the first two decades of rapid development. But in examining the experience of particular industries special interest lies in the manner in which Belgium carved out those niches in foreign trade which are essential for a small country. Some were of long-standing, like glass and linens, some based on supplying semi-manufactures to neighbours with wider market opportunities, yarn and zinc for example, some based on technological innovation like coke ovens, many protected in the end by cartels, for a small exporting country can do nothing through tariffs. But there was virtually no speciality in agriculture, no processing of real note; certain improvements were visible but in general contemporaries threw up their hands in despair at Belgian rural life. It was a different matter in the Netherlands where opportunities for development more closely related to agriculture had to be sought out.

II. Economic Development in the Netherlands

We showed in our previous work how after a period of remarkable development which made them by 1700 one of the world's richest mercantile societies, the independent Dutch provinces grew more and more slowly in the eighteenth century.[24] Amsterdam remained the focal point of European finance but a general stagnation overtook the country affecting its cultural as well as its economic life, making a striking contrast to the brilliant years of the seventeenth century. The kind of industrialisation in a rural setting that was occurring in Belgium, Switzerland and elsewhere and which provided an important foundation for nineteenth-century industrial growth was almost entirely absent. The period of the French Empire only intensified the problems, for the northern provinces were cut off from their empire and world commerce and Amsterdam surrendered completely to London her primacy as a centre of finance. The period of the joint monarchy after 1815 seemed to benefit the southern

provinces more than the northern and indeed the Dutch monarch showed more concern for the development of the economy of the south than for the north. So when the rupture came in 1830 the Netherlands had benefited little either from trade or from imitation of the economic changes taking place elsewhere in Europe.

At no point in the nineteenth century did the Dutch economy enjoy the kind of impetus given to Belgium by the railway boom. An almost total deficiency of raw materials meant that her development would have to take a different course. The share of the labour force engaged in agriculture and that sector's contribution to national income were both considerably above those in Belgium prior to 1913 but even so they were among the lowest in Europe, constituting 16·3 per cent of national income and 28 per cent of the labour force. On the other hand the Netherlands was more dependent than any other country on the service sector, which accounted for 57 per cent of national product and 38 per cent of the labour force. Nor was this only a recent phenomenon, for even in 1860 no more than a quarter of national income came from agriculture and it may be supposed that, with industry much less developed at that time, the role of service income was very important. The share of national product derived from industry, about 27 per cent, was, even on the eve of the First World War, one of the lowest in western Europe, comparable with Norway. On the other hand, the share of the labour force employed in industry, 35 per cent, was higher than in most other countries, a fact which may reflect a concentration on labour-intensive forms of production (building is included in the calculation).

AGRICULTURE

The Netherlands consisted of several distinct agricultural areas. First there was the polderland near the coast running from Groningen to Zeeland, rich land, two-thirds of it under grass, the home of high yielding milk cows: this was particularly characteristic of Friesland, most of Holland and western Utrecht where 70–80 per cent of the cultivated area was under grass in 1914. Farms were largely owner-occupied, well to do, and of an average of 30 hectares in size. Here and there large-scale market gardening was to be found, around Haarlem, for example, which was also a centre for bulb growing. There were also some fertile clay soils where cereals as well as sugar beet were grown. Zeeland and Groningen, together with Limburg, had 40 per cent of the cultivated area under crops. To the south and east was a naturally sterile belt including Drenthe, Brabant, Limburg and parts of Overyssel, Gelderland and Utrecht; in the 1860s the area was still only partially cultivated, a land with swamps and peat bogs on all sides and islands of sand and heather. Here were found rye, oats, forage crops and potatoes which were also grown in the islands of the south-west and in Friesland. The land between the three rivers, the Maas, Waal and Lek, suffered from the infiltration of river water through the dykes and there were large areas of almost un-inhabited grazing grounds in the middle of the century. Finally in southern

Limburg there were fertile plateaux and verdant valleys supporting a sizeable agricultural population.

One of the most remarkable aspects of Dutch agriculture was the extent to which technological knowledge was used to increase the input of land in response to the demand for food. In 1856 there were 700,000 hectares of heath and waste compared with 757,000 hectares of ploughland, to say nothing of the possibilities of recovering land from the sea. In fact in the course of the nineteenth century some 450,000 hectares were reclaimed, in the west by pushing back the sea and in the east by attacking the moors. Extensive reclamation took place in North Holland. The Koegras polder was formed after the construction of the North Holland canal of 1824, between the canal dykes and the dunes. In 1847 the Anna Paulowna polder was created. The Zuidplas polder was drained during 1828–39 by a series of windmills and the Prins Alexander polder completed in 1874. Reclamation from the Haarlemmermeer to the east of Haarlem and Leiden began in 1840; the three main pumps went into action in 1849 and by 1852 the work was complete. As for the heaths, Overyssel had been largely enclosed by the 1830s. Population pressure, the abolition of feudal obligations in 1789 and the fragmented nature of the terrain gave particular incentive for action in that region, but full development of the heath area had to wait till much later in the century. The communal ownership of land, which much inhibited reclamation, was tackled by a law of 1886, permitting enclosure on the application of a single commune. The government had in fact begun this process of restoring land to private property in 1809 but the procedure was difficult and costly till the 1886 Act. Of 36,000 hectares of communal land outstanding in that year, 15,000 hectares had been enclosed seven years later. Even so, much common land remained – 68,000 hectares in North Brabant for example – although some was used for sheep grazing on a considerable scale. The process of reclamation at the end of the century was greatly assisted by two factors. In 1888 the Nederlandsche Heide Mij was formed as a non-profit making organisation to help reclamation and afforestation and to give technical advice to local landowners. Then came the artificial fertilisers which alone made the large-scale change to arable cultivation on the sandy soils possible. Great fields of grain were soon to be seen in the east, as well as newly developed forests. Altogether between 1833 and 1911 370,000 hectares of waste were made cultivable and 93,000 hectares rescued from the sea. But although the waste area had been reduced to 590,000 hectares in 1900, it still covered 44 per cent of the area of Drenthe, 26 per cent of Overyssel and 21 per cent of North Brabant, though now only 7 per cent of Groningen. Such, however, were the obstacles that nature had put in the way of Dutch development.

Almost all the small countries of north-west Europe suffered from economic recession during the three decades after 1815 and in most cases it was associated with population growth and the collapse or stagnation of some former branch of external trade – linen in Ireland and Belgium, timber in Norway, kelp and cattle in the Highlands of Scotland, iron in Sweden. In the Netherlands it was the decline of shipping and shipbuilding which caused a general stagnation. In all these countries agriculture suffered severely from these twin pressures and the Netherlands was no exception. However, rising prices for grain from the 1840s brought greater prosperity, especially on the farms of Groningen, and this in part accounts for the big spurt in canal building and reclamation between 1840 and 1870. Dairying and cattle raising also benefited from the abolition of the British duties in the 1840s, and there was a big increase in the export of Friesian butter via Harlingen. The Dutch corn duties, which had been raised to high levels partly through Belgian insistence, were modified after the split and a sliding scale established in 1835. In 1845–7 this was replaced by a flat rate, at a reduced level and thereafter steadily lowered until abolished altogether in 1877. Most of the plough land in 1850 was in fact grain land; the bulk of it was under rye and there was a small export trade in oats to Britain but nothing comparable with that developing in Sweden. A densely populated protected country, with limited areas suited to arable farming, had no surplus land for such a large-scale export operation. The consumption of potatoes, which became important for the poorer classes in the second half of the eighteenth century, rose quickly between 1815 and 1850; almost certainly this was in part responsible for the 38 per cent rise of population over those years. In the fertile province of Friesland there were more than 11,000 hectares of potato fields in 1844 compared with 9,000 hectares under rye. Edible potatoes were grown on the clay soils; those for fodder and factory processing on the sandy soils. Rural labourers rented small plots of land but used the labour of the whole family to cultivate potatoes intensively and stored enough to survive the winter without going on relief. The blight of the mid-forties hit the edible potatoes worst of all while at the same time the rye crop was reduced by rust disease. Distress was therefore acute. Yields on the clay soils remained low for many years as the fungus continued to do much damage, and a long time elapsed before it was found that spraying with Bordeaux mixture would conquer it. A partial solution was to shift cultivation to the sandy soils and in North Brabant the area under potatoes rose from 12,953 hectares in 1845 to 17,071 hectares in 1852.

The proportion of arable to grass in the Netherlands rose from 1:1·36 in 1833 to 1:1·28 in 1876. It was not that the protection given to cereals prevented any further development of dairy farming but rather that most of the land brought newly into cultivation was placed under arable crops. Then came those pressures on grain prices that affected all Europe. Free trade in farm products was retained. After 1880 the wheat and barley acreages fell sharply but the area under rye, the biggest cereal crop, remained stable and that under oats rose steadily, most of these grains now being used for animal fodder. Prior to 1914 only about a tenth of the rye output and a fifth of the oats were sent off the farms to the market, compared with three-quarters of the wheat and two-thirds of the barley. Table 31 shows the slow rise in home production and the much bigger increase in imports of grain. Wheat was grown mainly in the marshlands of Groningen, Zeeland and the Hollands where high yields were obtained by heavy feeding and the use of first-rate seed. However, all these areas were badly hit by the price changes, although high prices were received for both wheat and rye straw used in the making of cardboard. The rye and oats were grown on the sandy soils of North Brabant, Overyssel and north Limburg, with oats grown in Groningen too. New problems arose when the British market was closed to Dutch cows in the later seventies as a general measure against disease, and the German market for store stock was cut off too, ostensibly for the same reason. American competition sent down prices of cheese and margarine forced down butter prices on the home market.

Yet in a country with a high proportion of the farm area already under grass, the overall pattern did not change radically under these conflicting

Table 31   *Annual grain consumption in the Netherlands (000 tons)*

	Home produced	Imports	Total
1861–2	680	220	900
1890–3	790	650	1,440

Source: M. G. Mulhall, *Industries and Wealth of Nations* (London, 1896), p. 242.

pressures and in 1910 the ratio of crops to grass had fallen to only 1:1·4, or just below the 1833 level. This was due in part to the massive application of artificial fertilisers to grain crops on the sandy soils. But the economy geared itself more and more to imports of grain for bread, to home production of fodder grains, and imports of animal feeding stuffs and concentrates. There was therefore a great rise in the number of cattle and pigs, as Table 32 shows.

In 1914 the cattle population per 100 hectares was very similar to that in Denmark but the pig population was only 60 per cent as high. Given similar potential markets, some interesting contrasts with Denmark may be made. Much of the Netherlands could not be ploughed economically but a milder climate gave a longer grazing season than in Denmark. So Dutch livestock farming was based more heavily on grassland grazing using a large amount of fertiliser, whereas the Danes relied to a greater degree on feeding cereals to their animals. Also, whereas in Denmark the bulk of roots were fodder roots, in the Netherlands the principal crop was potatoes. In Denmark just before the First World War the total area under crops and grass was 30 per cent greater than that in the Netherlands, but the area under cereals was more than twice as high, amounting to some 40 per cent of the whole area as against a quarter. On the other hand, the area under permanent or rotational grass in Denmark was 28 per cent of the area compared with 56 per cent in the Netherlands. In both countries most of the cattle were dairy herds but in the Netherlands, because of the predominance of pasture, nearly all calvings were concentrated in the spring to take full advantage of the early grass and this led to a big fluctuation in the milk supply, something that was only tolerable where the bulk of it was processed. This largely accounts for the fact that the Netherlands remained a major producer of cheese rather than butter, which was Denmark's prime product; to be run economically, a cream separator for making butter must be utilised to near capacity all the year round. Consequently, the Dutch were less able than the Danes

Table 32   *Animal population of the Netherlands, 1861–1910 (000s)*

	Cattle	Pigs	Sheep
1861	1,335	281	870
1890	1,533	579	819
1910	2,027	1,260	889

Source: J. D. Robertson Scott, *A Free Farmer in a Free State* (London, 1912), p. 161.

to use skim milk from the separator as pig food and butter production was relatively less well developed. The less specialised nature of her industry seems to have allowed Dutch dairy farmers more flexibility than the Danish in switching between pure milk and cheese and butter production in accordance with shifts in relative prices. The Dutch were also bigger egg producers and exporters. Possibly the greater variety of her agricultural output was attributable at least partly to her bigger home market and denser population.

The cattle population was large in Friesland, the Hollands and Utrecht and in those predominantly grass provinces cheese was very important, as Table 33 shows. However, butter output was significant in the sandy districts, Overyssel, Gelderland and North Brabant, where cereals were grown for fodder. South Holland was best known for Delft butter and Gouda cheese, the latter made in isolated farmhouses and taken to market by water; North Holland was noted for Edam cheese made in factories off the farms. Friesland factory cheese was of the Cheshire or Cheddar type and was manufactured specially for export to England. The Dutch markets were different from those of Denmark too. In 1913 over one-half of the butter exports went to Germany and the rest was equally shared between Belgium and Britain; cheese exports were equally divided between the three. Roughly half of the cheese was exported and a lower proportion of the butter; this compares with the export of over 80 per cent of Danish butter. The first modern creamery was set up at Leiden in South Holland in 1879 and a year later came the first in Friesland; but the first co-operative had to wait another six years. Undoubtedly the Dutch were feeling Danish competition, for the quality of their butter was not high, but the new methods developed rapidly after 1890 and by 1911 there were 958 creameries (680 co-operative), though a third of these were very small,

Table 33   *Dairy industry in the Netherlands in 1910*

	Cattle per 100 ha of cultivated land	Factory butter (m. kg)	Farm butter (m. kg)	Factory cheese (m. kg)	Farm cheese (m. kg)
Friesland	114	15·0	0·2	28·6	nil
Overyssel	92	4·6	2·9	0·8	0·1
Gelderland	97	6·1	1·9	0·1	0·3
Utrecht	138	0·6	0·8	0·1	13·5
North Holland	103	1·4	1·7	9·8	9·3
South Holland	127	2·9	3·0	1·6	18·7
North Brabant	80	6·5	3·8	nil	nil
TOTAL		46·3	18·3	42·1	41·8

Source: Netherlands Ministry of Agriculture, Industry and Commerce, *General View of the Netherlands* (1915), vol. 1, pp. 22 and 46.

using only hand machines. Friesland was the centre of the larger dairies; farm butter was produced mostly in the less developed east, as Table 33 shows.

But if the Dutch butter industry did not compare with the Danish there was one area of food production in which she was much further advanced. This was the processing of foodstuffs on the basis of both home production and imports. In 1899, for example, there were sixty-three condensed and powdered milk factories which provided Britain with 80 per cent of her consumption. Sugar refining, using cane from Surinam, soon won back its important role when the French wars were over: after 1830 the exclusion of Antwerp from the East Indies trade and the improved canal route into Amsterdam made that port Europe's chief sugar centre. Dutch refiners were helped by an export subsidy and though they were hit by the Zollverein tariffs of 1837 and 1842, growing exports to Russia, England and the Mediterranean area more than offset the loss. Imports of raw sugar rose from 28 million kilograms in 1834 to 93 million kilograms in 1871. In the 1870s Dutch refiners ceased to enjoy preferential access to Javan cane which was increasingly exported direct to Britain and they turned more and more to the processing of local Dutch and Belgian beet. The cultivation of sugar beet was introduced on the heavy clay soils of the Zeeland islands and into western Brabant after 1850 when the cultivation of madder was ruined by competition from artificial dyes. The area under the crop averaged 6,600 hectares in the 1860s, 20,300 hectares in the 1880s, 45,000 hectares in 1901–10 and was 64,800 hectares in 1912. In that year out of 27 factories, 12 were to be found in North Brabant. The average output of those factories was high by European standards. Exports of refined sugar, mostly cane, stood at about 100 million kilograms by 1871 and fell to only a little above half that level by 1880, but there was a steady growth of beet exports to 140 million kilograms by 1906. Sugar was the Netherlands' second largest export to Britain, after margarine, and only Germany supplied Britain with more beet sugar. The first factory to process potatoes was established in 1841 but many more appeared in the sixties and seventies, especially in the Veendam area of Groningen. There they turned out sago, glucose, dextrine and starch as well as potato meal, all for export. There was also a considerable strawboard industry concentrated in Groningen where there were large cereal crops to provide the straw and where peat was available for cheap fuel. In 1912 these two industries together provided £1·25 million out of total British imports of manufactures from the Netherlands of £3·75 million. Based on imports from the colonies there was a large and specialised chocolate and cocoa industry. After the Napoleonic wars there were already twenty-seven chocolate factories, mostly in Zeeland. They produced a bitter chocolate containing a large proportion of fatty matter. Van Houten's method of preparing cocoa powder, perhaps the greatest Dutch invention of the nineteenth century, was patented in 1828. By it he managed to get a cocoa free of this excess fat but it took another forty years before the industry began to develop on a big scale. Net imports of cocoa averaged 203,000 kilograms annually from 1847 to 1856, 633,000 in 1867–76, 3·4 million in 1887–96 and 18 million from 1907 to 1911.

These industries were linked either to particular Dutch resources, potatoes for example, or more significantly to her colonial trade. The margarine industry, described in our previous work,[25] was also rooted in a Dutch historical pattern, for there was a close link between the butter and margarine trades. Dutch merchants had organised the collection of butter from all over northern Europe, principally for export to Britain, and the margarine makers were able to benefit from the same commercial experience and contacts. By 1913 Dutch production of margarine was 84,000 tons compared with 210,000 tons in Germany, but most of German output came from Dutch-owned factories. In the Netherlands some twenty-eight margarine factories employed 2,400 men by 1914 and at over £3 million it was the country's biggest export to

Britain. Another major difference between Danish and Dutch food exports was to be found in the fact that whereas the Danes concentrated heavily on the British market and on two foods, butter and bacon, which provided over 80 per cent of all exports, Dutch trade was spread more widely both geographically and by product. Sugar and margarine accounted for a third of exports to Britain, followed by condensed milk, strawboard, pork, cheese, butter, cocoa products, mutton, eggs, potato manufactures and potatoes, in that order, adding another 30 per cent to her exports.[26] All this reflected a more complex historical background, a more varied and poorer agriculture in some regions at least, a different geographical position and a larger home market.

A speciality of Dutch agriculture was the production of bulbs and flowers. In the eighteenth century the exporters had enjoyed a limited wealthy market for exotic flowers together with a regular business in young thorn and fruit trees. In the nineteenth century the flower growers looked more to the needs of the socially conscious towns of Britain and Germany, now laying out their parks with ornamental trees and shrubs as well as bulbs and looking for mass colour rather than special striped tulips. New flowers were introduced which were native to central and southern Europe. The industry began in the Haarlem area but then moved to South Holland, a province which was also well placed to satisfy Dutch urban demand for market garden products and was the centre of glass-frame and glasshouse cultivation.

Co-operatives in the Netherlands progressed slowly at first. The first co-operatives were set up for the purchase of feeding stuffs and fertiliser and spread quickly in the densely populated, sandy soil areas of the Catholic south, due partly to the leadership of the priests. The butter and cheese co-operatives were followed by similar organisations engaging in egg production, sugar refining, potato flour and cardboard manufacture. The smaller peasant co-operatives tended to give each member equal rights and unlimited liability; it was the liability rather than the reserves that constituted the credit base. The larger groups – dairies, potato flour and cardboard works – were organised with voting rights according to shares in the capital along company lines. Large single-product markets all emerged around the turn of the century – for butter, cheese, eggs, garden produce – and were chiefly remarkable for the degree to which they educated the peasantry in the advantages of quality of produce and honesty of description. By 1914, for example, the export of butter not subjected to quality control was prohibited. Co-operative banks modelled on the German Raiffeisen banks began in the 1890s as an essential adjunct to the sales co-operatives. They were connected to three central associations, one of the true Raiffeisen type at Utrecht and two Catholic organisations at Eindhoven and at Alkmaar in North Holland.

Table 34 shows that as in Belgium a large proportion of holdings were under 10 hectares. In Denmark 10 hectares was considered the minimum size for a farm but there were many smallholders and cottars who possessed less than that. It will be seen that the number of holdings under 5 hectares in the Netherlands rose rapidly between 1888 and 1910 and those of 5–10 hectares grew significantly too. The increase in these smallholdings was due partly to the bringing into cultivation of formerly unused lands and partly to subdivision under the pressures of population growth. This category includes part-time holdings and also market garden and bulb farms where the average size was around 4 hectares, but many farms under 10 hectares were ordinary mixed farms and there was a big rise in their numbers in Overyssel, Gelderland and North Brabant where a lot of heath was brought under cultivation. Many of these farms were taken up by labourers left unemployed by changes in the pattern of farming elsewhere and they engaged in subsistence farming for want of capital to do better. Large farms were found in the areas of high arable farming, in Zeeland and Groningen, and to a lesser extent all round the coast.

Table 34 *Distribution of land in the Netherlands by numbers of holdings, 1888–1910*

	1–5 ha	5–10 ha	10–20 ha	20–50 ha	50–100 ha	+100 ha	Total
1888	74,589	34,088	30,004	22,422	3,558	217	164,878
1910	109,645	41,547	30,819	23,800	3,275	216	209,302

Source: J. D. Robertson Scott, *A Free Farmer in a Free State* (London, 1912), p. 82; J. Fröst, *Die Holländische Landwirtschaft* (Berlin, 1930), p. 70.

Some of these were owned by the town bourgeoisie and rented out but there were few great landed proprietors, as the Dutch nobility were always more interested in trade than in agriculture.

About half the holdings in 1910 were owner-occupied; in 1888 the proportion had been 41·5 per cent. The level was highest, 63 per cent, for the very largest farms and lowest, 37 per cent, for farms of 50–100 hectares. It was on the sandy soils of the south and east that peasant proprietorship was most pronounced and it was least prevalent in the coastal provinces. The relatively high level of tenancy tended perhaps to check subdivision of holdings but the break up of farms into small scattered parcels remained a serious problem. In 1925 still over a third of the cultivated land in Drenthe and Overyssel required to be consolidated, 35 per cent in Limburg, 20 per cent in North Brabant. It was less serious in the west where there had been little open field farming in the eighteenth century and on polder land which was always distributed in single blocks.

The pattern of Dutch farming was in some ways similar to that of Belgium, although the quality of dairy farming and of the specialised activities was generally much higher – excepting the latter's chicory growing and production of edible grapes under glass. The natural rate of population growth was one of the highest in Europe and there was little emigration so that the pressure on land was acute. There was less domestic industry than in Belgium, though there were numerous agriculture-based industries offering employment to part of the family. There was also a considerable flow of seasonal labour to western Germany when work on the land was at a low ebb. Land prices and rents were high and rising; the land was heavily mortgaged. The average price of a hectare of pasture land rose from 2,171 to 3,610 marks between 1891–9 and 1913–14; arable land rose from 1,275 to 2,050 marks. The rent of an acre of pasture averaged 97 marks in 1896 and 195 marks in 1913–14. There was an unusually high proportion of farm labourers by western European standards. According to the 1920 census, 622,514 people were active in agriculture of whom 181,875 were landowners. For the remainder a clear distinction cannot be drawn between wage labourers and the members of landholders' families but it has been suggested that wage labourers numbered in the region of 380,000. They were mostly employed on farms of over 20 hectares or on very small garden establishments. It was those branches of farming that used least wage labour that produced Dutch agricultural exports: dairying, poultry, pig rearing, fruit and vegetable growing. Wage labour was most important to the large corn growing farms of the marsh lands. On the small farms of the sandy soil regions there were practically no wage labourers, however. The fact that in the Netherlands, as elsewhere, the self-employed landowner, working his own land, imputed to himself a far lower wage than would a wage labourer, goes at least some way to explaining the international competitiveness of Dutch agriculture. Intensive farming was essential and an extraordinary amount of fertiliser was used. Output per hectare was high but output per man was low and little mechanisation was applied to actual cultivation of the soil. The numbers engaged in agriculture continued to rise, from 460,000 in 1860 to 525,000 in 1890 and to 618,000 in 1910. Their share in the working population, however, fell from 37 per cent to 32 and 28 per cent respectively. The latter is a strikingly low proportion; only in heavily industrialised Belgium was it lower, at 23 per cent. In part this reflected the fact that agriculture could not absorb the very rapid growth of population. There were also alternative outlets available, particularly in the service occupations, where a remarkably high proportion of the population, 38 per cent, found a living. But all studies point to a high level of urban poverty in Dutch towns in the middle of the nineteenth century and a serious tax burden for poor relief was felt in towns like Haarlem and Leiden. Industrial opportunities widened as the century wore on, but the basic problem remained.

Putting together his figures for shares of national produce and shares of working population, Kuznets found that agricultural production per worker in the Netherlands was 57 per cent of the national average compared with 38 per cent for Belgian agriculture and 73 per cent for Danish.[27]

One cannot properly relate this to national income per head without assuming that family size was the same in all three sectors of the economy. But if we make such an assumption, agricultural income per head was 40 per cent above that in Belgium in 1910 but 25 per cent below that in Denmark.

What then did Dutch agriculture contribute to growth? The 'wealth' of farmers in the Netherlands as elsewhere was a relative concept. In some areas a farmer with debt-free land was wealthy, in others one with good heavy cattle. In many places cash hardly came into the matter. On the rich soils, especially in Groningen, there was always a wealthy farmer class. Evidently the prosperity of these grain farmers, at least up to 1870, helped bring about reclamation and other public works but it seems unlikely that, with the population rising so quickly, per capita farm incomes across the whole country helped to boost internal consumption greatly. On the other hand the rising rent of farm land may well have produced a greater stimulus. It seems unlikely too that such a small-scale industry did much to help internal capital formation; the mortgages on farm land stood at £5 million in 1913. It may be that the average Dutch farmer received a negative return on any investment he made, offset only by his low imputed labour income. Agriculture hardly released labour for use elsewhere as a result of technical change. Nevertheless after 1890 in particular the growth of exports of dairy products and of processed foods became a major element in the balance of payments. It was less significant than in Denmark but there was a much denser population to be fed off the land too. It was here that the importance of farming lay, rather than in any direct contribution to other sectors of the economy.

SERVICES

Service income was immensely important to the Dutch economy. In 1913 the Netherlands derived 57 per cent of its income from that source, far more than most other countries; only Norway with 51·5 per cent was in any way comparable. It is, however, a great difficulty of economic history that less is known about this sector than about any other. It employed 38 per cent of the Dutch working population, 9 per cent in domestic service, 11 per cent in trade, 7 per cent in transport, and one per cent in banking and insurance; the rest were engaged in the professions, schools, local government, medical services and the like. All that is possible is to offer an impression of the role of this vital sector by looking at developments in trade and transport.

– *Transport*

The modernisation of the ports was of the first importance in helping the country to recapture its former role in world shipping, whereas internal transport was crucial for the inevitable contest with Belgium for the European transit trade. Rotterdam had become almost a dead port as a result of the last Anglo-Dutch wars of 1780–4 followed by the devastating effects of the continental system in cutting off the port from its extra-European connections. The population rose but not its prosperity. The city, too poor to expand, was packed to overflowing, its docks largely deserted, its waterways silted up. The Voorne canal of 1823, running from one of the arms of the Maas to Haringvliet near Hellevoetsluis, remedied the problem of the approaches temporarily but the route became outdated as the size of ships rose. Amsterdam too was badly situated with shipping going through the Zuider Zee, a shallow inland sea strewn with mud banks. At the end of the eighteenth century a new sea port was built for the city at Nieuwediep near Helder; in 1819–25 this was linked with Amsterdam by the North Holland canal of almost 50 kilometres in length but it involved a long detour for ships coming from the south and was quickly obsolete too.

With the opening of the Antwerp–Cologne railway in 1843 a new threat faced the Dutch ports. Dutch capital was certainly very slow to move into railways. This was partly because good waterways were already available and these waterways were themselves a barrier to railways: there were to be ninety-eight bridges over water on the Amsterdam–Rotterdam line, for example. On the other hand the flat terrain helped, for few tunnels, curves and gradients were required. The Dutch Iron Railway Company was founded by a group of Amsterdam businessmen in 1837, opening a line to Haarlem which had been extended to The Hague and Rotterdam by 1847. William I urged the construction of a rail link between Rotterdam and the Rhineland but the city was unwilling to take positive action. Only after receiving the King's personal financial guarantee was the Netherlands Rhine Railway Company established. Using English capital and equipment, the first link with foreign rail systems was made at Maastricht in 1853 but it was not until three years later that there were through international connections from Amsterdam and Rotterdam to the frontier at Emmerich. By 1860 there were still only 335 kilometres of line open in the Netherlands. There were many gaps in the system, above all in Twente, Brabant and the agrarian north and in connections to Hamburg and Bremen. Many concessions had not been carried out and in 1860 the state decided to complete the network at its own cost, the operation of the lines being leased to private companies for fifty years. Belgian and French capital flowed in too and French firms received many of the construction contracts. At last in 1865 Rotterdam was linked at Cleves with railways on both banks of the Rhine. By 1870 1,400 kilometres of railway were open and in 1890 2,600 kilometres, only extended to just over 3,000 kilometres by 1910. So in forty years under state tutelage the network was completed. True, the density was only two-fifths that of Belgium but there were also three great rivers and 2,500 kilometres of canals. Nevertheless, the delay had allowed Antwerp to build up a powerful position, against which railways alone could not compete; the ports themselves were still in a poor state.

In 1863 a law was passed to authorise improvements to both Amsterdam and Rotterdam. The Netherlands Sea Canal was to be constructed westwards to connect Amsterdam directly with the North Sea, the contract being entrusted to a private company with the state offering a guarantee and sharing the cost. In the event the government had to contribute seventeen times the £250,000 originally estimated and the state took over full control of the waterway. For Rotterdam a canal was dug across the southernmost part of South Holland, known as the Hook, in effect giving a new mouth to the Nieuwe Maas river, and the river itself was improved from the port to the canal. By 1870 the first shallow draught vessels were using the new route and the current began hollowing and

Table 35   *Sea-going ships arriving in Dutch ports*

| | Rotterdam | | Amsterdam | |
	Number	000 net tons	Number	000 net tons
1879	3,244	1,585	1,504	693
1894	4,633	3,854	1,574	1,193
1911	9,815	11,268	2,355	2,593

Source: Commercial Department of the Netherlands Ministry of Agriculture, Industry and Commerce, *Trade and Industry in the Netherlands* (1912), vol. 1, p. 23.

deepening the bed just as had been planned. The Rotterdamsche Handelsvereeniging was set up by a private group, the Pincoffs, and with the agreement of the city began reconstruction of harbours and basins and the installation of new machinery. But while the old eighteenth-century port was being transformed a major problem arose. Nature was no longer working as had been hoped and the shoals on the new waterway were not disappearing. Fully opened in 1877, the canal's expected depth of 7 metres was soon halved by sand. The slow growth of trade helped bring the Pincoffs down and something of a panic set in. The States General, disillusioned by their experience with Amsterdam, refused to help at first but the city took over and completed the harbour work. The central government now provided the money for dredging and by 1886 Rotterdam had an adequate outlet, the New Waterway, which was only 34 kilometres from the sea compared with Antwerp's 88 kilometres. In 1892 Amsterdam was linked with the Rhine by the Merwede canal. Ambitious attempts were also made to overcome the difficulties of navigation on the Maas to reach the industrial area around Liège. The Wilhelmina canal from near Belmond to the Bergsche Maas at Gertuidenberg, passing through Tilburg, was opened in 1906.

Thus by 1890, after long delays and disappointments and with the help of government and foreign finance, the Dutch transport system was in a position to take advantage of the rapid growth of trade about to occur in north-western Europe. The expansion is shown in Table 35. In 1912 the ships entering and clearing Rotterdam totalled just over 23 million net tons. Only New York with 28·8 million, Hamburg with 24·9 million, London with 24·1 million and Antwerp with 23·9 million tons were bigger and the Belgian method of calculation exaggerated the traffic there by perhaps some 10 per cent. Over the years 1893–1907 the tonnage entering Rotterdam rose by 183 per cent compared with 138 per cent for Antwerp, 105 for Hamburg, 47 for Liverpool and 24 per cent for London.

The Rhine traffic between Rotterdam and Germany was 2·6 million tons in 1890, 7·8 million in 1900 and 17·7 million in 1910. The Rhine was navigable to Mannheim by vessels of 1,500 tons and to Strasbourg part of the year by vessels of 800 tons; inevitably it was bulk cargoes that were most economically sent in this way, above all ore and grain. Consequently Rotterdam gained considerably from her ability to handle the growing imports of iron ore into the Ruhr after 1890. Many grain and ore ships never moored at the quays at all but anchored in mid-river and there trans-shipped cargoes directly into the Rhine barges. Of the wheat entering Rotterdam in 1903, about half came from Russia and a quarter from South America. Rye and barley came from Russia and Romania, maize from New York, Russia, Romania and South America, oats from Russia. Rotterdam was also a major port for timber and petroleum; English coal was imported, partly for fuelling ships, and was loaded by Rotterdam firms on to sea-going lighters in British ports and pulled across the sea by tugs. A crucial element in the cost pattern of any port is the possibility of picking up export cargoes for return freights. So although, for example, handling costs were high in British ports, freight rates were low because there were many return cargoes. In this respect a greater industrial base gave Antwerp the edge over Rotterdam, which depended heavily on exports of German coal and coke as return freights for Spanish and Swedish ore ships. Rotterdam was, however, a bigger emigrant port; in 1907, for example, some 60,000 people left Europe that way.

It was partly fortuitous that the last decade of the nineteenth century saw such a massive growth of the bulk trades which so suited Dutch water traffic. However, the growth of the transit trade and the port development brought a resurgence in the traditional Dutch shipping and shipbuilding trades, something which did not take place in Belgium at all.

– Shipping

Dutch shipping recovered only slowly from the Napoleonic wars, the first sector to show any buoyancy being the freight runs to Russia and the

Baltic, but for many years the share of Dutch shipping in all the shipping in Dutch ports declined steadily. The Dutch were slow to move over to steamships too. Of 2,209 steamships using her ports in 1867, only 512 were under the Dutch flag. The first Dutch steamship was *De Nederlander*, built in 1823 with an English engine for the Nederlandsche Stoomboot Mij, a company later expanded with Belgian capital and with John Cockerill as one of the chief shareholders. Two years later the Amsterdamsche Stoomboot Mij bought an English ship to ply a regular service to Hamburg but the company was only able to continue this and its other shipping services with the backing of the profits on its machinery works and a small government subsidy. By the 1850s the two companies operated nineteen ships but for the second of them the growing German competition proved too severe and the company sold its last four ships in 1877. In the fifties, urged on by William III, the state offered subsidies and guarantees for a transatlantic run but there were no takers. In the sixties there was opposition to subsidies and argument also over which port was best suited for such a line. At last in 1873 a service was started from Rotterdam by the newly founded Nederlandsche Amerikaansche Stoomvart Mij (later the Holland–Amerika line) with two English ships, small enough to be able to pass through the Voorne canal. The long delay over the New Waterway did not help its progress and after 1900 the company was taken over jointly by the American International Mercantile Marine company and the two German shipping lines, Hamburg–Amerika and North German Lloyd. By 1910 it had a fleet of five transatlantic liners and nine cargo vessels of 130,000 tons altogether.

A second important Rotterdam shipping line was the Rotterdam Lloyd, whose origins went back to 1844. In 1880 together with an Amsterdam line, Stoomvart Mij Nederland, they established the Koninklijke Paketvaart Mij to meet the competition arising in the Far East, above all in the Dutch colonial trade, from John Holt's British 'Blue Funnel' line. The new company was to operate between the ports of the Dutch East Indies with services to Australia too and its success was obviously crucial to the future of Dutch trade in the East. It was greatly to the advantage of the parent lines to have a feeder service to bring the products of the East Indian islands to Java and so provide a channel of trade to Europe which would be an alternative to Holt's feeder service via Singapore. Holt reacted by setting up his own Dutch company, Nederlandsche Stoomvart Mij Oceaan, whose fleet consisted of a number of older 'Blue Funnel' ships but being under the Dutch flag could enter Javanese ports on equal terms with those of the Nederland and Rotterdam Lloyd lines. An agreement was reached eventually between the Dutch and English interests over the mainline Java trade, though the coastal trade continued to see bitter rivalry. Without doubt, however, the Dutch owners had shown great tenacity and efficiency during the struggle and were in no way worsted by the Liverpool firm. The Dutch shipping industry was showing signs of recovering its old mastery of its trade.

Lines were opened to Australia, to the West Indies and to South America and all these developments brought a marked switch in the Dutch fleet as Table 36 shows. The decline of total tonnage from 1870 to 1890 reflected the reduced competitiveness of sail and the slow growth of steam, aggravated by the ending of the monopoly of the colonial trade, the development of 'Blue Funnel' competition in the East and the difficulties connected with the New Waterway which inhibited lines operating from Rotterdam. Nevertheless, sail tonnage being much less productive than steam, the overall fall in tonnage did not indicate an absolute reduction of freight carried. The rapid growth after 1890 reflected the success in the shipping struggle in the East, the effects of considerable direct aid in the form of mail and other subsidies to develop communications between the Netherlands and her colonies, special grants to the Java,

Table 36 *Dutch mercantile marine, 1870–1913 (000 net tons)*

	Total	Sail	Steam
1870	389·6	370·2	19·5
1880	328·3	263·9	64·4
1890	255·7	127·2	128·5
1900	346·9	78·5	268·4
1913	687·6	40·2	647·4

Source: USA Bureau of Foreign and Domestic Commerce, *Government Aid to Merchant Shipping*, Special Agents Series 119 (Washington, 1916), p. 126.

China and Japan services, to Rotterdam Lloyd for its operations in South America, and to the Royal Dutch Steamship Company operating between European ports. It reflected, too, the growing power of the Holland–Amerika line with the infusion of foreign capital, but above all it showed the ability of Dutch shipping to capitalise on the expansion of the Dutch ports. At its base lay the great expansion of world trade and the strategic geographical position of the Netherlands but by this time the Dutch were well able to make full use of the opportunities offered.

In a more specialised field the Dutch also built up a reputation for port work all over the world, based largely on their local reclamation industry. The Waldrops, father and son, built many harbours in South America, in Japan de Rijke improved Kobe and Osaka, and in China and Siam too the Dutch were called in. Dutch seamanship found perhaps its highest expression in salvage and towage and Smit and Co. of Rotterdam were the world's most renowned operators of tug boats. In 1896 Smit performed the first of the operations for which they were to become best known, towing a dock of 2,000 tons from Hamburg to West Africa.

– Oil

We have no measure of the size of the invisible foreign earnings built up by these activities but another very important source of income, linked both with shipping and with the Dutch colonies, emerged with the new oil industry. Already in the 1860s it was known that there were deposits of oil in the Netherlands East Indies but all the early attempts to exploit them proved fruitless. It was in 1884 that Jans Zijlker began drilling in Sumatra and, with the tenacity of the Groningen farming stock he came from, showed the way to the establishment of a successful oil industry in the area. His efforts were rewarded by the foundation of the Royal Dutch Company in 1890 with the help of a small circle of financiers in The Hague and the support of the Royal Family. Zijlker died, worn out by the struggle, only six months later. The first oil flowed in 1892 and was refined at Panghalan Brandan. Money was always a difficulty and a serious crisis developed when oil prices in the East fell and Royal Dutch shares slumped badly as Marcus Samuel and his British Shell Company obtained permission to ship oil eastwards through the Suez canal. In fact by 1900 both Shell and the Royal Dutch were operating in much the same way. Royal Dutch began as a producing company but was forced to trade in Russian oil to hold a place in the eastern market. Samuel, originally a merchant in oil, protected his supplies by going into production in Borneo. In 1900 Deterding took over leadership of Royal Dutch and two years later formed a joint company with Shell to take charge of all the sales and transport activities of the two companies.

The crucial new development in the European oil situation at this time was the rising demand for petrol, previously burned away as the crude oil was distilled to leave kerosene and lamp oil. Now tankers carrying Russian illuminating oil to the Far East could carry petrol as a return freight to Europe, the petrol from Sumatra oil being of high quality. But to safeguard this position it was eventually necessary for Royal Dutch to take a big stake in the Romanian industry where petrol production was also very important. The ideal port for tankers bringing petrol from the East was Marseilles but the French had a high duty on refined oil to aid their own refiners and so most of the tankers sailed on to unload at Rotterdam, which was by that means given a powerful expansionary boost. It had been technically possible since the late 1880s for ocean-going tankers to discharge petroleum direct to Rhine tank lighters and this again gave Rotterdam an advantage, for the lighters were more economical than the rail tank wagons being run from Bremen and Antwerp. By 1890 the traffic through Rotterdam was exceeding that through Bremen by one million barrels and soon the Dutch port was to surpass Hamburg too, being situated on the more important river.

In 1907 Royal Dutch and Shell amalgamated and were soon controlling 75 per cent of the oil output of the eastern production area and nearly all exports from the region. Yields from the Dutch fields rose from 100,000 tons in 1900 to 150,000 tons in 1913. In 1912 the company took over from Rothschilds 80 per cent of their shares in Mazout, a major distributing company in Russia, and their interests just before the war were expanding into Mexico, the United States and the Near East. By 1913 the group's share in total oil exports, excepting the American continent, was just under 70 per cent, perhaps a little over a fifth of this being exports of Dutch East Indies oil products. Royal Dutch was more a tribute to Dutch tenacity and managerial skill than to her financial enterprise, for money was always grudgingly made available. It was certainly the most important new venture into the world economy that the Dutch made before 1914, though in an important sense it was traditional, being closely linked with colonial exploitation and shipping skills. As for the economy in general, no doubt by 1914 the profits in foreign currency from these operations were considerable and the earnings from oil carriage through and beyond the Netherlands were obviously significant too.

INDUSTRY

Among Dutch historians there has been much discussion about the timing of industrial growth in their country. During the later eighteenth century Dutch industry had experienced a period of relative stagnation and many sectors, shipbuilding above all, had suffered severely from the blockade of the Napoleonic wars. The exposure of her industries to competition from the much more developed industries in Belgium before 1830 also had severe consequences. There are those who point to the 1850s and 1860s as years when industry began to expand but the evidence in favour of this analysis is slight. Railway construction was undertaken and new machinery was introduced here and there, but in 1870 the mass of industry still remained unaffected by these changes. More recent historians see the maturing of Dutch industry coming in the last two decades before 1914, with a slow but distinct growth of capacity during the previous quarter of a century.

The pattern of growth is suggested by Table 37. The percentage increases shown for the early years are misleading unless it is remembered that they are made over very low absolute starting points, but the acceleration after 1890 is undoubted. It has been shown that the increase in iron and steel consumption in the Netherlands between 1876 and 1891 was much below that of western Europe in general but from 1891 to 1910 it was slightly above that average, thus bearing out the general analysis.

How do we explain this delay? Was it due to the absence of coal and other raw materials, to the suffocating effects of the development of surrounding countries, to the timing of development in agriculture and services or to certain psychological or institutional factors? Her close geographical proximity to the greatest industrial centres of western Europe, Britain, Belgium and the Ruhr, was of the highest importance. The rising income there had a significant effect on demand for Dutch goods and services and their output limited the areas of Dutch industrial expansion, especially since after the early sixties only revenue import duties were in force. The growth of exports of foodstuffs to those countries certainly helped to eliminate any balance of payments difficulties that might have arisen from the increased imports of capital goods. The absence of ore and coal in these circumstances virtually eliminated certain areas of industrial growth altogether, although this would hardly explain the slow development of the wool and cotton textile industries. There was not the

Table 37   *Investment in the Netherlands, 1876–1910 (1876 = 100)*

	1876	*1881*	*1891*	*1901*	*1910*
Capacity of steam engines	100	132	160	280	390
Net imports of machinery	100	128	150	248	390
Workforce in machine building	100	n.a.	140	330	540
Net imports of iron and steel	100	138	132	240	490

Source: J. A. de Jonge, *De Industrialisatie in Nederland tussen 1850 en 1914* (Amsterdam, 1968), table 35.

same background of metal working and manufacturing enjoyed by Sweden nor the same material basis for early industrialisation that that country derived from timber. Danish industrial growth accelerated towards the end of the century too but growth earlier had been encouraged by the injection of money and initiative from men like Tietgen in a way that was not found in the Netherlands. In fact the evidence indicates that the positive antagonism of Amsterdam financiers towards industrial investment was a considerable handicap. Her commercial traditions may well have had an unfortunate effect on industrial development, unlike Belgium whose shipping and commerce had been well nigh destroyed by wars and political settlements at the end of the sixteenth century. There does not seem to have been any shortage of capital; overseas investment, for example, doubled from 1·5 million gulden in 1850 to 3 million by 1880. Although net domestic investment seems to have risen from around 5 per cent in the 1880s to 10 per cent or more after 1900, there is no evidence that industrialisation was effectively promoted by new sources of funds. We have already seen that railways developed only slowly in the Netherlands and that in any case she enjoyed less benefit than many from their construction, as the lines and much of the rolling stock had to be imported. Heavy investment in opening up and improving the ports and their waterways came only in the late 1860s. In view of the quality of existing water transport, however, it is open to question how far earlier railway building would have given a permanent boost to the economy – as opposed to the short-run stimulus derived from the enhanced incomes of those engaged in construction – since there was nothing to be gained by the coal and iron industries.

An important consideration is the fact that wages were considerably higher in the Netherlands than in Belgium, where the labour : land ratio was always much greater – by as much as 50 per cent in 1815. In the eighteenth century this potential labour surplus had led to substantial rural industrialisation in Flanders and elsewhere in Belgium, whereas in the Netherlands this had not come about. An industrial survey made in 1819 showed that on the whole wages in the Northern Provinces were some 40 per cent above those in Belgium. They were at the Belgian average only in North Brabant and Overyssel where the beginnings of modern industry started in the 1830s. It is significant that the population of Overyssel rose sharply between 1675 and 1764 in contrast to most of the rest of the Netherlands. Thus the Netherlands did not enjoy the benefits of modern mass production methods arising out of domestic rural industry and suffered directly from higher wage costs.

With regard to internal demand Dutch historians suggest that in the late eighteenth and early nineteenth centuries purchasing power was shifting more and more towards those with higher incomes and that this was limiting the expansion of the internal market. Belgium also enjoyed an advantage, denied to the Dutch, by being incorporated into the French home market after 1795. There were Dutch markets in the colonies, where between 1815 and 1830 Belgian industry competed, but such demand could not give the kind of stimulus required for Dutch industry to find the right openings on the European market. The types of industry which dominated industrialisation after 1890 had to be those where her industrial neighbours did not have overwhelming advantages. These included new technologies, such as diesel engines and electric lamps, and shipbuilding boosted by orders from the new Dutch lines which were developing with the help of subsidies. There were also the food processing industries satisfying rising incomes in Britain and Germany. The technical and market sources for these developments were hardly present earlier. The rise of the ports and of the transit trade and the urbanisation that accom- panied this, as well as some of the more specialised trends in farming, created eventually a further impetus to the growth of industries supplying the home market and facing little external competition. So although there may well have been entrepreneurial weaknesses among both financiers and ·industrialists, the timing of Dutch industrial growth is understandable in the light of other factors, many of which were outside direct Dutch control.

– Textiles

The cotton industry seemed to make some headway during the Napoleonic wars in the Twente area, a centre of rural linen manufacture, where there was a move to turn out cloth with a cotton weft and linen warp. The effects of the post-war tariff of 1816 have been variously analysed, for although the industry was given protection, the heavy excise duties on soap, vinegar, potash and peat were a disadvantage. The general impression, however, is that the Belgian industry developed faster than the Dutch. In 1824 William I established the Nederlandsche Handels Mij to encourage trade with the Dutch East Indies but initially it purchased most of its cloth in Belgium and benefited Twente very little. After 1830 a duty of 50–70 per cent was placed on Belgian cottons entering the East Indies and some Belgian companies actually moved to the Netherlands and concluded agreements over sales with the trading company. But factory manufacture in Twente gained ground too, for the company passed regular orders to the manufacturers there and provided working capital as well as fixed capital to enlarge their works. The first small steam-powered machine spinning mill of 10,000 spindles had been set up just prior to 1830. With the help of an English engineer, Thomas Ainsworth, the new machinery became more generally known and in 1833, encouraged by a state subsidy, he founded at Goor a school to introduce young people to new methods. But now the less fortunate side of the operations of the NHM began to appear, for the company only wished to trade in coarse cloth and manufacturers were not encouraged to show initiative in design and technology. As a result the home market developed only slowly and foreigners made more and more inroads into it. Exports of dyed goods too received a setback when in 1839 the preference in the East Indian market was restricted to cloth actually woven in the Netherlands, so that Dutch dyers and printers were forced to use only inferior home-made cloth for that market. Sometimes English and even Belgian finished cloths were imported and sold to the East Indies as Dutch, for the workmen could not print to the required standard. Even so, the use of steam spread and in 1852 the first steam-powered weaving mill was set up in the Twente region.

After 1850 the industry escaped from the tutelage of the NHM. Abolition of the excise duty on fuel in 1863 may have helped while the gradual removal of the differential duties in the East Indies forced the industry to widen its range of activities and become more competitive. The industry gradually responded to the growth of incomes and of population at home and succeeded in developing an export trade, based largely on low income countries such as British India, China, Japan and the Levant. The general pattern of growth is shown in Table 38. The rapid increase in the use of modern machinery during the sixties was in part due to a fire which destroyed much of the capacity in the main production centre, Enschede, in 1862. It will be seen that there was no great increase in spindles for two decades after 1870 but both the 1860s and 1870s saw a distinct rise in their productivity. The 1880s were a period of stagnation in spinning but of great advances in power loom weaving. The technological base now firmly laid, the industry enjoyed after 1890 the kind of expansion experienced by Dutch industry as a whole. Table 38 shows that the industry was a substantial importer of yarn, for cotton consumption by the spinning section was normally less than half of the weight of yarn used by the weavers, in contrast to Belgium where the export of yarn was a speciality. This reflected a more general contrast between the two economies: Dutch industry on the one hand having a well-established base in processing of agricultural products or imported semi-manufactures; Belgium on the other hand being a more significant

Table 38   *Cotton industry in the Netherlands*

	1861	1871	1881	1891	1910
Steam-powered spindles (000)	55·8	229·6	212·2	264·7	487·0
Cotton consumption (000 kg)					
3-year averages	700	5,800	9,000	10,400	21,300
Average consumption per					
spindle	13	25	42	39	44
Power looms (000)	3·5	10·9	13·5	19·4	33·0
Yarn consumption (000 kg)					
Power looms	n.a.	11,000	14,900	24,200	46,000
Hand looms	n.a.	5,100	2,700	–	–

Source: J. A. de Jonge, *De Industrialisatie in Nederland tussen 1850 en 1914* (Amsterdam, 1968), tables 5 and 6.

producer of semi-manufactures. The Dutch cotton industry was small in comparison with the important European manufacturers but the structure was unusual. There were nearly four times as many employed in weaving (27,800) in 1910 as in spinning (8,200) so that although Belgium had more than three times the number of spindles, total employment in the two industries was very similar. The Dutch had as many spindles as Sweden but total employment was nearly three times as large and it was ten times the size of the Danish cotton industry. In the context of a small, relatively unindustrialised country, it was an important sector – more important than was the case with other small countries in Europe except Switzerland – for two-thirds of the output was exported, two-fifths of these exports going to the East Indies. This reflected a tradition of exporting to the East but it also showed an ability to hold these exports against strong competition. Although the industry was small in total size, it was concentrated into relatively large units, mostly in the Twente area. In 1911 there were 26,000 looms in Twente, half of them in the town of Enschede; the rest were to be found in the east of adjoining Gelderland and in the south-east of Brabant where work on cotton was often combined with wool and linen weaving. There were 450,000 spindles in Twente, 350,000 of them in eight mills in Enschede, and only 37,000 elsewhere. In 1911 there were nineteen factories in the Netherlands employing over 1,000 men, and seven of these were cotton mills. The other textile industries together employed only 24,000 people. The wool industry, which was concentrated around Tilburg, made some advance after about 1860 when younger men who had gained experience of the manufacture of fancy stuffs in Verviers, Aachen and elsewhere, came to the fore in the industry.

Before 1850 the industry in the traditional textile areas had been hampered by the high wage level there and in certain towns by the high local taxes due for the most part to the burden of poor relief. Government attempts to set up a protected industry based on exports to the colonies faced this unpleasant problem. Where the industry prospered it did so in those rural areas where wages were low and taxation negligible. But rural industry in general was never as important as in Belgium if only because this supply of low wage rural labour was not widely available. Either agriculture was more prosperous and offered higher wages or the surplus of labour moved to the towns. Exactly why expensive labour persisted side by side with urban poverty is difficult to determine. It may be that there was some inflexibility in wage movements from the good days early in the eighteenth century; possibly in the commercial trades wages included a risk element to counterbalance fluctuations.

There were certain specialised industries apart from food processing. The Dutch were enormous smokers and there was a large cigar making industry based on tobacco from Sumatra. The import of raw tobacco rose from 6 million kilograms in the early 1860s to 30 million kilograms by 1913: exports of cigars rose tenfold by weight over these years. In 1909 25,800 workers were employed, making special brands to order in quite small numbers and delivering specially to individual customers as well as satisfying bulk demand. The factories were concentrated in North Brabant and were particularly found around Eindhoven and Bois le Duc. The diamond industry had established itself in Amsterdam in the late sixteenth century, attracting there by its commercial standing refugees from Belgium and France and Jews from Poland and Portugal. Initially the stones came largely from the East, until in the eighteenth century they were found in Brazil where an Amsterdam firm obtained the monopoly of the trade. In the nineteenth century there was a gradual changeover from domestic to factory production as horse and then steam power were introduced: the first steam cutting was carried out in 1840, for example. Thirty years later the first stones from South Africa arrived but the formation of de Beers in 1889 restricted the growth of output and the Dutch trade was further hampered by an American import duty on polished diamonds.

By 1914 there were some 9,000 workers altogether in seventy different establishments. The owners of the works were not lapidaries themselves; they supplied power and let out wheels to craftsmen who did not in the main work for any particular employer. The potteries at Delft were historically interesting, though tile making had declined in importance as wallpaper became popular. Industrially, however, the Maastricht potteries were more important. The industry had been started by Pierre Regout who had begun importing Belgian glass and pottery after the split in 1830. His became one of the world's biggest works and in 1910 the three factories there employed 5,000 men as well as another 1,500 in glassmaking. In Delft only 250 were employed. The traditional paper industry, centred in the Veluwe in Gelderland and at Apeldoorn, saw some growth under the impetus of the new machine methods but it was much less important than printing, another traditional Dutch industry, which employed 14,000 people in 1910.

Most of these industries benefited from the growth of incomes and of urbanisation at the end of the century; some of them were influenced by the growth of world trade too. None of them, however, could be considered as true leading sectors of growth. This lead came from various quarters; in the first place from the food processing industries whose share in industrial employment rose from 11·5 per cent in 1859 to 15 per cent in 1889 at a time when textiles and clothing fell from 29·8 to 21·4 per cent. Over those years the share of metal working fell too. The other industries whose shares increased included furniture and printing but the greatest rise was experienced by construction and the manufacture of construction materials. These were the years when the groundwork for more rapid expansion of the economy was being laid. It was only after 1890 that machine building, electrical engineering, shipbuilding and employment in dockyards themselves began to develop, raising their shares from 11·8 per cent in 1889 to 15·1 per cent in 1909.

– Coal and Iron

In the development of heavy industry the country was hindered by the absence of materials. Dutch coal was mainly anthracite and not easily mined. In 1877 output was 55,517 tons from two collieries, in 1900 320,225 tons from three collieries. At the turn of the century Belgian, French and German interests began to seek mining concessions around Haarlem in the south of Limburg and four of these were granted, though after 1901 the state reserved all further rights to itself. By 1914 output had climbed to 1·8 million tons, of which 400,000 tons came from state mines. Nevertheless coal was available relatively cheaply from neighbouring countries and in 1913 17·9 million tons were imported from Germany and about 2 million from Britain.

The Dutch iron industry grew slowly to the middle of the nineteenth century on the basis of small ore deposits in Overyssel and Gelderland, though no puddling was carried out and no steam power employed till the 1830s. The iron was used in local foundries to make hearths, stoves, ballast blocks, cannon balls and the like but as demand expanded so imports of pig iron grew. This became more pronounced as the machine and shipbuilding industries developed but again the Netherlands was well placed to obtain supplies from the Ruhr, given the excellent water links available.

– Shipbuilding

The most important heavy industry to develop in the Netherlands was shipbuilding. It was an ancient trade and in 1780 there had been 2,500 men employed in it in Amsterdam alone. By 1814, however, there were only 900. William I offered subsidies on ships built for sale abroad with no great success but in 1824 the Nederlandsche Handels Mij was formed and was obliged to use Dutch ships for trading to the East. This assistance proved far more effective and the subsidies were soon removed. Yet more important developments were at hand. Gerhard Moritz Roentgen, a naval officer, born in east Friesland in 1795, was sent to England after 1815 to study shipbuilding and the iron industries there. In 1822 he joined with others to build the *Nederlander*, a paddle steamer, to operate on the Rhine and from this beginning went on to found the Nederlandsche Stoomboot Mij with John Cockerill as one of its main backers. In 1825 the company decided to build its own works to repair and construct steam engines at Fijenoord, an island on the left bank of the Maas. An agreement was made with two Prussian companies to organise the Rhine trade on a mutual basis, these companies undertaking to buy their ships in Dutch yards. In 1836 an offer by William I to take 200,000 florins worth of shares if the company would double its existing capital of 750,000 florins, was taken up. They built their first iron sea-going ship in 1837 and specialised in tugs for towing iron barges, supplying some for operation on the Volga, and later making machines and railway materials. The Amsterdamsche Stoomboot Mij, referred to earlier, also had a works where, in addition to iron ships, they made sugar mills for export to the East Indies as well as steam engines for diamond polishing and rice hulling mills. They also built half the early locomotives and most of the rails for the first Dutch railways. This last venture was not successful but after 1850 the works were the most important in the country. In 1876 ASBM was liquidated but the works continued independently until in 1891 they were taken over by Werkspoor, who gave up the shipyard.

In general, however, development was slow. This stemmed partly from the low demand of Dutch shipowners for steam tonnage, partly from the strength of British competition and partly from the poor state of canals with respect to inland shipbuilding and of harbour access for sea-going shipbuilding. There was for some years also the disadvantage of a tariff on imported materials. Friesland and Groningen remained important centres of shipbuilding up to 1870, constructing small sailing ships, mostly for the Baltic trade. However, they came increasingly under the pressure of German competition and with no metal industries in the vicinity and little hope of modernisation, quickly dwindled to small repair yards. So the industry concentrated in Rotterdam and Amsterdam. From the 1880s more progress was made as shipping developed and companies were given mail and other contracts which were conditional on the employment of Dutch-built ships. The Rhine trade boomed, harbours were opened, shipbuilding and ship repairing expanded rapidly. The output of new ships was 4,000 tons in 1880, 23,000 in 1890, 45,000 in 1900 and 71,000 in 1910. The growth after 1890 is again unmistakable. Undoubtedly the industry played a major role in the timing of the industrial boom in the Netherlands. In 1913 the biggest yard, the Nederlandsche, employed 2,000 men in Amsterdam. The Fijenoord yards had 1,500 men; there were 1,800 at the Wilton yards, mainly engaged upon repair, and 1,600 at the Schelde engineering and shipbuilding yards at Flushing. There were also many other smaller and more specialised yards. Most of the barges on the Rhine between Rotterdam and Mannheim were built in the Netherlands and the Dutch had a special expertise in building and operating tugs. There was also an advanced marine engine building industry led by the Nederland Fabriek van Werktuigen Spoorwegmaterieel (Werkspoor). The factors bringing about the success of the Dutch industry were discussed in our previous work.[28] An engine industry, to the fore in innovation, gave Dutch ships an edge over their competitors. Plates and sections could be transported from the Ruhr at a cost lower than that to any German port and German steelmakers charged lower prices in the Netherlands than in Germany, where the tariff sheltered them from competition. In 1910 the price of 1,000 kilograms of shipbuilding steel was 62·5 florins in Rotterdam and 78 florins in the north German ports and the same on the Tyne. So although before the war Dutch owners were placing perhaps 40 per cent of their orders overseas, the Dutch industry was able to offset this by winning orders for foreign ships. In 1913, 95 ships of 104,000 gross tons were produced compared with 89 ships of 176,000 gross tons in France and 162 ships of 465,000 gross tons in Germany, but like the German industry, the Dutch output had more than doubled since 1900, whereas that of France had grown by less than half.

– Engineering

Apart from the shipbuilding industry, however, engineering in the Netherlands continued only on a small scale and for very local purposes. In 1912 only two works, building ships' engines and locomotives, and two railway workshops, employed over 500 men. Most Dutch locomotives were bought in Manchester until the turn of the century when the Nederlandsche company began to make them. There were three or four small firms making carriages and wagons but this was a minor industry. The nature of the terrain made cycling popular; the number of taxed cycles was 94,370 in 1899 and almost 540,000 in 1910. There were at least seven works producing them but the largest employed only 350 men in 1910 and a high proportion of the machines were imported. Similarly there were four motor car works, but the largest, in Amsterdam, employed no more than 325 men.

The outstanding Dutch development in modern engineering came in the manufacture of electric lamps. Gerard Philips was for a time an agent of the German AEG company in London and then in Amsterdam. With financial help from his father who, among other activities, ran a gas works, in 1891 he set out to make electric lamps on his own account, taking over an old buckskin works in Eindhoven and manufacturing basically Edison's carbon filament lamp. Three years later he was doing so badly that he tried to sell out but failed to attract a reasonable offer. At that time Gerard was joined by his brother Anton who became the salesman for the company. In 1892 Philips had made 11,000 lamps; in 1895 output totalled 45,000 and some profit was forthcoming for the first time; by 1903 they were behind only AEG and Siemens Halske in Europe, and when a cartel was organised that year Philips were given 10·5 per cent of the sales. After some financial problems during the changeover to metal filament lamps in 1909, the firm continued to expand and produced over 4 million lamps in 1911, now employing 2,500 workers. How does one explain such a success? They had an initial advantage in that with no patent law in the Netherlands, Philips was the only maker in Europe not saddled with the burden of royalty payments to the Edison interests. There was a distinct gain from the low wages payable in the Eindhoven area and they were well located for selling in north Belgium and in Germany. Research costs were low as Gerard did most of it himself and undoubtedly Anton proved a most successful salesman, especially in Russia. It was a niche that two clever and well placed entrepreneurs carved out for themselves, and once they were established as leading manufacturers, provided they kept pace with technological developments, their future was assured by the rapid growth of demand.

– *Conclusion*

It is important not to exaggerate the degree of Dutch industrial development. Industry's share of the working population, though rising from 23 per cent in 1859 to 32 per cent in 1889, was still only 34 per cent in 1909. In 1900 manufactures made up 14 per cent of exports but they only provided 12 per cent of imports and, given the narrow range of home industrial output, this points to a relatively low level of internal demand. Special niches were established in food processing linked in part to imports of colonial materials, in electric lamps, shipbuilding and ships' engines. Industry was more impressive in the Netherlands than in Denmark where shipbuilding was less important and other specialities did not emerge. It was not comparable with Belgium where the resource base was different but where there was also a far more positive drive for industrialisation and industrial exports from the financial community. Possibly more relevant, it was not as important as in Switzerland.[29] There were deeper industrial traditions there and a greater readiness on the part of Swiss finance to move into industry. A more virile and specialised textile industry flourished in Switzerland throughout the century and, partly based on its requirements, there soon emerged workshops turning out textile machinery, steam engines and water turbines. These skills were then put to the making of locomotives and eventually to modern power engineering – steam turbines, diesels and electrical generators. In the Netherlands the lamp industry was an isolated success and the belated growth of ship-building after 1890 left it in 1913 still something of an enclave industry with only the Werkspoor company expanding in other directions. To some extent industrial development in the cities was hindered by the relatively high cost of labour and of prices there. Consequently there were either industries where labour costs were relatively unimportant or a migration of industries to inland areas where costs were lower.

The acceleration of industrial growth after 1890 seems to have been closely linked to the rise in rates of growth felt all over western Europe at this time.[30] Calculations made by Teijl show national product rising in real terms decade by decade after 1850 by 14, 21, 20, 20·5 and 19 per cent and from 1900 to 1910 by 31 per cent.[31] It is interesting to note, however, that according to Bos the share of agriculture in the national income declined most during the years of falling prices, from 1873 to the early 1890s, but in fact maintained its role during the period of very fast industrial growth after 1900.[32] The experience of the Dutch economy was therefore one of balanced growth between services, industry and agri-culture, a balance which was not greatly disturbed in the period of fastest growth because all three were in a position to respond to similar external forces. It is significant too that there was a long upward trend in housing construction which lasted from 1885 to 1905 and that the high level achieved in the last of those years was maintained to 1913 when 30,000 dwellings were completed compared with 14,000 in 1890. Undoubtedly a long investment boom of this kind greatly helped to sustain the economy over those years.

In a general consideration of the Low Countries it must finally be stressed how much the development of both economies was bound up with that of western Europe as a whole. Transit and the ports were vital elements in their expansion and much of Belgian industrial growth in particular was an integral part of the development of the coal and steel based industries of the Ruhr, Luxembourg, Lorraine and Pas de Calais area both as regards interchange of products, sharing of markets and movement of investment funds. Both, however, displayed the typical concern of small countries for market outlets, Belgium looking for colonial opportunities, the Netherlands seeking to exploit what they held; and both too bore evidence to the problems of overpopulation. Belgian growth, starting much earlier, was highly skewed towards heavy industry. The Netherlands did not follow the opposite path of high agricultural specialisation seen in Denmark but provided an excellent example of balanced growth between all three sectors, partly because of the greater size of the internal market and because the country's geography determined the continuing importance of the tertiary sector.

SUGGESTED READING

There is very little literature on Belgium and the Netherlands in English. Something may be gathered about Belgian rural life in the old book by S. ROWNTREE, *Land and Labour* (London, 1910) and about the Netherlands in J. ROBERTSON SCOTT, *A Free Farmer in a Free State* (London, 1912). P. LAMARTINE YATES, *Food Production in Western Europe* (London, 1940) has more up to date material and is far more analytical; A. M. LAMBERT, *The Making of the Dutch Landscape* (London, 1971) is also useful. H. R. C. WRIGHT, *Free Trade and Protection in the Netherlands, 1816–1830* (Cambridge, 1955) is valuable for the Netherlands up to 1830, and there is an account of industrial growth in the Netherlands in E. SCHIFF, *Industrialization without National Patents* (Princeton, 1971). Much more valuable, however, is J. A. DE JONGE, *De Industrialisatie in Nederland tussen 1850 en 1914* (Amsterdam, 1968) which has a summary in English and a detailed translation of the contents of the many tables. An attempt to give a statistical framework to Dutch development is made in H. C. BOS, *Economic Growth of the Netherlands* (Portoroz, 1959). E. A. WRIGLEY, *Industrial Growth and Population Change* (Cambridge, 1962) briefly puts developments in Belgium alongside a more detailed examination of those in the neighbouring areas of France and Germany. R. CAMERON, *France and the Economic Development of Europe* (Princeton, 1961) and the chapter on Belgium in his *Banking in the Early Stages of Industrialization* (New York, 1967) are both useful. P. McKAY, *Pioneers for Profit* (Chicago, 1970) contains much information about Belgian investment in Russia. There are a number of books dealing with particular industries: on margarine there are the first two volumes of C. WILSON, *The History of Unilever* (London, 1954) and J. H. STUYVENBERG (ed.), *Margarine* (Liverpool, 1969). F. HABER, *The Chemical Industry in the Nineteenth Century* (Oxford, 1958) and *The Chemical Industry 1900–1930* (Oxford, 1971) are exhaustive on their subejct. For particular firms we have P. J. BOUMAN, *Wilton–Fijenoord History* (Schiedam, 1954) and the same author's *Philips of Eindhoven* (London, 1958). F. GERRETSON, *History of the Royal Dutch* (Leiden, 1953) consists of four long volumes in an old-fashioned descriptive tradition but there is much information for those prepared to search for it.

Some of the specialist books in French and German have been quoted in the text. There is a good general study of Belgian industrialisation by P. LEBRUN in CENTRE NATIONAL DE LA RECHERCHE SCIENTIFIQUE, *L'Industrialisation en Europe au XIXᵉ siècle* (Paris, 1972). An older work is F. BAUDHUIN, *Histoire économique de la Belgique* (Brussels, 1944). There is a considerable literature on Belgian banking and a brief but interesting survey is to be found in B. S. CHLEPNER, *Le Marché financier belge depuis cent ans* (Brussels, 1930), and R. DURVIAUX, *La Banque mixte* (Brussels, 1947) examines particular institutions in more detail. Older, but still useful, books on the Netherlands are E. BAASCH, *Holländische Wirtschaftsgeschichte* (Jena, 1927) and J. FRÖST, *Die Holländische Landwirtschaft* (Berlin, 1930).

More recent publications on Belgian and Dutch economic history are frequently reviewed together in *Economic History Review*. The serious student should consult copies of two journals, *Bulletin de l'Institut de Recherches Economiques et Sociales* and *Bulletin de l'Institut des Sciences Economiques*, for statistical studies of particular aspects of the Belgian economy. The *Revue belge d'histoire contemporaine* also has articles and reviews of interest; a whole issue in 1973 was devoted to questions of nineteenth-century Belgian agriculture. For the Netherlands besides *Economisch- en Sociaal-Historische Jaarboek* there are other journals, *Economisch en Sociaal Tijdschrift, Tijdschrift voor Geschiedenis* and *Tijdschrift voor Economie*, all of which contain articles on modern economic history from time to time.

NOTES

1 See A. S. Milward and S. B. Saul, *The Economic Development of Continental Europe 1780–1870* (London, 1973), pp. 438 ff.
2 The higher figure given for 1846 by other writers probably depends on the classification of domestic workers. P. Bairoch in his *The Working Population and its Structure* (Brussels, 1968), pp. 146–9, gives higher figures throughout. His definitions are different from those of Verhaegen but the trends are the same.
3 Anvers is used to refer to the province, the anglicised form, Antwerp, for the port itself.
4 S. Rowntree, *Land and Labour* (London, 1910), p. 148.
5 To put these figures in perspective, excluding holdings under 0·5 hectares, the average size of farm in Britain was 25 hectares, in Denmark 20, Prussia 13·5, France 10 and Belgium 6.
6 Although the most densely populated country in Europe Belgium was a country of small towns and as regards towns over 20,000 inhabitants one of the least urbanised in Europe. In large measure this was due to the daily movement from countryside to town and to the vitality of local domestic industries.
7 See A. S. Milward and S. B. Saul, op. cit., p. 452.
8 In part, of course, this was due to the fact that with protection grains were more widely grown in France and Germany and the range of yields was greater.
9 S. Kuznets, 'Quantitative Aspects of the Growth of Nations', *Economic Development and Cultural Change*, vol. V, 1957, appendix 6.
10 R. Devleeshouwer, 'Le Consulat et l'Empire; période de "take-off" pour l'économie belge?', in *Revue d'histoire moderne et contemporaine*, vol. XVII, 1970.
11 A. Madison, *Economic Growth in the West* (London, 1964), p. 28.
12 In J. Deharveng, *Histoire de la Belgique contemporaine 1830–1914* (Brussels, 1928), p. 347.

13 C. Carbonelle, 'Recherches sur l'évolution de la production belge', in *Cahiers économiques de Bruxelles* (1959), p. 360.
14 F. Baudhuin, *Le Capital de la Belgique et le rendement de son industrie avant la guerre* (Louvain, 1924).
15 The recent work of Lebrun bears out this analysis. He puts industrial growth at 4 per cent annually from 1850 to 1865 and 3·5 per cent from 1865 to 1910. Industrial production actually fell between 1873 and 1877 and again from 1883 to 1886. Otherwise a 3 per cent rate was maintained. P. Lebrun, 'L'industrialisation en Belgique au XIXᵉ siècle', in Centre National de la Recherche Scientifique, *L'Industrialisation en Europe au XIXᵉ siècle* (Paris, 1972), p. 150.
16 A. S. Milward and S. B. Saul, op. cit., pp. 443 ff.
17 ibid., pp. 446 ff.
18 ibid., pp. 183 and 228.
19 ibid., p. 442.
20 ibid., p. 450.
21 For example, there was no equivalent to the French requirement that shares allotted for a non-pecuniary consideration could not be sold for two years.
22 F. Baudhuin, op. cit., p. 26. Other estimates, however, put the figure nearer 5,000 million francs, and allowance has to be made for foreign capital in Belgian companies.
23 Daily rates for iron workers were 2·9 marks in Liège in 1890, 4·64 in Paris, 4·76 in Berlin and 6·48 in London. Average rates for miners were 3·72 in Belgium, 4·16 in France and 4·89 in the Krupp concern in Germany. Engine drivers earned 25 shillings a week in Belgium and 45 in Britain in 1909. P. van Noeske, 'Profit, Inflation and Belgian Industrial Expansion, 1830–1914', in *Tijdschrift voor Economie*, vol. IX, 1963, p. 315; S. Rowntree, op. cit.
24 A. S. Milward and S. B. Saul, op. cit., pp. 105 ff.
25 ibid., pp. 241–2.
26 These figures are from British trade statistics; Dutch statistics are so poor that no accurate breakdown by country or product can be given.
27 S. Kuznets, op. cit.
28 A. S. Milward and S. B. Saul, op. cit., pp. 220 ff.
29 ibid., pp. 455–62.
30 No worthwhile comment on Dutch foreign trade is possible as the figures are virtually useless.
31 J. Teijl, 'National Inkomen van Nederland in de Periode 1850–1900', in *Economisch- en Sociaal-Historische Jaarboek*, vol. XXXIV, 1971.
32 H. C. Bos, *Economic Growth of the Netherlands* (Portoroz, 1959), p. 10.

Chapter 4

The Economic Development of Spain and Italy, 1850–1914

PROBLEMS COMMON TO SOUTHERN EUROPE

A constantly recurring theme in our studies of economic development in western Europe has been the importance of the social changes brought about in the late eighteenth and early nineteenth centuries by the Enlightenment and the French Revolution. It was these changes which often enabled the smaller western European economies to respond so quickly to the rapid development of the larger economies in the nineteenth century. The most striking examples of this process are Denmark and Sweden which by 1914 had reached levels of per capita income almost as high as anywhere on the continent.[1] The increased demand emanating from the major developed economies, the diffusion of technical knowledge and of capital, the increasing volume of intra-European trade and the specialisation of function which this permitted, all seemed to suggest that, once the development of the larger economies was launched, the development of the rest of western Europe would inevitably follow provided no serious institutional obstacles stood in the way.

Two western European economies, however, Spain and Italy, which

215

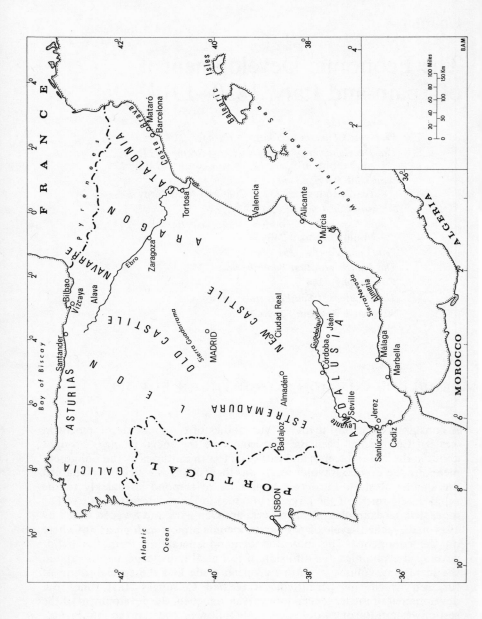

shared fully in the important institutional changes which began with the Enlightenment, and which were subject to the economic influence of the neighbouring developed economies, remained primarily agricultural economies until 1914. Their experience was not exactly parallel; after 1896 the growth of Italian industry distinguished it from the Spanish experience. In the last two decades of our period Italy began on a similar path of industrialisation to that of the other western economies and by 1913 its per capita industrial output was comparable to that of Norway. Nevertheless by 1913 agriculture still contributed 37 per cent of gross domestic product and the industrial sector only 26 per cent. Agriculture still employed 58 per cent of the labour force and industry only 24 per cent.[2] There are few statistical signposts through Spanish history and it is difficult to say anything about the composition and rate of growth of national income there. Estimates suggest that in 1914 38 per cent of national income still came from the agricultural sector and 26 per cent from mining and manufacturing. The contribution made by mining to this last figure is likely to have been high, since throughout the nineteenth century mining played an important role in the Spanish economy.

Yet Spain and Italy were countries which in the past had firmly belonged to the most advanced western part of the continent; indeed in earlier centuries they had been its richest and most influential representatives. It was in Italy that the techniques of banking and the use of long-term credit in international trade had first been developed. Spain had already become in the sixteenth century the centre of an extensive system of international trade and empire. Both were profoundly influenced by the philosophical ideas of the Enlightenment, some of its most distinguished representatives in the economic sphere writing in Italy. Both were then invaded and occupied by the French Revolutionary armies and under the influence of the Enlightenment the struggle for liberation from the French took, particularly in Spain, the form also of a movement to sweep away the institutions of the old regime. Those institutions whose survival was a handicap to the economic development of central and eastern Europe played no more important a part in Spain and Italy than they did in Germany.

The experience of the French Revolution and their long commercial history gave a modernity to liberal thought in both countries which served to make the consciousness of economic backwardness more acute. In Italy, as in Germany, backwardness could be attributed for the first half of the nineteenth century, although with less justification, to the political fragmentation of the country. But in Spain no such explanation was possible and Spanish liberal governments were early obliged to seek within the narrow confines of their philosophy for policies which would close the growing gap between their country's development and the rest of western Europe. In Italy these attempts were made only after 1870. Spain and Italy provide the first European examples of committed governments with little knowledge struggling unsuccessfully towards economic development, a pattern which grew more familiar later.

These efforts were more successful in Italy than in Spain, even if only at the very end of the period. This makes the example of Spain all the more interesting, for Spain had a notable advantage for development which we have identified elsewhere. She had the greatest of the American empires before 1800 and, although her transatlantic trade was smaller in volume than that of France or Britain, she nevertheless experienced the strong impulse to economic growth which the increase in that trade in the eighteenth century provided. A proportion of her manufactured exports was made in France or Britain but the connection between empire, trade and economic growth was still strong enough to produce the onset of mechanised production in the same way as in the other countries which benefited from this transatlantic trading system. A modern cotton printing industry developed in Catalonia, especially in and around Barcelona, based on a supply of cottons spun and woven in the rural areas, and Spain appeared to be following the same pattern of industrialisation as France. In 1792 the consumption of raw cotton in Catalonia was only about one-fifth of the French level, but as far as modernity of techniques went the cotton industry was little inferior to that of France. In eighteenth-century Italy the only activity that could be compared to this initial spurt of industrialisation in Catalonia was the growth in the export of thrown silk from Lombardy. But there was no successful attempt to manufacture the finished cloth in competition with Lyons.

This significant difference in eighteenth-century experience, however, proved in the long run less important than the similarities between the two economies. The arable agriculture of most of the countries we have so far considered was mainly practised on the well-watered lands of the temperate north European zone. The agricultural innovations of the eighteenth century were all designed for a climate with rainfall distributed throughout the year. One of the ineradicable characteristics of French agriculture, in fact, was the lower productivity and outmoded nature of farming in the Mediterranean zone where summers were hot and dry. This same arid climate covered the whole of southern Italy and Sicily and southern and eastern Spain. On the high plateau of central and southwestern Spain the summers are equally arid and the harsh cold winters have the additional effect of cutting down the growing season. Improvements in farming in such zones often required expensive irrigation works. These climatic differences perpetuated and exaggerated ancient patterns of land settlement which were distinctly different from those of the temperate European zone. Here the villages, hamlets and scattered cottages and farmsteads of most of Europe were often replaced by towns of considerable size the majority of whose inhabitants were farmers or agricultural labourers who travelled every day to distant estates or plots of land in the seemingly empty countryside.

In the more northern and temperate areas of both countries the pattern of land settlement had followed the most typical west European pattern of small or medium-sized peasant holdings. But in the southern areas the patterns of tenure were more varied and often differed widely from those further north. In Spain this was the result of the reconquest of the land from Islam. Large areas had passed into the control of the church, of military orders, noble families and townships. These areas had then been settled by cultivators who had so little land of their own that they were totally dependent on the labour provided by the estates. Such estates were frequently held in inalienable and indivisible tenures (mortmain). In the eighteenth century the proportion of church lands in the Kingdom of Naples has been estimated to have been as high as two-thirds of the total land area and large estates, owned by church and noble families, were the basis of cultivation in many areas of Sicily. The survival of such estates in Spain and Italy throughout the nineteenth century led to the existence in the southern areas of both countries of a growing and desperately poor army of landless labourers. And the singularity of agricultural conditions there both deterred industrialisation and created societies with their own customs and rules strikingly different from the rest of the continent, existing in a separate world uncomprehended and despised by the governing elites.

These fundamental differences of economy, history and thought were superimposed on other very strong regional differences which existed in both countries. Both are mountainous peninsulas whose southern extremities are a long way from the centre of the continent. There were no European countries where such great differences of climate, altitude, custom and pattern of settlement existed in such proximity to each other. In Spain these were exacerbated by the linguistic and cultural differences between the Basque provinces, Catalonia, Galicia and the Castilian heartland. In Italy there were no rival nationalisms although there were still important differences between the islands of Sicily and Sardinia and the mainland, but the great regional diversity of this varied country was exaggerated by the political disunity and by the differences in outlook of the governments of the different states before unification. These similar conditions in the two countries tended to militate against what was, from the standpoint of economic development, their earlier fortunate experience and created similar difficulties in their struggle for development.

To these disadvantages was added the crippling economic experience of both countries during the French Revolutionary and Napoleonic wars. The British blockade destroyed the flourishing transatlantic trade which Spain had built up during the eighteenth century; over a hundred ships left for South America in 1804, only one in 1807. The blockade struck at the economic base of the Catalonian cotton industry and nipped in the bud the first shoots of industrialisation. Afterwards, as the struggle turned into a guerrilla war against the French, conditions became even more difficult and much of the printing plant in Catalonia was destroyed. The colonial export markets passed under the domination of Britain and the United States and the support of those countries for the liberation movements in South America after 1815 meant that Spain's commercial loss was long-lasting, for British exports to this area grew especially rapidly. In the first half of the nineteenth century the evidence suggests that Spain's foreign trade declined, a complete reversal of the trend of the previous century and an indication of how severe the problems of readjustment were. Only three places of commercial importance remained out of the greatest empire the world had seen, Cuba, Puerto Rico and the Philippines. In Italy, the incorporation into the continental system produced effects quite the opposite of those experienced by the Low Countries and Germany. Italian manufactures could not compete in France, there were no raw material exports of the importance of Belgian coal, and the removal of protection exposed Italian domestic textile industries to competition from cheaper French cloths.

Furthermore, the incursion of the Revolutionary armies and the occupations brought profound conflicts of ideas in both countries to a head. In Spain these conflicts were so acute as to cause a succession of civil wars and changes of government and constitution which lasted until 1876. No country in Europe was so racked by internal dissension and saw so much fighting within its frontiers. Although these struggles did not always deter investors they did not provide a good foundation for industrial development and they held back the already backward agriculture. Faced in 1815 with the simultaneous tasks of devising a new commercial system and a new set of constitutional arrangements, while struggling still to hold on to her distant dominions, Spain emerged from the Napoleonic wars in a far less propitious position than she had entered them.

In Italy the ideas of the Napoleonic period crystallised into a struggle for liberation of the national territory which also involved similar constitutional disagreements. The return of the dynastic rulers there and in Spain did not stifle the liberal movements and this had an important effect on agricultural history. In most areas of Italy the work of dismantling the surviving feudal agrarian relationships was begun by legislation in 1808. In Spain the defence of the legislation passed by the Cortes of Cadiz in 1811, ending all feudal dues and incidences, became the programme of the liberal movement. In 1817 the Council of Castile pronounced in favour of the abolition of all seigneurial jurisdictions, for complete freedom of land sales and leasing, and for freedom of personal mobility. This early legislation was not very effectively enforced in either country and in Italy many elements of feudal tenurial relationships existed until the 1860s. But the impact of the French Revolution was to make the liberal movements in both countries direct their political energies against the ancient tenures which had preserved the large estates and particularly against the great landholdings of the church.

THE DEVELOPMENT OF THE AGRICULTURAL SECTOR

The failure of the agricultural sector to share fully in the development process was a cardinal fact in both countries. Spain was a less densely populated country than Italy and large increases in production could be obtained there merely by extending the farmed area. In 1800 the population of Italy was about 17·2 million, that of Spain only 10·5 million. As the population grew agriculture was able at first to respond to the increased demand in Spain without improvements in productivity by taking new land into cultivation. But this was a process with clearly finite limits which seem to have been reached by about 1870. Not much research has been done into Italian agriculture before 1870. The present picture appears to be one of a backward grain producing sector with extremely low standards of productivity existing side by side with a more efficient and developing sector producing specialised crops such as citrus fruit, rice and tomatoes. This picture may also be accurate for Spain but these specialised crops had only a local impact and in spite of the picture of agricultural improvement which is sometimes painted the overall standard of farming, in comparison with the rest of Europe in 1913, was so low that improvements in productivity before that date must have been slight.

The rate of population growth in Spain appears to have slowed down after 1860 but after 1900 rose steeply again. In Italy it remained high and between 1876 and 1900 an average of about 150,000 people a year emigrated. Between 1900 and 1913 this rose to 625,000 a year. After 1882 there were many years when over 100,000 people left Spain. Some of those who left both countries were not permanent emigrants and emigration itself was a regional effect, determined by local variations in the pattern of land distribution and in the habit of the community. But the result of population growth combined with such low levels of agriculture was to exaggerate the problems of the agricultural sector and make the need for economic development the more pressing.

– Agriculture in Spain

There are no reliable figures for the volume of agricultural output in Spain but the general outlines are clear. The output of grain increased between 1800 and 1860 perhaps by as much as 40 per cent and the increase in wine output was certainly much greater. As far as grain production was concerned there was a subsequent decline, the precise date of whose beginnings is hard to determine. Wine output continued to increase and by 1900 was almost double its 1860 volume. The increase in grain output in the first half of the nineteenth century shown in Table 39 can be compared with that shown for France in Table 27 of our previous work.[3] The total output of grain in France increased by about 50 per cent between 1815 and 1860. The increase in Spain between 1800 and 1860 was rather less than this. But in both countries the same pressures of a rising population together with improvements in communications and markets were at work, and in both cases the increase in output in the principal bread grain, wheat, was very similar. Superficially, therefore, the response of Spanish agriculture to the new conditions of production seems like that of France.

However, the similarity of trend between the two countries is misleading because the increase in output was achieved in very different ways. In France there was relatively little new land available to take into cultivation, except by converting from other types of farming, and increases in output depended on numerous small improvements in factor productivity. In Spain the increased output of agriculture seems to have been achieved almost entirely by the extension of the arable area. The productivity of grain farming declined over the period while it was improving in northern Europe. Table 39 suggests that the yield per hectare of grains may have been lower in 1860 than in 1800. In part this was the result of taking into cultivation so much new land, a lot of which in Spanish climatic conditions must have been very marginal. The ability of agriculture to feed the growing population depended entirely on changes in land use and on increasing the area of settlement; the quality of farming improved hardly at all. This, at any rate, is the interpretation now most usually accepted. But it should be said that the evidence on which it is based seems very flimsy: these isolated figures are no substitute for a proper series of statistics and until such quantitative information is forthcoming the argument were best regarded as unproven.

The increase in the cultivated area was mainly due to three processes. First, new legislation, beginning under the impact of French occupation with the sales of clerical estates between 1798 and 1808, released on to the market for the first time enormous areas of land previously held in entail and mortmain. Secondly, with the rise in grain farming the agriculture of the central plateau began to change. Its eastern areas had long been the most famous area in Europe for sheep rearing but its traditional economy based on the great flocks of sheep controlled by the sheep rearers' guild, the *Mesta*, was destroyed by the rapid social and economic changes including the dissolution of the guilds. Thirdly, there still existed in the less populated areas the possibility of new village settlements, for in relation to its land area Spain was an underpopulated country. These three processes were interdependent not separate. New settlement would often be on land previously used for pasture, and the evidence indicates that a relatively high proportion of immobilised church lands had been kept before their release in more or less permanent fallow. Disentailment and the breaking of mortmain tenures made possible an increase of 4 million hectares in the total arable area between 1818 and 1860. The new owners frequently turned pasture, woodland and waste into arable land or vineyards.

The legislation of the liberal ministry of Mendizabal in 1837 pronounced all remaining real estate of religious communities national property and initiated the second great period of disentailment and land sales. The main beneficiaries were bourgeois and noble purchasers. A down payment of one-fifth of the price was required and the remaining payment could be made either in cash over sixteen years at 10 per cent interest or in government bonds over eight years at 10 per cent. Such terms were greatly to the advantage of wealthier purchasers and middle-class bondholders and

Table 39 *Production and yield of grains in Spain, 1800–1900*

| | Output (m. quintals) | | | Crop area (000 ha) | | | Yield per ha per year (00 kg) | | |
	1800	1860	1900	1800	1860	1900	1800	1860	1900
Wheat	18·30	29·60	25·70	2,900	5,100	3,700	6·31	5·80	6·92
Other grains	39·50	55·75	51·54	6,100	9,000	7,000	6·47	6·20	7·06

Source: J. Vicens Vives, *An Economic History of Spain* (Princeton, 1969), pp. 645-6.

prohibitive to peasant purchasers. Most bonds were traded a long way below their nominal value but it was the face value which the government accepted as the purchase price for the land. In the province of Seville 76 per cent of the land sold was bought by 16 per cent of the buyers; 50 per cent of the buyers bought only 3 per cent of the land.

This was a typical result of the creation of an active land market and was to be equally true of the next and greater wave of land sales initiated by the General Laws of Disentailment of 1855 and 1858. In this next period the greater part of the land sold was communal land whereas before 1855 the greater part had been former church land. Roughly 60 per cent of the land sold was sold in the two periods 1836–49 and 1859–67. The new purchasers, many of whom were absentee landlords, were able especially in Estremadura and Andalusia to accumulate huge estates. Very little difference was therefore made to the overall geographical pattern of landholdings in Spain; it was merely the owners that changed.

At the close of the eighteenth century Spain had been a grain importing country. Decrees of 1820 followed the general western European pattern of that time in establishing a high level of protection for grain farmers. Only in very bad harvest years henceforward were imports necessary. After 1849 and until the decline in wheat prices after 1873 Spain was on balance a wheat exporting country. It is notable that these exports continued even after the sweeping reductions in tariffs in the 1860s. The conversion of land to ploughland continued until the fall in grain prices took effect. But after the legislation on disentailment of 1855 the extension of arable farming was taking place on more marginal land and returns may have been diminishing.

For its new owners the land was profitable and this, together with the small export surpluses, made it possible to ignore the clear warnings provided by the harvest failures of 1847, 1856 and 1867. In these years Spain suffered severe agricultural crises and the last two had a profound effect on the commercial and industrial development of the country. It had been assumed by governments that if the agricultural sector were freed from the inhibiting circumstances of feudal law and communal farming practice nothing else need be done to prevent it becoming a brake on industrial development. The crucial decades 1850–70 were to show how wrong this was. While feverish attempts were made in those years to industrialise the economy and while foreign investment poured into the country the agricultural sector remained largely uninfluenced by what was happening elsewhere in the economy, and eventually in the slump of 1867 brought the process of attempted industrialisation to a halt.

This had been foreshadowed by the agricultural crisis of 1857 which not only turned a financial panic into a general depression but showed how ill-equipped Spain was, unlike Sweden which greatly benefited from the same circumstances, to take advantage of the export opportunities suddenly provided by the Crimean War. The suspension of Russian grain exports and the bad harvest in Italy in 1855 saw a sharp upward movement in

Spanish grain exports. But as prices mounted towards the end of that year widespread demands were heard to suspend exports because of poverty and hunger at home. The following year saw a harvest inadequate even for domestic supply and by spring 1857 there were famines in many parts of the country especially in south-western Castile and in Estremadura. Certain areas such as the Ebro valley still had surpluses but distribution was difficult in the absence of railways. Prices were in fact generally lower around the littoral because of the arrival of imports. This was not a subsistence crisis of the severity of those endured in the late eighteenth century or in 1804–5 but it was confirmation that in spite of the great expansion of output Spanish agriculture remained at the mercy of the weather, and the economy at the mercy of the agricultural sector. This was made clearer in 1866 when harvest failures again produced famine conditions in the same areas in spite of the intervening period of extensive railway building. The crash which this produced was even more decisive.

As in most of western Europe the rapid increase of population in the eighteenth century continued through the first half of the nineteenth century to provide the driving force for the expansion of the cultivated area. The average annual rate of increase of population between 1797 and 1860 was 0·63 per cent and the population rose from 10·5 million to 15·6 million in that period. After 1860, again in apparent harmony with western Europe, the rate of population increase began to fall: from 1860 to 1900 it was only 0·44 per cent annually. But this misleading similarity disguises some significant differences of behaviour. The demographic expansion before 1860 was not related in any way to new opportunities presented by industrialisation. The gradual removal in agriculture of institutional obstacles to population growth, together perhaps with a decrease in epidemics, permitted an increase in population in a country which had been underpopulated in earlier centuries. The higher birth rates recorded in urban and industrial communities elsewhere in western Europe and the sharp distinctions between the fertility and life span of rural and industrial inhabitants are hardly noticeable in Spain. Until the end of the century Spain retained the high birth and death rates typical of an eighteenth-century economy. In 1900 the national birth rate was 33·8 per thousand, the death rate 28·8, and the expectancy of life at birth only 35 years. The fall in the rate of growth of population in the second half of the nineteenth century in Spain was not related, as it was in developed western Europe, to the emergence of a commercial and industrial society with lower birth rates and lower death rates. Rather it seems that by mid-century the population had begun to approach the limits to its growth imposed by the availability of resources, especially land. By 1900 the total growth of Spanish population, which had kept pace until 1850, was considerably less than the average for western Europe. Only after 1900 was there a noticeable decline in the death rate for the first time, with the birth rate also falling but more slowly. It may be that with the start of the twentieth century Spain was beginning to move towards the pattern of population growth established in developed European countries after 1870. But local fluctuations in grain prices continued to have a close correspondence to movements in the birth and death rates.

This rigidly Malthusian model of Spanish population growth should not be taken too literally. There always existed the outside world, not merely as a market for Spanish crops or as a source of grain but also as a target for emigration. Nor was the Spanish economy entirely unindustrialised. Modern industry, however, was confined to a few peripheral regions where the agricultural problems were less serious and before 1914 was never on a large enough scale to attract labour from other areas. Overseas migration from the Iberian peninsula was already important before 1860, and after 1880 this was one of the most important sources of European migrants. But migration never attained the landslide proportions that it eventually reached in Italy.[4] Until the 1870s there were restrictions on emigration from Spain, although reality compelled the government not to enforce them. Until 1882 the annual average number of emigrants to Latin America and Cuba was about 11,000. Thereafter it grew steadily to 1917 when it reached 113,994. In the last years of our period it was thus at about the same level as the increase in population, but there is much evidence that, as in the case of Italy, a high proportion of Spanish emigrants returned to Spain. We are presented with the paradox, not completely explained, that with the exception of Galicia most emigration was from areas where the population did not press so closely on the available land. No doubt among the causes were the need to have funds when emigrating, well-established patterns of land tenure which in Catalonia prevented farmers getting access to farms while permitting subdivision in poorer regions such as Galicia, and in the poorest areas attitudes of mind as yet ill understood.

In common with other mid-nineteenth-century western governments those of Spain had little interest in the role of agriculture. Until the 1866 crisis they were prepared to extend protection and keep up prices, but this did not lead to more investment in existing farms. The main reason for this was the pattern of landholding. There exists a fatalistic explanation which attributes this pattern to unalterable climatological facts but in truth much could have been done to change it given a different attitude by government. There are few reliable surveys of landholding in the period but the fragmentary figures that exist are confirmed by the official tax surveys of 1930. These reveal the comparative rarity of medium-sized holdings, between 10 and 100 hectares. Such holdings occupied only about one-quarter of the land area at that time. But in the most developed areas of the country, those with most manufacturing and with the highest levels of income, they were dominant; this was so, for example, in Catalonia, in Navarre and in Alava. Generally, the northern parts of the Mediterranean coast, an upland belt stretching from León to the Mediterranean, and the Basque provinces were free from the problems either of great estates or of landholdings which were too small.

In the north-western areas the proportion of medium-sized holdings was much lower and the proportion of holdings of less than 10 hectares in size was much higher. Galicia is a wet and not an arid region and the problems caused by an excess of small plots were less there than in the south. But the tiny farms did not lend themselves to anything more than self-sufficient family units; a cash surplus came only from the occasional sale of a calf or from migratory labour. By 1900 the hopelessness of the situation as population increased and the land was further subdivided led both to emigration and to a type of rural lawlessness familiar in Ireland and south-eastern Europe – rent strikes, the murder of land agents and so on. In southern Spain 53 per cent of the area was held in holdings of more than 500 hectares. By the side of these great estates existed numerous small-holdings about the same size as those of Galicia. In some southern areas the structure of landholding was even more distorted and consisted mainly of large estates cultivated by completely landless labourers.

Here crop fluctuations were severe and the land could seldom be sown more frequently than in alternate years. The landlords were usually the middle-class investors who had bought land under the liberal reforms rather than the older nobility, who had retained their position only in certain localities. The greater commercialism which the new owners into- duced could not overcome the fundamental embarrassment of an increas- ing swarm of labourers with no other source of employment. There were examples of tracts of fertile land used to rear fighting bulls, but the methods of farming on the big estates were in general no more inefficient than the peasant holdings elsewhere. Outside harvest periods there was a large labour surplus, and at harvest times migrant labour arrived from the areas of extreme subdivision in Galicia and from Portugal. The wages of agri- cultural labourers in Andalusia in 1902 were only one-third of the national average. The belongings of a family there even by 1914 might amount to little more than a cooking pot. A social system of extreme brutality, with absentee landowners, a mere subsistence income for the labour force, and cheap labour tending to discourage the adoption of less labour-intensive methods of cultivation, all created a climate in the south in which economic improvement seemed impossible without the development of alternative sources of employment in other regions.

The pauperisation of most of the population in the south-eastern area left them devoid of resources to meet natural disasters. This was to be shown by the famine of 1904–6. As in 1857 and 1866 the worst affected areas were those such as Andalusia in which the structure of landholding inclined most towards big estates. By 1900 rural revolt and disorder were as prevalent in these areas of Spain as in Russia. Violence, the attachment to myths, the escape into an unreal world of fervent dreams of the over- throw of the real world, and the widespread acceptance of revolutionary anarchism, kept society in a state of virtual civil war. The hopes raised by the commitment to political action, and the separate habits of thought produced by life in such a society joined with poverty to inhibit what was in the circumstances the only solution, emigration. More emigrants went from the south-eastern regions of Levante and Almería than from Andalusia and Estremadura, and even from poor Galicia the rate of emigration was higher.

Where agricultural improvement did take place it was limited to those regions where medium-sized farms were more usual or where irrigation projects had been successfully carried out. After 1860 the railways provided new marketing possibilities and so did the extensive programmes of road building. In 1906, after the famine, legislation deliberately fostered the growth of rural co-operatives. This had one useful result in making fertiliser more cheaply and widely available. But the co-operatives were successful only in those areas with a reasonable proportion of substantial peasant farms such as Catalonia and the Basque lands; even there land tenures were often not sufficiently firm, even though hereditary, for banks to provide mortgage capital. The long-term mortgage credits provided by the Banco Hipotecario and the Banco de España did not touch small farms and there was no administrative connection, as there was in France and Germany, between mortgage institutions and agricultural co-operatives. In the south and centre, the *pósitos*, ancient collecting centres for produce, were developed after 1877 to facilitate marketing and the *sindicatos agricolas* could everywhere organise bulk purchase after 1906. But until 1914 most Spanish agriculture remained under-capitalised and unmechanised. French copies of American reaping machines sold in Spain for about 50 per cent more than their price in France because of the high rail transport costs; only more elementary machines, ploughs and threshers, were made in Spain. Yet in spite of the higher purchase price of machinery its real costs would by 1913 often have been lower than the alternative labour costs in the central areas where labour was scarce. But for most peasant farmers there was no help with the initial purchase price of the machine, and in some regions labour was so abundant as to be starving, which effectively discouraged mechanisation.

So far Spanish agriculture has been discussed as though it had practically no connection with the outside world. But a high level of agricultural exports could have completely changed the situation. After 1880 grain exports were rare; the coastal areas attracted American grain in large quantities and American wheat sold more cheaply in Barcelona by 1887 than Castilian wheat brought by train. After the defeat in the war against the United States Cuba was declared an open market and the last vestige of Spanish grain exports, the monopoly trade from Santander to Havana, disappeared. The tariffs of 1891 and 1906 restored almost total protection to Spanish grain farmers and ended the attempt to stimulate exports through lower tariffs. The period of grain export had in fact been achieved at the expense of the loss of one eighteenth-century export, wool. Spanish sheep declined in number with the conversion of common and pasture and also sank in esteem as Australian and Argentinian breeders developed better strains from Spanish originals. The annual average level of wool exports from 1849 to 1880 was only one-third its level between 1749 and 1793.

But the impact of cheap transatlantic grain was temporarily cushioned in the 1880s by the success of one branch of Spanish agriculture which had flourished and grown since 1815, viticulture. Production of wine grew from 3·85 million hectolitres in 1800 to 21·60 million in 1900, and the crop area of vineyards increased more than threefold. The first Spanish railway concession was designed to improve communications between Jerez and the port of Sanlúcar to increase the exports of sherry to Britain. Catalonian wine had a less restricted market being sold throughout Latin America. Wine, grapes and raisins were more than one-third of total Spanish exports in the 1850s and remained the major export until eventually overtaken in the 1890s by ores. The importance of the foreign market gave viticulture a much more efficient air than grain farming. But this did not affect the central plateau until after 1860 because the vine was for a long time a crop of the peripheral regions where the climate was more suitable. When the phylloxera so drastically reduced wine output in France, French wine imports shot upwards showing a tenfold increase from 1877 to 1881. Spain benefited most; the Spanish share in them rose from 538,000 hectolitres to 5,435,000 hectolitres. France now became a market of vital importance and the volume of wine exports there continued to rise, reaching its record level of 9,394,000 hectolitres in 1891. But phylloxera spread to the country in the first years of the decade and by 1890 was at its most extensive just as it was being eliminated in France. The renewal of competition and the decline of wine exports to the French market produced a crisis in the wine trade so that by 1900 the volume of wine exports was again back to its level of the late seventies. Nevertheless the fortunes made in the wine trade did occasionally find their way into other forms of investment although vine-yards themselves for most of the century were one of the safest and most profitable investments in Spain.

Foreign markets also stimulated the cultivation of olives, especially the transatlantic market opened by large-scale emigration to Latin America. It was after 1880 that the two main zones of production, around Córdoba and in Lower Aragon, were formed. But lack of commercial and industrial skills meant that many Spanish olives were taken to Italy, where the trade was older-established, for processing into oil before export to Latin America. The irrigation of land to provide extensive orchards for fruit export only began on any scale after 1870. The small irrigated areas in the general sterility of the Levante became the most productive farming areas in Europe. Three to five crops of fruit a year were produced around Tortosa, Valencia and Murcia, and it was in such areas where there was a high degree of farming skill that export crops of almonds and vegetables were also first produced. Lastly must be mentioned one agricultural industry in which Spain dominated the world market throughout the period, the manufacture of corks. Its basis was the raw material provided by the Catalan cork forests. Its growth was tied to the increasing demand for high-quality French and German wines and to the general rise in European wine consumption. Whether the cork forests in other areas of Spain gave an inferior cork or whether the Catalan forests were simply, as seems likely, better managed and tended, is not established, but for over a hundred years cork exports gave employment and brought significant foreign earnings to the Costa Brava.

None of these export markets except that for cork was large or sustained enough fundamentally to change the backwardness of Spanish agriculture or to raise the level of incomes. The problems were intensely regional and the income from these foreign markets was regional also. Cork exports were in fact benefiting the most developed region and increasing the disparity between that and the others. But it is possible that the force of demand from Europe and America would have brought greater benefits had a better response been obtained.

– Agriculture in Italy

It is not possible as yet to make any certain pronouncements about Italian agriculture before unification. Even after unification its history remains one of the most neglected areas in European economic history. But the movement of output after 1861 is roughly known and is shown in Table 40. Its main features are an increase in all the main crops between 1861 and 1870, the slowing down of this growth in the next decade followed by a decline in grain output between 1881 and 1890, the continued expansion of grape and citrus fruit production in that decade, although insufficient to compensate for the severe decline in grain output, and finally the rapid increase in output of all the main products except wheat after 1901. The decline in grain production between 1881 and 1890 was a response to the invasion of cheaper grain from elsewhere. The increase in citrus fruits and grapes was a response to rising demand for such products in other European economies and the United States, a response facilitated by railway building in Italy. The annual average quantity of citrus fruit exported rose from 0·91 million tons in 1871–80 to 1·6 million tons in 1881–90 and to 2·0 million tons in 1891–1900.

The most valuable of the specialised crops, however, continued to be silk cocoons. After China, Italy remained the largest producer of cocoons although from the mid-nineteenth century onwards the silkworms were usually reared from eggs imported from Japan. Silkworm farming was, however, even more confined to certain localities than the production of citrus fruits, being heavily concentrated in the main centres of raw and thrown silk production, Lombardy and Piedmont. The overwhelming bulk of the production was destined for export to the Lyons market and it naturally followed closely the vicissitudes of the French silk industry. With the revival in that industry from the mid-1880s, and with the impetus which the same technological developments brought to the Italian silken cloth industry, the demand for Italian cocoons began to rise steeply. Here, too, the great industrial boom in Europe during the 1890s had an immediate effect on Italian agriculture. But the greater increases in agricultural output after 1901 are only partly explained by responses to change elsewhere; they also have to be seen in a long-run context. Throughout the whole period until 1914 silk, raw or thrown, was the leading Italian export, in value usually about one-third of the total of all exports, and the returns on these exports had been coming back to the northern provinces for a long time before the rate of growth of agricultural output accelerated. The production of raw silk and silk yarn represented the chief industrial base of the Italian economy until late in the nineteenth century and it was firmly erected on Italian agriculture.

The climatic conditions for competitive silkworm farming, however, were restricted to the north-western provinces at the foot of the Alps. The subsequent industrialisation of these provinces owed much to the cultivation and throwing of silk; indeed in the decade between 1855 and 1865 when the silkworm disease *pébrine* was at its worst there was a marked increase in the proportion of silk thrown into yarn. But these areas were much closer to Lyons and the Rhône valley than they were to central and southern Italy and if their ultimate industrialisation is seen as a balanced interaction between industry and agriculture in which the process of agricultural improvement was gradually fostered by the demand for a specialised crop, the improvements in technology and income which ensued were confined to the periphery of the country.

However, the improvements in agriculture after 1901 were more widespread and their origins more diverse. They were partly due to an increasing use of fertiliser; the value of fertiliser imports rose from 4 million to 60 million lire between 1887 and 1908–10 while the domestic output increased ten times. The value of imports of agricultural machinery increased twenty-one times between 1888 and 1910. There was practically no increase in the amount of cultivated land after 1887 while the labour force began to decline after 1897, all suggesting that in this last period farming became more capital-intensive. The improvement in the performance of the agricultural sector generally after 1896 seems also to be related to the spread throughout northern Italy of the type of credit, mortgage and co-operative institutions for peasant farmers developed elsewhere on the continent and particularly in Germany.[5] The 'popular banks' had begun as early as 1865 in Milan and Cremona under the influence of the propagandist Luigi Luzzatti who was himself strongly influenced by Raiffeisen. They acted as discount banks for village co-operative institutions. By 1908 there were 708 of them, the majority still in Lombardy. Frequently they provided a source of finance for collective leasing of land by associations of peasants and from them sprang not only the movement towards agricultural co-operation but also the movement to provide travelling teachers of agriculture.

Before 1890, and in the early 1890s, agriculture, except for a burst of increased output between 1861 and 1870, was slowing down the growth and development of the whole economy. In the 1880s, however, the increase in gross agricultural production, although slight, was actually as great as or greater than that in gross industrial production, so that by 1901 agriculture was making a slightly greater proportional contribution to gross national product than it had done in 1892. Government policy provided considerable help for agricultural interests. The duties on grain imports imposed in 1887 were high and by 1895, at least as far as wheat was concerned, Italy had a higher level of agricultural protection than any other continental economy. At the same time the commercial agreements signed from 1892 onwards with central European countries reduced import duties on many manufactured goods in return for a reciprocal reduction of their

Table 40   *Movement of agricultural production in Italy, 1861–1910 (annual averages, m. tons)*

	Wheat	Maize	Oats	Rice	Grapes	Citrus fruit	Wine[1]
1861–70	3·73	1·80	2·89	3·70	4·03	2·71	23·5
1871–80	3·98	2·45	3·54	4·91	4·59	3·77	26·9
1881–90	3·35	1·99	2·90	3·83	5·35	5·28	31·3
1891–1900	4·76	1·94	3·25	3·50	5·74	5·42	32·0
1901–10	4·57	2·49	5·02	5·69	7·66	8·21	44·1

[1] Million hectolitres

Source: Istituto Poligrafico dello Stato, *Sommario di statistiche storiche italiane, 1861– 1955* (Rome, 1958), pp. 106–10.

duties on Italian food exports. The increase in agricultural output after 1896 was in fact partly stimulated by an increase in food exports to Germany and Switzerland: Italian exports to Germany increased by over 50 per cent between 1898–1900 and 1911–13.

The great obstacle, however, was the south. In the absence of research accurate comparisons between northern and southern agriculture in 1860 are almost impossible to make. But the problems of southern agriculture were so long-run and deep-seated as to suggest that the south was already agriculturally a long way behind the north at the time of unification and that this lag caused it slowly to fall further behind after 1870 in spite of the good intentions of national economic policy.

Of all the areas of Europe for which we have evidence, southern Italy and Sicily present the lowest figures for crop yields, lower even than the Balkan states and Russia. The figures in Table 41, the only ones available, refer to the period 1923–8 and it would be reasonable to assume that before 1914 the yields would have been even lower. For wheat and maize the yields in northern Italy were about twice as high as in the south and the islands. These lower yields were clearly related to inferior methods of cultivation and these in their turn related in part to historical and institutional differences between the regions. If the growth of agricultural output in the south between unification and 1914 was accompanied by an improvement in methods and yields this can only emphasise how extraordinarily backward the region was in 1860 and how enormously long and difficult was the catching-up process.

The slow improvement in grain yields in the south, however, is only an indication of the quality of farming for the domestic market. As in Spain, export markets, could they be held for long enough, provided a faster way of raising agricultural incomes. But, again as in Spain, the efficient cultivation of a crop like citrus fruit sometimes required a level of capital investment, especially where irrigation projects were concerned, which was

Table 41 *Average yield of certain crops in Italy by region, 1923–8 (quintals per ha)*

	Wheat	Maize	Barley	Oats	Potatoes
North	17·2	22·8	12·5	15·6	93·3
Centre	10·9	11·7	10·3	12·0	64·1
South	9·5	9·5	8·4	9·1	51·7
Islands	8·9	10·3	9·5	10·2	67·8

Source: Associazione per lo sviluppo dell'industria nel mezzogiorno, *Statistiche sul mezzogiorno d'Italia 1861–1953* (Rome, 1954), p. 205.

beyond the capacity of the farmer. Where agriculture was able to specialise in this way it was in startling contrast to the large backward grain farms of Sicily and Basilicata. Wine was less demanding and more suited to small peasant farms. The great increase in wine exports in the 1880s brought a brief glimpse of comparative prosperity to Apulia which was able to participate in the national expansion of that decade. But the return to protection and the tariff war that resulted with France in 1887 showed how precarious the position was. With the French market closed wine exports from Apulia fell sharply, incomes declined and the situation deteriorated into a peasant revolt.

Lack of industrialisation in the centre, south and islands produced the same combination of cheap labour and technical backwardness as in Spain. Central Italy continued to be, as it had been in the eighteenth century, the area of Europe where sharecropping (*mezzadria*) was most common. In fact in an area like Tuscany, where the practice was almost universal, the sharecropper had a more secure position than in south-western France. But the fact that by custom his tenure was virtually hereditary did not necessarily make for better farming methods. The initiative came from the landowner and he tended to extract higher short-run profits from the system by putting up the share of gross output of the farm to which he was entitled by the sharecropping contract. By 1913 such contracts in Umbria and the Marches frequently reserved between one-third and one-quarter of output to the cultivator. The institutional arrangements of the great estates in the south and Sicily were often based on a system akin to sharecropping, because it enabled landlords to exploit the land hunger of an increasing rural population in order to ensure the cheap, albeit inferior, cultivation of their own land. Even Baron Ricasoli, the famous Tuscan agricultural reformer, retained sharecropping as a means of cultivating his estates. In Tuscany, where large estates were few, this resulted only in the stagnation of techniques. But further south where great estates prevailed their owners were able so to constrict the size of the sharecropper's plot and income, forcing him into agricultural labour, that the result was a society akin to that of Andalusia.

The larger peasant freehold farms in central Italy and Lazio tended to be confined to the poorer upland areas or to wine growing districts like the Monti Albani. The owners of the large estates, whether individuals or corporations, carried out their functions through 'merchants of the countryside' (*mercanti di campagna*), and leased their houses and lands, leaving the farming to sub-contractors who arranged the provision of agricultural labour. When the clerical lands were secularised in 1873 and subsequently sold in smaller lots it was these middlemen who acquired most of the new land. Government efforts to populate the countryside around Rome by expropriating recalcitrant proprietors after 1883 and dividing the estates into smaller units made little difference. Wherever similar areas of large estates predominated all observers were struck by the emptiness of the countryside, by the large apparently underpopulated and undercultivated areas in a country where the ratio of land to labour was comparatively unfavourable. Given a pattern of land settlement like that in Sicily where the agricultural population lived in towns of considerable size this was all the more difficult to change. The immediate surroundings of the town might be intensively cultivated but wide areas of the countryside were cultivated only in the most primitive way or even abandoned. Extensive tracts of land in the regions of Caltanisetta, Girgenti, Palermo and Catania were made up of contiguous great estates, short of wood, of water and of transport. Such estates either depended on day labour from the towns or were farmed by sharecroppers whose title to the land seldom lasted longer than the period covered by one rotation, five years at the most. The number and size of the Sicilian estates is hard to estimate but there were in the 1880s about 70 separate proprietors with more than 2,000 hectares each and whose total holdings measured more than 250,000 hectares. About 30 per cent of the island was held by 787 owners, each of whom had more than 200 hectares.

Of the 500 or more southern estates examined by the parliamentary enquiry of 1908–10 only 33 had any form of modern machinery, and those usually no more than a thresher. Their method of cultivation was on the same level as the poorest Russian peasant farm. In many cases three-quarters of the gross output went to the proprietors and what was left was so meagre that Sicily, like Russia and Romania, was one of the areas of Europe before 1914 where even bread was sometimes a luxury. The proportion of fallow land was very high. In highland zones or on the remoter areas of the great estates the scrub would be cut down and burned in summer, the land ploughed and sown to barley or wheat, and then left fallow for between four and eight years to recover. The more regularly ploughed areas, even when they were subject to a three-year rotation, would be sown to grain in only one of those three years, the other two being pasture and fallow. In the region of Bari in southern Italy there would be two grain years out of every three and this was perhaps more typical of mainland areas. But under that rotation yields of grain were declining because of soil exhaustion. The primitive wooden ploughs used over much of the south did not turn the soil sufficiently for most crops other than grain. There were no scythes in Sicily; the harvest was cut with sickles and threshed by the trampling of oxen.

The ratio of cattle to land was low everywhere in Italy, between a half and a third that in Germany, because of the lack of fodder. Only near to the towns did the peasant keep a few milk cows, whereas sheep and goats were still kept in large numbers. This made for a low level of supply of natural fertiliser. Once again the proportion of cattle was much lower in the south. Italy was in fact a meat exporter on a small scale but this was only the result of the extremely low level of meat consumption. In 1876–9, for example, per capita meat consumption in Piedmont and Lombardy was less than one-half its level in Germany; in the south it was about one-seventh. To these problems of southern Italy we shall return at the end of the chapter.

INDUSTRIAL DEVELOPMENT

In Italy, as in Spain, it was only in certain regions that agriculture offered a suitable basis for an increase in spendable incomes; on the national level it remained sluggish and backward, particularly the grain growing sector which provided the staple food of the population. The growth of industrial production depended on other sources of demand. The industrial history of Italy and Spain could be summed up as a long struggle to provide such alternative sources, a struggle which, in Spain, in spite of the promising developments in the cotton industry in the late eighteenth century, was unsuccessful, but in Italy did eventually meet with some reward. The textile industries grew only slowly because of the low level of incomes on the domestic market and in both countries governments attempted to speed up the process of industrialisation by the construction of a national railway network and the attraction of foreign capital, and then by high levels of tariff protection. In spite of its inconsistencies government policy was a strong impetus to industrialisation in both countries throughout the century.

- Textile Industries

Once peace was restored in 1815 the Catalan cotton industry recovered steadily from warfare and the loss of empire markets. It remained until 1914 the most important sector of Spanish industry, dominating the industrial scene in a manner characteristic of the less developed European economies. From a low base of 1815 output grew slightly faster than in the cotton industries of the major developed economies while remaining far behind them in absolute size. After 1903 its rate of growth slowed at the very time when the Italian industry was sharing in the cotton boom affecting larger west European economies. Table 42, though useful for general comparison (being misleading where a textile industry like that of the Netherlands had a relatively important sector weaving imported yarn), shows that until the 1890s the per capita consumption of cotton in the Spanish and Italian cotton industries was about the same as that in the low-income eastern empires whose production was destined almost wholly for the home market. Before 1880 the Spanish industry had higher per capita consumption than the Italian, probably due to the continued existence of certain Spanish colonial markets and perhaps also to a slightly higher level of spendable income amongst Spanish consumers. The surge in per capita cotton consumption in Italy after 1890 was related to the opening up of export markets in south-eastern Europe and Turkey and to the increase in incomes derived from a more rapid development of other industries after that date.

In general, however, the cotton industry in Spain and Italy grew slowly until the 1890s because it was held back by the low level of consumer incomes there. It was unable to export on the same scale as those of Belgium and Switzerland where per capita cotton consumption on average was twice as high. Being confined in this way to the home market also meant that the industry was less innovative than those in the countries with a greater proportion of exports since the market was less competitive. This was a situation common to textile industries in all the less-developed economies, as can be seen throughout this volume, and its implications were important. It meant that even though the cotton industry might, as in Spain, be the most important part of the industrial sector by almost any method of measurement, it did not play the dynamic role in the economy that it had in the early stages of industrialisation in countries like Switzerland or France. The technology was often outmoded and imported from

Table 42 Estimated total consumption (A) and per capita consumption (B) of raw cotton in some less developed European economies (A = 000 tons, B = kilograms, ten-year averages)

	Austria-Hungary[1]		Italy		Netherlands		Russia[2]		Spain	
	A	B	A	B	A	B	A	B	A	B
1860-9	30·8	0·86	7·2[3]	0·29	2·2	0·61	32·5	n.a.	16·8	1·07
1870-9	53·0	n.a.	24·4	0·91	8·9	2·22	76·6	n.a.	33·5	2·01
1880-9	80·3	2·12	68·0	2·39	11·9	2·64	139·1	n.a.	49·0	2·79
1890-9	118·5	2·76	111·7	n.a.	14·1	2·76	197·6	1·56	65·6	3·62
1900-9	163·2	3·61	167·8	5·17	22·6	3·86	299·0	n.a.	80·1	4·31

[1] Excludes Lombardy after 1860 and Venetia after 1866; Dalmatia only included from 1861
[2] Excluding Finland
[3] Nine-year average excluding 1860

The population is taken at the nearest census to the middle of the decade and, if censuses fall only at the first or final years, at the first year. Where no census takes place in the decade no calculation is made. The apparent per capita consumption of raw cotton in 1900-9 in Germany was 6·75 kilograms, in France 5·29 and in Switzerland 9·41

Source: National trade and population statistics; B. Mitchell, *European Historical Statistics, 1750–1970* (London, 1975).

the more developed economies and the levels of productivity lower. It was only in a merely quantitative sense that the textile industries in the under-developed economies could be counted as the 'leading sector'.

It was only in 1820 in Spain that the total output of printed cottons again reached its level of 1792 and it was not until the 1830s that the mechanisation of spinning began on any scale. It was not completed until 1860, a half century later than in France, and the out-of-date mule was until mid-century the machine mainly used. Mechanised weaving did not lag so far behind; it began in the 1840s and by 1861 45 per cent of the looms were mechanical. The onset of mechanisation in the 1830s may have been con-nected with a contraction in the labour supply caused by the lower surplus of births during the war period twenty years earlier.

The most rapid period of growth came between 1869 and 1878, after which growth slowed down once more. It is curious that growth should have persisted in the late seventies, a depressed period for European industry almost everywhere. It may be, however, that the boom in wine production and exports in Catalonia caused by the ravages of the phyl-loxera in France[6] brought about an increase in spendable incomes there. In an attempt to safeguard the higher quantity of output Catalan manu-facturers agitated for increased protection. From 1882 exports to the West Indian colonies were treated as coastal trade for revenue purposes and from the end of 1891 Spanish textile exporters acquired a complete mono-poly of the Cuban market. The proportion of output exported rose steadily with these provisions until in 1893–7 it reached its highest point, 17 per cent. But with the war against the United States and the independence of Cuba in 1898 the industry was once again gradually thrown back on to the internal market by American competition, and Spanish exporters were not subsequently able to find new foreign markets.

Although the cotton industry remained principally confined to north-eastern Catalonia, two of the largest and most modern firms were in Málaga. Other textile industries also tended to be restricted to Catalonia as the century ran its course. In terms of employment they were all more significant than cotton until mid-century, but they were less mechanised and gradually lost ground. Mechanisation of the woollen industry began only after 1860. By 1900 there were 226,000 woollen spindles, of which 130,000 were in Catalonia, and 120,000 worsted spindles, all in Catalonia. Linen was replaced by mass-produced textiles but the remnants of a silk industry survived in Barcelona against French competition, though without making any real contribution to development.

The failure of the Spanish cotton industry to make headway against foreign competition in the nineteenth century was matched for a long time by the history of the Italian silk industry. It was not cheaper raw material which had made Lombardy the main region of silk yarn production in eighteenth-century Europe but greater technical expertise and higher productivity in every stage of yarn production. These advantages were maintained throughout the nineteenth century. Both the cheapness and quality of yarn were superior to France. On this comparative advantage was based the most important Italian export trade to all the developed economies and particularly to France, Germany and, later, the United States. But in spite of this the weaving side of the industry showed no development; it was more or less abandoned in face of the competition from Lyons. Only with the invention of mechanised weaving methods in the 1890s were mechanical looms gradually introduced into Italy. Why weaving did not develop in Italy is not at all clear; the obvious poverty of the domestic market cannot be the only explanation, for French silk weavers usually exported over a third of their output.

The late burst of growth in the Italian cotton industry was related to complex changes in the Italian economy which we shall discuss later. For much of the period the greater size of the Italian cotton industry was simply a function of the greater number of consumers in Italy. In spite of the initial encouragement provided by the immigration of Swiss entrepreneurs and mechanics the industry was technically even more backward than in Spain. The finished cloths were almost all of the coarsest and cheapest varieties and the growth of output was very slow. Water power provided the main source of energy and this limited the number of spindles in each mill. Production was mainly concentrated in Piedmont and Lombardy, chiefly in the Alpine valleys where water power was regular and plentiful. There were about 240,000 spindles in Lombardy and Piedmont in 1850. By 1877 there were still only 880,000 spindles over the whole country but thereafter the industry began, with the help of a high level of protection, to take a larger share of the domestic market. Even so the real growth only came after 1892. Between then and 1913 the number of spindles rose from 1·68 million to 4·6 million, by which date the industry was only slightly smaller than that of Austria-Hungary. Mechanical innovations were retarded and derivative, mule jennies were little used before the 1840s, self-actors before the 1870s. About 90 per cent of the machinery was still imported from Britain even after 1900. Much the same pattern could be observed in the woollen industry. Before the protective tariffs which began in 1878 it was confined to the traditional cloths and few worsteds were made. As late as 1900 about half of the looms were hand looms. At the time of unification the industry supplied only about half the domestic demand. After protection it gradually expanded so that by 1914 it more or less satisfied the whole of the home market. Worsted spindles increased from 94,000 in 1894 to 433,000 in 1914 and woollen spindles from 251,000 to 400,000. Over the same period the number of mechanical looms increased from 6,500 to 17,000.

– Coal and Metallurgy

The other main props of western European industrialisation in the nineteenth century, coal mining and iron manufacture, saw much less change in Spain and Italy than textiles. Italy had virtually no coal and Spain very little. Manufacturing costs in most metallurgical processes were high and the use of steam engines spread only slowly. Until 1832 imports of coal into Spain were nominally forbidden and after that date the import duty was very high. After 1837 individual entrepreneurs were allowed reductions in import charges but until 1869 these were personal favours. Coal output was only 1·5 million tons a year in the early 1860s. The size of Spanish and Italian cotton mills meant, however, that the high price of coal was no great obstacle. They almost all worked on water power and the first mill in Spain to install a steam engine did not do so until 1832. Indeed the small size of coal output in Spain for a long time was probably attributable to lack of demand. In mid-century the coal mines in Asturias had difficulty in marketing their coal and actually exported small quantities.

Spain was a suitable port of call for British colliers trading down the west coast of France and the price of British coal on the northern Spanish coast was not high, and often indeed cheaper than Asturian coal. The iron manufacturing industry in Bilbao used British coal until 1914 because the colliers had a return cargo in the shape of iron ore from mines opened up in northern Spain by British capital and could thus offer cheap freight rates. After 1860 domestic output accounted for about half the total consumption of coal, the proportion remaining more or less the same until 1901 when it began to rise. Total coal consumption increased from 4·2 million tons in 1861–5 to 19 million tons in 1911–13 and Spain was a scarcely less valuable market for British coal than France. There are no sound reasons for supposing that cheaper and more widely available coal supplies would have boosted industrial development. The Bilbao iron works were built on the ore deposits and made no attempt in their siting to secure Asturian coal more cheaply. A large part of the demand for coal in mid-century must in fact have come from steam engines used to pump mines for other metals. But this argument cannot apply to Italy which was less favourably placed for imports. Coal consumption per capita in Italy, even after the industrial boom of the 1890s, was still in 1910 less than one-third that of Sweden. The amount mined did not reach half a million tons until after 1905 and even the localised use of steam engines which was possible in Spain was often too expensive in Italy.

There were iron ore mines in Italy in the Val d'Aosta and on the island of Elba but the total output of iron was insignificant. Spain was richly endowed with iron ore and in two areas, the Basque province of Vizcaya, near to the river and harbour of Bilbao, and in the south-east in Almería and Murcia, these deposits were within easy reach of the coast. In the early nineteenth century the annual output of iron was quite large, about 20,000 tons, a figure not consistently surpassed in Italy until after 1900. The first signs of modernisation came in 1832 when Manuel Heredia erected puddling ovens near Marbella on the coast of Málaga province. In 1843 he began the first experiments with the use of coal but they were a failure largely because Asturian coal was too dear and he was unable to get tariff concessions on the import of British coal. There had been experiments with coke smelting in Asturias in 1808 but they were not commercially success-ful until 1849. After 1864 output of iron in Asturias began to leave behind that of the charcoal based industry of Málaga because of the Asturian advantage in cheaper fuel. By 1876–80, however, the annual average output of cast and forged iron in Spain was still a meagre 67,000 tons; in Italy it was only a quarter of that.

Yet these were the years in which the railway network was built in Spain and begun on a large scale in Italy. The iron industry was quite inadequate to cope with the initial burst of demand from railway builders, unlike the industries of Belgium and France which were already geared to large-scale regular output when the demand for iron rail moved upwards. Even the traditional demand from the agricultural sector was very weak. Metal ploughs were uncommon and Heredia's main market at the start of his enterprise was iron hoops for cooperage for wine exports. As the textile industries grew a few machine manufacturers began business in Barcelona and in 1836 a steamship works was opened there. The machine shops opened in 1841 in the same city by Nicolas Tous were to become in 1855 the biggest Spanish machine firm, La Maquinista Terrestre y Maritima. But none of this was enough to establish an industry of sufficient size to cope with future demand. Even in so indigenous an industry as cork manufac-ture the machinery came almost entirely from France. In such circum-stances it was understandable that as an incentive to foreign investment in Spanish railways duty-free imports of rail should have been allowed. This was what was done and after 1857 Spain was deluged with imported iron products which remained free of restrictions until 1864.

The turning point in both countries was reached at about the same time but by different processes, a difference which sheds an interesting light on subsequent developments in Italy. Whereas the modern metallurgical industry in Spain arose gradually out of the accumulation and reinvestment of profits from the export of iron ore, the Italian industry was the direct and artificial creation of the government. In order to encourage British capital into iron ore mining the Spanish government removed the export duties on iron ore for ten years in 1870. The Vizcayan ores were not too distant from Britain, were easily mined, rich and non-phosphoric. By the end of 1875 twenty-two companies had been founded in Britain to mine them and by 1882 exports had reached 4 million tons, three-quarters of them to Britain. Over the period 1895–9 exports from the port of Bilbao averaged 4·6 million tons annually. After 1900 Vizcayan ore exports began to decline in relation to exports from southern Spain but the profits from this burst of exports formed the investment capital for an important industry.

The price of a ton of British pig iron was three and a half times that of the two tons of Spanish ore from which it was made, and the price of the rail into which it could be made seven times greater. Since the ore was on the coast coal could be brought either from Britain or from Asturias. The cost of British coal was brought down by the fact that the colliers had a return freight in iron ore. Taking advantage of these circumstances the Basque iron industry began to surpass the southern region in output. The opening of a new works with coke fired blast furnaces at El Desierto in 1879 marked the point of transition. In 1882 it was followed by the Sociedad de Altos Hornos y Fabricas de Hierro y Acero in Bilbao which installed the first Bessemer converters and Siemens–Martin furnaces in Spain. The market for these firms was in steamships and rolling stock, but it was so restricted that economies of scale were not possible. Total steel production in Spain in 1899 was only 113,000 tons. In spite of the equal production costs of steel ingots the cost of Siemens–Martin steel plate in Vizcaya between 1886 and 1890 was 50 per cent more than in a British works. The factory was in fact heavily supported by government naval orders and other forms of disguised subsidy. It was also in 1882 that another iron firm, La Vizcaya, was founded with profits from the ore trade. In 1902 the two firms were merged. Both firms produced on a much greater scale than the firms in the older iron regions so that between 1880 and 1913 66 per cent of Spanish cast iron was made in the province of Vizcaya. But although the disguised subsidies in the form of naval contracts cost the Spanish government dearly the industry was unable to manufacture steel of adequate quality for the hulls of warships which had still to be imported from Britain.

In Italy the long attempt by the government to use the Elban deposits as the basis of a modern industry bore some fruit in 1880 when the Banca Generale financed three small works, Ferriere Italiane, but they could survive only with subsidies and protection even though a fixed proportion of the ore mined in Elba had to be made available at a lower subsidised price. It was not until a Belgian company began to build the blast furnaces at Portoferraio in 1899 that the Elban site was successfully used for manufacturing. The first successful modern steel works was that built at Terni in 1884. Several major banks were involved but they were backed unequivocally by the government which also chose the site, an inland one for strategic reasons, and reorganised the existing small iron works there. The new works was guaranteed a succession of government orders, especially for armour-plate, at high prices. The technology chosen was the Siemens–Martin furnace which overcame some of the high costs of raw materials by permitting a much greater use of scrap. The conditions for the future development of the Italian steel industry had been decided. Until 1914 it remained, even more than in Spain, a wholly artificial creation sustained by the government for patriotic reasons. At the same time it was forced by the high costs of production into being an industry specialising only in the highest-grade and dearest steels made either by the Siemens–Martin or by the electric arc processes.

RAILWAY CONSTRUCTION

The railway was regarded as an indispensable basis for economic development in both countries and as the main force for industrialisation. These opinions found their fullest expression in Spain in the Railway Law of 1855, a deliberate attempt to integrate the Spanish economy more closely with the industrialisation boom in western Europe which had begun in 1852. The law created a special and extremely favourable status for railway companies in order to attract foreign investment, allowing them privileges of company formation denied even to joint stock banks, extensive tariff concessions and hidden subsidies. The great hopes pinned on railways were exaggerated still further in Italy by the national sentiment called forth in the battle for a united country. Here, as in Germany, a national railway network was understood as a symbol and instrument of national unity. Before 1848 Cavour had already publicised the plans of Carlo Petitti for an Italian network and after unification the task of linking together the small separate systems of the different states and extending them into southern Italy was always seen as the prime task of a truly national government, whatever the cost involved. As in Spain there was no possibility that this could be done from the state's own resources. The real cost of even a simple complete network would have been three times the estimated revenue of the new national government. After 1861, therefore, Italy followed the Spanish pattern of providing long-term guarantees to private capital, of which a high proportion, again as in Spain, was foreign capital, together with guaranteed interest rates and minimum yearly revenues.

These policies made Italy and Spain the first recipients on a massive scale of foreign investment, although this investment was not all confined to railway companies. Until 1870 Italy and Spain were the two biggest recipients of capital from France. Between 1815 and 1851 500 million francs had been invested in Spanish government bonds and 50 million in industrial and commercial shares. By 1858 about 280 million francs had been invested in the railways of Savoy and Piedmont. By the time a united Italy had been created, therefore, the pattern was well established and after unification French capital flowed even more readily into providing the framework of railways, roads, administration and defence of the new Italian state.

Such ready access to foreign capital meant that the slow beginnings of railway construction in both countries were overcome and a network of railways created with little difficulty. By 1855 only 500 kilometres of track were in existence in Spain, the first line, from Barcelona to Mataró, only having been begun in 1848. But between the Railway Law of 1855 and 1868 5,000 kilometres were built. The rate of construction and the size of the network in this period easily eclipsed those in Scandinavia or the Low Countries. Almost one-quarter of the whole system as it existed in 1900 was built in the period 1861–5. It is, however, easy to be misled by the size of the system into assuming it to be the equivalent of other western European systems. The gauge, as in Russia, was different from the rest of the continent. The lines often passed far from towns and because the system was conceived as a set of main lines radiating from Madrid to the periphery the intervening space seems to have been treated merely as a waste to be crossed. The equipment was poor, the track built too cheaply to be adequate, and the trains were unbelievably slow. Nevertheless the decade 1855–65 in Spain saw one of the most remarkable railway building achievements of the nineteenth century and the collapse of the railway boom marked a decisive turning point in the development of the economy.

Italian railways before unification had been constructed piecemeal within the separate states and by 1860 there were about 2,000 kilometres of unconnected systems in existence. Cavour's faith in the railway is revealed by the fact that Piedmont, still almost wholly rural, had over one-third of these lines. Another 520 kilometres had been built by the Austrian government in Lombardy and Veneto. Most of the remainder were in Tuscany; south of Rome there were still only about 100 kilometres of track. The main trunk routes were allocated in 1861 to a variety of French and Italian interests. The French company, Società Vittorio Emanuele, which had built the Piedmontese railways handed them over to the Italian government in return for the main line concessions in Calabria and Sicily; another mainly French company acquired the concessions for the main lines in the territory of the former Papal States, and although national agitation demanded that a nominally Italian company should build the main line down the east coast from Ancona to Brindisi it is clear that in reality a lot of its capital had French origins, perhaps from Rothschild and Talabot, who had been forced to relinquish the original concession. About 4,000 kilometres of track were completed between 1860 and 1870, most of it before the end of 1868.

Both countries, therefore, were able to follow the pattern of western European development even though the costs involved in government borrowing, especially in Italy, were very high. But the railway did not do what Cavour or the Spanish liberals of the 1850s wanted it to do. The consequences of building these large railway networks were not what they had been in Belgium, France and Germany. The railway proved not to be the magic key to progress and economic development. For Spain and Italy it was an expensive and possibly harmful investment. It diverted domestic funds away from other industries and from agriculture where they might have been placed to greater purpose, although foreign capital would not, perhaps, have been so available for other tasks. It obsessed government thinking and policy, built up severe balance of payments problems and, because the lines were mostly unprofitable, committed the government to paying for them in the future. There must have been some benefits in the reduction of transport costs, but the multiplier effects which railway construction had had in more developed economies were for the most part absent in Spain and Italy and these large railway networks remained only as social overhead capital on which the real gain was confined to the cost reducing effects on the economy as a whole. For such a costly investment they had little impact on iron manufacture, engineering, coal mining, or any of the other industrial and commercial activities which railways had previously stimulated elsewhere. Given the extravagant hopes which the passenger railway had inspired it was perhaps inevitable in the climate of mid-nineteenth-century opinion that foreign investors should so eagerly have seized these opportunities in Spain and Italy. But the true end of the European railway age came with the financial crash of 1867 which brought down the Crédit Mobilier in France and whose first origins were in the incontrovertible evidence that not even main line railways in Spain and Italy were profitable investments. It marked the end of the more extreme liberal hopes in both countries and the failure of what had been a simple and unquestioning attempt to copy the pattern of economic development of their neighbours.

From the start of the 1860s profits were low but investment was sustained by the belief that once the networks were complete higher dividends would follow. The two biggest companies in Spain, the Madrid–Zaragoza–Alicante and the Norte, paid no dividend after 1864. In that year the Madrid–Paris connection was opened, in the following year that to Málaga, and in 1866 the lines to Santander and Portugal. When still no dividends appeared a financial panic turned the boom into a paralysing crash. The Italian national network fared no better financially. It was divided among four major companies in 1865 but of these only the Società dell'Alta Italia, which operated the northern lines, made a profit. The companies operating the lines in the centre and south became immediately dependent on borrowing from the government. Over the country as a whole the gross revenue per kilometre showed a slight falling tendency. The slump of 1867 emphasised this; in that year revenue on the Bologna–Ancona line was less than one-third its 1860 level and three-quarters of the guaranteed revenue of the southern company (Meridionali) was coming from the taxpayer.

The provisions of the Railway Law of 1855 in Spain and the absence of any but the smallest and most antiquated iron works in Italy meant that throughout the first peaks of railway construction and for some time afterwards rail was an imported commodity. Spain did not build her own wagons until 1882 and continued to import most of her rolling stock until 1914. In Italy linkages to the rest of the economy from railway building were formed earlier but it was not until after 1880 that they could be said to have had any measurable impact on the growth of the economy. Rolling stock was made, almost from the start of large-scale construction, by three firms in Milan and by the Ansaldo works in Sampierdarena. The concession for the southern railway stipulated that it should open its own engineering works in the former Pietrarsa arsenal at Naples. Ansaldo built its first locomotive in 1854 and soon afterwards the Naples works followed suit. But by 1878 only 39 of the 641 locomotives bought by the Alta Italia had been made in Italy.

The 1867 crash produced a slowing down in railway construction. At the same time it threw the burden of future construction squarely on government finance. After 1875 construction recommenced in Spain at a steadier speed; the length of track reached 8,931 kilometres in 1885 and 14,675 kilometres in 1910. The Italian government, however, as in its earlier negotiations, persisted in its determination to use railway construction as an instrument of public policy. This was partly because the railway seemed to be vital for the integration of southern Italy into the nation. The system reached 9,000 kilometres by 1880, 16,000 kilometres by 1890 and 19,000 kilometres by 1913, with two important peaks of construction in 1885–95 and 1905–13. This persistence did eventually make a small contribution to the growth of the economy. Peaks in railway investment roughly coincided with upward movements in aggregate industrial output but the actual contribution of the railways to this total output does not appear to have been statistically significant except in the 1880s. They did provide an important market for Terni and the other steelworks which followed but the market provided by defence expenditure and by shipbuilding was more important. The engineering works which grew up with the railways did help in the dissemination of technological expertise: the output of the engineering industry grew at about 20 per cent annually from 1880 to 1887 and this may have been related to railway construction, but it then stagnated until 1898 although railway building continued. After the railways were nationalised in 1905 a massive capital investment programme for re-equipment and repairs again boosted engineering output but by that time railways were doing no more than adding to a boom in engineering caused by other and more powerful forces.

PUBLIC EXPENDITURE, FOREIGN CAPITAL AND BANKING

The very slow development of the economy in both countries accompanied by the attempts of governments, intermittent in Spain and incessant in Italy, to change this state of affairs produced a perpetual crisis in the public finances. The financial needs of the Spanish state increased with the foreign wars and the numerous civil wars, with the losing battle to maintain the Empire and with the mounting costs of national defence. In Italy the creation of a national state was a still greater and less evenly distributed burden; there were huge budget deficits in every year after unification until in 1866 the deficit was actually bigger than government revenue. The chronic public debt gave French banking circles a powerful hold over government economic policy because it was only through their intermediary operations on the Paris money market that foreign loans could be secured to sustain these high levels of government expenditure. The amount of Italian national debt in foreign hands rose from 640 million lire in 1851 to 1,700 million lire in 1865, the year in which it reached its peak; the bonds had a guaranteed interest rate of 7 per cent, much higher than the French *rente*. By that date there was a further 1,000 million lire of foreign capital privately invested in Italian transport, industry and commerce. Although much public borrowing went to provide the necessary infrastructure of the economy, especially railways, the railway was also one of the two main causes of direct foreign investment, by-passing the mechanisms of the national debt. The other attraction was the interest of foreign firms in the opening up and control of mines which would guarantee their sources of raw material. In the first case the relationship between railway companies and foreign lenders remained subject to legal definition by the government. With both forms of investment subsidiaries of foreign banks often acted as intermediaries, and in doing so they also helped to lay the foundations of a banking system in both countries.

A high rate of interest on government borrowing encouraged high interest rates elsewhere in the economy. Capital was difficult to obtain and discount markets were rudimentary. The Spanish national bank, the Bank of San Fernando, founded in 1829, was mainly concerned with diverting funds to the Treasury. The first bank intended expressly to support business ventures, the Bank of Isobel II, an issuing bank, opened in 1844 and copied many of the contemporary innovations in France such as banknotes of smaller denominations and branch banking. It also copied them by collapsing in 1848. The Bank of Barcelona, founded at the same time, was more successful as a local discount bank, but its business was very small. Italy had an extensive network of local savings banks to which after 1864 was added the secondary network of co-operative banks. The savings banks were not allowed extensive commercial and industrial discount or investment but in the early 1870s their credit services were used by industrialists because the wealthy Italian private bankers continued to concentrate their activities on foreign trade and the manipulations of the public debt and foreign lending.

The necessary complement to the Railway Law of 1855 in Spain were the decrees on banking in 1856. They specifically provided for 'credit companies' of the type of the Crédit Mobilier and allowed them to start business with a paid-up capital of only 10 per cent of the nominal figure. The purpose was to channel foreign investment into building the railways. The Northern Railway was financed by the Péreire interests and the Madrid–Zaragoza–Alicante by the Rothschild group. Between 1856 and 1858 14 'credit companies' and banks were founded. Three of the largest companies were entirely French. The largest of them, the Crédito Mobiliario Español, a branch of the Péreire interests, had a paid-up capital in 1864 more than twice that of the Bank of Spain and equivalent to one-fifth of the central government's revenue. The Rothschilds had the Sociedad Española, a smaller and more cautious institution, to safeguard their railway and mining investments, while the third French bank, the General de Crédito, had three-fifths of its total investments in railways, the same proportion as the Crédito Mobiliario, 60 per cent of whose investment at the end of 1856 was still in the Northern Railway.

The same international financial groups were behind railway construction in Italy in the same period. The collapse of the hopes placed on railway building dealt an almost mortal blow to the new banks and produced a banking crash in France. In Italy the consequences were just as drastic. A run on gold to pay panicking foreign lenders led the government to decree in 1866 the inconvertibility of banknotes, the *corso forzoso*. Effectively this meant that the lira was devalued on the foreign exchanges since foreign dealers continued to measure its external value against specie. The devaluation produced the usual short-term beneficial trade effects but its effect on foreign lenders was naturally the reverse. A similar process took place more gradually in Spain where the peseta fell in terms of other currencies almost until the end of the century with an equally dampening effect on foreign lending. After 1867 the inflow of foreign capital to Spain

Table 43 *Capital of joint stock and limited liability companies in Spain, 1859–66 (m. pesetas)*

	Companies in manufacturing industry (*paid-in capital*)	Railway companies (*paid-in capital*)	Credit companies
1859	99·8	343·9[1]	93·3
1866	66·5	698·9	229·2

[1] Nominal capital

Source: Servicio de estudios del Banco de España, *Ensayos sobre la economia española a mediados del siglo XIX* (Madrid, 1970), p. 170.

and Italy was cautious and faltering and became gradually less important. The end of the 1860s was a climactic experience in both countries and the way forward seemed now much more difficult and obscure.

The activities of foreign banks and railway financiers had diverted capital during the peak periods of investment from other forms of industrial activity towards railway systems which in the event did not greatly contribute to the growth or industrialisation of the economy. It is difficult to be categorical about this because the cotton famine caused by the American Civil War discouraged investment in the most important industry in both countries. Table 43 does, however, show the extent to which railway building monopolised and diverted investment capital in Spain.

– *Mining in Spain*

If inflows of foreign capital into railways were of only limited use, what was their value elsewhere? Manufacturing industry was still too feeble to attract such investment and the only other area worth exploiting on any scale was the rich mineral resources of Spain. After textiles the most important contribution to industrial output in Spain came from the mining sector. The nearness to western European metallurgical industries made the mountainous tracts of Spain, rich in metalliferous rocks, seem like a new El Dorado. Mining boom succeeded mining boom and unlike the situation in the textile industry the capital usually came from abroad and thé ore mined was almost entirely for export. Very little of this ore was processed in Spain and the benefits of foreign capital investment in this area were mostly confined to the foreign exchange earnings of the exports. But in a situation of great financial stringency these were usually welcome to the central government whatever its reservations about foreign control of Spanish resources.

The main ores exploited were those of lead, copper, sulphur and iron. A gradual relaxation of state controls over mining rights culminated in new mining laws at the end of 1868, very favourable to foreign capital and introduced because of the government's acute financial problems and its need to promote exports. In 1913 foreign capital, mainly British, French and Belgian, accounted for half the capital in those mining companies whose capital value is known. By 1900 minerals and metals had come to represent about 30 per cent of all exports.

Large-scale lead mining and exports of pig lead had developed even before the decrees of 1868. Andalusian lead exports were already about 8 per cent of total exports in the 1830s and for a long period they were second only to wine. After the new laws Spain became for thirty years the world's largest producer of lead. It was mined and smelted in many areas, around Jaén, Badajoz, Córdoba and Ciudad Real, and most of the new mines were sunk and operated by British, French, Belgian and German capital. Firms like the British company La Fortuna or the French La Cruz mines and foundries were on a completely different scale from the original Andalusian operations. The first big copper mines were sunk by a French engineer near Huelva and operated by a Paris company. The pyrites found there also contained sulphur and it was the demand from the British chemical industry for sulphuric acid in the 1860s which was the main factor in further copper and sulphur mining. From 1866 to 1909 the Glasgow company Tharsis Sulphur and Copper Mines recorded an annual average return of 20 per cent on its mining operations in Spain. In 1873 the richest of the concessions, the state-owned Rio Tinto mines, was leased to an Anglo-German-French consortium and within six years was not only the most prolific copper and pyrites mine in the world but was paying dividends of 70 per cent on the invested capital. The famous Almadén mines remained a major source of mercury in spite of new discoveries in America and Italy. In the early nineteenth century sales were controlled by the Rothschilds at great profits as part of their operations with the public debt and at several points in mid-century the family came close to establishing a world monopoly in the metal. Until 1914 the state was only the nominal owner of the mine and the major share of the profits went to the bankers.

TRADE AND TARIFFS

After the disasters of the revolutionary period the more developed economies increasingly drove Spanish exports out of the markets of the former Spanish American colonies. There was no real recovery in Spanish foreign trade until the 1850s when the increase in mineral exports and a few good harvests provided an occasional trade surplus. After that exports again stagnated until 1870 when they began to move upwards at an accelerating rate mostly under the influence of rapidly increasing wine exports. When the wine boom collapsed exports again became fluctuating and uncertain, showing a sharp upward movement with the boom in iron ore shipments to Britain followed by a contraction before 1913 as iron ore exports again began to fall. For most of the century the balance of trade was in deficit and the deficit tended to increase with the level of industrialisation. The accounts were balanced by the loss of metal currency, by remittances from emigrants and above all by imports of capital. Although the rate of capital imports from France slowed down after 1867 investment still continued and some of it was reinvestment of profits earned in Spain. Loss of bullion to finance trade deficits meant that Spain, unlike the rest of western Europe, moved away from a gold standard.

The failure of the attempt to develop along liberal lines in mid-century inevitably strengthened the protectionist movement but until the 1890s manufacturing industry was too weak to bring any effective pressure to bear on the government. The loss of the colonies in the American war was the turning point. Catalan textile manufacturers deprived of their guaranteed markets now demanded a more general protection at the same time as they launched a publicised campaign to find new export markets. At the same time the capital repatriated from the West Indies flooded on to the Bilbao stock exchange producing an investment frenzy in 1900 and 1901. In those years the value of the nominal capital of new companies was twice that of all new companies founded in the period 1902–14. Most of the new capital found its way into four main sectors, banking, shipbuilding, hydro-electricity and sugar refining. Sugar refining was now based on beet rather than on West Indian cane and soon led to requests for protection. Shipbuilders demanded government subsidies and in 1907 were rewarded with an expensive battleship building programme. The iron and steel industry supported this campaign. The ultra-protectionist tariff of 1906 was specifically designed to foster national industry. The period between then and 1914 is too short to measure the effects of this change but the earlier Italian experience of protection showed that, for all its many drawbacks, it was a necessity if any real industrial advance was to be made.

Modernisers and entrepreneurs in both countries in the early nineteenth century hoped to follow the example of Britain and make free trade a stimulus to more dynamic competition among the archaic industrial activities surviving from the eighteenth century. Cavour's political domination of Piedmont saw the introduction of low tariffs, railway building and an internationalist economic policy whose purpose was to increase the level of economic development of that small state. In reality Piedmont remained an agricultural state and there was thus a more realistic economic argument in favour of free trade for a country which depended for development on agricultural exports. But the forces supporting free trade were by no means merely economic. Free trade was closely associated with political liberalism since it was seen also as a force for modernising political society by sweeping away the many privileges accorded by autocratic regimes in the pursuit of their own less internationalist ideal of economic development. Misguided though free trade may have been as an economic policy for some countries, the idea that the modernisation of the state and the economy could most efficiently be achieved through free trade commanded the respect of most liberal statesmen and intellectuals. This can only be understood in terms of the fascination and domination exerted by the society and economy of Britain, although the importance of liberal thought in eighteenth-century Italy and Spain of course strengthened this tendency. It was through putting into practice the course of action suggested by this facile and misleading analogy with Britain that Cavour and the group of modernisers around him hoped to create a modern developed Italian national state.

The tariffs adopted when a united Italy was formed were about 80 per cent lower on average than those which had been maintained by the southern states and too low to offer any effective protection to Italian industry. The situation, however, was complicated by the *corso forzoso* which stimulated exports and produced an improvement in trade balances during the years of industrial stagnation after 1866 which was not due to the shrinking of imports but to a vigorous increase in exports, 35 per cent between 1865 and 1869. The biggest contribution, however, was made by foodstuffs, and given the low quality of agriculture and the rapidly growing population this could hardly be sustained long enough to solve the balance of payments problems which the public policy of the first years after unification brought about. The strength of national feeling lent considerable force to demands for industrial protection. The tariff of 1878 did give protection to the textile industry but otherwise the Italian market remained a relatively open one, the more so because Italy remained integrated into the mesh of western European tariff conventions. The increase in volume and value of manufactured imports was in fact greater in the decade after 1878 than before. With the end of the *corso forzoso* in 1882 some element of protection was actually removed from Italian industry while tariffs elsewhere were being increased.

With the fall in the price of food exports after 1873 the justification for this policy became less clear, the more so as the government's need for revenue was now urgent. Italian agriculture could offer no effective competition; not only did agricultural exports fall but grain imports increased almost ten times between 1881 and 1887. Low tariffs were abandoned from the start of 1888 although the general tariff level remained lower than that of France. All textile industries and the iron and steel industry received a very high level of protection; the Terni steelworks of course had just been opened. Duties on grain were increased. The intention was to use these high tariffs as a bargaining position in further agreements but the French government flatly refused to treat and applied its highest tariffs to Italian exports. The immediate consequences were everything the supporters of free trade had feared. Imports did not significantly decrease but exports of wine fell from 3,582 hectolitres in 1887 to 904 hectolitres in 1890, of flour by the same proportion and of silk yarn from 14,600 kilograms to 2,200 kilograms.

Protection coincided with the financial crash of 1887. The immediate cause was over-speculation in the construction industry but the deeper causes were more complicated and lay mainly in the sluggishness of the domestic market on which Italian industry depended. The banking system was virtually destroyed and had to be reformed in a different pattern. But in retrospect it can be seen that Italy no longer had much to gain from free trade and during the 1890s the cotton and woollen industries did in fact make considerable progress in eliminating foreign competition on the home market. But the problems of readjustment were bound to be so acute that the tariff war with France, the main export market, was a crippling aggravation. The period from 1889 to 1896 saw most of the promising developments of the 1880s undone. Successful tariff negotiations after 1892 began to redirect agricultural exports towards central and eastern Europe but these concessions were usually obtained at the expense of reductions in the tariff on manufactured goods. Protection did not stimulate an industrial recovery from the crash of 1887. The level of steel output achieved in 1889 was not again reached until 1904. The years between 1888 and 1896 were a period of industrial stagnation, of no significant growth, and a period when the overall importance of the agricultural sector in the economy actually grew. Neither low tariffs nor protection could be argued by 1896 to have done anything much to promote economic development. Nevertheless the intellectual break with free trade and the idea of stimulating economic development through the free movement of factors was a crucial and necessary turning point in Spain and Italy. To be effective, however, protection had to be combined with firm internal policies. But in Spain, except for the period of the American War, government policy remained deflationary and cautious; in Italy it became more positive.

THE INDUSTRIALISATION BOOM IN ITALY

The picture so far drawn is one of Italy's almost total failure to develop.

A scarcely perceptible industrialisation was taking place against the background of an agricultural sector inadequate to support the process of economic growth. In spite of massive emigration the proportion of the labour force in the agricultural sector, whose levels of productivity were as low as anywhere in Europe, was not declining; indeed, as Table 44 suggests, it was even growing. The import of capital and modern technology and a vigorous support for programmes of modernisation by the state had made little impact; tariff policies were ineffective, and both Spain and Italy had fallen far behind the rest of western Europe and much of central Europe in economic development. After 1896 the tide suddenly turned in Italy. The country experienced a vigorous industrialisation and a clear break with the previous economic pattern. What happened there is perhaps the most remarkable of all the economic changes we have explored between 1850 and 1914.

Table 44 *Percentage distribution of the labour force by sector in Italy, 1881–1913*

| Sector | % of labour force | | |
	1881	1897	1913
Agriculture	59	64	58
Industry	24	20	24
Services	17	16	18

Source: G. Fuà, *Formazione, distribuzione e impiego del reddito dal 1861: sintesi statistica* (Rome, 1972), table 2:8.

By the First World War national income per capita in Italy is estimated to have been about 523 lire (francs) at current prices, not much over half the level in France. But a great part of this growth may have taken place in the period after 1896; the Central Statistical Institute estimated per capita income in 1896–1900 at a mere 333 lire.[7] Other evidence suggests that only in the last two decades of the period did Italy cease to be one of Europe's poorest countries. Kuznets estimates that industrial production per capita doubled between 1901 and 1913.[8] All measurements agree on the timing and general dimensions of the burst of rapid growth after 1896. The compound annual rate of increase of total value added (at constant prices) between 1861 and 1897 was 0·7 per cent and between 1897 and 1913 2·7 per cent.[9] It is possible to be even more precise in the timing because all measurements also agree that the rate of economic growth after 1907 slowed down slightly. The period beginning in 1897 seems in most respects to represent a break with the previous period, a phenomenon not unlike the industrial revolution in Belgium or Germany, but lacking the previous long experience of economic development which explains so much of that phenomenon there. It is difficult, however, to be categorical about this since there is considerable contradiction in the statistical evidence relating to the previous period.

The figures of the Central Statistical Institute show a period of rapid economic growth after unification until 1871–5 followed by a long period of stagnating or declining per capita national income until economic growth was again resumed in 1896. But this is not confirmed by other estimates. Fuà's figures suggest a period of slow economic growth between 1881 and 1887 followed by a sharp drop in gross domestic product after that year and virtual stagnation until 1896. The indices of industrial production of Gerschenkron and Golzio show a marked increase over the period 1881–8 and Gerschenkron actually characterises those years as a period of 'modern growth'.[10] They are represented in his index by a 4·6 per cent average annual rate of growth of industrial production. Both these indices, however, also agree that the slump of 1887 ushered in almost a decade of no growth for the Italian economy. It is the experience of the 1880s before that slump that is in dispute. The weight of circumstantial evidence and the statistical evidence from single industries make the Central Statistical Institute's figures hard to accept. And since there is not much dispute over the movement of output in the agricultural sector, although there too the figures may not be as reliable as seems to be assumed, we may deduce that 1881–8 was a period of growth when output throughout the economy was increasing.

The pattern after that is clear. Gerschenkron's index shows an increase in industrial production of only 0·3 per cent annually between 1888 and 1896 followed by a 6·7 per cent annual increase between 1896 and 1908. Fuà's calculations, based on more industries, show an annual average growth rate of industrial output of 4 per cent from 1896–8 to 1915. Accompanying the industrial boom was a distinct improvement in the performance of the agricultural sector. Agricultural output had grown very slowly over the period from 1871 to 1897; its compound rate of growth was a mere 0·4 per cent a year. Between 1897 and 1914 its rate of increase jumped to 2 per cent. After 1897, therefore, the growth of the economy was more balanced. If the figures in Table 44 are correct the growth of per capita incomes over the period 1881–1913 could hardly have come from an improvement in industrial productivity alone. Given the size of the agricultural labour force the increase in its productivity, even if much less than in industry, was of equal importance to the growth of the economy as well as in providing the essential background to a more sustained industrialisation. After 1897 savings rose steeply as the share of consumption in the national income dropped. Before 1897 gross domestic saving was 9 per cent of gross national product; during the period 1897–1913 it rose to about 16 per cent. But that other, and probably more important, forces than an improvement in agricultural incomes were at work after 1897 can be seen from the changes in the composition of industrial output. Capital goods output became much more important, accounting for 28 per cent of the industrial output in Gerschenkron's index in 1896 and for 43 per cent by 1908. This was the reflection of a decisive increase in investment in industrial plant and equipment. Fuà's calculations show that in two periods 1883–7 and 1897–1908 the increase in fixed investment was the biggest factor operating on the change in gross domestic product.[11] In the first of these periods this investment was mainly in buildings and in social overhead capital. But in the second period it was mainly in industrial plant.

There is very little to support Romeo's well-known explanation of these movements, that the earlier period was one of capital accumulation which laid the basis for the subsequent industrial boom.[12] The rate of saving in the 1880s was low and not noticeably increasing. The growth of those years

Table 45 *Percentage contribution of the major sectors to gross domestic product in Italy (at constant prices), 1862–1913*

Sector	1862	1897	1913
Agriculture	46	42	37
Industry	18	21	26
Services	36	38	39

Source: G. Fuà, *Formazione, distribuzione e impiego del reddito dal 1861: sintesi statistica* (Rome, 1972), table 1:6.

probably owed more to the end of the *corso forzoso* and the return to convertibility of the lira. In order to achieve this change the government borrowed heavily, funds flowed into the economy and there was an inflationary boom which was led by the construction industry in the bigger cities especially Rome and Naples. There was no properly functioning central bank and no attempt at sound monetary management. The consequence was a series of flagrant public scandals involving corruption on a large scale and the spectacular bank crashes of 1887. Although the boom was reflected in national output calculations it was some way removed from being the sound foundation of the later industrialisation of the country and what happened after 1896 needs a better explanation. It is the more puzzling because of the relative unimportance of foreign capital. In fact between 1894 and 1906 Italy seems to have been a net capital lender. Table 45 shows how rapidly the importance of the industrial sector in the economy grew between 1897 and 1913.

In the period 1896–1908 the rates of growth of output of several modern industries, electrical industries, chemical industries, engineering and iron and steel manufacture, were higher in Italy than in other countries for which we have evidence. Concurrently the textile industries continued to expand their output under the influence of protection until they supplied the greater part of the home market. The increase in output of all industry between 1901 and 1913 was 87 per cent, in spite of the slowing down after 1908, a rate not achieved again until after 1945. We are dealing of course with industries starting from very low levels of output but, with this proviso in mind, Table 46 does suggest that the explanation of what occurred in Italy after 1896 must in part lie in the history of those industries showing the highest growth rates, industries which had scarcely been established before that date. But as with all such calculations the

Table 46 *Average annual rate of growth of industrial production in some sectors of Italian industry, 1894–1913*

Sector	1894–1913	1896–1908	1908–13
Electricity	15·0[1]	17·0[2]	10·5
Chemical industries	12·9	12·9	3·5
Iron and steel	10·7	13·8	5·0
Engineering	7·5	12·2	2·0
Wool	5·3	5·3	4·9
Cotton	3·5	4·7	−0·2
Silk	−0·4	1·0	−2·5

[1] 1898–1913   [2] 1898–1908

Source: J. S. Cohen, 'Financing Industrialization in Italy, 1894–1914', in *Journal of Economic History*, vol. XXVII, 1967.

main reason for the low growth rate of the textile industries is simply their greater size of output in 1894. In 1913 textiles and foodstuffs industries still represented about 60 per cent of the total value added in manufacturing industry and accounted for 60 per cent of the industrial labour force in 1911. Some part of the industrialisation boom is therefore also to be explained by developments in these older industries.

In fact the explanation of what occurred is very complex, as might well be expected of such a surprising change. In the first place the Italian experience suggests that the sheer persistence of government policy was important. The long sustained determination to modernise the country did eventually bring success, but only because other economic developments became favourable. The purpose of the tariff of 1888 was unequivocally stated to be to 'further the evolution of Italian industry'. Its early consequences, as we have seen, were damaging but it was behind this barrier that the textile industries came to occupy the domestic market and the uncompetitive steel industry to achieve such a high rate of growth. Behind the tariff a close alliance of government, industrialists and bankers formed a small powerful coterie of industrialisers able to push modernisation forward. When a world liquidity crisis in 1907 stopped the banks playing their part government accepted the implications of what had happened and took over the bankers' role to keep investment flowing to the steel industry. By its armaments orders to steelworks, by its subsidisation of shipbuilding, by its rescue of the railways after 1905, government gave support at crucial moments and provided the necessary background of confidence for investors.

In the second place investment banks based on German models and with initial support from German capital were able to operate successfully within the atmosphere created by these circumstances. They provided the impetus and financial knowledge necessary to reorganise the electrical, chemical and metallurgical industries into large units often closely allied with German firms and financial groups. Such larger units could operate as oligopolies within the protected domestic market and with the help and favour of government circles.

Thirdly, the development of hydro-electric power offered particular opportunities at the right time and they were eagerly seized. Italy had no coal, but in the Alpine regions and at the foot of the Alps, where industry had already made its tentative beginnings, there were ample water resources for the manufacture of cheap electric current. The advantages of cheaper power were felt throughout manufacturing industry and not least in the older textile sector.

Fourthly, the balance of payments difficulties which might have been expected to scotch these developments did not materialise. Much of this was due to the extraordinarily heavy emigration and the flow of funds which the emigrants sent or brought back to Italy. Some was due to the increasing flow of tourists into the country. At the same time, as we have seen, there was a sharp improvement in the performance of the agricultural sector, and the increase in food imports which might otherwise have resulted from the increase in per capita incomes was, as a result, restricted. Furthermore the textile industries began for the first time to export a significant proportion of their output and this also reduced the deficit on commercial account. This favourable turn in the foreign accounts provided a much happier background for the operations of government, bankers and industrialists.

The major changes in the rate of growth of industrial output were determined by changes in the rate of capital goods production; the rate of growth of consumer goods output was much more even. These abrupt fluctuations in capital goods production seem to be related to changes in government policy. This does not necessarily mean that specific acts of policy, such as protection or subsidies, were responsible but that the general sentiment that certain governments favoured the industrial sector rather than relying on agricultural exports as the main route to ultimate industrialisation produced sudden upward movements of entrepreneurial confidence in industries like engineering. Thus the growth of industrial output in the 1880s was related to the way in which the Depretis government favoured industry, as shown by the degree of protection accorded in 1878, although the increased level of protection in itself made little difference. The subsequent slump after 1887 was partly a reaction to the investment encouraged by this switch of policy because the engineering sector was still so small that there was little need for any replacement of fixed capital created in the growth of the early 1880s. But the impact of government policy was not felt only through the changes in entrepreneurial confidence which it produced. Some sectors such as steel and shipbuilding obtained specific legislation in their favour, and ultimately almost all industry received a substantial level of protection. Whether these more direct acts of policy were useful in furthering the industrialisation process is a more complicated issue.

The main benefit which protection brought to the textile industries was the opportunity to develop and mechanise the weaving sectors. The discovery of satisfactory mechanical weaving methods in the silk industry coupled to the availability of cheap electrical power permitted some small breaches to be made in the long domination of Lyons. The number of hand looms began to fall after 1898 and by 1912 there were 15,000 mechanical looms as against 5,000 hand looms. This growth in the weaving sector also produced a return on exports. Exports of silk cloth were only 6 per cent of silk exports in 1885 but amounted to 17 per cent in 1913. In all textiles, however, the main force for growth was the reinforcing effect of industrialisation in other sectors and the increase in spendable incomes which it provided. In a country with so low a standard of living much of the increase in incomes went on clothing. An index of real wages shows them standing at 79 in 1901 and at 100 in 1913. The number of mechanical looms in the cotton industry rose from 65,000 in 1896 to 115,000 in 1912. The level of technology still remained below the level of the bigger producers but the same gains in exports were registered as in silk, exports of woven cotton goods increasing ten times between 1895 and 1913. The main markets were in Latin America, particularly in Argentina, and in the Balkan countries and Turkey. Very little yarn was exported even by 1913 but the increase in cotton spindles reflected the greater command over markets which the industry now exercised. There were 1·9 million spindles in 1898 and 4·6 million in 1914. In the woollen industry protection brought the development of worsted spinning and weaving whereas previously only the coarsest woollens had competed against imports.

When the Terni steelworks were founded in 1886 it was the government orders placed even before the completion of the works which enabled private industrialists and bankers to participate with confidence. But until 1899 when the blast furnaces at Portoferraio were built there were still only two steelworks in the country. In 1902 the Terni and Elba works jointly established another plant at Savona. Ultimately in 1905 the major steel groups all combined to finance the Società Ilva to make steel at Bagnoli near Naples. Once again the pressure to combine came from government policy which, until the agreement, reserved 200,000 tons of Elban ore a year to be used in a steelworks to be built in the south. The financing of all these operations was undertaken by the Banca Commerciale and the Credito Italiano in liaison with government policy. After 1906 these banks extended their control over the independent iron and steel works in the north until only Ansaldo was out of their hands. Average prices for Italian steel were about one-third higher than those in France and Germany, output was still small, in 1914 a mere 911,000 tons, and imports were still competitive. The price of protecting the steel industry was, however, dearer metal for the engineering industry which otherwise was more competitive internationally. The consequence was that the growth of the engineering industry was sustained also by government orders for ships, armaments and railway equipment and became closely tied to the nationalist aggressive foreign policy of the government.

The two main markets, armaments and shipbuilding, had to be highly protected. In the first it was obviously a matter of strategic prudence but direct government intervention in the shipbuilding industry produced a complex of steelmakers, bankers and shipbuilders able to survive with government support in the face of much more efficient foreign competition and independently of a wider market. The government introduced subsidies for regular shipping services in 1877 and in 1885 added special bounties for construction, which provided for a rebate of the duties on imported materials. This was the start of a long series of government measures intended to produce an Italian merchant navy. In terms of international comparisons it was not very successful; the total steam tonnage under the Italian flag in 1912 was only 760,000 gross tons, the sixth fleet in Europe, and less than a third of this tonnage had been built in Italy. In terms of Italian industry, however, this aid and support was not so negligible. The same can be said of government railway policy after 1905 when almost all rolling stock orders, which were on a much larger scale than before, were directed to Italian firms.

The connection between banks, steel and government orders drew so close that the situation of the banks became precarious. In the financial crisis of 1907 one bank, the Società Bancaria Italiana, could not disengage itself from these investments enough to meet the demands for liquid capital. It had to be saved by the recently created central bank which provided 20 million lire to rebuild the bank's finances and to turn it from a bank largely dependent on foreign capital into an Italian bank. The purpose of the operation was to maintain the pace of development in the metallurgical industries when orders for their output were flagging.

The biggest of the investment banks was the Banca Commerciale Italiana founded in 1894 by a combination of German banks. Even in its foundation the hand of government could be seen. The tariff war with France after

1887 led the Italian government to seek an alternative source of foreign capital. This was arranged by diplomatic contacts between the government and the Bleichröder bank. The total equity capital of the Banca Commerciale Italiana, formed out of these contacts, was 20 million lire, greater than that of any existing Italian bank. It was jointly provided by Bleichröder, the Deutsche Bank, the Dresdner Bank, the Diskontogesellschaft, the Handelsgesellschaft and the Bank für Handel und Industrie. By 1910 the bank had 40 per cent of the total assets of all the ordinary credit banks in the country. One year later, in 1895, another German consortium transformed the Banca di Genova into a similar institution operated on German lines, the Credito Italiano. But the evidence suggests that after the initial foundation of the two institutions a high proportion of the capital soon became Italian in origin. In fact the leading personnel of these two banks were very similar to that of the earlier 'mixed' banks, the Banca Generale and the Credito Mobiliare Italiana. Both of these banks had suffered from the same weaknesses as the German joint stock banks of the early 1850s and the Crédit Mobilier in France; their investments had been too heavily tied to a small number of developments in railway companies and construction. It was this which had brought about their downfall but the experience gained was once again to be deployed after 1896 and it is a mistake to assume that the techniques used then were borrowed from Germany; they had been painfully acquired in Italy. But the new foundations were more closely backed by the major international financial consortia, and their investments, partly because of this, but also because of the greater diversity of the Italian economy itself after 1896, were more widely spread. Indeed Italy was in the unique situation after 1900 of being both a capital importer and a capital exporter of some importance. The Banca di Roma, which after 1900 copied the operations of its German-Italian counterparts, conducted much of its investment activity in the Balkans and Turkey. The Società Bancaria Italiana, formed from two Milan and Turin banks in 1903, effectively lasted only four years in its original form, but after being reconstructed by the Bank of Italy, continued like its predecessor to pursue a vigorous policy of industrial investment with active government co-operation. The importance of these institutions lay probably less in the capital they brought in than in the managerial knowledge and international financial and business contacts which they had at their disposal. The success of these banks in stimulating industrial growth where the international financial consortia of the 1860s had failed has to be seen in the context of the changed situation of the Italian economy. The investments of the new banks were in industry rather than in social overhead capital because protection and government backing gave them the necessary support to finance the transfer of technological and managerial innovations from Germany to Italy within a small group of rapidly developing industries. The success of their activities is explained by the same factors which led to the success of the whole economy in this period.

The proportion of total credit extended to the private sector of Italian industry and commerce by the commercial and investment banks was always high, about one-quarter in 1895–9 and two-fifths in 1910–14. Over the same period the amount increased by three and a half times. The exact proportion of foreign capital in this total is not known but most calculations suggest that the intermediary financial operations which the investment banks performed were done by mobilising Italian capital. Most of the bigger companies which expanded after 1894 used the services of these banks for loans, for floating new securities, for transforming firms into joint stock companies and for financing technological innovation.

Their most active sphere of operation was in the electrical industry. The Banca Commerciale from its earliest origins underwrote a massive increase in the equity capital of the biggest electrical firm, Edison, and three years later performed the same operation again. The Edison Company in turn, under its director Carlo Esterle, participated in the foundation of a further series of electrical companies so that by 1914 one-quarter of its assets were in securities of similar firms. Esterle himself became an important member of the Banca Commerciale and the bank's support was clearly implicit behind the founding of these new companies. In fact the bank had a special holding company, the Society for the Development of Electrical Firms in Italy, which controlled the policy of almost all new firms in the industry. Another member of the Banca Commerciale group, Giuseppe Orlando, had originally brought his family shipyards into a combination with the bank when they were formed in 1906 into the Cantieri Navali Riuniti, the biggest shipbuilding firm in Italy. In turn he became a member of the board of the three biggest steel companies.

The sudden massive investments needed in the electrical industry if hydro-electric power was to be properly exploited also provided a demand for the services of investment banks reminiscent of their role in the spurt of growth of metallurgical industries and coal mines in Germany after 1852. The great interest in electrical power is shown by the early building of the first central power station at Novara in 1883 but it was only with the construction of hydro-electric power stations that an escape from the constraints imposed by the high price of coal was possible. International technology reached the right level of development at the right moment; the first hydro-electric power station was built at Paderno on the Adda in 1898. A further sixteen were built between 1900 and 1904, and twenty-seven between 1905 and 1909. The growth of Turin as an industrial centre was directly related to the supply of hydro-electric power from the nearby Alps. In 1862 steam power provided only 13 per cent of the energy used by manufacturing industry in the city and many factories used the waters of the Dora Riparia. The biggest factory in 1898 had only 300 workers. The founding of the SA Elettricità Alta Italia in 1896, at the same time as the city's tramway system, made hydro-electric power more cheaply and generally available than anywhere else in the country. In 1914 over half the current sold was sold to manufacturing industry and some firms, like FIAT, financed the generation of current themselves. By 1911 30,000 were employed in metallurgical and mechanical industries in the city, almost 6,000 in the chemical industry, and one firm, Michelin, employed 2,000 workers.

But the connections between industrialists, bankers and government certainly do not explain developments in all industries. Some sectors of the engineering industry and in particular the car industry seem to have owed nothing to government encouragement, apart from what they gained indirectly from the encouragement of other industries. The springs of industrial growth were diverse. One element was the gradual development of rolling stock manufacture relying on semi-protected markets. A more important element was the demand for new types of capital goods to meet the requirements of the electrical and chemical sectors. But it is significant that many of these new demands could now be met by Italian machine manufacturers themselves whose response is often traced to the previous growth period of the early 1880s. Nebiolo began to make printing machinery at Turin in 1880, Franco Tosi founded the justly celebrated steam engine and turbine works at Legnano in 1882. After 1898 the climate was such as to encourage more such ventures, like the typewriter works begun by Camillo Olivetti at Ivrea in 1911. The car industry shows this background of confidence most clearly. As everywhere it was an industry started by mechanics in a small way with little capital and catering for a luxury market. The first Italian car was exhibited by Michele Lanza at Turin only in 1898. But the availability of cheap electric power after that date was important in providing new manufacturing possibilities. Giovanni Agnelli was able to open his works the following year on a site in the bourgeois quarter of the city, an important consideration in marketing. In 1903 he made 150 cars; in 1914 FIAT, as his company had become, made 4,500 cars. The concentration of the industry after the 1907 crisis still left six other car makers in the city and in addition there were five pneumatic tire manufacturers, three headlight makers, two chassis makers, two wheel makers and several other accessory firms. In the early stages most of the engines were imported from France but Italian firms soon made their own engines and exported finished models; 1,283 in 1907, with a value of about one-tenth that of the total value of French car exports. The car industry and its accessory suppliers employed over 9,000 people in Turin by 1911, an astonishing growth. FIAT itself had a labour force of about 3,000, Itala about 1,000 and Lancia about 500.

All of these developments would have been slowed down and perhaps brought to a standstill by the effect of the greater demand for imports on the balance of payments. It was mounting import demand which partly provoked the crisis of 1907 and the subsequent slowing down of growth. The total import bill rose three times between 1892 and 1910 while exports only doubled. The export performance was another clear break with the past; between 1892 and 1910 manufactured goods were the most rapidly growing export, growing at an annual average of 7·2 per cent. But imports of coal and cotton went up four times in the same period and this increase was accompanied by a surge in machinery imports. But against a deficit on commercial account of 10·2 million lire over the period 1901–13 were offset invisible earnings of 12·3 million lire, of which more than a third came from tourism and more than a half from emigrants' remittances. It is worth remarking once more that here, as in the case of Switzerland, the lack of studies of the early tourist industry is astonishing considering its present-day importance for economic development. But the new factor which tilted the balance was the remittances from the 626,000 emigrants a year between 1900 and 1913 and also the funds they brought back when they returned. By 1911 about 5·8 million emigrants had left Italy, about 44 per cent to go to Latin America and 37 per cent to North America. The avalanche after 1900 came from southern Italy and almost all of them were transoceanic migrants. Such emigrants by living cheaply in the United States reckoned to save between 1,000 and 1,500 lire for a year's work whereas their daily earnings as an agricultural labourer in southern Italy would at the highest have been about 700 lire a year. Such sums if sent or brought back were a substantial capital accumulation. Deposits in postal savings banks reflecting these remittances increased as a percentage of total savings until 1913; the south had 66 per cent of these deposits in 1906 and 83 per cent in 1913. The other financial intermediary was the Bank of Naples which opened branches in the emigrant areas to facilitate these transfers. After 1907 it was given a monopoly of the business. Of the total sum which it handled in remittances between 1902 and 1913 69 per cent came from the United States and 17 per cent from Argentina. The long-run effects of increasing the total proportion of Italian savings held in the south were only seen after 1914 but their immediate value in financing imports was very useful and at some stages decisive. They enabled, for example, the interest rate on Italian public debt held abroad to be reduced in a major conversion in 1906.

CONCLUSIONS

The main lesson to be derived from Italian industrialisation after 1896 is how wide a range of forces had to combine at an opportune moment to achieve a breakthrough in such generally unpropitious circumstances. The complexities of the Italian situation after 1896 have been discussed in some detail so that it may be easier to comprehend the failure of Spain or other underdeveloped countries to achieve a similar breakthrough. And what was achieved in Italy also laid up many serious problems for the future, not least that of fitting so uncompetitive an industrial sector into the framework of the European economy. It is hardly needful to explain why a similar pattern did not emerge in Spain. The government was less purposeful and less consistent, the slower growth of population meant there was no comparable surge of emigration, the investment banks with their foreign connections subsided into relative quiescence after 1867, protection came later and was not accompanied by the same positive aids to development although it did promote some industrial developments which had been stifled by free trade, the agricultural sector does not seem to have shown the same sudden improvement as it did in Italy and the trend of international technological innovation was less favourable.

The share of national income contributed by industry in both countries by 1913 was the same as in the Netherlands, although the proportion contributed by manufacturing processes as opposed to mining in Spain was probably decidedly smaller. Yet national income per capita had in each case attained only about 60 per cent of the Dutch level. All three countries saw their industrial development quickened by the accelerated growth of the major European economies during the 1890s and, although Spain was less able to share in these developments, it was only from that date in all three that there was anything that could be described as sustained industrialisation. The proportion of the labour force in industrial production in Italy, 24 per cent, was much lower than in the Netherlands and this confirms the more circumstantial historical evidence of greater capital intensiveness in Italian industry where many new firms after 1900 were manufacturing on a scale rivalled by only one or two Dutch companies. There is not much evidence about industrial wages in Italy but it does not suggest that they were so low as to account for the differences in income. These must rather be explained by the differences, equally striking, between other sectors of the economy. The high contribution of services to national income in the Netherlands and the much lower proportion of the labour force employed in agriculture throughout the century in fact enabled the Netherlands to compensate for the smaller scale and more labour-intensive pattern of its manufacturing industry. The fundamental weakness of both the Italian and Spanish economies lay in the agricultural sector where the level of agriculture remained so low as to prevent all possibility of balanced development. This it was that held down per capita income and presented the gravest obstacles to what seemed to optimists an easy, automatic process of the spread of economic development from the other developed western European economies. In such circumstances the type of industrial development which took place in Italy from the mid-1890s did seem one possible way forward. It laid the foundations, given continued propitious international circumstances, for a more extensive transformation of the economy through the industrial sector, but, in opposite circumstances, those which after 1918 did apply, it was a less satisfactory and more dangerous basis for further development.

THE PROBLEM OF SOUTHERN ITALY

By 1914 the industrialisation of Italy was still concentrated in the northernmost provinces. These were the areas where the Italian national state had been forged, where railway building had been first begun on a large scale, where access to French, Swiss and German capital and ideas was easier, the areas into which the roads and railways from the rest of the continent debouched. The south and Sicily were at the time of the unification of the country a little known and neglected area. To what extent the south was actually more backward than the north and centre in 1860 is difficult to establish precisely but the difference was probably less marked than in 1914. Employment figures, though likely to be inaccurate, show a higher proportion of the labour force in industry and handicrafts in the south than in the north until 1881 and a roughly equal proportion in agriculture. In 1911, however, when less than 52 per cent of the north's population was

Table 47   *Vital statistics of Italian regions, 1881–1910 (per thousand)*

	1881–5	*1891–5*	*1901–5*	*1906–10*
North				
Birth rate	36·1	34·5	32·7	32·2
Death rate	26·1	24·1	20·9	20·2
Centre				
Birth rate	36·2	36·3	30·1	30·3
Death rate	26·4	25·4	20·5	19·4
South				
Birth rate	40·2	38·9	33·3	34·3
Death rate	29·4	28·2	24·1	22·3
Islands				
Birth rate	41·1	37·2	33·6	32·7
Death rate	27·6	26·4	22·5	24·1

Source: Associazione per lo sviluppo dell'industria nel mezzogiorno, *Statistiche sul mezzogiorno d'Italia* (Rome, 1954), p. 67.

employed in agriculture, the proportion for the south was still 60·6 per cent. There are certain indicators that the south was already behind in 1861. It had fewer roads relative to its area and fewer railways. There were still only about 100 kilometres of railway in the territory of the Kingdom of the Two Sicilies in 1859. There was no industry or export to compare with the making of silk yarn in Lombardy. Table 47 shows that demographically the south in the early 1880s, when accurate population statistics became available for the first time, was already showing the marks of a less developed economy, a higher birth rate and a higher death rate, although the difference became less marked by 1910.

In spite of the convergence of demographic trends the industrialisation over the last two decades before 1914 greatly increased the economic and social disparity between the two parts of the country. The increase in industrial employment after unification was heavily concentrated in the north: by the 1911 census 64 per cent of the total industrial labour force was employed there, 15 per cent in the centre and 21 per cent in the south. This was more than a question of employment. Modern mass-productive methods were even more concentrated in the northern area: the north and centre had 83 per cent of the installed horse-power in 1903, the south and islands only 17 per cent. Government policy struggled against this tendency. By 1909 the south had almost the same length of railway as the north and expenditures on road building over the period were greater there. Commercial policy favoured southern agricultural exports such as citrus fruits. It was all to little avail.

The problems of the south of Italy are now usually discussed as though they were a unique European phenomenon. But although they had their distinctive aspects they were typical of a problem common to the whole continent before 1914: the extreme localisation of industrialisation and the great regional inequalities of income which resulted from this. Such regional inequalities were just as marked in Spain, Austria-Hungary and Russia. Their prevalence does not, however, diminish their seriousness. In Spain they still add strength to vigorous movements for regional autonomy and in Italy, where the economic dividing line between the more prosperous and the poorer regions was simply drawn across the middle of the country, they still remain unsolved. The per capita income of Piedmont in 1928 was 4,071 1938 lire, of Lombardy 3,717 and of Liguria 3,784. The corresponding figure for Calabria was 1,554 lire, for Sicily 1,824 and for Basilicata 1,751. The level of per capita income in the south and islands was by that date less than 70 per cent of the average for the whole country. In the north alone it was more than 20 per cent above that average.

To attribute these differences simply to the greater degree of industrialisation in the north would be wrong. Their origins were more complicated and stretched further back into the past. In spite of the isolated examples of successful agricultural development in the south, especially in the production of citrus fruits, economic development in the north was more balanced and in general agriculture developed more successfully there after 1896 than in the south. Of course the spurt of economic growth in the north after that date did raise incomes and increase the demand for food and make a higher level of capitalisation of agriculture possible. But the ways in which this was done were hardly possible in the southern society of large estates and sharecroppers. Agricultural output by 1911 in the north, despite the years of falling grain output, was almost 300 per cent above its estimated level in 1861; in the south the increase was only 228 per cent. The south, it is clear, was in no way stagnating, but it was falling further behind the north agriculturally as well as industrially. In the period 1880–4 it provided almost half of Italian wine production; over the period 1905–14 only 39·5 per cent. The inferiority in yields of the main crops leaps to the eye from Table 41. These differences in productivity were extremely important. When the internal per capita consumption of wheat was rising slightly between 1870 and 1890 the north showed also a slight upward trend in per capita wheat production. But there was a sharp fall in southern production because of the inability to compete with imported grain. The greater cheapness of imports in such a poor society hardly liberated greater spending power for the consumption of non-agricultural products, the price of most of which was in any case considerably higher in the south.

On the other hand emigration was possible and it was the flow of remittances returning mainly to the south which was responsible for keeping southern agriculture moving forward, though more slowly than in the north. Economically, therefore, the problem was perhaps being solved in the long run by the free play of economic forces which encouraged such massive population movements. But in the meantime the deeper social problem remained and had more serious consequences. The growth of agricultural output in the north had been due to the changes in attitude associated with the origins of the popular banks and the movement towards agricultural co-operation, already under way in the first decade after unification. South of Rome there were practically no village banks nor peasant co-operatives. The initiative and responsibility needed to operate such local institutions was replaced in the south by a widespread communal apathy, a general sense of resignation in the face of fate, and a dependence on others in intricate systems of kinship and local power for getting things done, of which *mafia* was the final expression.

Patterns of land tenure had established the single nuclear family as the unit of land ownership and within the pursuit of the economic self-interest of that family the peasant sought his defence against a distant and arbitrary state and a brutal and calamitous life. Even in 1958 Banfield could still write of Montegrano, an agricultural township in Basilicata, that 'the parent knows that other families will envy and fear the success of his family and that they are likely to seek to do it injury. He must therefore fear them and be ready to do them an injury in order that they may have less power to injure him and his.'[13] There were enormous cultural as well as economic barriers to the spread of co-operation and agricultural improvements into such a world, and these cultural barriers were increased by the emergence of an industrial society in the north with a wholly different outlook and a wider set of horizons. This was not unique to Italy. In southern Spain the sufferer escaped from reality by embracing a political creed of fantastic revolutionary hope promising the overthrow of all organisation which oppressed him; in southern Italy he adopted the other defence of a realism so narrow that it precluded the effort of imagination needed for change. Such were the ultimate consequences of the extreme regionalisation of nineteenth-century European economic development.

SUGGESTED READING

The best general survey of Italian economic development in the period was left unfinished, covering only the period 1861–94. It is G. Luzzatto, *L'Economia italiana dal 1861 al 1914*, vol. 1 (Milan, 1963). A portion of the work exists in English, 'The Italian Economy in the First Decade after Unification', in F. Crouzet et al. (eds), *Essays in European Economic History*, published for the Economic History Society (London, 1969). A more comprehensive but now out-of-date survey is S. B. Clough, *The Economic History of Italy* (New York, 1964). Beyond these works the student is best advised to turn to recent articles in journals. Of particular value are S. B. Clough and C. Livi, 'Economic Growth in Italy: an Analysis of the Uneven Development of North and South (1800–1950)', in *Journal of Economic History*, vol. XVI, 1956; J. S. Cohen, 'Financing Industrialization in Italy, 1894–1914: The Partial Transformation of a Late-Comer', ibid., vol. XXVIII, 1967; R. S. Eckaus, 'The North–South Differential in Italian Economic Development', also ibid., vol. XXI, 1961; and S. Fenoaltea, 'Railroads and Italian Industrial Growth, 1861–1913', in *Explorations in Entrepreneurial History*, vol. IX, no. 4, 1972.

A useful summary of most of the recent arguments is a collection of essays: A. Caracciola (ed.), *La Formazione dell'Italia industriale* (Bari, 1969 edition), and there are valuable contributions of a similar nature in Biblioteca della rivista Economia e Storia, *L'Economia italiana dal 1861 al 1961* (Milan, 1961). A few indications of the richness of recent monographs in Italian may be derived from the excellent G. Doria, *Investimenti e sviluppo economico a Genova alla vigilia della prima guerra mondiale*, 2 vols (Milan, 1973), the equally good F. Bonelli, *La crisi del 1907: Una tappa dello sviluppo industriale in Italia* (Turin, 1971), and the volumes in the series *Archivio Economico dell'Unificazione Italiana*, published by the Istituto per la Ricostruzione Italiana.

There are two general studies of Spanish economic development in English of high quality, the older J. Vicens Vives, *An Economic History of Spain* (Princeton, 1969) and the excellent J. Napal, 'The Failure of the Industrial Revolution in Spain 1830–1914', in *The Fontana Economic History of Europe*, vol. 4, part 2. Of more detailed work in English there is G. Tortella Casares, 'Spain, 1829–1874', in R. Cameron (ed.), *Banking and Economic Development* (New York and London, 1972); S. G. Checkland, *The Mines of Tharsis: Roman, French and British Enterprise in Spain* (London, 1967); M. W. Flinn, 'British Steel and Spanish Ore 1871–1914', in *Economic History Review*, vol. IX, 1955–6; and R. J. Harrison, 'British Armaments and European Industrialization, 1890–1914: The Spanish Case Re-examined', in *Economic History Review*, vol. XXVII, 1974. The early part of a work dealing with a later period, E. E. Malefakis, *Agrarian Reform and Peasant Revolution in Spain* (New Haven, 1970), is indispensable.

Beyond that the student must read in Spanish. Some works are fundamental, for the literature in English only skims the surface. These are J. Nadal, *El fracaso de la revolución industrial en España* (Barcelona, 1975) and *La población española* (*siglos xvi a xx*) (2nd edn, Barcelona, 1971); J. Vicens Vives, 'La industrialización y el desarollo económico de España de 1800 a 1936', in *Première conférence internationale d'histoire économique* (Stockholm, 1960); N. Sánchez Albornoz, *España hace un siglo: una economía dual* (Barcelona, 1968); and Banco de España, Servicio de Estudios, *Ensayos sobre la economía española a mediados del siglo xix* (Madrid, 1970). Few works touch on the important changes after 1906. This could be described as one of the least studied aspects of Spanish development were it not for the more astounding paucity of modern research on the most important topic of all in this period, the history of agriculture.

Recent research on economic history is scattered among the numerous historical journals and the various economics journals published in Italy, but one journal, *Economia e Storia*, specialises in the subject and reviews all works on Italian economic history. The best journal for modern work on Spanish economic history is the little known *Recerques*, published in Catalan. But there is also, in Spanish, the useful *Moneda y Crédito*.

NOTES

1 A. S. Milward and S. B. Saul, *The Economic Development of Continental Europe 1780–1870* (London, 1973), pp. 531 ff.
2 There is a wealth of conflicting macroeconomic statistical evidence for Italy. Much of it, including the evidence published by government institutes, must be wrong. The most one can do is to select those figures where there is more detail on the method of derivation or where the calculations are better borne out by other evidence. Those chosen here are from G. Fuà, *Formazione, distribuzione e impiego del reddito dal 1861: sintesi statistica*, Istituto nazionale per lo studio della congiuntura (Rome, 1972).
3 A. S. Milward and S. B. Saul, op. cit., p. 355.
4 A. S. Milward and S. B. Saul, op. cit., p. 148.
5 We have adopted the system used in official statistics of referring to the regions of Italy by the provinces shown here.
   North: Piedmont, Liguria, Lombardy, Veneto, Emilia.
   Centre: Tuscany, The Marches, Umbria, Lazio.
   South: Abruzzi, Molise, Campania, Apulia, Basilicata, Calabria.
   Islands: Sicily, Sardinia.
6 See above, p. 110.
7 Istituto Centrale di Statistica, *Indagine statistica sullo sviluppo del reddito nazionale dell'Italia dal 1861 al 1956* (Rome, 1957), p. 42.
8 S. Kuznets, 'Quantitative Aspects of the Growth of Nations', *Economic Development and Cultural Change*, vol. V, 1957, appendix.
9 G. Fuà, *Notes on Italian Economic Growth 1861–1964* (Milan, 1965).
10 A. Gerschenkron, 'An Index of Italian Industrial Development', in *Economic Backwardness in Historical Perspective* (Cambridge, Mass., 1962); S. Golzio, *Sulla misura delle variazioni del reddito nazionale italiano* (Turin, 1951).
11 G. Fuà, *Formazione, distribuzione e impiego del reddito dal 1861: sintesi statistica* (Rome, 1972), table 1:18.
12 R. Romeo, *Breve storia delle grande industria in Italia* (Bologna, 1963).
13 E. C. Banfield, *The Moral Basis of a Backward Society* (New York, 1958), pp. 110–11.

Chapter 5

The Economic Development of Austria-Hungary, 1850–1914

THE NATURE OF THE COUNTRY

Sprawling eastwards from the Swiss Alps to the crests of the Carpathian
mountains, crossing those mountains in the north-east and descending
into the north European plains of Poland, in the north-west reaching to
the lower forested mountains which separated it from Prussian Silesia
and Saxony, spreading south-eastwards down the warm Adriatic coast
and southwards over the snowbound high Alps into the fertile plain of
northern Italy, stretched the second largest country in Europe. Within
its boundaries in 1914 lived one-eighth of the continent's population. The
centre of the country was the plain of Hungary, in the early nineteenth
century one of Europe's main stock rearing areas, by the end of the
century one of its major grain growing areas. The river Danube linked all

271

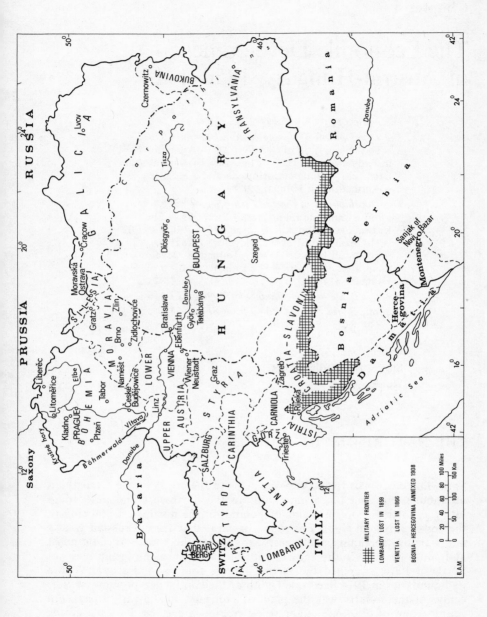

the central parts of the country but it was not easily navigable upstream towards Vienna and Germany, and its mouth in the Black Sea was far from the main trade routes of Europe and not within the Imperial frontiers. The diversity of circumstance which had brought this vast area of almost every possible kind of terrain under the rule of the Habsburg family was preserved in the nineteenth century by a diversity of constitutional patterns and the Vienna government was never able to create from these territories a unitary and centralised state. The area is now divided between Austria, Czechoslovakia, Hungary, Yugoslavia, Poland, Romania, the Soviet Union and Italy.

The Empire embraced eleven major language groups each aspiring to national independence either under the rule of the dynasty or by secession and union with their fellow peoples outside its borders. The Italian provinces were in fact lost, Lombardy in 1859 and Venetia in 1866 after two major wars. Except for the period between 1850 and 1867 Hungary, in whose territory lived six language groups, exercised almost complete constitutional independence. The Habsburg emperor in Vienna ruled Hungary through a separate constitution as king. In the intervening period after the bloody suppression of a nationalist revolt in Hungary an attempt was made to bring the country under the direct control of Vienna, but after the military defeat by Prussia and the exclusion of the Empire from the new German state the Hungarians once again asserted their constitutional independence. In no other European country was there so complex an interaction between political and economic decisions, nor such differences of cultural pattern or of levels of economic development. Almost every theory of the economic development of Europe yet advanced is exemplified by one part or other of Austria-Hungary, but none fits the whole.[1] It is not only the size of the country which makes the history of its development so interesting but also the fact that it serves as a model for the development of the whole continent.

THE DEVELOPMENT OF THE AGRICULTURAL SECTOR

– The Dissolution of Serfdom

The attempts by Joseph II to reconstruct the legal and financial basis of the old regime had not ended in complete defeat in 1790. Although the economic arrangements of the old regime, including compulsory labour service, survived everywhere in the agricultural sector until 1848 except in the free peasant smallholding communities of Vorarlberg and Tyrol, in the Austrian and Czech provinces they were no longer backed by the legal concepts of personal bondage.[2] Joseph's reforms had, however, left the Hungarian lands untouched so that it was only in the western half of the Empire that there was any labour mobility and a satisfactory system of bequeathing or selling former serf and domain land. In 1848 serfdom was swept away by separate revolutions in Vienna and Budapest, and after the defeat of the revolutions the Vienna government made no attempt to undo this their most notable achievement. The brief revival of Joseph II's centralising and unifying policies which followed the defeat of the revolutions brought no unification of the social structures in the agricultural sector. The great differences in development which had existed at the end of the eighteenth century between Austria and Hungary had been exaggerated by the important institutional differences preserved between 1790 and 1848. The terms on which serfdom was then abolished in the two parts of the Empire acknowledged these differences and did nothing to remedy them. The outcome was that no country had such extreme differences from one area to another within the agricultural sector in patterns of landholding, in methods of farming and in levels of output and productivity.

In the western half of the Empire before 1848 pressures built up from the nobility to complete the abolition of serfdom and to farm their estates with wage labour. This they hoped would speed up the abandonment of the system of common fields and allow them to farm a larger part of their domain land as a separate commercial enterprise. Without such a thorough-going institutional reform there was no way in which the larger farmer could emancipate himself from communal practice. In Hungary, however, where the pattern of settlement had led to a much stricter separation of the domain lands from the rest, the existence of a plentiful supply of servile labour had the opposite effect and impeded any demand for change in agricultural methods. In Austria many of the smaller dues in kind which the peasant had to pay were abolished in 1836 and the conditions of sale and inheritance of peasant land were further improved while the legal powers of the noble were greatly curbed. By 1848 labour service there had been widely commuted into money payments to meet the noble's increasing demands for working capital as his farming methods improved.

The Act of 7 September 1848 abolished all obligations of serfdom in German Austria and the Czech lands. In most areas the serfs received not just their own land but part of the domain land which they were cultivating. The lords were compensated for the loss of labour services but for only a small range of other dues, mainly because in German Austria many of these other dues were no longer collected. The compensation was shared between state and emancipated serfs but the proportion paid by the latter could not rise above 40 per cent of the cadastral value of the land obtained. The lord received his compensation in the form of interest bearing bonds from a bank, the Landeskreditanstalt, set up for the purpose in 1851. In Hungary serfdom was abolished by the bill of 18 March 1848. But the noble in this case, partly because his domain land was more easily separable, retained almost the whole of the domain. About 3 million joch (1·7 million hectares) of land in the regular use of serfs was not declared peasant property. Over half the new 'peasant' population received no land other than their serf plot, if they had one, with their personal freedom. The patent of March 1853 then gave full compensation to the nobles for all dues and obligations surrendered, whereas estimates for Austria suggest that only about two-thirds of these losses had been taken into account. At the same time the weaker economic position of the former serfs in the east was acknowledged and the servicing of the compensation funds was not shared but borne solely by the central government, not just in the Hungarian lands but also in Galicia and Bukovina.

The break, therefore, in Hungary was sudden and drastic. In Austria the peasant had a maximum of forty years in which to redeem his share of the noble's compensation; in Hungary he was emancipated immediately. For the Hungarian nobility the terms were very generous. They too were emancipated, with their estates more intact even than those of their Prussian peers and, because the proportion of peasants with little or no land was also larger than in Prussia, with an abundant supply of still captive labour. How lord and peasant adapted to this new situation will be examined in the next section, but it is important to note that these changes came as a result of economic pressures from the more developed parts of the Empire coupled with political demands for a more universal social justice. In the more backward parts of the Empire, however, the social relationships of the old regime were still solidly based on economic realities. Once they were dissolved peasant and lord alike had to recreate them in new forms.

In some areas these relationships were not completely dissolved. Along the 'Military Frontier' of the Empire with Turkey, an east–west strip of territory stretching from Wallachia along the southern boundary of the Hungarian lands through the Voivodina and Croatia and thence curving in a wide arc south-eastwards to the Dalmatian coast, the pattern of land settlement had been determined by purely military considerations and these gave rise neither to large estates nor feudal dues but to the obligation on all settlers to bear arms in return for their land. This area was untouched by the reforms of 1848–53 and the system of land tenure was only gradually demilitarised between 1869 and 1886. After the military occupation of Bosnia and Hercegovina in 1878 an area where the land was encumbered with a similar military set of obligations came under the control of the Empire. The 'nobility' there were muslim military landlords and the obligations on the peasant (*kmet*), though not servile, obliged him to finance the military needs of the local landlord and of the Turkish overlord (*Beg*) to whom the landlord owed, in his turn, military service. The *kmet* paid on average about one-third of the gross yield of his farm in obligations so that the burden on him was comparable to the feudal obligations of western Europe, which had originated in the same way. Some peasants in fact did perform compulsory labour services. From 1879 onwards these tenures were gradually changed to modern freehold tenures by agreement but by 1911 only 32,700 new tenures had been created, a small proportion.

The system of landholding in these former Turkish areas was so well established that the imposition of modern western European legal arrangements served only as a veneer to a quite different type of society. Most lords had had between eight and ten *kmet* and the *Beg* in his turn depended on the yield of 400 to 500 *kmet*. Each *kmet* had only between 5 and 10 hectares at his disposal. Local custom and the pressure of the obligations had brought *kmet* households together in extended kinship networks, the *zadruga*, by which the cultivation of these small plots was carried out in common. The dissolution of the old tenures implied a substitution of the nuclear family for these older and wider bonds. After the founding in 1909 of the Bosnian and Hercegovinan Agrarian and Commercial Bank, the long-term credit necessary to create even very small separate peasant farms out of the older system became more available and legislation in 1910 took advantage of this to offer better terms to all parties to the contract and thus to speed up this reconstruction. Nevertheless although a further 13,400 tenures had been created by the end of 1915 almost a third of the peasants were still living in these provinces under a regime which, economically, was essentially the same as that which had prevailed over most of western Europe before the French Revolution and which, socially, was in striking opposition to the assumptions on which most European land and property legislation was based.

Elsewhere in Austria-Hungary the dissolution of serfdom left only the owners of large estates with an adequate supply of working capital which they could always augment by trading their redemption certificates. Thus in an area like Transylvania where there were a large number of new 'peasants' with little or no land the owners of medium-sized estates who had not enough liquid capital to hire labour entered into a type of share-cropping arrangement whereby the smaller peasant cultivated his own and part of their land in return for providing them with a fixed share of the proceeds. The rules governing these contracts were strict and the proportion of gross yield which the peasant retained no larger than what he had retained when still a serf. Similar developments took place in all the Hungarian lands revealing how unwarranted in such areas were the economic assumptions of the revolutionaries of 1848 that every man should and could hold his land in freehold. In Transylvania even in 1896 many of these 'contract peasants' were still doing up to thirty days' free labour service in return for their dwelling, and an equivalent amount of wage labour was often also compulsory. For the same economic reasons a similar situation persisted in Dalmatia. The nobles here followed the Mediterranean pattern of exercising no agrarian function but living in towns like Ragusa (Dubrovnik) off their rent-roll. Their peasants, however, continued to owe them certain free services until 1878. Inland a system akin to that in Bosnia prevailed, the peasants coming together in wider groupings but with only a temporary right of use over the ploughland and with a proportion of their gross output, between one-third and one-half, continuing to go to the landlord. In 1902 42·5 per cent of all landholdings in Dalmatia were still governed by these tenures (*kolonat*). Even in Bohemia, which was to be after emancipation the showplace of Austrian agriculture, a proportion of the resident labour on the large estates received payment partly in kind and entered into new obligations. There survived for a long time a class of house and farm servants who were bound to the estate for long periods by the law. Over this unfortunate group legislation in 1866 gave the lords new rights of punishment and compulsion.

The reforms of 1848–53 were thus only the beginning of the restructuring of agriculture in Austria-Hungary. Unlike the Russian government the state, except in the Serb areas, withdrew after 1853 from its paternalistic functions and confined itself to legislation supporting contracts between the strong and the weak. In doing so it also created a situation in which the pattern of fields and method of farming could more quickly and easily be changed if the capital and initiative were forthcoming. This withdrawal meant that the great differences which existed in landholding and agricultural practice from one part of the Empire to another were still further emphasised between 1848 and 1914. Some areas did have both capital and initiative and the brutal changes which took place there resulted in a consistent growth in the agricultural sector. Other areas had no chance of a similar response and were to all intents and purposes abandoned to fend for themselves inside the protective shield of the Empire's tariffs. Thus in spite of the extraordinary diversity of agricultural development which took place over the next seventy years the inescapable fact remained that, whatever the growth of output and productivity in the developing areas, the national figures were always kept at a relatively low level by the existence of large areas where hardly anything had changed except that the population had increased.

The size of the Empire meant that in any case there was a great diversity of climate and terrain. But what might in another country of similar size be considered as accentuated regional differences in agriculture were made more profound by the great racial and cultural diversity of the country. Differences in patterns of land tenure and farming methods were not only expressive of different levels of economic development superimposed on adaptations to climate and soil but also expressive of cultural distinctions deriving from a long history of separateness. The variety of patterns within which the old regime was dissolved helped to preserve such distinctions. Over half those 'peasants' with little or no land created by the reforms in Hungary were, for example, not of Hungarian race.

– *Agriculture in Alpine Austria*

A significant part of the total land surface of Austria, excluding Galicia,

Bukovina and the Serb lands, was Alpine or sub-Alpine in character, consisting of uplands with long snowy winters. In this zone which covered much of Salzburg, Styria, Carinthia, Tyrol, Vorarlberg and over half of Lower Austria and Carniola most of the agricultural land was grassland. Livestock farming predominated and the extensive forests and the high mountain pastures were essential to supporting the quantity of livestock. The high proportion of grassland and pasture in these areas may be seen from Table 48. A typical routine, although this would vary with altitude and location, was to feed the animals in stalls for four months during the winter, for three months in the home meadows, for a further three in the forests, and for two on the uppermost mountain pastures when they were free of snow. Any change in this cumbersome and unproductive pattern was difficult to bring about because the amount of arable land was limited and what there was in the more northerly areas after being sown to grain for three years would then have to revert to grass for the same period. The most typical grains were rye and oats, but in all these areas their crop was smaller than that of potatoes. The pattern of landholding over the whole area was that of the peasant farm with insufficient capital to break out of these routines. Compared to many areas of Europe these farms were quite large. Table 49 shows that farms of 20–50 hectares made up over 17 per cent of all farms in Upper Austria, Salzburg and Carinthia in 1902. But the scarcity of arable land meant that much more land was necessary for the farm to be profitable. In fact the retention of arable areas on these farms was itself a measure of the backwardness of this area and its failure to specialise. In these upland areas farmers could be a long way from any consumer market and transport was difficult. Milk was mostly consumed on the farm, for making cheese or feeding pigs. Milk yields were low and the number of cattle to the hectare was also lower than in some other parts of the Empire. The peasant therefore clung tenaciously to his bit of ploughland although his yields of grain were low by comparison with those elsewhere. In these provinces the older domestic handicrafts still flourished and flax was frequently grown to provide employment and income in winter.

In the lower-lying foothills and in the most southerly of the Alpine areas the situation offered opportunities for improvement. The eastern foothills were the most important area for rearing calves sent annually to markets in the Austrian lowlands of Bohemia and Moravia. In the southerly valleys of Carinthia and the Tyrol wine became the important cash crop and these two provinces together with Vorarlberg produced 1·5 million hectolitres in 1912. The small vineyards fitted well into the structure of peasant enterprise especially in the Tyrol where 73 per cent of all landholdings were under 5 hectares. But the changes which took place over the area as a whole were very few; the only force generating much economic change after emancipation was the growth of population and in this area that tended to be absorbed into the expanding labour market of Vienna and Lower Austria.

Table 48 *Land use in Austria, 1902 (per cent)*

	Arable	Grassland and pasture	Alpine lands	Vineyards	Woodland	Wasteland
Lower Austria	43·4	14·8	0·4	1·9	34·3	3·6
Upper Austria	35·1	20·4	0·6	0	34·0	7·4
Salzburg	9·2	13·2	29·0	0	32·4	15·0
Styria	18·9	17·6	6·2	1·4	47·9	6·9
Carinthia	13·7	15·4	17·1	0	44·1	4·2
Carniola	14·8	33·0	1·4	1·1	44·4	9·5
Görz	15·6	42·7	4·5	2·4	22·9	11·7
Istria	11·3	39·0	0	9·4	33·2	3·4
Tyrol	5·2	10·2	25·7	0·5	38·9	19·1
Vorarlberg	3·0	23·8	33·8	0	25·9	12·1
Bohemia	50·5	15·0	0	0	29·0	3·4
Moravia	54·8	12·7	0	0·5	27·5	3·1
Silesia	49·4	12·0	0	0	34·2	3·1
Galicia	48·4	20·3	0·4	0	25·8	3·5
Bukovina	27·6	22·6	2·4	0	43·2	3·3
Dalmatia	10·7	47·1	0	6·4	29·7	2·2

Source: Agricultural Co-operation and Rural Credit in Europe, Information and Evidence Secured by the American Commission, 1913. Senate Document no. 214, 63rd Congress, 1913.

Table 49 *Relative percentage of landholdings by size in Austria, 1902*

	0–5 ha		5–20 ha	20–50 ha	5–50 ha	+50 ha	
	a	b	a	a	b	a	b
Lower Austria	56·5	9·3	31·0	10·7	53·5	1·7	37·2
Upper Austria	49·7	6·8	31·2	18·2	62·4	1·5	30·7
Salzburg	37·5	1·8	35·9	9·5	23·2	2·9	57·0
Styria	55·8	7·9	31·7	19·9	44·3	8·3	47·7
Tyrol	73·5	6·5	18·4	5·2	18·5	2·8	74·9
Vorarlberg	68·7	13·0	25·3	3·2	24·5	2·8	62·5
Carinthia	39·0	n.a.	32·7	19·9	n.a.	8·3	n.a.
Bohemia	70·5	12·5	22·7	5·8	46·3	1·1	34·8
Moravia	73·6	16·2	21·7	4·0	45·8	0·6	37·5
Silesia	73·2	23·5	21·3	4·7	41·2	0·7	39·9
Galicia	80·3	n.a.	18·0	0·8	n.a.	0·7	n.a.
Bukovina	85·7	n.a.	12·1	1·4	n.a.	0·8	n.a.
Carniola	51·0	n.a.	39·1	8·5	n.a.	1·4	n.a.
Istria	71·1	n.a.	25·5	2·6	n.a.	0·7	n.a.
Dalmatia	87·4	n.a.	11·4	0·9	n.a.	0·3	n.a.

a = % of total landholdings   *b* = % of total land area

Source: Derived from S. Pascu et al., 'Einige Fragen der landwirtschaftlichen Entwicklung in der österreichisch-ungarischen Monarchie', in *Mitteilungen auf der Konferenz der Geschichtswissenschafter, Budapest, 1964* (Bucharest, 1965).

– The Areas of Agricultural Crisis

In no other part of the Empire could the growth of population be so easily accommodated. The south-western areas, Görz, Istria, Dalmatia and, after the annexation, Bosnia-Hercegovina, and the north-eastern areas of Galicia and Bukovina experienced like central and southern Russia an acute economic and social crisis as the agrarian basis of their economy proved increasingly inadequate to absorb the increase in population. The sharp rise in the rate of growth of population in these crisis areas in the late nineteenth century was attributable to a sudden and steep fall in mortality combined with a much earlier average age at marriage for women than in most of western and central Europe, producing a much greater excess of births over deaths. The decline in mortality was probably due to medical and sanitary improvements in these areas but the low age at marriage was perhaps more directly related to cultural patterns. In the south-eastern Slav provinces the rate of natural increase of the population rose more than threefold in the 1880s over its level in the 1870s and thenceforward it never fell below 14·5 per cent in any quinquennial period until 1910. For the fact that the average age of women at marriage was between 20 and 21, and for the high number of children born to each woman, the continued existence of communal farming and extended families may have had some responsibility. Where the economic upkeep of the children and even their rearing was not solely a matter for a unitary family but for an extended kinship network the pressures to restrict births were less. Furthermore, it was not necessary for men to have independent and adequate resources before marriage. But since a similar pattern of marriage is observable over much of eastern Europe this cannot be the sole explanation.

In the south-east and the north-east the consequence of this sudden surge in population was either an increasing subdivision of already inadequate peasant plots or an increase in the number of landless rural inhabitants. In Görz, Istria and Dalmatia the proportion of arable land on farms was extremely low, only about 12 per cent in 1913 (Table 48). The harsh stony terrain interspersed with rocky deserts did not even provide the natural meadows on which the herds of Alpine cattle were fed. Sheep and goats were the typical livestock of this region but even they grazed on the young trees and plants and worsened the quality of what grassland there was. The most commonly grown grain, even for a food crop, was maize. The yields of grain were only half the national average. Wine was the most useful cash crop, especially in Dalmatia, and was the only crop briefly to offer a solution to the agricultural crisis in this area. When the phylloxera seriously reduced Italian output between 1870 and 1890 exports from Dalmatia, as yet unaffected by the disease, began to develop. In the mid-1880s they amounted to about 650,000 hectolitres a year and vines‾covered almost one-third of the cultivated area. But before 1890 the phylloxera had reached Dalmatia and this, combined with the recovery of other wine producing countries, reduced Dalmatian exports to insignificance. Small beginnings were made with the growing of oil seeds as a cash crop and in Bosnia, where the Turkish taxation system had taken a portion of the grain output in payment, this discouragement from growing too much grain acted as an encouragement to grow tobacco. But none of this amounted to very much. The wool produced was of poor quality and often used for making the peasants' own clothing and in most of the southern Slav lands outside Dalmatia the only real source of cash came from the sales of skinny livestock driven long distances to market.

The income from a 10 hectare farm in Dalmatia was barely enough to sustain existence and yet one-quarter of all landholdings there in 1902 were between 2 and 5 hectares. In fact less than 4 per cent of all holdings were of 10 hectares or larger, compared to 27·6 per cent in Styria. The high proportion of landholdings under 2 hectares (Table 49) is a measure of the way in which the extended family unit provided economic shelter at a low level of existence for its members. Peasants with holdings so small had to combine in groups of five or six to have cattle to pull the plough or to make it worthwhile to own the simplest machines and in this way the extended family both fulfilled an important economic purpose and at the same time acted as a force to preserve subdivision and discourage migration. The proportion of the population in such relationships fell from 43 per cent in 1895 to 31 per cent in 1910 but their absolute number, because of the growth of population, did not fall.

In Galicia and Bukovina the fundamental problems were the same, but for the Empire much more serious because these provinces represented one-third of the area and the population of Austria. In fact the two westernmost provinces of Galicia, Cracow and Sandomir, were much closer agriculturally to Silesia and Moravia and it was in the easternmost two-thirds of Galicia that the combination of population increase and agricultural backwardness assumed the gravest proportions. Here the growth of population took place in an area where population was already dense and where there was much less uncultivated land than in the southern Slav provinces. By 1910 the density of population in Galicia, 102 people to the square kilometre, was not exceeded in any unindustrialised area in Europe and 40 per cent of the Austrian agricultural labour force worked there. Eighty per cent of the units of landholding were less than 5 hectares in size; in Bukovina they were 85 per cent. Galicia more than anywhere else was the land of the 2–5 hectare farm, containing 360,000 of them. But it was also an area of large noble estates and about one-half of the area was held in estates of between 50 and 200 hectares. Estates and peasant farms alike were sown to grain. All the grains were cultivated but winter wheat was the most common. In Bukovina maize was the dominant crop. Where grain did not suffice to sustain the wretched existence of the Galician peasants it was replaced by potatoes, and as the population continued to grow, potato patches came after 1900 to cover a greater area than wheat. Rotations and root crops could make little headway in this situation and together with the concentration on arable cultivation this meant that the population of cattle was low and the milk yield of a Galician cow little more than that of a goat. The Galician peasants, like those in the Russian Ukraine, remained attached to horses as farm animals and the density of the horse population was far higher than elsewhere in Austria-Hungary. With little natural manure and insufficient income to purchase fertiliser it is not surprising that grain yields were so low; for most grains they were between a half and three-quarters the level of those obtained in neighbouring Silesia and Moravia. The level of mechanisation was the lowest in the Empire and the use of agricultural machinery was only permitted by the existence of the large estates. Even these were farmed on a miserably low level but of the 511 steam-driven agricultural machines in Galicia in 1902 505 were on farms bigger than 50 hectares. As for other machines there was one for every 1,973 landholdings; in Austria proper the proportion was 1:342. In many years in spite of its concentration on arable farming Galicia was dependent on imports of grain from other provinces of the Empire.

In 1910 73 per cent of the population of Galicia and Bukovina was still employed in the agricultural sector of the economy as against 55 per cent for the Empire as a whole. Land remained the vital resource and a hunger to acquire it permeated the whole society from top to bottom. In this struggle the middle and larger landowners slowly lost land to the peasants. Nevertheless about three-quarters of the total mortgage business done in Austria was transacted in Galicia, most of it with the larger landowners. The interest rates they paid for capital were sometimes as much as 5 per cent above those paid elsewhere in Austria. The smaller peasant, relying on usurers, paid even more. The Galician Credit Society founded in Lvov in 1865 was deliberately based on the Prussian model and was not concerned with the financing of peasant farming operations. The Raiffeisen banks founded later made little impact in Galicia, partly because of the desperate competition for more land which kept the credit rating of most peasants at a very low level and partly because the banks themselves were usually making more loans than they took in deposits: this was true also of their operations in Dalmatia, with the result that they were themselves seeking credit in a highly competitive market.

The chief factors in the mounting economic crisis in these areas of the Empire were the unbearable pressure which the rapid increase in population put on backward and inadequate agricultural systems while industrialisation, largely because of the low and sometimes falling level of incomes in the agricultural sector, went ahead far too slowly to improve the situation. In the more unfortunate areas industry did not grow rapidly enough to attract a sufficient number of migrants from the crisis areas to ease the situation. Although in its general outlines the situation was akin to that in Russia it was distinguished by the fact that in the Habsburg Empire the crisis areas were part of a country where other important areas developed a level of industrialisation comparable to that of western Europe. Cheap surplus labour did not enable the crisis areas to benefit from higher incomes elsewhere because labour costs were not an important consideration. In spite of the fact that all these territories belonged to the Austrian part of the Empire (although Dalmatia was separated from Austria by Hungarian territory), the successful development of other regions of Austria left them far behind and the differences in level of economic development, and the consequences thereof, between Galicia and Bohemia were like those between Sicily and Lombardy or Ireland and England.

The only answer to the situation would have been migration, but extreme poverty and subdivision also acted as a brake on this. Seasonal movement of agricultural workers to Bohemia and even to Germany was common after 1860, and after 1880 as pressure on the land mounted permanent emigration became important, rising to almost half a million people between 1901 and 1910. The demand for labour elsewhere in the Empire grew slowly and was met by shorter range migration. A large industrial city like Vienna attracted permanent migrants to the industrial labour force from the neighbouring regions of Moravia and Bohemia but seldom from as far as Galicia. In the last decade of the period the tensions erupted in reaping strikes, rick burning, and refusals to pay rents and taxes. Nothing could better illustrate the important intercommunications between agriculture and industrial development than the existence side by side in the Empire of areas like Bohemia and Upper and Lower Austria which had the employment structure of developed economies as well as the most productive and profitable agricultural areas and Galicia and Dalmatia which were wholly unindustrialised and had an agriculture whose levels of productivity and methods of farming were among the poorest in Europe.

– Bohemia, Moravia and Silesia

This point emerges more clearly from a consideration of the striking and rapid improvements in agriculture in Bohemia, Moravia and Silesia. This area had important advantages over those we have just considered. In the first place the rate at which the population grew was more gradual. The age of females at marriage was higher and the average number of children to each household little more than half that of the south Slav provinces. It is sometimes suggested that one influence operating strongly here was the strictly maintained primogenitural inheritance laws; before 1869 the subdivision of peasant farms in Bohemia was forbidden by law. By the time subdivision was permitted a pattern of population growth more like that in industrialised societies had become established. Nevertheless the pressures after 1868 were still such as to make subdivision quite widespread. The population of Bohemia increased by 40 per cent between 1869 and 1890; but by 1870 in Bohemia and by 1890 in Moravia half of the labour force was no longer employed in agriculture and the existence of other sources of employment meant that the new population did not go into the agricultural sector. Thus although the number of farms increased between 1869 and 1890 the number of people employed in agriculture fell slightly. Before 1914, however, the decrease in the absolute number of the labour force in agriculture was small. One further outlet was emigration; in two five-year periods, 1881–5 and 1901–5, it exceeded 40,000, but this was less than the number emigrating from Galicia or Hungary. Before 1880 internal migration was more significant than emigration abroad, with peasants from the poorer areas of Moravia and southern Bohemia particularly gravitating to Vienna and its environs.

In the second place the nearness of the commercialised agriculture of Prussia and German Silesia set an example which the noble estate owners of the north-western provinces were in a position to follow. Climatic and soil conditions were similar and the chief lines of communication as well as of economic influence ran towards Saxony and Prussia. It was in fact along the valleys of the Elbe (Labe) and the Vltava that the most commercially competitive estates developed. Czech historians describe the agriculture of Bohemia and Moravia as developing on 'the Prussian model' and the analogy is a good one. But the early development of alternative sources of income in the Czech lands provided an outlet for surplus labour nearer home than it had done on the large estates of Prussia and Mecklenburg. Furthermore the influence of ideas of peasant protection spreading in an earlier period from north-western Germany, and still expressed in the legislation forbidding subdivision of the peasant holding below a certain size, gave the pattern of landholding a less monolithic aspect than in Germany east of the Elbe. There was a substantial proportion of medium-sized farms which consisted of good arable land. Over 17 per cent of the Bohemian farms were of 10 hectares or more. On these farms sufficient capital could be gradually acquired to adopt better farming methods and together with the larger estates they were responsible for the great superiority of grain yields in the north-western provinces. But the innovations in agricultural practice began on the larger estates and it was the entrepreneurial activities of their owners using the very large number of tiny landholdings to provide a plentiful source of cheap labour which sustained the pace of change in Czech agriculture.

Between a quarter and a third of the land of Bohemia was held in large indivisible entails, mostly by the nobility, in 1890. Not all of this was productive arable land. There were twenty-nine holdings of more than 10,000 hectares, including the vast estates of the Schwarzenbergs and Lichtensteins, but these were often made up of large game forests. It was rather on the holdings of around 200 hectares that the most commercial farming methods were adopted. Estates between 200 and 500 hectares made up about 18 per cent of the land area of Bohemia and Moravia and this proportion seems to have remained fairly constant after 1860. At the other end of the scale 48 per cent of the landholdings in Bohemia and Moravia were less than 2 hectares. Two-thirds of these supplemented the income of people with other occupations, and 55 per cent of those owning farms between 2 and 5 hectares also had a supplementary occupation. This was the source of the wage labour on the large estates. Leasing was more common than in Galicia and many of the smaller plots shown in Table 49 were leased out to be coupled with other plots. Most farms over 10 hectares would employ wage labour and on the bigger estates when sugar beet became an important crop after 1850 the method of farming was very labour-intensive. The legal survivals of the old regime still gave the noble certain rights over the labourers on his estate and a certain amount of the basic farm work was done by servants who were legally bound to the noble household, but with growing industrial employment the estates came to depend almost entirely on a large hired labour force.

The third and most fundamental advantage of north-western agriculture lay in the higher level of economic development of the area. The existence of important domestic textile industries in the Erzgebirge (Krušné Hory) and in Silesia in the eighteenth century and the mechanisation of these industries early in the nineteenth century provided not only an urban market for foodstuffs but also the social overhead capital so noticeably lacking in the poorer areas. In these industrialising areas agriculture and industry developed in a balanced way with valuable interactions. Whereas, for example, there were on average in the whole of Austria 40·45 kilometres of roads for every 100 square kilometres, in Bohemia and Moravia there were 62·0 and in Silesia 77·2. And although grain remained the main crop, specialised crops such as sugar beet and hops developed which not only had a local industrial market and were in part financed by these local industries but whose increased consumption was also partly a function of the rise in incomes generated by industrialisation. The extensive cultivation of sugar beet in its turn enabled more cattle to be kept by means of stall feeding so that not only were grain yields higher but the density of the cattle population was as high as anywhere in Europe. This stock of cattle in turn provided milk for the local markets.

Sugar beet, as elsewhere in Europe, made a brief appearance during the continental blockades and then disappeared to be revived as a crop in the 1830s. The first sugar refinery was built in 1837 on the northern railway at Zidlochovice in Moravia. The previous year pressure by the noble landowners had caused the government to cancel its plans to lower the tariff on sugar, but the restraints imposed by the old regime prevented any extensive changes. The terms on which the old society was dissolved gave the larger estate owners their opportunity. The compensation for loss of rights provided a supply of investment capital, especially for those with the largest estates who received the largest sums. Their initial investment often went in building a small refinery and it was some time before the raw material supply was sufficient to enable these refineries to be used to full capacity. In 1859 three-quarters of the beet was grown on the estate properties of the refiners and the total area of beet was still only 11,500 hectares. By 1869–70 it had expanded to 64,400 hectares and it then almost doubled again by 1872–3. The total output over the same period grew by 45 per cent so that although Bohemian sugar output was still much smaller than that of France it had almost equalled that of Germany. Sugar consumption per capita in Austria-Hungary, however, was much lower than in western Europe and after 1864 this growth of output was sustained increasingly by exports; by 1870–1 about 30 per cent of output was exported. By ploughing back their profits into the refining process the estate owners made Bohemia and Moravia temporarily the centre of technological research in sugar refining, lowering their manufacturing costs and improving the final quality at the same time. At the peak of the boom in 1873 the industry employed 40,100 workers. The economic crisis in 1873 burst the bubble and led to massive withdrawals of capital from sugar. The area sown to beet shrank by 20,000 hectares in one year and did not again reach the extent of 1872–3 until 1878. The recovery depended even more on exports; between 1870–1 and 1880–1 they increased seven times more than domestic consumption. It was in this faltering period that German sugar output began to leave that of the Empire far behind and that the lead in refining techniques passed to other countries. In 1885 a slump of similar dimensions hit the industry and again it took four years before the crop returned to its earlier output. Nevertheless with an annual average output of 64 million quintals of beet in the last decade before the First World War Austria was still one of the world's major producers and more than 90 per cent of the output came from the north-western provinces.

The relationship between large estate agriculture in this area and brewing seems to have many similar aspects. The output of beer in Bohemia between 1850 and 1865 increased by more than half and it was in this period that some of the larger farms began to specialise in growing high-quality barley for brewing. In the brewing industry also Bohemia, particularly the town of Plzeň, became a centre of technological innovations. After 1875 the area devoted to hops more than doubled, in this case providing a useful crop for the larger peasant farms.

The tendency of some recent Czech and Hungarian historiography has been to see the history of the food and drink industries after the dissolution of serfdom as constituting an industrial revolution of a kind unique to central-eastern Europe, but we have already seen how important food processing industries were in western European industrialisation. Like the textile industries they responded sharply to marginal increases in consumer incomes and the same process explains much of what happened in the Czech lands after 1850. Davis estimated a threefold increase in real wages of agricultural labourers in Bohemia between 1855 and 1876, and even if the figure is exaggerated it is clear that the results of emancipation were fortunate both for lord and serf.[3] In any case the concept of a Czech industrial revolution based on foodstuff industries ignores the leading role played for most of the century by the textile industries.

The importance of these industrial crops should not be exaggerated. Bread and fodder grains remained by far the most important crops except on the large number of small plots which, as in Galicia, were planted with potatoes. It was not the specialised crops which distinguished the north-west, for Galicia still produced considerable quantities of flax, but the much higher level of productivity of all crops. This was mainly a function of the generally higher level of development of the whole economy, of

Table 50   *Average yield of grain crops in Austria, 1902–5 (quintals per ha)*

	Wheat	Rye	Barley	Oats	Maize
Austria (average)	13·3	13·0	14·0	11·5	12·0
Bohemia, Moravia, Silesia	16·8	14·8	17·0	12·9	15·3
Galicia, Bukovina	11·6	10·7	10·7	10·2	11·9

Source: S. von Strakosch, *Die Grundlagen der Agrarwirtschaft in Österreich* (Vienna, 1906), pp. 49, 75.

which the connections of the sugar and brewing industries with agriculture were one symptom. The north-western provinces were the chief source of rye, oats and barley. Until the 1870s there were still grain surpluses to export to other parts of Austria. Uncultivated land, 21·6 per cent of the land surface of Bohemia in 1848, was only one per cent of the area in 1908. Meanwhile every type of livestock except sheep increased significantly in numbers and quality over the same period. In the survey of 1902 49 per cent of farms in the area were recorded as using machines, including virtually all those over 5 hectares in size. The most and best cultivated provinces of the Empire were also those in which the importance of the agricultural sector in the regional economy was diminishing most rapidly. Agriculture accounted for 40·5 per cent of the labour force in Bohemia in 1890; by 1910 for only 32·1 per cent, a pattern comparable to that of France and Germany. Moravia was less industrialised but the figures for Silesia are akin to those for Bohemia. In Galicia at the same date, a region with the lowest agricultural productivity, only 6 per cent of the labour force was employed in manufacturing industry.

– *Agriculture in Hungary*

The role of the big estates in disseminating better farming practice, in generating employment, and in investing both in agriculture and industry in Bohemia as in the eastern provinces of Germany, does suggest that given adequate access to markets the noble landowners could, as many of them had realised before 1848, benefit from the dissolution of the old regime. Their ability to do so was in striking contrast to the continued impoverishment of the supposedly emancipated peasants of Dalmatia or Galicia. The same process, with less happy results, can be seen at work in a more backward setting in Hungary, which more than any other country in Europe was dominated by the large estate.

Table 51   *Distribution of land-holdings in Hungary, 1914*

Size (jochs)[1]	% of total area
0– 200	49·1
200– 1,000	11·3
1,000–10,000	20·3
+ 10,000	19·4

[1] One joch (hold) = 1·421 acres = 0·575 ha

Source: S. Eddie, 'The Changing Pattern of Landownership in Hungary, 1867–1914', in *Economic History Review*, vol. XX, 1967.

Estates over 575 hectares in size covered 39·1 per cent of the area of Hungary in 1867. Included among these were many vast latifundia of families like the Esterhazys which were greater than 6,000 hectares in size. Side by side with these estates a system of partible inheritance had already created large classes of smallholders and of landless labourers. Farm holdings of 2·87 hectares or less accounted in the same year for 14·2 per cent of the land area. Real political power in Hungary after 1867, particularly in local government, remained firmly in the hands of the larger landowners, uninhibited by secret ballots or simple forms of universal suffrage. This, and economic forces, caused the very largest category of landholdings to grow in size from the mid-1880s to 1914. Thus in the latter year estates over 5,750 hectares in size which had accounted for 8·5 per cent of the land area in 1867 now accounted for 19·4 per cent. At the same time smaller landholdings also grew in area. The growth of the latifundia took place at the expense of the gentry estates of between 57·5 and 575 hectares. When grain prices fell after 1873 farms of this size, which had often specialised in producing wheat, the commodity whose price fell most, survived temporarily by leasing out the worst parts of their land but could not sustain themselves by this means for the whole length of time preceding the rise of prices in 1896. The latifundia had more varied resources and greater capital reserves, the peasant farmers had less overheads. By the twentieth century, therefore, Hungary had become even more the country of the great estate and the peasant smallholding.

In the early nineteenth century the owners of these estates had no opportunity to follow the trend set by their Czech peers. On the Hungarian plains transport was lacking and at any distance from the valleys of the Danube and Tisza the patriarchal life of the estate remained little affected by the great changes which were taking place on the continent. There were no towns of any size outside Budapest, and towns like Szeged were in reality only overgrown village settlements in which the agricultural population had originally crowded together for protection. A large part of their population was still agricultural, consisting of estate owners and their labourers who travelled long distances to their work. Into this self-sufficient world the steamship and the railway brought a measure of change as sudden and great as that seen anywhere in the history of Europe in the nineteenth century. Prior to these changes the Hungarian plains were one of Europe's major stock rearing areas and arable agriculture was little practised. By the end of the nineteenth century the Alföld had become one of the continent's greatest grain growing areas. The founding in 1831 of the Danube Steamship Company may be taken as the starting date of these changes. The main Hungarian export before 1848 was wool but after 1844 it began to decline in importance in the face of foreign competition, and in the doubling of the value of Hungarian exports to Austria between 1831 and 1845 there was a marked increase in the relative importance of wheat and rye. Although railway construction proceeded only slowly in Hungary, at an average of only 135 kilometres a year between 1848 and 1868, it provided a further means by which demand from the growing urban markets of Austria could be met. One of the first acts of the Austrian government after the suppression of the Hungarian revolution was to abolish the customs barriers between Hungary and the rest of the Empire and in this act they were expressing the clear intention of fixing permanently Hungary's 'colonial' status as an exporter of primary produce. The irony of this act of centralisation could be appreciated in later years. After the establishment of dual control free trade was maintained between the two countries by mutual agreement for successive ten-year periods and this free access to the Austrian market was to become the pillar of Hungary's agricultural economy and thus of its political society. The railway, the abolition of serfdom and internal free trade all arrived together.

The terms on which serfdom had been abolished gave the Hungarian nobles a competitive advantage within the Empire by providing them with better compensation and cheaper labour than their Austrian peers. The readiness of their response, made easier by a strong national sentiment to develop a Magyar state, is summed up in the remarkable career of a man like Count István Széchényi, an early nineteenth-century pioneer of better stock breeding, of the use of agricultural machinery, of improved navigation on the Danube, and of commercial and mortgage banks. The history of the Hungarian economy until the end of the century is largely that of the attempts of the nobility to develop a modern commercial agriculture in a setting of economic backwardness. Their control of political power enabled them to overcome some of the inevitable consequences of the absence of previous development. They were able, for example, to subsidise agricultural exports and credit for large estates with little political opposition. They were able to manipulate freight rates in their own favour, and to exercise a formidable control over their labour force. The history of Hungarian agriculture provides a fascinating and unique example of an attempt to overcome the severe problems of economic backwardness common to all eastern and east-central Europe by the forced development of agriculture within a customs union with a more developed economy.

The central problem was always the lack of industrialisation and it was this that made the situation so different from that in the Czech lands. As late as 1910 60·1 per cent of the total labour force was still employed in the agricultural sector. Given the political nature of the Magyar state, industrialisation constituted in some ways a threat to the holders of power and their attitude to economic development in its fullest sense for much of the period was ambivalent. But with such an inflexible pattern of land distribution the growth of population could only result in increasing landlessness which in its turn could only be met by an increased demand for labour on the estates or by emigration, unless employment opportunities were created outside the agricultural sector. The use of mechanised farming methods, more easily adopted on such large landholdings, however, reduced the demand for agricultural labour. In the Hungarian plain the harvest provided between 40 and 60 days employment in the 1860s, but only from 14 to 21 days by 1900.

In spite of the relatively high birth rates the growth of the Hungarian population was less dramatic than in the Slav lands, although this may be explained partly by the high emigration and partly by the abnormally high death rates of the early 1870s. The annual average growth of population was 0·75 per cent between 1869 and 1910, most of this growth occurring after 1880. The net emigration from Hungary in the period 1869–1910 was about 1·26 million, more than one-fifth of the natural increase. The acceleration of population growth after 1880 eventually produced an avalanche of emigrants and more than half the number leaving after 1869 left after 1900.

The evidence available suggests that real wages of agricultural workers certainly did not rise between 1870 and the mid-1890s, although most of this period was one of falling food prices, and that they may even have decreased. In the last decade before the war more rapid industrialisation and massive emigration led to an increase in real wages, but for most of the period total surplus purchasing power did not grow. This not only had the effect of restricting industrialisation but also exaggerated the social tensions inherent in the state, dominated as it was by large landlords ultimately governing in their own interests. The total agricultural population grew at an average rate of about 0·36 per cent between 1869 and 1910 and after 1880 was growing more quickly. The declining demand for labour on each farm was to some extent compensated for by the great extension of the cultivated area. Railway building, land improvement and irrigation schemes all provided extra employment but after 1890 seasonal unemployment was so serious that handicraft instruction was given out with charity. The harvest strikes of 1897 and 1906 were symptomatic of the bitter poverty and brutal labour relations which persisted in the countryside. The reaction of the landowners was to make strikes illegal and to import more harvesting machinery. But by this time the experiment of forced agricultural growth had been greatly modified and the government had begun also to attempt a policy of forced industrialisation.

The history of Hungarian agriculture in this period is a striking example of the contribution which the agricultural sector could make to growth and development. The volume of agricultural output grew, so did output per employee and so did the volume of agricultural exports. The cultivated area grew and methods of cultivation and the yields obtained improved steadily. These changes were of course mostly confined to the larger farms but they stand out in contrast to the continued inadequacy of the agricultural sector elsewhere in eastern and south-eastern Europe. Calculations of the annual rate of growth of agricultural output between 1867 and 1913 put it between 1·8 and 2·5 per cent.[4] This compares favourably with any large economy in Europe over the same period, although the growth of course was taking place from very low levels. The higher of these figures would give an annual increase in output per employed person of 0·5 per cent, which, particularly because it is the most optimistic calculation, is less impressive. The figures for average yields of crops are conflicting but all indicate a high rate of improvement. By 1890–4 the average wheat yields had improved by 75 per cent and those of potatoes by almost the same proportion over their level of the 1870s. But by 1913 the yields of most of the grain crops were nevertheless still below the European average and far below those for Germany.

The main concentration of arable farming was in Hungary proper rather than in Croatia-Slavonia or Transylvania, and there the proportion of land ploughed rose from 33·5 per cent in 1846 to 47 per cent in 1895. This increase was achieved at the expense of fallow land, of pasture and of forest. Through the increasing use of rotations the ploughland itself was less often left fallow; 21·5 per cent of it lay fallow in 1870, 8·4 per cent in 1910. By that date the frequency of fallowing and the amount of fallow land were about the same as in Germany and France, although in Transylvania the proportion was still much higher. Four-fifths of the arable acreage was sown to grain and grain output more than doubled between 1870 and 1912. The output of certain other crops, grass, fodder and sugar beet, grew more rapidly. Sugar beet as an important crop was at first confined to the western border but the improvements in yield, consequent on the spread of better techniques from Bohemia, meant that the output of sugar beet was increasing at 7 per cent annually after 1870. More specialised crops were severely limited by the constraints imposed by transport and markets. Wine was the only significant exception but like Dalmatia Hungary suffered severely from the phylloxera. The vineyard area fell by more than 40 per cent between 1885 and 1895. Except for sheep the numbers of livestock also increased, the increase being mainly in cattle on the big farms and pigs on the smaller peasant farms.

But the development of Hungarian agriculture rested on the improved production of wheat and maize. The sources of these improvements are not only to be found in the introduction of crop rotations and better strains of crop, factors common to the whole continent, but in the advantages which these large grain farms had in adopting certain kinds of agricultural machinery and in the financial support given by the government. The extent of mechanisation of farming on the large Hungarian estates is often exaggerated – an estate of similar size in Germany would have had two or three times the machinery – but the large and level farms of the Hungarian plain were in certain circumstances well suited to cumbersome steam driven machines which were of less use elsewhere. Before 1865 the British firm of Clayton and Shuttleworth had provided about 400 steam threshers for Hungary. Afterwards the number of these machines and of steam tractors increased so that by 1895 there were about 900 of each. Beyond the plains this process was much less in evidence; in 1902 there was 50 per cent more cultivated land to an agricultural machine in Transylvania than in Hungary proper and 68 per cent more in Slovakia. Machines were also concentrated on the large estates, the simpler machines as well as steam engines: at the same date three-quarters of the sowing, drilling and reaping machines in Hungary proper were on farms over 50 hectares which formed just over one per cent of all landholdings.

The most difficult and persistent problem involved in this rapid transition was the shortage of credit. It was here that the government made its greatest effort to overcome the inherent problems of economic backwardness. The poor methods of farming discouraged the flow of short-term credit to farmers. Even in proportion to the anticipated lower yield the sum which a farmer could borrow against the future harvest was only about one-third of what could be borrowed in Germany. The rates of interest set by moneylenders in the 1850s were between 18 and 20 per cent at their lowest. The usual method of overcoming some of these difficulties by creating institutions which would provide long-term mortgage loans was made more difficult by the vagueness of many land tenures and by the complicated entails and trusts used to hold the large estates together, making them inalienable and therefore poor security for a mortgage. At the same time the demand for capital was much higher because the level of capital equipment was so low compared to western Europe. There were no ancient barns or byres, the result of the lack of economic development in previous centuries; there were practically no buildings other than dwellings and churches.

The opening of a mortgage loan department in the National Bank in Vienna in 1857 was the first step in remedying this, but it had to be taken in conjunction with a massive programme of verification and registration of tenures. The land books took about fifteen years to prepare and until they were ready proof of tenure was hard to establish. Loans could not be less than 5,000 florins and in fact were usually much higher, which effectively restricted them to wealthy landowners. By 1882 about half the total loans had in fact gone to Hungary but it is clear that these facilities were still inadequate. Ditz calculated the ratio of mortgage debt to the value of the land in Hungary in 1866 to have been only between a quarter and a third of that in Italy and less than a third of that in Austria.[5] In an effort to free themselves from Vienna the Hungarian landowners themselves created the Hungarian Land Credit Institute in 1863. The new bank lent at a lower interest rate, 5 per cent, but loans were still large and confined to half the 'real value' of the estate. Since these 'real values' were calculated from land tax returns the loans were in fact much lower. The bank's capital was provided by over 200 estate owners whose own resources acted as a guarantee for the unsubscribed nominal capital. As in Bohemia the model chosen was that of Prussian agriculture and its similar credit institutions. But in Hungary the demand for loans could only be satisfactorily met if such credit institutions attracted large funds, since the more backward state of Hungarian agriculture required heavier capital investment than in Prussia or Bohemia. The government helped with favourable loans, by giving the bank exceptional legal powers to overcome the tenurial difficulties and by exempting its mortgage bonds from taxation. But in the last resort the success of any such institution depended on the interest of foreign capital lenders in Hungarian fixed interest securities, and that was variable and never sufficient.

Smaller landholders were first helped in 1879 by the National Small Holdings Land Mortgage Institute organised on similar lines to the Land Credit Institute, but it suffered from the universal weakness of such institutions, never being able to raise as much capital as a bank for larger landowners. Six years later Raiffeisen banks and co-operatives spread into Hungary. As might be expected they were carefully controlled by the wealthier landholders and had none of the regenerative social aspects of their German counterparts. Even so by the time they were organised into a central body with the help of government funds in 1898 they had 700,000 members. In 1911 all these mortgage and co-operative institutions were amalgamated into a national federation. The new body was provided with larger sums of public money to cope with what was now acknowledged to be the severe political problem of the inequality of land distribution, especially by organising the division and leasing or sale of parts of the big estates held in entails and mortmain. In 1912 alone it bought 7,400 hectares of estate land for sale and leased a further 13,000 hectares. The idea was not merely to appease popular land hunger but also to provide financial support for the large estate owners by helping them to handle the worst and most legally encumbered parts of their estates. With all the restrictions imposed by lack of capital, by law and by the political structure of the country, these credit institutions still played a vital role. The use of machinery on medium-sized farms would not have been possible without the creation of credit institutions of this kind nor without the association and co-operation of smaller farmers which accompanied it.

The whole process of agricultural development depended on the ability to sustain agricultural exports, which at the end of the period were still 51 per cent of all exports. Until the extension of arable agriculture, wool and wood had been the main export commodities. Animal products formed over 40 per cent of exports in 1840 and grains only 18 per cent. As in most of Europe the sheep flocks declined in the face of wool supply from outside the continent. Wood remained a crucial factor in the economy of the large estates, especially those in Croatia. But three-quarters of all exports in 1910 went to the Austrian part of the Empire, and the structure of exports had to accommodate itself to the nature of Austrian demand. When after 1870 non-European and Russian grain at lower prices brought competition to Hungarian farmers they were partly sheltered from the need to readjust by the free market which they enjoyed inside the protective tariffs of the Empire. After 1890 exports of grain outside the Monarchy virtually ceased although the overall level of wheat exports showed only a slight falling trend. Whereas in 1882 68 per cent of grain exports went to Austria, after 1895 the proportion always exceeded 90 per cent. Flour exports followed the same trend and 85 per cent went to Austria by the end of the century. The large estate owners in fact exploited the political arrangements of Austria-Hungary to preserve their income and, since the total output of wheat remained steady after 1895, may also have been exploiting their secure hold on the internal market to keep up prices by restricting output.

It is true that an increasing proportion of this grain was milled into flour and that Hungary derived a valuable impetus to industrialisation from the development of an important flour milling industry. But the question must also be asked whether the existence of so high a level of tariff protection did not in effect serve actively to discourage social and political change by keeping the grain price in Vienna and Budapest so far above world prices. After 1882–4 the rate of increase of exports of meat, pigs and poultry was much faster than that of grain and flour, but because of the high price of animal feeds these exports were equally confined to markets within the Empire. By 1909–13 live animals had come to have an equal value with grain in the composition of agricultural exports. At the same time as the customs union provided an important mechanism for furthering the expansion of agricultural output and exports in Hungary it also became a conservative force, not only discouraging changes in the economic relationships between Hungary and Austria but also helping to maintain the distribution of economic and political power within Hungary.

THE DEVELOPMENT OF THE INDUSTRIAL SECTOR

– Industrialisation, an Overall View

How far had Austria-Hungary in fact gone along the path of industrialisation by 1914? Calculations of the rate of growth of industrial product are by no means complete, but the figures that exist suggest that the annual rate of growth of per capita industrial product between 1841 and 1885 was about 3·2 per cent. After 1880 we are on slightly surer ground in estimating it at 3·4 per cent. These relatively high rates are not to be explained away entirely by the fact that they start from low absolute levels. Industrial output in 1841 was not negligible. National product per capita was roughly 75 per cent of that in the Zollverein, but the gross value of agricultural output per capita by contrast was only about half.[6] Most of the indicators that we might use to suggest the comparative level of industrial development – horse-power of steam engines in use, consumption of coal, output of pig iron and so on – would put Austria-Hungary below the Zollverein in that year with one important exception, the greater size of the Austro-Hungarian cotton industry. But industrialisation began early in the Habsburg Empire and continued, if national aggregates only are considered, successfully but erratically to promote economic development throughout the century. If compared to Germany after 1850 the disparity in the size of per capita industrial output increases sharply until 1890 after which date industrial output in the Austro-Hungarian economy grew at a rate similar to Germany's although the growth rate in Germany was by then achieved on much higher absolute levels of output. This of course, though the obvious political comparison, is the most unfavourable one. Comparisons with earlier industrialising economies like France or Britain would suggest that, certainly after 1890, as far as the industrial sector was concerned Austria-Hungary was closing the development gap. But how wide that gap had become may be judged from the fact that Austria-Hungary produced in 1913 only about 6 per cent of Europe's total industrial output although it was the fourth largest industrial producer on the continent. In terms of per capita output it was behind the Scandinavian countries, Belgium and the Netherlands.

Over the years 1911–13 the agricultural sector was responsible for 49 per cent of the national product. Industry contributed 37·9 per cent and trade and transport 13 per cent. In 1890 62·8 per cent of the population still depended on the agricultural sector for their livelihood, in 1910 55·1 per cent. The proportion of the labour force in industrial employment is more difficult to estimate, but it seems to have increased from about 19·7 per cent in 1890 to 22·6 per cent in 1910. Although Austria-Hungary exhibited most of the obstacles to economic development associated with eastern Europe it was a much more developed economy throughout the nineteenth century than all the other eastern European economies and the main force in that development was the persistent growth of industry. There is also evidence that productivity in the agricultural sector, in spite of the areas of agricultural crisis, was also higher than elsewhere in eastern Europe.

The contribution of different industrial sectors to total industrial output indicates a high contribution from consumer goods industries. The early onset of industrialisation is shown by the relative weight of the textile and clothing industries in 1841 when they contributed 41 per cent of all industrial output. At that date food and drink contributed 18 per cent, industries based on stone, earth and glass 15 per cent and metal producing and working industries 14 per cent. The glass industries of Bohemia and Venice produced high-value luxury products not easily capable of adaptation to wider consumer markets and their overall contribution fell in the nineteenth century. By 1880 textiles and clothing contributed 36 per cent, foodstuffs 28 per cent and metals 13 per cent. In the industrialisation boom after 1890 metallurgical and engineering industries, as everywhere, increased their importance so that by 1911 they contributed 20 per cent; foodstuffs contributed 25 per cent and textiles and clothing 24 per cent. The exploitation of oilfields in Galicia in this last period sharply increased the contribution of the chemical and fuel industries from 4 per cent in 1880 to 10 per cent in 1911. Until 1900 about two-thirds of total industrial production consisted of consumer goods, whereas in France and Germany only about 45 per cent fell under that heading. In spite of the changes brought about by the final boom, 67 per cent of the value added in Austria in 1911–13 was still accounted for by the foodstuffs and textiles industries. There is no support here for the argument that the economic conditions of eastern Europe created a unique market structure; the composition of industrial output in Austria-Hungary was rather an exaggerated version of that of western Europe.

In spite of the persistent industrialisation of the economy the situation in 1913 offers much less cause for optimism both to contemporaries and to the historian than the national aggregate figures would suggest. Especially is this so because of the importance in total output of consumer goods, which were almost entirely dependent on the domestic market where incomes grew only slowly. A more detailed study of industrialisation shows that these national aggregate figures disguise regional differences as enormous as those in the agricultural sector and that the areas of industrial backwardness coincided with those of agricultural backwardness. In large areas of the country the process of industrialisation was so weak that it was unable to drag the agricultural sector after it so that the contribution of some large regions to gross national product remained very small. Only in an abstract sense was economic growth a national phenomenon in Austria-Hungary. These great disparities of regional per capita income suggest that in so protectionist an economy it would have been very difficult to increase or perhaps even sustain the rate of expansion of industrial output. These suspicions are only deepened by observing how spasmodic the process of industrialisation was; for example, the average rate of growth of industrial output for the period 1841–85 includes one period, 1873–8, when industrial output seems to have declined, and these fluctuations were directly related to the lack of buoyancy in the domestic market.

– *The Beginnings of Industrialisation*

In spite of the survival of serfdom until 1848 the legal and governmental framework of Austria from the mid-eighteenth century was more favourable to industrialisation than that of most German states. Serfdom indeed, as may be seen from the example of Russia, was no absolute barrier to industrialisation, particularly the kind of quasi-serfdom which existed in Austria after the reforms of Joseph II which permitted labour mobility. Enlightened despotism had done its work here almost as effectively as in western Europe and by the late eighteenth century Austria had internal free trade and the principles of a common commercial law. The powers of the guilds had been so weakened that entry into most occupations was unrestricted and the struggle for a declaration of *Gewerbefreiheit* did not in any sense have the economic and legal importance which it assumed in Prussia. Cotton printing was declared a free industry in 1773. Within this framework of rationalisation the government extended subsidies and market privileges to foreign and native entrepreneurs in a painstaking attempt to encourage 'manufactures'. The same attitude was responsible for the founding of the technical schools in Prague in 1806 and Graz in 1811 and the Vienna Polytechnic in 1815, the first such institutions outside France.

Most of these 'manufactures' had no more impact on later industrialisation than in Germany, although in the 1830s the woollen industry did draw on the labour and skills which these state-encouraged enterprises had acquired, and the Bohemian glass industry fostered by these means remained important until well into the nineteenth century. But several of the greater Bohemian and Austrian landlords were encouraged to use the capital resources at their disposal to finance industrial enterprises, which they often did to such effect that, as in Prussian Silesia, their estate income became essentially non-agricultural. In Bohemia in particular the great landowners became also the first important group of industrial entrepreneurs. Many of their early attempts at creating their own 'manufactures', such as the cotton cloth production established on his estates at Kosmanos by Count Joseph von Bolza or Count Haugwitz's woollen manufacture, did not die the death of noblemen's hobbies, but survived to become the first factories of the new age. In fact Haugwitz's works at Naměšt became one of the early builders of woollen spinning machinery. Of similar importance were the glassworks of Count Bouquoy on his estate at Gratz or the first large Bohemian sugar refineries, centres of technological experiment, on the lands of Count Salm and the Count of Thurn and Taxis.

But the origins of industrialisation in Austria, although much helped by the actions of an enlightened government and by the response of some of the magnates, were fundamentally a familiar repetition of events in France and Switzerland. Rural domestic textile industries grew up for the same reasons, changed in the eighteenth century to using cotton, began to be mechanised during the continental system, and after a lull caused by the peace in 1814 and the onslaught of cheap British exports, recovered again in the 1820s to pursue once more the path of mechanisation. The important difference is that the Austrian cotton industry was not catering for an export market but for a low-income domestic market and this made for differences in the structure and size of output and the speed of mechanisation.

In the more mountainous districts of Bohemia, the Erzgebirge and the Böhmerwald which separated it from Saxony and Bavaria, the population by the 1760s was already much denser than in the more fertile lowlands. As in western Europe it was in the less fertile areas that domestic industries developed and income from spinning and weaving in many households became more important than agricultural income. Spinners and weavers would pay their servile dues for a licence to collect and distribute yarn and from this position began to perform the entrepreneurial activities of the 'putter-out'. The use of cotton had been actively stimulated by privileged government manufactures in the early eighteenth century and by the start of the Revolutionary wars it was already well-established. The sudden removal of British competition led to the establishment of the first mechanised spinning mills in Bohemia in 1797, using smuggled British machines. They were closely followed by Austrian spinning mills. The Pottendorf spinning mills set up in 1801 had 38,900 spindles in 1811 and were rivalled in size by the Lower Austrian mills at Schwandorf and Klosterneuburg. Vienna was the source of capital and also an important yarn distribution centre. The finishing processes, however, were still performed in rural Bohemia. In fact the flow of mechanisation was on the British rather than the French pattern, starting from the spinning process at the bottom and not flowing downwards from printing. Whereas Alsace and Switzerland in order to get a niche in the export market specialised in finer fabrics than the British producers, only about 5 per cent of Austrian yarn output was in the finer counts because it was destined almost entirely for the lower-income home market. In these circumstances there was none of the striving for technological advance which drove mechanisation forward so rapidly in Alsace, and the subsequent mechanisation of the industry was derivative and leisurely. It was an industry mainly interesting for its relatively large size, but this only reflected the large number of consumers on a protected market.

This protection was not enough to keep out the stream of more cheaply produced foreign yarn after 1814 and from that year until 1820 there were no new spinning mills founded. From the early 1820s onwards, however, the industry resumed its slow but steady development. Land and labour were cheap, the market was there, and machinery easily obtainable from just over the Saxon and Swiss borders. In the province of Vorarlberg cotton spinning was virtually a dependency of the Swiss industry and by this means several Swiss entrepreneurs entered the Empire market. The mills at Neunkirchen which soon became the largest of the Lower Austrian factories, were rescued from collapse in 1819 by a Swiss manufacturer, Vaucher du Pasquier. Several Austrian works bought their machinery from Escher Wyss at Zürich, Bohemian mills bought from Saxony, but the Pottendorf works was making its own spinning machines in the 1820s and also manufacturing for other firms. Hand spinning was not eliminated straight away as in other areas where this process occurred, and lingered on until the 1840s. The spinning mills founded after 1820 were restricted in size; the biggest cotton mill in Bohemia in 1848 employed only 410 workers. The total horse-power of steam engines used in Austria-Hungary by 1841 was still only 1,845 – much less than in Russia. But the number of cotton spindles was greater than in Russia or the Zollverein: in 1843 they were concentrated entirely in the three industrialising areas, 387,500 in Lower Austria, 354,000 in Bohemia and 141,000 in Vorarlberg. A rough calculation, however, suggests that the output per spindle and per worker in the Zollverein was considerably higher than in the Empire so that the lower Zollverein tariffs, while restricting the size of the industry, by permitting foreign competition had also resulted in higher productivity.

The weaving, finishing and printing trades only became established in a small way in Lower Austria. Almost three-quarters of the value of their total output in 1841 came from Bohemia. The largest of the printing works were in Prague and Litoměřice but in other areas there were numerous smaller works where the newer techniques of roller printing came in only slowly. Mechanised weaving came even more slowly being scarcely in evidence at all before the 1850s. But cheap labour and lack of competition, although they acted to preserve domestic weaving, could not save hand spinning which by the end of the 1840s had almost disappeared. Yet even here Hübner calculated that if cotton spinning had operated at British levels of productivity it would have employed 3,625 persons rather than the 23,600 full-time workers it actually employed.[7]

The mechanisation of woollen spinning followed the same timing. It was a process in which the older-established Bohemian urban industry played a more important part. The first recorded machines were smuggled from Britain into Brno in 1802 followed one year later by Cockerill machines from Verviers in Liberěc. As the industry of these towns grew and with it the related activities in the countryside the relative importance of the older state 'manufacture' at Linz declined. It was not the market which gave the advantage to Bohemia and Moravia, for Vienna remained the chief marketing centre where goods were transported to Hungary or elsewhere. The growing branches specialised on coarser cloths whereas the state 'manufactures' had aimed more at prestigious quality production. As with cotton, wool spinners gradually put together enough capital to embark once more on the path of mechanisation in the early 1820s, and those that were in this second wave sometimes became the dominant firms in the industry until 1914. Many of them, typically, were foreigners: the Schoeller brothers who set up their works in Brno in 1820 and had the machines built on site by imported workmen were from Düren in the Rhineland; John Thornton, who had started the Pottendorf works, was from Manchester. Much of the early spinning machinery in Liberěc was made there by the British firm of Thomas and Bracegirdle, already an established business in 1830. It was easier to be assimilated in Austria-Hungary than anywhere else on the continent, while the districts in which these changes were mainly concentrated were both linguistically and economically almost a part of Germany and thus particularly accessible to the operations of financiers and manufacturers from the Zollverein states.

The tendency of most Czech historians has been to overlook the long survival of antiquated methods of production and to see their country as experiencing an industrial revolution like that of Britain early in the nineteenth century. But the pace of mechanisation in wool was slower even than in cotton. In Liberěc in 1841 there were still only two steam engines with a total of 40 horse-power at work. Not until 1880 were there more mechanised woollen spindles there than hand spindles. In Brno in 1850 five-sixths of the output still came from guild workshops. The largest mill in Liberěc, although it had about 3,000 looms at its disposal in 1841, had only 40 mechanical looms, and mechanical weaving remained much less important than hand looms until the 1880s. What happened was a pattern of industrialisation like that in France and Britain but its development was so gradual as to lack any true resemblance to the events of the industrial revolution in those countries. In the iron industry too the important technological changes in western Europe were initially adopted at an early date in Moravia but replaced the older techniques much more gradually.

Bohemia and Moravia established themselves before 1848, because of their early advantages, as the manufacturing centre for the whole of the Empire market. There were already 51,000 woollen spindles in Liberec in 1832 and Brno was a larger centre of production. But per capita incomes were lower in the Empire than in the west and there was no larger export market to compensate. As long as these conditions obtained two consequences followed: that the industrialisation of the Czech provinces would be very protracted, and that it would prevent a similar process occurring in any other province apart from Lower Austria where Vienna was situated.

– Railways

To change this situation it was open to the state either to invest its own resources more heavily in the development of the country, or to try to compensate for the weakness of the consumer goods market by deliberately creating a demand for capital goods. The railway provided a means of combining these alternatives; as in all the more backward economies it was early and eagerly appreciated as a means of catching up with the more industrialised states.

The 53 kilometres of railway built in 1832 from Linz on the Danube to České Budějovice on the Vltava, intended to provide a direct freight link to the Elbe and thence to Hamburg, can lay good claims to being the first railway of any length on the continent. But until 1854 it was operated for its whole length by horses. Even so the alacrity with which it was financed by Viennese private bankers showed that in a more backward setting such private banks would be less reluctant to finance railway developments than their fellows in Paris and Frankfurt. Sporadic private initiatives of this kind had provided 473 kilometres of track by 1841. The main venture was financed by the Rothschild group – the Nordbahn linking Vienna with the German railway system through Silesia. But anticipating the railway legislation in France and Prussia, the state intervened in December 1841 reserving to itself the planning, building and operating of a network. The Nordbahn, completed in 1848, remained private, but until 1854 most construction was undertaken by the government. By that date the government had built 1,000 kilometres of the 1,433 kilometres in use. But the rate of increase by now was much slower than in France and Germany. After 1854 policy was reversed. Private concessions were awarded for ninety-year periods and a minimum rate of return on the investment guaranteed. The state began to sell off its own lines.

The railway boom of the 1850s was financed in Austria-Hungary in the same way as in western Europe, with the creation of large new joint stock financial institutions copying the example of the Crédit Mobilier; so also was the second great spurt of railway building from 1867 to 1873. The state's only contribution was to subsidise rail imports. This was the period in which all the major main lines were built. From the start of 1867 to the end of 1872 over 7,600 kilometres of new track were laid down, a greater rate of building than anywhere else on the continent. By 1873 all the main towns of Austria-Hungary except those of the Dalmatian coast were connected with Vienna, Budapest and the outside world.

The stock market crash of 1873 brought railway building to a standstill by cutting off the stream of private investment. So great had the importance of railways become in the economy that the government was soon persuaded to attempt to reverse the falling trend of industrial production by financing railway construction directly and once again taking the system under state control. The railway programme of 1875 allocated 23 million kroner of state credit to build the Danube bank railway, the Arlberg line and the so-called Bohemian transversal railway. The responsibility for construction now fell directly on the government and after 1877 it began to buy back the private lines which were in the worst difficulties. By 1913 over three-quarters of the system was government-owned. After 1873, therefore, railway finance was mainly provided by means of the public debt of the government, a large part of which continued to be owned by the Viennese bankers but some of which was owned by foreign banks and individuals.

State involvement after 1875 sustained the rate of railway construction at a high level; 8,000 kilometres of track were added to the system in the 1880s, which was as much as the net addition between 1850 and 1870. With an equivalent addition in the following decade the Austro-Hungarian system became almost as large as that of France by 1900 and, by 1913, with 43,280 kilometres, was surpassed in size only by those of Russia and Germany. Much of this later development was in Hungary where the government provided greater incentives for building. This mixture of private and state financing, while it was unable in mid-century to equal the achievements of the western powers, produced by 1913 a network which, judged on length and density alone, was little inferior. The lines were by no means equally distributed. There were 10 square kilometres of area to each kilometre of track in Bohemia in 1914, 28 in Galicia and more than 100 in Dalmatia. But, on a national level, railway construction did achieve many of the desired multiplier effects.

Moravian iron works were already producing rail in 1840 and the Carinthian works followed ten years later. Almost from the outset a high proportion of the locomotives was built in the country, although at first often by foreigners such as Joseph Hall who organised the Graz locomotive works for the Südbahn and John Haswell, a Scottish engineer, who organised and ran the workshops of the Nordbahn at Tabor. There were also native machine manufacturers who converted to locomotive construction, the most important being the Wiener Neustadt works of W. Günther. These developments also, however, were confined at first to Lower Austria and the Czech lands. No rail was made in Hungary until 1867 and the first locomotive only in 1873.

The multiplier effect of railway construction did not in any case operate in ratio to the length of track constructed. The Austro-Hungarian railways, as Table 52 indicates, used less rail, because there was more single-track line and fewer sidings, used less locomotives and rolling stock and carried less freight in relation to their length than the western systems. The weight of freight traffic transported in any year after 1900 was far less than on the German system and the costs of carriage were higher. In part this reflected the awkward shape of the country, in part the irrationalities imposed on the network by national rivalries and in part the attempt by the state to recoup the costs of construction in a situation where on certain long hauls which were strategically and politically necessary the traffic was inevitably light. Some Vienna firms could deliver goods more cheaply in Buenos Aires, shipping them via Hamburg, than in Czernowitz

Table 52 *Amount of rolling stock per 100 km of railway track in certain countries, 1911–13*

	Locomotives	Passenger cars	Goods wagons
Austria (1913)	33	67	652
Hungary (1913)	20	43	465
Germany (1912)	47	106	1,066
France (1911)	33	76	886
Britain (1911)	61	141	2,091
Belgium (1911)	98	182	2,060

Source: F. Hertz, *Die Produktionsgrundlagen der österreichischen Industrie vor und nach dem Krieg* (Vienna, 1917), p. 68.

(Chernovtsy) in Bukovina. Rivalry between Austria and Hungary prevented any direct rail link between Austria and Dalmatia or Bosnia, and made impossible all the plans for constructing a network in Bosnia and Hercegovina to forward the development of those provinces. The foreign trade of the Czech regions went in any case through Germany to Hamburg. All circumstances combined to make the question of railway rates one of nightmarish complexity and prevented the railways from being used in any straightforward way to further the development of the whole country. The benefits of building this large network were for all these reasons less than had been hoped for.

– *The Iron and Steel Industry*

The most obvious impact of railway construction was on the production of iron and the consumption of coal. The Alpine provinces were an old-established centre of European iron manufacturing with a large trade in sickles, scythes and bar iron. Styria and Carinthia remained responsible for about 60 per cent of the value of iron output in Austria-Hungary until 1880, but for the whole of that time charcoal smelting remained the basis of their operations and the traditional market in agricultural implements was vital to them. Technological change began in a smaller area of production, Moravia. The first experiments with the puddling process took place in the Czech lands in the 1830s and in 1836 the Vitkovice works successfully put into operation the coke smelting process in two blast furnaces. This important step was directly related to the beginning of railway construction; the necessary changes were financed by the Rothschild group to cater for their Nordbahn and the Vitkovice works henceforward became tied to their large railway interests in Austria-Hungary. Once again the briskness of these beginnings was not matched by the pace of later developments. It was not until 1856 that there was another coke smelting furnace, at Kladno, and between 1844 and the mid-1860s the proportion of pig iron smelted by coke remained fixed at about one-quarter. Foreign iron was sold more cheaply than domestic iron, the native ore supply was not satisfactory and the coking coals had to be transported from the Ostrova field in Austrian Silesia. Total output of pig iron in 1865 had risen only to 292,000 tons.

Only a small breakthrough came with the great spurt of railway building between 1867 and 1873. In 1873 pig iron output had climbed to 535,000 tons. This was still only about 60 per cent of total consumption but the effects of the increase in demand could be seen from the introduction of the first Bessemer converters, in 1866 in Vitkovice and in 1869 in Kladno. These developments were forced on the manufacturers by the demand for steel rail in a protected economy, although the only suitably non-phosphoric ore resources were to be found in Styria. The numerous experiments in de-phosphorisation were not very successful. When the crash of 1873 came the effects were disastrous; pig iron output fell by more than half between 1873 and 1877 and although imports now diminished after the surge of rail imports at the start of the 1870s it was not until 1881 that domestic output again reached its 1873 level. The collapse of the market for rail meant that charcoal-smelted iron, responsible for about one-third of total output in Moravia and Silesia in 1875, accounted for almost 60 per cent in 1877. The growth in output there had basically depended on rail and castings for railway construction and only as the government's deliberate stimulation of railway construction began to take effect did it recover. It needed the buoyancy of railway construction in the 1880s to complete the technological changes which had started almost fifty years before.

This revival of the market coincided with the introduction of the Gilchrist–Thomas process permitting the use of the local Bohemian and Moravian low-grade high-phosphorous ores for steelmaking. Both

Kladno and Vitkovice were among the first European firms to use the new process, one year after its invention, and the same period saw a start on the exploitation of the Nučič ore beds in Bohemia. At the same time the Alpine industry resumed its experiments with coke smelting which had been cut short in 1873. The small firms were reorganised under bank pressure into a large combine, the Österreichisch-Alpinen Montangesellschaft, in order to cope with the transition to the new processes. Charcoal smelting did not die out; the new iron works built at Vares in Bosnia in 1891 was designed to use charcoal, but wood was very cheap there. After 1880 Austria-Hungary rapidly developed a large modern iron and steel industry using the Gilchrist–Thomas and Siemens–Martin processes almost exclusively. The output of Bessemer steel declined after 1880. Total output of steel reached one million tons in 1895 and by 1913 was over the 2 million ton mark. The shift to the Gilchrist–Thomas process and low-grade Bohemian ore also meant a great shift in the importance of the regions. In 1878 Bohemia and Moravia still only made 23 per cent of Austro-Hungarian pig iron; in 1897 they made 57 per cent of the much larger quantity manufactured and this proportion was slightly increased by 1913.

But if this cheap steel industry is compared with a similar contemporary development, that in Lorraine, its success even after such long travails is clouded. The cost of making a ton of comparable Gilchrist–Thomas steel at Vitkovice in 1899 was 23 per cent higher than the average for Lorraine and Luxembourg and at Kladno 18 per cent higher. Only in the works built in 1897 at Servola near Trieste to use imported ores were manufacturing costs comparable to France or Germany. The Moravian works used local coke but the Bohemian works imported coke from German Silesia and the Styrian works had to pay the haulage on coke from Austrian Silesia. Conversely the Moravian works imported ore from a wide variety of sources, only the Bohemian works using the Nučič beds. Without the high level of protection and the market provided by government stimulation of railways from the mid-1870s and by rearmament and naval building after 1890 these changes could not have taken place so rapidly and completely. Supplies of raw materials were of course deficient, but coal was relatively cheap in most parts of Bohemia and Moravia throughout the period, and by 1856 was used for all refining processes. The forge owners were often large landlords with capital also invested in the production of wood and charcoal and the forges remained after 1880 on the same sites and not very conveniently placed for coal. But it was the narrowness and uncertainty of the market that spun the process out so long. Even in 1883 rail production accounted for 40 per cent of pig iron output and it was only after that date that industrialisation developed sufficiently to provide a more general demand for the industry's output. Until then the more traditional demand from the agricultural sector never warranted the largest part of the Austro-Hungarian iron industry abandoning the charcoal smelting process.

– Coal

The small number of steam engines before 1850 and the perseverance with charcoal smelting meant that the railways had an even more direct impact on the demand for coal. Their consumption was supplemented by the demand after 1850 from sugar and iron refiners. Some writers suggest that Austria-Hungary, in spite of its size, was actually deficient in raw materials and that the lack of coal in particular retarded the industrialisation process. Such an argument cannot easily be sustained. The combined output of coal and lignite surpassed that of France in the 1880s and was always larger than that of Russia, amounting to more than 50 million tons annually before 1914. In the industrialising areas the price of coal to manufacturers was, apart from the price of labour, almost the only

Table 53   *Annual percentage rate of growth of output and consumption of coal in Austria-Hungary, 1831–1913*

	Rate of growth of Austrian consumption	Rate of growth of Hungarian consumption	Rate of growth of Austrian output	Rate of growth of Hungarian output
1831–73	9·6	n.a.		
1831–50	8·6	n.a.		
1851–73	10·4	11·5	10·3	11·3
1871–1913	3·8	5·5	3·7	4·5
1882–1900	4·1	7·3		
1900–13	3·6	4·8		

Source: N. Gross, 'Economic Growth and the Consumption of Coal in Austria and Hungary 1831–1913', in *Journal of Economic History*, vol. XXXI, 1971.

element in their costs which was not higher than in western Europe. The most industrialised areas were virtually self-sufficient in coal until after 1900 when with the increasing pace of industrialisation net imports of hard coal developed, though these were offset by exports of lignite from the Most area across the border to Saxony. However, the attempts by the Hungarian government to foster industrialisation did eventually necessitate coal imports to satisfy Hungarian needs. Table 53 shows that in the Austrian lands coal production kept pace perfectly with consumption even when consumption was growing most quickly, but in Hungary after 1896 production was only two-thirds of consumption.

The level of coal consumption in Hungary was only about one-fifth of the national total so that net coal imports into the Dual Monarchy were not high. The high internal freight rates acted to modify the high rate of tariff protection so that in coastal and border areas German coal could sell more cheaply than domestic coal, and as the coal mining booms in Germany and Britain after 1906 kept coal prices relatively low the tendency was for even Austrian imports to grow. In 1911–13 net hard coal imports into Austria of 8·3 million tons were balanced against net lignite exports of 3·6 million tons. It is true that domestic coals, excepting those from Silesia, were not well-suited to the coke smelting process, but there were certainly more important factors than this holding back that particular change. Only in 1880 did the total horse-power of steam engines in the Austro-Hungarian economy surpass that in Russia and at that time it was still less than half the steam horse-power employed in France, both of which were countries no better endowed with cheaply mined and conveniently situated coal supplies.

– Foodstuff Industries

Railway building, although it did eventually give rise to important steel and coal industries, only did so on any scale after 1880, in contrast to the rapid developments in the Zollverein where these industries became leading sectors in growth after 1852. In Austria-Hungary the process of industrialisation continued to depend after mid-century on the gradual growth of consumer goods production, with all the limitations which the low level of per capita incomes implied. But that there were possibilities of continuing development on that basis is shown by the changes which took space in some food processing industries.

Of these the industry that offered most possibilities was sugar refining, which provided a valuable export over a long period of time. It was an excellent example of the power of autonomous development, springing as it did from the natural agricultural conditions of Bohemia, and apart from its foreign trade value it also had a valuable multiplier effect on the economy. Julius Robert, the son of the founder of the first refinery at Zidlochovice, discovered there the diffusion process in 1864, the technological basis of the modern beet industry. By the end of 1867 the new process had spread to a further twenty-seven refineries. It was accompanied by a variety of mechanical changes – better filters, more efficient washing plant and so on – most of which also originated in Bohemia. In this field, therefore, Czech machine makers were able to establish a brief but clear advantage and before 1870 were exporting sugar refining machinery to Germany and France. This was the basis of what was later one of the two largest Austro-Hungarian engineering firms, Danek, which between 1862 and 1872 built eighty-six new sugar refineries. Average sugar production per refinery rose from about 1,000 tons in 1871–2 to 6,481 tons in 1913–14. The new technology also instigated a great increase in the demand for hard coal. The total output of sugar beet after its setback in the mid-1870s continued to rise, averaging 9·5 million tons annually in the last decade of the period. Of this output the proportion refined into sugar for export continued to increase, reaching 58 per cent in 1883 and 72 per cent in 1910. After wood sugar was the second most important export of Austria-Hungary: 3·6 per cent of exports in 1875 and 9·3 per cent in 1910. After 1870 sugar refining also developed in Hungary but the weight of production remained in Bohemia, reinforcing there both industrialisation and higher agricultural productivity.

In Hungary similarly autonomous developments took place in flour milling. As wheat cultivation spread, Budapest, as the market whence it was shipped to Vienna or Bohemia, became an important milling centre. It was also the place where Romanian wheat with the same destinations was milled. This type of development was universal in nineteenth-century Europe and Budapest was only repeating a pattern which had evolved earlier in Austria. The flour mills built by the Schoeller brothers in 1853 at Ebenfurth in Austria were at that time the biggest on the continent. This again reflected the size of the market, but in capturing this market Budapest had the advantages of good transport and of being the financial and business heart of the greatest wheat growing area. To these natural advantages was added an element of deliberate subsidisation by the Hungarian government. Millers were allowed duty-free wheat if it was for export, and shipments to Austria were counted as exports. The first of the mechanised Budapest flour mills was built in 1839. In the 1850s five more large flour mills were built in the city and between 1862 and 1867 five more. The early mills made very high profits out of which they financed further expansion so that their total capacity in the 1870s would have been sufficient to mill one-third of Hungary's grain harvest. This striving after size developed an important engineering industry in the city to cater to the millers' needs. It was in the first of the large mills that Ganz, founder of the city's most famous engineering works, came to work and later it was the manufacture of milling machinery for export that first built his firm's reputation.

Only a small proportion of the flour was for export outside Austria-Hungary. The rapid growth of the flour milling industry in Budapest was in fact precisely the type of regional specialisation that tariff protection of a common market might be expected to encourage, although it was not without help from the Hungarian government. The proportion of Hungarian flour 'exports' compared to wheat 'exports' continued to grow until 1900 when, like the amount of wheat grown, it seemed to hit a ceiling which may well have represented a point of stability, satisfactory to Hungarian interests in the closed economy. Viennese and Bohemian grain millers were unable to compete adequately after the mid-1850s and the Budapest millers took an undisturbed hold on the market, beginning the slow industrialisation of another region. From 1882–6 to 1892–6 total flour shipments out of Hungary, as Table 54 indicates, showed their greatest increase since the start of the industry and after that date remained higher than shipments of wheat.

Developments of this kind tend to indicate that per capita incomes were growing, although not necessarily in all regions. The output of beer in Bohemia from 1850 to 1870 grew by 54 per cent and this developed a brewing industry there which by the latter date was no longer merely an ancillary process of the agricultural sector. The use of steam engines and certain technological improvements in the production of chilled lager beer made Plzeň one of the main centres of European brewing. But this change was once again confined to the north-west where most of the structural changes and improvements in the market were taking place.

Table 54 *Shipments of flour out of Hungary as a proportion of shipments of wheat, from 1882–6 to 1897–1901 (per cent)*

1882–6	1892–6	1897–1901
59·5	99·0	133·5

Source: Derived from P. Sándor, 'Die Agrarkrise des 19 Jahrhunderts und der Grossgrundbesitz in Ungarn', in *Studia Historica*, no. 51, 1961.

– Industrial Development after 1880

After 1880 this autonomous development of consumer goods industries continued at the same slow pace, but now came together with a number of other economic forces, the growth of a larger capital goods market caused by the increase in railway construction, the drive by the Hungarian government to industrialise the Hungarian lands, and the exogenous impetus to development provided by foreign capital. The result of these forces was to bring about an average rate of growth of industrial output for Austria-Hungary until 1913 of 4·05 per cent annually. This growth was not free from strong cyclical fluctuations but no more slumps as bad as that of 1873–8 occurred. The Austro-Hungarian economy benefited greatly in this respect from its close connections with Germany, which was by far its most important trading partner. The fact that the decade of the 1880s was a period of economic expansion in Germany helped to insulate Austria-Hungary from the depressed business climate elsewhere in Europe over these years. Furthermore the less violent nature of cyclical fluctuations in the German economy between 1880 and 1914 tended also to even out the fluctuations in Austria-Hungary and to provide a slightly less volatile setting than in earlier years. Cartels and similar devices to restrain competition became even more firmly established in Austria-Hungary than in Germany since there was less foreign competition on the internal market and their effect was to smooth out the swings of the trade cycle. In 1885 industrial production fell slightly after slowing down in the previous year. The fall, and the preceding boom of 1880–3, seem to have been mainly occasioned by fluctuations in sugar exports and the output of the foodstuffs industries, which could still not be counterbalanced by the newer developing industries. But from the recovery in 1888 there was a continuous growth of industrial output, which slackened from 1900 to 1903 but was followed by a great surge of growth over the period 1903–8. The consumer goods industries showed no faster growth over this period than between 1880 and 1900 and the main contribution was made by capital goods industries, especially metallurgy and engineering. From 1880 to 1900 in Austria the annual average rate of growth of output in the engineering industry was 13·3 per cent and in metal industries 8·3 per cent; by contrast foodstuff industries grew at 3·7 per cent a year and textile industries at 2·7 per cent. But the growth of the textile industries was in fact concentrated almost wholly into the decade of the 1880s. It was the capital goods industries, responding to government construction programmes and to foreign capital, which after 1890 were becoming the driving force in the economy. Although the combined rate of growth of the two major consumer sectors was only slightly below the average rate of growth of Austrian industrial product, the scanty figures for Hungary suggest that if they were included they would bias the national aggregate results much more in favour of the capital goods sector.

But the basic weaknesses which had produced the crash in 1873 still produced fluctuations in industrial output. The slowing down in 1900 was associated with poor harvests. The upswing of 1903 was associated with an improvement in agricultural incomes. The textile industry in Austria grew at 4·1 per cent annually from 1905 to 1912; it was also in this period that most of the growth occurring in the foodstuffs industries after 1900 was concentrated. Engineering and metals now grew at a slower rate – just over 5·0 per cent annually. But at the height of the boom, 1904 to 1908, the capital goods industries still grew much more rapidly than consumer goods and kept the economy buoyant. Employment in iron and steel in this period grew by 33 per cent and in engineering and metal goods production by 40 per cent. The basis of this was Prime Minister von Koerber's costly railway and public works programme. It seems that the two sectors of industry were still affected by different conditions, the output of consumer goods being still basically determined by conditions in the agricultural sector while the main force for growth was the response of the capital goods sector to the activities of the state. After 1903 this distinction was less clear because of the more rapid growth of the cotton industry; nevertheless by 1914 the spasmodic growth producing activities of the state were still being held back by the low level of per capita incomes on the domestic market and the brake which this imposed on consumer goods production.

The growth of the engineering industry after 1880 was mainly based on an increase in the output of those products already produced. There was not much that was new, and specialised machines, mainly from Germany, were a large item on the import bill until 1914. The annual average number of locomotives built in Hungary over the years 1874–83 was less than eight; over the years 1884–94 it was sixty. Sugar refining and milling machinery were likewise produced in larger quantities after 1880. Breitfeld, Danek, one of the biggest companies, employed 1,300 at most in the early 1890s and 4,500 by 1909. An equally rapid expansion was that of the Škoda company, which began as a firm manufacturing mainly sugar machinery and went on to make steel in 1889 and armaments in 1890. Henceforward it was intimately connected with the growth of the Austro-Hungarian armed forces and became one of the major European armaments firms. On the outbreak of war in 1914 it was building a new steel mill in Russia for the Nevsky armament works. Following a similar path the Manfred Weiss food canning company in Budapest, founded in 1884, had become by 1900 an important munitions manufacturer. One firm, however, was particularly innovative, the Budapest firm of Ganz, but the mainsprings of their innovation came from Germany. German was the language of engineering and in the Hungarian Technical University was the language in which the subject was taught; it was also the language of the Ganz firm and of Abraham Ganz himself, originally an immigrant from Switzerland. When the firm first began to produce electrical machinery in 1878 it was closely following similar developments in German companies. By the 1880s it had become a leading European manufacturer of turbines, making about forty a year in the 1880s and sixty a year in the 1890s. Four-fifths of the electrical machinery made was exported and the firm built the first power stations in Milan and Rome. By 1895 it employed over 6,000 workers.

The expansion of the electrical and chemical industries in Germany inevitably brought a surge of activity in the same sectors in Austria-Hungary. The supply of electric power to Vienna was undertaken by the German firm Siemens-Halske and it was the operations of such firms that created the market for engineering companies like Ganz. But in the chemical sector Austria-Hungary had one resource, crude oil, which attracted wider interest. Crude oil output in Galicia showed a steady upward trend from 32,000 tons a year in 1880 to 97,000 tons in 1889; by 1901 it had risen to 452,000 tons and in 1909, the peak year, had reached 2 million. The first refinery had been built in Vienna in 1862 and its small output exported to Germany but it was only after 1890 that the international oil companies began to finance developments in Galicia on a large scale and a market developed for drilling and refining equipment.

However, these newer industries remained by 1914 relatively unimportant beside the expansion of the older sectors.

The number of cotton spindles in Austria increased only gradually from 1·33 million in 1851 to 2·17 million in 1885. After that date it grew much more rapidly, reaching 4·96 million in 1913. In Hungary the textile industries remained very small and this suggests that the growth of per capita incomes was still not sufficient to break the fixed pattern of regional specialisation in consumer goods production in Austria-Hungary which had grown up early in the century. The spinning industry in Vienna survived because of the market there but the cotton by now often came through Bohemia from America and the spun yarn went back to Bohemia. Cotton, coal and labour were cheaper in the Czech lands. In fact in the boom after 1903 there were still examples in the German areas of Bohemia of small entrepreneurs successfully developing medium-sized spinning firms by ploughing back profits, a process reminiscent of the early nineteenth century.

The rate of increase in cotton consumption per capita between 1901 and 1913, although much more rapid than in Britain or Germany, was equalled in France and exceeded in one or two more backward countries, particularly in Italy. The output still remained concentrated on coarser cloths for the domestic market. Wages were lower than among the larger producers and, except for some parts of Britain and the Rhineland, coal was cheaper. But machinery and transport were more expensive. There never developed in Austria-Hungary the network of wholesale cotton trading and exporting houses that might have distributed Bohemian cloths in larger quantities on international markets. This had serious internal effects also. Weaving remained for a long time under the control of the Vienna yarn dealers with the consequence that cotton firms were less frequently integrated than elsewhere, weaving remaining a specialised and smaller-scale activity. The increase in spindles was not accompanied by a corresponding increase in finished output and by 1913 about 30 per cent of the yarn produced was exported, a lot of it to the cheapest markets, Turkey, Romania and Serbia. The export value of finished cottons in 1913, in spite of a steep increase after 1911, was just over half the value of Italian exports, less than one-fifth those of Germany and one thirty-sixth those of Britain. Since more expensive cloths as well as cotton were imported the net export surplus produced by the cotton industry was extremely small, again distinguishing Austria-Hungary from all other significant producers except Russia.

In the other consumer goods industries growth was less and the major changes still concentrated in the north-east. In 1905 Tomaš Bata returned from the United States to his native Moravian town of Zlin and using German machines and American production methods began to corner the cheap footwear market of the whole Empire. Even this striking example of entrepreneurial initiative was only repeating the pattern of the industrialisation of one region at the expense of others which the restrictions of the domestic market had imposed on Bohemian cotton spinners a century before. The fundamentals of the economic situation had not changed.

– The Industrialisation of Hungary

Before 1867 industrialisation in Hungary was virtually confined to the milling industry and to a few early metallurgical ventures sponsored by the railway companies. In 1870 only 8·6 per cent of the labour force was employed in the industrial sector. But by 1910 this had risen to 17·1 per cent and the structure of the Hungarian economy had become significantly different from that of the other undeveloped territories of the Dual Monarchy. Dissatisfied with the slow pace of development generated from the agricultural sector the Hungarian government turned increasingly to promoting industrial development. The pattern of industrialisation showed significant differences from that elsewhere. Firstly textiles were less important than in any other industrialising country so far considered; secondly the importance of state action in stimulating growth in the capital goods sector was greater. These two facts raise certain issues about the development of eastern European economies in general which are discussed later in the chapter, but because of the existence of the customs union it would be wrong to compare the structure of Hungarian manufacturing industry too closely with that of other states. Hungarian industry tended to develop in areas where the competition from the rest of the Empire allowed it to develop, except in the few fields where government protection could shelter it despite the absence of a tariff.

The real importance of the market created by the state emerged during the railway boom of 1867–73. The output of iron ore and coal doubled in this period and the first steelmaking processes were introduced. The building of a new Siemens–Martin steelworks at Diósgyör was financed by the Hungarian government in 1868 to meet the increased demand for rail and by 1913, when it employed 8,000 workers, it had become only a part of the State Iron Works, the second largest steel producer in Hungary. From the earlier period the Staatsbahn still owned large iron ore and coal mines, rail making plant and carriage shops. Together with the Danube Steamship Navigation Company the nationalised railway system owned for a long time most of the hard coal mines in Hungary. The first locomotives were made in 1873 by the State Railway Machine Works. It is estimated that by 1907 the government purchased 13 per cent of industrial output in Hungary and in the machine building sector as much as one-third. In fact the importance of the railway and of Danube shipping may be seen from the fact that two-thirds of the output of machinery in 1900 was represented by transport equipment. Private railway investment was of course still continuing but it is clear that the government's railway building programmes were now the prime force in industrialisation in Hungary; it was often only through government intervention that the multiplier effect of railway building functioned.

Furthermore in Hungary it was only government intervention and support that created a textile industry. In 1881 the state had first made its intention to subsidise and encourage industry in its own territory explicit by legislation offering tax exemptions to entrepreneurs establishing new factories. As it became increasingly clear that spontaneous development from the agricultural sector would not proceed fast enough to keep Hungary abreast of other western European economies this programme of state action expanded until it embraced policies which are now frequently adopted by underdeveloped countries. By 1890 interest-free loans were available and by 1899 tax rebates and loans for extensions to existing works. By 1907 the state had given itself a free hand in subsidising all developments it wished to encourage even to the extent of buying and holding shares in new enterprises. It took from entrepreneurs the burden of providing workers' houses, roads, schools, sidings and all the other forms of social overhead capital which were still so short in Hungary. In the allocation of these subsidies 57 per cent of those for new enterprises went to the textile industry. Numerous foreign and Austrian entrepreneurs were attracted and the number of cotton spindles increased from a mere 110,000 in 1900 to 500,000 in 1913. The government's intention was to use these subsidies in lieu of a tariff to promote import substitution, and in this it was successful. The textile industry, which covered only 14 per cent of domestic consumption in 1900, could meet 70 per cent of the demand by 1913. The two industries showing the biggest increase in employment after 1899 were clothing and textiles.

Yet the modernity and interest of this type of government legislation can easily lead to an exaggeration of its importance at the time. At the height of the programme, 1900–14, state subsidies were still only 6 per cent of the capital invested in joint stock companies. Their total sum was less than that of the volume of 'foreign' (including Austrian) capital invested in Hungary over the period when this legislation was in force. Nevertheless the state was, by its actions, forcing the growth of industry within those patterns it desired to create and at the same time providing a much more favourable climate for unsubsidised private investment. On the other hand it was also introducing an element of protected irrationality into the otherwise rational allocation of resources which the customs union theoretically encouraged. In doing so its motives were unashamedly nationalistic: the promotion of an independent and developed Hungarian national economy.

How far had this aim been achieved by 1914? The average annual rate of growth of industrial production between 1870 and 1900 was 6·2 per cent; from 1900 to 1913 5·1 per cent, which was faster than in the rest of the Empire. The gap in per capita incomes between Hungary and Austria closed between the mid-century, when Hungarian incomes were about 60 per cent of Austrian incomes, and 1913 when they were about

75 per cent. By 1914 the country produced about 13 million tons of hard coal, 89 million tons of lignite and 800,000 tons of steel within its own territories. Within the Dual Monarchy it was now responsible for between a fifth and a quarter of total industrial output, which, although by European standards it left Hungary a quite insignificant producer, had laid the basis for a separate industrialised economy. This determined effort at national economic development posed several difficulties for the Empire as a whole. One of the most serious was its effect on the regional pattern of industrialisation which had been established within the framework of an overall Imperial self-sufficiency. In spite of the fact that the expansion of manufacturing industry in the Empire as a whole after 1880 ultimately reduced dependence on manufactured imports and helped the balance of payments, in the periods of rapid growth in Hungary the cost of manufactured imports into the Empire rose. Austrian industry could not supply all Hungary's needs, especially in machinery, and at the same time Hungarian industrialisation was eroding the quasi-monopolistic position of Austrian industrialists.

FOREIGN TRADE AND THE BALANCE OF PAYMENTS

The lowering of tariffs in Austria-Hungary after 1852 and the subsequent involvement in European trade treaties had little effect on foreign trade and its per capita level remained very low. At least ten European countries, including Italy, had a higher level of exports per capita in 1913. The return to protection and to autonomous tariffs was a return to the long tradition of the Empire and after 1873 this was only momentarily disturbed by the reductions in German tariff levels in 1891. But the idea of a central European customs union embracing Germany and Austria-Hungary could never again be buried after the Austrian attempts to instigate it in 1850, so that throughout the period of high Austro-Hungarian protection the concept of a 'Germanic' common market was still widely and publicly canvassed, reinforced by Germany's domination of Austro-Hungarian foreign trade. In 1891 Germany (excluding Hamburg) took 47 per cent of the Empire's exports, and in 1913 38 per cent. In the intervening period the proportion of exports to Britain and her colonies and to Turkey and the Balkans increased, each of these regions taking about 14 per cent by 1913. Throughout the whole period Germany supplied between 30 and 40 per cent of all imports. For all the major export commodities except yarn, and that only for the last decade, it was the German market that counted and Germany in turn dominated in the supply of semi-manufactured and manufactured goods to the Empire.

But the rock on which the common market proposals always foundered was the growing disparity in per capita income levels in the two countries;

the Austro-Hungarian market was simply not a good enough market for Germany really to gain from such sweeping tariff adjustments. Faced with this fact the Empire could only revert to the tradition of development on the basis of its own resources. Such a policy was by no means entirely fanciful and even in a rapid period of growth such as 1867–73, in spite of the surge of rail imports, there were no serious balance of payments problems arising to slow down that growth.

Until the end of the period the structure of Austro-Hungarian trade was still one in which the most valuable exports came from the agricultural sector, particularly sugar and wood. But the structure of imports showed more clearly the changes that had taken place during the century. Cotton was the most valuable import after 1875, with wool also very important, the two textile fibres together accounting for 5·5 per cent of imports in 1875 and 7·7 per cent in 1910. With the growing industrialisation after 1880 imports of coal and coke and of machines became larger than imports of 'colonial' goods such as coffee. This was mostly due to the extra demand from Hungary which was far from self-sufficient in industrial raw materials and rail. After 1909 there was a substantial trade deficit, and balance of payments difficulties were now only averted by the heavy inflow of foreign capital and the great increase in emigrants' remittances which followed the mass emigration from the poorer areas after 1890. After 1911 emigrants' remittances were the largest single credit item on the balance of payments.

The balance of commodity trade became negative both because of the increased demand arising from industrialisation and because, as industrialisation continued, the Empire ceased to be self-sufficient in food. The export surplus of agricultural produce and processed foodstuffs developed after 1867 and reached its peak in 1889. By 1897 it had sunk again to its level of the mid-1870s. By this time the diversification of production had led also to a diversification of exports so that in spite of the continued drop in agricultural exports total exports continued to increase, with the exception of the period 1907–11. Between 1876 and 1891 imports had grown at only half the rate of exports, but after this date they began to grow faster than exports, particularly after 1900. The Empire was becoming a net importer of raw materials. The penalties of slower economic development throughout the century were felt particularly acutely because of the close trading relationship with Germany. German mining output was more than six times greater than that of Austria-Hungary and German exports of raw materials to the Empire were growing after 1900 almost as quickly as those of manufactured goods. In constant prices imports of industrial raw materials into Austria-Hungary between 1903 and 1913 increased by 76 per cent whereas into Germany, where the rate of increase of industrial production was similar, they increased by only 46 per cent. At the same time output in the agricultural sector was neither providing sufficient exports to obtain foreign exchange nor even keeping pace with increasing domestic demand. At the very least this was one contributing factor to the deteriorating balance of payments after 1900.

CAPITAL, BANKS AND THE ROLE OF THE STATE

We have laid stress throughout this chapter on the importance of state activity in generating an increase in capital goods production. At the same time we have also stressed that in consumer goods production most of the development which took place was self-generated. It is frequently argued that the possibilities of economic development in Europe should be seen in terms of a west–east continuum: the further west the country the easier the possibilities of self-generated, autonomous economic development; the further east, the greater the need for the state to intervene directly in the process of development by subsidising industrialisation and even by functioning as an important consumer of what was produced. If Hungary is regarded as a separate national entity, rather than as a region in a customs union, this west–east difference may certainly be observed within the Habsburg Empire itself because the role of the state's actions was more crucial in Hungary. This general view of the problems of European economic development is expounded in its most sophisticated form by Gerschenkron.[8] He suggests that only in Britain was economic development entirely self-generated. Elsewhere in western and central Europe the lower level of capital accumulation and the greater volume of capital investment therefore required necessitated the prior development of large new financial institutions, the investment banks, which could collect capital and bear the risk of modernising the economy. In eastern Europe, he suggests, not even this solution was possible because of the greater backwardness. There the only answer was for the state itself to undertake the task of economic development.

It has to be said in the first place that this is a very simplified view of what happened in western Europe and in Germany. The role of the state in Germany, as indicated in our earlier work, was important in a different way, in eliminating the obstacles to self-generated economic development. We suggested also that the importance of large investment banks was mainly determined by the type of technology on which development was based. They were crucial in Germany because of the vital role played by the nexus of coke smelting blast furnaces, deep coal mining and the railways, demanding a high level of capital investment over a short period of time. Where the main force in industrialisation came from the textile industries their importance was much less and confined to financing railway construction, which in its turn also had a less significant impact on the economy. Furthermore the importance of the state in promoting railways and creating favourable conditions for railway investment was considerable, both in France and Germany.

In Austria-Hungary the state, in creating the railway system, played a similar role to that of western European governments, but because private investment was more sluggish the impact of the state's activities was greater; this no doubt held true also for the impact of the state's military expenditure. But in general the pattern of state activity and intervention throughout the economy did not differ from the western European pattern except in the case of Hungary where the capital disbursed directly by the state in subsidising economic development made only a marginal difference. Between 1850 and 1873 the state withdrew from direct involvement with development, partly because of the heavy military expenditure involved in the frequent wars. The financial reforms of Bruck after 1854 in fact reduced the note circulation and it remained contracted until the mid-1860s. The war with Prussia was financed by avoiding the rules governing the control of the note circulation by the central bank and issuing supplementary *Staatsnoten*. This sudden expansion of the note supply was certainly not intended to stimulate development but some historians argue that it was the root cause of the boom of 1867–73 and thus that the state's only real contribution to economic development in this period was accidental. It is curious that the immediate aftermath of a crushing defeat should have been a great spurt of economic growth, but the outcome of the war did settle many vital political and economic issues, particularly over the relationship with the German market and the future levels of tariffs, which must while undecided have deterred much investment.

As far as the sources of capital were concerned Austria-Hungary was a microcosm of the whole of Europe. In the Czech textile industry the main source of capital was the ploughing back into the firm of accumulated profits; in other industries such as iron and steel or engineering where sudden changes in technology imposed the need for large capital investments, the main sources of capital were investment banks based on the model of the Crédit Mobilier or the Darmstädter Bank. Where these did not suffice, as in railway construction after 1873 for example, the state itself entered the arena and used its own greater credit resources to finance investment.

But this is a somewhat crude assessment of the state's importance. Except in those industries where growth was possible on the basis of internal capital accumulation foreign capital was more important for longer periods of time than in western Europe. And in providing a satisfactory framework for foreign capital investment, whether merely by creating good investment conditions or by guaranteeing the rate of return, as it did with railway investment, or by subsidising foreign investment, as it did in Hungary, the state was in numerous ways, sometimes subtle and indefinable, performing a range of functions beyond the scope of even the most international of the investment banks. The role of the state, therefore, was perhaps not diminished but rather enhanced by the proportion of total capital investment coming from abroad.

– The Role of the Banks

Some historians have rejected this view and attempted to fit Austria-Hungary into the west–east continuum by arguing that it properly belongs to that category of central European countries where development would not have been possible without one necessary and vital institutional change, the evolution of the joint stock investment bank.

The state bank provided only the most limited discount facilities although it did function as an umbrella organisation for the growing land mortgage business after the abolition of serfdom. Discount banking for local business was first put on a sound footing with the foundation of a number of regional intermediary institutions, the Niederösterreichische Escomptegesellschaft in 1853, the Banca Commerciale Triestina in 1859 and the Mährische Escompte-Bank in 1862. But of these institutions only the first functioned on any scale as a bank promoting industrial development rather than providing only working capital. But the early interest in railways of the private bankers in Vienna bore fruit with the support of the more forward-looking governments after 1850. The Péreire brothers tried energetically to install a branch of the Crédit Mobilier in Vienna in the early 1850s and in so doing forced their great rivals, the Rothschild group, to obtain government support for a similar institution. This bank, the Bodencreditanstalt, founded in 1855, was to remain the greatest of the Austrian investment banks. Anselm Rothschild's main partners were other members of the Viennese merchant banking circle with the exception of the Württemberg banker Louis von Haber who had close connections with the Darmstädter Bank. But by its joint stock constitution and its enormous capital resources the Bodencreditanstalt was designed to play a quite new role in the economy. It was in fact a railway bank of the same kind as the Crédit Mobilier, and was a prime agent in financing the main line railways built before 1873, including the important Nordbahn and Südbahn.

Its success encouraged a proliferation of similar institutions although all had less capital and were less committed to railway financing. The Anglo-Austrian Bank founded in 1864 financed the line from Lvov to Czernowitz. The Živnostenská Banka began as a liaison bank between the large number of local savings banks in the Czech lands and the central bank, but eventually began to function as an investment bank on the German model. The General Hungarian Credit Bank (Magyar Altalános Hitelbank) was an offshoot of the Rothschild group in Budapest and supported their railway and industrial investments in Hungary. In 1869 came the Wiener Bankverein and in 1870 the Union Bank. The 1860s in particular echo the burst of joint stock bank foundations in the Zollverein after 1852. The purposes of these foundations were broadly similar and the rush of new banks came ever faster in the railway boom of 1867–73. But the failures of 1873 showed that the economic foundations on which these banks were built were highly inadequate.

The crash on the Vienna stock exchange in that year was the most spectacular in modern history after the Wall Street crash of 1929. In the year before the crash speculation reached crazy heights and a complicated edifice of ramshackle financial constructions which involved many of the investment banks took the place of investments in real railways and real factories which they had been set up to undertake. Of the thirty-three banks founded in the Czech lands in 1872 all went bankrupt in 1873. The loss of confidence bit deeply into the economy. In the period 1867–73 the government gave 1,005 concessions to form joint stock companies, 376 of them in the one year 1872; in the period 1874–80 only 43 were granted. No other European country suffered such a traumatic financial experience in the nineteenth century. The heroic age of private railway investment came to an ignominious end and in its collapse drastically altered banking policy; as a result during the subsequent years when the greatest industrial growth took place, the banks could not be said to have been especially important in financing it.

One reason for the limitation on bank participation was technical. The law made it much more difficult to become incorporated as a joint stock company in Austria-Hungary than in the other major European economies. Since the change to an easier method of incorporation had not been made before 1873 proposals for such change thereafter were naturally met with deep suspicion. Furthermore, the system penalised limited liability companies as against other firms. The most likely occasion for a bank to become deeply involved with an industrial company was when that company was extending its range of activities over a short time. The conversion of the Škoda plant to armaments manufacture, for example, was undertaken by the Bodencreditanstalt and the Böhmische Escompte-Bank, an operation which involved converting the company into a joint stock company. With a much smaller proportion of joint stock companies such opportunities were fewer. Even in the iron industry the early conversion of the Vitkovice works to coke smelting by the Rothschild group long remained an exception. When the Prague Iron Company was created from three smaller companies in 1857 it was done with only a little help from the Diskontogesellschaft and no permanent change in relations with the bank.

Between 1880 and 1912 short-term credit formed 80 per cent of all the assets of the major joint stock banks in Vienna and Prague and the other banks had their main interest in mortgages. This reflected a situation where the banks still provided mainly working capital for the day to day operations of the firm. In doing so they may of course often have liberated other funds for longer-term investment; the evidence available indicates that firms allocated their own capital and reserves to investment in fixed capital while drawing heavily on the banking system for short-term capital. But this is no indication of a capital shortage in Austria-Hungary as compared to western Europe. There was a high ratio of bank deposits to national income in the German and Czech areas, as high as in the developed western economies. An extensive network of savings banks throughout these provinces transferred loanable funds from areas with a low demand for capital to areas with a high demand and dealt also in short-term lending, especially to meet the seasonal rhythm of the textile industry. The rate of interest on capital provided to industry between 1904 and 1912 was lower than in Germany and before this it was seldom much higher. This was not the situation in Hungary, however, where the banking system depended much more on the inflow of capital from the major Vienna and Prague banks. The importance of the investment banks in Austria-Hungary as a whole has certainly been exaggerated but if Hungary is regarded separately their role there may be said to have been more important.

After 1900 relationships between banks and industry began to change as the extreme cartelisation of industry came to involve the banking system. High tariff protection and a low level of efficiency were the main motives in forming cartels. There were very few examples of the type of German cartel based on vertical integration of the firm to secure cheaper raw material supplies. Most cartels were horizontal agreements aimed at restricting competition between firms making similar products, and their intention was often to achieve the economies of specialisation in a low-income market which were otherwise not possible. One great influence on the firms seems to have been the pressure to emulate the German companies with whom they were often so closely connected, but not much is yet known about the origins of cartelisation in the Empire and even less about the operations of that unique European institution, the Kontrollbank, founded as a cartel bank by a cartel of all the major bankers.

– Foreign Capital

Although the banks were partly responsible for the inflow of foreign capital, especially in the period of private railway development, the primary responsibility was the state's. It was mainly towards railway construction that foreign capital flowed. In Austria, Bohemia and Moravia in 1901, 12 per cent of industrial shares and debentures were foreign-owned, compared with 75 per cent of railway bonds. By that date very few of the major Czech and Austrian joint stock companies had foreign participation, but it is possible that foreign capital had been more important here in the earlier period. In banking and in insurance companies it was about 20 per cent of the nominal value of shares. Even here, however, foreign participation was more directed towards mortgage institutions. France was the major source of the capital flowing into the railway system from the construction of the Südbahn onwards. It was likewise from France that foreign capital came into the banking system. The Länderbank, which reorganised the Alpine iron industry after 1880 to meet the conversion to coke smelting, was a subsidiary of the ill-starred Paris bank, Union Générale. Over 90 per cent of the foreign capital after 1900 was in railway bonds or state loans, and with the greater involvement of the state in railway construction the distinction between these categories was in reality rather blurred. Although, therefore, foreign capital probably played a greater role over a longer time than in western Europe it tended to fulfil the same functions, building up the infrastructure of the economy and occasionally providing an initial impetus in new industrial directions.

If Hungary is considered as a separate entity the role of foreign capital there was much more important. Over half of the shares of the major Budapest banks were owned outside Hungary, though mainly elsewhere in the Empire. But the third largest bank, the Hungarian Discount and Exchange Bank (Magyar Leszámitoló-és Penzváltó Bank) was closely tied to the Länderbank, the Banque de Paris and the Société Générale. It was not alone in being at the end of a chain of capital which started in Paris rather than Vienna. The Hungarian Commercial Bank of Pest (Pesti Magyar Kereskedelmi Bank) was also built into an important institution by the Banque de Paris et des Pays Bas. As late as 1900 over 40 per cent of the share capital of Hungarian manufacturing industry was owned outside Hungary, much of it in Austria. The proportion of 'foreign' investment originating outside the Empire is difficult to determine. In 1872 between 7 and 8 per cent of Hungarian state loans were owned in France and after that date the proportion fluctuated between a peak of 10·3 per cent in 1900 and a trough of 2·9 per cent in 1890. There were also some direct French investments; the company which exploited the Tatabánya coalfields after 1890 was French, and French participation in 1913 probably accounted for about 6 per cent of industrial and mining share capital. After 1900 German capital and German direct investments became increasingly evident in Hungary, especially in the links which developed between the powerful German joint stock banks and the Budapest bankers.

CONCLUSIONS

Why did Austria-Hungary develop so slowly after the early beginnings of industrialisation? Many of the conditions which led to the industrial revolution in north-western Europe were present and most of the phenomena associated with that event can be observed at an early date in the Habsburg Empire. Moreover, as our chapter has suggested, none of the obstacles habitually cited as impediments to economic growth were particularly significant there subsequently. The endowment of raw materials and labour was not deficient. Capital was not in short supply. Institutional difficulties, such as the high taxation imposed on joint stock companies, were present but so they were everywhere, not least in Germany. There were, furthermore, the closest of connections with the rapidly growing German economy and market. But the growth of the economy after 1850, except for the brief period 1867–73 and the period after 1903, seems to have been slower than that of the other large economies which had industrialised early, and over much of the last four decades slower also than that of Russia.

To understand this, one phenomenon common to all the less-developed lands in the late nineteenth century should in the first place be appreciated. A relatively lower level of industrialisation carried severer penalties than in the first half of the nineteenth century. It had a self-reinforcing effect, especially in a country which was so commercially dominated by the one country that reaped the greatest advantages of rapid and concentrated technological change, and in doing so nullified some of the other advantages which Austria-Hungary derived from the German connection. This self-reinforcing effect may be seen in the chemical industry which benefited from a complicated network of other industrial processes and technologies spread throughout the economy. German chemical firms, for example, got sulphuric acid, a basic input, at low cost because it was a by-product of the metallurgical industries; in Austria-Hungary it was still made in the old way from high-cost imported Spanish pyrites. Such effects could be seen throughout the economy. Exports of wood from Austria-Hungary in the last decade before 1914 were eleven times greater than exports of cellulose and wood pulp and the country was unable to make the same transition to domestic processing of the raw material as the Scandinavian countries. The German market continued to attract untreated wood from Austria-Hungary because the lower level of manufacturing costs at each stage of the German paper industry resulting from better technology and economies of scale enabled it to pay higher prices for wood than the domestic processers could bear.

Rapid industrialisation tended to create its own markets in the late nineteenth century through the process of rapid urbanisation. The market created by urban electricity supply and tramways was crucial to the electrical industries, for example, and there are many similar examples to be observed in fast industrialising countries and especially in Germany. But slower industrialisation over a long period deprived Austria-Hungary of all these benefits. The forty-eight German towns with a population of more than 100,000 in 1910 may be compared with the seven towns of that size in the Empire. Vienna equalled the German rate of expansion and Budapest exceeded it; between 1880 and 1910 400,000 people moved to Budapest creating there a vast collection of national monuments, packed urban housing and public transport systems which is surely Europe's most impressive visual image of the nineteenth-century economy. But every other town in Hungary remained small. There were fewer towns in the Empire, their small population grew less rapidly, the incomes of their inhabitants were lower and grew only slowly, their habitations were smaller and their consumption of gas, electricity, building repairs and public transport less. The same conditions applied to an even greater extent in other underdeveloped lands, such as Russia, Spain or the Balkan countries. Once a slower pattern of development had been established it became harder to break the mould.

Austria-Hungary also suffered from its cumbersome political system and the extreme irrationalities introduced into the logical economic framework of the customs union by the nationalist movements. Economic developments were more and more encouraged because they were specifically Hungarian, Czech or Polish. As the dissolution of the political unit into its component parts, none of which had any real economic basis for separatism, grew more likely, this at least had the advantage of encouraging the government to direct public expenditure towards the underdeveloped areas in an effort to equalise the pattern of development. State expenditure on the infrastructure of the economy was more than three times as large a proportion of estimated national income in 1913 as in 1869 and almost all the increase was spent on trying to keep the country united by providing roads, railways and harbours in the most backward regions. But these laudable activities could not overcome the unfortunate fact that the shape of the transport systems, including the main railways, was distorted by non-economic considerations arising from nationalist pressures. The plans to develop Bosnia and Hercegovina could never be implemented even in their simplest form because the most trivial economic decisions aroused bitter political tensions between Austria and Hungary, which were usually buried again by doing nothing. Hungary's own industrialisation was itself in part a subsidised distortion caused by national sentiment. Such rivalries were no less on a microeconomic level. The Živnostenská Bank, distinguished by the purely Czech origins of its capital, was repeatedly refused normal facilities by the central bank and by the German banks in Vienna. For a long period its own connections were with the sugar refining industry and this reinforced the idea of a peculiarly Czech industry, producing a middle-class group whose political aspirations were narrowly nationalist.

But the fundamental weakness of the Austro-Hungarian economy and the most important cause of the slower development was the lower level of agricultural productivity, aggravated by the enormous regional differences, and the great and ineradicable inequalities in regional per capita incomes which this produced. The political rivalries and discontents fed on these regional inequalities and they became not regional but 'national' injustices. The area with the highest level of agricultural productivity – Bohemia, Moravia and Silesia – was able to sustain the self-generated industrialisation typical of north-western Europe, but more slowly and only because with the rest of the Habsburg territories at its disposal it had a much larger market than that of the region itself. But throughout the rest of the territory agricultural productivity mostly remained so low that the growth of per capita incomes there was much less than in the Czech lands and the market as a whole grew so slowly that it was unable to induce further industrialisation outside the region where it had first taken place. Almost all the subsequent industrialisation was confined to the region where it had begun so that by 1914 Bohemia and Moravia had the social structure of a developed country while Galicia, Dalmatia and Bosnia had the social structure of completely undeveloped countries. The differences which existed in employment patterns in the regions are shown in Table 55 and the differences in regional per capita incomes in Table 56. Table 56 suggests that the most populous region, Galicia, had a per capita income only one-third that of the German

Table 55 *Population by employment in the regions of the Habsburg Empire, 1910*

	% in agriculture	% in industry, trade and transport
Upper and Lower Austria and Alpine Provinces	35·02	46·01
Lower Austria separately	17·85	60·27
Bohemia, Moravia and Silesia	34·22	51·46
Galicia and Bukovina	72·74	18·63
Carinthia and Istria	53·87	31·34
Dalmatia	82·48	9·40
Hungary and Transylvania	62·41	25·06
Transylvania separately	71·71	18·26
Croatia	78·82	13·42

Source: S. Pascu et al., 'Einige Fragen der landwirtschaftlichen Entwicklung in der österreichisch-ungarischen Monarchie', in *Mitteilungen auf der Konferenz der Geschichtswissenschaftler, Budapest, 1964* (Bucharest, 1965), appendix.

provinces and contributed only 13·7 per cent of the national income. The reason appears in Table 55; three-quarters of its population depended for their livelihood on hopelessly inadequate farming.

It is sometimes argued that outside the world of the great landed estates Hungary, like Bohemia and Moravia, may be regarded as an example of balanced growth. There is little to sustain this argument; the insignificance of textile industries there until government subsidisation became effective shows how sluggish was the Hungarian response compared to that of the Czech lands. In any case the proprietors of the landed estates were still until 1914 'the Magyar nation'. Hungarian development makes no sense if those estates are regarded separately. Nor, indeed, does it make sense unless understood as depending on the market of the whole Empire.

Where there was any structural change towards manufactured goods in the commodity composition of Hungarian exports it was to be seen more in foreign trade with the outside world than in exports within the Imperial customs union. The growth of Hungarian sugar exports in the 1880s, for example, occurred mainly to destinations outside the Empire; the growth of incomes within the Empire was not sufficient by itself to sustain Hungarian industrialisation at the desired rate. By 1913 53 per cent of the exports outside Austria consisted of manufactured goods; of the exports to Austria 60 per cent consisted of agricultural produce.

Outside the Czech lands and Upper and Lower Austria it was only where the state itself intervened to speed up the industrialisation process by stimulating capital goods industries that there was any change in

Table 56 *Estimated per capita income in the different regions of Austria, 1911–13, and regional contribution to Austrian national income*

Region	Estimated per capita income (kroner)	Regional share of national income (%)
Alpine Provinces including Lower Austria and excluding South Tyrol	790	33·8
Bohemia, Moravia and Silesia	630	42·8
South Tyrol, Trieste and Istria	450	4·8
Slovenia and Dalmatia	300	3·3
Bukovina	300	1·6
Galicia	250	13·7

Source: Derived by H. Matis, *Österreichische Wirtschaft, 1848–1913* (Berlin, 1972), p. 436, from F. Fellner, 'Das Volkseinkommen Österreichs und Ungarns', in *Statistischen Monatschrift*, vol. XXI, 1917; and E. Waizner, 'Das Volkseinkommen Alt-Österreichs und seine Verteilung auf die Nachfolgestaaten', in *Metron*, vol. VII, 1928.

the pattern of a slow growth in consumer goods production consequent upon the low level of incomes derived from the agricultural sector. The reasons for the inadequacy of that sector were discussed in the early part of the chapter and many of them go back to the separation between agricultural methods in the eighteenth century when those of the Empire stagnated by comparison with the rapid improvements in north-western Europe.[9] It does not necessarily follow, therefore, that a more vigorous programme of state intervention would have been able to solve this problem. However, the state, except on the Hungarian plain, concentrated its activities almost entirely on the industrial and transport sectors, attempting to drive development forward mainly by railway building and later by implanting manufacturing industries. Its activities in the agricultural sector were mainly concerned with protecting and sometimes subsidising the low levels of productivity, as in the tariff increases after 1888 which were introduced to keep out the produce of the even less productive agriculture of the Balkan states.

In this situation the low level of foreign trade made the pattern harder to break. Behind the tariff barrier the Hungarian farmers after 1900 did not increase their output, content with their control of the Empire market. Exports were too low for foreign markets, even that of Germany, to make any substantial difference to the sluggish growth of domestic demand. Only a few industries such as sugar, porcelain and glass exported a significant proportion of their total output. The rest were confined to the domestic market, costs were high and the impetus to technological change was weak. The great cultural differences within the Empire meant that this internal market was less amenable to standardisation; even such things as scythes and window frames were different in different areas. But this hardly mattered when compared with the low levels of per capita consumption. Annual sugar consumption was 13 kilograms per person in 1912–13, compared with 21·6 kilograms in Germany, and 42·2 kilograms in Britain. Beer consumption in 1912 in Austria was 74·4 litres per capita, as compared with 10·5 litres in Hungary and 108 litres in Germany. Paper consumption in 1913 was 11·3 kilograms per capita in Austria, 6·1 in Hungary and 27·3 kilograms in Germany. How unsatisfactory these low consumption levels were as a foundation for development was shown after the crash of 1873. Between 1873 and 1880 the population of Vienna increased by 70,000 but the consumption of most foodstuffs either remained stationary or declined.

It was not in Vienna or Prague that the crisis finally came, but in the underdeveloped areas where the rate of population increase rose after 1890. Given time, it is possible that this slow development within the framework of a customs union, coupled with a high rate of emigration, would have been successful in attaining higher income levels. The expansion of employment in the industrialised areas might have then continued gradually to absorb the surplus agricultural population of the other areas and the slow, if unequal, increase in per capita incomes have been continued. But would the population have moved in such numbers even to escape the grinding poverty of agricultural work in Hungary? Hungary was not only a region, it was also a country, with distinctive speech, habits, traditions and aspirations, like the other regions. And how much longer could this slow development be tolerated? There were more people in Galicia than in Bohemia and they were breeding more rapidly. In answering our question why the development of the Austro-Hungarian economy was so slow we come face to face with a disturbing conclusion. In spite of the great increases in output and national aggregate wealth in Austria-Hungary, it is possible that we are not merely looking at a case of less successful economic development but at a case where economic development was unlikely to continue even at its own slow pace. In some regions indeed we are faced with something yet more serious: the failure of economic development to take place at all, and these regions were in many ways typical of other areas of Europe.

SUGGESTED READING

The bizarre turns which national sentiment imposes on economic thought can nowhere be better illustrated than in the historiography of the Habsburg Empire. There is no economic history of the country as a whole but several authors have undertaken the more dubious task of compiling economic histories of parts of it. Hardly anyone is prepared to regard it as what it was, one economy. One work which surmounts the problem by seeing the Habsburg Empire as a part of a wider region with some common problems is I. T. BEREND and G. RÁNKI, *Economic Development in Central and South-Eastern Europe in the Nineteenth and Twentieth Centuries* (New York and London, 1974), a knowledgeable work and the best introduction to the subject. The same authors have made many original contributions in several languages to the economic history of Hungary, some of which are now conveniently summarised in *Hungary: A Century of Economic Development* (New York, 1974). Their work may be supplemented by N. T. GROSS, 'The Industrial Revolution in the Habsburg Monarchy, 1750–1914', section 5 of volume 4 of *The Fontana Economic History of Europe*, which does not, however, circumvent the limitations imposed by its title and so has to omit half the story.

On the pre-1848 period in Austria there is J. BLUM, *Noble Landowners and Agriculture in Austria, 1815–1848* (Baltimore, 1948), and a useful article by the same author, 'Transportation and Industry in Austria', in *Journal of Modern History*, vol. XV, 1943. A different version from our own of the industrialisation of Bohemia is discussed by J. PURŠ, *The Industrial Revolution in the Czech Lands* published in *Historica*, vol. II, Prague, 1960. From that vast volume, J. TOMASEVICH, *Peasants, Politics and Economic Change in Yugoslavia* (Stanford, 1955), may be quarried information valuable to both historian and economist. There is also P. F. SUGAR, *The Industrialization of Bosnia-Hercegovina, 1878–1918* (Seattle, 1964), a book whose title is misleading. What remains in English is mainly confined to more rigorous articles on narrow topics. From the recent contributions by S. EDDIE may be singled out 'Agricultural Production and Output per Worker in Hungary, 1870–1913', in *Journal of Economic History*, vol. XXVIII, 1968; 'The Changing Pattern of Landownership in Hungary, 1867–1914', in *Economic History Review*, vol. XX, 1967; and 'The Terms of Trade as a Tax on Agriculture: Hungary's Trade with Austria, 1883–1913', in *Journal of Economic History*, vol. XXXII, 1972; and by N. T. GROSS, 'Economic Growth and the Consumption of Coal in Austria and Hungary, 1831–1913', in *Journal of Economic History*, vol. XXXI, 1971 and 'An Estimate of Industrial Product in Austria in 1841', in *Journal of Economic History*, vol. XXVIII, 1968. On the beginnings of industrialisation there is A. KLÍMA, 'The Role of Rural Domestic Industry in Bohemia in the Eighteenth Century', in *Economic History Review*, vol. XXVII, 1974, but this is only the briefest summary of his detailed study *Manufakturní obdobi v Čechách* (Prague, 1955). One of the best works in English is in course of publication: the University of Wisconsin Ph.D. thesis by

R. L. RUDOLPH, 'The Role of Financial Institutions in the Industrialisation of the Czech Crownlands' (1968), much richer than the brief summary of its conclusions in 'Austria 1800–1914', in R. CAMERON (ed.), *Banking and Economic Development* (New York, 1972).

It will be seen that the work in English is very sporadic. In other languages it is no better. The best of several old-fashioned economic histories of Austria is H. MATIS, *Österreichische Wirtschaft 1848–1913: Konjunkturelle Dynamik und gesellschaftlicher Wandel in Zeitalter Franz Joseph I* (Berlin, 1972) and a lot of the same ground is covered by E. MÄRZ, *Österreichische Industrie- und Bankpolitik in der Zeit Franz Joseph I* (Vienna, 1968) which incorporates a history of the Bodencreditanstalt. A useful study is V. SÁNDOR, 'Die grossindustrielle Entwicklung in Ungarn 1867–1900', in *Acta Historica Academiae Scientiarum Hungaricae*, vol. III (Budapest, 1956). A good summary which throws clear light on other less illuminating work is B. MICHEL, 'La révolution industrielle dans les pays tchèques au XIXᵉ siècle', in *Annales*, vol. 20, 1965.

Sad to say some of the best works on the economic history of the Habsburg Monarchy were written before 1918. Particularly useful are F. HERTZ, *Die Produktionsgrundlagen der österreichischen Industrie vor und nach dem Krieg* (Vienna, 1917); J. SLOKAR, *Geschichte der österreichischen Industrie und ihrer Förderung unter Kaiser Franz I* (Vienna, 1914); H. DITZ, *Die ungarische Landwirtschaft, Volkswirtschaftlicher Bericht an das königl. bayerische Staatsministerium des Handels und der öffentlichen Arbeiten* (Leipzig, 1867); and S. VON STRAKOSCH, *Die Grundlagen der Agrarwirtschaft in Österreich* (Vienna, 1906).

The latest research is published intermittently in the English language journals mentioned before. But two journals are especially important: *Studia Historica*, published by the Hungarian Academy, and *Historica*, published by the Czechoslovak Academy. Both publish contributions in several languages. Specially valuable is volume 62 of *Studia Historica* which contains the invaluable study by L. KATUS, 'Economic Growth in Hungary during the Age of Dualism, 1867–1918'.

NOTES

1 We have chosen for convenience to call the country 'Austria-Hungary' throughout the period. 'Hungary', unless otherwise qualified, means all the territory of the crown of Hungary and not just present-day Hungary. 'Austria', unless otherwise qualified, means present-day Austria plus Bohemia, Moravia, Silesia, Istria, Trieste, Dalmatia, Galicia and Bukovina.

2 A. S. Milward and S. B. Saul, *The Economic Development of Continental Europe 1780–1870* (London, 1973), pp. 61–5.

3 K. Davis, 'The Modern Condition of Agricultural Labor in Bohemia', in *Journal of Political Economy*, vol. VIII, 1899–1900.

4 L. Katus, 'Economic Growth in Hungary during the Age of Dualism, 1867–1918', in *Studia Historica*, no. 62, 1970; I. Berend and G. Ránki, 'Nationaleinkommen und Kapitalakkumulation in Ungarn 1867–1914', in ibid.; S. M. Eddie, 'Agricultural Production and Output per Worker in Hungary, 1870–1913', in *Journal of Economic History*, vol. XXVIII, 1968.

5 H. Ditz, *Die ungarische Landwirtschaft* (Leipzig, 1867).

6 The statistical basis of these calculations depends solely on the work of A. Kotelmann,

Vergleichende statistische Übersicht über die landwirtschaftlichen und industriellen Verhältnisse Österreichs und des Zollvereins sowie seiner einzelnen Staaten (Berlin, 1852).

7 O. Hübner, *Die Zoll-Einigung und die Industrie des Zollvereins und Österreichs* (Leipzig, 1850), pp. 18–19.

8 A. Gerschenkron, *Economic Backwardness in Historical Perspective* (Cambridge, Mass., 1966).

9 A. S. Milward and S. B. Saul, op. cit., pp. 71–83.

Chapter 6

The Economic Development
of Russia to 1861

PROBLEMS OF RUSSIAN DEVELOPMENT

The examination of the development of the Russian economy in the nineteenth century is essential to our understanding of the process of change over the whole continent for it unites in a striking manner most of the elements of economic backwardness and the positive barriers to development identified in a less concentrated form in other countries. Russia was a country of immense size, even before the acquisitions of the eighteenth century, with a population no larger than 12–13 million in 1700. Yet such was the pace of population growth over the next two centuries that, despite the expansion of the land area, the pressure on land resources in certain parts of European Russia became acute. It was the country where serfdom lasted longest and where it was found in its harshest form. The crucial periods of Russian development, at the beginning of the eighteenth century and at the end of the nineteenth, were the result of feverish efforts to match the advances of the west. The consequence of this combination of sporadic bursts of development superimposed on a framework of society deeply rooted in the past left in simultaneous existence in Russia social, economic, political and cultural forms which in western Europe seemed to belong to different stages of civilisation and were regarded as incompatible with each other. In Russia elements of a servile feudal and of a capitalist society continued to exist side by side and this anomaly could not help but set up new tensions. That cultural patterns existed which seemed incompatible with modern economic growth elsewhere does not mean that they were to be incompatible in Russia too. However, it did mean that unusual and often drastic measures had to be taken to surmount the difficulties they posed.

Russia was a land of extremes – of climate, of luxury and indigence, of a primitive agriculture and the most modern steel industry in Europe, of the most sophisticated thought and the most antiquated superstition, of uninhibited freedom and untempered oppression. It is these contradictions that make the study of Russia so fascinating: modern growth theorists are inclined to lay down ideal conditions for rapid economic growth and often, as policy makers, seek to create such circumstances as far as possible. In Russia such conditions were largely unobtainable and a series of substitutes and compromises had to be adopted instead, although the social tensions that they generated finally proved to be too intense for the capitalist system to survive.

Such is the scope of the subject. In this and the next chapter we can only establish a general perspective, eschewing detail and ignoring often vital regional differences except where these are crucial to an understanding of the general process of change. In this chapter we consider the nature of the economy and the factors determining its rate of change between 1700 and 1860. In the second chapter a more detailed account is given of Russia's move towards a more industrialised society over the half century following the emancipation of the serfs in 1861.

THE PHYSICAL ENVIRONMENT

Nature had not been kind to European Russia; it was not a rich land. There were only limited deposits of minerals and these were inconveniently located in the Urals to the east and in the Donbas region far to the south, part of which was only acquired towards the end of the eighteenth century. The severe climate allowed only a short growing season: in summer in the southern region rainfall was low. The unending plains provided no sheltered, well-watered valleys and when difficult weather conditions produced a poor harvest, it tended to be widespread, leaving little hope of effective relief. The rivers, frozen for six to seven months in the north and three to four in the south, were often dried up in the summer, after a short but serious flood period when the winter snows melted all at once on the flat terrain. The soils in the region around Moscow and to the east and north were poor. The most fertile lands were those of the black earth region stretching west-south-west to east-north-east between the poor soils to the north and the dry steppes to the south. The black earth zone covered most of the Ukraine, the valley of the Don, the western part of the north Caucasus, the western parts of the lower and middle Volga and thence stretched into the southern Urals and into Siberia. The zone reached a maximum width of 600 miles at the basin of the Don River, narrowing steadily to some 200–250 miles wide in Siberia. The low rainfall and big variations in temperature made the whole area prone to periodic harvest failures. For some 150 miles to the north the middle Russian zone was a land of vast open spaces broken by patches of woodland, with the soil varying from very poor in the north to the black earth of the south; the climatic conditions, however, were generally favourable for farming. South of the black earth belt lay the brown soil land of the dry steppes covering a large area in the south-east to the north of the Caspian Sea and stretching along the lower Volga, through the steppe region of the Crimea and on to Romania. This was a land less fertile than the black earth, but superior to the northern regions and suited both by soils and climate to extensive grain cultivation. Much of this region to the south was conquered from the Turks during the reign of Catherine the Great (1762–96). The successive partitions of Poland in 1772, 1793 and 1795 also added to the Russian Empire in the west. The first partition gave Russia a substantial part of White Russia, the second yielded the rest of that area, the Ukraine, Podolya and the eastern part of Polesye and Volhynia. By the third partition Russia acquired Lithuania together with Vilna and Grodno and the remainder of Polesye and Volhynia.

Distance was a major problem both for communications within Russia itself and because of Russia's isolation from the trade centres of the rest of Europe. Given the inadequate forms of transport available in the eighteenth century, there was no such thing as a national market in Russia any more than in any but the smallest countries elsewhere. Goods were gathered together and exchanged, for the most part, at local fairs; more important regional fairs were held at convenient points on the great arteries of transport, the rivers. There were important urban centres such as Moscow and St Petersburg (Leningrad) and export markets were available but many export products originated far from the ports. Isolation hindered specialisation and the rise of population in the eighteenth century therefore brought about no significant development in the country's internal market. For such a country transport improvements were to be more than usually significant.

PETER THE GREAT

In many ways the basis of modern economic development in Russia was laid during the reign of Peter the Great (1689–1725). This is not to ignore the importance of the establishment of a unified and less troubled state by the Muscovite Tsars in the seventeenth century and the growth of trade and industry that went with it. But such activity was carried on only at elementary levels; most advanced products were imported and foreign trade was entirely in the hands of foreigners: over a half of all large industrial plants before 1700 had been established by foreigners with Dutch entrepreneurs to the fore in iron manufacture. Throughout the seventeenth century Russia's military weaknesses were constantly exposed; so serious were the depredations that by the end of the century Russia's only outlet by water was the White Sea. Peter's aim was to redress this military balance and to do this he had to make a series of decisive breaks with the past. He needed to reform his army, to improve the internal administration of the country and rapidly to increase its productive resources and tax revenues. To achieve this he was forced to make radical innovations in many aspects of social as well as economic life. The state became interested in the economy in a wide sense, not only acting directly on its own behalf, but indirectly encouraging private investment too.

To increase industrial output the basic requirements were to bring about an accumulation of capital, to create a class of industrial workers, to develop a market and to provide for the acquisition of industrial technologies. Some late-nineteenth-century Russian writers accused Peter of not making sufficient use of the existing handicraft industries and of forcing Russia into what they saw as 'unnatural' channels of industrial growth. But iron, guns and sailcloth could not be produced on the scale Peter wanted by petty hand workers, nor had they the means of acquiring the new expertise and machinery that would be needed. Of their own volition, the rich merchants were unlikely to act. So the state was forced to take the initiative. One method was the direct creation of state industries. Capital came from new taxes; military demand for arms, clothing and sails provided the market, and labour was mobilised forcibly from rural districts, from the ranks of conscripts and runaway serfs and from the poor. State metallurgical and munitions industries were first created near Moscow at the height of the struggles with Sweden and Turkey in 1709–10 but shortly afterwards they were concentrated in the Ural mountains near the local iron ore supplies. In this way Peter established an iron industry which by the beginning of the nineteenth century had become the world's largest. Textile works were built around Moscow to make army clothing, sail cloth and the like and other state plants were created for the manufacture of leather, glass and lumber, among other industries. The lack of technological knowledge was supplied by inducing specialist foreign workers to migrate to Russia. After his first voyage to Europe in 1697 Peter persuaded over 600 Dutch and English workers to migrate to Russia. Germans were given top posts in administration, the army and heavy industry, the Dutch and English dominated commerce and the navy. Foreign entrepreneurs obtained privileges concerning taxes, exemption from billeting soldiers and such like. Russians were sent to the west too and in Moscow Peter established the Academy of Sciences to foster the understanding and diffusion of new scientific ideas. Inevitably progress was slow; Russians abroad were puzzled by what they found and hindered by the cultural and language barriers. More often than not they returned home to act as translators rather than to make an independent contribution to knowledge. The Academy was dominated by foreigners. It could scarcely be avoided: Russia was not yet able to afford the use of precious resources for experimentation in search of new technologies. Nationalists might complain of dependence on foreign ideas but the economics of the situation required it. As it was, Peter achieved far more in terms of the expansion and organisation of industry than in changing its primitive techniques.

Later in his reign Peter began to show more enthusiasm for private investment. The expansion of Russian industry at this time in fact owed a great deal to the advanced level of the commercial, as opposed to the industrial, capitalism of pre-Petrine Russia. The new entrepreneurs in the main came from the merchant classes and even though they were given state aid they had to supply a large share of the capital for themselves. It was the initiative and the incentives that were new. By a decree of 1721 Peter allowed merchants (as opposed to nobles) to buy fully inhabited villages for their factories, even to buy serfs running away from their noble masters, so long as the labour remained bound to the factory, not to the present owner. The workers became known as possessional or assigned peasants. State loans were granted, state factories handed over to merchants until even in the Urals private capital predominated. Peasants who had enjoyed a relatively untroubled life as state serfs in that sparsely populated region now became serfs to private masters and suffered exploitation of an unusually vicious kind even for Russia in the ironworks and mines. Most spectacular among the Petrine brand of private entrepreneurs was Nikita Demidov. Originally a maker of weapons in Tula, he was helped by Peter to enlarge his works and then eventually moved to the Urals where by the end of the century the family dominated the Ural industry, employing tens of thousands of serfs in their twenty-nine factories and on their estates. Russian pig iron output rose from 150,000 poods in 1700 to 800,000 in 1725.[1]

Peter imposed high tariffs on imports, for revenue more than for protection. Building his new capital at St Petersburg, he used it to encourage direct trade overseas and constructed his own merchant fleet, placing lower duties on goods carried in Russian ships. He encouraged the establishment of commercial agents in foreign countries and sought particularly to extend trade with Persia and China. He embarked on a programme of public works, building canals, wharves, harbours, military works as well as his new capital. This and the needs of the army involved a huge mobilisation of labour and inevitably the financing of such heavy real investment was a major burden on the population. He used the age-old techniques of increasing the money supply and debasing the currency but also raised real revenue threefold over the first quarter of the century. There were many new and ingenious taxes but the main weapon was the soul tax, a fixed per capita impost regardless of income, replacing an older tax on households levied according to capacity to pay. The new tax posed no problems of assessment and was fiercely regressive. One estimate has it that in 1710 the total tax burden was equivalent to 64 per cent of the grains harvested by a peasant household.

Economically Peter's programme was remarkable in its originality, breadth and coherence, though not without inconsistencies in detail. For example, though he centralised administration, he continued to permit the disruption of the market by internal duties, for revenue needs were held to be paramount. But together with these innovations went a determination to preserve, and indeed to intensify, the existing social structure. He showed little interest in agriculture as a productive agent and at the same time went out of his way to strengthen the bonds of serfdom. The strain of waging war and of increasing industrial output called for the full mobilisation of all elements of society from the gentry to the common people. Labour was scarce and an adequate supply could only be achieved by increasing the role of forced labour. In addition the nobility had to be sustained and rewarded, not for their ancestry as in many other countries, but for the service to the state that he required. This obligation was intended to be a real one, beginning at the age of 15. It could be civil or military but only one-third of any family could choose the civil service. These requirements were imposed not for political reasons but because he needed more officers and administrators than the old system could supply. Admittedly enforcement was always difficult, but the requirements were exacting. In 1736 the period of service was reduced to twenty-five years beginning at the age of 20 but registration and examinations were required at intervals before service began. In return the nobles were exempt from taxation and corporal punishment and enjoyed the right to manufacture, trade and own property. The control over serfs was strengthened by giving the noble the duty of collecting the head tax and to this end the passport system was introduced to impose stricter control over the internal movement of the peasantry. In addition Peter began the transfer to private ownership of crown and state lands along with the peasants living on them, a process that reached its apogee in the first months of the reign of Paul (1796–1801). So began the eighteenth-century intensification of serfdom in Russia which contrasts so sharply with the policies followed by Joseph II and Maria Theresa in Austria and the abrupt termination of serfdom in Denmark, to give but two examples.

In essence much of what he did had already been anticipated by rulers since Ivan III in their attempts to match the military development of their neighbours, but this culminating effort was of a different order of magnitude. Although Peter tried superficially to impose western modes of dress and behaviour, he was essentially Russian in character and temperament and his policies were in the national mould. He sought to mobilise his country both to fight an immediate war and to create a basis for future economic and military strength. Low productivity would be offset by the sheer size of Russia's resources provided these were mobilised effectively.

Because his reforms were enforced with unprecedented ruthlessness, because Russian resources were potentially so great and because Peter was prepared to intensify the system of forced labour rather than follow the gradual relaxation occurring in the west, the Russian experience of state intervention in industry was much more impressive than that of other states in Europe, and for the next century Russian arms were to win great successes. But progress occurred not only in that industry. Successive rulers sought to modernise the country by building canals, ports and cities. Research and teaching institutions like the University of Moscow flourished. But for all that the intensification of bitterness was to become a serious hindrance to further economic development, at a time when such development was to proceed in the west at hitherto unknown speed. To 1860, Russia enjoyed growth but the rigid social structure precluded thoroughgoing development. True, Peter's concept was one of mutual service, noble to state and serf to noble. There was nothing new in the idea; what was new was the refined and intense application it received; what turned out to be short-lived was a sense of obligation to the contract on the part of the nobles.

The kind of intensive development that Peter the Great forced through inevitably entailed great sacrifices and for this reason, if for no other, the pace could not be long maintained. Even so, the decline of abnormal state expenditure after Peter's death in 1725 did not herald the complete collapse of his new industrial structure. About 180 new factories were founded during Peter's reign, a half by the state. There were 40 arms and iron works, 15 for non-ferrous metals, 23 sawmills, 15 cloth mills, 13 tanneries. Some were very large – a sailcloth mill in Moscow employed nearly 1,200 workers – but most operated on a small scale. By 1750 86 per cent of the ironworks and about three-quarters of the textile mills still survived and iron output had risen fourfold. In part this was helped by the continuation of the system of protective state control of entry, investment and size of operations initiated by Peter; in part perhaps it was due to a modified tariff system that put more emphasis on the negotiation of trade agreements than on outright protection; but above all it points to the depth of the roots of the Petrine industries. No new dramatic mobilisation of resources was now attempted; the state retained its interest but began to express it in different ways. Yet there were always limits to what could be achieved by personal magnetism, by mere organisation and exploitation. Long-term growth called for a transformation of the basic productive element in the Russian economy, and this in turn required a complete reform of the social structure.

SERFDOM IN RUSSIA

The degree and nature of serfdom varied considerably from place to place. By 1794–6 the serfs accounted for 53 per cent of all peasants and 49 per cent of the total population. They formed the highest proportion of the population in the area around Moscow, above all in the provinces of Kaluga, Smolensk and Tula, and a rather lower proportion in the black earth regions further to the south. The acquisition of territory in the eighteenth century resulted in a considerable increase in the number of serfs. The severe form of serfdom found in White Russia and Lithuania was continued and serfdom was brought to the Ukraine in 1783 to reconcile the gentry there to the loss of political autonomy. At the same time it was introduced in the southern steppe regions and the Caucasus. In the nineteenth century policy changed. Finland, annexed in 1808, did not have serfdom forced upon it; it was not pressed upon Siberia as the population gradually expanded there; Estonian and Latvian serfs were freed in 1816–19 and it was not forced upon the Jews in the south-west. In 1807 the liberation of serfs was proclaimed in the Grand Duchy of Warsaw created by Napoleon out of part of the former territory of Poland and when part of that area came under Russian control after 1815 the peasants retained their freedom.

As regards the estate serfs, their obligations were of two kinds. There were *obrok* serfs whose services had been commuted to payments in money or in kind and *barshchina* serfs who were obliged to provide man and team services on the domain. The village community, the *mir*, held the right of disposition of the land of the community and had become the agent of the noble for implementing his decisions. The origins of the *mir* became a key issue in debates in the nineteenth century on the future development of Russia. Some saw it as the spontaneous natural product of folk culture and something, therefore, to be preserved. Others saw it as a later, less desirable creation of the state and serf owner. Modern scholarship tends to take the view that to the fifteenth century the commune managed common property, divided the tax burden and collected taxes, but that each man controlled his own holding. In the sixteenth century, however, serfdom began to strengthen its hold as the Tsar, his country weakened by the depredations of the Tartars and others, sought to control more effectively the use of its sparse labour supply and to reward his servants. The *mir* now came more and more to work for the serf owners, beginning the process of periodic distribution of land and equalisation of holdings. The soul tax, however, gave a powerful boost to the role of the *mir*. The noble was made responsible for seeing that the tax was paid and it was in his interest to ensure that the peasant had the wherewithal to pay it. So the *tiaglo*, or peasant labour unit, was created as the unit of payment. Land was distributed according to the size of this family group and periodic distribution of land was carried out to maintain this relationship between land and labour. It became common first in the central regions. By the end of the eighteenth century it was standard on court and imperial family land, in many state communities and on much private land. In the southern and south-eastern regions which had been most recently colonised redistribution was only introduced on the eve of serf emancipation in 1861 and in

White Russia, Lithuania and the Ukraine it was little known. The time between redistributions was rarely less than six years and often much longer. The plots were scattered all over the village area and there were several divisions of land based on fertility and distance and on the almost universal two- or three-field systems. On the *barshchina* estates the peasants occupied about a half of the arable land; three days' work on his lord's land and three days' on his own was the general rule for the peasant, though here and there work for the lord rose until the peasant became in effect a slave with no time to work on any land of his own. The seigneurial plots were scattered about the village lands too but were not normally subject to the same process of redistribution. The amount of land available to the peasant varied widely; in the 1850s a male serf averaged 4·3 dessiatines in the non-black earth regions and 3·2 dessiatines in the black earth area, more for *obrok* and less for *barshchina* peasants, but the rise of population had almost certainly caused this to decline from the eighteenth-century level.[2] On average a peasant family might own 9 dessiatines, quite high by European standards, but deviations from this average were very wide. Regular repartition, or redistribution of landholdings, seriously inhibited the raising of agricultural productivity by halting the process of technological improvement begun elsewhere through concentration of holdings. It also left the peasant with little or no incentive to limit his family, but at least it maintained a degree of social equality between the peasants and largely eliminated the landless labourer, though differences could and did emerge in the accumulation of animals and personal possessions.

There has been much dispute over the division between *obrok* and *barshchina* peasants, the reasons for such distribution and the changes over time. *Obrok* was the more flexible form of economic relationship. In the less fertile regions many such peasants obtained permission to leave the village and take work elsewhere as gardeners, masons, carpenters, waiters, drivers, factory workers, paying their obligations to the *mir* out of their wages. Many also migrated seasonally to help with the harvest, especially in the southern regions. Some *obrok* serfs were able to set up enterprises of their own, employing other serfs or even free men. The state exercised control over the movement of all people. In the nineteenth century it was still common to find even gentry without the right to reside and travel where they pleased and the right to live in cities was limited by police regulations. In 1757 over one million passports were issued but it is easy to exaggerate the degree to which such movement resolved the problem of supplying a labour force for the non-agricultural sectors of the economy. Whether the state or a noble was the employer an *obrok* serf had to surrender part of his wages and consequently tended to offer his labour only when wages were high and his stays were generally of short duration. Only rarely did he become a factory labourer in the sense of being a permanent employee, divorced from the land. For the serf entrepreneur the ever-present danger of recall made his operations particularly hazardous. *Obrok* was appreciated by the noble who lived away from his estate, who wished to opt out of farming operations himself and required a money income rather than his keep in kind. Not surprisingly, it tended to be preferred by those with estates in relatively infertile areas.

Barshchina was generally found on medium-sized estates where supervision and administration were relatively easy. Field *barshchina* was sometimes supplemented by work in the noble's factory. For the peasant it meant a complete ban on movement. The lord derived part of his income in kind direct from the estate and depended on the state of the market for particular farm products for the rest. *Barshchina* was least prevalent in the northern non-black earth regions and proportionately most common in the Ukraine and White Russia. In general it was most employed in fertile areas but there were other forces at work which help to explain the complicated movements between the two systems. Throughout the eighteenth century mixed systems grew up, requiring both forms of payment from each peasant or dividing the peasants on the estate between the two, giving freedom of movement to some but not to others. For most of the eighteenth century it appears that *obrok* gained ground through its introduction into mixed systems where previously only *barshchina* existed. As the economy slowly developed, wider opportunities for *obrok* serfs emerged and the mixture was a way of adapting the old regime to new forces. Around 1780, however, the trend seems to have been reversed, either by wholesale return from *obrok* to *barshchina* or, possibly more commonly, by the growth of new mixed systems once again. The improvement of communications with canal construction and the growth of non-agricultural incomes encouraged more and more direct exploitation of local markets with the result that, although these were poor soil areas, *barshchina* came to be particularly important in the region of St Petersburg and Moscow. Moreover many nobles lived on estates there and could more easily supervise the *barshchina* operations. The rise of grain prices towards the end of the century led nobles to believe that they could make short-term gains more easily by direct exploitation than by raising rents. The fact that their simple accounting systems rarely involved any calculation of costs but identified the benefit from any sale directly with the price received for the merchandise, only intensified this trend. The choice between *obrok* and *barshchina* was rarely clear cut for the growth of the market economy can be said to have encouraged both in some way. Combination of the two systems was therefore the logical solution within the structure of the serf economy.

Barshchina was not confined to work in the fields; there was the carting obligation which in a land of such distances and appalling means of communication took up perhaps 30 per cent of the serf's working time in winter when the use of sledges over frozen soil provided the best form of transport. The *mir* also had to supply conscripts and to outfit and transport them. The serf was totally at the mercy of his master so far as justice was concerned. Laws against maltreatment were poorly enforced; fines, corporal punishment, exile were all regularly used. The lord's consent for serf marriage was required by almost universal custom if not by law. A serf could not own real estate and needed permission to contract financial obligations. Well into the nineteenth century serfs were sold without land as if they were slaves. In return the lord had an obligation to his serfs during famine, an obligation he usually tried to carry out since they were his source of income. Each estate was in effect a small local autocracy; the only redress was by petition and this was taken away at the end of the eighteenth century. It is not surprising, therefore, that the peasantry so often turned to murder, revolt, suicide, flight and drink.

In addition to these two classes of serfs there were enormous numbers of household serfs – possibly the harshest form of all serf labour – totalling about 1·5 million in 1858 or 7 per cent of the serf population. Many of these were simply servants but many too were skilled labourers, maintaining the buildings and equipment of the estate. There were also the possessional serfs who worked in the merchant factories instituted by Peter the Great. In 1762 further acquisition of serf villages for such factories was forbidden although the *ukase* did not affect the existing workers and their descendants, some 67,000 peasants.

In 1858 40 per cent of the peasants were not serfs at all in the true sense. The definition of these 'state peasants' tends to be very general and comprises various types of free peasants such as the foreign colonists. They predominated in the less densely populated northern regions and a few southern provinces, in Siberia and in particular central provinces such as Kursk and Moscow. In general they were found most where gentry landownership had never developed or where it came late. They paid the soul tax and a levy equivalent to the *obrok*; they owed obligations with respect to carting, road building and recruiting but in general they were better off than most serfs. Certainly their tax arrears were less. Serf laws forbidding renting of land and sale of property did not apply to them. They had civil and political rights: they could buy and sell land and renounce their peasant status and move to towns, although communal responsibility for taxes and for providing recruits inhibited their movement. Many took jobs as service workers, hauling sledges or peddling. The ever prevalent money lending led to turnover of land and the rise of richer peasants as the poor borrowed to pay their taxes. But all the same the state peasants were restrained by the general backwardness of agricultural techniques and of the economy as a whole. Worse still they faced the possibility that the state might hand them and their land to private individuals and so enserf them. From 1740 to 1801 1·3 million male peasants and their dependants were given away, mostly by Catherine and Paul. Some were transferred to servitude on the imperial family estates and though these practices were much reduced in the nineteenth century, they did not cease sufficiently to provide a sense of complete security. It has been suggested by some writers that the existence of large numbers of state peasants shows that serfdom was not at the root of Russia's economic problems. However, the argument is not convincing. These were not free men; taxes, *obrok* and other obligations took a great slice of their incomes. Their patterns of cultivation and technology followed those of the rest of the country and it was unlikely that new enterprise and investment income would emerge from their ranks.

It is difficult to give any precise account of changes in the peasant burdens over time, though it is clear that arrears of payment of the head tax rose rapidly. Table 57 gives some indication of the situation at different times in the eighteenth century. The rye prices are included to allow some assessment of the real tax burden though there is reason to believe that these rose faster than prices in general. Such figures are so inaccurate that only relatively large differences or changes carry any weight at all. The total real burden of rent and taxes did not rise much in all probability; that of

Table 57   *Russian peasant tax burdens in the eighteenth century* (*kopecks*)

	Serfs			State peasants		Index of rye prices
	Soul tax	Obrok	Total	Rent	Total	(1730s = 100)
1730s	70	60	130	40	110	100
1770s	70	250	320	200	270	273
1790s	100	500	600	450	550	606

Source: A. Kahan, 'The Costs of Westernisation in Russia', in *Slavic Review*, vol. XXV, 1966, pp. 51 and 54.

soul tax fell sharply in real terms but that of the *obrok* rose. The accumulation of tax arrears, therefore, would have to be explained by the fact that the noble collected his own rents before those of the state. In the nineteenth century the soul tax continued to fall in real terms and the burden of the *obrok* remained roughly stable. Obligations such as the period of military service certainly were reduced. But there were great variations in peasant welfare from one area to another according to land fertility, the peasant's ability to grow alternative crops and the pressure of *barshchina*, so it is not surprising that visitors came back with conflicting accounts of the wellbeing of the Russian peasants.

THE NOBILITY

But if serfdom oppressed the serfs, it hardly enriched the nobility for they were imprisoned between the inefficiency of the agricultural system and a fear of revolt which pushed them towards conservative social policies. The difference between noble and peasant in an agricultural sense was quantitative rather than qualitative. The typical noble had the mentality of a small exploiter and the serf system forced him to farm always after the manner of a small farmer. The great estates were in general not farmed in large-scale fashion but simply as a collection of small farms. There were exceptions, such as those nobles in the south-west who ran sugar refineries and distilleries on their estates employing many thousands of migratory workers. The system of serf agriculture was inflexible and inefficient but open to substantial improvement where the will and incentive were present. A simple three-field system was almost universal; the land was badly ploughed and inadequately manured. The usual inefficiencies of open-field agriculture were compounded by the sapping of incentive for improvement caused by the periodic redistributions. Grain yields comparing the amount harvested to that sown have been calculated at a ratio of about 3·5 for both wheat and rye in the first half of the eighteenth century when already they were over 7 in Holland and the gap was to widen rapidly thereafter. Peter the Great tried and failed to stop the practice of equal inheritance by which sons were given equal shares of the estate, each daughter one-fourteenth and the wife one-seventh of real property. Only the availability of new land saved many families from complete disaster in the face of such division. Noble accounting practices rarely allowed any true assessment of costs and revenues in different branches of activity, nor did they differentiate between investment outlays and the mass of other expenses. Such a system could lead to regular losses without revealing the real causes; even the most austere could be ruined by it. The most common remedy was to try to sell even more and the result was even greater losses. In the end the only solution was to exploit the serf more intensively; good or bad landlords were an irrelevance, for losses made them all exploiters. Another motive behind this feudal reaction was the gentry's pressure for new income to spend on imported western goods and travel to the west. But unlike many other parts of Europe that experienced the same reaction, it seldom led to more effective farming. The serf system inhibited change and the noble was rarely aware of the most effective farming system for him to adopt. He was incapable of developing new patterns of farming which would entail rearrangement of human, physical and financial resources.

After the death of Peter the pressures he created were released and the country drifted into a period of reaction and disorder, compounded by the fact that there were six occupants of the throne between 1725 and 1762. The struggles for the throne lessened the power of the autocracy and increased that of the nobility who steadfastly aimed to shake off the burdens of service and strengthen their position over the serfs. Nevertheless, it has been argued that the decline in service requirements was a result of the state's efforts to bring the supply and demand for military officers and civil servants into balance. In peace time particularly there was much to be said for reducing the state's obligation to employ the nobility. Efforts were also made to improve the quality of state servants by training. So one implication of the final emancipation from service in 1762 was that the state could now afford to pick and choose. After this emancipation the nobility won confirmation and extension of their rights and monopolies in trade, their freedom from taxes and quartering of troops, and complete freedom in disposition of property. Under noble pressure Catherine prevented further extension of the merchant factories, although at the same time allowing foreigners to buy serfs for the purpose, and this was followed by a marked rise in manorial factory production. A common procedure was to unite small, independent, part-time serf craftsmen into centralised estate manufactories, mostly for the production of wool and linen, cloth and leather goods. The serf soon became a full-time worker and lost his land. An official report showed that early in the nineteenth century 78 per cent of woollen factories, 64 per cent of mining activities, 60 per cent of paper mills, 66 per cent of glass works and 80 per cent of potash works were manorial establishments. Such industries were most successful where the raw material was produced on the estate and the techniques were simple. Thus, manorial wool and linen manufacture was much more successful than cotton. The serfs could be employed to cart the output to market too. Some nobles rented out their serfs to manufacturers or labour agents who drove them to their workplaces under close guard like cattle. Possibly the most profitable of the estate enterprises was distilling. The investment was small, skills low, the raw materials, barley, rye and malt, locally available, merchants were excluded from the trade and the government contracts provided a guaranteed market. However, only a small minority of nobles were involved in manufacturing. The lands of the southern steppes, conquered from the Turks, were offered to men of noble birth on generous terms, and being relatively fertile land it gave an excellent opportunity for profitable exploitation of the market. The gentry's desire to take over the church estates was frustrated; instead the state chose to make grants and loans which were rarely called in. By 1800 these debts already totalled 45 million roubles and 700,000 serfs had been mortgaged. In 1859 two-thirds of all serfs were so mortgaged, though an unknown proportion of these debts must be attributed to a desire on the part of nobles to invest in improvements to their estates.

None of these measures brought any long-term benefit to the financial position of the nobility apart from staving off ruin. Much less did they benefit the peasant or make any significant improvement to the productivity of Russian agriculture. In some measure a basic contradiction emerged. Those small changes which improved the state of the economy, such as the growing employment of *obrok* serfs in factories or the expansion into the southern regions, by bolstering noble incomes permitted the survival of a social institution that inhibited long-term growth. On the other hand it could be argued that the growing use of money transactions put continually increasing pressure on the rigidity of the serf system. The problem was that the nobles were not convinced that the changes in techniques and organisation required to raise agricultural productivity were worthwhile. The peasant for his part saw that enclosure often led to labour-intensive innovations such as the abandoning of unplanted fallow, thereby increasing the burden of his services and at the same time depriving him of his common rights. But this was true to some degree in all parts of Europe and usually the state had to provide encouragement and leadership by reforming ownership patterns, sponsoring experiments and the like. But none of this was the Russian state willing or able to undertake.

There were huge differences in noble wealth. In 1760 there were some 50,000 nobles. Some had no serfs and had to work in the fields; of the rest, around 1780 a third owned less than 10 serfs each, a quarter 10–20 serfs, another quarter 20–100 serfs and the remaining 16 per cent more than 100 each, though an influential 4–5 per cent owned two-fifths of all the serfs. The richest, Count Sheremetev, owned 185,000 serfs of both sexes at the end of the century. There were those few who worked at plans for comprehensive reform, who saw serfdom as sapping all initiative, as retarding the development of trade and industry by keeping down incomes by its inefficiency and its brake on mobility, as preventing the nobles from prospering and hindering the growth of the middle class. But they were a small minority. The vast majority took little direct interest in their estates and left them in the hands of stewards. These men, serfs themselves, were their lords' *alter ego*. They carried out the administrative duties of the village, delivering passports, checking absences, administering minor justice, keeping order, arranging for recruits and, above all, collecting taxes. They needed every virtue of hard work, patience and honesty and yet they might be severely punished for shortcomings, often unavoidable especially where tax collection was concerned. The way out of this uncertainty and the excessive burdens of the office was to exact more from the peasants, for the steward usually had the right to any taxes collected above a certain minimum. The ultimate victim was, as ever, the peasant and the lords themselves rarely enjoyed the benefits of a well-administered estate. The obvious solution to this dilemma was more delegation of power, more independence for the *mir*, but the logic of the serf relationship prevented this, so the situation deteriorated.

We must not ignore the fact that within the constraints of the serf system some noteworthy economic progress was made in the eighteenth century. The mere opening up and colonisation of the sparsely populated southern lands offered the possibility of producing a substantial market surplus there. Acquisition of the Crimea, the Sea of Azov and passage rights through the Dardanelles made Russia potentially a much greater sea power and a much more significant trading nation also. But these were marginal gains. Russia enjoyed a degree of development but little of that radical growth which alone could produce the rapid progress seen in the west.

INDUSTRY IN THE EIGHTEENTH CENTURY

We have already pointed out that the factories set up under Peter did not collapse with the end of his reign. Estimates for the creation of new capacity after 1724 vary considerably but by 1762 the number of factories had risen at least threefold and some say by twice that amount. Between 1762 and the early 1790s they increased three times yet again. Of course, a factory is a variable unit of measurement but the evidence of progress is indisputable. It has been suggested that the manorial factories, which multiplied after mid-century, were about 16 per cent of the total in the 1770s and much the same proportion fifty years later. They produced, however, in 1770 about one-third of the total output. The figures are merely orders of magnitude but they indicate that the merchant industrialists quickly overcame the ban on further possessional factories by switching to the use of hired labour. The labour problem eased as factories gradually created their own supply, helped, too, by the growth of *obrok*. The ban on merchant serf industry was useful in forcing one entrepreneurial group in the direction of a more efficient mode of production. The possessional factories were subject to an unusual degree of labour unrest even by Russian standards. The government continued to exercise supervision over their activities and would not allow serfs to be laid off in slack times. This was inevitable given the social system but it was impossible for the factory owner in those conditions to adjust his operations to market conditions. He had to make the same qualities, use the same methods, pay the same wages. This problem was partly resolved in 1840 when owners of such factories were allowed to release their assigned peasants and take full control, in effect abandoning the inefficient possessional system which had become obsolete and unprofitable in a changing industrial environment.

The Urals iron and metallurgical industries, manned entirely by forced labour, experienced the fastest growth. The industry covered a large area 800 kilometres north to south and 500 kilometres east to west though the only large town was Ekaterinburg (Sverdlovsk) named after the wife of Peter the Great. The need for wood prevented any significant centralisation of the industry. Peter founded 12 factories there; by 1790 there were 165. Output rose from 800,000 poods in 1725 to about 8 million poods in 1790. The growth of British demand was the dominant element in this expansion, so much so that by the last decades of the eighteenth century half of the output of iron was being exported, with 80 per cent of that going to Britain. Of the remainder about two-thirds was sold on the domestic market and one-third was bought by the state. This industrial region, which also produced 90 per cent of Russia's copper, was notorious for cruelty and oppression although there is evidence that the most skilled workers enjoyed a high standard of living there even measured in western European terms. Its advantages lay in the juxtaposition of ore and wood supplies with water power easily available too but its technology was unchanging and its labour costly in terms of productivity; it was typical of the unprogressive nature of the industry that all exports of iron left Russia as unprocessed pig iron. Transport was a serious problem too. Dams were built each spring to ensure enough water to float the accumulated production to the nearest navigable waterway. Much of the iron for domestic distribution was disposed of at the Nijni Novgorod (Gorki) fair; that for export went via the Volga and the canal systems to St Petersburg and the whole trip from factory to port might take six months and often much longer. The iron could well be sold four times on the way, its price rising each time to cover the merchant's profits. The industry remained competitive only so long as British demand continued to rise rapidly and technological problems prevented British ironmasters from exploiting their own resources more fully to satisfy local needs. Once these difficulties were overcome at the end of the eighteenth century, the Urals industry was unable to offer an effective response partly because of lack of resources – the lack of coal, the depletion of local timber supplies – and partly because of the distance to urban markets and the industrialists' inability to shed the mentality of serf exploiters. The problems of adjustment to a new technology were possibly greater for the Russian than for the Swedish iron industry as the latter had already concentrated on producing high-quality iron.[3] Russia offered a larger home market but this was growing only slowly and simply allowed the highly protected Urals industry to survive, stagnating on the basis of the past rather than flourishing on the prospects of the future.

Of the merchant industry the most important sector was the manufacture of textiles. Between 1725 and 1765 the number of workers in these industries rose from 10,000 to 54,000, some two-thirds being in linens, about 30 per cent in woollens and only a very few making silks. Export demand was the basis for the growth of linens, Russia being a major world supplier of sail cloth; the woollen cloth was purchased mostly for military use. The view of Soviet historians is that in its concentration, division of labour and use of water power, textile manufacture in Russia in the middle of the eighteenth century was at the level of that in western Europe. This is not a surprising conclusion, since factory production everywhere in Europe at that date consisted of no more than bringing machinery used in domestic manufacture of textiles together under one roof. Those technological changes which were to be the essence of the industrial revolution had yet to make themselves felt anywhere. Factory production of cottons in Russia began with calico printing in the middle of the century but by 1767 there were only seven mills with 491 workers. The new machine technology for spinning was brought to the Alexandrovsk mills in St Petersburg in 1798 but rapid development was still some years ahead.

The supply of labour for this textile industry was not easily obtained. As long as it remained a small industry, centred on Moscow, it was possible to hire local workers who in some way had severed their local ties. But the industry spread and grew and unauthorised migration became more difficult, as the authorities clamped down to aid recruitment and protect noble revenues. For a time merchants showed some interest in acquiring possessional serfs but eventually they came to rely on village workers with passports, though the supply was much less easily and quickly available than they would have liked. One important group of entrepreneurs were the Old Believers, who had broken away from the orthodox Russian church and had been persecuted from time to time since the mid-seventeenth century. They brought qualities of honesty, perseverance, thrift and mutual support in their business activities together with a feeling of moral superiority brought about by their isolation. They were most prominent in the Volga grain trade but were to be of considerable importance in the early growth of the modern textile industries in the Moscow area. Serf industrialists also made a significant contribution and a few became owners of very sizeable enterprises. The serf entrepreneur was a paradox, of course, but such paradoxes may be important in development for they are typical signs of a transitional phase. As opportunities for industrial development made their appearance in Russia this unusual form of entrepreneurship came to substitute for the capitalists of the west, springing from the difference in social systems. However, the response of the serf entrepreneurs, though in many ways remarkable, was inadequate to bring about any major industrial transformation. Much the most important function performed by serfs as independent entrepreneurs was to be found in the conduct of internal trade and in operating the craft (*kustar*) industries. The former activity was carried on with the encouragement of their masters, though for much of the eighteenth century it was of dubious legality. Most were small-scale pedlars but some traded on a substantial scale and paid huge sums in *obrok* to their lords as a result.

The craft industries reached the peak of their development in the first half of the nineteenth century. Many of the crafts were very old and some of the output was used for direct *barshchina* payment in kind – textiles, utensils, soap and spirits, for example. In the eighteenth century more and more of this output came on to the market. Particular districts and even villages were known for their specialities and their output was marketed at the great fairs which were often held long distances away. Although these craft industries were helped by the slow growth of factory industry, the *kustarny* industry was to play a basic role in Russian industrial growth not only because it provided a reservoir of labour skills, but also because it played an important supplementary role to the growth of factory production, *kustar* manufacture mushrooming around factory industry in the eighteenth century and sometimes competing successfully with it. This was partly because for a long period factory production, in weaving for example, simply involved groups working by hand methods under one roof, using virtually no new technology. The factory owner tended to change to a putting out system to save the cost of building and other overheads, and some *kustars* then went further, buying their own raw material and becoming independent.

Ivanovo, east of Moscow, in the eighteenth century was an important centre for the dyeing and printing of cloth, mainly linen. The work was carried out by domestic labour. But as the century wore on calico weaving began and the cotton cloth was printed there on a growing scale. The finishing processes were the first to be mechanised but after some early experiments with factory production, large-scale cotton weaving gradually disintegrated as it was taken up by individual peasants coming from mills elsewhere or from a mill set up locally. By 1850 small-scale weaving was the leading peasant industry of the Central Provinces. From 1836 to 1857 the workers in cotton weaving mills fell from 95,000 to 75,000 while the import of cotton rose fourfold. Only later with technological change did factory weaving fully establish itself. In cotton, only spinning was from the first a factory process; the rest emerged out of the peasant craft roots. Linen weaving seems to have followed similar trends. In the metal industry the growth of iron mills gave rise to a varied *kustar* industry for processing iron. Unfortunately this very success of the *kustar* gave rise to the belief at the end of the nineteenth century that he could survive and even replace factory industry, but by then technological progress had in most major industries created cost advantages for centralised large-scale production which made his decline inevitable.

DEVELOPMENT IN THE NINETEENTH CENTURY

The first six decades of the nineteenth century brought Russia to the fringes of industrialisation, even though a radical change in the system was required before rapid modernisation could take place. New technologies made their appearance, canals and railways were built on a modest scale, institutions for technological training and research began to appear and if foreign engineers and capital were responsible for many new developments, the same was true in other European countries too. It is instructive to compare Russian and German development at this time, for at the beginning of the century it is doubtful if industry in Germany was any more advanced. Why did Germany advance so much more rapidly after the middle of the century? Mobility of factors, comparative income levels and income distribution, education standards, administrative and commercial practices, location of resources all played their part, although it is hard to attach relative weights to these factors. But the Russian disadvantage of remoteness should not be underestimated. With the most exciting events taking place in the west, it was not surprising that transmission of men, machines and money occurred most readily between neighbouring countries with cultures that were not too dissimilar. But Russian remoteness took another and more serious form: genuine intellectual doubt as to the desirability of industrialisation or the form it should take. Russian intellectuals showed intense concern for the welfare of the peasant and a deep distaste for the obvious evils of factory and urban life. They expressed a hatred for the bourgeoisie and a horror of what they believed was a dehumanised factory proletariat in Britain. The Slavophils, as they were known, fell into the error of romanticising the Russian rural way of life but they held firmly to the view that each culture was a unique historical phenomenon and, reasonably enough, feared the shattering consequences of industrialisation for Russian culture. It was not necessary to be a romantic or an anti-westerner to realise that the transitional effects of industrialisation were bound to be much worse in Russia than in the west, given its degree of backwardness. In France or Britain, for example, development came relatively slowly, and, with a much less rigid social system, the transition was less painful. For Russian intellectuals, concentrating on the misery of the peasant, the grimmer prospect was intolerable. Their answer came through an adaptation of the ideas of the French Utopian Socialists into a form of Russian populism which would make use of that unique element in Russian life, the *mir*. Through the *mir* it was hoped to achieve a direct conversion to a socialist society without having to suffer the evils of a capitalist period. They believed that associations of workers, based on the *mir*, would engage in industry as well as in agriculture and still be able to employ the relevant elements of advanced technology. At the same time the pattern of worker control would enable them to avoid the horrors of proletarianism and domination by the bourgeoisie.

In so far as the Slavophils and, later, the Narodniks argued that Russia's backwardness made it impossible for her to modernise, they were to be confounded by developments in the closing decades of the nineteenth century, where in some sectors of the economy at least, this very backwardness was to prove an advantage. Many more thinkers were not against industrialisation as such, however, but questioned whether Russia must follow the pattern of the west. They exaggerated the power of the *mir* to respond to the demands of both industrial and agricultural technology but the essence of their argument concerned the quality of life rather than technology as such. Events were to show that, if anything, they underestimated the cataclysmic social consequences of industrialisation. The dilemma they faced in choosing between a way of life and higher productivity remains unresolved today in advanced as well as undeveloped areas of the world.

The arguments between the Slavophils and the Westernisers had nothing like the impact of those between the Marxists and the Narodniks two generations later. The direct influence on policy was slight, but indirectly the Slavophils gave comfort to those who disliked any kind of change and the debate renewed the fears of danger to the established order which might arise from congregations of disaffected workers in large industrial towns. Count Kankrin, Minister of Finance to Nicholas I (1825–55), was a prime example of the inconsistency of thought and paralysis of will which beset ministers when faced with the need to make positive decisions over industrial policy. He feared the social tensions; he feared dependence on overseas supplies of raw materials; he feared that Russia might lack the skills necessary for the successful creation of advanced industries, yet he had no positive alternative. His actions were inevitably half-hearted. His tariffs protected what existed but did not foster further industrial development. He opposed railways until overruled by the Tsar. He gave some small help to technical education but blocked the development of banking. For such a man the arguments of the intellectuals served to intensify his own irresolution. All this was in sharp contrast to Prussia, for there the opposition to industrialisation came only when it was already under way and there the arguments of the intellectuals were more positively put aside.

During the early years of the nineteenth century there was a considerable growth in the number of institutions for general and technical education, following the establishment of a Ministry of Public Instruction, although it represented only the slightest of inroads into the all-pervading illiteracy in Russia. During the reign of Nicholas, however, restrictions were imposed on university entry, the emphasis on science and technology was reversed, and further expansion of the educational system halted. In addition the intellectuals were able to influence many university students not to prepare themselves for practical work or economic activity of any kind. From the middle of the 1850s these restrictions were eased but though some foundation had been laid, the flowering of scientific training and technological achievement had to await an era more conducive to modernisation. All this, let it be remembered, is not to argue that those pressing for modernisation were in any sense 'right' and the Slavophils 'wrong'. It is simply to say as objectively as we can that these were the consequences of their conflicting attitudes for the process of industrialisation, whatever one's opinions may be of the social consequences of this process.

TRANSPORT AND THE INTERNAL MARKET

We mentioned earlier the problems nature had posed for Russian economic expansion: the distances, the terrain, the climate. Roads were as bad as in most other parts of Europe except that the size of the country made this even more of an obstacle to growth. In areas of severe winters, however, the sledge proved to be the most convenient form of transport, despite the immense physical hazards it entailed. The rivers inevitably were the prime arteries in summer, above all the Volga, navigable for the greater part of its length, and whose landing places, Astrakhan, Kazan, Nijni Novgorod, Rybinsk, Tver, were among the great centres of distribution in the country. In 1815, 400,000 boatmen worked the river. But the rivers froze in winter and the huge spring floods suspended all activity in the affected areas for six to eight weeks. Little could be done to mitigate these natural hazards but Peter the Great had initiated a programme of canal building to link St Petersburg with the interior river systems. More work was started during the reign of Paul, and the early years of the nineteenth century saw a further burst of construction and improvement so that by 1830 Russia could be said to have one of the most extensive systems in Europe. The Volga was linked to the Baltic by a series of rivers, lakes and canals 1,450 kilometres long; in the 1820s the Volga and the White Sea were joined, then the Baltic to the Dnieper, the Dnieper to the Niemen, the Niemen to the Vistula and eventually the Vistula to the Dnieper and the Bug, offering a link from the Black Sea to the Baltic. For bulky goods such as grain, iron, hemp or lumber water offered a most economic form of transport, though up to 1860 only token attempts were made to bring steamboats to the major routes. Even so the isolation of markets led to huge differences in internal price levels. To give one example, the price of grains in St Petersburg province during 1847–53 was on average about five times what it was in Orenburg, the most distant grain supplying province.

The extent of the canal system was used as a powerful argument against the building of railways. Cost, weather, low population density were all urged together with the general arguments against any form of industrialisation. The first short line to the Tsar's summer palace outside St Petersburg was built in 1837 as a result of personal intervention by Nicholas. In some ways it was an expensive toy but it was not without value in offering experience of construction and operation and giving the lie to those with no faith in the new technology. Most of the early advocates of railways thought purely in terms of their value for distributing agricultural surpluses, seeking to link the Black Sea regions more closely with the rest of the country. Only later did they come to realise the industrial and, above all, military implications. The Tsar again overrode his advisers in going ahead with the St Petersburg–Moscow line opened in 1852: 650 kilometres of double track over difficult, swampy terrain, it was a notable feat of construction. The cost was high in money terms but not comparable with the burdens of the serfs who were conscripted to lay it. Foreigners were employed to build the rolling stock in Russia. The Alexandrovsk foundry was hired out to two American engineers who were to run the plant for eighteen years, first assembling imported parts and then manufacturing more and more locally. In all 165 locomotives, 2,500 freight wagons and 76 passenger coaches were built for the railway. The immediate cost of this equipment was high and the quality of the output poor but the long-run contribution to the development of heavy engineering in Russia was substantial. The St Petersburg–Warsaw line, undertaken immediately upon the opening of the Moscow line, was built mainly for military considerations. Then with the outbreak of the Crimean War planning and construction came to a halt. To 1860, therefore, although some useful technical experience had been gained, railways had had virtually no impact on the Russian economy.

These, therefore, were some of the limitations to the opening up of the internal market. The total population of European Russia rose by 1·14 per cent per annum between 1811 and 1851 and the urban population from 4·4 to 7·8 per cent of the whole. But low incomes limited the benefit of this for internal trade, though the growing commercialisation of agriculture helped to boost internal spending power. Only the biggest towns had regular markets and functioned as producing, consuming and trading centres with a permanent demand and circulation of goods. Traded goods came from the estates but the reverse flow was small because of limited incomes and the existence of household craft manufacture. The number of fairs rose from 4,000 in 1812 to 6,500 in 1850. Most of these were local fairs: there were about 200 regional fairs and some 30 national fairs conducting internal and external trade. In 1852 the Nijni Novgorod fair with a turnover of 54 million roubles was easily the most important; its turnover more than

Table 58 *Consumption of manufactures per head in 1850 in Russia, Britain and France (kg)*

	Pig iron	Wool	Cotton	Leather
Russia	3·9	0·8	0·35	0·68
Britain	56·5	3·7	3·3	1·4
France	17·8	1·4	1·25	0·89

Source: M. L. Tegoborski, *Commentaries on the Productive Forces of Russia*, vol. II (London, 1855), pp. 6, 61, 98, 123.

doubled between 1830 and 1860, most of the growth coming in the 1850s. Second in size of turnover was Irbitz in Perm province with 29 million roubles, the chief fair for inferior and out of date goods, and after that Kharkhov (12·8 million), Poltawa (9·2 million) and Kursk (3·4 million). The growth of internal trade to 1850 had thus been insufficient to make any radical change in the prospects of manufacturing industry or the old structure of markets.

Textiles and metal products in 1852 comprised 61 per cent of the Russian products sold at the Nijni Novgorod fair. The output of cottons and woollens in particular grew sharply after 1820 but the absolute level of production was still extremely low in 1860. The contrast with more developed countries emerges vividly in Table 58.

INDUSTRIAL DEVELOPMENT TO 1860

The most striking developments in industry came in the manufacture of cottons. Some idea of the rate of growth can be derived from Table 59.

The first private cotton spinning works was set up in 1808 with machinery from the state's model factory at Alexandrovsk but the occupation of Moscow in 1812 saw the destruction of all the new mills. The private mills emerged again towards the end of that decade but they were working with inferior French and Belgian machines. To the 1840s, therefore, the industry was expanding mostly on the basis of weaving and finishing imported English yarn. Russian-made yarn was normally used as weft along with English warp. With the ending of the ban on exports of British machinery in 1842 there was a rapid rise in mechanical spinning of cotton in Russia and a corresponding fall in imports of yarn. By 1860 over 90 per cent of the yarn consumed was home produced. Weaving and printing of the finer fabrics, where special skills and designs and close supervision were required, were usually carried on in factories, above all in

Table 59 *Imports of cotton yarn and raw cotton into Russia (000 poods)*

	Yarn	*Raw cotton*
1812–20	165	55
1831–40	574	235
1851–60	167	1,877

Source: P. Lyashchenko, *History of the National Economy of Russia* (New York, 1949), p. 334.

Moscow, whereas common cloths were woven by the domestic peasant industry. It has been estimated that by 1860 there were 18,000 cotton looms in factories and 80,000 operated in peasant homes. The distribution between factory and domestic production was not very different from that to be found in Germany and Austria at that date, though Russia possessed some unusually large fully integrated mills employing over a thousand workers. There were some 2 million cotton spindles in Russia (including the still embryonic Polish industry), a number surpassed only by Britain, France, Austria and the USA, but in general the quality of output was very low and sales restricted to a highly protected home market. Efforts were made to find markets in the Middle East, Central Asia and the Far East and total export of cottons rose from an average of 786,000 silver roubles in 1824–8 to 2,544,000 silver roubles in 1852–3, the latter figure representing something like 5 per cent of gross output. On the other hand, imports of cotton manufactures in that year came to 4,570,000 roubles. Total output was only a tenth of that in Britain and technologically the Russian industry could not in any way compare with great European centres such as Lancashire and Alsace.

Nevertheless, in their essence the processes of industrial change were much the same in Russia as elsewhere. Mechanical spinning and the use of steam power required repair shops and the offshoot of this engineering activity was to be seen in the growth of Alexandrovsk as a centre of iron foundries and machine shops, making a variety of products from iron bolts to railway turntables, bridges and locomotives. From these origins there developed a range of metal industries near St Petersburg, using imported coal and pig. Many depended on foreign capital and management and were a constant source of annoyance to nationalist Slavophils. The cotton industry near Moscow grew under the direction of a group of half-anglicised German importers who controlled the supply of yarn from Britain and, later, of raw cotton from the United States. The most famous of these was Ludwig Knoop, a native of Bremen who went to Moscow as the clerk of a firm of Manchester yarn spinners in 1839. In the course of time he came to monopolise the market for raw cotton and to hold a dominant position in the supply of yarn from his own mill on the Narva. He ruled the machine trade too, bringing in what was required from Platts of Oldham together with steam engines from Hargreaves of Bolton. English skilled workers, foremen and managers were employed everywhere. Nevertheless this foreign influence was due to exceptional circumstances – the trade in imported yarn and the technical superiority of British textile machinery makers throughout the nineteenth century in Europe – and in branches of industry other than foreign trade foreigners were much less frequently found.

Almost all the labour in the cotton factories comprised hired *obrok* workers and they provided the first significant experience in Russia of the problems of managing labour on a large scale. Wages in cotton factories for full-time workers were said to be at least as high as those in German mills in the 1840s, though possibly 10 per cent on average went to *obrok* payments. Certain basic drawbacks were unavoidable. These workers retained close ties with the land, took no share in the educational systems of the cities, enjoyed no family life there to speak of, rarely adjusted well to the discipline of factory life and considered themselves mainly as a temporary work force. Such labour might grow in numbers but hardly at all in quality. Some argued that the peasant links proved their value when demand for cottons and, therefore, for labour slackened off. There may have been some truth in this but even so from a technical point of view this kind of labour was far from ideal.

At the end of the eighteenth century the woollen industry was in a very backward state. Mechanisation was rudimentary, dyes were poor and costly, and it was burdened by expensive middlemen who sorted and washed the wool. State-protected, subsidised and regulated, it lived on the orders for military cloth which were five times as large as private sales. But after the Napoleonic wars there was a gradual change. The restrictions were removed and private demand rose until by 1850 it was at least three times that from the government. Although as in cotton the *kustar* weavers flourished, there emerged too in Moscow a considerable number of factories making good and medium-quality cloths or concentrating on manufacture for export to the Far East. These exports through Kiakhta for the Chinese trade had risen sharply to some 6 per cent of home production by 1850. In the 1840s the manufacture of worsteds began in Moscow too. As a result of these developments the proportion of wage earning workers in woollen factories rose from under 10 per cent in 1804 to 60 per cent in 1861, encouraged by the relative decline of government woollens for which forced labour was almost exclusively employed. So this industry too began to reap some of the benefits of the technological changes originating in the west, of growing numbers of consumers at home and of new markets abroad, of protection and of the emergence of a force of hired factory workers. In contrast linen manufacture remained almost wholly domestic and changed little technologically, yet it must be remembered that, though it suffered from the competition of cottons, the value of its output was more than that of woollens and cottons combined. Exports of linens and hempen goods, sail cloth and other strong fabrics, grew from 77,000 pieces to 251,000 between 1758–62 and 1793–5 yet by 1847–53 had fallen back to 69,000 pieces and the average price received fell markedly too. Competition from British manufacturers and some substitution of cottons were the prime cause.

The biggest employers of non-hired labour in Russia in 1860 were the mining and metallurgical industries, centred mainly in the Urals. New technologies such as rolling and puddling were belatedly introduced from the mid-1820s onwards but in 1860 the industry was unique in Europe in making no use of the waste gases from the blast furnaces to provide a hot blast. At a period when iron technology was changing rapidly and costs declining sharply, the Urals industry was unable to make the necessary adjustments. These competitive pressures were severe enough for all charcoal producers, as the Swedes found. For a remote industry that had grown on the basis of what was virtually slave labour such a quick response to market forces was impossible. The state mills, thirteen in number in 1860, were the smallest and most archaic of all. The possessional mills faced suffocating regulations on quantity and quality of output and tight restrictions on the deployment of the labour force; consequently they found it not worthwhile to undertake new investment even supposing they could raise the money. The private factories in 1860 were the sources of such innovation as there was. Many owners were uninterested in change but those who continued to take a direct managerial role found themselves hampered by the poor quality of labour – such was the evil reputation of the area that voluntary immigration was negligible – by the absence of coal, by the growing cost of wood fuel as the nearer forests were cut down and by the general problems of transport. The cost of importing new machinery for the industry from the west was well-nigh prohibitive. The export market largely disappeared; at home there was high protection but even so, when the first Russian railways came to demand unusual quantities and precise shapes and qualities of iron, the Urals industry was unable to make effective tenders. Between 1836 and 1865 seven-eighths of the rails needed were imported as well as much iron for bridge work and the like, despite the fact that the home industry was offered prices twice as high as those given to foreign exporters. Some progress was made in the re-rolling of used rails but this was carried out in foundries in the north-west and not in the Urals area. Output of pig iron rose slowly from something like 8 million poods in 1790 to 10·5 million in 1831–3 and 12·6 million in 1849–51. In 1860 Russian pig iron output was now only one-tenth that of Britain and in the output of manufactured iron, where the industry had always tended to be weaker, her output was exceeded by six other European countries as well as by the United States. In Russia as everywhere else, the effect of tariffs varied. It seems probable that protection helped the cotton industry to establish itself during the 1820s and 1830s – a time of severe British competition – and encouraged foreign investment too. In the Urals, however, it had no such dynamic effects but only nurtured inefficiency. Much depended on the entrepreneurial climate as well as the objective economic obstacles. The social pattern in the Urals was one where local iron-masters were unlikely to respond quickly and where outsiders found no home at all.

If Russian industry did not stand still in the first half of the nineteenth century, it cannot be said to have flourished. The fact that almost no significant contribution to technology emerged from Russia at this time is unsurprising and unimportant, for borrowing of technology was the logical course of action at this stage. Whether or not one can justifiably write of the beginning of an industrial revolution in Russia at this time is meaningless without a precise definition of that phrase. Certainly by 1860 industry had changed the face of the suburbs of Moscow and St Petersburg and that of the entire countryside in the triangle of the Volga, Oka and Moscva rivers. But beyond this there was only the Urals metal industry and the beet factories of the Ukraine. If the phrase implies a condition in the economy from which rapid development of the industrial potential will inevitably follow, this clearly had not come about. If it simply means that one or two industries were slowly moving towards a partial application of modern technology then this was the case. But the latter is a very exiguous definition of a revolution. Such industries might well be classified as leading sectors fulfilling some of the many pre-conditions that come about in an economy before an industrial revolution in the first sense could hope to get under way, but even this would not apply to Russia for the real leading sectors of growth were to come from quite different sources twenty years or more after emancipation.

THE RURAL ECONOMY TO 1860

Progress in industry and transport, therefore, was modest and variable and in 1860 over 90 per cent of the population still lived in rural areas where change was slow to come about. One of the most significant elements in the agrarian economy of Russia now was the very rapid growth of population. The provinces of Petrine Russia which held 14 million people in 1724, had risen to 29 million in 1796 and to 45 million in 1859. But there had also been a huge migration to those areas annexed during the eighteenth century, and a population of 7 million in 1796 had risen to 29 million in 1859. Indeed, the colonisation of new lands greatly helped to support a population growing more rapidly than anywhere else in Europe and with little outlet as yet in urban areas. Even so, the pressure on land resources in some regions was already acute; in some northern regions, such as the provinces of Tver and Pskov, peasants were in dire straits. The persistence of peasant uprisings tells the tale most vividly: from 1826 to 1861 there were 1,186 revolts in the Central districts and the Urals alone.

During the eighteenth century the centre of Russian agricultural production had shifted southwards from the Muscovite area towards the steppe lands and by 1800 over a half of European Russia's sown area was in the black earth region. In the following decades the process continued with a great enlargement of the sown area in New Russia and the Volga provinces. The concentration on grain growing was extraordinary. Some calculations put output in 1850 at 9 hectolitres per head of the population; the next highest in Europe was Sweden with 6·5 hectolitres. But this gives no indication of productivity; at that date spring cereal yields ranged on average from 14 hectolitres per hectare in Belgium and Holland to 9·3 in France and Sweden and 6 in Russia. One would expect to find lower land yields in cases of extensive cultivation but except in the steppe lands of the south, Russian farming was highly intensive, so the comparisons are particularly significant. Rye dominated the north and central regions down to the 52 degree line, with oats an important crop also; to the south wheat was dominant. Everywhere the crops grew in vast, flat, open, unfenced fields, oppressing outside observers with their monotony. Rotations designed to restore fertility other than by fallowing were virtually unknown; manure might be applied in the less fertile northern regions but even there it was quite inadequate to maintain full fertility.

It is estimated that early in the nineteenth century 90 per cent of the grain for the market came from estate lands, though the peasant had a greater share in the production of surplus flax and hemp, the most important crops after cereals. The central black earth regions were excluded from the export trade by poor communications and by the cultivation of rye which was almost wholly consumed at home. So the region concentrated on the home market. Wheat exports came mainly from the steppe and Volga regions through the ports of the Black Sea and the Sea of Azov; other grains and flour went through the Baltic ports or overland by the western frontier. It is difficult to present a true picture of grain exports as they varied greatly according to the Russian harvest and conditions in western Europe. Exports reached 1·8 million hectolitres in

1771–3 and over 4 million in the first five years of the next century. The average from 1824 to 1844 was 4·8 million hectolitres, indicating no spectacular expansion. The average for the next ten years was 12 million, though trade was much helped by good harvests and bad years in the west.[4] Nevertheless this was the beginning of a rapid long-term expansion. But if cereals were the main crop they were also the main problem. Techniques of cultivation were among the worst in Europe; one complete and two partial crop failures could be expected each decade and miserable transport facilities made it difficult effectively to mitigate such crises. The serf system was too rigid to permit the majority of landowners to adopt alternative measures in accordance with agricultural prices even had they sufficient knowledge of their costs to be able to make rational decisions. The typical noble's inclination was not to shift between crops but to move from one degree of exploitation to another; his response to low returns caused by low productivity was to squeeze the peasant further. The lord's lack of direct interest in his estate, the ignorance of a totally uneducated peasantry and the absence of significant market forces created a dead weight of inertia over much of Russian agriculture. Where commercial farming with more advanced techniques was carried on in the southern steppes it helped to relieve certain pressures in the north by providing opportunities for seasonal work but it made little difference to the techniques and patterns of farming elsewhere.

In spite of the general backwardness there were areas where more change was apparent. Parts of the Ukraine provinces annexed in 1793–5, on the west bank of the Dnieper river, consisted of large holdings farmed directly by Polish nobles and there techniques were relatively advanced. The three-field system gradually gave way to other rotations, manuring was more extensive and sugar beet growing and refining proceeded rapidly after 1840 with the beets forming part of relatively sophisticated rotations. By 1860 85 per cent of beet sugar was produced in refineries equipped with modern machinery and driven by steam. In Congress Poland much barren land was reclaimed, forests cut and fallowing reduced. Between 1820 and 1865 the area tilled rose by 50 per cent and that actually sown by 111 per cent. It was in the new Russian provinces of the south that agricultural machinery was first used on any scale – not surprisingly given the sparse population, the absence of serfdom and a more capitalistic farming structure than in most other areas. Threshers, iron ploughs and mowing machines were all imported; the first native makers, Butenop Brothers, were established in 1833 and by 1850 there were nineteen such firms, though the mass of peasants continued to use the most rudimentary equipment. It was in the south also that the most interesting developments in animal husbandry took place. Foreign immigrant farmers, lured by offers of vast tracts of land and loans on easy terms, not only grew grain but introduced sheep rearing, especially of merino sheep, on a large scale. By 1840 there were 7 million sheep in the south and 11 million two decades later. Every summer large numbers of sheep and cattle were driven north to the urban markets of Moscow and St Petersburg; as early as the 1830s 100,000 were said to have moved each year. Potatoes were little grown until the 1840s when yet another crop failure caused the Minister of State to order them to be planted on common lands of state-owned property, and with a great deal of propaganda accompanying the order the crop spread quickly. Even so it was a late start and in 1880 potatoes still only comprised 2 per cent of the sown area; only in Estonia did they become a major crop.

THE PROSPECTS FOR DEVELOPMENT

In assessing the nature and importance of the development of Russian agriculture in the early nineteenth century we have to look at two related though distinct issues. What lay behind the general stagnation and low level of productivity? Did these and other factors produce a crisis in the serf economy which forced the introduction of emancipation in 1861? It is difficult to distinguish the direct effects of serfdom on agricultural methods from the debilitating effects of a social system in which serfdom was a central feature. There were intelligent landowners interested in new techniques, operating reasonably accurate accounting systems and seeking to adjust to the most profitable pattern of farming. They were inevitably inhibited in doing this by the *mir* and the *tiaglo* which made it difficult for them to eliminate inefficient communal farming practices or to redistribute land to the more efficient farming families. But outside the new regions few of the gentry were farming actively. How far such inertia on the part of the Russian gentry was due to the rigidity imposed by serfdom and how far due to a cultural barrier which dissociated landowners from actual farm work is hard to say. The fact is that, despite the trends towards modernisation here and there, most progress was thwarted by the nobility's sense of position and administrative incompetence, whether their concern was farms or factories. They had taken the place of the bourgeois entre-preneurs without being able to do their jobs. But modernisation was also impeded by the suspicions and prejudices of the peasantry who were hostile towards outside influences. From 1835 onwards, under the ministry of Count Kiselev, considerable efforts were made to improve the lot of the state peasants. Surveys and valuations were undertaken with the object of changing to a more equitable form of taxation; some peasants were moved to less populated areas; modest programmes of education, public health, fire insurance and technical instruction were undertaken. But Kiselev shrank from the basic problems of tenure and repartition and by so doing failed to tackle the very elements that alone could have influenced pro-ductivity significantly. Perhaps most serious of all, the immobility imposed by serfdom inhibited the redistribution of population either within the agricultural sector, where Kiselev's movement of 160,000 peasants was trivial in the national context, or out of it permanently to other sectors. Of course, serfdom was not incompatible with growth of total output so long as there was new land to be taken up, nor incompatible with some degree of regional specialisation; after all, the black earth regions supplied grain to northern areas that specialised in flax, hemp and potatoes. But again this commerce was all marginal to total agricultural output; there was no substantial rise in productivity except in certain isolated regions outside the main serf areas. Stagnation in agriculture did not mean that industrialisation was totally inhibited; there is no one model for economic growth. The development of the agricultural sector – through the demand arising from higher rural incomes, through the food surpluses for urban workers and for export, through the release of surplus labour and surplus capital – was the usual and often the least painful road, but the resources for development outside agriculture could if necessary be obtained by pressure on agriculture rather than through progress in agriculture. The rise of agricultural productivity and the fall of peasant real incomes were in a general sense historical alternatives in Europe. But the second was an infinitely more arduous and socially destructive path even compared with the dispossession of peasants that sometimes preceded the first.

As it was, with two-thirds of all serfs mortgaged in 1860 there can be no doubt that the estates were not covering their outgoings. The numbers mortgaged rose from 2 million in 1823 to 6·5 million in 1843. The rise may well reflect Count Kiselev's increased willingness to lend, thereby encouraging noble extravagance, more than the fact that the nobility faced any particular crisis in the 1840s and 1850s. It is sometimes suggested too that the growth of the grain trade after the 1840s brought a great urge for investment on the part of some nobles in the main wheat growing regions and hence a greater incentive to mortgage their serfs. Heavy debt is as much a feature of efficient farming as of extravagant consumption. The fact that such borrowing deprived the commercial sector of funds by lowering the lending power of the government's Commercial Bank is, in this context, irrelevant. But there is no evidence that the landowners themselves felt that abolition of serfdom was necessary to resolve their economic difficulties. An intensification of internal competition through major improvements in transport might have precipitated such a crisis but this had not occurred by 1861. It is one thing to argue that serfdom held back the growth of agriculture and made the whole process of development more difficult but another to see the immediate urge for the abolition of serfdom as rising from the same roots.

The economy was not entirely stagnant and governments not entirely unaware of their responsibilities. Tsar Peter had tried to force the economy to modernise a century and a half before, but in so doing had left a troublesome legacy. Ever since his time, as the economy developed, the social system deteriorated. The state itself was too poor and too committed in other directions to be able to afford to do very much. There was a huge war machine to finance and the condition of the budget made borrowing overseas out of the question. The nobility would not contribute significantly to tax revenues without a major social upheaval. The basis of those revenues – the soul tax, liquor duties, salt monopoly and customs duties – were typical of a backward country, particularly in their inelasticity. So investment in communications, in education and in the supply of credit for commerce and industry, all lagged.

As far as government intervention was concerned the basic problem was indecision. Tsars and ministers were worried by the misery and discontent of the peasantry but yet more alarmed by the prospect of towns seething with an industrial proletariat. They feared that Russia would not be able to overcome the disabilities of a weak internal market; they feared the consequences of the lack of the requisite industrial skills. Moreover, Russia's nearest neighbours, Austria-Hungary, Prussia and Turkey, were not industrialising rapidly either before 1850 and past military success bred confidence and complacency. Encouraged in these apprehensions by the distaste of the intelligentsia for industrialisation, they took refuge in reaction. Why then did reform come in 1861? There was no immediate economic crisis different from those that had oppressed the country for so long, nor any general conversion to a belief that serfdom was an obstacle to development. There were those who held this opinion but their influence was slight and, indeed, the document of reform itself embodied the hope that the country could continue to live within the traditional structures of rural society. The Crimean War was a shattering blow to Russian pride; it drained the country's finances, revealed its technological shortcomings and laid bare the inadequacy of the transport system. Apart from these economic problems, many now began to feel that it was only possible to create a modern army with trained reserves from a body of free men. Military defeat certainly influenced the government towards reform, but the Tsar's basic motive was political. After the abortive Decembrist rising of 1825, when a group of guards officers attempted to seize power, the danger was recognised in all its ominousness. If these men could not be trusted, who could? Only Nicholas's paralysis of will prevented earlier action. The oft-quoted opinion of Alexander II (1855–81) that it was necessary to free the serfs from above before they freed themselves from below still expresses the true motives better than any other: the Crimean War may have provided the immediate occasion for reform but the real roots lay in fear. The supreme irony was that in the event reform failed to stave off the revolts that had been so widely and deeply dreaded, yet it formed the basis for that very industrialisation that so many had wished to avoid.

NOTES

1 1 pood = 16·2 kilograms or 36 pounds.
2 1 dessiatine = 1·092 hectares or 2·7 acres.

3 A. S. Milward and S. B. Saul, *The Economic Development of Continental Europe 1780–1870* (London, 1973), pp. 482–3.
4 After 1850 the figures also include exports from Russian Poland which were excluded previously; wheat provided more than 60 per cent of these exports and rye about 20 per cent.

Chapter 7

The Economic Development of Russia, 1861–1914

EMANCIPATION AND ITS CONSEQUENCES

The Russian serfs gained their personal liberty with the publication of the Emancipation Statute on 5 March 1861 and through it received rights of property and private activity which constituted the most progressive aspects of the reform. Even though emancipation was politically motivated, it could not fail to have far-reaching economic consequences. The terms of reform would determine to a marked degree the future level of productivity in agriculture and the ability of farmers and farm workers to respond to changing economic opportunities. This, together with the distributional aspects of reform, would in turn affect the level of internal demand; add to these the effects of reform on labour mobility and it is obvious that the edict would have a profound influence on the course of industrialisation. But there was far more to it than this. The conditions under which serfdom was abolished were to be of the highest significance in determining the degree of internal political stability for the next few decades. Expectations play a large part in the process of investment and views on the likelihood

365

European Russia in 1911. Regions: 1. Far North; 2. North; 3. Baltic; 4. Central Industrial; 5. Central Agricultural; 6. Ural; 7. Lower Volga; 8. Little Russia; 9. New Russia; 10. South west; 11. White Russia; 12. Lithuania

of internal peace, formed in Russia and abroad, would certainly have an appreciable influence on the level of capital investment. However, these two elements necessary to the future of Russian society, development and political stability, conflicted with each other. The solution of 1861 sought stability at considerable cost to the prospects of growth and development, and thirty years later lagging industrialisation had to be forced forward at such a pace that the internal tensions created built up inevitably to the revolts of 1905–6 and to the revolution of 1917.

What the edict fundamentally determined was the form in which land would be made available to the peasant once he had been freed. It was possible to aim for a landless proletariat and there were those, especially in the north-west regions where estate agriculture was well developed, who advocated this course. But there were overwhelming objections. The age-old belief of the peasantry was that the land was theirs even if their souls belonged to their masters. Anything short of complete division of all land among them was likely to be seen by the peasants as a betrayal; anything approaching expropriation would precipitate the very upheaval emancipation was designed to avoid. Furthermore, the heavily indebted landowners of the northern regions wanted cash, not land, whilst those from the southern steppes wanted to give former serfs some land to bind them to their places of abode and so provide a local labour force. Whatever path was chosen the emancipation of certain types of serfs who had no close attachment to the land would create a large reservoir of landless labour: these were the vast numbers of domestic serfs, serfs belonging to landless nobles, serfs working in manorial, private and state factories and serfs in military service. There were some 3 million of these of both sexes and another million who would receive very small plots of land. The alternative of expropriation of the gentry offered insuperable political as well as budgetary problems. In the event, by juggling with land prices and land allocations between one area of Russia and another, the government sought to conciliate the gentry as much as possible. Certainly the peasant was not to be given land on grounds of equity; emancipation was not proposed as a liberation, nor was it received with any great show of joy. It was a careful calculation of areas, values and rents with political considerations always uppermost. The peasants gained most where the landowner was either the state itself or one of a noble party that was politically out of favour.

In general, however, a landowning peasantry was created and, taking Russia as a whole, the peasants lost some 4 per cent of their land to the gentry compared with the pre-1861 division. But the losses were not spread evenly. The largest peasant gains were concentrated in the eight Polish provinces and the loss of land in the rest of Russia amounted to some 13 per cent. The gentry were particularly anxious to retain land in the fertile black earth regions and there the peasant loss reached 23 per cent; in Samara and Saratov it was as high as 42 per cent. Some gains were made by the peasants in the non-black earth regions, most notably in Minsk, Kovno and St Petersburg provinces. The landlords also retained more often than not the better, more conveniently situated land. Temporarily the land was made over to the peasant in return for work services and *obrok* payments but after two years could then be redeemed at the wish of either party.

When such redemption became obligatory in 1881 about 15 per cent of the peasants were still in a state of temporary obligation. The government provided the peasant with loans of up to 80 per cent of the redemption value of the land and 6 per cent of this was to be paid annually for 49 years, equivalent to a rate of interest of 6 per cent on the capital sum outstanding. The peasant had to find the remaining 20 per cent of the redemption value, usually from moneylenders, unless it had been the lord who had requested the redemption.

Equally as important as the amount of land granted the peasant was the value placed upon it, and in general the higher the proportion of his former holding the peasant obtained the greater the price he paid for it. In the non-black earth regions the redemption value on average exceeded by 90 per cent the average value of land over the years 1863–72; in the black earth regions it was some 20 per cent higher. Only in the western provinces, where the conditions of liberation were generally most favourable to the peasant, did he pay less than the market value. Sometimes the lord gave the peasant his land free but then he only received a quarter of the normal holding for the area. This appealed to peasants where there was land available for leasing.

Former state peasants were more generously treated; they lost no land and simply continued their old payments to the state under another name. They were allowed to buy their land but few did so until it was made compulsory in 1887. All land in the use of the 850,000 imperial peasants was transferred to them in ownership. Their average holding of 4·2 dessiatines per person and that of 5·7 dessiatines of the state peasants were both greater than that of the former private serfs. Three-quarters of the old private serfs received less than 4 dessiatines. In the southern provinces 3 dessiatines was the norm and only in a few of the northern provinces did it average more than 5 dessiatines.

In other countries a pattern of emancipation such as this, where the peasant received less land and a high rent valuation, would have encouraged him to sell up, provide himself with a little capital to start a new life and move away. In Russia this was rarely possible, for the peasants were still attached to the village commune, which they could leave permanently only in very special circumstances, and they held their land in use from that body. After emancipation these communes covered 80 per cent of peasant land. They were not found in the Baltic areas and were rare in the Polish provinces; in Belorussia and the left bank of the Dnieper region they covered some 40 per cent of the area but in the east Ukraine, the Greater Russian area and the eastern steppes they were universal. The *mir* was preserved both as a convenient administrative and tax unit and above all because it was believed to promote political stability, being culturally deeply rooted in the Russian past; it was also recognised as minimising migration which might lead to the growth of politically dangerous urban concentrations. Whatever its role as a bastion of conservatism, the *mir* was certainly a powerful bar to economic change. The periodic repartition of land, in which many communes indulged, discouraged attempts to improve that land. Since holdings depended on family size, every effort was made by the family to obstruct movement of its members away from the *mir*. Several writers have pointed to the absurdity of a situation where the abundant factor, labour, was retained to ensure possession of the scarce factor, land. Enclosure of the open fields and commons was discouraged, but as far as economic development was concerned it was the restriction on mobility that was potentially most damaging. It inhibited the redistribution of labour within the agricultural sector to ease the growing pressure on the black earth region, for example, while other sectors of the economy found themselves with a reduced supply of labour totally divorced from the land. It is not clear how serious this second problem was, however. There was, as we have seen, a considerable supply of landless labour and labour could move from those areas where there were no communes. Studies have shown that by the end of the century the bulk of the labour force in the factories equipped with modern machinery was in fact divorced from the land. It was the technologically less advanced industries, outside the largest urban centres, that were manned by labour which had temporary leave from the communes and which often returned to their villages for weeks on end at harvest time. It could therefore be argued that a shortage of labour at the margin held back the growth of modern industry, though when such growth was induced after 1890 the results do not indicate that industry was likely to have proceeded more rapidly under easier labour supply conditions. In fact the census of 1897 showed that long-distance migration to the big towns had been much less than that to other rural areas; the steppes and the eastern regions gained more than St Petersburg (Leningrad), Moscow, Lodz or Warsaw. The fundamental weakness of the economy was the low productivity of the peasant. This perpetuated a low level of income and provided inadequate purchasing power for the stimulation of internal industrial growth. Redistribution of the labour force in agriculture and reduction of the numbers on the land would have raised productivity there, whilst the policy of repartition according to family size was likely to give no encouragement to limitation of population; it remains possible, however, that underemployed labour in the villages would have simply become unemployed labour in the towns.

Nonetheless emancipation did have its benefits. The cash payments to the serf owners helped to extend the money economy within Russia, even though a high proportion of these payments were withheld to pay off the gentry's existing mortgage debts to the state. By 1871 about 248 million roubles out of the total sum of 543 million roubles for gentry redemption money had been used for this purpose. It was the small and medium-sized estates that found their redemption monies swallowed up most completely in this way. The big estates generally retained a large surplus, though it is not clear how much of it was used for estate improvement. In so far as gentry land was better cultivated and geared more to the needs of the market any increase in their share of the land was economically beneficial, but often the great landowners preferred to invest in banks and railway companies and many came to feel that the great estates were at the root of many of Russia's troubles. They were not particularly well managed and became the source of much violence and anger. The 1861 Act was followed three years later by another establishing the *zemstvos* as units of local administration now that the local landowners had ceased to perform these functions. These were assemblies in which peasant communes, landed proprietors and tradesmen were represented in proportion to the extent of their lands or value of their property, and they were responsible for education, public health, jails, local trade, emergency stores, charity and so forth. Politically they were subordinate to the central government but they soon became organisations of great social significance, with a mass of employees of their own and creating growing numbers of progressively minded professionals closely in touch with the realities of rural problems.

Certainly there was a delay of a quarter of a century before the economy entered an era of rapid growth and development, for although serfdom was the major obstacle to such growth before 1861, the economy was extremely backward in other respects too and no legislation, however firmly geared to economic ends, could have brought a rapid transformation of the structure and attitudes of Russian society. It can at least be said that the pattern of society created by reform did not prevent a faster growth rate occurring from the later 1880s onwards. But apart from its economic deficiencies, emancipation gave the peasant a deep sense of grievance. What had been seen for centuries as his inalienable right to the land had been ignored, and the working out of emancipation itself contained elements of unfairness, amounting sometimes to fraud, which left the peasant with little respect for property rights of any kind. Before 1861, for example, peasants had often bought and sold land for themselves but in the name of and with the consent of their owners who had an interest in seeing serfs increase their economic strength. Yet the legislation refused to acknowledge any such transaction made more than ten years before. After the French Revolution clearly defined and agreed sets of assumptions about legal rights in property had seemed an essential feature of the modernisation process. But in Russia government and peasants were unable to make anything approaching the same assumptions and were each working towards different ends. The government assumed that all land belonged to the nobles and for the area they did not retain they were entitled to compensation. Peasant land was said to belong to the *mir*. Some peasants enjoyed the mutual protection the commune provided but others were frustrated by the limitations it imposed on the use and disposition of land. All deeply resented paying for land they believed was by right theirs, and above all were aggrieved at the loss of land they had previously tilled, the so-called *otrezki* or 'cut-off' land. Such feelings made it easy for groups such as the Marxists to posit other assumptions about property rights and work towards different goals.

The burdens imposed by shortage of land, high taxes and the rapid growth of population gave little hope of investment and improvement in much of Russian agriculture; indeed capital depletion, most of all of live-stock, became more and more common. One answer to land shortage was to adopt a more intensive pattern of farming, but this called for capital, knowledge, security of tenure, local urban markets and suitable climatic conditions which were rarely available except in the most favoured regions of the north-west. The average size of holding for the peasant was not low by western standards; it was climate, technology, capital and markets that were deficient.

In the Polish provinces the pattern of emancipation was different. An *ukase* of May 1861 ended all labour services with fixed rates of commuta-tion. Then, following an insurrection in 1863, decrees settling the agrarian question were promulgated in March 1864. All lands farmed by peasants on state or private estates passed to them as freeholds and compensation came not from the peasant as in the rest of Russia, but from a state fund and the landlord was excluded from any part in the administrative or judicial affairs of the peasant community. In addition 130,000 small-holdings were created for landless peasants from government estates. So 700,000 families got farms on terms far more generous than those granted in Austrian or German Poland and on better and less complicated terms than those in the rest of Russia. But giving power over landholding to the peasant in this way had the unfortunate consequence of leading to rapid subdivision of the land and an intensification of rural poverty, although it also eased the creation of an industrial labour force. Whatever form emancipation took, it seemed to have grave shortcomings. In any case, it is important to realise that there were limitations to what legal emancipation could do by itself. Prussia's problems were not solved only by better or more efficient terms of emancipation but by the more com-mercial farming of the nobility, who were satisfying longstanding and developing export markets, and by emigration and internal migration on a larger scale than in Russia. The terms of emancipation made it more or less easy to exploit opportunities, but the existing economic background was fundamentally important also.

The pressures upon the rural community in Russia proper after 1861 can be seen most vividly in increased indebtedness, in the rise of land values and in the growth of repartition as population expanded. A study of 6,830 communes has shown that whereas in the 1880s 65 per cent did not practise repartition, by 1897–1902 only 12 per cent were not doing so. Some attempt was made to check this trend by a law of 1893 which required a two-thirds majority on a decision to undertake repartition and a minimum interval of twelve years between one repartition and the next. Whatever one might think of it as an economic institution, the *mir* certainly retained its vitality, though it seemed more likely to ensure that all starved in common than that any progress was made. Already by 1876–80 the tax arrears stood at 22 per cent of the annual assessment; in some areas they constituted almost one-half. Thereafter the situation deteriorated rapidly. In Kazan province, for example, arrears rose from 4 per cent in the early 1870s to 418 per cent in 1898, in Tula from 3 to 244 per cent and in Samara from 48 to 363 per cent.

The rise in land prices can be seen from Table 60. One curious consequence of this inflation was that land values were now above what had been considered very high redemption values and so it became possible for a peasant to consider repaying his debt to the commune and selling his land as a compact plot at a good price. Not many did so, for it was a complicated operation, but in 1893 the government intervened by laying down that permission of two-thirds of the commune would be required. The authorities were still determined to preserve the commune as far as possible though by exercising greater control over repartition, decreed in the same year, they hoped to bring about better farming practices. But the commune

Table 60 *Land prices in Russia*
(*roubles per dessiatine*)

Regions	1860	1889
Moscow	22	55
South west	43	120
Ukraine	34	99
Central agricultural	43	111
Middle Volga	30	67

Source: G. Pavlovsky, *Agricultural Russia on the Eve of the Revolution* (London, 1930), p. 110.

was many things to many people. To the state it was a bulwark of stability as well as a tax collecting agency. Some saw it as possessing the germ of socialism; the Narodniks hoped it would offer a uniquely Russian route to industrialisation; some believed it provided a useful degree of economic security; the Marxists saw it as an obsolete institution which held back but would not prevent the inevitable growth of capitalism. Above all it was thought to contain the essence of old conservative Russia. Internal disorder had always been recognised as the fundamental Russian problem. As tensions mounted towards the end of the nineteenth century it was reasonable to feel that the supreme need was to preserve at all costs such an agency of stability. The Marxists accepted the inevitability of chaos when further reform came because they believed it would suit their ends, but most other reformist thinkers time and again retreated from the logic of their ideas because of this deep dread of internal disorder. Such fears seemed to be well-founded; peasant uprisings were not simply the result of poverty and hunger. The worst revolts at the beginning of the twentieth century came in good harvest years such as 1902 and 1905. Relatively well-off peasants often took part and the young immigrants into New Russia in the south were particularly subject to the influences of revolutionaries. There were no easy solutions in such an environment.

For the rural community, the costs of this stability were enormous. Agricultural prices fell, taxes and population rose. Some move was made to reduce the tax burden in the 1880s by abolition of the poll tax and by reduction of redemption payments. Although these were to be abolished entirely in 1907, in one province the burden of redemption at its worst rose by 40 per cent from 1883 to 1895 and the land available to each peasant fell by 27 per cent. The prices of rye and oats fell by 58 and 44 per cent respectively between 1881 and 1894 and wheat began to drop heavily in the late 1880s, although it should be remembered that many peasants were purchasers of food, especially those engaged part-time in rural industries, and so benefited from low prices.

The total population of Russia rose from 74 million in 1860 to 126·4 million in 1897, rising to about 170 million in 1913. The total population rose by about one-quarter between 1877 and 1905 and the average size of the village allotment fell accordingly. The increase in population in Russia in the second half of the nineteenth century was the fastest in Europe except for Bulgaria. To counter this disastrous trend the peasants turned more and more to leasing and buying private land. In 1877 the peasants owned 6·5 million dessiatines privately in addition to their allotments from the *mir*; by 1887 this had risen to 12·6 million and by 1905 to 23·6 million. Of this last figure over a half was held by private individuals, the rest by private associations of peasants and by the communes. Even so, of 11 million peasant households in 1905 under 500,000 held private plots, though about one million participated in peasant associations and 800,000 in acquisitions by the *mir*. Some of these households no doubt were involved in more than one type of acquisition though the extent of this is not known. In 1882 the Peasant Land Bank was established to assist the transfer of land in this way. Its activities were much restricted in the first decade of its existence and in some regions municipal land banks were for a time more effective. The leasing of land by peasants was yet more important than outright purchase, though estimates of its extent vary considerably. One suggestion is that 37 million dessiatines was so leased in 1900, equivalent to 38 per cent of all private land (that is to say not peasant allotted or state owned land) and 24 per cent of peasant landholding, with the division between private and group holdings again about equal. As a result the peasants may have been cultivating nearly 80 per cent of all farmland by 1905. Leasing of estate land was rare in the south-west where intensive farming was the rule; it was more common in the south-eastern grain area and most usual in the densely populated central regions. In the black earth region the peasant leased arable land; further north it was meadow land that fetched the highest rents. Whether this leasing was carried out mainly by subsistence farmers or concentrated among the richer peasants who grew crops for the market, has been much discussed. Certainly Lenin and other contemporary observers had no doubt that the latter were the dominant force and considered this the prime feature of differentiation of the peasantry. As regards the relatively sparsely populated areas of the south and east Lenin was undoubtedly right, but in central Russia there was much more subsistence leasing, some on a share-cropping basis and some involving work on the estate fields as part payment. Even as regards the purchase of land by peasants, Lenin himself noted a similar difference between provinces such as Saratov and Samara where nine-tenths of such land was held by less than 2 per cent of the households and those like Orel and Voronezh, for example, where the division was less marked. It is probably true that the small peasant accounted for the largest number of leases but the larger peasant land-holders held the biggest area of leased land. In any case, leasing served to intensify peasant anger, as they disliked paying for land they believed theirs by ancient right and objected to the middlemen who inevitably came into the transactions. But as regards the wider problems of poverty in Russian rural society, mere redistribution of land in these ways could only be a minor element in any final solution. For this, reform of the whole nature of tenure, of the technology of agriculture and of the pattern of internal mobility would be required. Some relief was derived from bringing new areas into cultivation – the southern steppes and the lower reaches of the Don, areas of low rainfall. Many peasants illegally took up state land and in Kherson alone over 70,000 peasants had settled an area of 120,000 dessiatines by 1882.

Undoubtedly these trends in prices, population and taxation caused a serious impoverishment of the small farmers and this was worsened by the effects of periodic famines which were tending to die out in western Europe but remained acute in Russia where one harvest might still be less than half of its predecessor. They also suffered from the heavier indirect taxes imposed during the industrial boom of the 1890s though, on the whole, in the last quarter of the century state taxes on land fell by more than the increase of those exacted by the *zemstvo* and *mir*. There was, however, much variation between one province and another. As for the decline in the size of family holdings, the smallest were to be found in the south-west and the Ukraine, though there were good opportunities for outside earnings in those areas. The crisis was worst in the central agricultural region and the middle Volga where population pressure was most intense. But size alone does not tell the whole story; productivity also was extremely low. A dessiatine lot might have as many as fifty parcels of land and it was not rare for these to be from five to fifteen kilometres from the village and of inconvenient shape, perhaps a kilometre long and 20 metres wide. The two-field system of cultivation had been replaced by the three-field in most areas, though in the south and east it was common to follow a series of years of cereal cultivation by an equally long period of fallow. In 1887 37 per cent of the cultivated land was held fallow and in 1901 the proportion was still about 30 per cent.

For the peasant in the central region the quickest way out of his difficulties was usually to plough as much as possible, regardless of erosion and loss of potential manure from pastured animals. By the mid-1880s the arable acreage in the black earth region had risen by 50 per cent over the previous twenty years, though some of this was newly cultivated land. In the east and south-east there were still opportunities for wild grazing, and big herds of beef cattle were to be found although they were being pushed further east by the inroads of cereal farming. In the Baltic and western provinces and in the northern industrial region dairy cattle were raised. The number of cattle in Russia rose slightly between 1901 and 1913 though this was offset by an equal decline in their average weight. Feed roots were hardly grown and almost all livestock was raised on grass and on the by-products of grain production. Outside the areas of nomadic grazing almost no cattle were raised for meat alone. The best beef came from work oxen fed on the residuals of sugar beet production but most beef was a by-product of milk production and cows were rarely fattened before slaughter. Yet Russia exported 1·5 million tons of bran and oilcake on average in 1911–13, partly because of the remoteness of the processing areas but also owing to a failure to realise its worth. The great herds of merino sheep on the southern steppes, which reached over 12 million in 1881, declined in the face of falling prices for wool and the advance of cereal farming to just over 2 million in 1910. By western European standards the animal population was low in relation to the land area and little effective manuring was carried on. Very small quantities of artificial fertiliser were used and almost all of this was applied on the landed estates. The plight of the peasant can be measured by the depletion of perhaps his most important stock of capital, the horse. In 1887 27 per cent of peasant households had no horse and in 1900 the figure had climbed to over 30 per cent, at which date 43 per cent of the households had only one horse. By contrast, the more successful development of agriculture in the south and south-east and in particular the use of machines such as mowers, rakes and potato sowers caused a big shift from the use of oxen to horses.

Very little was done in the way of educating peasants to better methods, although some local governments did give credit for seed and machinery and offered technical advice. Sharp differences could be seen in the adoption of new rotations, for example, between areas otherwise similar in farming practice, according to the degree of encouragement offered by the local *zemstvos*, though admittedly all such gains were marginal. In the central agricultural regions 80 per cent of the farmland (excluding forests) was under the plough and with little forage produced for livestock the three-field system was a blind alley, offering no solution to land hunger or poverty. None of the usual prerequisites for modification of the three-field system was present to a sufficient degree, neither enclosure, freedom of cultivation nor capital. There was a widespread belief that partial reform of the system was not possible due to the interdependence of the whole and total reform was too hazardous for social reasons. Certainly partial change was difficult because of the extreme subdivision of holdings, repartition and poor tools but it was this, not the rigidity of the three-field system itself, that prevented change. There were some complicated rotations to be sure, some so sophisticated that they caused chaos in communal systems, but in European Russia in 1913 only 4·4 per cent of the planted area was devoted to roots, and though this fell below 4 per cent in the black earth region, over the rest of Russia it was still under 6 per cent. True, there was an overall increase in the area under crops in European Russia but this was achieved mainly in the south-east where the population was not dense and colonisation still in progress. Permanent emigration, the traditional palliative to Russia's agricultural problems, was no longer possible in the areas where the crisis was worst, though hundreds of thousands of workers migrated to carry out seasonal work in the southern steppes every summer.

The typical peasant was a man in poor health, living in a tiny hovel crowded in winter with animals, infested with vermin of all kinds except in the very poorest homes where it was said that there was nothing for the cockroaches to eat; cleanliness was rudimentary, the diet a matter of bread, porridge, cabbage and potatoes with meat and fish only on feast days. In years of good or average harvests he managed, but disaster hit him all too often. The likelihood of any improvement seemed remote; the only realistic aim of policy at the end of the century was to avoid any further deterioration.

The role of the larger landowners gradually diminished. In 1877 the nobility owned 73·1 million dessiatines of land and only 53·2 million dessiatines in 1905. The more resourceful among them bought land, improved techniques and generally sought to reap the profits offered by a growing internal and external trade in agricultural products. The wealthiest had the greatest opportunities and some adapted to capitalism easily but they were exceptional even among their own class. Emancipation posed real problems of organising labour and supplying capital; many found it hard to adjust to a new form of economic life. As the poet Nekrasov wrote of emancipation: 'The great chain burst asunder, and one end hit the master, the other the peasant.' The nobility continued their old ways of borrowing on mortgage for current expenditure although now it was land, not serfs, that they pledged. In 1860 they were in debt to the sum of 425 million roubles; by 1880 300 million of this had been paid off but new debts contracted with private mortgage banks had brought their total debt in 1881 to 396 million roubles. The Nobles Land Bank was founded to help their financial difficulties by lending on mortgage and also by arranging for land sales. Some of the money doubtless went to estate improvements, some of the nobility followed middle-class practice by investing in industry and using dividends to support themselves, but for the majority the sales simply went to finance a way of living which their own sources of income were insufficient to maintain. It was paradoxical that the new methods of farming were most suitable for proprietors who had the money to invest and the freedom to use their land as they wished, but many saw their personal prosperity as a reason to make no change. Even nobles on the verge of ruin were unable to save themselves in this way, partly for want of resources and partly for want of the right attitude of mind. However, although in 1905 the nobility owned considerably less land than immediately after emancipation, the value of their holdings had risen by approximately one-half. A large part of noble land was in the hands of between two and three hundred very wealthy families but there were also 50,000 small estates averaging about 100 dessiatines each. In 1905 a quarter of privately owned land was in holdings of over 10,000 dessiatines though much was rented out to the peasantry. Some 9,700 peasants had farms of over 200 dessiatines too and therefore were themselves in the category of grand proprietors.

THE PATTERNS OF AGRICULTURAL PRODUCTION

Large-scale farming was carried on in the south-west, in the Baltic provinces and on the southern steppes. The south-west was an area of commercialised farming, abundant labour and low wages. There the growing of sugar beet was particularly important; the acreage rose from 100,000 dessiatines in 1860 to 369,000 in 1896–8. Sugar beet processing originated in the central provinces, Tula and Orel, but made only slow progress until it shifted to the warmer climate of Kiev province in the 1840s, soon spreading over the whole south-western region. Output rose from 1·2 million poods in 1848 to 46·8 million in 1898 and with that expansion went great improvements in factory production. The average annual output of the 380 factories of 1841 was 3,200 poods; the 238 factories at the end of the century averaged over 185,000 poods. The yield (sugar related to weight of beet) rose from 1·5 per cent to 10 per cent. The growing of beet and the processing plants associated with it undoubtedly represented one of the most advanced sectors of Russian estate agriculture. New Russia in the south was an area of cereals, high wages, seasonal labour and increasing mechanisation. The use of harvesters expanded rapidly after 1900 but this did not stop the flow of seasonal workers. Rather, it helped increase the cultivated area and ensured that crops would be fully harvested in even the most bountiful years. In the north and west the large farmers catered for the local urban markets. There was a big rise in the area under potatoes grown largely for distilling purposes. They formed 8 per cent of gross crop output on the larger farms after 1900 but only 2 per cent on the peasant holdings where they were hardly a cash crop at all. In part the patterns of farming reflected climatic conditions: the rainy northern provinces needed drainage and heavy manuring, while the dry southern lands could only be farmed extensively. Even more the patterns reflected different market conditions. The St Petersburg region had the lowest percentage of land under cereals in all Russia and the highest under field crops. There lucerne, sainfoin and clover were basic elements in rotations and fallow had almost completely disappeared. There was a considerable amount of dairy farming in White Russia to meet the demands of the big Polish cities and other townships in the province; pigs were bred for export to Germany.

Russia played a role in the world supply of flax as dominant as that taken by the United States in cotton. It was principally a peasant crop. In the north flax was usually grown as a spring crop in a three-field system and then separated into seed and fibre; in the south only the seed was used. In 1912 exports of flax amounted to 108 million roubles and of linseed 20·4 million roubles. In 1913 Russia also provided more than a third of world timber exports and timber accounted for 11 per cent of all her exports, 165 million roubles. These exports grew rapidly after 1900 when Swedish trade began to decline. Nearly half of Russia's exports came from Finland and almost all the remainder from the five northern provinces of Archangel, Vologda, Perm, Olonets and Viatka. Two-thirds of the exports went to Germany and Britain; Germany took largely unprocessed wood, transported by way of the Niemen and Vistula rivers to be finished in the mills of Tilsit, Memel (Klaipeda), Danzig (Gdansk), Stettin (Szczecin) and Königsberg (Kaliningrad). Britain imported processed wood. The home trade in timber was possibly three times as large as the foreign. The industry in Finland began using steam saws in the late 1850s and with removal of export duties too, exports began to rise rapidly. Then came the expansion of pulp and paper manufacture, mostly for the Russian market. The number of workers in that sector rose from 2,600 in 1885 to 9,900 in 1905, while those employed in sawmills rose from 7,300 to 21,600. In 1910–14 timber, pulp and paper provided 71 per cent of Finland's exports outside Russia.

At the southern extreme of the country, in Turkestan, the state fostered the growing of cotton. In the 1870s government experimental stations began bringing in good American varieties; the tariff on imported cotton was raised in 1887 and 1894 and railways came to open up the market. The sown area rose from 17,000 dessiatines in 1880 to 88,000 in 1887–91 and to 466,000 dessiatines in 1912–16. After 1900 cotton was grown in all provinces of Turkestan and in most regions comprised about a third of the cultivated area. The share of Russian cotton in total home consumption had reached more than a half by the outbreak of the First World War.

But grain growing was the key to Russian agriculture and the country's major contribution to world trade. Wheat and barley were the cash grains and the most heavily exported grains; oats and rye were grown mostly for home consumption, though so huge was the total crop that the small proportion exported was a significant element in world trade. The surplus of these last two grains was produced in the east and flowed from the Volga ports of Kazan, Simbirsk (Ulyanovsk), Samara (Kuibyshev) and Saratov to Moscow and St Petersburg, to the Baltic ports and to the western land border into Germany. The Russian rye harvest virtually determined the basic European price, but not so that of wheat where Russia was only one of several major world exporters. The commercial wheat and barley areas were found above all in the south and east and in the Trans-Volga region – in Kherson, Bessarabia, Taurida, Don, Ekaterinoslav, Saratov, Samara and Orenburg, an area of large estates and relatively high mechanisation. Since the 1880s all the increase in the grain area had been devoted to wheat and barley. In 1913 wheat took 32·3 per cent of the crop area, rye 29 per cent, oats 18·6 per cent and barley 11·9 per cent. To the 1890s grain was grown on the European steppes regularly year after year and the land then left idle for up to fifteen years and animals pastured on it. Thereafter pressure of population could not allow such a high proportion of the land to lie idle for so long and the period of fallow was gradually shortened. Some big landowners sowed lucerne there and cultivated more winter wheat than the peasants. This required better tillage, which helped keep up the fertility of the soil, but in many areas no effective rotation was to be found. In the black earth regions the rotation consisted of winter rye, oats or spring wheat and fallow but the fallow was not ploughed until mid-summer despite the fact that earlier ploughing would have increased the yield by 30–40 per cent. The reason was that with so much ploughing up of meadows for cereals, use of the fallow was the only means of pasturing livestock. On average in 1900 the peasant used 0·43 poods of fertiliser per dessiatine compared with 10·2 in Germany. The output of agricultural machinery factories grew rapidly after the turn of the century – its value was 5 million roubles in 1890, 10·4 million in 1900 and 60·5 million in 1913 – while imports rose from almost nothing to 15·9 million and 59·5 million roubles in these years respectively. The machines were largely employed in the area of extensive farming in the south and east. In 1910 two-thirds of all the ploughs in use were still wooden and half of these were of the most primitive type, though it was in the north that most of them were to be found. Only some 2 per cent of peasant households used seed drills in 1910.

With such a primitive technology both in the use of implements and in rotations, and with cereal growing so widespread, yields were inevitably low. The return to cereals all over Russia in 1870–4 was only 4 : 1, that is to say four units reaped for every unit sown, similar to the position in western Europe during the middle ages. The dry climate inevitably meant that yields would be low anyway, but in the years immediately before 1914 the yield for wheat in Hungary where the climate was similar was 60 per cent higher than the Russian average. More significantly, the output of wheat and rye did not keep pace with the rise of population. Taking per capita output in 1870–4 as 100, in 1886–90 it was 92·3 and in 1896–1900 it was 97·2. Deducting exports, the figures were 86·1 and 94·5 respectively. Eventually the pressure of home demand began to have its effect in reducing the relative importance of the export surplus. The reduction in transport costs associated with railways greatly stimulated internal trade and reduced price differentials between regions. There was, too, a marked switch to the production and export of barley whose price was more favourable. Most of that grain went to Germany, where low transport costs allowed it to compete with maize from the United States, and to the Danube region as feed grain for livestock. Particularly after 1906 the German tariff favoured barley over maize and this in part accounts for the changeover to barley in the south-eastern steppes just before 1914.

The relative decline in the importance of wheat exports is shown in column three of Table 61 and column four shows the sharp rise in per capita consumption. The share of output marketed at home rose from 22 to over 30 per cent between 1891–5 and 1906–10: this was largely due to

Table 61 *Production and sale of the bread grain crops of European Russia, 1897–1913*

	Production	Exports	Percentage exported	Quantity retained per capita (quintals)
	(*m. quintals*)			
Wheat				
1897	102·7	34·6	33·7	0·6
1907	143·2	40·2	28·1	0·8
1913	180·7	43·9	24·3	1·0
Rye				
1897	193·0	12·5	6·7	1·7
1907	202·2	11·9	5·9	1·6
1913	225·9	7·9	3·5	1·6

Source: V. P. Timoshenko, *Agricultural Russia and the Wheat Problem* (Stanford, 1932), p. 372.

the relative increase of urban population who tended to eat more wheaten bread. The per capita consumption of rye fell, in part due to the rapid growth of the rural population in the south-east and Siberia, where wheat was the main bread grain. Nevertheless the share of output marketed at home rose from 10 to over 20 per cent. Russian bread consumption in 1913 was 195 kilograms per head compared with 186 kilograms in Austria-Hungary and 244 kilograms in France. Of course, the grains were different and bread was a different proportion of the diet in each country so that the figures tell us little about living standards. The overall consumption of grains by the Russian peasant was extremely low, however, largely because so little was used to feed to livestock.

Grain was moved internally over very long distances and this posed great problems of transport and commercial organisation. Both rye and wheat faced an average freight haul of over 700 kilometres and grain raised in the east and exported through the Baltic travelled 1,000 to 1,600 kilometres. The trade required an army of intermediaries, a lot of capital and much storage capacity. By 1914 public silos were being erected but there remained a serious deficiency and grains left at collecting points one autumn were frequently there the next. One of the earliest of the functions of the railways was to collect grain from the central agricultural and the black earth areas and take it to Moscow and St Petersburg. Subsequently a line was built to connect the Volga region with the Baltic ports. But in the 1890s a quarter of the grain still moved by internal waterways and in 1911–13 the proportion was one-fifth, mainly going by the Volga to internal markets, though some was taken from the milling areas at Nijni Novgorod (Gorki), Yaroslavl and Rybinsk, downstream to Tsaritsyn (Stalingrad, Volgagrad) and thence by rail to the Black Sea.

The marketing of crops was naturally a matter of great importance. Far more wheat than rye left the farms; in 1913 a quarter of the rye harvest was marketed compared with 60 per cent of the wheat. The large estates marketed far more of their output than the peasants and the richer peasant, the *kulak*, a greater proportion than the small peasant. As urbanisation proceeded and the need for exports became more urgent, the question of increasing the marketed surplus became more and more pressing. In part it could be achieved through a larger total output, either as a result of greater productivity or from ploughing up more land; encouragement of emigration to Siberia played an important role in this. In part it could come from imposing higher taxes on the farming community, forcing it to market more so as to be able to meet the taxes; this was very much a feature of the policies of the Finance Minister, Count de Witte, during the 1890s. Finally it might be brought about by shifting control over land towards those who tended to market most – in fact from smaller to larger landowners – and this was in effect the aim of policy after 1906.

The internal market was satisfied above all from the central agricultural provinces. In the years before 1914 provinces such as Riazan, Orel, Tula, Kiev, Poltava, Kharkhov, Kursk, Voronezh, Tambov, Saratov and Samara, where a lot of rye was grown, were disposing of more than half their surplus grain at home, moving it in particular to the grain deficiency areas further north. Regular exports of grain began in the late eighteenth century when Russia obtained access to the steppes around the Black Sea and the fertile regions of the west Ukraine and after the partitions of Poland – though Polish exports through Danzig had been important throughout the eighteenth century. The growth of the Russian trade and its distribution between various crops is shown in Table 62. Between 1861 and 1917 Russian wheat comprised between a third and a quarter of world trade. In the first half of the nineteenth century most of Russian wheat was distributed to Europe via Constantinople (Istanbul) and the north Italian ports. Then in the 1860s and 1870s the bulk of it began to go to Britain through the Black Sea and at its peak was providing 30 per cent of

Britain's requirements. But the market was poorly organised, the supply unstable, the grain badly cleaned and as other sources of supply materialised Russia declined to being Britain's marginal supplier when other crops fell short or when large Russian crops brought low prices. Germany became the main customer for Russian soft wheat and the hard wheat, which was grown in the semi-arid areas of the south, went to markets in southern Europe. There durum wheat, which was grown only in small quantities outside Russia, was prized for the manufacture of semolina, macaroni and spaghetti.

Table 83[1] shows Russia's share of world trade in all grains before the war. She was now dependent on the German market, which took one-third of her wheat, three-quarters of her barley and two-thirds of her rye, though German rye also competed with Russian in the Scandinavian market.

Table 62 *Annual average Russian grain exports, 1820–1913 (m. quintals)*

	Wheat	Rye	Barley	Oats	Total
1820–39	1·51	0·49	0·18	0·21	2·39
1840–9	4·23	1·21	0·23	0·34	6·01
1860–9	8·89	2·64	0·82	1·39	13·74
1880–9	21·54	11·38	6·93	9·07	48·92
1890–9	28·76	10·5	14·33	8·16	61·75
1900–9	33·37	13·55	21·84	10·88	79·64
1910–13	40·12	6·73	37·49	10·55	94·89

Source: V. P. Timoshenko, *Agricultural Russia and the Wheat Problem* (Stanford, 1932), p. 472.

Russia exported very little flour as the quality was not up to western European standards. However, the exports of bran alone – husks left after milling – were about the same as those of oats and rye, amounting to 33 million roubles. These exports were of immense significance to the economy. In the 1870s they provided 56 per cent of all exports and in the years prior to 1914 still only slightly less than one-half. There were, nevertheless, huge fluctuations from year to year because poor storage facilities made it impossible to control outflow. Indeed concentration on grain to this extent raised several serious problems. The urge to plough up the land reduced the animal population and in some areas such as the central agricultural and middle Volga regions this, together with the rise of population, led to soil exhaustion and a fall in the marketed surplus. The lack of internal demand for livestock products also left the farmer with little chance to adjust to the relative prices of grain and non-grain products. As grain prices fell in the 1880s and early 1890s, except near the large towns there was no option but to try to produce more grain in the hope of making good the losses sustained through lower prices. Even so, capitalist agriculture in Russia was undoubtedly boosted by the opportunities offered by the international market after emancipation. The organisation of the trade, largely in the hands of Jewish merchants, for all its shortcomings, was effective enough for the output and variety of cereals to respond reasonably quickly to international demands, as may be seen in the shift to barley before 1914, the growth of shipments of wheat from Siberia and the way in which Russian oats supplanted Swedish oats in the British market.

Despite these developments, however, the basic point remains that technically Russian agriculture was backward and undiversified. The rise of population and the pressure of taxation helped to produce a growing volume of marketed crops but helped, too, to keep the mass of the peasantry in abject poverty. The internal market for manufactured goods, therefore, received little boost from all this activity and the problem of peasant unrest remained as serious as ever. Not until after 1900 were significant attempts made to come to grips with these fundamental problems of Russian agriculture.

There was therefore no possibility of achieving economic progress in Russia through a balanced development of the agricultural and other sectors. The size of the problem and the Ministry of the Interior's fear of the social consequences of any positive action paralysed policy completely. But there were as many obstacles to an unbalanced development depending primarily on industry, so that again only positive action by the state could hope to make an impression on the extreme backwardness of the economy.

THE STATE AND ECONOMIC GROWTH

The cultural and institutional handicaps to growth, the problems of the agricultural sector and the extent of the effort needed to make good what was now a rapidly growing gap between Russia and western countries, meant that rapid industrialisation would only come about under some unusually powerful stimulus, external or internal. Yet it could hardly be thrust upon an unprepared economy. The terms of emancipation were scarcely conducive to industrialisation but even had they been more favourable, there was bound to have been a period of only modest development while the infrastructure of a more diversified economy was created. Judicial and administrative reforms in the wake of emancipation were essential; essential also was the improvement of communications. The problems of labour supply resulting from the preservation of the commune in 1861 have almost certainly been exaggerated but undoubtedly the quality of much of the labour was poor and skilled workers were in very short supply. Standards of commercial honesty were low; capital for long-term industrial investment was extremely hard to come by. Consequently the likelihood of rapid expansion of industry under private initiative was slight, even had there been no shortage of entrepreneurial talent. Most problematic of all was the question of the spur to industrial growth; where would the demand come from?

Historical experience shows that there were no single answers to these difficulties, though the more acute they were the more drastic the solutions needed to be. Technology and special skills could be imported, as could capital, for the more ambitious investment projects. Capital-intensive technology could be substituted for scarce skills in many cases; the organisation of industry into large units might make it possible to economise on the supply of entrepreneurial talent. The demand problem, which seemed so intractable given a negligible growth of rural incomes, could be overcome, initially at any rate, by government spending on a large scale.

In these ways the obstacles created by Russia's historical background and by the mode of emancipation could be surmounted. Indeed, there was a marked acceleration of industrial growth during the 1880s only a quarter-century after emancipation, though it is always well to remember the low absolute level of output on which these gains were made. The peak of growth and, far more important, the rapid development of the more modern sectors of industry came during the 1890s. A great deal depended on the drive of ministers like de Witte but determined though they might be, there was a limit to what they could accomplish in such a huge and widespread economy and there were always those about them who were not of the same mind. The twin demands for order and progress were never entirely reconcilable; the very magnitude of the problems of rural society set up tensions which brought down ministers, created contradictions in economic policies and culminated in internal unrest both in country and town. Added to this were the notorious vagaries of the Russian harvest and the complications of international politics and wars. The achievements of the three decades before 1914 in this most difficult of environments are therefore the more astonishing.

Demand was the key to growth and here government fiscal policy was to play a crucial role. The problems, however, were complex; the government would have to provide a substitute for the weakness of internal demand by placing direct orders with industry, supplemented by subsidies, protection and other favours. This expenditure would have to be covered by taxes as far as possible, for there was no conscious idea of deficit financing. The nature of this taxation would in turn affect the level of internal demand. Furthermore, military expenditures were high and not easily controlled and spending on education was at last beginning to rise significantly too. On the other hand there was the important question of the relationship between the state of the public finances and the exchange value of the rouble, for foreign investors would need to have confidence in the currency if they were to be induced to invest in Russia on any scale. So Russian finance ministers faced problems not altogether unlike those plaguing some western European countries a hundred years later. The requirements of long-term expansion conflicted with the short-term need to preserve the rouble and to balance the budget. Recent writers have shown that both the finance ministers of the 1880s, Bunge (1881–7) and Vishnegradsky (1887–91), unduly restricted the money supply to achieve these ends and so hindered expansion. It is argued that the danger of inflation was not great, the budget deficit at worst less than one per cent of national income and so the policy entirely misconceived. But such an argument is untenable in its historical context. Ideas of sound finance demanded a balanced budget and finance ministers running a deficit would have fallen long before any beneficial consequences could have appeared. Foreign confidence in the rouble demanded orthodox fiscal policies. A country with as many problems as Russia, with a basically weak currency, could hardly flout international conventions.

The level of government expenditure for the whole period from 1885 to 1913 was no more than about 13 per cent of the national income, a modest figure for the time, but there seems little doubt that the tax burden was regressive. With 22 per cent of the national income earned by 0·9 per cent of the active population in 1909–10, a significant increase in revenue could have been brought in by direct taxes aimed at the relatively small number of big incomes. Politically, however, it was out of the question and the authorities faced immense administrative as well as political difficulties in their attempts to tap different sources of revenue. In part taxation was kept high by the level of military expenditure; from 1866 to 1885 it accounted for 32 per cent of total outgoings. An expenditure of 148 million roubles was incurred in 1869, for example, compared with 114 million roubles spent by France in 1870, and 77 million by the North German Confederation in the same year when the two were at war. The actual expenditure on pay and equipment per head was much below that of the other countries but the number of men under arms was more than twice that in either France or Germany in 1872. The Turkish War of 1877–8 had further serious consequences for the budget and this, together with a number of other factors, made overseas borrowing very difficult. Foreigners were unwilling to lend to a country with a depreciating currency unless interest and capital were guaranteed in gold terms, but this might result in intolerable costs of servicing the debt if the rouble did in fact fall. Two attempts to fix the exchange rate of the rouble and adhere to the gold standard after the Crimean War failed. Furthermore the balance of trade worsened in the early 1880s as the fall in price of Russia's grain exports turned the terms of trade against her, but in the late years of the decade good harvests helped to build up a trade surplus and the rouble appreciated again. Since after 1877 all import duties were collected in terms of the gold rouble, both the revenue and the level of protection were enhanced by the fall in the value of the paper rouble. It has been suggested that this raised protection by a third and the duties were increased by a further 20 per cent in 1885.

N. K. Bunge, who was finance minister from 1881 to 1887, tried to tackle some of the wider problems of Russian society. He reduced the tax burden on the peasantry by abolishing the notorious per capita soul tax and the tax on salt, recouping the revenue in part through higher import duties. He looked to the needs of the growing proletariat with the first comprehensive Russian factory legislation. Through the Peasant Land Bank and Nobles Bank he sought to facilitate the transfer of land and, from an economic point of view most significant of all, he brought the state into the business of constructing railroads at its own expense on a considerable scale. Eventually the problem of providing financial support for these projects and the steady decline of the rouble brought his downfall but some progress in creating the environment for expansion had certainly been achieved.

He was succeeded by I. A. Vishnegradsky, a new type of administrator interested in science and technology, enjoying close connections with business and finance. His methods were rigid, even brutal, but by the standards of the time remarkably effective. He raised indirect taxes and curtailed government expenditure wherever possible. He stimulated exports by differential rail rebates and by putting pressure on the peasants to pay their taxes. In 1891 tariffs were drastically increased, partly for fiscal reasons but also undoubtedly with the object of stimulating home industry. The prospects of overseas borrowing were much improved by the political entente with France. Russia had previously been dependent on Germany for most of her borrowing but after this link had been severed by Bismarck in 1888, the finance minister was able to convert the 5 per cent Mendelssohn bonds of 1877, subscribed mainly in Germany, to a French loan at 4 per cent, thereby inaugurating a new era in Russian finance. The trade surplus averaged 311 million roubles in 1887–91 compared with 68 million during 1882–6, but Vishnegradsky was not able entirely to stabilise the rouble, largely owing to speculation carried out in Berlin, but also being content himself to let it depreciate to stimulate exports. He had not consciously sought to bring about a rapid expansion of the economy and indeed some would argue that his measures to balance the budget and bring down the note issue were positively harmful but, by putting both the budget and the balance of payments in a healthy condition and creating the conditions favourable to foreign borrowing, in an important respect he laid the foundations for what was to come.

De Witte, who followed Vishnegradsky when his term of office was ended by the disastrous harvest and cholera epidemic of 1891, had been a railway promoter and administrator and was much influenced by List's ideas of state-fostered industrialisation. It was therefore not surprising that his attention should be focused on railways, and that his actions should be supplemented by an intensification of protection. No doubt these tariffs raised the costs of capital outlays, but in so far as they were at least partly instrumental in bringing about a rise in the output and efficiency of the metallurgical industry in Russia and in encouraging the emergence of a machine building industry with its attendant skills, it was probably worth while. Certainly there is no evidence that the tariff inhibited technical change, though by eliminating imports it undoubtedly encouraged price fixing agreements. Direct subsidies for industry were unimportant but further help came through tax remissions, profit guarantees and government orders at favourable prices, the latter being most vital of all to the steel industry. Yet de Witte's third line of attack, the encouragement of foreign investment, was seen by him as one means of attracting new technology and of cutting into the monopoly profit of inefficient Russian businesses. De Witte did what he could to mobilise Russian resources through the medium of the State Bank and through the encouragement he gave to savings banks by easing the conditions under which they could be established and by creating more confidence in the currency. In 1890 there were 871 such banks with assets of 111 million roubles; by 1900 there were 4,781 with deposits of 608 million roubles. In aggregate the bulk of capital accumulation during his period came from Russian sources. But foreign capital went into those vital sectors where new technology was being introduced, giving much of the impetus to rapid growth after 1890 and in turn helping to stimulate an upsurge of purely Russian investment.

De Witte, as we have seen, needed to support his industrial policies by measures to bring in more revenue and to stabilise the external value of the rouble, measures which had serious consequences for the well-being of the mass of peasants. For much of the time the 1890s were good years for borrowing abroad because the rate of interest was low; by converting expensive home loans to cheaper foreign loans de Witte was able to reduce expenditure by over one thousand million roubles. But he faced a dual problem; despite that windfall he still needed to increase income to balance his budget, where expenditure on railways had risen appreciably, and he also had to face a deteriorating balance of payments as grain prices fell to their lowest in the early 1890s. Yet he needed to build up the gold reserve so as to be able to go on to the gold standard and strengthen Russia's ability to borrow. To balance the budget and stimulate exports he therefore turned to higher taxation. By raising taxes and requiring payment in the autumn, he forced the peasants to market more and more of their crops; under de Witte 15·7 per cent of the grain was exported compared with 14·3 per cent from 1887–92. He concentrated too on direct taxes, arguing that under Russian conditions the rural masses were largely self-sufficient and that consequently the taxes hit most those who could afford them. It is hard to know whether de Witte believed this but by taxing basic goods such as salt, tobacco, matches, lamp oil and sugar, he placed a heavy burden on the masses. He kept up the redemption payments and put heavier duties on liquor, ostensibly to curb drunkenness, though in fact his revenue from vodka rose by a quarter. The budget and the balance of payments came to depend on the peasant not eating his fill.

Table 63 Russian foreign trade, 1890–9 (m. roubles)

	Exports	Imports	Surplus	Gold imports		Exports	Imports	Surplus	Gold imports
1890	693·4	416·0	277·4	2·2	1895	689·1	538·5	150·6	36·2
1891	707·4	379·3	320·1	76·9	1896	688·6	589·8	98·8	116·3
1892	475·6	403·9	71·7	109·1	1897	726·6	560·0	162·6	130·9
1893	599·2	463·5	135·7	24·0	1898	732·7	617·5	115·2	85·4
1894	668·7	559·6	109·1	86·7	1899	630·0	650·5	−20·5	21·0

Source: Parliamentary Papers, Statistical Abstract for Foreign Countries.

Nevertheless, it is important to note that revenue rose in part because of increased demand for taxed goods from the urban population: in 1911 urban demand for kerosene was twenty times that of the rural areas, and demand for vodka three times as great. The rouble was stabilised de facto by exchange control and by counter-speculation against Berlin from 1894 onwards, the State Bank receiving orders to keep movements of the currency within narrow limits. For the sake of stability the bank held very high reserves relative to its note issue; notes were really gold certificates and the issue was much below the maximum safe level. Over the later years of the decade as a result of this policy the circulation did not rise nearly fast enough to cover the needs of a rapidly growing economy, which was bringing sector upon sector and area after area more into the money economy. The stabilisation of the currency, though inhibiting development in this way, did help to bring about a large inflow of foreign capital. The export surplus actually fell as a result of the big rise in imports of manufactures and the fall in the price of grain exports, as Table 63 shows. But this deterioration was covered by overseas borrowing to a degree sufficient to bring about a substantial rise in the gold reserves although one-third of the total increase during de Witte's regime was due to Russian output of gold which in these circumstances was entirely retained at home.

Eventually, in 1897, following a good harvest in the previous year, Russia returned to the gold standard. The cost of achieving this was a huge burden of additional taxation, of extra forced exports and the immobilisation of the reserves. The gain came in the form of stabilisation of the exchange rate and the easier borrowing conditions overseas that followed from this. So firm an achievement was it that the rouble even weathered the upset of the war with Japan in 1903–4 and the uprising of 1905, though it had to face heavy international speculation. But help from foreign banks was requested and was forthcoming.

De Witte's policies and the massive inflow of foreign capital and technology were not the only force behind the expansion of Russian industry at this time. Mechanisation of certain sectors and the emergence of the Ukraine as a new centre of industrialisation were already well under way before he came into office. International conditions, cheap money early in the decade and a worldwide boom later, also helped. But the force of de Witte's various policies is undeniable. He sought to identify growth sectors and to stimulate them in a variety of ways. He saw, too, the penalties of illiteracy and lagging technical education. Vishnegradsky had earlier established a system of independent schools and de Witte followed this by setting up commercial and trade schools with the intention of educating a cadre of intelligent businessmen. The fear of the disruptive effect of popular education on the part of other ministers thwarted his efforts, but already the *zemstvos* were beginning to see this as their responsibility and in the first decade of the new century there was a marked rise in expenditure on elementary education both by the *zemstvos* and the Ministry of Public Instruction.

There were, of course, limits to what de Witte could achieve in a short space of time, especially as he was working in an increasingly hostile atmosphere in both royal and government circles. He was unable to take any significant action to change the pattern of rural life and farming techniques. This was partly because of lack of the necessary political support and partly because till after 1900 he was against radical change and believed unbalanced growth would eventually force change in the lagging sectors. In this he was clearly mistaken. The social unrest which developed as workers migrated to the growing industrial towns he was forced to treat largely as a police matter. In 1903 de Witte was forced to resign but by that time not only had Russian industry been given a major boost, but subsequent events were to suggest that the main object had been achieved; growth was to continue with a momentum of its own on the basis more and more of private internal demand and Russian entrepreneurial initiative.

But if industrial progress was ensured the twin problems of social unrest and rural poverty began to grow even more serious, culminating in the storm of uprisings in 1905. Piotr Stolypin, who became Prime Minister after the 1905 revolt, now undertook a major reform of rural society and sought to create a new basis of political solidarity for the regime among the more enterprising peasants, who were given the opportunity to improve their positions by being freed from the control of the *mir*. Given time, it is possible that his radical approach, together with the opportunities offered by industrialisation for raising the standard of living in the cities, might have provided the basis for a more stable social system, but events overtook him in 1917.

The half century after 1861 had seen Russian governments seeking to resolve their twin problems of stability and backwardness, of short-run budgetary and long-run expansionary requirements. If the final solution eluded them, it is wrong to ignore their successes. We now turn to see in more detail how the economy reacted.

THE SUPPLY OF CAPITAL

The potential for private capital investment in Russia began to develop after 1861 primarily because of the great rise in the grain trade, but such internal sources were not likely to be large and venturesome enough to press forward economic development by direct investment, especially in new areas of industrial technology, until the ground had been prepared by alternative sources of finance. To 1861 banks had played little part in industrial finance. After emancipation the situation began to change. The first joint stock bank, the St Petersburg Private Commercial Bank, was opened in 1864 and was followed by others of the same type in the north-western area, some with the participation of German and Austrian capital, until by 1873 there were 73 banks altogether. Some collapsed in the depression after 1874 and the State Council sanctioned new ones grudgingly. A policy requiring high minimum reserves served to encourage concentration too, so that by 1900 there were only 43 banks, 6 of them carrying 47 per cent of the liabilities. In 1914 there were 50 with about 750 branches altogether. Until the 1890s these banks largely confined themselves to helping industry with working capital; the railways were mostly financed by the state and the new industries in the south by direct foreign investment. Only after the breakthrough to more rapid industrial growth did the Russian banks turn to investment banking of the German type. The problems inherent in this type of banking are well known and in Russia, where the viability of industrial companies was generally far lower than in Germany and the economy more vulnerable to cyclical fluctuations and to the effects of international speculation, the dangers were great and became particularly acute during the recession that began in 1900. The banks had large holdings of industrial securities for which there were no buyers. They also found themselves deprived of the short-term credits provided until then by foreign banks.

At this moment de Witte brought in the State Bank to play a vital role in state financial policy. The Bank set about rescuing the commercial banking system. It gave prompt and liberal advances, lowered its own interest rates to encourage funds to move to the private sector, supported a syndicate to buy shares and bolster the market, gave loans to firms in temporary difficulties so as to free the assets of the private banks and even took over the weakest banks so as to maintain confidence in the financial community. Such action was always open to charges of corruption and favouritism and of bolstering up inefficiency, but these dangers, though real, were of little moment compared with the effectiveness of its actions in maintaining the momentum of industrialisation. The depression of 1929 was to call for similar action in more developed western countries; that of 1900 was a less severe crisis but the future of the Russian economy was at the same time more delicately poised.

To 1900 a great deal of capital for new industrial ventures, and above all for the coal and metallurgical industries of the south, came from abroad. In 1900 45 per cent of the capital investment in common stock in Russian industry was foreign, though it must be remembered that only the larger concerns issued stock in that way. France had 692 million francs in joint stock companies in Russia and some 100 million in Belgian-owned companies operating in Russia. Belgian and German investment was nearly as high. Regionally French and Belgian capital dominated in the Donetz, French and German in Poland; there was some French capital in the Urals while German capital predominated in the chemical and electrical industries in the northern and Baltic areas. The patterns of such investment varied a great deal; some came from existing manufacturing concerns in the west such as Cockerills of Belgium; less frequently one would find individual western promoters of new industries in Russia. Then there were promotional groups usually led by banks such as the Société Générale in Paris whose activities in Russia went back to 1872. The reasons for such investment varied. It was usually directed towards new types of industry or to backward sectors where foreigners were seeking to exploit a technological gap. They were attracted by the solicitous attitude of the Russian government which offered contracts, subsidies and other favours, especially where railway building was concerned, and at the same time they were influenced by the high tariffs placed on imports, certainly an important consideration for firms like Cockerills which had enjoyed a large export trade to Russia. Their sales were over 5 million francs in 1877 but after the imposition of high tariffs these had slumped to 300,000 francs by 1886. Foreign investors were given confidence by the orthodox fiscal policies pursued by the Russian government and they were greatly attracted by the high rates of return which many of the early investors enjoyed. The major part of French finance was placed in state and state-guaranteed bonds and such investment was much encouraged by the activities of banks such as the Crédit Lyonnais which made large commissions out of placing Russian issues, by the more friendly political climate between Russia and France and by the stability of the rouble consequent upon the return to the gold standard in 1897.

In the boom that followed the world depression of 1907–8, however, Russian banks and foreign capitalists came to finance Russian industry in a partnership quite different from that obtaining during the de Witte period, though the share of foreigners in Russian joint stock companies actually rose slightly and the absolute level of this investment doubled between 1900 and 1914. Much of this money came from development within existing firms and in part because profits were ploughed back. Active foreign management declined and there was a big rise in foreign portfolio investment, especially the purchase of shares of Russian banks, possibly because foreigners appreciated the help that had been given by the State Bank after 1900. By 1916 foreign participation provided 44 per cent of the capital of the joint stock banks in Russia. French banks now began to form syndicates with the Russian banks to finance industry. Russian banks sought out the opportunities for investment and the syndicates placed the shares simultaneously on several international stock exchanges. Many financial reorganisations were brought about which offered notable profits to those financing them but there was true innovation too. Whereas in the 1890s Russian businessmen had been at a disadvantage as against the foreigner in seeking to tap foreign funds for their own use, by 1914 all this had changed. Russian banks tracked down the opportunities, organised studies and the acquisition of expertise and then looked to the foreigner to help convert these to advantage. In the years just before the war the Russians were thus showing signs of conquering their remaining major deficiency, the lack of managerial and technical enterprise. The banks were taking over the role played by the government in the 1890s by promoting industrial growth, an important indication that industrialisation was achieving a momentum of its own. The banks had also rectified a more general institutional weakness for they were now able to use for these purposes the large sums which were lying dormant with them on deposit owing to the poor market for direct personal investment. The links between the banks and industry were now strong and immediate therefore, the bulk of them contracted by a few very large organisations. In 1914 twelve of the banks, nine of them in St Petersburg, comprised four-fifths of all bank capital and dominated overseas business and that of the main industrial sectors. The most recent was the Russo-Asiatic Bank established in 1910 with two-thirds of the capital French. By 1914 it had 102 branches, 17 per cent of all banking assets in Russia and representatives on the boards of sixty-two concerns. Its chairman, Putilov, had close links with the Russo-Chinese banks, was director of Prodamet, the major syndicate in the metallurgical industry, and was the chief shareholder of many big firms

Table 64   *Foreign investment in Russia,*
1890–1915 (m. roubles)

	1890	*1900*	*1915*
Belgium	24·6	296·5	318·7
France	66·6	226·1	687·9
Germany	79·0	219·3	436·1
Britain	35·3	136·8	535·4
USA	2·3	8·0	114·0

Source: P. Lyashchenko, *History of the National Economy of Russia* (New York, 1949), p. 538.

such as Putilov Arms, Bryansk Steel and Neva Shipbuilding. It was the St Petersburg banks who conducted their business on lines closest to those of the great German banks, overshadowing the Moscow banks who continued in the main to carry on deposit banking closer to the British model.

In 1914 total foreign holdings of Russian securities came to 7·8 million roubles, about 36 per cent of the total. However, foreigners held very few mortgage bonds. The large proportion of native Russian capital directed to mortgages may be considered a weak feature of the economy if much of the money was used for consumption outside the country, though we lack definite evidence of this. It would suggest again that capital supply was not so much deficient as misdirected. Foreign holdings therefore amounted to 47 per cent of all other securities: 49 per cent of state and state guaranteed bonds, 39 per cent of joint stock shares, 55 per cent of joint stock debentures and 74 per cent of municipal bonds. Foreign investment in Russian industry, including financial institutions, has been put at 2·2 thousand billion roubles amounting by sector to roughly 830 million roubles in mining and metals, 390 million in metal working, 260 million in public utilities, 240 million in banks, 190 million in textiles and 85 million in chemicals. By country the distribution amounted to approximately 33 per cent from France, 23 per cent from Britain, and from Germany and Belgium about 20 per cent each. The statistics for the development of total foreign investment in Russia are given in Table 64.

LABOUR

The supply of labour for industry was not greatly eased by the terms of the emancipation edict and yet large numbers of workers, unattached to communes, were available for factory employment, especially in the north-west and western regions. Alternatively, it was possible for long-term passports to be issued to peasants to leave their villages for extended work in factories. In course of time a labour force was created with varying degrees of attachment to the rural community. There were those peasants who slept and ate at their places of work during the week, returned home for holidays and worked in the fields during the summer. There were those who left the commune but preferred to retain a similar way of life by attaching themselves to an *artel* under a foreman who negotiated with employers for the group as a whole; such men lived communally at their places of work but left their families back in the village. Then there were those who were housed with their families in the factory towns but who might still have a plot left in the village, rented out but available for them to return to in their old age. Finally there were those with no village contacts at all.

How far this multifarious labour force fell short of requirements in both quality and quantity is difficult to say. Certainly, there was a shortage of the highest skills but for many industries the level of skill required of the ordinary worker was not high and, as we have suggested earlier, an ill-educated workforce that was not easily bored was a distinct advantage in some mass production industries. Supervisory personnel were the hardest to find and in the textile and metal industries this vital work was frequently carried out by experienced foreign workers. The spatial distribution of labour for industry was unequal. In southern Russia it was hard to find workers and even harder to hold them the year round; in the Donetz wages were as high as in Belgium for example, much higher than in the north where skills were more plentiful and the workers more settled to factory life. Foreign entrepreneurs had little to complain of about the metal workers in St Petersburg and Moscow, and in the Baltic provinces where the commune had always been weak they considered the workers outstandingly good and cheap. It is hard to be precise about the nature of the labour force but Tugan Baranovsky, quoting an investigation of 18,576 workers in the Moscow region in the mid-1880s, showed that a distinct and important class of factory workers had emerged there. Fifty-five per cent of the sample had fathers who worked or had worked in a factory. In the modern steam powered cotton and wool mills only 8 per cent of the workers left for summer work in the fields. It was in the hand weaving mills, the tanneries and the small establishments of various kinds that the largest proportion of labour was lost in this way. In hand dyeing and cotton printing one-third went away and of those doing so 30 per cent went for as long as two or three months. Study of a calico printing firm in Moscow in 1898 showed 12 per cent leaving for field work, 61 per cent not leaving but with families still living in villages and the rest with no rural ties at all.[2] It has been suggested that by 1900 possibly one-half of all industrial workers were sons of fathers who had themselves been factory workers. Yet the pattern varied a good deal. In 1893 in the Moscow industrial area, of nearly 2 million workers over the previous decade four-fifths on average had worked the full year. For all Russian factories the proportion was more like 72 per cent; in St Petersburg it was 90 per cent but in Kiev only 42 per cent. The greatest amount of seasonal work was found in the mineral extracting industries carried on in largely rural areas where the figure was 24 per cent and we must assume it was the rule in the mass of small rural industries. A labour force hovering between field and factory was the product not so much of the emancipation settlement as of the seasonal nature of Russian industry and the unwillingness of the peasant to divorce himself from the land except as a last resort.

De Witte once wrote that Russian labour was the free gift of nature. The gift was unevenly distributed and its very abundance encouraged wasteful use in some areas, but de Witte's view helps to explain why so little was done for so long to nurture the gift. Only minimal efforts were made to help the peasant adjust to factory life, protect him from exploitation there, give him some means by which he could air his grievances or educate him so that he might have the opportunity of becoming a more effective worker. The periods of rapid industrial development in Russia inevitably created severe emotional tensions throughout the nation as the workforce shifted in a short space of time from one way of life to another. The contrast between country and city was matched by that between the huge factories and tiny workshops the peasant would find side by side in St Petersburg and Moscow. Both contrasts caused extreme confusion. For the employer the unwillingness of local authorities to take any action themselves threw upon him the responsibility and cost of providing houses, schools, hospitals and churches, though after 1900 public expenditure on education rose sharply. The large numbers of workers with families in the villages and the few with no stake at all there indicate the complexity of the adjustments required. A man's father might have worked in a factory but he himself might have been born and raised in the village and eventually had to migrate too. If, therefore, the immediate problems of factory labour supply arising out of the terms of emancipation were not serious, it was the great increase in the labour force from 1890 onwards that brought immense social as well as economic problems. The difficulties were those of assimilation not of supply. The mass of workers remained backward, superstitious, hostile to outsiders, deferential towards the factory owners, suspicious of the radicals. But a more educated workforce had begun to emerge, at first in the large machinery, steel and railway works. A survey suggested that by 1910 the young factory workers in Moscow, for example, were almost completely literate. From this elite leaders were to emerge who were far more receptive to new ideas concerning the organisation of society.

For twenty years after 1861 the government did nothing about factory conditions. A law of 1845 treated strikes as uprisings against the state; workers could petition the Tsar for action but it was a dangerous and usually fruitless thing to do. The owner of a factory was sovereign; he could fine his workers or beat them. The workers could not legally organise or take action to defend themselves. Essentially such a patriarchal system was part of the existing pattern of social relationships; the employer was supposed to look after his workers and if he misbehaved it was the Tsar, not the workers, who was expected to act. But events rarely went according to rule and were less likely to do so the faster the industrial sector expanded. The laws against strikes were hard to enforce collectively and publicity often aroused sympathy for the strikers. So punishment by the employer was preferred to judicial action and a network of spies dealt with the most active agitators.

In theory emancipation was intended to break up this old social pattern but revision came very slowly. In 1882 laws were passed to regulate child labour and to provide for factory inspectors. Three years later schooling, women's work and night work were controlled. Industry was depressed at the time and the effects were not immediately felt. Employers in St Petersburg were more disposed to support the legislation than those in Moscow; wages there were higher, factories better equipped and in fact the laws were advantageous to well-run works where the extremes of exploitation were absent. In 1886 the finance minister Bunge obtained a comprehensive law on employer–employee relationships covering matters such as length of contract, payment in money and limitation of fines. By this means the worst excesses were curbed but the scales remained unevenly weighted: breach of contract by the worker was still criminal, as were strikes, and the worker was consequently poorly placed to deal with the many forms of exploitation such as low wages not covered by the law. Enforcement of the law was difficult and workers were often terrorised into not testifying. De Witte raised the number of factory inspectors from 143 in 1894 to 257 in 1899 but at the end of the decade there was a return to repression. Special police units were set up in factory towns and de Witte's attempt to persuade the Tsar that workers' organisations should be a normal feature of the industrial scene failed. So the legislation failed to halt the growing alienation of the working class and police intervention in industrial relations usually offended the employers also. It was not so much that the worker was exploited more than in the village, where there were *kulaks* and landlords instead of factory owners, but that the social gap seemed so much greater; in the towns there was no contact of any kind. The industrial system was also subject to wide fluctuations but no help was provided for those unemployed who had cut their ties with the rural community. Because of this the severe depression beginning in 1900 brought matters to a crisis, though strikes were already multiplying in the period 1894–1903 and were accompanied by much peasant discontent, aggravated by famines in 1891–2, 1897, 1898 and 1901. The strikes were often not prolonged and possibly commoner in summer when the loss of earnings was more easily borne, but the bigger the works the greater the sense of common action and the more serious the strike. Two ministers and two provisional governors were assassinated. The culminating point came after the final defeat by Japan early in 1905 when a strike at the Putilov works in St Petersburg spread through the city. A hundred and fifty thousand people marched peacefully on the Winter Palace to put forward their grievances; they were fired upon and a blaze of revolt flared up. Soldiers, sailors, peasants and professional men joined the industrial workers and by autumn what amounted to a general strike paralysed the country. But the regime was by no means defeated yet and the effectiveness of the old repressive measures is shown by the rapid fall in the number of strikers: 3 million in 1905, one million in 1906, 400,000 in 1907 and 64,000 in 1909, though a revival of business activity no doubt played its part too.

One branch of industry strongly affected by the coming of new technologies and new methods of production was the traditional peasant *kustarny* industry. The skills which had been accumulated in peasant crafts over many generations proved to be of great value to the process of industrialisation, especially in the metal working industries. The *kustarny* industries themselves had varied experiences. Where the advantages of large-scale production were great, the *kustar* was inexorably driven out. For instance, after 1860 mechanical weaving of cotton became more and more important. In 1866 there were 94,000 workers in mechanical weaving shops and 66,000 *kustars*; by 1894 only 20,500 *kustars* were left compared with 240,000 in the factories. On the other hand flax and hemp preparation and weaving were still largely *kustar* in 1895 mainly because the raw material came from the peasant farm. Mechanisation of processes such as rope and net making proved difficult too. *Kustar* production of nails had died out by the mid-1890s with machine competition; locksmiths and knife makers suffered a similar fate. As factories developed, *kustar* manufacture by peasants brought together in small workshops declined but individual peasant home work often increased as factories put more work out. The pressure of competition eroded the *kustar* entrepreneur's profits and led to individuals being exploited directly by the factory manufacturers. Samovar production, for example, became divided in this way with part of the operation taking place at a main plant and the rest of the work given out to the *kustar* workers. But sometimes the *kustar* workshop itself developed into a small factory; much depended on the nature of the technology and the speed of growth of factory output. If the technology was such that the power element could be adapted for use in small production units, the *kustar* often survived. Declining standards of living in the overcrowded agricultural areas encouraged the peasant to maintain an industrial income even though it might be very low. Cheap labour and fuel in the forest regions took industry there too. The populists pointed with pride to the rise of these new *kustarny* techniques and to other *kustarny* activities which fed special materials to factories – braid for factory-made wool cloth for example – but these were marginal developments dependent on a large factory sector and as often as not these patterns of production emerged because of the very low incomes the *kustarny* workers were prepared to accept. It was in that sense the very opposite of a positive form of industrial development. Much discussion took place in the 1890s about the decline of *kustarny* industries and the exodus of men and women from the peasant villages. It is possible to show a striking correlation between literacy and the level of such migration. Yaroslavl, for example, had a very high level of literacy, 85·5 per cent in 1896, and there emigration was more common. Possibly those best informed and qualified, such as the *kustar* workers, were most ready to go; possibly too the word got back that the better educated did better in town. Yet in 1914 the *kustar* still provided the essential needs of the people for all manner of consumer goods and petty luxuries. To some extent he survived because of the limited size of the market for mass consumer goods; modern industry in Russia was still very regional in its impact and many areas were hardly affected by it at all. Finally one must remember that the most famous of the *kustarny* products were not goods for local consumption at all: ikons, musical instruments, boots, nets, sledges and toys were distributed throughout Russia and even sent to foreign markets.

As mentioned in the previous chapter, the desirability of industrialisation itself was a point of much philosophical dispute. As the industrial revolution went forward a great public debate developed between the Populists and the Marxists over the future of capitalism in Russia. The influence of the Marxist groups in Russia was slight until Lenin began to co-ordinate their activities in the 1890s and public acknowledgement came through the movement's attacks on the Populists. The issues were similar to those which had worried the Slavophils and the Westernisers two generations before but this debate was not simply for a select few; it was one which absorbed the intellectual life of the country. In the optimistic days after 1861 a new group of Populists led by Mikhailovsky sought through their Narodnik Socialism to build a bridge between old and new in Russia.[3] They wished to turn their backs on western example and looked to the commune as the only acceptable means of conducting business and trade: the commune to them made for the harmonious development of the individual and this to them was more desirable than the narrow outlook created by the industrial way of life. It was a utopian movement with little concern for political activity but with a deep faith in the traditional ways of the Russian folk.

But Russia continued to follow the capitalist path. Construction of railways, growth of heavy industry, urbanisation, investment by foreigners called for a more sophisticated form of opposition. Some had hoped that Russia would escape the miseries of the industrial revolution in the west but they were rudely shaken by accounts of the extreme distress of Russian factory workers. Opponents of industrialisation now argued that capitalism in Russia was stillborn. Russia lacked capital, entrepreneurship and a bourgeoisie. Capital-intensive industry could not absorb the surplus rural labour force and the low purchasing power of the masses would deprive industries of active markets. Russian goods were too inferior to be sold overseas and Russia was too weak to gain captive colonial markets. The climate and the long distances between urban centres were also held up as unfavourable factors. Meantime, it was agreed, the peasant was being ruined by factory competition. Industrial capitalism was a contradiction in Russia; industry would fail through overproduction and the peasant, deprived of his side earnings, would farm more intensively and ruin the soil as the famine of 1891 seemed to prove.

Russia should therefore evolve its own transformation, for the Populists were at one with the Marxists in believing that some form of revolution in the organisation of the economic structure was inevitable. They envisaged a move to socialism through the commune and the creation of the craftsmen's *artels*. There the application of the latest technology to peasant crafts would form a viable small-scale peasant industry, though there would need to be a nucleus of government-owned heavy industry. If this left Russia weak in international power politics, she should stand aloof from military conflicts and struggles for markets; such a solution would free her also from the influence of foreign bankers and industrialists. The Populists believed that Russia could shape her own economic future through her own institutions. They saw Russia as a peasant country without a proletariat: the revolution would be a peasant uprising offering a direct transition to socialism, a movement the intellectuals hoped to lead and direct.

Like many others of the time the Populists were deeply afraid of the chaos that might ensue if the communal basis of Russian society was allowed to disappear. Yet their hope of adopting new forms of technology within the framework of the old institutions was presented in only the vaguest terms. For the reasons put forward in the last section such peasant industry seemed likely to be of only marginal importance and in some cases would survive not because it was progressive but because it offered an effective form of exploitation. Furthermore the speed of industrial growth during the de Witte era seemed to confirm the Marxist view that capitalism could and would develop as inevitably in Russia as elsewhere. Around

1893 Lenin came to the conclusion that the emergence of capitalism in Russia was no longer a problem; it was a fact and was already the basic feature of Russian agricultural as well as industrial life. Some now began to appease their consciences by accepting the costly and ruthless process of Russian industrialisation as an iron law of development. The Marxists for their part did not fear the social chaos resulting from the industrial changes, for they were confident that out of it the industrial proletariat would emerge as the prime revolutionary and governing force.

COMMUNICATIONS

The improvement of communications was vital to Russian growth, as a means of extending the internal market and bringing new resources into the economy and also as a stimulus to industrial growth derived from the actual process of construction itself through the direct purchases of materials and the payment of wages to the workers. Before the 1860s railway construction had been slow and sporadic but after the Crimean War there was a surge of interest. The earlier tendency for state promoted lines was abandoned on budgetary grounds and the existing state railways were sold to private companies. By 1880 only 60 kilometres of line were under state control. A considerable amount of German capital went into Russian railways at the time and a lot of the rolling stock was bought in Germany. Nevertheless, the state did badly out of the transactions, for the lines were sold on poor terms at a time when profits were beginning to mount as traffic expanded. Moreover, the private railways proved to be incompetently run, so government policy was reversed. In 1882 the state repurchased a quarter of the system, mainly bankrupt lines, and with large-scale construction programmes in subsequent years owned 55 per cent of the railway mileage by 1914.

The first post-emancipation boom in construction paralleled a similar burst of activity all over Europe from 1868 to 1874. These years saw the laying of the radial system near Moscow, connecting the city with the grain surplus areas of the central agricultural region, and also the building of grain export lines linking Tsaritsyn to Riga. Later in the 1870s other such lines, connecting with the Black Sea ports, were built in a second boom which reached its peak in 1877-8. After several sluggish years a rising trend from 1883 brought another peak at the end of the decade, although the level of activity was below that of the early 1870s. The main plan now was to develop the interregional connections; for example, the first Urals railway was completed in 1878 and the Urals linked to Moscow in 1892. New lines linked Moscow and the central agricultural region with the middle and lower Volga areas and extended to the southern steppes and to the south-west, all developments of great significance for the internal grain trade. There were also lines intended to promote development in the northern Caucasus and central Asia and, most important of all, because it linked the coal and ore resources of the region, the Donetz railway was completed in 1886. The 1890s under de Witte were a continuous period of expansion and between 1894 and 1903 25,300 kilometres of line were completed, including almost all the Trans-Siberian railway. The network was improved and new lines built in border regions such as Archangel and the Caucasus. In 1901 the Orenburg to Tashkent line was started, to bring cotton from central Asia to the Moscow mills. Finally there was another boom during 1906–8 which saw the connection of the lower Volga and southern Urals and the linking of the Urals to St Petersburg. Just before 1914 a line was run to Murmansk, lines in Siberia were taken to the Kuznetsk basin and the Trans-Siberian railway was re-routed to avoid going through Manchuria. The details of construction are given in Table 65

Table 65 *Railway construction in Russia, 1838–1913 (annual average length of line, km)*

1838–63	141	1874–8	1,231	1889–93	688	1904–8	1,584
1864–8	653	1879–83	335	1894–8	2,307	1909–13	835
1869–73	1,884	1884–8	1,057	1899–1903	1,750		

Source: E. Ames, 'A Century of Russian Railroad Construction, 1837–1936', in *American Slavic and East European Review*, 1947, p. 60.

though naturally the five-year intervals used do not necessarily coincide with the timing of the main peaks and troughs in construction.

Before the coming of railways Russia had an extensive system of navigable waterways and for some types of traffic these remained extremely important. This was particularly true of the shipment of grain and oil from the southern region up the Volga and along connecting waterways to the central industrial areas and for shipping grain relatively short distances from the southern steppes to the Black Sea. In 1907 grain and flour comprised 15 per cent of railway freight by weight. Coal provided 21 per cent and indeed the highest density traffic was the interchange of iron ore and coal on the Krivoi Rog–Donetz line and the transport of coal and metals from the Donetz itself. However, if the weight of freight is divided by the distance hauled grain and coal each took 18 per cent of the traffic because grain, on average, was hauled some 40 per cent further than coal. Timber and firewood provided another 9 per cent of the railway freight and these three commodities, wood, coal and grain, comprised nearly one-half of all the railway freight in Russia. In fact the timber export lines, built in the 1890s, were a good example of the combination of rail and water transport; the logs were floated down the Volga from the northern forests to Tsaritsyn and then loaded on railways to take them to the Black Sea or to the Donetz where they were in great demand for pit props. The railway made a significant impact upon the pattern of internal trade in Russia, intensifying the trend towards the creation of larger centres of trade, production and consumption, so much so that the turn-over at the great annual fairs began to decline after 1881 even though the overall rate of growth of the economy began to accelerate after that date. But for the railway the exploitation of the southern ore and coal could not have come about, nor would the economy of Siberia have been opened up in any appreciable way. On the other hand some new trades such as the transport of oil were able very effectively to use water transport, especially with the application of oil motors to the barges.

Before 1860 Russian industry had made a certain amount of progress in producing its own rolling stock but from the boom of 1868–74 onwards much more rapid advances were made, helped by tariffs, subsidies and conditions embodied in railway charters. The number of locomotives built in Russia rose from 38 in 1870 to 334 eight years later and throughout the 1870s the value of home production exceeded that of imports by about 50 per cent. Of 5,196 engines delivered in the 1890s only 826 were imported. Capital, skill and technology were brought in from France, Germany and the United States, though the largest works, that at Kolomna, was of local origin. In 1906 there were eight major locomotive factories catering for all internal requirements. Local production of rails caused more difficulty until the emergence of the steel industry in the Donetz in the late 1880s. Thereafter with the imposition of a penal tariff, virtually all rails were made there. That the rails and equipment were of higher cost than material available overseas is undoubted. On the other hand the balance of pay-ments benefited from import saving at a time when marginal increases in exports were not easy to bring about. Furthermore, metallurgical and engineering activities of this order gave a boost to heavy industry in Russia which had extensive secondary benefits, above all through the dissemination of much needed engineering skills. Railway tariffs were manipulated to help particular industries, to facilitate colonisation, to discriminate in favour of long hauls and to help famine areas. They were lower for exports than for internal trade and protected the black earth region from Siberian grain by raising the grain freight beyond Cheliabinsk, though still helping exports from Siberia.

In 1913 Russia had less than one kilometre of railway for every 100 square kilometres of territory and its railway system still remained one of the least used and least effective in Europe (see Table 93).[4] Such com-parisons must be used with care but when allowance is made for the sparseness of population and the huge land area the fact remains that despite the massive efforts of the previous four decades, the rail network was still not large enough by 1914 to bring such a widely scattered people within a national economic structure.

THE GROWTH OF INDUSTRY

The course of industrialisation in Russia after 1861 is indicated in Table 66 which shows the pattern of timing and degree of industrial growth. There was very rapid expansion during the 1890s and significant progress, too, during the 1880s. The depression in 1900 terminated growth for some years but from 1906 to 1913 it was almost as fast as during the 1890s. From 1888 to 1913 the rate of growth was faster than that of either Germany or the United States on a per capita basis, though the absolute level of output was much lower and Russia was still on that basis one of the least industrialised nations in Europe in 1910. Although such a conclusion partly reflects the relative size of the rural population, given the backwardness of that rural sector it is obvious that in 1914 Russia had a long way to

Table 66 *An index of added value in manufacture and mining in Russia, 1860–1913 (1900 prices)*

		(1900 = 100)			
1860	13·9	1890	50·7	1905	98·2
1870	17·1	1895	70·4	1910	141·4
1880	28·2	1900	100·0	1913	163·6

Source: R. W. Goldsmith, 'Economic Growth of Tsarist Russia, 1860–1913', in *Economic Development and Cultural Change*, vol. IX, 1961, p. 462.

travel before she would achieve anything like parity with the developed European economies.

The advance of modern technology in Russia before 1861 had been confined almost entirely to cotton spinning, printing and sugar refining but these industries had not acted as leading sectors for further development. Emancipation dealt a severe blow to the old serf industries; iron output fell by 15 per cent between 1860 and 1867; the gentry woollen mills were already in decline and the reduction of output was less severe in that industry for that reason. Although railway construction went ahead rapidly, most of the rails were imported. It was consumer industries that really led industrial expansion until the mid-1880s.

– Cotton

After initial difficulties connected with a shortage of raw cotton during the American Civil War, the cotton industry continued to make steady progress. Its fortunes were largely determined by the state of the home market though some efforts were made to push exports to the east. In 1900 exports of cloth amounted to 324,000 poods whereas home production of cloth was 11,700,000 poods; of the exports 44 per cent went to Persia and 33 per cent to China. After the turn of the century the export share began to rise slowly to reach between 4 and 5 per cent by 1913. The overall progress of the industry is shown in Table 67. It will be seen that though cotton manufacture was not particularly fostered by de Witte, its fastest period of growth came during the 1890s with output rising at over 8 per cent annually. With a workforce of 365,000 in 1899 it covered 15 per cent of industrial labour and was the largest single employer. Three-quarters of the workforce were to be found in factories of over a thousand employees. By this time mechanical weaving had become almost universal. The *kustars* either went into factories or became adjuncts of factories,

Table 67   *Cotton industry in Russia, 1870–1910*

	Spindles (000)	Looms (000)	Cotton consumption (m. poods)		
			Russian	Foreign	Total
1870	2,000				4·0
1890	3,457	87	2·0	6·0	8·0
1900	6,646	151	6·1	9·9	16·0
1910	8,306	213	11·3	10·9	22·2

Source: United States Bureau of Manufactures, *Cotton Goods in Russia* (Washington, 1912), p. 9.

assigned the intricate work most suited to hand looms. It has been shown that in 1899 per capita consumption of cottons was 36 arshin compared with 23 arshin in 1890.[5] This apparent rise in average living standards raises an important question of interpretation, since previously we have emphasised the poverty of the mass of the peasantry: the figures relate, however, to factory output of cottons so that the rise was mainly due to the rapid increase in the number of factory workers who did not make their own cloth in villages or buy linen and woollen cloth locally. Peasant demand for cheap cloths rose, therefore, because of the differentiation of the peasantry and the growing wealth of a small proportion of them. It was also encouraged by the improvement of internal communications and by the elimination of *kustar* production. Even so, per capita consumption of cloth in 1900 was still very low by western standards precisely because the masses were so poor. With population growing there was still room for further expansion of the industry and consequently output was not seriously affected by the depression beginning in 1900.

The industry was concentrated around Moscow and in the central areas where in 1910 over 300,000 men were employed. In Moscow province 23 per cent of the yarn and 22 per cent of the cloth was produced, and in Vladimir and Petrovsk another 36 and 48 per cent respectively. In Kostroma, an area well located for importing cotton from the east and for sending goods along the Volga to Nijni Novgorod, the proportions were 9 per cent and 14·5 per cent. Wages were half those in St Petersburg and it was there that the industry had grown most quickly since 1900. Vladimir had gained over Moscow for similar reasons. The cotton industry in the Kingdom of Poland, centred upon Lodz, produced 20 per cent of the yarn and 17 per cent of the cloth. This sector of the cotton industry was the most developed in a technical sense.

Growth had been greatly stimulated in Poland by the abandonment of customs duties on exports to Russia soon after the protective tariff had been introduced in 1877 and by the improvement of internal communications, though the tariff placed on imported cotton to help the native Russian cotton growing industry was particularly unfortunate for the Polish industry, which was dependent upon imported cotton. In 1891 there had been 473,000 mule spindles in Lodz but by 1904 there were over 1·1 million mules and 143,000 ring spindles and the number of workers had almost doubled. By 1910 there were some 50,000 workers in the Polish industry. The factory wool textile industry began in Poland around 1870 with the immigration of Saxon workers; by 1900 it employed about the same number of workers as the cotton industry but its relative position, in what was a considerably smaller industry over Russia as a whole, was much greater. In St Petersburg another 34,000 workers were to be found in cotton manufacture. Here it was a highly integrated industry and mills were of large size, though few did dyeing and printing as well as spinning and weaving. Knoop's Krenholm mill, seventy-five miles from St Petersburg, was the largest in the world, located on the river Narva, where its fall of twenty-seven feet as it flowed into the sea provided a great source of power; in 1910 it employed 12,000 workers on 475,000 spindles and 3,700 looms. It was managed, as were many mills, by Lancashire men; all carding and spinning machinery was imported but some looms were made locally. There the finest yarn was made and in the mid-1890s output per man was about 400 roubles compared with less than 150 in Moscow and Vladimir.

The average number of spindles per mill in 1910 was 78,000 in the Baltic region, 66,300 in the central regions and 24,000 in Poland. One reason for this large size was the frequent need to provide housing and other facilities for the workers. One estimate was that for every 100 roubles spent on equipping a mill, 40–50 roubles were spent on these external requirements. One large mill, for example, had a school for 1,800 children and employed thirty-five teachers. In the central districts outside Moscow individual mills were located in isolated places up to fifteen miles from the nearest large settlement and so these other facilities had to be provided. Though Knoop remained a major figure in the industry on account of his own manufacturing and his role as chief importer of machinery, his influence gradually waned with the growth of industry in the Moscow area. There the indigenous bourgeoisie was dominant and the influence of foreign capital less powerful. Many of the great cotton industrialists were of serf origin, men who gained their freedom early in the nineteenth century. The best known were the Morozovs who employed some 50,000 workers altogether before 1914.

Despite the use of modern machinery labour productivity was not high by western standards and costs were increased by the external investments which could not be avoided. But low labour costs tended to offset the low efficiency and the best mills were at least competitive with those in Germany and the United States for cheap cloth and yarn. Low labour costs in Russia, as elsewhere, ruled out the introduction of automatic looms but concentration on low-quality yarn led to a switch from mules to rings for spinning. In 1890 77 per cent of the spindles were mules; in 1910 the proportion was down to 45 per cent. Quality production was more important at Lodz and mules continued to be much more widely used there.

The cotton industry was one of the first in Russia to modernise and to enjoy rapid growth. It was much the most important factory textile industry, its output in 1912 being four times that of the wool textile sector, but its significance for the overall process of industrialisation was less than that of other sectors whose effect in spreading new technologies, seeking new modes of finance and supplying new skills was greater. It borrowed a specialised technology but did not seek to advance it within Russia, benefiting neither metal nor engineering industries, and the skills required of its operatives were low. The impetus of the new industrial era came from elsewhere.

– Coal and Steel

We have seen how for most of the century the technology and organisation of the iron industry in the Urals stagnated, although output slowly increased. Above all with the growth of railway construction, home production of iron fell more and more behind demand and in the early 1870s Russia was meeting only 45 per cent of her needs. Tariff protection gave some encouragement to iron production in Poland. German industrialists in Upper Silesia were forced to set up processing plants over the border after the introduction of the 1868 tariff and the higher duties of 1877 compelled them to build their furnaces there too. But protection did little more than offer higher prices to the Urals ironmasters, hampered as they were by distance, the absence of local coal deposits, the growing shortage of convenient wood supply and their own conservatism. Output responded slowly. Of 195 furnaces in Russia in 1885, 88 were not using the hot blast technique almost universal elsewhere; in 1870 there were 425 puddling furnaces but still 924 of the older type of refinery. Only in 1893 did the number of puddling furnaces come to exceed that of the refineries. Experiments with the Bessemer process for making steel were not followed by regular production until 1877, seventeen years after Britain. Demand too remained limited; little iron was required for houses, few agricultural implements were manufactured of metal, ovens were made of stone, utensils of earthenware, spoons and forks of wood.

Coal had been known to exist in the Donetz basin for some time but it was in a region remote from other industrial centres. The Kursk–Kharkhov railway (1869) linked these fields to the interior of Russia and later railways carried the coal to the Black Sea area. Output rose from 2·6 million poods in 1870 to 57 million in 1880 and to 147 million in 1890. Before 1888 Donetz coal was used mainly as fuel for the railways and for the southern sugar refineries. For the manufacture of iron the coal was difficult to use because of its high sulphur content and local ore supplies were deficient, although some inferior ores were used without much success in an attempt to smelt iron in the 1860s. In any case further exploitation was discouraged by the concessions given to European-financed railway companies to import iron duty free. In 1871 John Hughes took up a concession of coal and ore bearing crown lands in the area and founded his New Russian Company. Born in South Wales in 1814, he had set up his own works at Ebbw Vale before becoming director of a company supplying iron for the construction of a Russian battleship and through this connection became interested in the development of the industry in southern Russia. He was given the right to build a railway from his works to the Kursk, Kharkov and Azov railway and the government provided a ten-year subsidy on rails made by him for Russian railways. The factory was built near Mariupol and the settlement named Yuzovka after the founder; later it became Stalino and then Donetsk. The difficulties of setting up a works in the uninhabited steppe region were enormous but by 1874 it was in full production, employing 2,000 men and producing 6 per cent of Russian pig iron output. But despite his enterprise and persistence, Hughes soon lost his technological lead as Polish mills and Putilov in St Petersburg adopted new techniques for producing steel rails. By 1884, of the 25,000 kilometres of steel rails laid in Russia 8,400 kilometres were domestically rolled, but probably three-quarters of these used imported semi-manufactured steel.

The true transformation of the southern industry began with the building of the Donetz railway, linking the coal with the rich iron ore deposits at Krivoi Rog, some 300 kilometres to the west. The ore was located in a narrow zone 250 kilometres long and running north–south, having an iron content as high as 60 per cent in parts though that most easily mined on the fringe of the field was under 40 per cent. The ore had been discovered twenty years earlier but could not be exploited until Alexander Pol, a rich landowner who spent many years urging the importance of these natural deposits, was able to raise money in Paris to have the railway built. It was then found that between the ore and the coal lay also rich deposits of manganese ore at Nikopol.

The completion of the line in 1886 was the signal for a rush of investment in mining and metals in the area, induced also by further protection and government support. By 1887 pig iron output had scarcely doubled over the 1870 level, yet from 1887 to 1890 southern pig iron output rose from 4·2 to 13·4 million poods while that in the Urals grew from 23·8 to 28·2 million poods. Railway building was not at its peak at that time, though it was above the level of the previous seven years, but imports of pig fell from 17·5 million poods in 1883 to 4·8 million in 1887. From the 1890s onwards demand rose for steel for rails and machinery, and for use in factories and cities and in the oil industry. Only between 1894 and 1899, when a great deal of metal was required to build the steel mills themselves, were imports significant. By 1898 there were 17 large smelting works with 29 blast furnaces, and 12 more building in southern Russia, and only one of these works, a minor one, was entirely Russian owned. French and Belgian investment was primarily responsible for the growth of the industry and in 1900 French money also controlled one-third of the output of coal. Firms such as Cockerills of Belgium who invested in coal and steel (in partnership with the Warsaw Steel Company) brought technical and management skills as well as finance. They built plants embodying the latest proved techniques. The size of blast furnace in the south compared with the newest in Europe; their output was even greater because the ore used was so good. Thus furnaces in the south in 1910 were charged with 1·73 tons of ore for every ton of pig produced; in western Europe the average was more like 2·55 tons. The average yearly output per blast furnace was 60,000 tons in Russia and only 50,000 tons in Germany. Total steel output in Russia rose from 48·3 million poods in 1890 to 247·4 million poods in 1913 and the share of the southern mills from 18 per cent to 57 per cent: their share of pig output reached 67 per cent. Western methods of organising coal mining were introduced with double shafts, a labyrinth of tunnels, equipment for washing and sorting coal at the pit-head and modern coke ovens, though little attempt was made to use mechanical cutting before 1914. This use of modern technology was the rational answer to the nature of the labour supply; it might be possible to substitute labour for capital in handling steel but in making it the proved technical optimum was the most economical. Experiments would be carried out by the experts in plants in Germany and Belgium but the latest ideas were soon transferred to their Russian plants. The result was a high level of productivity; in 1913 the annual output of pig iron per worker was 299 tons in southern Russia, 209 in all Russia, 243 in France and 411 in Germany. It is likely that capital costs in Russia were higher in view of the distance steel making machinery and plant had to be carried, for it was all imported, the higher cost of putting it into operation and the fact that for much of the time the mills were run below capacity. The basic problem of the Russian industry remained its fuel costs: with ore and coal so far apart, transport costs were a serious handicap. With a long haul overland to the final markets, prices for steel products such as girders, rails and plates were almost twice as high in St Petersburg as in Britain or Germany before the First World War.

– Oil

The development of the oil industry in Russia is discussed in its international context in Chapter 9. Before 1872 the government had used a 'lease' system for operating wells and extracting crude oil, 'assigning' peasants for the purpose. From 1872 an auction system was substituted; the parcels of land sold for exploitation were small and a mass of individual producers worked the main field near Baku. Foreign capital concerned itself mostly at first with the processing and transport of oil and only later moved into actual prospecting. It was the Nobel brothers who first realised the true importance of transport for the oil industry; they set up the Nobel Naphtha Extraction Company in 1879 and soon established a virtual monopoly of transport from Baku by sea to the Volga and up river to the railheads. By 1912 petroleum products comprised over one-third of all the Volga traffic. They established pipe lines, tanker ships and tank wagons on railways and it was in a bid to break their hold that foreign capital was brought in to build a railway line from Baku to Batum. Output of oil rose from 2 million poods in 1870 to 241 million in 1890 and 631 million in 1900. De Witte quickly recognised the possibilities of the new industry; in 1896 he imposed royalty payments as well as an auction for new extraction rights. He placed a tax on illuminating oil but encouraged its export by helping to finance a pipe line and build a new harbour at Novorossisk. State revenue from the transport of oil products rose. He ordered the universities to direct research into the area of chemical engineering and with some success, for to 1914 Russian technical handbooks were highly valued by refiners in all parts of the world. Russia's advantage lay in low raw material and refining costs, her disadvantage in high transport costs. Her share of world output, over a third in 1900, dropped to one-sixth by 1913. This was partly because the yield of the wells began to diminish, while the mean depth of borings rose by 25 per cent, and partly because of the riots of 1905, which had resulted in great damage to oil installations in Baku. Thus, whereas oil produced 6·5 per cent of exports in 1900, its share had fallen to 2·3 per cent in 1912.

INDUSTRIAL DEVELOPMENT IN THE 1890s

The developments in metallurgy, coal mining and oil production in the Ukraine and the Caucasus, together with the mechanisation of the textile industries and the revival of railway construction, marked an important stage in Russian industrialisation and provided a springboard for the rapid expansion promoted so energetically by de Witte. Industrial production grew 7·9 per cent annually during the 1880s compared with 9·7 per cent during the 1890s though obviously the starting point in 1880 was much lower than in western European economies.[6] The basic statistics on Russian industrial growth during and after the de Witte era are shown in Table 68. During the 1890s alone pig iron output rose by 190 per cent compared with 18 per cent in Britain and 72 per cent in Germany; Russia was the world's seventh largest producer in 1880, sixth in 1890, fifth in 1895 and fourth by 1900. Such was the pressure of demand that Krivoi Rog ore rose sharply in price at the end of the 1890s and Belgian companies were encouraged by this to open up the poorer Kerch ores on a peninsula of the Sea of Azov. British coal output rose 22 per cent over the decade, German

Table 68   *Industrial output in Russia, 1887–1913 (m. poods)*

	1887	1900	1908	1913
Pig iron	36·1	176·8	171	283
Coal	276	986·4	1608·5	2215
Oil	155	631	529	561
Cotton consumption	11·5	16	21·2	26
Sugar	26	48·5	76·7	75·4

Source: R. Portal, 'The Industrialisation of Russia', in *Cambridge Economic History of Europe*, vol. VI, part II (Cambridge, 1965), pp. 837 and 844.

52 per cent and Russian 131 per cent. The number of British cotton spindles increased by 4 per cent, continental European by 33 per cent and Russian by 76 per cent. The import of machinery and tools, which averaged a little over 20 million roubles in the 1880s, rose to 33·7 million in 1891–5 and was 59 million in 1896. The value of the output of chemicals almost doubled and the workforce rose from 28,000 to 35,000: German and Swiss firms were forced by the tariff to begin to manufacture chemicals in Poland. But of course the absolute levels of Russian output were still low; for example, coal production stood at over 17 million tons on average from 1900–4, compared with 156 million tons in Germany. Such was the growth of internal demand that Russian coal imports rose from 95 million poods in 1877 to 108 million in 1890 and 196 million in 1898, this last figure representing approximately a fifth of total consumption in that year, most of it being used in the north-west and in Poland where the steel industry came to use Silesian coke exclusively. Domestic pig iron, however, supplied 67 per cent of home consumption in 1883, 90 per cent in 1893 and 99 per cent in 1903. There were striking increases in productivity

in the new industries too. Whereas in cotton the increase in the value of output was accompanied by an equal rise in the number of workers, in mining and metal production output rose 152 per cent from 1887 to 1897 and the workforce by 39 per cent; in metal manufacturing output rose by 176 per cent and employment by 107 per cent. Of all industrial enterprises in 1900, 40 per cent had been founded since 1891. The railway network grew by almost a half and the quantity of freight doubled, while the general expansion of the economy carried other industries along with it, most of all those concerned with construction such as bricks and cement. Despite these remarkable new developments the highest rates of growth were found in the older food and textile industries and it was the smallest works, employing under fifty workers, that were growing most quickly.

The 1890s saw the full industrialisation of the Ukraine. In 1899 the three largest steel companies, two on the bend of the Dnieper and one at Yuzovka, had 15 blast furnaces, 24 Siemens furnaces, 42 puddling furnaces and

Table 69   *The iron and steel industry in Russia, 1890–1900*

| | Urals | | South | |
	1890	1900	1890	1900
Pig smelted per plant (000 poods)	250	436	1,491	3,192
Horse-power per plant	135	244	1,530	6,159
Pig smelted per worker (poods)	194	297	990	1,714

Source: P. Lyashchenko, *A History of the National Economy of Russia* (New York, 1949), p. 532.

23 rolling mills; the Bryansk Company alone was employing 4,000 men. There was also an inrush of new concerns concentrating on more specialised metallurgical activities, producing sheet metal and rolling steel. Indigenous industries expanded also: sugar refining, distilling, flour milling, and the manufacture of agricultural machinery. Though still not the largest, the Ukraine was the most progressive industrial area in Russia, growing most at the eastern and western extremities, in the provinces of Kharkhov and Ekaterinoslav. Despite the influence of foreign capital there emerged here, as in Poland, a small but powerful group of Russo-Jewish bankers – sugar barons, railway kings and the like – closely linked with both industrial and international investment. The iron and steel industry in the Urals expanded only slowly and by 1900 there were still only five joint stock companies there, the rest being state or family run concerns. Its technology was still dependent on charcoal and, as Table 69 shows, the industry's performance was in no way comparable with that in the south. In 1913 it produced 20 per cent of Russia's pig iron and 17 per cent of her iron and steel.

Growth was by no means confined to the Ukraine. Industry in the central regions was most influenced by the developing market for capital and consumer goods and, helped by improved internal transport, was expanding faster than in the St Petersburg region. In Moscow itself the number of factory workers rose from 67,000 to 100,000 during the 1890s. Using some local ores in the Moscow area and imported pig in St Petersburg these two regions in 1900 still produced 20 per cent of Russia's iron and steel. In the St Petersburg area industry was spread less widely through the region, being concentrated in a few industrial towns. Metallurgical industries predominated, with larger and more modern factories than elsewhere and a greater proportion of foreign investment. It was there that the newer industries such as electrical engineering, rubber, dyestuffs and motor cars were to be concentrated after the turn of the century. Factories in Poland were generally more mechanised than those in Russia proper and

Table 70 *Regional industrial output in Russia in 1896 (m. roubles)*

Region	
Six provinces of Moscow region	755
(Moscow province)	(403)
St Petersburg	317
Three Polish provinces	335
Krivoi Rog and Donetz	246
Kiev and Podolsk	135
Urals	85

Source: P. Lyashchenko, *A History of the National Economy of Russia* (New York, 1949), pp. 538–9.

fuel supplies were easier, but discriminatory freight and tariff measures had been intensified in the 1880s to reduce the competition they offered to other Russian industries. Gradually, however, the struggle became less tense as Polish and Russian firms began to concentrate on different markets for textiles – Poland specialising in finer fabrics and prints and Moscow in calicoes – and as financial links between firms in Poland and the Ukraine brought Poland more firmly into the Empire. The growth of industry during the de Witte era was reflected too in the renewed building of railways by private investors in Poland. By 1913 the region was producing 10 per cent of Russia's iron and steel, 12 per cent of its sugar, 13 per cent by value of cottons, 43 per cent of woollens, 20 per cent of flax and hemp and 12 per cent of its silks. Coal output at Dombrovo rose from 109 million poods in 1885 to 426 million in 1913, although the product mined was not good coking coal; this compared with a rise of output in the

Donetz from 115 million poods to 1,507 million poods. Table 70 shows the relative importance of the major industrial areas in Russia and indicates the continued dominance of the historical centres of industry near Moscow, St Petersburg and in Poland. The rise of new industries was important principally for the introduction of new techniques and by 1900 had only marginally modified the distribution of total industrial output, which remained unaltered to 1914.

CRISIS AND RECOVERY

Inevitably such a burst of expansion could not continue unchecked. In the late summer of 1899 difficulties built up in the money market as similar crises began to sweep through western Europe. Interest rates rose and share prices fell. Two major industrial and banking groups went into liquidation. The banks restricted loans to protect their reserves and working capital became hard to find. The State Bank entered the market to try to rescue those banks with the most serious problems but the effects on prices and output were acute. Pig iron was 70–80 kopecks at the middle of 1900 and 45–48 kopecks by the end of the year; coal was 9–10 kopecks at the beginning of 1900 and 6–7 kopecks by the end of 1902; crude oil was 17–18 kopecks in 1900 and 4–6 kopecks at the beginning of 1902. Pig output fell from 177 million poods in 1900 to 149 million in 1903; Donetz coal output was 691 million poods in 1900 and 642 million in 1902. In 1899 325 joint stock companies were founded with a capitalisation of 363 million roubles; in 1902 only 68 companies capitalised at 73 million roubles. Heavy industry was now suffering from overproduction, for the growth of steel output was supported only by railway demand and by the industry's own demand for steel. Underlying the whole crisis was the exhaustion of the tax paying powers of the rural population. Government expenditure could not maintain the rate of acceleration needed to keep capital expenditure at an even level. By the nature of the expansion there was little help to be expected from a rise in internal demand except for the textile industries which were not leading forces in growth. Unrest began to develop in hitherto peaceful rural areas. De Witte altered course, hoping to gain strength from modernisation of the rural economy, but he achieved little. The sources of industrial growth were further sapped by the war with Japan in 1904–5, by the internal disturbances of 1905 and the short but profound world depression in 1907–8. The output of capital goods stagnated while production of coal remained virtually unaltered during 1900–5, though rising by half over the next three years largely because of the sharp decline in the output of petroleum and the consequent rise in oil prices.

One consequence of the depression was the formation of syndicates in many sectors of Russian industry, above all in those dominated by foreign capital, with the aim of holding prices and controlling competition. Their methods varied; some took over the allocation of orders to economise on transport and selling costs, some exercised control of terms of credit but essentially the syndicates were sales agencies and only on occasion intervened to regulate output. Many of the smaller syndicates – in cement, tobacco and matches, for example – were simply local elements in big international cartels. The best known of the large groupings were the Prodamet syndicate in the metallurgical industries and Produgol in coal. By 1908 Prodamet, founded six years before, was marketing up to three-quarters of the output of the fifteen biggest companies, though Hughes and some Polish firms never took part. Produgol emerged in 1906 out of a reorganisation of the Donetz coal industry and soon came to control 75 per cent of all domestic production. Eight of the nine locomotive makers joined in a cartel; the ninth was owned by the state. One result of their efforts to control the forces of the market was that from time to time their works were grossly under-utilised. From 1909 to 1913, for example, the state works produced a mere six engines a year. Such organisations were not new in Russia and, after all, de Witte himself had acted deliberately to maintain prices when in 1899 he made agreements with six firms over the supply of rails for three years ahead at that year's prices. As in Germany there were bitter rivalries within industries which served to curb the worst excesses of this form of monopoly. Action was limited also by dissension between industries as, for example, in the steel producers' reaction against rising coal prices. Prodamet found itself in competition with the Krovlia cartel established by the leading Urals steel manufacturers, awakening from their slumber at last. Other opposition came from Baltic industrialists who resented paying monopoly prices for steel and other manufactures so much higher than those tendered by firms abroad with which they were in close contact. Yet others objected to what they saw as the regulation of Russian industry by foreigners. In any case a more effective way of rationalising the internal affairs of Russian industries soon came through the activities of the investment banks discussed earlier, which had their origins in the same post-1900 depression; their emergence signified a much healthier development for Russian industry. The control over important sectors of the Russian economy apparently exercised by foreigners through the syndicates was in fact very limited. The power of the state, exercised through the State Bank as creditor of the investment banks, was a formidable check and any monopolistic activities were limited by the open competition between the banks themselves.

After 1905, but more particularly after 1908, Russian industry expanded again at a rapid rate. From 1910 to 1913 industrial production rose at 7·5 per cent per annum compared with 9 per cent from 1894 to 1899. To some extent this expansion was helped by the excess capacity in plant established before 1900: from 1900 to 1909, for example, the steel industry was only operating at approximately 50–60 per cent of capacity; the coal industry in 1913 was still only working at three-quarters of capacity. Even so, there was a real rise in demand to take up this slack and to encourage further expansion. Now, however, the impetus came from different sources. No longer was it directly inspired by the government. War and revolution had strained the budget and it was neither possible nor desirable to squeeze the peasant further. The years of depression had been sustained in part by the completion of railway projects already begun but the five years prior to 1914 saw relatively little new construction undertaken. Now it was the investment banks who took up the government's former role, tapping foreign investment but deploying it mainly now through Russian channels. The industrial sector now had a greater stock of technical knowledge and a more permanent labour force whose economic position was slowly improving. Russians took over more senior management roles: in the Donetz this tended to bring more Poles into technical management and Russian Jews to occupy commercial positions. With grain exports rising too, the internal market showed a hitherto unknown buoyancy; the cotton industry gained from the increased demand arising from the increase in grain prices after 1897 and the cancellation of redemption payments in 1907. Employment in the Moscow industry rose 16 per cent from 1909 to 1913. Towns were growing fast and from this came demand for construction materials and incomes to be spent by construction workers. There was heavy investment in public utilities, backed by foreign, mainly Belgian, capital. Many Russian cities, for example, never had gas lighting and were now able to install electricity from the start. Agricultural reform created greater confidence in the prospects of Russian industry.

So rapid was the growth that oil, coal and metals became relatively scarce and the government had to suspend certain tariffs on the import of pig iron. There is little evidence to suggest that these shortages were the result of the activities of the syndicates; they arose rather from the disproportionate growth of construction. Expansion was still dominated by the basic industries though they conspicuously failed to develop in important new directions, such as in producing quality steels for the engineering industry. Indeed the maturity of Russian industry can best be assessed from the growth of the machine building industries. Thus in 1913 more than a half of the electrical machinery going into service was built in Russia. The Swedish Ericcson plant now employed 1,275 men making telephone equipment and the German Siemens-Halske works used 750 men to build electrical machinery. Westinghouse were manufacturing in Russia too through their French subsidiary. The Singer Sewing Machine works at Podolsk, forty kilometres south of Moscow, established in 1901, was employing 2,000 workers eight years later and the firm had 3,000 outlets for sales and servicing throughout the country. In 1912 Russia imported steam and internal combustion engines to the value of 20 million roubles (excluding duty) whereas Russian production of engines and parts came to just under 17 million roubles. Perhaps a third of the home requirement for machine tools was now satisfied from Russian makers, though this partly reflected the limited demand of home industries. Most significant of all was the manufacture of agricultural machinery. By 1908 there were 800 plants, not including local individual peasant makers, though some no doubt were very small repair shops; together they employed 39,000 men. The biggest was the International Harvester plant in Moscow with 2,000 employees but manufacture was extensive at and around Berdiansk (Osipenko) in southern Russia where possibly 7,000 men were at work in the industry. In 1913 the supply of agricultural machinery in Russia was about equally divided between home production and imports. However, the absolute level of output in the Russian machine industry was low by western standards; only the poorest quality machines were manufactured. Machine building was held back by the small market and consequent lack of specialisation, by the high cost of iron and the absence of many of the requisite skills.

Of over 2 million workers in factories of above twenty employees, over 40 per cent were in establishments employing more than 1,000 workers. This may be compared with the United States where of over 6 million such workers only 20 per cent were in 1,000 worker plants. In part this derived from the nature, timing and technology of southern Russian industry and reflected too the weakness of the specialised machine and consumer goods sector in Russia, which were usually smaller scale industries. The urban population expanded rapidly, rising from 5·5 per cent of the whole in 1850 to 12·7 per cent in 1880 and 14·6 per cent in 1914. However, many small factories were located in the countryside and an analysis of occupations has suggested that some 22 per cent of the population could be classified as 'non-agricultural' in 1913. Yet the historical pattern of industry shown in Table 66 had still not been greatly modified. The central industrial region in 1912 accounted for 43 per cent of factory labour and 36 per cent of total output and this proportion had risen somewhat since 1900. The predominance of textiles there and the relatively rapid growth of that industry after the crisis of 1900 were important factors in this trend, though there was a considerable growth in the manufacture of machinery and railway equipment too. The Donetz area produced 87 per cent of the coal output, 74 per cent of pig and 63 per cent of steel produced in the Russian Empire, excluding Poland, by the outbreak of the First World War but on the basis of these supplies of fuel and semi-manufactures industrialisation essentially took place within the bounds of the old geographical framework.

This, then, was the Russian achievement in industrialisation before 1914. For all its shortcomings, compared with that of the great powers of western Europe the speed and magnitude of the change were amazing. The pattern was in all its essentials that of pure capitalism, not surprisingly in view of the large contribution of western capitalists and industrialists. In detail, however, Russian industrialisation followed paths all its own; substitutes had to be found for the more usual processes of demand creation and accumulation of capital. Yet even by sacrificing ways of life that many held dear and by placing well-nigh intolerable strains upon the mass of her people, Russia was unable to escape from her dilemma. Whatever the Narodniks imagined, her proximity to Germany could not but implicate her in the power struggles of European politics and this necessitated further economic development. She was still heavily dependent on foreign capital and particularly dependent on Germany for the supplies of machinery essential for further development. Resentment of the evils of industrialisation was to be found all over Europe but in Russia it was not appeased by rising living standards as it was in the west. So the internal crisis developed and at the same time, for all her efforts, Russia remained unable to match the growth of her potential enemies. It is often asked whether, if war had not broken out, the existing regime would have avoided the revolution as a result of improvements in living standards brought about by a longer period of industrial growth. There is, of course, no answer to such speculation though most commentators seem to hold that internal unrest had become so acute that a cataclysm was inevitable. The revival of industry after 1909 brought some recovery in the position of workers, although the real wage level of 1903 was not again attained. Strikes tended to be directed towards achieving yet more material gains rather than for political ends, though continued harassment by the police intensified the bitterness of any strike. The growth of industry brought thousands into the towns and closer to the centres of discontent. Lenin at least believed that his most acute problem was one of preventing premature revolution by the working classes. However this might be, there is no doubt that the economic and political future depended greatly on the feelings of the peasantry and how they reacted to the immense if belated reforms in the pattern of rural life that came soon after de Witte's fall.

FURTHER REFORM IN AGRICULTURE

In 1903 as in 1861 there were conflicting views on further reform of Russian agriculture. There were those like de Witte who saw rural backwardness as an obstacle to industrialisation but there were others, and the architect of eventual reform, Piotr Stolypin, was one of them, to whom it was still primarily a political problem. The peasants had been quite peaceful after emancipation; there were local conflicts with landlords but pro-peasant groups such as the Narodniks were disgusted at their failure to rouse the peasantry as a whole to agitate for radical reform. From the later 1890s, however, the conflicts became stronger and more widespread, culminating in the storm of 1905 when there were serious riots in the black earth region aimed at dividing up estate land. The liberals and the Narodniks were also in their different ways looking to the small peasant farmer as one solution of Russia's social and economic problems. Even if it had been politically possible, such a hope was absurd and paid no heed to the enormous climatic and market differences between eastern and western Europe. Stolypin sought to divert the peasants from their agitation for the division of noble land by offering them direct control of their own land and redistribution through market processes for the benefit of the more prosperous and the go-ahead peasants. The *mir* had not prevented the uprising of 1905 so he was content to see it go, urging instead that the regime should trust to the more prosperous peasantry as its main basis for support. The consequences might also be beneficial for agricultural productivity but this was a secondary consideration.

One of his first actions was to abolish redemption payments altogether in 1907 and with them the corporal punishment that had frequently been used against defaulters. By then only about one-third of the originally scheduled amount had been repaid. Land reform proper began in 1906 with legislation allowing the peasant to claim his share of hitherto communally owned land as his own private farm and at the same time to retain his rights in communally owned meadows and woodland. It also gave him the right to press for consolidation of his holdings. By a two-thirds vote a commune practising regular repartition could be abolished; this was modified to a simple majority vote under the law of 1911. Land in communes not repartitioning since 1861 was declared private property, a recognition of an existing situation. At the same time the powers of the Peasant Land Bank were greatly strengthened to encourage the sale and exchange of plots. The government believed that the peasant was only ready for the simplest of reforms and consequently did not try to force consolidation. The eagerness with which the peasant began to press for it, therefore, came as a surprise and the officials administering the reform had to work out their policies experimentally as they went along. Their actions then came to be codified into the legislation of 1911. In 1905 there were 12·3 million peasant households of which 9·5 million were under communal tenure. By 1915 2·8 million households had applied for conversion to private tenure and the process had been completed for about 2 million. Another 100,000 had left the commune through wholesale conversion under the two-thirds vote provision. About 3·5 million households in non-repartitioning communes qualified for certification as private owners but less than 500,000 had actually been so certified. To this 2·5 million that had actually converted to private tenure must be added approximately 0·5 million households that left the commune as part of the process of consolidation of land after 1911, making 3 million altogether to add to the 2·8 million already under private tenure in 1905. Yet the total number of communal households was much the same in 1915 as in 1905 because of the growth in the total number of households. Clearly by no means a half of peasant households were under private tenure in 1915 as some writers have suggested.

Consolidation of strips, however, was not as rapid as conversion to private property. In 1917 new consolidated holdings covered about 10 per cent of all peasant land; the highest proportions were to be found in the outlying areas in the west, in the Ukraine, in the east and above all in New Russia. Knowledge of new agricultural techniques and the degree of commercialisation of farming were the vital factors in bringing this about. Thus in the west the peasant had the example of his neighbours in the Baltic provinces and Poland and of German and Czech settlers; the western districts and the eastern steppes farmed heavily for the market. The *khutor*, or consolidated farm with the house on the farm out of the village, was most common in the north and north-west. Typically the owner of such a farm was a man with a big family, literate and well provided with capital stock. Altogether such farms made up perhaps 3 per cent of peasant households. A more common compromise was the *otrub* holding which consisted of two or three scattered plots, the peasant continuing to keep his house centrally in the village. Distances, costs of land transfer and water shortages in arid areas made the peasant prefer this to the more radical solution of a single compact plot with the peasant's house located upon it. *Otruby* was common in the south and eastern parts of the black earth area where water was only to be had in the village. The Stolypin experiment was least effective in the central agricultural and middle Volga regions where the problems of rural poverty were worst.

The move to leave the commune reached its peak in 1908–9 and then declined and the evidence seems to be that two types of peasant took most advantage of the opportunity. There were those, mainly with little land, who wished to leave farming and sold out, and the more prosperous who wished to buy more land, though by no means all these wanted to leave. Often it was more profitable to stay and dominate the village, to pasture stock on the common land, run the store and rent land from those leaving. It was the hard core of 'middle' peasants who remained attached to the *mir*. Apart from tradition, their unwillingness to move was due to fear of losing the element of 'group insurance' in the communal way of life and also to a lack of capital. Those who left did so partly at the expense of those remaining and resentment built up: the commune was bound to decline but the process would be slow. Former state peasants were less concerned to move than former serfs partly because their holdings were larger and their communes had greater vitality but also because many were to be found in the northern regions where farming was more or less a part-time activity.

Under Stolypin the Peasant Land Bank became the main agency for land settlement and colonisation. Lending conditions had been eased by de Witte in the 1890s and the Bank allowed to deal in land on its own account. With loans below 90 per cent of the cost of purchase it tended to help the well-to-do rather than the poor peasantry and in this way anticipated the Stolypin philosophy. The Bank was now allowed to buy land itself without restriction. It encouraged the purchase of land in enclosed holdings and was empowered to lend up to 100 per cent of the cost of such land. It always sold its own land in that form and its example in areas where enclosed holdings had not previously existed had considerable effect. Table 71 shows the big increase in the activities of the Bank after 1906, though it should be remembered that the riots of 1905 threw many land-owners into a state of panic and much land was put up for sale: nearly 2 million dessiatines were disposed of in 1907 alone. The price of land over 1906–15 was double that of the previous ten years. Altogether in that time the peasants bought over 10 million dessiatines and in 1917 they owned two-thirds of the land in European Russia that was not owned by the state. The influence of the reforms can best be seen through the change in the direction of sales by the Bank. In 1906 96 per cent went to communes and associations of peasants; by 1912 87 per cent was sold to individuals. In addition money was made available by the state for experimental stations, agricultural schools and implements and seeds. Such appropriations rose from 15 million roubles on average in 1898–1902 to 20·9 million roubles annually in 1903–7 and 58·7 million roubles in 1908–12. The expenditure of the *zemstvos* rose too. The number of co-operative credit

Table 71 *Annual average transactions of the Peasant Land Bank in Russia, 1883–1912*

	Land bought through Bank (000 dessiatines)	Advances (m. roubles)
1883–95	185	6·3
1896–1905	586	41·0
1906–12	1,081	120·0

Source: G. Pavlovsky, *Agricultural Russia on the Eve of the Revolution* (London, 1930), pp. 155–6.

institutions rose from 837 in 1901 to 14,500 in 1915 with some 9 million households taking part. With this increase in the sale and reorganisation of land and the ending of the *mir*'s veto over passports came a marked rise in peasant mobility generally.

There has been some argument over the real nature of Stolypin's motives in framing the reform as he did. It is said by some that as the reform evolved largely in response to peasant pressures it is unfair to accuse him of favouring one class of peasant over another. It is argued that his intention was not to assist those who were already strong but to aid those smaller peasants of strong character and ambition sufficiently to permit them to achieve the progress they desired. Even so, the inevitable effect of his legislation was to help the already rich peasant to acquire more land and more power, whatever small gain there was to the poorer individual. From an economic point of view the reforms brought much needed mobility into the economy: easier movement of people within the agricultural sector and from one sector to another, and faster transfer of land. Whatever the motives and political consequences, greater concentration of land into larger holdings increased efficiency, above all in the major grain growing sector, and increased the share of output going to the market. One estimate of this conspicuous increase in efficiency in agriculture in the early twentieth century suggests that from 1900 to 1913 output in constant prices rose by a third.

But reform was only part of the story. Prices were rising, the weather was generally favourable and industrialisation was offering a growing internal market. Internal grain shipments rose from an average of 297 million poods in 1896–1900 to 429 million poods in 1911–13, taking a steadily rising share of the grain trade. Just as after 1900 industry seemed to be gathering its own momentum of growth without constant injection of government demand, so this same industrialisation provided a boost to agriculture which the Stolypin reforms made all the more effective. On the other hand, it must be remembered that some of the increase in output was due to the bringing into cultivation of new land, mostly outside European Russia. Livestock per capita continued to fall and striking percentage increases in co-operatives, machinery and use of fertilisers reflect more than anything the very low base level in 1900.

Can we now argue that the reform would have succeeded in staving off internal revolt had it been given the full chance to work? In economic terms it made much sense and had a powerful and immediate impact; yet much of the country remained untouched by it and there is no doubt that the impetus of change slackened after 1910. Conservatives and liberals both disliked the attack on the *mir*, for different reasons. The mass of peasants, faced by the growing power of their stronger brethren, were hardly persuaded that redistribution of their land was an acceptable substitute for expropriation of noble land. The revolts continued throughout the years from 1906 to the war and Stolypin himself was assassinated in 1911.

The most striking new development of all was unquestionably the colonisation of Siberia.[7] A land of forests to the north and of deserts to the south, it had a central band of highly fertile soil, a monotonous plain similar to European Russia, starting some 200 kilometres beyond the Urals, of some 2,000 kilometres in length and 200–600 kilometres wide; it was an ideal place for new settlement. In both the pure steppe land and the wooded steppe to the north the black earth soils predominated, though the climate was less satisfactory than in European Russia, the southern regions in particular being extremely arid.

Yet at the end of the eighteenth century it was still sparsely populated land, peopled by Turks, Tartars, Eskimos and nomads of various kinds. Early in the next century the state began to think for the first time of establishing more than political and military control in the area and of planning orderly settlement and development. But only in the 1850s was permission to leave the commune granted on such terms as to allow more than a mere few to migrate. Even so, the numbers migrating remained small. In part movement was held back by ignorance, by distance and lack of transport and by the severity of the winter climate; to some degree too Siberia was ignored until the 1880s because there was still enough land available nearer at hand, above all in New Russia. Gradually the rules were relaxed further; the migrant was given longer to discharge his obligations to the commune. Extension of the Urals Railway in the 1880s made possible the journey from the Volga to Tomsk by rail and river without the need to walk. The main rivers of Siberia, the Ob, Yenussi and Lena, flow north to south but the east–west course of their tributaries helped the trans-continental movement considerably. The new migratory law of 1889 aimed to give the right to move to all who were under economic necessity to do so and migration officials were established in Siberia to allot land, based on a norm of 15 dessiatines per adult male, though there were far too few officials to cope with the influx and most emigrants had to fend for themselves. A licence system was established giving a peasant the right of preliminary sale of allotment lands in European Russia – something which became universal in 1906 – and the right to receive state lands in Siberia. Then came the Trans-Siberian railway, feeding the wooded steppes more than the land further south, for the projected connecting lines in the Altai were not completed before 1914. The bad harvests of the early and late 1890s, government assistance and the Stolypin reforms all transformed the tide of migration into a flood. The annual average of reported migrants was over 120,000 in the 1890s, 230,000 in the next decade and 180,000 from 1911 to 1914. A total of well over 4 million people migrated and the numbers returning were small, many of these being scouts who went back to fetch their families.

All emigration to the area from 1896 to 1915, as a percentage of the population in 1896, was 11·8 per cent for the western provinces, 12·8 per cent for the Ukraine, 10·5 per cent for New Russia and 8·4 per cent for the central agricultural area. In absolute terms the largest number left from the Ukraine and the central regions. Land hunger, the small size and poor location of existing holdings, a desire for greater opportunities for outside earnings – few went from the Moscow and St Petersburg areas for example – all played a part in encouraging the move. But so acute was agricultural overpopulation in 1900 that even migration of this magnitude could have only a marginal effect in the worst areas of Russia. The highest rates of migration were well under a cumulative one per cent per annum of the 1896 population. Thus the provinces of Vitebsk and Minsk in the west lost the highest proportion of the 1896 population, 17·2 and 14·4 per cent respectively, but these rates are equal to 0·86 and 0·72 per cent per annum whereas the population was rising at a cumulative rate of about 1·5 per cent.

As for Siberia itself, the area under cultivation rose quickly from 3·4 million dessiatines in 1897 to 7·5 million in 1917. To some degree the colonisation was simply a transfer to the east of the agricultural techniques of the black earth region and where this was so soil exhaustion soon set in. Until the great rush after 1895 most immigrants were accepted into local communes as there was plenty of room and local inhabitants wanted to avoid the problems arising from illegal squatting. Up till this time new-comers usually had animals and land well in excess of what they could hope for in the west. Their homes were rough but clean, not providing shelter for the animals as they commonly did in European Russia. Later settlers too found higher standards of living if they were allowed into communes but the proportion so welcomed fell off sharply and the out-siders found themselves generally much less well off.

By comparison with the west there was greater concentration in Siberia upon livestock farming, partly because the level of transport costs to western markets was less onerous on goods of relatively high value : weight ratio. The number of sheep, cattle and pigs per head was twice that in European Russia. More significant yet was the establishment of creameries on the Danish pattern along the route of the Trans-Siberian railway. By 1911 there were 3,102 such plants, including 1,318 co-operatives. They used Danish and Swedish dairy apparatus and Danish officials to supervise the installations. Most of the butter went eventually to Britain though not a little went through Denmark and changed its nationality on the way. Exports reached one million poods in 1900, 2 million in 1905, 3 million in 1906 and 4·3 million in 1910. The butter trains ran every day picking up their ready-loaded ice trucks at each transit centre. The dominant elements in the co-operatives were *kulaks* who owned considerable herds of cattle; the dairy work itself was the least satisfactory part of the industry, for the sanitary arrangements left much to be desired, but the whole opera-tion brought a unique element of modernity to Russian agriculture. By 1911 the grain harvest in Siberia was calculated to have been double local consumption and 50 million poods were exported from the region com-pared with 400,000 poods in 1894. In the arid areas the pattern was to grow grain for six to twelve years and then to leave the land fallow for a slightly longer time. Only in the regions of western Siberia near the railway and where the animal population was higher was a three-field system to be found with fertiliser in use. Except for such areas of advanced farming, however, the pattern of farming remained as primitive as in the west. The reforms of Stolypin and his predecessors had enabled men to move but it had not given them either the money or the knowledge with which to improve their ways. The problem of monoculture and soil wastage that cast its shadow over most of the rural life of European Russia became just as real in the east.

CONCLUSIONS

What in measurable terms had been achieved in Russia since 1861 ? The population grew from 74 million in 1860 to 170 million in 1916, a net rate of 1·5 per cent per annum, the numbers emigrating out of the country making very little difference. Agriculture, which supplied rather more than half the national income in 1913 and employed two-thirds of the working population, had increased its output at about 2 per cent per annum due equally to an increase in the area under cultivation in the south and in Siberia and to an annual one per cent rise in yield per hectare. Industrial production grew at 5 per cent per annum, though in 1913 it provided still only a little over 20 per cent of the national income. Total output, including transport, trade and services, rose at 2·5 per cent per annum, thus exceeding population growth by one per cent, though from 1880 to 1913 growth was more like 3 per cent. After the period of preparation for growth following upon emancipation, from 1880 onwards Russia's industrial growth matched all but the fastest in Europe. However, in 1913 real income per head in Russia must have been only a little above one-third of that in Germany. Such comparisons are of limited implication where one economy has such a large subsistence sector, but they do indicate the distance Russia had still to travel. Economic development in such a huge economy, functioning in such diverse environments under an archaic social system, called for unique as well as herculean efforts. In no other major country was the state called to do so much: in no other was it more ill-suited for the role. Although much had been accomplished, it was the very size of the problem that brought defeat. Russia was a vast land, varied in fertility and hostile in climate, where natural resources were widely dispersed and least available in the west; its population was so large and growing so quickly that movements that were huge in other contexts had little economic effect; above all its backwardness was so profound that even intense programmes of reform and innovation made little impression. Against such a background it would be rash to assert that any alternative policies within the framework of a Tsarist political regime would have brought any substantial modification and acceleration of development growth before 1914.

SUGGESTED READING

Though biased in some respects, P. LYASHCHENKO, *A History of the National Economy of Russia* (New York, 1949) is the best single account. This can be supplemented by works of a more or less general nature dealing with particular periods, such as W. L. BLACKWELL, *The Beginnings of Russian Industrialisation* (Princeton, 1968) and W. M. PINTNER, *Russian Economic Policy under Nicholas I* (Ithaca, 1967). More briefly there is the pamphlet by M. FALKUS, *The Industrialisation of Russia, 1700–1914* (London, 1973). For the eighteenth as well as the nineteenth century J. BLUM, *Lord and Peasant in Russia* (Princeton, 1961) is invaluable. Two outstanding works on rural society have been published by M. CONFINO, *Systèmes agraires et progrès agricole* (Paris, 1969) and *Domaines et seigneurs en Russie vers la fin du XVIIIᵉ siècle* (Paris, 1963). Another specialised work of importance in French is R. PORTAL, *L'Ourale* (Paris, 1950). On the nineteenth century two contemporary works of great interest are M. L. TEGOBORSKI,

Commentaries on the Productive Forces of Russia (London, 1855) and P. TUGAN BARANOVSKY, *The Russian Factory in the Nineteenth Century*, now published in English (Homewood, Ill., 1970). Nor can one forget V. LENIN's remarkable book *The Development of Capitalism in Russia* published in Moscow in 1899 and available in English in a Moscow edition of 1967. Neither of these last two works is an objective study but both contain material of great value. All students should read A. GERSCHENKRON's brilliant chapter in the *Cambridge Economic History of Europe*, vol. VI (Cambridge, 1965) dealing with emancipation and its consequences, and R. PORTAL's informative study of industry over roughly the same period in the same volume. The reader will also gain a great deal by studying the various collections of essays by GERSCHENKRON: *Economic Backwardness in Historical Perspective* (Cambridge, 1962), *Continuity in History* (Cambridge, 1968) and *Europe in the Russian Mirror* (Cambridge, 1970). As regards agriculture there are a number of older works still of merit, above all G. PAVLOVSKY, *Agricultural Russia on the Eve of the Revolution* (London, 1930) and to a lesser degree G. T. ROBINSON, *Rural Russia under the Old Regime* (London, 1932). More recently there is W. S. VUCINICH (ed.), *The Peasant in Nineteenth-Century Russia* (Stanford, 1968). Of a more specialised character is V. P. TIMOSHENKO, *Agricultural Russia and the Wheat Problem* (New York, 1972). T. H. VON LAUE, *Sergei Witte and the Industrialization of Russia* (New York, 1963) deals with a crucial period in Russian development in a way that has aroused the ire of Gerschenkron for no apparent reason; it can be criticised for suggesting a degree of discontinuity in development not borne out by the facts but even so it deserves careful study. D. W. TREADGOLD, *The Great Siberian Migration* (Princeton, 1957) and, much more persuasively, F. X. COQUIN, *La Sibérie* (Paris, 1969) deal with that area of non-European Russia. J. N. WESTWOOD, *A History of Russian Railways* (London, 1964) and N. HANS, *A History of Russian Educational Policy* (New York, 1964) are unexciting but present useful information. Foreign investment in Russia has excited a lot of interest. The most valuable works are J. P. MCKAY, *Pioneers for Profit* (Chicago, 1970); J. MAI, *Das deutsche Kapital in Russland 1850–1894* (Berlin, 1970) and R. GIRAULT, *Emprunts russes et investissements français en Russie: 1887–1914* (Paris, 1973). The most useful work in Russian, especially for its statistics, is P. A. KHROMOV, *Ekonomicheskoe razvitie Rossii v XIX–XX vekakh* (Moscow, 1950).

Besides the general economic history periodicals referred to elsewhere there are some specialised English language journals which occasionally publish relevant articles. The most important of these are *Slavonic and East European Review*, *Slavic Review* and *Soviet Studies*. These journals should also be consulted for reviews of works in Russian. The reader who possesses a knowledge of Russian will find much of interest in the pages of such major historical journals as *Voprosi Istorii*, published by the Historical Section of the Academy of Sciences of the USSR, and in *Istoricheski Zapiski*. An excellent guide to Soviet literature published before 1953 is *Istoriya SSR. Ukazatel' Sovietskoi Literaturi 1917–1952*, 2 vols and index (Moscow, 1956–8). This can be supplemented for more recent research by reference to section 6, 'History', of the standard Soviet bibliographical guides *Knizhnaya Letopis'* for books and *Letopis' Zhwal'nikh Staatei* for periodical literature.

NOTES

1 See page 479.

2 P. Tugan Baranovsky, *The Russian Factory in the Nineteenth Century* (Homewood, Ill., 1970), pp. 356–61.
3 *Narod* means 'the people'.
4 Statistical appendix, p. 541.
5 1 arshin = 71 centimetres.
6 These figures are from Goldsmith, op. cit. (see Table 66). Those of Gerschenkron are lower and offer a more marked contrast between the two decades. A. Gerschenkron, 'The Rate of Industrial Growth in Russia since 1885', in *Journal of Economic History*, vol. VII, 1967, p. 146.
7 A. S. Milward and S. B. Saul, *The Economic Development of Continental Europe 1780–1870* (London, 1973), pp. 153–6.

Chapter 8

The Economic Development
of South-Eastern Europe, 1850–1914

THE INTERNATIONAL SETTING

In our discussion of economic development in Austria-Hungary we drew
attention to the extreme differences in regional levels of development
which existed there. We also pointed to the great gap in development
between the eastern and south-eastern provinces of the country on the
one hand and the German and Czech provinces on the other. This gap
was mainly the result of long-existing historical circumstances which had
created in eastern and south-eastern Europe a large area where the
obstacles to economic development were, by European standards, unique
and severe. The important improvements in agricultural techniques had
been confined to northern, western and central Europe resulting in a
much lower relative level of agricultural productivity in the south-east
and that fact together with the lower level of external commerce had
created an area where per capita incomes were too low to promote the
indigenous growth of manufacturing output on a large enough scale.
Whilst the process of rapid industrialisation went ahead elsewhere on the
continent, south-eastern Europe remained a backward area displaying

before 1914, as far as can be estimated, hardly any of the increase in per capita incomes which industrialisation ultimately brought to most of the continent. The survival long into the nineteenth century of a number of institutional obstacles to development, such as serfdom, none of them fundamental but most of them no longer existing on the rest of the continent, exaggerated this gap in development and made it harder to close.

Although the historical legacy of the Balkans[1] meant that the area had no chance of repeating the earlier pattern of economic development of other European countries, this did not necessarily condemn the region to a state of permanent underdevelopment. There were possibilities of progress which, although they had many permutations, could be roughly divided into three main categories. Firstly, the state itself could force a more rapid rate of industrialisation by dominating the flow of investment and forcing it into channels which would create a more rapid expansion of capital goods production. This was the route most vigorously pursued in Russia when de Witte was Minister of Finance, and it was ultimately the solution adopted by communist governments in the Balkans. Secondly, the economy could be thrown open to foreign capital and foreign entre-preneurs to the greatest possible extent or, carrying that solution to its logical conclusion, merged in a larger economic unit; this was much more unlikely than in Russia whose apparently limitless resources exercised a fascination for western investors which a small Balkan state could not match. Serbia and Bulgaria did agree on a commercial and monetary union in 1905 but were prevented from implementing it by Austria-Hungary. Those parts of underdeveloped eastern Europe which did form part of a wider economic unit, Galicia, Dalmatia, Bosnia and Transylvania, did not in fact benefit to any degree from being included in Austria-Hungary and it may even have been to their detriment. But there remained the possibility of association with a much greater trading power and source of capital. In some commercial circles in Germany, a possible candidate, this idea was actively explored and cast an ominous shadow across Europe, a shadow which sprang into life in 1915. Thirdly, everything could be staked on the encouragement of agriculture; once brought to sufficiently high levels of productivity, and combined with access to foreign capital and to the rapidly expanding network of international and intra-European trade, it would induce a slower and more balanced growth than would spring from distorted concentration on the industrial sector or on special sections within industry. Even if it was possible, how-ever, that type of solution needed time and peace. In the event neither was available.

In Russia and Austria-Hungary these problems were tackled by the two largest European states with ample resources at their disposal and to outward appearances still great and independent powers. But in south-eastern Europe the gradual break up of the Turkish Empire left behind a collection of small, ill-endowed client states of the greater powers to cope with these problems. There the resources of the state were far less than in the great eastern empires. This made not only the first but also the second solution more difficult because it affected the possibility of attracting foreign capital and capitalists. A country like Bulgaria had little to tempt the western investor and could attract capital only with the most watertight and humiliating guarantees. There were on the other hand certain advantages: much less capital was needed and the population was small enough for the economy soon to feel the benefit from the sort of sustained increase in export income which went nowhere in Russia. But the lack of any real political autonomy meant that all choices of economic policy were severely circumscribed by the attitudes of the great powers. This was felt most acutely in the lack of independence in tariff policy and even, for some periods in Greece and Bulgaria, in internal fiscal policy. The major European importers saw the whole area merely as a source of raw material supply and they intended to keep it that way. While Russia and Austria-Hungary, with both good and bad results, maintained high and autonomous tariffs the Balkan states for much of the period had to suffer something akin to free trade.

The many limitations imposed on the exercise of full sovereignty by the international treaties which recognised the autonomy of the Balkan states took in each case many years to circumvent. Serbia, for example, was not recognised as a completely independent state until 1878. When Bulgaria won independence from the Turkish Empire the great powers continued to impose on her the same restrictions on autonomous tariff policies which they had enforced against Turkey. Because the bulk of exports from these countries was agricultural produce the ruling groups were for a long time themselves inclined to favour low tariffs, and the protectionist movement, in spite of its close identification with nationalism, did not gather real political force until the answer to the problem of development came to be seen as accelerated industrialisation. The Greek tariff for fifty years after independence was very liberal, and early trade treaties by the other states, such as the Romanian treaty with Austria-Hungary of 1875, were primarily designed to push agricultural exports into central Europe by mutual lowering of tariffs. The tide turned in the 1880s, partly because the balance of commodity trade moved sharply against the Balkan countries with an increase in manufactured imports, partly because falling grain prices dimmed the hopes of development based on agricultural exports alone, and partly because the industrialised continental economies themselves veered sharply towards agricultural protection thus exposing the economic and national weakness of the Balkan countries. 'Western Europe', wrote one of the leaders of the Romanian protectionist movement, Alexander Xenopol, 'leaves us with the heavy and wearisome burden of agricultural labour, reserving for herself the less labour-intensive and more profitable work of industry. In other words, we in Romania, in terms of European society as a whole, have to bear the burden of the most menial work and endure a degrading social function which would be more appropriate for animals or mindless machines; we are reduced to the status of helots of civilisation.'[2]

During the 1880s there began in all these economies a determined effort to impose tariff protection and, where this was diplomatically too difficult, to encourage by a wide variety of other devices national industrial production. The first Greek protective tariff came in 1884, although at first it applied only to existing industries, and by 1904, when the duties were collected at artificially high exchange rates, Greece had become a high tariff country. The Bulgarian trade treaty with Britain in 1890 was the first diplomatic acknowledgement of the country's right to conclude independent agreements. In successive steps in 1894 and 1897 the general duties were raised and in 1906 Bulgaria applied specific high ad valorem duties to all the many countries with which she had no tariff convention. The results of protection were far from impressive but after 1873 it had become an essential defence of the weak balances of payments of these economies. There is nothing to say in favour of the commercial policies of the great powers towards the Balkan states; they were petty, mean, short-sighted and misguided and their consequence was an intensification of economic nationalism in the states themselves.

Yet it would be wholly wrong to lay the blame for the failure of economic development in the Balkans on the great powers. They did nothing to help, indeed their actions made the situation worse, but the general and specific obstacles to development intrinsic to the economies of the states themselves were a greater hindrance. The constant threat and occasional reality of war, coupled with the rapid development of other European economies after the mid-1890s, meant that all hopes of a slow, balanced growth were abandoned by men of every political persuasion. After the 1880s governments floundered between a mixture of the two more drastic solutions, both of which raised enormous difficulties, and discovered that their inherited intellectual traditions and the example to be derived from the experience of other states were alike inadequate to cope with problems peculiar to the history of their own region.

THE INDUSTRIALISATION PROCESS

The thirty years before 1914 appear to be dominated in the Balkans by continuous government encouragement and stimulation of industry. But it is important to remember that by European standards the industry of these economies by 1914 was still so undeveloped that it would be pointless and misleading for us to analyse the industrialisation process in the way we have done in other countries. The total horse-power of all forms of energy used in industry in all four economies was far less than the horse-power of steam engines in use in Prussia alone in 1861. There were only 16,000 workers in modern manufacturing industry in Serbia in 1911 and a similar number in 1909 in Bulgaria. But what this actually meant may be judged from the fact that in the slack season in Bulgaria only 10,500 of these workers were in employment. The 'factories' from which such statistics were taken were still in many cases part-time workshops whose labour force returned to agricultural work in the harvest.

There were only twenty-six firms in Bulgaria in 1909 employing more than 100 workers. The gross per capita output of all private industry and mining in Romania, the most industrialised of the countries, on the eve of the Balkan wars in 1912 was about 111 lei (francs) per inhabitant. The comparable figure for Italy was about 158 francs, that for Germany almost three times the Romanian figure; for Serbia the figure was about 77 dinars (francs) and for Bulgaria about 45 leva (francs). The Romanian population was much larger than that of the other countries: 7·2 million in 1912 compared to 2·9 million in Serbia in 1910, 2·6 million in Greece in 1907 and 1·3 million in Bulgaria in 1910. To some extent therefore Romania was more industrialised than the other south-eastern countries but may still properly be grouped with them.

The industrial sector was responsible for only about 15 per cent of Serbian gross national product in 1911 and for 14 per cent of Bulgarian gross national product in 1912; estimates for the other economies would not differ greatly. By the end of the period 75 per cent of the population in Bulgaria and Romania depended on agriculture for their incomes and the percentage was higher in Serbia; the figure may have been slightly less in Greece but that was attributable to the fact that in 1907 16 per cent were dependent on commerce rather than to any greater level of industrialisation there. Whereas the proportionately small industrial sector in Russia could show in certain industries the most modern mass-productive technology because of the size of the domestic market, the small size of the market in the Balkan countries prevented such a development. Thus, for example, the first two machine shops in Bulgaria were opened only in 1907 and at that date there were only three foundries in the country. There was nothing to compare with the textile industries of the bigger eastern empires; the total number of cotton spindles in Bulgaria in 1910, 15,600, would not have formed one medium-sized Russian mill. In Serbia wool was more important than cotton but there were only 9,500 spindles in 1911. After 1905 there was a sharp increase in the rate of growth of industrial output. Per capita output in large-scale private industry in Romania increased at an annual average rate of 5·3 per cent in the period 1902–15 and in mining between 1901–2 and 1912–13 at 12 per cent. In Bulgaria between 1904 and 1911 per capita output in large-scale private industry increased at 12·7 per cent a year, and in Serbia between 1901 and 1911 at 10·5 per cent. But these rates of growth were based on such low levels of production that the most interesting question is why the output figures were so low. Some clues can be derived from an examination of the structure of the industrial sector in these economies.

– *Indigenous Industries*

The structure of industry throughout the Balkan states was remarkably similar once the chance distortions produced by raw material finds such as oil in Romania and mineral ores in Greece are discounted. The great mass of industrial output remained domestic handicraft production. This was by no means confined to local markets; before independence Bulgarian woollen weavers had supplied Turkish army uniforms and Romanian domestic textiles had been widely sold through the Turkish Empire. But these domestic industries existed on more irregular markets than the eighteenth-century domestic textile industries of western Europe, were much less capitalised and much less under the control of merchant entrepreneurs. Nevertheless they did not immediately decline in the face of competition from industrialised Europe. They continued to supply the peasant market and to increase the volume of their output until about 1880 when an avalanche of cheap European cloth overcame the conservative preferences of peasants for their traditional attire. Nevertheless textiles and clothing in most of south-eastern Europe was one of the only two industrial sectors where native entrepreneurs were able, by using cheap imported yarn, gradually to build up small factories. Although the size of these works remained very small and their productivity very low there was a thread of continuity between domestic industries and the newer modes of production. The difficulties were formidable. The second mechanised woollen factory in Bulgaria was set up in 1875 with machines brought from Brno; the machines took months on the journey and half the cost of transport was incurred inside Bulgaria. The 8 looms and 350 spindles were destroyed two years later by Turkish soldiers. But a small mechanised woollen industry did ultimately develop in the very towns, Gabrovo and Sliven, which had been the main centres of the handicraft industry.

The other sector to develop was that of foodstuff processing. With textiles it completely dominated the industrial structure, even after allowance is made for the extractive industries which in most cases were the product almost entirely of foreign capital and whose output was almost wholly exported. Of the total capital stock in Bulgarian 'factory' industry in 1909 40 per cent was in foodstuffs industries and 19 per cent in textile industries. Capital in foodstuffs industries in Romania was 32 per cent of all industrial capital, excluding the construction industry; in textiles and clothing industries it was 22 per cent. In fact the range of foodstuffs industries was very narrow. Sugar refining was little developed. Where there were modern sugar refineries, as in Bulgaria, they usually supplied only a small part of domestic consumption and were owned by foreign companies; only Serbia refined her own sugar. Flour milling made up most of the total output of the foodstuffs industries, and the value added in milling being low and gross output much higher than net output, foodstuff industries actually accounted for 67 per cent of Bulgarian gross industrial output in 1911, and 43 per cent of Serbian output in 1910.

In Greece the large number of island communities and the great difficulty which the mountainous terrain imposed on inland transport gave shipping a sufficient importance for it also to be considered an indigenous industry.

It was only in Greece that an important proportion of foreign trade was carried by native ships; indeed in Bulgaria the proportion was as low as 8 per cent in 1911. By cutting costs and using second- or third-hand vessels Greek shipowners were able to get the least profitable part of the Mediterranean tramp shipping trade. The comparison with Norway where, for similar geographical reasons, a similar development took place is instructive.[3] In the last years before 1914 earnings from shipping were contributing between 25 million and 30 million francs annually to the Greek balance of payments, more than covering the cost of the annual imports of grain. But the development of this relatively large shipping sector was more erratic and less impressive than in Norway. In 1875 the total registered tonnage was just under 300,000, a total reached by 1850 in Norway, and it then grew only very slowly until 1883 when it fell again by 1892 to its 1875 level. The problem was the conversion to steamships, a transition for which Greek shipowners did not have the capital in sufficient quantities. In 1890 only 44,684 registered tons consisted of steamships, and since there were 97 such ships their small size can easily be seen. After 1895 however the problems of conversion to steam were eased by the start of the traffic in emigrants who provided the outward cargo for the first regular transatlantic voyages by Greek shipping companies, and by the increase in availability of used steamers. Even so the total tonnage of the merchant fleet was still only 433,662 registered tons in 1912. Greek shipping provided no basis for a native shipbuilding industry. The vessels remained small, out of date, mainly used in non-specialised tramp shipping operations, and except for the very smallest, purchased at knock-down prices from elsewhere. It was usually reckoned in the late nineteenth century that the only market for a steamship that the Norwegians could no longer use was Greece.

It might seem that, had the world been peaceful, the textile and foodstuff industries would constitute a base from which the Balkan countries could have generated a slow and balanced industrialisation, capitalising on the rise in the rate of output that began after 1905. But such a conclusion is unrealistic. The increased rate of growth of industrial output in the last decade was not in fact the result of an increased rate of growth of output in textiles and foodstuffs industries but was caused by the first stirrings of larger-scale production in other industries. These were often related to the activities of newly founded banks acting as intermediaries for placing foreign capital. Per capita output in mining, a sector almost entirely controlled by foreign capital, rose from 5 to 13 per cent of total Serbian industrial output between 1901 and 1911 because of French investment in local copper mines. The most obvious example of this process was the sudden invasion by foreign capital of the small old-established oil industry in Romania. In these bursts of growth the industries which depended on native capital investment responded only sluggishly. The annual average real growth of gross output in the Romanian foodstuffs industries between 1901–2 and 1915 was only 4·5 per cent compared to an average for all industries of 7 per cent. Nor were the textile industries a good basis for industrialisation; they depended heavily on imports and were restricted by the narrowness of the market. Their growth rate in Romania over the decade before 1914 was about the same as that of industry as a whole.

Foodstuff industries were less open to this reproach. They did use domestic raw materials and the small quantities of flour exports from these countries meant that foodstuff industries made a positive though small contribution to the balance of payments, whereas the textile industries were usually before 1914 making a negative one. Romanian flour exports in the period 1910–13 were, however, only 6 per cent of unprocessed wheat exports. Moreover, in brewing and flour milling technology did not fall as far behind the levels of productivity prevalent elsewhere in Europe as it did in the textile industries. Indeed so low was the level in textiles that it must be a further argument against supposing that any process resembling the indigenous industrialisation of other areas through the medium of textile industries was taking place in the Balkans before 1914. Furthermore, the narrow range of activity of the foodstuff industries prevented them from playing an equivalent role. Three-quarters of the sugar consumed in Bulgaria in 1909 was still imported owing to the inadequacy of Bulgarian agricultural methods of sugar beet cultivation.

This was the common Balkan pattern. The raw materials produced by the agricultural sector could not sustain the textile and foodstuff industries. The Bulgarian wool industry used only one-quarter of the domestic wool clip and depended for most of its raw material on imports. The leather industry imported 68 per cent of its hides, the wood industries about a third of their wood. Everywhere small textile industries with low levels of output and productivity dependent on imports of cheap yarn existed side by side with small food processing industries, particularly milling and brewing, operating at higher levels of productivity, but still making no contribution to the economy comparable to that of sugar refining and flour milling in Austria-Hungary. It would be pointless to stress the reasons why this was so: Balkan factories laboured under almost every disadvantage, shortage of capital, poor labour, lack of technical knowledge, high fuel costs, high transport costs and, above all, a small and impoverished market.

– Industries Created by Foreign Capital

In contrast to the indigenous industries there existed the small sector of industry where output grew under the promptings of foreign capital largely to meet foreign demand. Of this kind the best example is the Romanian oil industry. Oil had been extracted by primitive methods for centuries and during the 1840s it began to be refined in small local refineries. But by 1898 the total output of crude oil was only a meagre 134,185 tons, enough to supply lamp oil, street lighting and additional fuel for some industrial purposes. Attempts at deep drilling copying the methods used in North America had been unsuccessful. The lands on which the deposits were found were often divided into numerous small peasant tenures and this combined with the smallness of the domestic market and geological difficulties to deter banks from providing the large injection of capital needed to turn the industry into something closer to the Russian model. Hand-dug pits still provided over 80 per cent of the output in 1900.

But once the international oil companies decided to use Romanian sources of supply the swiftness and scale of developments outstripped comparison. Foreign capital at first confined its interest to the refining process because of the difficulties with land tenure. There were three foreign-owned refineries in 1894 out of more than seventy, but they already processed over half the oil extracted. The Mining Law of April 1895 was designed to overcome difficulties in the way of capital investment in extraction and to develop a resource which for its plentifulness was unique in the Balkans. The law permitted the state to exploit mineral resources where the owner of the land was unable and to lease out its newly acquired rights to a third party while retaining government control over royalties and the size of concessions. The law was not as favourable to the oil companies as it seemed because the state could still control the railway freight rates from the oilfields to the sea, but the lower cost of extraction and refining in Romania compared to Russia immediately brought an influx of capital. The Hungarian Commercial Bank of Pest brought in British and Austrian capital to transform a small Romanian refining and distributing company into Steaua Română, the first integrated exploration and marketing company in the region. By 1899 it already produced more than 60 per cent of all Romanian output. In that year was formed the Română-Americană, a subsidiary company formed by Standard Oil of America in an attempt to regain the position in the western European market which it was losing to European companies operating in Russia. The German banks Diskontogesellschaft and Bleichröder founded another large new company, of which a third of the capital was French, and their rival institution the Deutsche Bank bought up and enlarged Steaua Română in 1902. Two years later a combine of the Dresdner and Schaffhausencher banks opened up a new oilfield in the Câmpulung area, and finally Royal Dutch Shell was forced to enter Romania to stop Standard Oil monopolising the output of gasoline for which western European demand was beginning to mount.

In 1902 the total capital investment in the chemical sector of Romanian industry was about 31·5 million lei out of a total industrial investment of 247 million lei. In 1915 total industrial investment was estimated at 636·5 million lei and of this total 404 million lei was now in the chemical sector, almost entirely in oil. Very little of this sudden surge of investment came from inside the country. By 1914 Romanian-owned capital accounted for less than 5 per cent of capital in the oil industry; over 70 per cent of it was nominally in German, Dutch and British ownership. What the foreign companies did was to systematise exploration, introduce Canadian drilling methods, and build much bigger refineries producing to much more exacting specifications almost entirely for export. The earlier small refineries continued to produce for the home market at relatively high prices, within a compulsory cartel forced on them by the government. The nine biggest refineries were all foreign-owned and by 1913 their exports of petroleum products exceeded one million tons. The output of crude oil had already reached that level in 1907. This transformation was responsible for a 15 per cent annual average rate of real growth of gross output in the petroleum industry after 1901 which was the major influence in the rapid rate of growth of national industrial output. Because of the speed with which it took place and the boost it gave to exports it was a more promising development than the slow industrialisation in the other sectors. But in relation to the rest of the economy it provided no more than a few small extra markets for engineering products. And the social and political tensions which resulted from the operations of multinational corporations in an intensely nationalistic country flared up to a serious political quarrel as early as 1902 when the government was prevented by a national agitation from conceding long leases of oil reserves on crown lands to Standard Oil as an incentive to the company to invest more heavily in extraction in Romania. Thereafter disputes over freight rates were common, and more critically, a quarrel broke out with the oil companies over whether priority on the railways should be given to grain exports or to oil in the harvest season. Furthermore the small proportion of Romanians employed in senior posts by the oil companies, in spite of legislation to improve the situation, was a constant reminder of the risks involved in this type of solution to the problem of development.

In fact no other south-eastern European economy had a resource so attractive to foreign investors as Romanian oil. Although foreign investment formed a much larger part of total investment than in other European economies, direct foreign investment was attracted only rarely and then under the most stringent of guarantees. The usual route for foreign capital to enter Balkan industry was through banks which themselves were creations of, or drew much of their capital from, the major banking institutions of industrialised Europe. Of the eight largest banks in Romania five were founded with foreign capital and over half of the permanent capital and reserve funds of these eight banks came from banks in othes European countries. Inevitably some of these funds found their way into industrial development, but well over half the foreign-owned share capital in Romania was in the oil industry alone. In Greece in 1910 35 per cent of fixed investment in industry and 38 per cent of working capital was foreign, and most of it was from foreign banks. The revealing analysis by Michailov of the disposition of foreign capital in Bulgaria in 1909 shows a pattern just as lopsided as that in Romania.[4] In the 261 biggest firms 22 per cent of the capital was foreign-owned. In the electrical industry

96 per cent of the capital was either foreign-owned or of mixed origin and in mining (excluding the state-owned Pernik coal mines) 71 per cent. In textiles and foodstuffs the percentages were far lower, standing at 10 per cent and 16 per cent respectively; in metallurgical industries it was lower still, amounting to only 7 per cent. The generation and supply of electricity to the few south-eastern cities was invariably undertaken by the large German companies who found profitable outlets for their equipment there. Mining of anything but coal was invariably financed by foreign firms as a way of securing sources of raw materials. But many industries which governments struggled to develop, engineering and iron manufacture in particular, attracted no extra resources of capital from abroad. If they did it was usually in return for sweeping concessions. The Belgian-owned match factory in Bulgaria had a monopoly of supply to the state match monopoly; the British-owned Prince Boris cotton mill had a marketing monopoly over north Bulgaria; the German fertiliser plant in Burgas had monopoly concessions for every type of artificial fertiliser in southern Bulgaria.

– Government Aid to Industry

Faced with these harsh facts governments could not abandon, even had they wished to, the more gradual pattern of development based on the growth of indigenous industries. In Serbia there was a strong movement to pursue that avenue of development alone because it was thought a more nationalistic solution; restrictions were imposed on village stores as late as 1891 to prevent their selling imported clothing or utensils. In Bulgaria officials were obliged to wear Bulgarian-made clothes and shoes; the law of 1883 promoting the leather industry insisted on the wearing of the traditional Balkan sandals, *opinci*, and for some time this was also the law in Serbia. Although this of course was romantic nonsense, legislation encouraging industry together with the raising of tariffs inevitably favoured the textile and foodstuff industries chiefly.

Legislation of this type was not, as many writers imply, copied from the Hungarian model. It came earlier and was a rational response to the situation. The Balkan countries after all had a chance of manipulating tariffs, whereas Hungary had none. A Serbian law of 1873 exempted certain new factories from import duties and direct taxes and in the same year Romanian legislation granted tax exemption for twenty years, freedom from import duties on machinery and freedom from stamp duty on shares to new sugar refineries. Piecemeal legislation of this kind, selecting certain industries suitable for development, remained the pattern for some time but achieved little success. In 1881 similar concessions were offered to new flour mills in Romania, but for the first one founded the king himself had to participate in the placing of the shares. They were placed with members of parliament who had immunity from debt, yet the state bought practically the whole of its output. These acts were changed in Romania in 1887 to a generalised system of industrial aid. Every firm with a fixed capital of at least 50,000 lei (francs), using 'machines', and employing at least 25 'specialist' workers, of whom two-thirds had to be Romanian, could apply for tax exemption, 5 hectares of free land, customs duty exemption on imported machinery and raw materials (providing they could not be found in Romania), and a reduction of up to 45 per cent on rail freight rates. Foodstuff industries such as breweries and flour mills were exempt because of the qualifications on the origin of raw materials. The sugar industry received a production subsidy of about 15 per cent of the retail price and these conditions attracted several large foreign companies after 1897. By this stage the legislation had ceased to resemble the frantic mercantilistic efforts of small German states in the eighteenth century and had begun more to resemble the co-ordinated development policies of underdeveloped countries in the mid-twentieth century. It was to be widely copied in the Balkans, particularly in Bulgaria.

Bulgarian concessions in the acts of 1894 and 1897 also demanded that firms had a certain minimum capital and adopted the provision stipulating a minimum number of 'specialist' workers: 20 in this case. Serbia added to her legislation in 1898 exemptions from railway freight rates. In all three countries aid was channelled towards firms employing mechanical motive power above a certain capacity, since this was regarded as a proxy for productivity. The Romanian codification of the industrial law in 1912 raised the proportion of the workforce which had to be Romanian to three-quarters and the express intention, as in many African countries now, was gradually to phase out all foreign workers. A fixed period of time was laid down within which in each firm a stipulated proportion of the technical and managerial staff, between 25 and 60 per cent, would also have to be of Romanian origin. There was in fact almost no technical education in Romania and the intention was to force foreign companies to provide on-the-job training.

What did such legislation achieve? Of the total output of the 266 factories receiving state aid in Bulgaria under the codified industrial legislation of 1909 25 per cent were in the textile industry, 23 per cent in flour milling and 19 per cent in other foodstuffs. In Serbia after the legislation of 1898 there were 54 factories taking advantage of the concessions by 1905, but again over half the concessions were to foodstuffs or textiles firms. On the whole legislation of this kind encouraged low-productivity enterprises; over a quarter of the Bulgarian firms meeting the motive power requirements used water power. Nor did such legislation fill the gaps in the industrial structure left by the erratic distribution of foreign capital. But one useful aspect of this aid seems to have been overlooked; it did enable some firms to export a proportion of their output. About one-quarter of the output of Romanian firms receiving aid in 1904 was exported, only about one-twentieth of the output of firms not receiving aid; yet the output of the two sectors was about the same. To that extent it served the same purpose as the concealed export subsidies given to flour millers in Hungary.

If this legislation achieved so little one reason was that relatively little money was involved in it. State subsidies to industry in Bulgaria between 1900 and 1914 were only about 4·3 per cent of all investment in industry; in Serbia they were even less. This bore little resemblance to the state-promoted drive to industrialisation required to produce development. But subsidisation of industry in this way was by no means the only policy of state aid to industrialisation which Balkan governments followed. There was always the railway. Such development, however, had to depend on foreign capital and it can only be studied within the context of foreign capital movements and the attitude of Balkan governments to them.

THE STATE AS BORROWER AND INVESTOR

It was impossible for governments with such meagre revenues, no matter how severe the fiscal burdens they imposed on the population, to build from their own resources the railway networks on which they pinned so much hope. But the importance of the railway as an instrument of national economic development seemed so great that the construction of a national rail network was always, with the exception of Serbia in the early period, one of the highest economic and political priorities. There were no railways at all in the area before 1860 when a British company built the short line from Cernavoda to Constanţa in Romania to avoid the river journey through the still unregulated Danube delta. In attempting to remedy what was only the most visible symptom of the economic backwardness of the Balkans compared to the rest of the continent the state was certainly ignoring the more profound economic problems. Nevertheless it was in this area that the Balkan governments made their greatest effort, one more remarkable and determined than historians have allowed. In doing so they were able to unite advantages from the alternative solutions to the problem of underdevelopment outlined above by using the diplomatic resources and higher credit-rating of the central government to attract foreign capital by means of guaranteed loans and directing this stream of capital into the construction of a railway system.

There were few lines in this area whose strategic implications did not actively concern the foreign policy of the great powers. By playing off international rivalries and exploiting these strategic implications the smaller state could often force a greater power to provide implicit and even explicit backing to major European financial groups who would have found the construction of Balkan railways, as a private venture, an unattractive proposition. For there were few medium-sized towns in the area and Constantinople (Istanbul) was the only large city; internal trade was small and passenger movement negligible. Indeed the railway to Constantinople would probably have remained the sole focus of interest of western investors, apart from occasional short lines for the transport of raw materials or grain to ports, had the state not played so active a role. Serbia and Bulgaria were each bound by the terms of the Treaty of Berlin in 1878 to complete through their territories the railway from Belgrade to Constantinople. A long stretch in Bulgaria lay in so-called East Roumelia, which the powers kept separate from Bulgaria until it was annexed in 1885, and was owned and operated by the western-owned Orient Railway Company. The company soon fell foul of the Bulgarian government which in any case wanted its foreign trade to go through the Bulgarian port of Burgas rather than through Constantinople and for this reason was eager to complete an east–west railway link on its own territory. Most railway building plans in Bulgaria therefore hinged on constructing a parallel line providing an all-Bulgarian connection to Burgas by Stara Zagora and Yambol. This line was blocked by the western powers because of its threat to the Orient Railway but the government was eventually able to raise funds in Vienna in 1889 to complete the line. Three years later the same sources financed the Pleven–Sofia–Kyustendil line. But Austria-Hungary was no less interested in the strategic implications than Britain and France and refused further funds for an extension of the network in accordance with Bulgarian plans. By raising funds from the Banque de Paris et des Pays Bas the state was able to launch further lines and by threatening to turn wholly to a French source, the Crédit Lyonnais, it was able to twist the arm of the government and bankers in Vienna to re-open the line of credit.

There are many such examples of playing off one group against another and the diplomatic activities of the Balkan state make the model of its operations subtly different, and of course much more dangerous, than that of the Russian government under de Witte. The implicit guarantees to western financiers could be implemented because the Balkan states were so weak militarily. By operating in this way the state was accepting the implication that it was in some respects only a diplomatic plaything of the more important European powers. There was no successful struggle to withdraw from these conflicts into neutrality as in Switzerland or Belgium; indeed the reverse had taken place as nationalism sowed the seeds of savage inter-Balkan conflicts in which questions of railway construction were also involved. It followed therefore that raising foreign capital in this way for railway building soon led to raising foreign capital for war. Indeed the military expenditure of the Balkan states eventually came to consume greater sums of foreign capital than railway building. The many writers who deplore this fail to see that these uses of foreign capital were not always alternatives; defence did not always get in the way of railway building. They were often complementary, forming part and parcel of the same risky state operation. Furthermore the multiplier effects of defence expenditure could in certain circumstances be as valuable economically as railway expenditure.

Nothing could better illustrate the power which the railway still exercised over governments in the late nineteenth century as an instrument of development. Balkan railways, apart from the numbers they employed in construction, had only a limited impact on the economy. No locomotives or rolling stock were built there, and no rail. The Bulgarian locomotives came from Germany – from Henschel, Maffei and Hanomag – and the Romanian locomotives from the Staatsbahn workshops in Austria; there were not many of them, and the railways were ill-equipped as well as badly built. Bulgaria had only 196 locomotives in 1911, compared with the 2,393 of the Bavarian State Railways in the same year, but the import cost of these inadequate railway systems was still very great. Ultimately the economic, diplomatic and military risks run for such results show that all that was left of the liberal ideology which had sustained economic development in Europe in mid-century was now a nationalist ideology, whose economic calculations were, inevitably, less nice.

Compared to the length of track constructed elsewhere on the continent the Balkan railways may seem insignificant, and indeed are usually so treated. Serbia, for example, still had no railways in 1883 and only 929 kilometres of track in 1910. But that is a superficial view. For countries with such slender resources the construction effort was enormous and sustained. When it flagged the state often intervened more directly by taking over the system or diverting other public funds. After 1875 the Romanian state took over the building of the railways and in 1882 their operation; Bulgarian railways were nationalised in 1884 and Serbian in 1889; in Greece by 1914 only the main line had been taken over but it is estimated that 58 per cent of the construction costs of the whole system were met by the government. The rate of construction, as Table 72 shows, was very erratic. In Bulgaria construction was at a standstill in the period 1900–6 because no more foreign capital could be found. But no small western European economy achieved significantly faster rates of growth of railway construction than did the Balkans at its periods of boom. It is difficult to be more precise as the only contemporary official statistics are for Romania; for that reason Table 72 is compiled also from other sources and shows considerable differences from the reconstructed official statistics. The exact statistical truth remains to be determined.

In countries where even carts were not common the cost reducing effects of railways could be dramatic and without more thorough investigation of these effects it is perhaps wiser not to condemn this concern with railway building too harshly. It was not exclusive of other forms of transport improvement as it had usually been in western Europe. The network of paved roads in Greece grew from 1,625 kilometres in 1867 to 4,012 kilometres in 1910 and the Corinth canal was cut with government funds. In Romania the length of officially maintained roads rose from 1,910 kilometres in 1876 to 41,000 kilometres in 1900 and the canalisation of the Danube at the Iron Gates was completed in 1896. But transport costs were still very high in spite of the manipulation of freight rates, partly because more revenue per kilometre had to be recouped by higher charges if the systems were to attempt to pay the interest on the foreign capital which had built them. Revenue per kilometre on the Piraeus–Athens–Peloponnese railway, the most important Greek line, was in 1911 about one-quarter that of the Chemins de Fer de l'Ouest, the most rural and unprofitable part of the French network. Even the Romanian network with its heavy grain and oil freights still fell short of that level.

Table 72 *Length of railway line in Balkan countries, 1867–1913 (km)*

Greece		Bulgaria		Romania		Serbia	
Date	Km	Date	Km	Date	Km	Date	Km
1867	8	1888	384	1869	171	1884	253
1880	206	1894	529	1873	938	1890	540
1892	712	1900	1,174	1878	1,300	1895	540
1900	1,009	1906	1,176	1890	2,424	1900	571
1909	1,548	1908	1,589	1900	3,080	1905	707
		1911	1,931	1910	3,437	1912	976
		1913	2,109				

Source: N. Aguelopolos, *Le Rôle des capitaux étrangers dans la construction de la Grèce moderne* (Lausanne, 1969), passim; J. Dantschoff, *Das Eisenbahnwesen in Bulgarien* (Leipzig, 1917), passim; G. Cioriceanu, *La Roumanie économique et ses rapports avec l'étranger de 1860 à 1915* (Paris, 1928), passim; B. Mitchell, *European Historical Statistics, 1750–1970* (London, 1975).

The proportion of Bulgarian state expenditure which went on building and running the ports and railways was 13·1 per cent in 1887 and averaged 17·9 per cent over the period 1907–11. If to that is added the proportion of state expenditure on 'other forms of communications and construction' the totals are increased to 24·5 per cent and 26 per cent. At least one-quarter of government income was therefore committed to improvements in the infrastructure of the economy. A larger definition would incorporate education because between one-half and three-quarters of the population there, as everywhere in the Balkans, was illiterate in the 1880s. Expenditure on education was 6·8 per cent of state expenditure in 1907–11, but even this addition would only raise the proportion of government revenue spent on the infrastructure slightly above that devoted to military expenditure – one-third in 1887 and 26·4 per cent in 1907–11. Of the capital raised in foreign loans by Serbia 41 per cent went to finance military expenditure.

The other great item of public expenditure was the servicing of interest on the public debt whether owned by nationals or foreigners. We have drawn attention elsewhere to the way in which this became institutionalised in the relationships between borrowing and lending states so that large loans were often raised purely to pay the interest on earlier loans.[5] Balkan states particularly found themselves in this position. Greece was only allowed back into the international capital market in 1878 on condition that it repaid interest still owing on the original Rothschild loans of the 1830s which had financed the first years of independence. The automatic consequence for all south-eastern countries was that servicing the public debt took up an ever greater proportion of expenditure and together

Table 73   *Public debt per capita in   certain   underdeveloped capital-importing countries, 1911 (current francs)*

Portugal	662·1
Spain	498·0
Italy	368·5
Greece	328·0
Romania	299·6
Serbia	238·8
Norway	188·0
Russia	186·8
Bulgaria	149·2

Source: K. Popov, *Stopanska Bulgariya*, pp. 497–8.

with the burden of military expenditure reduced the proportion of borrowed capital available for economic development. Debt payments rose from 4·3 per cent of expenditure in Bulgaria in 1887 to an average of 20·7 per cent over the period 1907–11.

The estimates of the size of public debt per capita in 1911 in Table 73 show that the per capita burden of debt payments in the Balkans was lower than in Portugal, Spain and Italy. But the figures are no indication of the proportion of foreign capital per capita in these countries and it is impossible to calculate the exact contribution which foreign capital made. At the end of the nineteenth century it was not making as important a contribution in Spain and Italy as it had in mid-century and the implication of Table 73 is that Balkan governments might have used their national debts even more vigorously for financing development. But the institutionalisation of intra-European loans by the major banks tended to increase the national debt of debtor countries with time and the lower figures for the Balkan countries partly reflect their shorter history on the international capital market. A fairer comparison might be with Russia, where the Balkan countries emerge favourably.

But foreign capital entered the country not only through the public debt; the attitude of the state also affected its inflow through banks. The development of the Romanian oil industry was the obvious example of this process. Of the eight biggest banks in Romania in 1914 only three had been founded with Romanian capital. Undoubtedly one thing which attracted such banks to Romania more than to the other states was the state's encouragement of the activities of the international oil companies there. However, it does not seem that they invested their funds with any vigour in any other industries. The Banca de Credit Român, a subsidiary of the Länderbank, provided, for example, only 12·5 per cent of its short-term credits to industry. The native Romanian bank, Banca Marmarosch-Blanc, had as large a direct participation in industry as all the bigger foreign banks.

Direct foreign capital participation in Balkan industry was nevertheless important. Its main sources seem to have been smaller investors, especially from Austria-Hungary, whose resources were tapped by native joint stock companies. In 1914 80 per cent of industrial shares in Romania were owned by non-citizens, although some proportion of this must have been owned by Jews resident in Romania who were not allowed citizenship. Foreign capital was responsible for 41 per cent of the fixed investment in Greek industry in 1906 and over 60 per cent of the working capital. The terms on which foreign capital was obtained were stiff and interest rates were as high as 8 per cent when to other borrowers in Paris and Berlin they were a mere 3 per cent. The state could exercise little influence on this process and with the more rapid industrial growth after 1900 it may have been superseded by the more positive attitude of the banks. After 1905 in Serbia the rate of growth of fixed investment in industry corresponded quite closely with the increase in bank capital there. The tariff war with Austria-Hungary in 1906 pushed the foreign-owned banks such as the Banque Franco-Serbe and the Srpska Kreditna Banka, owned jointly by the Comptoir d'Escompte and the Länderbank, towards industrial and mining investments and away from foreign trade which had been their previous main interest. In Bulgaria too the big expansion of the credit structure came with the entry of foreign banks after 1905. Since the railway systems were largely a creation of foreign capital the conclusion is inescapable that foreign capital, even though its achievements were feeble and its methods of operation not always in harmony with the best interests of economic development in the Balkans, was largely responsible for the important developments in communications and such minor industrial development as took place there.

That is not to say that standards of consumption did not fall. With the long fall in grain prices to the 1890s much of the population was faced with producing more to maintain incomes or cutting consumption. In this situation the Balkan governments, however inconsistent their policies, did not fail to understand the urgency of economic priorities. By their actions they evolved a different model for European development, using their financial resources and strategic position to act as brokers between capital lending countries and by this means to obtain capital. Although we may still attach some criticisms to these governments, particularly to the nationalistic belligerency of their foreign policies, and although we may feel sceptical about the methods of operation of foreign capital, neither government nor lenders were responsible for the failure of industrialisation before 1914. To explain this we must look elsewhere, and in particular at the failure of the domestic economy to supplement the meagre imported resources which Balkan governments obtained by such great efforts and at such great risks.

AGRICULTURE IN SOUTH-EASTERN EUROPE

– The Ratio of Land to Labour

In all four countries three-quarters of the population still depended on the agricultural sector for their income before 1914. In three of them, Bulgaria, Greece and Serbia, rural society was largely made up of small independent peasant farmers. During the Turkish administration large areas of fertile lowland had been left uncultivated by the indigenous inhabitants who at the time of the invasions had moved into the mountain regions. In the eighteenth century the recolonisation and cultivation of the more fertile areas began on a large scale. The ratio of land to labour in these countries in the first half of the nineteenth century was still very favourable and for much of the century the Balkans were an advancing frontier of cultivation. There was a powerful feeling that once the Turkish yoke and its quasi-feudal system were thrown off these societies would be free to develop as egalitarian peasant democracies with each household having at its disposal a satisfactory supply of the principal resource, land. When the Turks were expelled the landlord class lost all importance, except in Romania, and rents and dues for a long time took little of what surplus income the peasant had. The Serbian war of independence was a war against the dues owed to the Turkish landlords and it resulted in a seizure of the land by the peasants so that after 1830 they held this land in freehold. In Bulgaria the former Turkish estates were jointly purchased by government and peasant through a compensatory annuity to Turkey regulated by the Treaty of Berlin, and the same system applied to the extra territory which Serbia acquired by that treaty. In old Greece the situation was legally analogous to that in old Serbia but the government itself retained a high proportion of the former Turkish estates as crown domain. Only with the acquisition of Thessaly did Greece again acquire large private estates. The possibilities of an idyllic peasant nation, distinct from other European societies, received due expression in the Serbian legislation of 1833 which created for each family a protected indivisible farm of a minimum size in perpetual tenure.

The major force extending the frontier of cultivation was population increase. Nevertheless in spite of the wide availability of land the rates of population increase before 1880 were no more than and perhaps below the continental average. After that date the rapid drop in death rates unaccompanied by a corresponding fall in birth rates sent the rate of population increase in the Balkans far above the European average. In some areas of Romania the birth rate even showed a rising trend. The age of marriage for females was everywhere low and the frequency of female marriage very high. Only one per cent of the females in the age group 40–49 in Serbia and Bulgaria had not married in 1900 compared to 11 per cent in Germany. The existence of extended kinship units rather than nuclear families as the unit of farming in some of the Slav areas encouraged marriage and reproduction. The rate of natural increase of the population in Bulgaria rose from 9·7 per cent over the years 1891–5 to 18·2 per cent in 1901–5 and stayed at that high level until the end of the decade. But although the standard of agriculture was as low as in European Russia or the crisis areas of the Habsburg Empire the situation was less desperate because of the availability of land. At the time of emancipation in Romania in 1866 about 3·9 million people cultivated 2·5 million hectares of arable land; in 1909 about 6·8 million people cultivated 5·4 million hectares. The area of land cultivated in fact doubled between 1838 and 1862 and again between 1862 and 1880, mainly through taking into cultivation the steppe lands (the Bărăgan) of Wallachia. In Bulgaria as in Romania the area of land ploughed grew quickly enough to maintain the size of farm units; it increased by 39 per cent between 1897 and 1911. There were 84·8 hectares of cultivated land for each hundred inhabitants in 1904 and 92 hectares by 1912.

With falling grain prices and a rapidly growing population after 1880 the ready availability of land no longer served automatically to sustain income levels for most of the population. Until that time, however, Serbian and Bulgarian peasants seem to have enjoyed a rising standard of living. Their political power enabled them to devolve a greater share of taxation on to the townspeople and it was their relatively fortunate economic position which sustained the handicraft industries so long. Even after 1880 there was nothing corresponding to the heavy pressures to subdivision and to emigration existing in the more crowded areas of

Table 74 The pattern of landholding in Bulgaria, Serbia and Romania

Bulgaria (1897)			Serbia (1897)		Romania (1907)		
Size of farm (ha)	% of all farms	% of total farmed area	Size of farm (ha)	% of all farms	Size of farm (ha)	% of all farms	% of total farmed area
0–2	29·8	3·9	0–2	21·0	0–2	30·3	4·3
2–5	27·2	14·9	2–5	33·6	2–5	46·9	21·5
5–10	25·4	28·8	5–10	27·5	5–15	18·2	14·5
10–20	13·5	29·3	10–50	17·5	15–50	3·7	8·9
20–50	3·7	15·9	50+	0·3	50–100	0·3	2·1
50+	0·4	7·2			100+	0·6	48·7

Source: Derived from C. Abajieff, Die Handelspolitik Bulgariens, Staats- und sozialwissenschaftliche Forschungen, vol. 143 (Leipzig, 1910), p. 104; G. D. Creanga, Grundbesitzverteilung und Bauernfrage in Rumänien, Staats- und sozial-wissenschaftliche Forschungen, vol. 129 (Leipzig, 1907), pp. 32, 167.

eastern Europe. Emigrants from the Balkans were few. One important exception was the return migration of Turks from Bulgaria, about 350,000 between 1877 and 1912, which relieved the pressures caused by the high rate of natural increase over those years in Bulgaria. After 1900 Greece provided a substantial number of transatlantic emigrants; the number passed 10,000 in 1905 and reached 27,000 in 1910. They were almost entirely men and not for the most part permanent migrants. There was already a century-long tradition of emigration from Greece to Anatolia and the Aegean islands and there is no evidence that Greek emigration was the result of a land shortage at home. With 41·6 people per square kilometre in 1911 Greece was less densely populated than Serbia. Serbia itself was a target of migration throughout the nineteenth century, receiving 400,000 immigrants in the period 1876–1912; about half the skilled labour in Serbian industry in 1910 was provided by immigrants. Until 1880 and perhaps even later it is more appropriate to consider Balkan agriculture in terms of labour scarcity than labour surplus.

Although the situation in Romania was fundamentally the same, there could scarcely be any greater contrast in Europe than that between the agricultural society of Romania and the peasant lands to the south. In the peasant lands, with few contacts with the outside world, neither labour surplus nor labour scarcity meant much; the labour performed on the peasant farm was determined by the economics of that farm alone. But the simplicity of Serbian and Bulgarian society was replaced in Romania by a much more complex social system. Here landlords and large estates had survived. Political power was in the hands of the richer landed proprietors and because of the scarcity of labour they used their power to acquire and retain a sufficient labour force on their estates. The outcome was a set of agricultural and social problems unique on the continent. Whereas the typical south Slav peasant had a relatively large landholding the typical Romanian peasant had a very small plot and supplemented his income by indentured labour on the large estates under a legal system more resembling that of eastern European serfdom.

The difference in the distribution of landholdings between Romania and the two Slav countries leaps to the eye from Table 74. There are no such exact figures for Greece but apart from Thessaly its pattern was close to that of Bulgaria and Serbia. In the Slav countries the number of landholdings over 50 hectares was negligible; in Romania landholdings over 100 hectares covered almost half the farmed area. The typical Bulgarian and Serbian farm was the 5–20 hectare unit although the number of smallholdings in the 2–5 hectare category was also high. In Romania adequately sized peasant farms were much less common than 2–5 hectare smallholdings. Romania was a land of very large and very small farms. In spite of the wide availability of land the institutional arrangements were such as to prevent the biggest share of the population acquiring an adequate stock of it and this meant that the pattern of consumption there and the problems of economic development were quite different.

– The Romanian Frontier

The fertile lowlands of Moldavia and Wallachia were a natural target for settlement from the late eighteenth century as population grew. With easy river transport to the Black Sea by the Danube, Prut and Siret they were areas of grain export. At first exports went to Turkey, but as land settlement was extended in Wallachia, they went in greater quantities to the Mediterranean and to western Europe. Mounting demand from western Europe after the 1820s increased the volume but to take advantage of these commercial possibilities the landlords needed to have a regular supply of labour and to attract settlers for the purpose.

To meet the needs of the grain trade the customary pattern for the settlement of new land in Moldavia had been incorporated into the law by the eighteenth-century Phanariot rulers. After 1770 the landlord provided every newly married couple with arable land, pasture and a vegetable garden out of his estate. In return they worked his land with their own labour and their animals for a 'rent' regulated by the state. These rents were seldom paid in money but calculated in days of work on the land remaining to the landlord, or, in produce, which resulted in a situation analogous to sharecropping, or in a mixture of produce and work. The Organic Regulation framed by the Russian occupiers in 1831 for both Moldavia and Wallachia allowed the landlord to hold permanently for his own use one-third of his land regardless of future demand. It also put firm limitations on the number of peasant cattle for which the landlord would henceforth be required to provide pasture and limited the amount of arable land the landlord had to provide to new households against 'rent'. The right of the state to control these 'rents' was curtailed so that effectively the remaining two-thirds of each estate, potentially future peasant settlement land, was now under the landlord's control outside government regulation.

At the same time two ideas were spreading from western Europe which were to complicate the situation further. One was the firm nineteenth-century belief that individual freehold property was one of the foundations on which all social and economic progress was built. This ideology of private property was responsible for sweeping away many obstacles to economic development in western Europe, but when imposed on eastern Europe it produced curious results; the landlords (boyars) came to be thought of as freehold proprietors of their estates, a tendency fostered by the Organic Regulation. The second idea influencing development was the interpretation of east European agricultural arrangements in the light of western history. The land settlement relationships in Romania came to be seen as a type of European feudalism. The interpretation was economically sound; they had their origins in the need to cultivate the land in a situation of labour scarcity and with no implements but men's hands.

The Romanian peasants came to be thought of as the equivalent of serfs, and their 'rents' as feudal dues. The Act of 1864 which altered these relationships is still usually referred to as the Act of 'Emancipation' and Romania described as the last country where serfdom survived in Europe. But these 'serfs' had always been free to inherit and to own land and property in perpetuity. Their serfdom consisted in being bound to the estate. But this was not merely a judicial situation, they were bound to the estate by their economic needs and the Act of 'Emancipation' in 1864 as modified by subsequent laws did nothing to change the fundamental economic relationship between boyar and peasant. The laws of 1831 and 1864 were both in fact framed to assure the landlord a continued supply of labour and farm animals to work his estate and sustain the expansion of arable cultivation in a basic situation of labour scarcity. They did this by forcing the peasant into a situation where he could survive economically only by acquiring more land than his small customary portion and where he could get that extra land only by providing labour services to the landlord.

The legislation of 1864 gave the peasant freehold ownership of that portion of the estate for which he had formerly paid rent or services, thus completing the transition to concepts of private property. For this the peasants paid fifteen annual cash instalments. A high proportion of the landholdings created were, as Table 74 suggests, too small for survival at the low standards of agriculture in Romania. Three-quarters of all landholdings were of 10 hectares or less, whereas to sustain existence at a very low level and have a reserve to cope with harvest failures the peasant family needed at least 6 hectares of land. Probably only about 18 per cent of the families had so much under the 1864 legislation; the rest had to lease extra land from the estate to survive. Since newly married couples in future could only obtain freehold land by inheritance the natural tendency was for holdings to be reduced still further by subdivision. The pattern of holdings was yet more fragmented because such inheritances usually involved two widely separated pieces of land. It was in the economic interests of the landlord to encourage both subdivision and fragmentation because it strengthened his economic grip over his workforce. The peasant farms were declared inalienable in 1864 so that sales and readjustments of peasant landholdings, as well as raising credit on them by mortgage, were practically impossible making it even more difficult for the peasant family to leave the estate, and preventing the emergence of any group of larger and better-equipped peasant farms. Nevertheless the relative scarcity of labour might still have gradually broken down this pattern had not the landlords in absolute control of local administration used the law and various extra-legal methods to ensure a regular supply of labour on the portion of the estate which remained to them. The Law of Agricultural Contracts of 1866 initiated a series of acts providing a separate summary legal system based on the local administration to enforce all landlord–peasant contracts involving labour services.

Although they were guaranteed cheap labour few of the landlords had the capital to take advantage of the continued expansion of grain exports. Increasingly, they formed commercial partnerships with land agents, who functioned as financiers and traders and provided the capital, commercial contacts and storage facilities to export the grain to western markets. The estate would be leased for a number of years to an agent of this kind, the *arendas*, frequently Jewish or Greek, whose returns depended on extending as much as possible the area of arable cultivation. This he could only do by squeezing more contract labour out of the peasant and his animals. By 1900 over half the land in Moldavia was leased in this way, much of it in large continuous areas to financial trusts like that of Mochi Fischer, the largest and most infamous. The obvious way to increase the area of arable cultivation was to raise the price in labour of the extra portion of land which the peasant family needed to rent from the estate in order to maintain existence. The expansion of arable also increased the price of the pasture which the peasant required to feed the animals necessary for fulfilling his contract to the estate. The estates themselves owned very little livestock; in 1900 87 per cent of the cattle were kept on peasant farms, and more than half on farms which owned no more than two head of cattle.

The great estates therefore functioned as a frontier for the peasant population, providing them with a continuous supply of land and credit. But the effect of this process on peasant income and on the standard of agriculture of noble estate and peasant holding alike was exactly the opposite to that of the Siberian and American frontiers. The Romanian frontier held down peasant income and fostered labour-intensive methods of cultivation. The social and legal arrangements of the country nullified its greatest economic advantage.

Under labour contract laws the peasant had to fulfil his labour obligations on the estate first. As grain cultivation spread across the Bărăgan, everything depended on the timing of farm operations to catch the last of the rains before the summer heat. The inevitable neglect of the peasant farms produced periodic harvest failures which could almost eliminate the peasant crop. In the famine of 1904 the peasant population had to be largely fed on maize imported from the Argentine. The fact that the contract depended on power relationships based on a flagrant inequality of land distribution kept the peasant in perpetual debt, and debts incurred in village taverns or to moneylenders were transmuted into further labour obligations to the estate lands. A common system of cultivation was to rotate the land between wheat and maize. The extra land leased to peasants was usually sown to maize, the peasant's staple food. The peasant's wheat crop would have to be grown on his own hereditary land. Because the peasant's lease in such a system ran for only one year he had no interest in improving the leased land, and his maize yields were very low while his hereditary land was increasingly exhausted by the unrelieved cultivation of wheat. The increasing shortage of pasture meant that cattle were of dismal quality and with so little capital in the system there were few shelters for them. In the treeless Wallachian plains they died in large numbers in winter. Boyar and peasant alike were raping the frontier and, as the stock of new land began to decline, gradually using up their capital assets. Falling wheat prices on the international market only encouraged this process: it was necessary to cultivate more land to sustain the same income. Romanian wheat was of poor quality and its price was low, falling from an average of 205 lei (francs) a ton in 1870–1 to 163 lei a ton in 1890–1.

In this situation it may well be that the boyars realised that their days were numbered and that there was no point in a policy which attempted to conserve their assets. The relative scarcity of labour meant that even this policy demanded extreme brutality. There were about 10·5 workers to each hectare of cultivated land in Romania; in a comparable area of great estates in Germany, East Prussia, there were 14·6 and in a peasant area like Württemberg about 21·5. The daily wages of migrant workers in Romania were between four and seven times greater than the wages of those peasants residing on the estates who were paid cash. Inevitably such a situation required the use of constant coercion. There were occasional feeble attempts to ameliorate social conditions. In 1882 the length of labour contracts was limited to five years. Other laws in the 1880s began in a small way the creation of a medium-sized category of farmsteads. But despite such tinkering what evolved in Romania was a socio-economic system unique to modern Europe, a manorial economy like that of early medieval western Europe but enforced in a wholly commercial setting. There were peasant revolts in 1888, 1889, 1894 and 1900 and, most violent of all and suppressed with appalling callousness, the revolt of 1907.

Without wishing to defend the nasty reality of rural Romania or to gloss over its inhumanity the fundamental criticism of this unique society is not its unpleasantness but the fact that it impeded the process of economic change which might have brought some amelioration. The system came into being and was maintained for economic reasons: to colonise the land and to push Romanian wheat exports on to European markets. Romanian wheat was the only Balkan primary export commodity which was of real quantitative importance in international trade; her wheat exports in 1911–13 were 8·3 per cent of world wheat exports. Short of revolution, it was only a questioning of its basic economic value which could subvert the system; this eventually is what happened. As industrialisation on the basis of forced agricultural exports made so little progress between independence and the late 1890s the state turned its attention again to the internal market. There the evidence seemed convincing that while the spendable income of so large a part of the population was being reduced by the social system there was little hope of developing indigenous industries. Protective tariffs were in fact the first nail in the coffin of the Romanian landlords. From the moment they were established attention inevitably turned to creating an internal peasant market for

Romanian textile and foodstuff industries, and that in its turn implied some measure of land reform as a step towards income redistribution.

Such land reform when it came, however, did not copy the egalitarian distribution of land in Serbia and Bulgaria. It closely resembled Stolypin's reforms in Russia with their deliberate attempt to encourage the development of a middle stratum of prosperous peasants while driving the smaller farms out of business. There was, indeed, nothing in the economic development of the other Balkan countries to suggest that their pattern of landholding, although more just, was better suited to development. Inevitably the growth of population led also to subdivision there, and in Serbia where the peasant farms were inalienable and indivisible, to the emergence by 1914 of a landless class. In the other Balkan countries the provision of new land for settlement became increasingly a matter for state intervention. The Greek government after 1871 distributed about 265,000 hectares of the former Turkish land it had retained to create new peasant farms. After 1907 the Agricultural Bank broke up a further 106,000 hectares of entailed land to create over 7,000 new farms. But when the Romanian government pursued the same process, influenced by the failure of the de Witte system in Russia and the beginning of Stolypin's 'wager on the strong', it made a much more determined effort to follow the Russian path.

An Act of 1903 regulated and controlled the Popular Banks which had begun to develop in the countryside as the peasant movements became more politicised and organised. The intention of the Act was to transform the inadequate network of rural credit into an extensive supply of credit for more progressive farmers and farmers' associations. An older state institution, the Agricultural Credit Society, acted as a central discount bank for the Popular Banks and in its turn it was given discount facilities by the National Bank. The legislation was specifically designed to encourage the Schulze-Delitsch type of peasant bank with its higher interest rates, its tendency to support the wealthier peasant and its freedom from the democratic egalitarian control of the village. The law of 1904 on village co-operatives was designed to support this policy. Co-operatives would be provided on certain conditions with funds from the Popular Banks to bid against the land trusts for leases of estate land. The hope was that by excluding the poorer and riskier members of the community the co-operative associations would themselves function as a middle stratum landholding group and help in the break up of the estates.

The impact of the 1907 revolt did not change government policy. Indeed by enabling the state to limit the size of land trusts it tended to further it. But as in Russia the speed at which changes in landholding were made was quite insufficient to provide an effective alternative route towards the economic development of the country. In 1913 the area of land leased by the co-operatives was only 10 per cent of the total arable land available on estates of more than 100 hectares, and only 35 per cent of co-operative land was in fact leased from private estates, the rest coming from government and charitable foundations. In any case the events of

1907, following so hard on the Russian revolt of 1905, indicated quite clearly that a new and powerful political force had entered the scene and that the agricultural sector would no longer be content merely to be manipulated in the interests of industrialisation.

– Possibilities of Development through the Agricultural Sector

The essential problems with which the agriculture of the other Balkan lands was faced need not be rehearsed. They were in certain respects similar to those of most of underdeveloped Europe. The growth of manufacturing industry elsewhere cheapened essential items of consumption such as clothing and kitchenware, destroying as it did so most of the handicraft industries by which the income of the Balkan peasant family had been supplemented. The standard of cultivation remained so low that a far larger farm unit was needed to sustain even self-sufficiency than in western and central Europe, whereas peasant families, because of the rapidity of the economic changes taking place around them, became less and less self-sufficient. Meanwhile the level of income generated by the peasant farms was inadequate to provide any but the smallest market for national industries. With inadequate capital resources the peasant could not adequately redirect his farming operations away from self-sufficiency towards producing cash crops, much less towards producing competitive agricultural exports.

But the consequences of low agricultural incomes should have been easier to avoid than in Austria-Hungary or Russia. In spite of the rise in population there were still only 10 million people in the three peasant countries in 1911. In Romania there were only 7·2 million so even there the size of the problem was much less than that which faced Stolypin. A sufficient measure of growth in other sectors of the economy would soon have moved a significant proportion of such small numbers into higher-productivity occupations. This, as we have seen, proved impossible in spite of government encouragement of industry and foreign investment. On the other hand Stolypin's policy of promoting development in Russia by increasing rural spendable incomes was based on the fact that there was already a sizeable amount of industrial employment in Russia. But what would have happened to the landless proletariat to be created by the Romanian reforms? In retrospect, had Balkan governments not been dazzled by western images and patterns of industrialisation they might have achieved more by concentrating on the agricultural sector, not merely as an instrument but as a source -- in the early stages perhaps the best source – of economic growth. By directing more investment at an earlier date towards the agricultural sector might not the indigenous industries, brewing, flour milling and textiles, have been put in a position to utilise more domestically produced raw materials instead of the imports on which they were mostly based? Alternatively, might not such investment have enabled Balkan countries to find long-run stable markets at better prices for better quality agricultural exports? In such small economies this would have raised per capita incomes in the agricultural sector in a way that was impossible in the east European empires. Following this second path manufacturing specialisation based on growing foreign trade in the indigenous industries might have developed as it did in Hungary.

The objection to such solutions with their emphasis on prior investment in the agricultural sector was the same as the objection to industrialisation by way of the indigenous industries: there may not have been enough time. This objection was probably valid if the Balkan states were to be left to fend for themselves. For such solutions to work an international economic system more sympathetic and responsive to their development needs would have had to exist. In the last resort the responsibility for the failure of economic development in the Balkan countries rested not only with their heritage of economic backwardness but with the failure of major European economies to create, in their own interests, an international economic system which would have helped such small economies towards economic growth and development. It must, however, be admitted that the Balkan governments themselves showed little interest in these agricultural solutions to the problem of development, except in the period after Romanian independence and before protection when it was assumed by Romanian industrialisers that grain exports would provide the answer.

The social consequences of this last assumption were so grim as to make it very doubtful whether Romanian society was in fact better constituted for growth along these lines. But at least the situation in Romania was such as to keep agricultural problems in the forefront of attention. Elsewhere their neglect was almost total. In Greece in 1907 there was still no ministry of agriculture; the chief sector in the economy was the responsibility of four people in the Ministry of the Interior. In Bulgaria expenditure on agriculture and commerce together was never as much as 3 per cent of total budgetary expenditure. There were two agricultural colleges in Bulgaria and some agricultural tuition was provided to army conscripts. The main interest everywhere, however, came to be to provide agricultural credit along lines similar to, but less purposeful than, those in Romania. In Serbia a government credit institution, Uprava Fondava, was reorganised in 1898 into a land mortgage bank, Hipotekarna Banka, but half its credits were made available for buildings in Belgrade. In Bulgaria an older Turkish mortgage institution was transformed in 1904 into the Agricultural Bank which operated more successfully than its Serbian counterpart. The mortgage debt of the original bank was 6·9 million leva in 1904 whereas by 1912 it had a debt of 38·3 million leva.

Much of the new settlement everywhere in the Balkans was at the expense of livestock farming and the consequence was an agriculture devoted almost exclusively to grain. Because yields were so low it was difficult, except in Greece where climatic conditions discouraged grain farming, for specialised industrial crops to develop. Grain covered 83·5 per cent of the arable area of Romania in 1911; vegetables, fruit, industrial crops and root crops only 6·4 per cent. In Bulgaria grain covered 76 per cent of the arable area in 1912. In Serbia the output of maize and wheat more than doubled between 1889 and 1910 but it is estimated that the per capita availability of meat and animal products fell between 1859 and 1905 by as much as 60 per cent. Everywhere grain was cultivated by the most antiquated methods; the means of cultivation and the implements used were quite unaffected by the great changes in northern and central European agriculture since the sixteenth century. The wooden ploughs used universally in Greece had not substantially changed from those recorded in the first century BC. Such ploughs, which barely turned over the soil, made the cultivation of most root crops such as sugar beet impossible; they accounted for 85 per cent of the ploughs in Bulgaria in 1905 and about two-thirds of those in Serbia. In Romania, however, iron ploughs were much more common, amounting to almost two-thirds of those in use, and it was from there that their use spread southwards across the Danube into Bulgaria after 1900. No doubt the better methods in Romania were attributable to the earlier existence of a more commercialised farming sector there, but even these methods were primitive. It was possible to use steam engines for threshing and even ploughing on such big units of landholding and the shortage of labour should have encouraged it, but in 1905 although there were 4,600 threshers there were only 55 steam ploughs. In the other countries of course such machines were rarer; only 100 mechanical threshers were counted in Bulgaria in 1912.

Although there was a rapid increase in imports of agricultural machinery in the first decade of the twentieth century, in response to the wider dissemination of agricultural credit, the agricultural base of the Balkan economies was not such as to make them capable without considerable capital investment of becoming a growth sector. The extensive methods of farming at low productivity levels also diminished their ability to generate a consistent stream of primary exports. Agricultural exports were the vital factor in the balance of payments of Balkan countries and the ultimate backing for their foreign loans. But except in Greece these exports were increasingly composed of grain whose international price for most of the period was falling. From 40 per cent of Romanian exports in 1866 grain rose to 80 per cent by 1911, of which more than four-fifths was wheat. Exports of untreated and processed foodstuffs were 87 per cent of Bulgarian exports in 1911, mostly wheat and maize. Only in Greece were agricultural exports, 70 per cent of all exports after 1900, composed of more specialised crops. Greece was in fact a grain-deficiency country and grains were responsible for 30 per cent of all imports. In Serbia the older livestock export trade survived longer than elsewhere at an important level and one new export, that of plums, developed strongly. Between 1896 and 1906 grain and livestock were each responsible for just over 40 per cent of exports; however, the ban on the import of Serbian cattle into Austria-Hungary in the latter year virtually blocked all livestock exports and finally tilted the balance towards grain. In doing so it was only speeding up an inevitable trend; after 1890 Serbia regularly exported about one-fifth of her wheat crop and after 1900 the same proportion of her maize. Until the upward movement in prices after 1896 Balkan grain exports were sustained by the tendency of domestic consumption to fall as well as by the cultivation of new land. Romanian wheat exports were 37 per cent of the total harvest in 1871–6 and 51 per cent in 1886–95. Without improvements in farming the same equations applied everywhere and by 1914 the potential limit of grain exports must have been very nearly reached.

Apart from Romanian wheat Balkan agricultural exports were unimportant except within the Balkans themselves and were at the mercy of diplomatic and political crises and shifts of tariff policy in the bigger economies. Romanian livestock exports suffered a catastrophic fall after 1882 when they were excluded by the same sort of bogus veterinary restrictions imposed by Austria-Hungary that were later imposed on Serbia; they fell from 7·9 million francs in 1881 to 1·3 million in 1889. Both Austria-Hungary and Russia were highly protectionist states and both exacerbated the problem by using tariff policies as an instrument of their foreign policies in the Balkans. The western markets were at the end of long sea voyages which raised the transport costs of exports to the point where they were not always competitive.

Poor agriculture in any case led to harvest failures and irregularity of supply which made the problem worse. This was particularly the case with Romanian wheat whose total export quantity fluctuated widely. This and its low quality tended to drive it out of most markets as a regular commodity and it was increasingly exported to Belgium and the Netherlands to be held in store against occasional last-minute deficiencies in supply on other markets. These difficulties also hit a more specialised exporter such as Greece with particular force. Currants often represented over half of the value of exports and the expansion of the currant trade between 1875 and 1889 was responsible for an increase in output from 102,000 tons to 171,500 tons. But the western markets then began to close again, partly because of the recovery of western grape-growing countries from the phylloxera. In 1892 only 120,000 tons could be exported from the same level of output and the consequence was a typical overproduction crisis which led almost directly to the suspension of interest payments on foreign debt and the international control of Greek finances. The levies from production which the government took to stimulate distilling and wine making were only a palliative and by 1909 peasants were being paid to uproot vineyards.

The differences in social structure between Romania and the other lands tend to diminish in economic importance when seen against the background of the international difficulties common to them all. Romanian agriculture was marginally better equipped, the returns to the economy in foreign exchange were marginally higher but equally insecure, and the general standard of agriculture slightly higher but still very low. In return for these slight advantages the distribution of income was so unequal as to remove all chance, if there had ever been any, of a gradual development of the internal market. In the last resort more important than these differences in internal social structure were the international opportunities available. For although there were better possibilities of growth in the agricultural than in other sectors of the economy they depended on the international setting for their realisation.

THE INTERNATIONAL ECONOMY AND THE BALKANS

The exports of the Balkan countries were, it must be stressed, very small. Furthermore, the per capita value of their exports was also very small; except in Romania it was still among the lowest in Europe, even lower than in a large self-contained economy like Austria-Hungary. With the oil boom in Romania after 1900 Romanian per capita exports became twice as high as those of the other countries. By 1914 oil accounted for 18 per cent of Romanian exports and that, together with the increase in grain prices after 1896, changed a substantial trade deficit into a substantial trade surplus after 1901. Bulgaria's trading balance was in deficit from 1879 to 1892 and showed almost no surplus years thereafter except in the period 1900–5. The years of surplus coincided with the complete stagnation of railway building; once imports of rail and machinery began again on a large scale the balance once more moved into deficit and stayed there until 1914. Greece had a deficit on commercial account every year; there was no chance there of sudden export windfalls through exceptionally good harvests. After 1900, however, Greek deficits were covered by shipping earnings and emigrants' remittances. Serbia usually had small trading surpluses because her import needs were lower. Almost all manufactured goods had to be imported and foreign capital lenders found it easy to acquire powerful positions in supplying imports. After 1904 an increasing proportion of the foreign capital raised by Bulgarian state loans was retained abroad to cover imports, and again the larger economies were able to establish powerful positions. Serbia was the most helpless because of her geographical position; between 1891 and 1900 88 per cent of Serbia's exports went to one country, Austria-Hungary, which in turn supplied 57 per cent of all imports. This was the most extreme example, but in 1911–12 the United Kingdom took 34 per cent of Greek exports and supplied 41 per cent of imports. Bulgaria's trade was more complex: her small textile manufacturing sector exported mainly to Turkey and the agricultural exports were widely distributed but her imports were dominated by manufactured goods from Austria-Hungary and Germany, the principal suppliers of machinery and railway equipment.

Not only were the terms of trade until 1896 against Balkan exports but where their imports were linked to foreign investment they could not be bought in markets as highly competitive as those in which their exports were sold. Even where imports of manufactures were not dominated by the main foreign capital lender there was often little true competition. From the early 1880s onwards for example Krupp dominated the supply of rail to Bulgaria and another German firm dominated the supply of rolling stock. When the American steel firm, Carnegie, tried to undercut Krupp's prices to secure contracts for the parallel railway to Burgas, German diplomatic pressures, such as the refusal to facilitate Bulgarian public loans, kept the market, with the tacit agreement of the European firms in the rail cartel, in Krupp's hands at the original price. The contract for the railway was awarded to a British firm, Vulcan, who agreed beforehand to subcontract most of the rail manufacture to Krupp.

With the two nearest large economies, Russia and Austria-Hungary, the two most protectionist states on the continent, the Balkan economies were driven to rely on central and western European markets. But as the terms of trade improved these markets became more difficult to breach. The 1892 tariff in France had a legal basic minimum rate which could only be secured by offering preferential treatment to French exports; the German tariff of 1902 imposed a high level of agricultural dues. Unable to exercise any leverage in international trade, dependent on foreign capital which seemed only to finance more imports, and having to fight against all possible obstacles to place their exports, the Balkan countries failed to derive from the gold standard the benefits it offered to the developed economies. The sums of foreign capital which they were able to borrow were only a very small proportion of total capital export in Europe and, as we have seen, the impact of foreign capital on their economies was limited. In return for this the gold standard often imposed restrictions on domestic economic policy. The commission which supervised Greek finances after 1898 forced the central bank to reduce to par the 68 per cent premium payable in drachma for other European currency backed by gold, something it could only achieve by a long and drastic reduction in money supply in the Greek economy. Adherence to the gold standard usually meant restriction of the domestic money supply and elimination of export subsidies. The only real hope of promoting development by stimulating growth in the agricultural sector lay in more satisfactory international arrangements which might have brought foreign capital and technological skills into the agricultural sector or guaranteed long-term markets for primary exports.

CONCLUSIONS

The dance of death in Russia in 1905 and its reappearance in Romania two years later shocked Europe into an awareness that for large numbers on the continent the economic changes of the nineteenth century had brought little improvement and for some indeed conditions had worsened. The murders wreaked by the Romanian peasantry, the bloodthirsty land struggles in Ireland, Galicia and Andalusia and the turmoil in Russia seemed to belie the hopes which the nineteenth century had placed in industrialisation. At the same time they awoke again an interest in land reform and in the agricultural foundations of economic development, a subject neglected since the late eighteenth century.

The typical pattern of peasant expenditure in the Balkans was for one-third of gross income to go on the staple food, grain. The state's concentration on providing an economic infrastructure and promoting industrialisation, together with the large sums devoted to military expenditure, made heavy and increasing demands on remaining funds. Before 1880 the peasant lands remained unaffected but eventually the increase in military expenditure took away even there much of the marginal increase in peasant income derived from the new roads and railways and prevented any further expansion of the internal market. In Romania this had always been the situation and when the redemption payments ended in 1879 there was a sudden rise in textile imports for the peasant market. Indirect taxes on everyday articles of consumption, matches, salt and tobacco, increased with the government's modernisation efforts and tariffs on textiles and household articles also increased. From contributing 16 per cent of government revenue in Bulgaria in 1879 indirect taxes and monopolies rose until they contributed 42 per cent in 1911. By 1905 in Romania they contributed almost one-half of revenue. Over the last forty years of our period Bulgarian peasants paid a proportion of their income in taxation rising from 15 to 20 per cent, and although nowadays such a proportion may not seem high, it must be remembered that in a good harvest year much less than half this proportion was available for items of consumption other than food. In fact the per capita consumption of the staple food in Romania, maize, showed a steep fall from 194 kilograms to 150 kilograms between 1886–90 and 1896–1900. This no doubt was the cause underlying the increasingly violent peasant revolts of those years. At the same time there was an increase in diseases such as pellagra caused by malnutrition. With better terms of trade the decline in consumption slowed down and there are indications that after 1905 in Romania, and perhaps elsewhere, it was beginning to improve.

But attention was turned too late to the agricultural sectors of the Balkan economies, and still with no appreciation of the sector's own capacity for growth rather than its use as a mere base for industrialisation on the apparent western model. Zane's calculations for Romania show that the cost of a Saks iron plough from Germany was one-third of the annual income of a comfortable peasant family in 1905.[6] Since that income was almost wholly committed to necessities the purchase was difficult. But even a fraction of the government aid which went to other sectors, if only in modification of the tariff, could have made all the difference. Faced with the failure of development based on industrialisation either by means of foreign capital or by the extension of the domestic market for the products of indigenous industry, Balkan governments never consistently pursued the alternative path through the agricultural sector.

Estimates of per capita national income for the Balkan countries are few and unreliable. Those that exist suggest that per capita national income for all four countries varied between 238 current francs, the lowest estimate for Serbia, and 378 francs, the highest estimate for Bulgaria. This would give them each a per capita national income of about one-half to two-thirds that of Italy or Spain in 1914. But Popov's high figure for Bulgaria is surely wrong. The most reliable figures are probably those for Romania which suggest that gross national product per capita was barely more than 300 francs.[7] This is especially interesting because of the rapid increase in industrial production in Romania after 1901. However bad conditions in Romania were in the two previous decades, it seems improbable that they could have been so bad as to leave Romanian national income after the last decade of expansion still below that of any of the other three countries. So it may well be that Lampe's recent estimate of gross national product per capita in Serbia at 310 dinars (francs) is also rather high.[8] His calculations do suggest, however, that for purposes of international comparison, these magnitudes are reasonable.

Pazvolsky puts the contribution of industry and handicrafts to Bulgarian national income in 1911 at 14 per cent only[9] and estimates for Romania suggest that it was responsible for 15 per cent there in the same year. Existing figures which suggest a rapid rate of growth of national income in Bulgaria after 1892 and Romania after 1901 have to be seen against the small number employed in industry. It is difficult to see where such growth could have come from in Bulgaria. But whatever changes were taking place after 1900 the Balkan countries still constituted in 1914, in spite of all their efforts, an undeveloped and unindustrialised area of the continent: they were infant states and infant economies. The other undeveloped European countries all carried a long and complex history with them into the late nineteenth century and this legacy inevitably determined to some extent the path of development which they followed. The Balkan lands at the moment of emancipation from Turkish control were economically a clean slate on which almost anything could have been written. But by 1914 only the most blinkered patriot could have felt any optimism about their economic future.

The economic history of the Balkan countries refutes even the most historically sophisticated theories of economic development in Europe, those of Gerschenkron. He argues that for those economies with the worst heritage of economic backwardness development had to take place through the positive intervention of the state in creating demand and in installing the most modern technology. Only in this way could the necessary break with the past, essential to the process of modernisation, take place. He himself argues that in respect of Bulgaria had government intervention been more sophisticated and had tariff policy especially been used to promote industries more capital-intensive than textiles and foodstuffs, this departure could still have been effected.[10] Even had the state intervened more strongly and consistently to promote industrialisation, however, it could not in such small economies have had sufficient resources to function as a driving force in the same way as the Russian state did in the 1890s. Most of the meagre industrial developments that occurred and most of the social overhead capital that was created were in fact due to the active policies of the state in trying to promote industrialisation and modernisation, but they were insufficient. Balkan governments cut their coat according to their cloth and combined an active policy of economic development by the state with strong incentives and encouragements to foreign capital. This was an uneasy compromise which meant that neither policy was taken to its logical extreme. In highly nationalistic and recently independent countries subservience to foreign capital could hardly be expected, whilst on the other hand their political weakness could impose much greater limitations on their freedom of action than was felt by the major east European powers.

Nevertheless, with such small populations it did not require a great measure of economic change to affect the whole economy. It was of course difficult for Balkan governments to avoid simplifying the economic history of other European states and this was the source of their failure to understand the important role played by change and growth in the agricultural sector in the initial stages of economic development over almost all the continent. What would have been far too long-term and costly a policy in Russia might have been more feasible in the Balkans. But nineteenth-century ideologies and theories of industrialisation had little to offer to this part of the continent that was relevant to its economic situation; the assumption that economic development, modernisation and industrialisation were equivalents led to a dangerous neglect of the agricultural sector.

Yet even if Balkan governments had pursued different policies they would still have met a serious obstacle. A more balanced development, based for an initial period on an intensification of agriculture, would have received no help from the international economy. The amount of capital still necessary to provide the sort of communications and ports provided in Denmark, for example, after 1864 would have been much harder to acquire and also of course needed in greater quantities. From the standpoint of the Balkans the international trading and payments network in Europe, which worked so well for the developed countries after the evolution of the gold standard, could even be seen as inimical to economic development. Without some better way of obtaining capital and without more guaranteed markets for primary exports sustained growth in the agricultural sector would have been difficult. And without a more generous agricultural tariff policy by the developed continental states and an awareness that the economic fate of all the European states hung together Balkan economies would for a long time have faced almost insuperable obstacles. Although to many European observers before 1914 south-eastern Europe seemed a lost and negligible corner of European civilisation it was not so at all and the failure to solve its economic problems was to cost the whole continent dear.

SUGGESTED READING

The only attempt at a general study of this area exists in English: I. T. BEREND and G. RÁNKI, *Economic Development in Central and South-Eastern Europe in the Nineteenth and Twentieth Centuries* (New York and London, 1974). Only a small part of the volume deals with the Balkans and it does not include Greece but it is an indispensable introduction. D. WARRINER (ed.), *Contrasts in Emerging Societies* (London, 1965), is a book of readings designed to stimulate further interest in the subject. J. R. LAMPE, 'Varieties of Unsuccessful Industrialisation: The Balkan States before 1914', in *Journal of Economic History*, vol. 35, 1975, is a valuable review article. A few specialised monographs exist in English. J. TOMASEVICH, *Peasants, Politics and Economic Change in Yugoslavia* (Stanford, 1955), covers the agrarian history of Serbia before 1914. Three interesting works deal with Romanian agriculture: I. L. EVANS, *The Agrarian Revolution in Roumania* (Cambridge, 1924); D. MITRANY, *The Land and the Peasant in Rumania* (Princeton and Cambridge, 1930), and P. G. EIDELBERG, *The Great Rumanian Peasant Revolt of 1907: Origins of a Modern Jacquerie* (Leiden, 1974), which, although narrow in its interpretation, makes a valuable contribution to Romanian history. M. PEARTON, *Oil and the Romanian State, 1895–1948* (Oxford, 1971), although also circumscribed, is a useful pioneering study. J. R. LAMPE, 'Serbia 1878–1912', in R. Cameron (ed.), *Banking and Economic Development* (New York and London, 1972), is almost the only substantial work in English remaining to be mentioned. It can be seen that Balkan economic history has been almost completely neglected by English and American scholars. It has received little attention from others.

Bulgaria alone can lay claim to a modern work synthesising the country's economic history before 1914: Z. NATAN et al., *Ikonomikata na Bulgariya do Sozialistitscheskata Revolyuziya* (Sofia, 1969). Two older economic histories of the country still have their uses: I. SAKAZOV, *Bulgarische Wirtschaftsgeschichte* (Berlin, 1929) and W. WEISS-BARTENSTEIN, *Bulgariens volkswirtschaftliche Verhältnisse* (Berlin, 1917). There is an out-of-date but comprehensive economic history of Romania: N. RAZMIRIŢA, *Essai d'économie roumaine moderne 1831–1931* (Paris, 1932).

For Romania, however, there is now a wealth of specialised monographs published under the auspices of the Romanian Academy. Most research is concentrated at the moment on the period before 1850. To understand the large contribution to knowledge that has been recently made it is necessary to read Romanian but a proportion of the works are translated into French, and more rarely English, in the series *Bibliotheca Historica Romaniae*. Particularly interesting for the period after 1850 is G. ZANE, *L'Industrie roumaine au cours de la seconde moitié du XIXe siècle* (Bucharest, 1973), volume 43 in the series. The student who is able to read Romanian will find a comprehensive bibliography of Romanian economic history published by the Institute of Economic Science of the Romanian Academy: *Istoriografia Economică Românească* (Bucharest, 1970). The curious arrangements of nineteenth-century Romanian agriculture provoked several interesting analyses which have not yet been superseded. G. D. CREANGA, *Grundbesitzverteilung und Bauernfrage in Rumänien* (Leipzig, 1907); D. B. IONESCU, *Die Agrarverfassung Rumäniens, ihre Geschichte und ihre Reform* (Leipzig, 1909), and M. SERBAN, *Rumäniens Agrarverhältnisse* (Berlin, 1913), still make valuable reading.

In the other countries economic history is less well served. A fundamental work for Bulgaria remains the remarkable K. POPOV, *La Bulgarie économique, 1874–1911: études statistiques* (Sofia, 1920), a compilation from his earlier statistical analyses in Bulgarian. Most other work deals with the country's relationship to capital lenders and the student who is able to read in Bulgarian or Russian will find a now rather dated bibliography in Z. NATAN et al., op. cit. In other languages S. TODOROVA, 'Die deutsch-bulgarischen Handelsbeziehungen in den 80er und 90er Jahren des XIX Jahrhunderts', in *Etudes historiques*, vol. 3, 1968, and 'Aspekte der industriellen Entwicklung Bulgariens vom Ende des XIX Jahrhunderts bis zum Ersten Balkankrieg', in *Etudes historiques*, vol. 5, 1970, are useful. Useful also are the back volumes of *Bulgarsko Ikonomitschesko Druzhestvo*. But it is difficult to recommend anything further on the economic history of Serbia or Greece; J. KIRKNER, *Die Industrie und Industriepolitik Serbiens* (Halle, 1913) and Z. NATAN and A. STANOJEVITCH, *Die Landwirtschaft in Serbien* (Halle, 1913) seem to have had no successors. The most tolerable book on Greek economic history is X. ZOLOTAS, *Griechenland auf dem Wege zur Industrialisierung* (Leipzig, 1926), probably the most optimistic of all the titles we have cited. Commentaries and articles on the latest research are published in *Revue roumaine d'histoire* and, for Bulgaria, in *Etudes historiques*. Both are published in several languages. A journal which has the special merit of encouraging the study of the area as a whole is *Revue des études sud-est européennes*, published by the Institute of South-Eastern Studies in Bucharest.

NOTES

1 There has never been precise agreement on the extent of the 'Balkans'. We have used the term here for practical reasons to cover Bulgaria, Greece, Romania and Serbia although, strictly speaking, Romania is not in the Balkans and the term seldom includes Greece.
2 A. D. Xenopol, *Studii economice* (Craiova, 1882), p. 187.
3 A. S. Milward and S. B. Saul, *The Economic Development of Continental Europe 1780–1870* (London, 1973), pp. 524–6.
4 N. Michailov, 'Nasurchavanata ot durzhavata industriya prez 1909', in *Revue de la Société Bulgare d'Economie Politique*, no. 17, 1914.
5 See below, p. 496.
6 G. Zane, *Industria din România in a doua jumătate a secololui al XIX-lea* (Bucharest, 1970), p. 30.
7 N. Jordan, *Venitul național al România* (Bucharest, 1930).
8 J. R. Lampe, 'Serbia 1878–1912', in R. Cameron (ed.), *Banking and Economic Development* (London, 1972).
9 L. Pazvolsky, *Bulgaria's Economic Position* (Washington, 1929).
10 A. Gerschenkron, 'Some Aspects of Industrialization in Bulgaria, 1878–1939', in *Economic Backwardness in Historical Perspective* (Cambridge, Mass., 1962).

Chapter 9

International Trade and Investment

THE NATURE OF INTERNATIONAL TRADE

Essentially international trade is only a special form of interregional trade. We know a great deal about it because the movement of goods over the frontier was always recorded by every nation for revenue purposes, though not always very accurately. It was the subject of different and varying degrees of national regulation and national budgets and taxation could alter the relative prices of goods on different sides of the frontier, but essentially the same factors were at work as between different regions of the same country. Areas specialised: some grew faster than others. The lagging regions would find their industries tending to wither under competition and might experience what were really balance of payments problems as money flowed out of the area: on the other hand, the rise of incomes in the more competitive parts of a country tended to increase demand for imports from other areas. The main differences between internal and external trade lay in the greater ability and willingness of governments to control trade with outside countries and in the ability to vary exchange rates with the outside world.

Trade has generally been considered to be primarily the means by which countries take advantage of the benefits of specialisation. Regions previously isolated and self-contained begin to concentrate on those forms of activity where they are relatively most efficient and exchange this output for goods in which others enjoy a comparative advantage. Similarly, men and money move to those areas where they are likely to achieve the highest rewards. This is the theory and it is important to bear it in mind, for where such division of activity did not come about we need to ask why. Actual interference with the free flow of trade stemmed from two basic motives, one defensive, the other offensive. Defensively a country might hinder the movement of goods (and also of men and money) internally as well as externally, in order to preserve existing interests and existing ways of life. Such measures might be taken for reasons of national security, to preserve certain industries or certain natural resources, to maintain manpower or defend the balance of payments. They might be taken in favour of certain powerful political groups – peasants, businessmen, unemployed workers. Sometimes these actions were intended to preserve the status quo and sometimes to provide a sound basis from which a positive but controlled adjustment could come about. It is here that the defensive merged into the offensive. The difficulty about the idea of comparative advantage and the doctrine of free trade, with each country specialising where it is relatively most efficient, is that it assumes these advantages are given. But in an age of considerable technological change such as the nineteenth century it was possible for countries to create comparative advantages for themselves. The question was whether they could do this without some form of interim protection against the competition of those with an existing comparative advantage. Beyond that was the problem of whether and in what circumstances such protection would stimulate the desired change or merely allow farmers and industrialists to sit back in the now more cosy environment.

Whatever the answers to these problems, for all countries the early stages of growth brought considerable risks because their foreign trade was inevitably narrowly based. Countries with small populations had no option but to seek growth through an extension of their overseas markets. Some believed on the other hand that larger market areas such as that available to the German states, once they had eliminated the barriers to trade between each other, could cut themselves off from overseas trade. In the event, reductions in transport costs, the opening up of new areas of trade and international investment led to an increased emphasis on foreign trade throughout Europe. Trade became a major engine of growth, the means by which the demands arising from increased incomes in the rapidly growing industrial countries were transmitted to others and brought about structural changes and increased incomes there too. Such transmission was worldwide, but within Europe commercial life came to depend primarily upon the levels of activity in Britain and Germany. Trade allowed a region to escape from the constrictions of income levels within its home markets. Economists write of the existence of diminishing returns to scale but whatever the case today, historical examples are hard to find. Consequently the export sectors tended to enjoy the highest gains in productivity. The smaller a country or region, the more important this was. This is not to say that countries inevitably developed first on the basis of foreign trade, and contemporary writers such as List most certainly did not believe that growth would best be achieved initially that way. Import substitution was just as powerful a force as exporting but except in the very largest countries world markets were generally necessary for the full exploitation of any major industry's potential. The smaller an economy the greater its reliance on trade was likely to be, partly because its natural resources would be limited and partly because of the difficulty of achieving economies of scale from the home market.

THE SIZE AND GROWTH OF FOREIGN TRADE

In general the ratio of the value of foreign trade to national income grew as a country entered the international economy, as specialisation and exchange increased, though this was less marked for big countries where such developments might be largely internal. But if this was the major trend, there were other influences present to offset it. One was the process of import substitution through technological change. Furthermore, if imports consisted mainly of foods and fibres and if domestic production consisted mainly of the manufacture of complex articles, then the latter tended to grow faster than the former for which demand was relatively more inelastic. Also, as production shifted to what were, by their very nature, home market activities, then imports inevitably became less significant; such activities included the building of roads, ports, schools, houses, the growth of service industries and the development of local industries which faced little foreign competition – brewing, baking, carpentering, brick making and such like.

The smaller, relatively developed countries such as the Netherlands and Belgium were most heavily dependent on foreign trade. Norway and Sweden were less so: for the former, this is partly a matter of statistical definition in that a high proportion of her 'exports' took the form of 'invisible' shipping income which is not included in the calculation; as for Sweden the lower proportion derives partly from the protection offered to her agricultural and to her industrial sectors. After them came the larger industrial economies, France and Germany, and then the more undeveloped and highly protected economies such as Italy, Austria-Hungary and Russia. Some of the relevant statistics are given in Table

75. Of course, foreign trade might involve great danger if too many eggs were put in one basket but generally a high level of concentrated trade was better for growth than a low level of diversified trade. In any case, countries such as Sweden and Denmark showed a remarkable ability to adjust to changing economic advantages. To them and to many others the critical factor was that Britain maintained a free-trade policy and as the major importer in Europe gave suppliers the chance to adjust in accordance with the free operation of market forces.

World trade began to expand sharply from the 1820s onwards. It rose by 10 per cent per decade in real terms to the forties and fifties when it grew by more than 60 per cent each decade. During the next two decades the increases exceeded 50 per cent. The rate of growth fell during the 1880s, in part because of the revival of protection in Europe and elsewhere

Table 75 *Ratios of exports of European countries to national product, 1909–13 (per cent)*

Germany (1910–13)	France (1908–10)	Italy (1911–13)	Norway (1905–14)	Sweden (1911–13)	Denmark (1910–14)	United Kingdom (1909–13)
17·9	16·9	11·4	22·4	19·7	29	18·8

Source: S. Kuznets, 'Quantitative Aspects of the Growth of Nations', in *Economic Development and Cultural Change*, vol. XV, 1967, pp. 96–111.

and because of the slow rates of growth experienced in Britain and France and associated slower rates in countries such as Sweden during that decade. The sharp depression of the early 1890s kept growth for that decade down to 25 per cent but after 1900, with industrialisation going forward rapidly throughout continental Europe and the United States and with international investment at unprecedented heights, it moved back to a decadal rate exceeding 45 per cent between 1906 and 1913. What accounted for this extraordinary expansion of trade? The answer is partly technological. Advances of this kind gave opportunities for specialisation, created new goods for trading, lowered costs and thereby increased demand. Developments in transport were most important in encouraging this flow of goods and specialisation, although, of course, they were as vital for internal as for external trade. Economic growth itself, deriving from all the factors we have discussed as well as technological change, inevitably increased the volume of world trade, whether such growth was faster or slower than the growth of internal economies. Both were expanding very fast by all previous standards.

TRADE IN THE MID-NINETEENTH CENTURY

Until the middle of the century foreign trade was influenced most of all by the growth of the British economy and by Britain's gradual shift to a more liberal trade policy and by the anxiety of some western European countries first of all to absorb the fruits of British technology and then to protect their growing industries against it. Within Europe the formation of the Zollverein was a major step in removing the barriers to foreign trade. Generally restrictions which had confined the trade of colonies to the mother country died away; those on the British colonies in North America disappeared after the War of Independence, those on the Spanish colonies of South America during the Napoleonic wars. In the next three decades or so, trade with India, China and all the British colonial possessions was freed. The non-industrial world markets were, even at this time, too large for Britain, despite her great technological lead, to be able to fill by herself. France exported textiles and finished metal goods to the poorer countries of Europe; Switzerland and Saxony exported their textiles. The formation of the Zollverein allowed more trade to develop within the customs union. Belgium's situation was different: she began to seize markets not with traditional goods but with iron and machinery because of her early development, particularly exporting iron rails which were soon to become a major item of trade throughout Europe. The Zollverein was crucial to her and to Switzerland because it lowered and standardised tariffs over a wide area. The Zollverein also imported British yarn, iron and machinery and then began to develop competitive exports with the help of lower wage costs. At first most countries made use of the network of British overseas export houses to distribute their own goods but independent expansion came quickly. The German states, exporting traditional products such as woollens, glass and hardware, had over 340 export houses outside Europe in 1845. More than half of them were in the United States and Mexico but, interestingly enough in the light of later developments in German trade, there were already 100 in South America.

In 1854 British imports from Europe amounted to about £50 million, over £16 million from the German states, about £11 million from France, £6 million through the Netherlands, much of that no doubt originating in Germany too, and over £4 million from Russia. Almost every country sent some grain. There was wood from Norway, Sweden and Prussia, flax and hemp from Russia and Belgium, wool from Germany, live animals from Holland, wines and spirits from France, Spain and Portugal, fruit and oil from the Mediterranean countries, but apart from Swedish iron, the only significant quantities of manufactures were silks and woollens from France and Belgium. It was the typical relationship of a developed with an undeveloped region but a similar kind of link could also be found between France and the rest of continental Europe. Up to the middle of the century a half of France's exports consisted of textiles sent mainly to neighbouring countries and she imported much the same kind of commodities from the rest of the continent as did Britain. A distinct world-wide pattern was beginning to appear in French trade already: her exports to distant low-income countries such as India and Russia were much smaller than her imports and she financed such deficits by export surpluses with her neighbours, Britain, Switzerland and the German states. The rate of expansion of French trade at this time was very striking. Exports to Britain rose sevenfold between 1837–46 and 1857–66, vividly illustrating the role British trade was playing as an agent of economic development at this time. To a smaller degree the same was true of French exports to the United States until the Civil War and to Germany after the mid-fifties. Exports to Belgium rose very quickly though there was an even greater increase in French imports, particularly of coal. Belgian

Table 76   *Value of exports per capita in European areas (constant $)*

	1820	1840	1860	1880	1900
Britain	3·6	7·25	20·7	31·0	36·2
Western Europe	1·7	3·2	7·3	14·8	25·9
Rest of Europe[1]	0·9	1·3	2·8	4·3	5·9

[1] Russia, Balkans, Greece, Turkey, Italy, Spain, Portugal

Source: J. R. Hanson, *The Nineteenth-Century Exports of the Less Developed Countries* (Ph.D. thesis, University of Pennsylvania, 1972), p. 24.

special exports (exports of Belgian goods) rose slightly in the 1840s compared with the average of the previous decade but the average for the 1850s was more than double in value that of the 1840s and, for the 1860s, the average rose by another two-thirds. Table 76 shows how rapidly Europe's trade expanded in real terms to 1860 even excluding the effects of population growth, though it was slower in eastern Europe than elsewhere partly because these economies remained undeveloped and because their populations were now expanding very rapidly. According to Bairoch[1] the rate of growth of German special exports (goods originating in Germany) was at its highest for the century at 6·7 per cent per annum during the 1860s but this was from a very low absolute level. He finds similarly high figures in the 1860s for Belgium (6·4 per cent), France (5·7 per cent) and Sweden (7·3 per cent) which were not exceeded later.

From 1815 to the middle of the nineteenth century most countries maintained relatively high tariffs and any trend towards liberalisation was offset by the impact of falling prices on specific tariff rates. Specific duties are not proportionate to the value of imports but are fixed according to weight or quantity. Consequently, as the price per unit falls, the burden of the fixed tariff automatically rises. The 1850s saw gradual moves in the direction of freer trade in France and elsewhere following the lead set by Britain. Then in 1860 came the Anglo-French Treaty of Commerce followed by a whole network of treaties between the countries of western Europe, Scandinavia and central Europe. All subsequent treaties were modelled on the Franco-Belgian treaty with its simple most-favoured-nation clause. This provided that any tariff concession made by either party to a third party would automatically apply to the other signatory of the treaty. With a whole collection of similar clauses in operation, any one reduction in tariffs which was negotiated applied immediately throughout Europe. Even though the general drift towards freer trade was reversed during the 1880s under pressure from both farmers and industrialists, the treaties, with only minor exceptions, prevented outright discrimination between countries.

EUROPE'S TRADE IN MANUFACTURED GOODS AFTER 1860

Both the volume and the value of world trade more than trebled between the late 1870s and 1914 and western Europe enjoyed the lion's share of the expansion. Table 77 shows the changing shares of European countries in world exports of manufactures. We should remind ourselves first of all that, interesting though this is, of itself it tells nothing about total production of manufactures in the countries concerned. The sharp increase in the share of Germany and the relative declines of France and Britain are the chief features. There are no statistics to allow us to take the analysis further back than 1880 but we may reasonably assume from what is known of the general pattern of German trade that her share, of a much lower total trade of course, was considerably below 19·3 per cent in 1860. The contrasts between the three major countries arose partly from differences in competitive skills, though it was most unlikely that France and Britain, however competitive they might be, could long retain the two-thirds share of world trade they held in 1880 once other countries began to grow. But their relative decline was also due to the fact that France and Britain were big exporters of textiles and this was the area of world trade growing most slowly by this time. In 1913 both France and Germany exported about $330 million of textiles and clothing but this was equivalent to 42 per cent of French exports of manufactures and only 18 per cent of German exports. It will be seen that only exports from Germany and Sweden grew faster than world exports after 1899. Italy, however, increased her exports by increasing her share of the stagnating world textile trade. Germany was particularly dominant in two areas by 1913: she held 37·6 per cent of world exports of steel and 40 per cent of trade in chemicals. She was also the largest exporter of machinery, though followed here closely by Britain.

Table 78 analyses this trade in another way, dividing it between those sectors growing most quickly (machinery and transport equipment), those whose share of world trade in manufactures was fairly stable (metals and chemicals) and those whose share was declining (textiles and

Table 77 *Percentage shares of world exports of manufactured goods amongst European countries, 1880–1913*

	1880	1899	1913
France	22·2	14·4	12·1
Germany	19·3	22·4	26·6
Belgium and Luxembourg	5·0	5·5	5·0
Switzerland	n.a.	4·0	3·1
Sweden	0·8	0·9	1·4
Austria-Hungary	8·0[1]	n.a.	5·0
Britain	41·4	33·2	30·2

[1] This figure is approximate

Source: S. B. Saul, 'The Export Economy 1870–1914', in *Yorkshire Bulletin of Economic and Social Research*, vol. XVII, no. 1, 1965; A. Maizels, *Industrial Growth and World Trade* (Cambridge, 1963), p. 189.

Table 78 *Percentage shares of exports of manufactures by groups, 1913*

	Germany	France	Italy	Belgium and Luxembourg	Switzerland	Sweden
Expanding	16·9	10·0	7·6	9·3	11·8	18·8
Stable	33·6	15·6	8·4	29·9	11·3	35·9
Contracting	49·5	74·4	84·0	60·8	76·9	45·3

Source: A. Maizels, *Industrial Growth and World Trade* (Cambridge, 1963), appendix A.

the miscellaneous group) and showing the distribution of each country's exports by these classifications. It will be seen that France, Italy and Switzerland were poorly placed, with three-quarters or more of their exports in the contracting groups, whereas Sweden and Germany, with a greater concentration on exports of machinery of various kinds, were in a much more favourable position.

Germany's great advantage was her ability to dominate the markets of her neighbours. If proximity to the sea conferred a comparative advantage in the eighteenth century, now it was the railway network that gave Germany a supreme trading advantage in central Europe, completely offsetting, for example, the Ruhr's geographical remoteness from the east. Her neighbours were developing quickly, though belatedly, and offered a rapidly rising demand for machinery, in particular, which they were unable as yet to satisfy for themselves. By 1913 Germany had a larger share than France in the imports of every significant European importer except Belgium and Spain. Germany's exports boomed because their distribution by both product and market gave them a high-income elasticity of demand. In 1912 over a quarter of her exports of electrical machinery went to Russia, Austria-Hungary and Italy, over 40 per cent of her machine tools to the same countries and another 27 per cent to France, Belgium and Switzerland. Of her exports of agricultural machinery, 35 per cent went to Russia alone. She did not neglect overseas markets,

Table 79 *Percentage import content[1] of supplies[2] of manufactures, 1913*

	France	Germany	Italy	Belgium and Luxembourg	Norway	Sweden	Britain
1899	12	16	11	26	n.a.	8	16
1913	13	10	14	24	35	14	17

[1] Import content = imports of finished and semi-finished manufactures
[2] Supplies = gross value of production of non-food manufactures plus imports of manufactures

Source: A. Maizels, *Industrial Growth and World Trade* (Cambridge, 1963), p. 136.

particularly South America and the Near East, but continental Europe was her real source of strength. Looking at the position in a slightly different way, in 1913 Germany held 28·5 per cent of the world trade in manufactures conducted between manufacturing countries compared with 19 per cent held by Britain. Of world exports of machinery 55 per cent went to such markets which were, for the most part, located in Europe.

Germany was also, in absolute terms, the biggest importer of manufactures in Europe, though compared with total German consumption of manufactures, the share was one of the lowest in Europe as Table 79 shows. The highest figures reflect different factors: the Norwegian proportion was high because this was a small economy concentrating heavily on the production of primary products. Belgium was an important but specialised producer of manufactured goods dependent upon imports of certain semi-manufactures, such as steel from France and Germany, and also imports of certain important types of finished goods such as textiles. Countries beginning to industrialise, such as Italy and Sweden, saw their import proportions rising, though protection and, possibly, relatively low demand from the still substantial agricultural sectors helped keep the absolute level low. British imports were the most significant from Europe's point of view. In 1913, for example, such imports were half as large as the whole intra-continental European trade in manufactures and half as large again as Britain's exports to Europe. As we shall see in a later section this imbalance played a vital part in forming the whole pattern of European settlements. The United States played a minor role at this time: in 1913 she supplied 15 per cent of the imports of manufactures into western Europe (France, Germany, Netherlands, Belgium, Denmark, Norway, Sweden) but almost a half of this consisted of semi-manufactured copper; imports of American machinery were relatively small.

It is difficult to determine the effects of industrial tariffs on this trade, especially as the increases were carried through gradually and were accompanied by rapid technical progress. A League of Nations study of the trend of imports of manufactures and industrial production in Germany, France, Italy and Sweden found that the return to protection in the 1880s temporarily halted the growth of imports but that once imports had adjusted themselves to the higher level of tariffs, they began to rise afresh alongside industrial production at much the same rate as before.[2] Of course, the pattern of such trade would be altered; after the drastic Italian tariff of 1887, British exports of textiles fell but her trade in machinery developed rapidly. One objection to tariffs much voiced by free-trade countries was the opportunities they offered for the dumping of surplus production. A German manufacturer could sell his steel in Britain at a price lower than the price at the German port to the extent of the level of the tariff and the cost of shipping the steel back to Germany again. If he sold it at a lower price it would then be possible for a British importer to buy the steel, ship it back, pay the duty and still undercut the ruling price in Germany. German manufacturers were very prone to dump overseas in times of poor business and indeed it was logical for them to do so; as long as the price received was above the level of variable costs, some contribution was being made to fixed costs. It was to avoid such dumping that many international agreements and cartels came into being. Possibly the first international cartel was a salt agreement established in 1867 between the Société Saline de Neckar and the Syndicat des Salines Françaises at Nancy. In 1870 there was a bismuth cartel and in 1884 the first international rail syndicate including most producers in Germany, Britain and Belgium. Thereafter, the numbers multiplied rapidly until by 1914 there were over 110 known combines and no doubt many other informal agreements. There were 19 in chemicals alone, 18 in transport, 15 in textiles and 26 in coal, ores and metals. Some allowed producers control over their home markets, some divided up export markets, some restricted output. Obviously, wide areas of international trade were no longer subject simply to the normal forces of competition.

Throughout Europe there were wide differences in the patterns of exports, as Table 80 shows. Switzerland relied on exports of manufactures more than any other country, followed by Germany and France: Denmark was the least dependent on them in the west but her food exports were highly processed, very different from the trade of the massive grain exporters of eastern Europe. Exports of lumber and pulp gave Norway, Sweden and Finland the lead in category II, though Austria-Hungary had a high proportion there too. The large share of Belgium's exports coming into category II reflects a very high level of exports of semi-manufactures. Care must be taken to allow for different absolute levels of trade in interpreting this table. Sweden's figure of 63 per cent in category II is less significant to total European trade than Germany's 26·3 per cent

Table 80 *Percentage shares of exports of European countries by category, 1913*

	I	II	III		I	II	III
Germany	10·4	26·3	63·3	Russia	56·1	38·8	5·1
France	12·2	27·0	60·8	Romania	71·4	27·7	0·9
Italy	30·0	38·0	32·0	Serbia	74·1	24·0	1·9
Belgium	10·0	49·1	38·7	Bulgaria	71·5	18·1	10·4
Switzerland	14·6	11·1	74·3	Greece	61·3	38·0	0·7
Austria-Hungary	27·2	40·4	32·4	Spain	43·8	30·9	23·3
Sweden	12·8	63·1	24·1	Portugal	68·0	20·4	11·6
Denmark	83·7	11·0	5·3	United			
Norway	36·6	50·5	12·9	Kingdom	6·1	33·9	60·0
Finland	14·8	65·3	19·9				

I = food and drink
II = raw materials and semi-manufactures
III = industrial manufactures

Source: Compiled from national trade statistics of relevant countries.

with her massive exports of coal to France and of semi-manufactured steel to Britain and other parts of the west. Similarly, Germany's 10·4 per cent in category I is in absolute terms a very large amount: her trade in rye, oats, wheat, flour and sugar was very important for other parts of Europe.

TRADE IN PRIMARY PRODUCTS

Table 81 illustrates the important and growing share of continental Europe in world imports. The share of the United Kingdom in world imports of primary products fell from 29·7 per cent in 1876–80 to 19 per cent by 1913: the contrast therefore is very clear. A considerable part of the growth, of course, was intra-European trade. Looking more specifically at these primary products, in 1913 continental Europe accounted for nearly a half of all world trade in foodstuffs and as much as 61 per cent of trade in cereals.

All of Europe was much affected by the changes in the prices of bread grains which came about during the last quarter of the nineteenth century. Steam transport, new farm machinery, the opening up of new areas of production within and without Europe, all increased the supply of grains faster than population growth and the increase in demand caused by the rise of incomes. Over the previous quarter-century prices had shown a rising trend, helped by the opening up of the British market. Prices of animal products followed an even more favourable trend and encouraged some shift in agricultural activity in the west, but where this was difficult grain growing for export was still eminently profitable.

The changes in supply conditions after about 1870 affected wheat most of all and presented almost every country with pressing decisions on whether to protect the farmers or not. A minimum was set to the prices of both rye and wheat by the use of marginal supplies as feed grains.

Table 81   *Share of continental Europe in world imports, 1876–1913*

	1876–80	*1896–1900*	*1913*
Total world imports	43·8	47·5	49·9
World imports of primary products	50·5	55·4	55·4

Source: P. Lamartine Yates, *Forty Years of Foreign Trade* (London, 1959), pp. 33, 51.

The amounts involved were too small compared to total feed grain supplies to influence those prices much but inevitably the price of wheat came to approximate much more closely to that of the other grains. Table 82 shows the prices of grains in one open European market: it will be seen that the prices of feed grains were relatively well maintained whereas those of rye and, above all, wheat fell drastically. The smaller countries of north and west Europe took only nominal action to cut off the cheap imports. Between 1902 and 1914 the Netherlands produced only 16·5 per cent of her wheat needs and Belgium 22·5 per cent; these were the smallest proportions found on the continent and compared closely with Britain's 21 per cent. Elsewhere protective duties were imposed and the acreage under the crop rose slightly but still there were considerable increases in imports. From 1902 to 1914 France and Spain produced about 93 per cent of their home consumption of wheat, Italy 80 per cent and Germany about two-thirds.

Though large quantities of wheat came into Europe from Canada, the United States, Argentina and Australia, Russia remained the world's largest exporter and for the whole period from 1860 to 1914 provided a quarter to a third of world trade. The pre-war world exports of wheat are shown in Table 83. To the 1870s most of Russian wheat went through the Black Sea ports to Britain but then there followed a gradual shift in trade patterns as Russian wheat was pushed out of that market and began to play a more important role in central Europe, entering the German market through Rotterdam, for example, and replacing Hungarian wheat there. At the same time Russian hard wheat, grown in the new lands of the northern Caucasus, the lower Volga and western Siberia, was sent to southern Europe where it was used for making food pastes such as macaroni, spaghetti and vermicelli. In the 1860s and 1870s much Hungarian wheat was exported to central Europe, but by 1900 virtually all of it was consumed within the Austro-Hungarian Empire. Prior to 1914 Romania was exporting about 60 per cent of her total wheat output, the highest proportion in the world. The staple food there was maize and, as in Russia, the low levels of income and grain consumption served to stimulate

Table 82 *Prices of grains in Copenhagen* (*kroner per 000 kg*)

	Wheat	Rye	Barley	Oats
1855–64	18·9	13·4	12·5	11·9
1885–94	12·8	10·5	11·3	11·5

Source: J. Pedersen and O. S. Petersen, *An Analysis of Price Behaviour* (Copenhagen, 1938), p. 244.

a high export level. To the 1880s much Romanian wheat went up the Danube through the Budapest mills to central Europe, but a tariff war with Austria-Hungary diverted these supplies down the river and then by the maritime routes to western Europe, first to Britain but eventually, as with Russian grain, more often to Belgium and the Netherlands.

Rye, essentially a European crop, was more important for home consumption than wheat in northern and eastern Europe up to 1914. Russia and Germany were the chief exporters, but in 1909–13 world rye exports were only one-ninth those of wheat by volume.

Maize was the first feed grain to reach the deficit countries of Europe such as Belgium in large volume as international trade developed and as the former grain producers of western Europe moved more towards animal husbandry. It came first from the United States and, as European farmers were not accustomed to it, had for a time to be dumped at low prices. By 1914 Romania was the world's principal exporter and large supplies were forthcoming from Russia and Argentina too. After 1900, however, there was a significant increase in European trade in barley as a feed grain.

This was largely due to the creation of an extensive trade between Russia and Germany as the German tariff was made to favour such imports over maize coming from America and the Danube region; indeed, from 1909 to 1914 Russian barley exports were almost as high as her wheat exports. Table 83 gives the volume of world trade in all these grains in two periods and the shares of the two most important exporting regions in Europe. This immense flow of grains into Europe from its eastern regions and from the outside world was perhaps the largest single influence determining the patterns of world trade in the years to 1914.

Protection against imports of meat was far more effective than that against grains and it was the high prices for meat which helped to keep much of Europe closely wedded to a cereal and potato diet. Countries

Table 83   *Average annual world trade in grains, 1884–1913*

	Exports (m. tons)		Percentage share of Russia		Percentage share of Danubian countries	
	1884–8	*1909–13*	*1884–8*	*1909–13*	*1884–8*	*1909–13*
Wheat	9·5	19·7	25·3	22·3	18·6	15·8
Maize	2·6	6·8	15·0	11·2	30·9	23·9
Barley	1·9	5·5	43·6	67·1	26·2	12·2
Oats	1·4	3·0	66·0	35·8	10·1	11·7
Rye	2·0	2·4	68·7	27·3	14·0	20·3

Source: R. M. Stern, 'A Century of Food Exports', in *Kyklos*, vol. XIII, 1960, pp. 58–61.

such as Belgium and Switzerland that allowed grain in free, raised substantial tariffs against meat imports; only the Netherlands and Denmark in the west adhered fully to free trade. The comparison with Britain is remarkable; over 1909–13 on average Britain imported 95 million tons of meat annually while the rest of Europe imported 89 million tons – Germany 33 million, Belgium and Switzerland 13 million each. There were movements of live animals from the Netherlands, Russia and Denmark across the borders to neighbouring countries but these were insignificant in the context of total world trade.

In addition to these trends in foreign trade in manufactures and basic foodstuffs, industrialisation in Europe brought about large increases in imports of raw materials from non-European countries – cotton, wool, silk, jute, tin, rubber, oil, fertilisers and much besides. Rising incomes brought with them increased demand for foodstuffs such as coffee, tea and rice from outside Europe, though most European countries deliberately fostered home manufacture of beet sugar in preference to imported cane. Some of the largest exports of the primary producers found their biggest markets in Europe: Brazilian coffee and Chilean nitrates, for example. Hanson has suggested that exports from South America, Asia and Africa to western Europe increased ninefold in current prices between 1840 and 1900.[3] More specifically, Table 84 indicates the huge increase in imports into Europe from South America and these figures take no account of goods from those countries re-exported to Europe via Britain. This trade was dominated by coffee, fertilisers and wool, which comprised two-thirds of the total in 1900. Looking at countries within the British Empire (excluding the United Kingdom itself) and allowing for re-exports through the United Kingdom, their exports to all continental Europe rose from something like £42 million in 1890 to £126 million in 1912, a growth of

Table 84 *European imports from South America, 1890–1912 (£m.)*

	1890	*1901*	*1912*
Germany	17·96	26·92	61·74
Belgium	6·10	7·44	18·85
France	19·36	20·60	36·31
Switzerland	0·25	1·05	2·72
Italy	0·76	2·49	9·29
Austria-Hungary	1·83	3·07	8·00
Netherlands	1·45	6·90	13·62
TOTALS	47·71	68·47	150·53

Source: Parliamentary Papers, *Statistical Abstract for Foreign Countries.*

the same order of magnitude as that from South America. European countries took particularly large imports from their colonies in North and Central Africa and the East Indies; the Netherlands, for example, was one of the few countries on the continent open to imports of cane sugar from Java.

With world trade growing so quickly and so concentrated in north-western Europe, the ports in that region inevitably developed very fast. The Dutch, for example, after a prolonged depression following the end of the Napoleonic wars, began to resume their position as the carriers of Europe. Rotterdam became the link between the Rhine–Meuse systems and the outside world, above all with Britain. Clearances from the port rose threefold between 1846 and 1870. By 1912 11·5 million tons of shipping entered Rotterdam, the tonnage of cargo cleared alone having risen another nine times since 1870, the fastest rate of growth in Europe.

However, trade through Antwerp, helped by the earlier and greater development of the Belgian economy itself, was fractionally larger at 13·7 million tons, though there are some doubts as to the method of calculation. Further up the North Sea coast Hamburg maintained its historic role in the German overseas economy and the volume entering was 12·3 million tons. Only New York had a greater volume and no other port on the continent was in any way comparable; next came Lisbon (8·7 million), Marseilles (8 million) and Naples (6·3 million). Even London cleared only 10·8 million tons and Liverpool 7·3 million.[4] The ports inevitably became major centres for the processing trades, shipbuilding, all manner of commercial and financial activities and, based on these staples, achieved their own momentum of growth. On the whole continent, in 1910 only Moscow, St Petersburg (Leningrad), Berlin, Paris and Vienna had populations greater than that of Hamburg, for example.

PATTERNS OF TRADE SETTLEMENT

The commodity statistics for most European countries show that in the thirty years to 1914 their foreign trade balances in manufactured and semi-manufactured goods were improving and those for primary products were deteriorating, as Table 85 shows. Most countries increased their export surpluses of the former and their import surpluses of the latter. Both Sweden and Italy reduced their surpluses of imports of manufactures and Sweden's surplus of exports of primary products became a deficit. The exceptions were those countries that were major suppliers of primary products and yet had either very limited levels of industrial activity,

Table 85 *European trade balances, 1881–1914 ($m.)*

		1881–5	1911–13			1881–5	1911–13
Germany (a)[1]		− 332[2]	− 1,477	Russia	(a)	+ 72	+ 331
	(b)	+ 329	+ 1,158		(b)	− 46	− 172
France	(a)	− 455	− 788	Austria-	(a)	− 27	− 207
	(b)	+ 220	+ 461	Hungary	(b)	+ 70	+ 55
Italy	(a)	+ 21	− 196				
	(b)	− 61	− 39				
Sweden	(a)	+ 2	− 22				
	(b)	− 20	− 7				

[1] (a) = primary products   (b) = manufactures
[2] A positive figure shows an export surplus and a negative an import surplus in each category of trade

Source: National trade statistics.

Spain and Romania for example, or were industrialising so fast as to require heavy imports of capital goods, like Russia. Austria-Hungary lay somewhere between these two, increasing imports of primary products but also slightly reducing the net surplus in exports of manufactures, making it the only country in Table 85 whose balance of trade deteriorated in both sectors.

One result of all this was that the industrial countries of western Europe began to build up large deficits with outside primary producers. The most important are shown in Table 86 but smaller deficits were also incurred with China, the Dutch East Indies, West Africa and the West Indies, Ceylon and the Straits Settlements. Although Germany in particular developed a thriving export trade to South America, it was not sufficient to cover her own imports, let alone those of the other industrial European countries. Exports to British possessions were much harder to achieve and,

Table 86 *Trade balances of western industrial Europe*[1] *with primary producers* ($m.)

	Argentina	Brazil	Australia	India
1880	−14·6	+4·9	−4·9	−53·5
1910	−92·5	−73·0	−131·5	−263·0

[1] Austria-Hungary, Belgium, France, Germany, Netherlands, Italy

Source: S. B. Saul, *Studies in British Overseas Trade, 1870–1914* (Liverpool, 1960), p. 53.

partly for that reason, the deficits were more substantial. To some degree the deficits in South America were offset by income from investments and the remittances of emigrants and by the visible export surpluses earned there by Spain, Portugal, Italy and Switzerland. However, these were not enough to alter the basic pattern which became one of the prime elements in European and world trade settlements at this time.

Trade across the north Atlantic was more complex. In the 1880s exports of manufactures from industrialised western Europe were slightly in excess of its imports of American primary products and, with a small net invisible income too, that part of Europe probably enjoyed a surplus with the United States in normal years of the order of $50–80 million. As for the rest of Europe, a small trade deficit with the United States was more or less compensated for by invisible receipts. Prior to 1914, although these patterns had been modified in detail, the basic relationship remained much the same. Western industrial Europe had developed a sizeable trade deficit but a rise in invisible income had more than offset this. As for the rest of Europe, American trade deficits with the Mediterranean countries and with Norway, Sweden and Switzerland were offset by a large surplus with Russia. The overall figures are given in Table 87. Both in the 1880s and the pre-war years, therefore, continental Europe financed some of its imports from overseas primary producers through a surplus with the United States deriving from the heavy invisible income earned from that country.

To 1900 the remainder of Europe's imports from primary producers was financed by the trade surplus with Britain. In the 1880s Britain had trade deficits with France, Spain, Russia and the Scandinavian countries and was in balance with Belgium, Germany and the Netherlands as a group, though Britain undoubtedly was a net earner on invisible account

Table 87 *United States balance of payments with Europe, 1908–9 ($m.)*

	Western industrial Europe[1]	Rest of Europe
Trade and gold	+205	−15
Interest	−127	—
Tourism	−97	−29
Remittances	−102	−29
Freight	−10	−5
Capital	+88	—
Balance	−43	−78

[1] See Table 86

Source: S. B. Saul, *Studies in British Overseas Trade, 1870–1914* (Liverpool, 1960), p. 53.

in Europe. To the end of the century these deficits grew quickly, most of all those with Scandinavia, France and now also Germany, as Britain imported foodstuffs and primary products across the North Sea and manufactures from France and Germany, and faced growing competition and tariffs in her attempts to export in return. By the end of the century Britain's trade deficit with Europe reached almost $500 million. But thereafter the deficit with industrial Europe in particular began to fall rapidly, largely because of the increase in Britain's coal exports, and by 1911–13 the trade gap with industrial Europe was only $88 million compared with some $240 million at the turn of the century.[5] Since Europe was all the time increasing its deficits in Asia, South America and Australia, the falling surplus with Britain prompts the question as to how these changing balances were financed after 1900. The answer must be by rising invisible income which not only modified these deficits with the primary producers but brought a sharp improvement in Europe's balance of payments with the United States, which we must presume was more unfavourable in 1900 than it was a decade later.

These were the worldwide patterns then, with continental Europe as a whole financing its deficits with primary producers through surpluses with Britain and the United States. Intra-European trade (including Britain) comprised one-third of all world trade in 1880 and still 27·5 per cent in 1913. In 1913 Germany, France, the Netherlands and Switzerland all sent about two-thirds of their exports to other European countries; Belgium and Austria-Hungary about 80 per cent, Sweden 84 per cent and Denmark 95 per cent. The basic pattern was simple; there were two great surplus countries, Germany and Russia. Both had surpluses with almost every country in Europe. Russia also had a balance of payments surplus with Germany but these Russian surpluses had to cover not only trade deficits with the United States, India, China and Persia but also interest payments

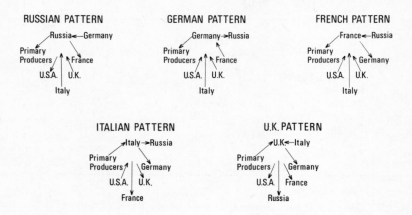

on foreign loans which must have exceeded $150 million in 1913. Possibly two-thirds of this sum went to France and, allowing for some reinvestment, France alone in Europe probably had an overall surplus with Russia in 1914. France in fact was a European surplus country, for her trade deficit with Germany was small and those with Norway, Sweden and Austria-Hungary offset by invisible income. The Scandinavian countries seem to have used their surpluses with Britain to cover deficits with most of the rest of Europe. Italy was unique in having a deficit with every country in Europe, including Britain, but she financed these through exports to South America and invisible income from there and the United States. Hers was the direct opposite of the normal European pattern, though of course the balances were quite small.

Small diagrams (shown above) may make the pattern of multilateral trade clearer; the arrows point to the surplus country of any pair. 'Primary producers' refers, in this context, to non-European countries.

The information is not accurate enough to allow us to give precise values to these balances but certain central aspects should be stressed again. Although a high proportion of European trade was conducted between European countries, industrialisation inevitably saw the growth of deficits with overseas primary producing countries, though, because of Europe's big invisible income there, not with the United States. These deficits were offset by a huge surplus with Britain who in turn enjoyed a surplus with the primary producers, her Empire countries in particular. In a much smaller way Italy played the same role as Britain by having deficits within Europe and surpluses outside. The critical role of the United Kingdom is obvious; not only was she an excellent market for the foodstuffs and materials of countries such as Denmark, Sweden, Norway and Russia, but her free-trade policy and high income levels gave ample opportunities for French and German industrialists. The surpluses so earned made possible payment for the import of raw materials fundamental to the industrialisation of Europe.

THE TERMS OF TRADE

This rapid growth of trade in manufactures and primary products raises the question of movements in the relative prices of such goods, of changes in the terms of trade. Many factors determine such price changes and much discussion has centred around the possibility of there being a long-run trend in favour of one kind of exporter or another. Some have suggested that as incomes rise demand for food and raw materials rises more slowly than that for manufactured goods and so the terms of trade will move in favour of industrial countries. Others stress the fact that primary production is more subject to diminishing returns and so the terms of trade will tend to favour such producers. There is little validity in either argument so far as Europe was concerned. Historical experience shows that there were huge variations in this process between one commodity and another; each European country had its own mix of exports both within the category of primary products and between these and manufactured goods: witness France's iron ore exports and the complex pattern of Swedish exports, for example. More significant than these alleged long-run trends was the short-run instability of primary product prices. Output was less responsive to price changes than that of manufactured goods, supply was relatively price inelastic and prices often rose and fell with great sharpness in the course of either boom or slump. It was this instability, together with the fact that many primary producing areas were dependent on one crop or material, that posed the most severe difficulties. The terms of trade might move unfavourably because the real cost of imports had risen but they might also do the same because the real cost of exports had fallen. This was the case, for example, with the exports of wheat by many producers after 1870. In such circumstances there may well have been a gain to exporter as well as importer, for though more goods in a quantitative sense had to be exported to pay for a given amount of imports, it was the real cost of producing the larger volume of exports that was relevant and this may well have fallen. Sometimes the terms of trade moved unfavourably because supply tended to overshoot demand; this seems to have been the case with Australian wool exports in the 1880s, for example. The opposite was often the case at the peak of a boom. During the early 1870s the supply of coal and iron to Europe from Britain became very inelastic and prices soared, making the German terms of trade temporarily unfavourable and the British very favourable indeed.

Some interesting comparisons can be made by studying the prices of particular exports. The export price of German chemicals in 1900, for example, was only 25 per cent that of 1872 and in 1913 only 45 per cent that of 1900. In some measure this was due to sharp cost savings achieved by German chemists but it was also due to changes in the relative

Table 88 *German terms of trade, 1880–1913 (export prices : import prices, 1913 = 100)*

1880 = 125·5	1901 = 120·9
1882 = 136·6	1905 = 110·5
1890 = 125·7	1913 = 100

Source: W. G. Hoffmann, *Das Wachstum der deutschen Wirtschaft seit der Mitte des 19. Jahrhunderts* (Berlin, 1965), p. 548.

importance of particular chemicals within that general group – a factor which makes calculations of the terms of trade always very hazardous. On the other hand the opposite happened with machinery exports; in 1900 their price was 16 per cent above the 1872 level and by 1913 31 per cent up again.

In general most European countries experienced a fall in their import prices of some 25–30 per cent between 1872 and 1900. Germany, who was a considerable exporter of grain as well as of manufactured goods, saw export prices fall more than this and the terms of trade deteriorated as Table 88 shows.

In contrast Sweden and Denmark, whose special types of primary products were in much greater demand, saw distinct improvement in their terms of trade. From 1900 to 1913 import prices rose again. Sweden continued to enjoy improving terms of trade, the gain from 1872 to 1913 being in the order of 50 per cent. Denmark gained too. As for Norway, although she enjoyed favourable commodity terms of trade, for the whole period shipping freights fell in relation to import prices. Only between

1895 and 1904 were her total terms of trade (goods plus freights) favourable. Again, the German terms of trade deteriorated sharply as Table 88 shows; her export prices, held back by the low chemical prices, rose by far less than her import prices. This does not necessarily mean that she suffered severe economic disadvantage, since one reason for the relative price fall was higher productivity in the chemical industry. Nonetheless, for the whole period Germany's terms of trade contrasted with those of Britain and with those of Belgium which tended to improve after 1875 partly because Belgium was willing to import heavily those grainstuffs whose price fell so sharply. French terms of trade were not as distorted as the German by the import boom of the early seventies but from 1890 onwards they exhibit the same unfavourable trends. Those countries that erected tariffs against imports of foodstuffs naturally turned the terms of trade against themselves.

Table 89 *Price indices of certain products, 1872–1913 (1913 = 100)*

	Timber and products	Coal and coke	All primary products
1872	123	122	126
1900	102	110	86
1913	100	100	100

Source: C. P. Kindleberger, *The Terms of Trade* (New York, 1956), p. 266.

Broadly we can say that differences in the terms of trade are to be looked for in terms of specific goods and not as between primary products and manufactures. Table 89 exemplifies this: both coal and timber prices held much better than those of all primary products between 1872 and 1900 but thereafter they continued to fall when prices in general were rising again.

FINANCING WORLD TRADE

The rapid growth of world trade called for ever greater sophistication in methods of finance. In earlier times payments for traded goods had been made in gold or silver coins and traders would negotiate loans to help carry on their businesses as the opportunity arose. The eighteenth century saw a momentous change come about with the increasing use of the bill of exchange. Such a bill was in effect a loan by the seller to the buyer. The latter signed the bill and agreed to pay in, say, thirty or ninety days' time. The seller could get his money earlier than that by persuading an intermediary to let him have the money right away, paying a small rate of interest for the privilege. Such bills might pass from hand to hand until they fell due (matured), the ease with which this took place depending upon the repute of those who had successively signed (accepted) the bill. Gradually there emerged throughout Europe a number of firms specialising in this and other forms of trade finance. These merchant bankers, as they were called, were foreign trade bankers. They bought and sold bills, collected debts, gave advances on consignment of goods, changed money, shipped bullion and so forth. Hopes, Bethmanns, Speyers, Barings, Erlangers were some of the best known of them. After 1815 London became the centre of this kind of activity and throughout the nineteenth century most of world trade was conducted in sterling, though towards the end of the century German traders made some not very successful attempts to finance more of their activities in marks from Berlin. The rate of discount in London was usually one per cent below that in Berlin and with a complicated pattern of multilateral settlements such as we have described it was useful to have one financial centre as a kind of clearing house. It is estimated that by 1913 the total amount of this short-term credit outstanding was something in the region of $3,000 million. By the last part of the nineteenth century most important banks had branches or correspondent banks in London and through them the whole of the pattern of world multilateral trade was financed. Through the transactions of banks on behalf of multitudinous traders, all the deficits and surpluses would be offset in the accounts of the financial institutions in London. Actual settlements were made through cables from bankers to their London principals. Nearly all the exchange business of the primary producing countries went through London directly or through the overseas branches of British banks. There was no need at all to remit bullion for particular transactions but of course each country's balance of payments with the rest of the world tended to move into surplus or deficit from time to time. If, say, Germany was in deficit this meant that the demand for marks to buy German goods was running below the supply of marks as Germans imported other countries' goods. Since the mark had a price like every other commodity, its exchange value would tend to fall. What would happen then?

To answer this we need to know more about the nature of international currencies. If the value of the mark were allowed to fall, this would make exports cheaper and discourage imports by making them dearer and so possibly rectify the situation, though other factors might modify this process. For example, dearer imports would tend to raise industrial costs and offset the benefits of devaluation to exporters, or demand for the country's exports might be of such a nature as not to be affected much by price adjustments and home demand for imports might be similarly price inelastic. Nonetheless, some countries, such as Spain, allowed the external value of their currencies to fluctuate in this way throughout the period. Russia and Austria-Hungary restored the redeemability of their currencies in silver at new, fixed, if devalued, parities after the Napoleonic wars, but during the 1850s wars and revolutions pushed both of them off the silver standard and left the currencies floating to the end of the century. By the last quarter of the century most of the major countries had adhered to the gold standard and this meant following a different procedure. Simply speaking, the gold standard involved keeping the value of the currency fixed in terms of gold, allowing unrestricted movement of gold in and out of the country, and maintaining some link between the stock of gold and the internal money supply. This could possibly come through adjustment to the stock of gold coins in circulation but these were important only in Britain, France, Germany and, after 1897, in Russia. More important were the constraints imposed on the note issues of central banks which were related to the level of the special reserves. In Britain, Norway and Russia all notes above a set maximum had to be covered by gold or foreign exchange holdings. In Belgium, the Netherlands, Switzerland and Denmark (after 1907) the note issue was directly proportionate to reserve holdings. Germany, Italy, Sweden and Austria operated a combination of those two systems. Only in France was it laid down what the maximum note issue should be at any time regardless of the level of reserve holdings.

As an international system the gold standard came into being in the 1870s. At that date only Britain and Portugal were adhering to gold. The price of silver was remarkably stable from 1815 to 1870: indeed the fall of the price of gold during the California discoveries of 1849–50 brought countries like Belgium, Switzerland and France to demonetise gold altogether. But then came the sharp fall in silver prices. Germany went on the gold standard in 1871, followed by the Scandinavian countries. Silver now came to be dumped in those countries still permitting its free coinage, above all France, Italy, Belgium and Switzerland who had formed the Latin Monetary Union based on silver and gold in 1865. In 1873 they too were forced to limit coinage of silver. Of course agricultural exporting countries saw the devaluation of their currencies under the silver standard as a way of maintaining internal prices as world prices for their exports were falling. This was the case in Austria-Hungary and Russia: the former abandoned silver in the 1880s, when wild oscillations in the price of silver began to cause heavy losses for farmers, and sought refuge in a more stable currency. Foreign lenders naturally opposed devaluation while borrowing states would be reluctant to see their obligations rise in terms of their own currency if loans were denominated in foreign currencies.

Each gold standard country denominated its currency in terms of gold; one ounce, say, would be bought and sold by the Bank of England for £4 and for 80 marks by the Reichsbank, giving an equilibrium rate of exchange of 20 marks = £1. But the prices of these currencies on the foreign exchange market would vary according to the demands for each to settle commercial transactions. Let us say that the mark was weakening and moving up to 21 to the £1 sterling. It would then pay a speculator to buy one ounce of gold for 80 marks in Berlin, ship it to London, sell the gold for £1 sterling and convert that on the foreign exchange market into 84 marks. It is simple economics that this kind of activity is always possible wherever two prices exist for the same commodity in free markets. The only restraint would be the cost of transporting and insuring the gold. However, once the mark had weakened enough to cover this cost, gold would tend to leave Germany in the way we have shown. This was the gold export point and the demand for marks in order to buy and export gold would prevent the exchange value of the mark from falling below that level. The same would apply when the mark was strong; gold would be imported and the sale of marks for the purpose would prevent the currency from rising further. Currencies on the gold standard could only fluctuate between the gold import and export points; when these were reached gold would flow in or out as the case might be. Here, then, was the automatic link between the whole mass of commercial transactions and the compensating flows of gold in and out of each country.

But countries did not have inexhaustible supplies of gold. What action could they take to protect their reserves, given that adherence to the gold standard ruled out further reduction in the exchange value of the currency? In the first place the interest rate could be raised in the hope of attracting short-term capital from other countries, thereby weakening the pressure on the home currency and pushing the exchange rate above the gold export point. If this were not enough, further measures would be taken to reduce internal credit in order to induce deflation into the economy. This, it was hoped, would lower prices and so stimulate exports and lower incomes, thereby reducing imports and releasing resources for the export industries. Also the direct link between the gold stock and the internal money supply meant that an outflow of gold was self-rectifying to some degree, since it would directly influence the level of internal activity. At least, that is the view of one modern school of economists and was certainly the contemporary view too.

It will be seen that the level of activity and of employment in the home economy was largely subordinated to the task of maintaining the rate of exchange. Furthermore, it appears that in the main industrial countries labour resisted wage cuts during deflationary periods with considerable success. The consequence of this was that adjustment of the balance of payments came to depend even more on creating actual unemployment. A stable rate of exchange removed one element of uncertainty from inter-national trade and, in particular, it encouraged long-term movements of capital across national frontiers, since investors had little fear of capital losses through exchange rate variations. Furthermore, it avoided the kind of speculation over movements in exchange rates which has been such a feature of the world economy since 1919. After that date holders of short-term funds tended to shift them about not so much in response to differences in interest rates as before 1914, but according to their anticipation of exchange rate fluctuations, anticipations which, if strong enough, could force the changes they were expecting. This is not to say that there was no speculation before 1914, but it was much less common. The United States was subjected to such attacks in 1893–6 when the agitation in Congress for the coinage of silver made foreigners wonder if the country could stay on the gold standard. Russia came close to being forced off in 1905–6 because of a heavy capital flight following the defeat by Japan and an outbreak of violent internal unrest. The situation was saved by a loan of 2,000 million francs from a consortium of European private banks. Such international co-operation was not common but several examples could be quoted. The Bank of France loaned 75 million francs to the Bank of England during the Baring crisis in 1890; in 1898 both these banks gave help to certain German banks that were in difficulties. Some central banks, under pressure, borrowed directly from private banks; sometimes they would borrow from their own governments as did the Swedish Riksbank, for example, in 1899 and 1907. After 1885 the central banks of Norway, Sweden and Denmark introduced a mechanism for co-operation that in effect eliminated the gold points for movements between the three countries.

Of course, the pressure on the home economy might be severe and it is a matter of opinion whether the gains outweighed the disadvantages. Adherence to the gold standard was less a matter of principle than of expediency. In Latin America where the ruling oligarchy consisted of landowners whose income derived from exports, currencies were generally allowed to depreciate. However, with a constantly expanding world economy, the disequilibrium of the balance of payments for any major country was never so severe as to require prolonged internal deflation. This is the great contrast with later years and is indeed the reason why the gold standard worked relatively smoothly for the industrial countries. Unfortunately, less developed countries did not possess money markets of such sophistication that short-term money could be attracted to ease the pressures. What tended to happen was that in moments of crisis the European money markets raised their rates and threw much of the burden on those borrowing countries which had no means of offsetting such action. They could only solve their balance of payments problems by deflation or, on occasion, by devaluation; hence, for example, the severity of the crisis of the early 1890s in Australia and Argentina.

We have discussed here only the procedures followed when a country was losing gold. When gold was moving in why should action be taken to check it? Many thought the authorities did so because this was one of the 'rules of the game'. But there were no such rules. Central banks took measures which tended to raise prices and promote internal activity, not to assist those who were losing gold, but in their own self-interest. They cut off the inflow of gold largely because they did not care to hold large amounts of an asset which earned no interest. Some made it a practice not to hold all their reserves in gold but to hold foreign assets – sterling, mark or franc bills of exchange. These earned interest and were quickly convertible if need arose. So in effect, when gold flowed in they immediately lent it out again by buying these foreign bills. It has been calculated that, by 1910, the reserve banks of the world were holding about 20 per cent of their official reserves in this way. Russia was by far the largest holder of foreign currencies in Europe but Finland, Germany, Greece, Italy, Sweden and Belgium all had substantial reserves in this form. Taking the world as a whole, sterling was the favourite currency, but within Europe sterling was not the major reserve currency. In 1913 Russia held 292 million in francs, 53 million in marks and only 24 million in sterling. Greece concentrated upon francs, Romania and Italy upon marks. Several European banks held Dutch guilders too. Only the Reichsbank and the Swiss National Bank held more sterling than any other reserve currency. The Bank of France held very large gold reserves in relation to its imports – 40–50 per cent before the First World War – and so did not need to take action to protect them nearly so quickly as the Bank of England which held very small reserves. The distribution of the world's gold held in central banks and treasuries in 1913 shows this contrast. The Bank of England held 3·6 per cent, 14·5 per cent was held in France, 16·8 per cent in Russia and 27·6 per cent in the United States. The series of gold discoveries after the mid-1880s much assisted the smooth working of the system – the world's stock trebled between 1867 and 1913 – but from time to time three were shortages, as after 1870 when many countries were struggling to build up stocks so as to go on to the gold standard and there were no new major discoveries for almost two decades. Many would argue that this relative shortage of gold was an important factor in bringing about the long fall of prices during the twenty years after 1873.

INTERNATIONAL CAPITAL MOVEMENTS

We have described the payments mechanism in terms of trade movements. Now we must say more of the second major influence on balances of payments, the international movement of capital. In the nineteenth century foreign investment was a means, along with foreign trade, by which the effects of development in one part of the world were transferred to others. The leading industrial countries themselves relied on outside capital to only a minor extent at the initial stages of their growth. As for their own investment abroad, from 1880 to 1913 between a third and a half of French domestic savings was invested abroad; for Germany the figure was below one-tenth from 1900 to 1913 and significantly above that level only in the early seventies and mid-eighties. About two-fifths of British savings went overseas from 1875 to 1914. In absolute terms the total stock of long-term foreign investment in 1914 was about $44,000 million of which $18,000 million was held by Britain, $8,000 million by

France, about $6,000 million by Germany and $5,500 million by Belgium, the Netherlands and Switzerland together. Of this, $14,000 million was invested in Europe, possibly one-third in Russia. But more to the point, 60 per cent of French and one-half of German investment was made in Europe.

As for the receiving countries, over considerable periods of time capital imports were always less important than domestic savings, but for certain short periods foreign loans might finance up to a half of domestic investment. This applied most of all to newly peopled countries outside Europe whose sources of internal savings were initially very limited. Australia, New Zealand and Canada, for example. In Europe the highest proportions were found in Bulgaria and Romania. In Sweden, too, foreign investment reached 45 per cent of gross domestic capital formation in the 1880s; for Norway it averaged one-third in the two decades before 1914 but in Denmark never more than 20 per cent. Capital imports into Italy reached 40 per cent of gross domestic capital formation during 1861–5 but then the proportion declined and from the 1890s onwards, though still receiving injections of foreign capital, Italy was a net lender abroad, a unique situation for a country on the verge of rapid industrial growth. Between 1880 and 1913 Russia borrowed abroad something like 5,700 million roubles, about $3,000 million, much the largest amount in Europe. It is not clear that this implies a proportion of domestic savings significantly higher than that of Denmark, however. In general, circumstances favoured foreign investment; exchange controls were non-existent, exchange rates were stable and labour moved freely across the continents, often in the direction of the capital flows. The supreme example of this was the huge export of money from Europe to the United States paralleling the movement of people.

The impact of foreign investment on the receiving countries is not easy to determine. Viewed in the aggregate imports of capital do not finance capital formation any more than they do consumption, or imports of capital goods more than consumption goods. Even where the funds are directly used for capital purposes they may release internal funds for consumption which might otherwise have gone into investment. The most that can be said is that capital imports make some contribution to the supply of capital assets but we do not know how much because we do not know to what extent increases in capital investment would have been reduced in the absence of foreign investment or maintained at the expense of consumption. The statistics given in the previous paragraph, relating capital imports to gross domestic capital formation, are interesting if only for the inter-country comparisons but do not have the direct significance for each country that is sometimes given to them.

But foreign investment is important in a qualitative sense, because of the sectors to which it flowed. Throughout Europe it was indispensable for the building of railways, for example, and in general it may be argued that at least in the initial stages of industrialisation some of the most modern sectors of industry were introduced by foreign capital. The French contribution to the industrialisation of Germany in the 1850s and 1860s was of importance not so much because of its size but because it was concentrated upon the coal, iron and engineering industries and because it carried with it that financial and technological experience which was at least as important as the money itself. The electro-chemical industries in Norway, ore mining in northern Sweden, steel in Russia, electrical engineering in Hungary are other important examples of this process. Because of the tremendous growth of international trade the costly construction of major ports in underdeveloped countries both within and without Europe came to have the same importance for their governments as the provision of airports nowadays. French investors, for example, financed the development of Bulgaria's two chief ports, Burgas and Varna; the Imperial Ottoman Bank, under French control, invested heavily in the port of Beirut. A high proportion of investment by European countries consisted of portfolio investment – the buying of shares in foreign enterprises. All the same, within Europe the amount of direct investment, or establishment of branch plants abroad, was significant and brought to the recipients quick access to technical and managerial knowledge and skills already created elsewhere. This applied most obviously to manufacturing industry but when French insurance companies opened branches in other parts of Europe, they too were using accumulated capital and expertise to fill gaps in the economic structure of the poorer countries. A further target for direct investment was found in the growing cities of Europe. The provision of gas, light and transport was a natural extension of domestic investment. Such investments were available in the more developed countries too; French companies, for example, played an important role in the beginnings of the London omnibus and underground system.

Where loans were for the purpose of armaments their value in fostering economic development was more disputable. Borrowing countries varied from those merely requiring funds to buy armaments to those who sought to install an armaments industry in their own country and with it an important area of modern technology. The competition for armaments contracts in either case was severe and confined to a small number of private armaments firms such as Schneider in France and the German firm Krupp. The contracts offered by the Russian and the Spanish governments after 1890 usually stipulated that the finished armaments should be manufactured in the country, as far as possible out of indigenous material and by the native labour force. Sometimes they were on such a scale that international co-operation was necessary to meet them. The Russian gun foundries and shipyards at Reval were built by the Scottish firm William Beardmore and Schneider in collaboration. In a period dominated by military alliances, international collaboration of this kind easily led to closer liaisons in an industry which was so dependent on an accurate appraisal of the latest techniques. French investors by the eve of the First

World War dominated the main private armaments manufacturer in Russia, the Putilov company. There were certainly important advantages to be gained from making battleships and large guns in an industrialising economy, especially through the effects of the learning process on engineering and metallurgical industries. But the question remains to be answered how far such contracts, drawn up with specific purposes of economic development in mind, were in reality fulfilled. The Spanish naval loans seem to have passed in no small measure into the pockets of ministers and their friends and the generally widespread corruption in public affairs in underdeveloped countries may well have nullified many of the more fruitful aspects of these loans.

Investment outside Europe brought returns to the home economies by opening new channels of supply for foodstuffs and raw materials. Directly and indirectly it encouraged exports, though only the minority of loans were tied to the purchase of supplies in particular places. Nevertheless, it did not always bring increased trade. Although an important part of business in Bulgaria, for example, was controlled by French investors, the main trading partner was always Germany. Whether the direct returns to investors were commensurate with those obtainable at home is hard to determine but certainly many of the opportunities were attractive, for the new areas offered cost advantages and a degree of effective control over existing resources to an extent not common in the contemporary world. Foreign investment by no means always coincided with political control over foreign territory. All the same, much of European investment had political overtones. In retrospect it would be astonishing that the French investor should have been willing to put so much money into Russia and the Balkans for a mere 4 per cent return if there were not other factors at work. French loans from the 1890s onwards had to satisfy the political requirements of the Franco-Russian alliance. Not only was money encouraged to go to Russia but Germany and, eventually, Austria-Hungary were stopped from borrowing in France. Loans to Italy were kept off the market until her alliances began to shift away from the central powers during the 1890s. Special pressures were sometimes applied too: in 1909 an Argentinian loan was not listed on the French stock exchange because that country had just bought arms from Germany; the French loan to Morocco in 1914 was tied to the construction by Schneider of the port of Casablanca; in 1910 Norway and Sweden were asked to reduce their duties on French wines as a *quid pro quo* for permission to float loans. But investment was not always safe, for on occasions even an apparently helpless government like that of Honduras could renounce its debts with impunity. Nor was it always profitable, for many losses were sustained in Latin America above all. Governments played a major role in obtaining concessions overseas for their investors, most notably in Turkey and China. Sometimes the terms of a loan specified that only the goods of the lending country could be imported if a special project were being financed; alternatively the same pressure could be applied by refusing permission to borrow again if this were not done. The French exerted heavy and successful pressure on Serbia to that end, for example, just before 1914. Borrowing countries could still try to play one set of investors against another or deliberately seek to reduce the influence of one. In spite of the dominance of French investors in Turkey, the Turkish government gave vital strategic railway contracts to Germany. The Austrian government backed the Vienna bank, Bodencreditanstalt, in a bitter campaign after 1880 to break French influence over the Staatsbahn railway company, which was eventually nationalised. The Bulgarian loan of 1896 led to a contest between Krupp and Schneider for artillery orders. The French insisted on orders as a condition of placing the loan in Paris but the orders were eventually divided between the two. Spain, at the same date, was feeling too beholden to the French and sought a loan in Berlin; the price was orders for Krupp and naval vessels from Stettin (Szczecin).

Once a country, Turkey for example, had become an international borrower on a vast scale the situation became institutionalised and took on an almost permanent aspect with loans regularly being raised to service the debt on the previous loans. About three-quarters of the French capital lent to Turkey went on making interest payments back to France, paying civil servants, some of whom were placed by the French government, and buying military equipment. It became familiar after 1890 for the principal purpose of an international loan to be to satisfy an earlier generation of investors expecting a regular fixed-interest payment. It does not follow from the greatly increasing volume of international lending that correspondingly more capital was being used for development purposes.

French investors had a much more marked preference for fixed-interest shares in public debts than German or British investors so that for continental countries the tendency for international loans to become subject to informal and formal institutional arrangements between Parisian banking institutions, the French government and the receiving government was inevitably strong. Because the choice of fixed-interest investment indicated a desire for security of return to the investor, the prime purpose of these institutional arrangements was to guarantee a regular stream of payment. In this way some borrowing countries lost their capacity for independent political action and found their internal economic decisions supervised and controlled by institutions representing French interests. Everything in the last resort depended on the differences in political and economic power and on the diplomatic bargaining power of the countries concerned. Far from being free to do what they would with foreign capital, most receiving countries, even if they had well-conceived and honestly administered schemes for development, which was rare, found their decisions closely confined and governed by the harsh realities of their international political weakness. Even in those cases where fixed-interest investment was actually for railways or ports the relationship was still one between the weak and strong. It was to all intents and purposes impossible to conceive a railway in the Balkans which did not directly affect the strategic interests of one of the greater powers, and the railway routes were not laid out and built through independent national action as they had been in western Europe. In our work on Belgium we stressed the importance for industrialisation of the government's decision to build a railway network, and also of the economically purposeful and rational design of that network. In spite of the easy access to foreign capital no such possibility of independent action was open to smaller eastern European countries after 1870; there were too many other powerful interests concerned with the Balkan routes and the fragmentary railway systems which did emerge often served foreign interests as much as national ones.

At its best, foreign investment was a means of transmitting resources and knowledge to the mutual benefit of both sides but it was not always so well directed or intentioned. At its worst, it fed on the cupidity and stupidity of rulers, bankrupted their treasuries, led to military action to enforce payments, reduced the borrowing country to being ruled in the interests of foreign bond-holders and left the economy and the people no better off than before. This was so above all in China and Turkey. Turkey was not allowed to modify existing taxes without the permission of the great powers, and after 1881 its budget and debt payments were supervised by an international body under Anglo-French direction. By 1914 Romania was the only Balkan state to have avoided international financial control on account of default or insolvency. Undoubtedly, one of the attractions of foreign investment was the belief that in many circumstances there was a greater degree of control of the environment in which the investment was taking place, not necessarily by the sending of gunboats to enforce payment but by the exaction of concessions or restrictive agreements from the borrower, each small in itself but having a powerful cumulative force. With the exception of particularly ill-conceived speculative loans and of complete political upheavals such as the Russian Revolution of 1917, investors were largely right. They were also able to assert in Asia and Africa a kind of cultural ascendancy which enabled them to demolish local behavioural patterns in a way that was satisfactory to the nineteenth-century moral sense of western Europe but which might have disastrous social consequences. Already before 1914 a reaction was setting in. Despite her heavy dependence on foreign resources and technology, in 1903 Norway enacted a series of laws limiting the rights foreigners might be granted over local resources, water power in particular.

Investment was not the work of individuals, nor, though they could exert pressure, of governments. Complex financial arrangements of this kind were the work of highly specialised financial houses. International investment banking emerged naturally out of the resources and experience of the merchant bankers. It began to grow at the beginning of the nineteenth century, largely as a result of the needs of the belligerent nations. Barings of London, Hopes of Amsterdam, Bethmanns of Frankfurt led the way. The unprecedented post-war operation of floating loans to enable the French government to pay her indemnities was, almost inevitably, entrusted to Barings and Hopes. Supporting them were firms which had grown up on the basis of wartime transactions and which were ready to help supply the money for reconstruction after 1815. They worked on the basis of their own private resources and the large deposits made with them by friends, relatives and major clients. The risk element for even the most powerful was always considerable and there were many who had to close their doors during troubled times such as those of 1848, when the essential element of public confidence was prone to ebb away more rapidly than in normal years. There was also a limit to the amount of lending that could be carried out in this way, as time was to show, but all the same it was often an extremely profitable exercise, provided one had the right contacts. For the generation after Waterloo it was the Rothschilds who reigned supreme in European finance. A family dynasty, originating in Frankfurt, in the first two decades of the nineteenth century they established houses in London, Paris, Frankfurt and Vienna. Among their more remarkable activities was the series of massive loans made in 1830, after the revolt in the United Netherlands, to secure the Société Générale, the bank which William I had established in 1822. Without doubt this action helped put the new Belgian state on its feet and Rothschilds were able to arrange issues in Paris over the next decade for many of the industrial concerns in which the Société Générale had holdings. After 1830 too it was railway finance that dominated the activities of almost all these houses, who used their resources in concert with specialist concession hunters and railway constructors. Here the Paris and Vienna Rothschilds showed more interest than the other two branches of the family. The Englishman, Thomas Brassey, was the outstanding example of a truly European railway builder of the time, working for syndicates who won the concessions and with international alliances of financial groups. Brassey himself was a sleeping partner in the Paris bank of Sir Edward Blount, one of the major railway bankers. Between 1841 and 1870 he built 4,500 kilometres of railway all over Europe, operating on an international scale. The Papal States railway, for example, was conceded to a Paris banker in 1857; he sold the stock mostly in France and Italy, the rails came from Newcastle, the locomotives from Brassey's works near Paris, the wheels from Belgium and the carriages were built in Italy. The East Hungarian railway of 1868 got its rails in England, its locomotives in Bavaria, coaches in Switzerland and Hungary and freight cars in Austria.

But the power of the private bankers did not long go unchallenged, for around the middle of the century emerged the finance companies – joint stock concerns, able to tap much wider financial sources and making investment banking their prime business. The French Crédit Mobilier is the best known of these but the idea was by no means new, as the example of the Société Générale in Belgium indicates, and an important element of continuity was always present in that the Crédit Mobilier was financed initially by prominent French private bankers. The merchant bankers were stirred from their conservatism, and astute enough to support the new venture rather than invite their own destruction by opposing it. In the ensuing battle for concessions between the Rothschilds and the Péreire brothers of the Crédit Mobilier, the former called on the resources of all its four branches while the latter acted in concert with other private bankers. Governments, for their part, enjoyed playing the two off against each other. It is significant, however, that one of the Rothschild victories was to win the right to found in Austria an investment bank of the Crédit Mobilier type, the Bodencreditanstalt. The bank was restricted to operations within the Habsburg Empire but Rothschilds were able to use it effectively as the base for their railway operations there. Even so they had to surrender some of the Austro-Hungarian railway concessions to a Crédit Mobilier group which included Mallet and André from the Parisian merchant banks. In Spain the railway spoils were divided fairly evenly; in Turkey Rothschilds were given the loans of 1854, but the opposition founded the Imperial Ottoman Bank. By the mid-1860s the Crédit Mobilier had been destroyed as an effective force in European finance but the trends were inevitable and other new figures like Gustav von Mevissen and David Hansemann forced the merchant banks forward. The new types of bank had greater power to attract savings and to market bonds and so further adjustments were made. Rothschilds, through the Berlin private house of Bleichröder, founded the Berliner Handelsgesellschaft after the model of the Crédit Mobilier. The Oppenheims of Cologne, the Mendelssohns and others from Berlin took similar action, though the Frankfurt banks and houses like the Hopes of Amsterdam showed less interest. Rothschild's part in the French war indemnity loans of 1871 was the last major independent action of the private banks.

Thereafter leadership passed firmly to the French and German joint stock investment banks, though co-operation with the private bankers was maintained since they possessed the flair and inside knowledge essential for winning the concessions in the first place. So one of them at least, either Rothschild, Bleichröder, Mendelssohn, Speyer or Warburg, always took part in the great syndicates. Quietly, informally and very effectively they worked through their contacts in social, political and military circles. This had always been their forte and the need for them remained; it was the scale of operations that changed. Examples of the work of these syndicates abound. The Italian loan of 1881, for example, was carried by a Franco-British-Italian group consisting of the Banque d'Escompte of Paris, Barings, Hambros and the Italian Credito Mobiliario. A group consisting of the Comptoir National d'Escompte, the Banque de Paris et des Pays Bas, the Société Générale, the Crédit Lyonnais and the Crédit Industriel et Commercial, all members of a syndicate that had wrested for itself a share of the indemnity loans of 1871, together with a group of German banks led by the Mendelssohns, moved in to control the Russian loan business in 1877. The Chinese government preferred to raise its railway capital for the Peking–Hankow railway in a neutral country, Belgium. But the Belgian Société Générale had already earmarked portions of the loan for the French Société Générale and the Comptoir National d'Escompte and these two French institutions were in fact bigger subscribers than the Belgian bank. Conversely, the Belgian bank was allocated a share in the founding of the Buenos Aires Provincial Railway Company in 1905 by the Banque de l'Union Parisienne. Alliances of this kind make the problem of deciding the exact origins of foreign capital difficult to resolve and much French capital may have been Belgian and Belgian capital French.

On occasion political pressures forced banks into competition for loans where their respective governments wished to extend their own spheres of influence. On the other hand the syndicates would often offer their loans simultaneously in different markets; the borrower would not get the best price as arbitrage would work against this to give the lenders the advantage, but at least in this way he avoided undue dependence on one source of money. Ignoring political considerations, however, the prime motive for engaging in foreign investment was the profit which accrued to the banks from the process of promotion and issue, not from the holding of loans. It was this which directed money overseas rather than the predilections of the individual lenders. There were also close links between many of the investment banks and associated industrial concerns, associated informally or, more frequently in Germany, through shareholdings and directorships. Large-scale electrification schemes, for example, would be financed on condition that the home firm got the bulk of the equipment orders and in this way the German electrical engineering industry was able to scoop orders for tramway and electric power schemes in many parts of the world. The Deutsche Bank, for example, promoted electrical works in Barcelona and Seville in 1894 and on the Rand in 1895; the Dresdner Bank promoted the Victoria Falls Power Company in 1896.

In some countries banks were able to attain positions of great political power. After 1904 the Moroccan government was so helpless against France that the Banque de Paris et des Pays Bas had first preference on all international loans. The total of the 1914 loan was in fact fixed by the budget committee of the French Chamber. The same bank managed three big loans to Bulgaria between 1902 and 1907 and acquired in the process some rights of supervision over the Bulgarian budget. This process reached its height in Turkey with the Imperial Ottoman Bank. It had been founded in 1863 as a Franco-British bank but by 1900 was almost exclusively French. Over the whole period it managed about 60 per cent of all Turkish international issues. This it did on the Paris money market through a combination of allied banks, the Société Générale, the Crédit Industriel et Commercial, and the Banque de Paris et des Pays Bas. Its usual system was to provide the money first to the Turkish government and then recoup the funds, together with whatever interest it could obtain, out of the loans.

It established a position in Turkey akin to that of the farmers-general of taxes in the eighteenth-century French state.

INDUSTRIAL INVESTMENT AND INTERNATIONAL OIL

One of the most remarkable examples of international investment is to be found in the oil industry where the activities of international producers and financiers completely outweighed the activities of local investors and where the complex machinery of production, transport and refining led at an early date to the formation of large multinational enterprises. At the end of the nineteenth century there were three major areas where oil drilling was being carried out in Europe, in Galicia, Romania and in Russia near the Caspian Sea; the older oil bearing lands in Europe such as Hanover, Alsace and parts of Italy had proved to have only small resources. Oil had been produced in Galicia for many decades from hand-dug shafts but this small-scale industry began to be transformed around 1882 with the introduction of new drilling techniques. But technical and financial success were different matters. Drilling was costly, the industry was hampered by high excise taxes on refined oil, by a low internal demand for kerosene, or illuminating oil, and by transport difficulties. Just before the First World War it was holding stocks equal to one year's shipment and consequently all new prospecting had ceased and output was falling badly. Exploitation there, as elsewhere, was an international operation: capital came from the Rothschilds and the Nobels, from the Deutsche Bank and the Diskontogesellschaft in Germany and from French banks in Lille and Roubaix but it was hardly one of the world's booming oilfields in 1914.

The Romanian industry grew very slowly until about 1895 when new techniques of drilling and casing were introduced. Laws were enacted to protect concession rights for foreign investors and a flood of capital poured in. First it was mainly German, the Deutsche Bank taking control of the largest company, the Steaua Română. Exports of Russian kerosene were by this time cutting into the European markets of Standard Oil and in 1904 that company organised its own subsidiary, Română Americană, and in the next year built the largest refinery outside the United States at Ploești. Royal Dutch entered with its Astra Română about the same time to compete with Standard Oil. The importance of Romanian oil after 1900 lay in the fact that it was very rich in volatile components and produced almost 50 per cent gasoline which was in rising demand. By 1914 39 per cent of the capital employed in Romanian oil was British and Dutch, 33 per cent German, 12 per cent French and Belgian and about 6 per cent American. Output of crude oil rose from

250,000 tons in 1900 to about 2 million tons in 1912. At that date output in Galicia was 1·2 million tons, though in 1909 it too had reached 2 million tons.

Significant though these were as examples of international exploitation of oil, they were minor compared with what took place in Russia. The modern development of the oil industry in the Baku region dates from the arrival of foreign capital in the mid-1870s. For a quarter of a century the industry grew very rapidly and in 1899 Russia was producing rather more than a half of the world's output and 35 per cent of world trade in oil products, though at this time something like two-thirds of Russian oil was consumed at home. The first foreign influence came from Sweden through the Nobels. They quickly learned the vital importance of transport and established a virtual monopoly in the movement of oil from Baku by sea to the Volga and up the river to the railhead at Tsaritsyn (Stalingrad, Volgagrad). The independent producers in Russia wished to break this monopoly by building a railway from Baku to Batum on the Caspian, and eventually invited Rothschilds to help them. Rothschilds were already distributing oil for Standard and had a refinery at Fiume (Rijeka) serving the Galician field. They put up the money to complete the railway, obtained mortgages on the independents' property and the exclusive right to buy their crude in Baku. The completion of the Trans-Caucasian railway in 1883 brought Russian oil to Europe in large amounts and to the east too, using the Suez canal and the improved tankers being built in Britain and Sweden. Both Nobels and Rothschilds established bulk storage and distribution systems in Europe, but even so to 1900 the bulk of oil production in Russia remained in the hands of Armenians and Turks, some of them with a legendary reputation for the manner in which they spent their enormous wealth. One of them, Mantachov, was said to distil his kerosene in platinum stills, though by all reports most of their excesses were of a less technological nature.

More foreign capital entered Russian oil after the turn of the century. In 1906 the Deutsche Bank and the Diskontogesellschaft took an interest in the Nobel enterprise. Royal Dutch Shell entered the field in 1910 and two years later procured 80 per cent of the stock of the Rothschild Caspian and Black Sea Company. British capital took a prominent part in the founding in 1912 of the Russian General Oil Company by a group of Russian banks and producers such as Mantachov and Lianosov. In 1913 foreign investment in Russian oil came to about $130 million; of this $90 million was British and Dutch, $26 million French and the rest German and Belgian; Russian investment stood at something like $85 million. The industry was now very concentrated, with six enterprises controlling 65 per cent of the output. Direct investment in Europe was paralleled by similar investment elsewhere and accompanied by the creation of a complex network of distribution and selling agreements. British capital was predominant in Mexico which became in 1911 the world's third largest producer. British and German companies fought bitterly for concessions in the Middle East. In 1903 British, Dutch, German, Russian, Nobel, Rothschild and Mantachov oil interests combined to form a marketing company in the east, East Asiatic Petroleum, largely as protection against the activities of Standard Oil. In 1906 in Bremen the Europäische Petroleum Union was set up in which the main parties were the Deutsche Bank, Nobels and Rothschilds, but the battle with British, Dutch and American interests for the European market continued unabated and it is interesting that in 1913 Germany still imported three-fifths of her oil from the United States. Such international action was not surprising in view of the enormous investment that was undertaken, although it called forth much unfavourable comment at the time. It was less the principle of international cartel action which was new than the scale; the level of investment in exploration, production, transport and local marketing was such that only giant companies could compete and the activities of such giants inevitably attracted much attention. At the same time, the countries where oil was found sought to control the use of their resources in their own interests, without, before 1914, having much success.

COLONIAL EMPIRES

A special manifestation of overseas investment in the second half of the nineteenth century was the extension by the major European powers of their colonial empires in Africa and the Far East. A wide range of explanations has been put forward to explain the phenomenon. Some, Lenin for example, saw it in terms of the need to find new markets as outlets for capitalist production and new areas of investment to offset the falling rate of profit at home. This narrow definition of imperialism is quite inadequate to encompass the many complicated aspects of the economic relations of the European powers with their colonies, although it does not give a wholly false picture. Some writers have stressed the way in which financiers and merchants were able to call in the state to defend their interests or to enforce their rights as an essential feature of imperialism. There is no doubt that such intervention occurred from time to time but it does not explain the circumstances in which the powers decided to go further and to take over formal control. It is not clear that statesmen were particularly anxious to establish such control over overseas territories and it is not true that state power was inevitably at the service of economic interests unless a major state interest would be served at the same time. Moreover, imperialism in the widest sense was not confined to the colonies; it was seen there only in its simplest and least sophisticated aspects. The bulk of German, French and Belgian trade and investment took place outside the colonies. At the same time, in some colonial ventures economic forces were relatively unimportant. In Algeria and Tunisia, in particular, political considerations were the dominant factors leading to French control. In Morocco the economic interests of a number of the powers prevented the casual allocation of the country to one or the other and preserved economic competition there for a long time; modification of this policy in favour of France after 1900 was determined primarily by political and military considerations.

But economic forces were often extremely important, although the tendency of modern writers is to stress not the motives of those in the homeland but events in the overseas countries as leading to the establishment of formal control. Traders and financiers operated in overseas countries and did not initially seek control, often being wary of the cost, but eventually they came to put pressure on the home government when events in the peripheral regions began to interfere with their activities. It cannot be argued that Samoan copper was vital to German economic well-being or investment in the Congo crucial to Belgian bankers, but it meant ruin to local traders if their activities were obstructed by native peoples or by rival Europeans and so the pressure for protective control would mount. As an extreme case, King Leopold II acted in the Congo as a private individual and really believed his company could be profitable on that basis alone. He made territorial claims only when he found that other European powers were about to assert their own. He was also forced to this conclusion when it became obvious that the cost of the infrastructure necessary for developing the territory was beyond private means. But the positive developmental view of colonies that Leopold held was rarely sustained by statesmen at home; Joseph Chamberlain agitated powerfully for it in Britain but he had few supporters. It was the general expansion of commercial competition after 1880 that was the moving force behind the extension of the formal empires, not any positive imperialist designs in Berlin or London, although it may be argued that such positive designs were more in evidence in Paris, possibly because of a stronger mercantilist outlook or a greater sensitivity to questions of prestige. But in general the growing significance of trade may be summed up by the difference in metropolitan attitudes, to which the key before 1880 had been 'trade if possible but no territory', but thereafter was 'trade in any case and territory if necessary'; we must always remember, however, that economic interests were rarely the whole story.

French policy in the Far East exemplifies this. In South China she did not seek the political control which she had established in Indo-China partly because it was against her economic interests to do so and also because there was not the same pressure for action from missionary interests. The Lyons silk industry wanted railways there but they had no concern for political intervention; theirs was the true voice of metropolitan imperialism, pragmatic and devoid of jingoism. Parisian bankers were willing to provide money to develop trade with China but the south was the least promising area so they left it alone. It is significant, too, that neither Britain nor Germany nor France tried to consolidate their holdings beyond the Chinese Treaty Ports into extensive colonies, partly at least because the system of free ports had given them interests all over China which they wished to preserve. In addition, they had made big loans to a central Chinese government which it was now in their interests to preserve intact.

Economic factors therefore played a major part in drawing the powers to establish formal empires but they tended to be factors operating in the remote regions themselves, bringing the home government, albeit often reluctantly, to undertake wider responsibilities. When, as in China, these pressures did not arise, the powers left the country alone. But investment in the colonies was always a trivial part of total foreign investment and though the home country invariably dominated trade with its colonies such trade was always a minor part of the whole. In 1912 German colonial exports were 0·5 per cent of her total exports and the figure for Belgium was 0·7 per cent. The French share was considerably higher at 10·8 per cent, a half of this consisting of exports to Algeria. Some particular industries found these markets very important – three-quarters of French exports of cottons went to the colonies and the Congo was the second largest market for Belgian cottons – but, in the main, they tended to offer soft markets to the less enterprising industries. The import of food and raw materials from the colonies gave some opportunity for profit on the re-export of these goods as well as the establishment of processing industries in the home ports. But such imports were no cheaper than supplies from any other part of the world and though some links, such as in the Dutch cocoa industry for example, were preserved for historic or technological reasons, as the century wore on further developments were a function of real economic factors rather than political ties. So, although the Dutch oil industry had its origins in the wells and refineries of Java, within a decade it was inextricably tied to the oil business of Russia and Romania. One positive advantage, however, was the opportunity of stimulating home shipping and shipbuilding through controls and subsidies to the colonial trade, but in no way did the colonial markets provide a major stimulus to economic development.

The colonies were not profitable in any strict accounting sense although the reality of the economic exploitation should not be understated. They provided ripe pickings for individuals though governments often had to bear the cost. But fundamentally we should not pay too much attention to these territories as colonies because it is meaningless to see them as a separate aspect of the history of trade and investment and to try to distinguish them from the economic relations with those countries not under political control.

FLUCTUATIONS IN ACTIVITY

We have been concerned in this book for the most part with the timing and the nature of economic growth in different parts of Europe but whatever the rate of long-term expansion, in all countries there were divergencies from the trend. At intervals there were spectacular crises which brought financial losses and sharp reductions of activity in many parts of Europe and the rest of the world. Those of 1857, 1873 and 1907 were particularly severe and a vast literature grew up on the causes of these calamities. Contemporary writers saw the changes of activity in terms of waves of optimism and pessimism, so-called 'manias'. Certainly, if a boom was receiving support from irrationally optimistic expectations it would be vulnerable to any kind of jolt. Such a setback might be political; or it might be economic if, at the end of a major investment project such as a railway, it became clear that investment had exceeded any reasonable expectation of returns. Speculation played its part too. Speculators buy with a view to resale, knowing that prices are rising because others are doing the same thing; all are aware that the process is risky but each hopes to beat the market before the crash. Such speculation took place in several markets, on stock exchanges on commodity markets and in real estate above all. A boom in share prices, for example, would lower the cost of finance to business firms and encourage investment, so that there was a direct link between speculation and real factors in bringing about the boom.

There seems no doubt that many cyclical downturns were a consequence of a collapse of speculation or of some other form of optimism. The crisis was a common nineteenth-century phenomenon, most severe perhaps in the United States where well-founded fears that banks would not be able to meet their obligations would now and then lead to a rush for liquidity. There was a general feeling that crises were caused by maladjustments and imbalances, by overextension of credit, overproduction or excessive stocks, and the solution was to purge the economy, liquidating those bad business commitments. Explanations in terms of 'crisis' tell us a lot about the upper turning point in a cycle but they do not indicate whether the crisis in confidence was the prime cause or the consequence of a downturn in activity. In fact only in those cases where speculation was the main force in a boom was the former true, though the depression of expectations would obviously intensify any contraction already under way. More often the crisis came after the upper turning point in business activity had already passed, and the business failures which brought about the crisis may have been due to a contraction already under way or to the increased monetary stringency associated with the end of a boom which the crisis would then intensify.

There is much controversy about the nature of the root causes of fluctuations, though the details of the arguments do not concern us here. There are those who argue that the supply of money was the critical factor; others suggest that this supply only responded passively to the needs of trade, although this is hard to accept when central bankers in the nineteenth century frequently stated that their aim was to keep the supply of money stable unless gold was moving out, in which case they took the accepted action and put up interest rates. In general, fluctuations are caused by changes in the level of total demand and these changes in turn are brought about by fluctuations in investment rather than in consumption. Some of these may be due to faulty knowledge or poor forecasting on the part of businessmen, so that from time to time they overshoot the market. This may not be a prime causal factor but it seems to have been important in the explanation of variations in the levels of shipbuilding and, above all, house building, both of which tended to fluctuate in a manner independent of the main cycles. Nevertheless, this argument, assuming the same kind of entrepreneurial error every seven to ten years, is basically implausible as a general explanation.

A more important explanation is one which sees waves of high investment as arising from a cumulative sequence whereby investment is high relative to its long-run trend in one period and this encourages it to stay high in the next period, so bringing about a boom. Such a process may be explained in several ways; it may be due to the kind of bunching effect that Schumpeter described.[6] He argued that major innovations, by breaking down bottlenecks in particular industries, encourage further investment in those and associated industries. This is an argument that probably applies in some industries more than in others; it seems likely that the building of railways, ports and other public utilities had this effect. The completion of hydro-electric power stations in Norway after 1900 led quickly to investment in power-using and allied industries but the bunching might simply derive from pure economic factors. The accelerator principle indicates that as income rises, the effect on investment goods industries is most pronounced as they add to their regular replacement output enough new machinery to keep the total stock of capital in line with the level of income. However, when income ceases to grow the effect on the investment goods industries will be unduly heavy since they will immediately revert back simply to replacement demand. This rise and fall of induced investment in critical sectors such as steel and engineering would have powerful effects throughout the rest of the economy. A basic element in this cyclical process is that while investment stimulates further innovation during the upswing, it also tends to bring about exhaustion of investment opportunities, either generally or through completion of innovating programmes in major sectors, so leading to a cumulative decline. The top of the boom may also see bottlenecks developing in the supply of output from certain industries, or shortages of raw materials; this was particularly the case in 1872, and such a situation may well make further investment seem unprofitable or, alternatively, businessmen may come to distrust such rapid price rises and begin liquidating stocks in anticipation of a fall. At the bottom of the cycle investment will again be stimulated by inherent forces. It will be necessary to build up stocks of materials again, or demand may increase because of a rising population, because technical progress has made some equipment obsolete or because the slump may have been so sharp that for a time investment was not even covering normal replacement demand. To the extent that these crises weeded out weaker elements in the business community, one might think it no surprise that the reduction of capacity, and possibly of price competition that this entailed, would eventually encourage the stronger members to invest more confidently again.

Cycles varied considerably in length. The four-year cycle was common in the United States but not in Europe. In Britain the so-called 'trade cycle' of about ten years' duration was very marked although it has been argued that it simply emerged out of the interaction of longer but not coincident swings in home and foreign investment. These long swings of twenty years have been well authenticated for Britain and the United States but less clearly seen in Europe. In general, phases of rapid growth rested on investment booms beginning in conditions of excess capacity and unemployment. Waves of development of transport facilities and of towns and cities were associated with movements from the farms to urban areas both within Europe and to overseas countries. American swings were determined predominantly by internal factors; those in Britain inevitably were much influenced by external factors affecting exports and the outflow of capital. German swings seem to have been dominated by endogenous home factors and turning points in home activity often preceded those elsewhere. Fluctuations in Norway, Denmark and Sweden were obviously much influenced by swings in the level of British activity since they exported so heavily there, yet emigration was equally responsive to long swings in the United States. Swings in population growth are well established and in certain countries these were correlated with swings in building activity.

We do not know sufficient about these long swings. It is clear that where peaks of swings coincided, the boom and subsequent depression could be severe. In Germany the coincidence of heavy home investment and capital exports contributed much to the high peaks of 1873, 1890, 1906 and the subsequent slumps. But when a large home boom reached its peak in 1898 it was followed by only a moderate recession because the building cycle did not reach its peak until six years later. The long swings in emigration from Europe and the export of capital have been associated with swings in the level of activity in the United States but there is much doubt as to the validity of this explanation because emigration had its roots in European conditions and at least in Germany swings in capital exports and in net emigration moved inversely to each other. Swings in capital imports might be expected to be correlated with upswings in activity in the receiving country but this hardly tells us what starts the process. In Sweden, one of the European countries most dependent on imports of capital, it appears that such swings in activity were not initiated by capital import swings but rather reinforced by them.

Amid this complexity of fluctuations one thing is reasonably clear, even 'though its explanation is in doubt. The economies of Britain, France, Germany and the United States were very different from each other in the pattern of their overall swings in activity. A high trend in Britain and, to a lesser degree, in France offset deep depression in Germany and the United States in the 1870s. In the next decade high prosperity in Germany and the United States offset a lower trend in Britain and Sweden and deep stagnation in France. After 1890 the German economy seemed to move more in parallel with the British and, as a result of this and the growing importance of German demand, countries such as Sweden tended to conform more closely to the general European pattern. From the mid-nineties to the turn of the century all Europe enjoyed a tremendous boom. We can judge the power of this boom from figures of steel output as a percentage of the previous business cycle: comparing the 1890s with 1883–90 Germany was up 80 per cent, Sweden 90 per cent and France 30 per cent; for the next two cycles the figures show Germany up 60 per cent in each, Sweden 50 per cent and 20 per cent and France 20 per cent for 1901–6 but 60 per cent for 1907–13.

Much was once made of the even longer swings in prices which were thought to have occurred in the nineteenth century, falling shortly after Waterloo to the end of the 1840s, rising to 1873, falling to 1896 and then rising again to 1913. The evidence for regular movements of this kind is slight and, at least till 1873, the existence of any but short-run cyclical trends is very doubtful indeed. The decline of prices from the early seventies to the mid-nineties is inescapable, however. It has been explained in a variety of ways. We have already mentioned the monetary explanation, the failure of the stock of world gold to keep pace with the growth of world activity. Possibly the fall in prices derived also from the effects of new transport facilities, the opening of new areas of production for primary products and other cost reducing innovations. As regards demand too, the slowing down of the rate of growth of the British economy had a powerful effect on world prices. This period has been given the name of the 'Great Depression' but it is an extremely misleading title. A fall in price levels did not necessarily induce depression in other sectors of the European economy, apart from the pressure on grain growers that we have discussed. Growth was below trend in several European countries at some time during these years but it was also very much above it in others. A spurious unity is given to the period by the fact that all European countries enjoyed an enormous boom to 1872 and many were in depression immediately before the boom of the mid-nineties. But the existence of two very different end-periods does not give any unique quality to the whole period they embrace. After 1896 prices on the whole moved upwards again; gold discoveries and a change in the balance of supply and demand for many primary products were two major world trends helping to bring about this change.

Whatever the fundamental factors behind these long swings, over the shorter 'trade' cycle the major European countries moved much more closely in parallel with each other, even if the degree of such fluctuations varied according to the power of the long swings. It has been found that from 1879 to 1914 Britain, France and Germany were in the same phase of the trade cycle for 83 per cent of all the months examined. Whatever the reason for this, it greatly eased the operation of the gold standard. As incomes, prices and imports in one country rose, thereby tending to bring about an outflow of gold, rising incomes and imports in the others brought a rise of exports for the first country, thereby mitigating its balance of payments problem and preserving a degree of underlying stability. Even so, the crises, when they came, were severe and, because of the interaction of trade and international investment, tended to become worldwide in character. It has been suggested that the nineteenth century witnessed increased instability, both because of the international character of the crises and because of a relative shift of activity from agriculture to more cyclically unstable industries. Certainly, the random shocks to the economies of western Europe caused by harvest failures became less important as the international exchange of foodstuffs developed but they remained very important in the east because these were major subsistence economies as well as big exporters of foodstuffs and also because, for climatic reasons, the failures tended to be far more severe than in the west.

The first world crisis is generally regarded as occurring in 1857. The complex events of the late forties, the harvest failure in the west in 1846–7 and the political convulsions of 1848–9, certainly had a serious impact throughout Europe but the crisis of 1857 was more clearly of the type of later crises. Within weeks of the crisis in the United States in August, resulting from a run on railway securities, all the world's major trading cities were paralysed. Merchant houses in Britain connected with the American trade began to suspend payments. Hamburg merchants who formed the link between northern Europe, Britain and the United States clamoured for support, making heavy use of bills drawn on London and imposing an additional strain. The Bank of England put its rate up to 12 per cent in November. Many Hanse merchants went into liquidation. Suspension of the Bank Charter Act in Britain created panic on the Paris stock exchange. Every centre in northern and central Europe was affected. Disappointment over railway investment in the United States, speculation in Germany, psychological panic in France, reduction of the money supply due to a drain of gold from London, the influence of external events such as the loss of gold from Britain to meet contingencies raised by the disorders in India, all these phenomena were to recur in the subsequent period.

All the same, recovery was not long in coming about and in this respect the crisis of 1873, possibly the worst of the century, was very different. In the first place it followed a powerful boom of investment and at its peak the prices of iron and coal soared to famine levels. Not only was there another railway mania in the United States as well as a general boom in construction, accompanied by the heaviest import of capital experienced up to that time, but there was a great wave of what proved to be extravagant investment in many other parts of the world too. Irrational optimism certainly played its part on this occasion. On the other hand, technological progress, particularly in steel, gave a powerful impetus to the boom, reinforced by the sudden demands of the belligerents during the Franco-Prussian War. The end of the war saw an orgy of company flotation in Germany, encouraged by a rash of newly founded investment banks, a process found on a smaller scale in Austria and Italy too. Mortgage banks and building societies, in Berlin and Vienna in particular, also encouraged heavy speculation in real estate.

The first break came in Vienna in May 1873. In September the house of Jay Cooke, American railway promoters who were heavily involved with the Northern Pacific railroad, closed its doors and precipitated a collapse on the New York stock exchange. This panic and the levelling off of activity in the United States came at about the same time and for once the crisis seems to have been of major importance in checking the growth of the economy, although there is general agreement that investment opportunities particularly in railways were temporarily exhausted. There was no big setback in Britain but at the end of the year the speculative boom broke in Germany; those countries which had been most subject to speculation, the United States, Germany and Austria, suffered much more seriously from the subsequent depression than in 1857. In its origins this crisis was not unlike that of 1857, but the degree of over-speculation was altogether greater. Britain and the Scandinavian countries suffered only slight recessions as did France, where the development of the joint stock company had been kept within bounds. The crisis and depression after 1873 seemed spectacular to contemporaries but in general the fall of prices was much more severe than the decline of production and in many countries by 1878, when the contraction was supposedly ending, real output was substantially higher than in 1873.

Not every local crisis had international effects. The failure of the finance house of Overend Gurney in Britain in 1866 passed largely unnoticed elsewhere, although the crash in the same year in Spain had long-lasting results there. The crash of the Union Générale in France in 1881 ushered in a long period of stagnation there but little affected the rest of Europe. But another world depression followed a complex series of events in the early 1890s. The first signs of difficulty were experienced in France with the collapse of the Panama canal venture and of the attempt to corner the world's copper. Money markets began to tighten and then in 1890 came the Baring crisis when one of the most famous merchant banks in Britain was unable to meet its obligations on Argentinian loans. It was saved from complete collapse by the Bank of England which in turn made borrowings in France and Russia. Interest rates tightened again and this was in fact the commencement of a depression in Europe, but the parallelism of activity between Europe and the United States was now broken. The disastrous harvests in Europe of 1891–2 which forced Russia to forbid exports and France temporarily to suspend the grain duty, brought considerable prosperity in America. However, the crisis there came in 1893; the action of Congress over the coinage of silver led to a serious loss of gold and fears that the country might have to leave the gold standard, although the outflow had the effect of bringing cheaper money in Europe. The process of downturn was therefore one of a slow decline of investment in Europe from 1890 onwards and a more sudden collapse in the United States in 1893. There was no major crisis in Europe in 1893 but the course of events had a serious impact on investors in London and a sharp fall in foreign lending precipitated the collapse of the land boom in Australia.

This, therefore, was a gradual world decline, one where a series of shocks of varying origins seem to have had a cumulative effect. It was in sharp contrast to the events of 1907–8 when the worst banking crisis in American history to that time resulted in a huge demand for gold from Europe, although a decline in activity had already been occurring for some months. Unlike the events of 1873, the crisis of 1907 certainly did not precipitate the downturn. Already there had been small stock exchange crises in Egypt, Italy and Japan and early in October severe liquidation began in Amsterdam where there had been much speculation on worthless American securities. A series of important failures in Hamburg and Bremen followed. There was an unprecedented drain on gold from London, over £6 million in one week, but a bank rate of 7 per cent brought gold back from twenty-four countries including France, Germany and Sweden and the British money market weathered the storm. Profound though the subsequent world depression was, with a fall of 23 per cent in pig iron output from the world's six largest producers compared with only 8 per cent in 1873–4 and 6·5 per cent in 1890–2, recovery came very quickly, possibly owing to the fact that agricultural prices were well maintained, at least compared with the 1890s when wheat prices completely collapsed.

Each downturn therefore had its own characteristics. That of 1857 was much affected by speculative factors; the early 1870s saw a severe reaction following tremendous activity stimulated by extensive technical progress and by war and its aftermath. The sudden breakdown of stock exchanges followed widespread company flotation and unwise overseas investment in many centres but investment opportunities were also temporarily exhausted in Germany and the United States if not in Britain and Scandinavia. In the 1880s productive activity suffered no major setback but the boom broke in the early 1890s under severe financial strain following a gradual slowing down of industrial activity.

Here we have merely given a summary of the main events of each cycle but in general not enough research has been carried out in detail to give us anything like a full understanding of the mechanisms at work. The interaction of a variety of long and shorter cyclical trends was obviously crucial in determining the power of booms and the subsequent reactions but precisely how these operated we do not know. In general, however, the forces promoting economic expansion throughout the world, the rise of population and technological progress in particular, prevented depressions from becoming intolerably severe. It was possible to preserve a system of fixed exchange rates because disequilibrium was never very prolonged or profound. Another factor which helped in this regard was that countries adopted the gold standard one after another over a gradual period of time. Each inserted itself into the system with an exchange rate which was almost always that dictated by economic and not by political factors; by so doing the existing rates of exchange of other countries were not disrupted. The contrast with the inter-war years in this respect is very clear. It is true that the primary producing countries outside Europe bore much of the burden of fluctuations since they had no money markets to attract short-term capital to help them ride the storms, but in the last analysis it was the stability of the major consuming countries that meant more to the primary producers than anything else.

SUGGESTED READING

There are no books dealing specifically with the general theme of this chapter though a mass of literature exists on various aspects. For a general introduction see A. G. KENWOOD and A. L. LOUGHEED, *The Growth of the International Economy* (London, 1971). S. KUZNETS, *The Economic Growth of Nations* (Cambridge, 1971) and C. P. KINDLEBERGER, *Foreign Trade and the National Economy* (New Haven, 1962) provide some basic statistical material as well as challenging insight into the role of foreign trade in development. See also LEAGUE OF NATIONS, *Industrialization and Foreign Trade* (Geneva, 1945). A. MAIZELS, *Industrial Growth and World Trade* (Cambridge, 1963) gives elaborate details of the role of individual countries in world trade in particular categories of manufactured goods. P. L. YATES, *Forty Years of Foreign Trade* (London, 1957) looks at world trade generally, including primary products, but in much less detail. C. P. KINDLEBERGER, *The Terms of Trade* (Cambridge, 1956) remains unrivalled as an analysis of that problem. The effects of German competition are evaluated in R. J. HOFFMAN, *Great Britain and the German Trade Rivalry* (Philadelphia, 1933) and in one market area by D. C. M. PLATT, *Latin America and British Trade 1806–1914* (London, 1972). The patterns of world trade are examined in the League of Nations monograph, *The Network of World Trade* (Geneva, 1942) and in S. B. SAUL, *Studies in British Overseas Trade 1870–1914* (Liverpool, 1961). Much of interest on the pre-war pattern of European trade is to be found in I. SVENNILSON's great study for the United Nations, *Growth and Stagnation in the European Economy* (Geneva, 1954). Views on the working of the gold standard have much changed of recent times. An excellent recent book is M. DE CECCO, *Money and Empire. The International Gold Standard 1890–1914* (Oxford, 1974). This must be supplemented by the pamphlets of A. BLOOMFIELD, *Monetary Policy under the International Gold Standard* (New York, 1959); *Short-term Capital Movements under the pre-1914 Gold Standard* (Princeton, 1963); and *Patterns of Fluctuation in International Investment before 1914* (Princeton, 1968). See also P. LINDERT, *Key Currencies and Gold 1900–1913* (Princeton, 1973). A more general monograph is R. TRIFFIN, *The Evolution of the International Monetary System* (Princeton, 1964). Details of foreign investment patterns will be found in the literature suggested for particular countries. A general study is H. FEIS, *Europe, the World's Banker 1870–1914* (New Haven,

1930) and for an earlier period D. LANDES, *Bankers and Pashas* (London, 1958), is an enthralling study. The theoretical literature on fluctuations is vast but a fine introduction is R. C. O. MATTHEWS, *The Trade Cycle* (Cambridge, 1959). See also the bibliography in S. B. SAUL, *The Myth of the Great Depression* (London, 1969), which contains a number of references to studies relevant in the wider context of comparative fluctuations in Europe. The recent work by D. K. FIELDHOUSE, *Economics and Empire 1830–1914* (London, 1973), gives a fair account of different schools of thought as well as putting forward an interesting personal viewpoint.

NOTES

1 P. Bairoch, 'Europe's Foreign Trade in the Nineteenth Century', in *Journal of European Economic History*, vol. II, 1973, p. 25.
2 League of Nations, *Industrialisation and Foreign Trade* (Geneva, 1945), pp. 88–9.
3 J. R. Hanson, *The Nineteenth-Century Exports of the Less Developed Countries* (Ph.D. thesis, University of Pennsylvania, 1972), p. 77.
4 These figures apply only to foreign trade. London, Liverpool and New York had a much larger coasting traffic than the continental European ports.
5 Since in 1911–13 $300 million of Britain's exports to Europe consisted of re-exports of goods from non-European sources, the real European surplus with Britain was that much greater and Europe's deficit with the primary producers greater to the same extent.
6 J. B. Schumpeter, *Business Cycles: a Theoretical, Historical and Statistical Analysis of the Capitalist Process* (New York, 1939), especially chapter 4.

Chapter 10

The Nature of Economic Development in Europe

INCOMES

By the years immediately prior to the First World War the variations in per capita income levels among European countries were beginning to conform to a regular pattern. Over the pre-war decade France, Germany, Belgium, the Netherlands, Denmark, Norway and Sweden all averaged something like $150 per head. The British figure was about $250. There is no point in pretending to greater precision than this because the figures are approximations but the order of magnitude is just. Indications are that, in France and Germany at least, the actual level by 1914 had risen to something like $200. Then came a group with distinctly lower levels; Spain, Italy and Hungary had figures in the region of $90. Last came Russia and the Balkan countries with figures considerably lower still: about $60, for example, for Romania. The statistics are poor but not so inaccurate as to cast serious doubt upon the general validity of these groupings. There were striking variations within countries too, especially large countries with distinct social and geographical differences. In the Alpine provinces of Austria, including Lower Austria, per capita income in 1911–13 was at the western level of approximately $150; in Bohemia and Moravia a little lower at perhaps $125. In both areas the share of the labour force engaged in farming was much the same. But in Bukovina and Galicia with a much higher proportion in agriculture, income was more like $50. The gaps in real income were not as great as at first appears because in general the cost of living was higher the higher the level of income. The figures also tell us nothing about the standards of living of particular groups in the population because they do not show how

515

income was distributed, how great was the tax burden and where its incidence was felt most severely. In general, however, it is probably true to argue that the distribution was most inequitable in the more undeveloped countries where surpluses of labour existed. These surpluses were somewhat reduced by migration to other parts of Europe and to other continents but the growth of population was such as to make this outward movement merely a palliative to poverty and no real solution. To what extent the gaps in real income were widening is difficult to say. That they grew during the long period of rapid development in the west until 1880 is certain. For the two decades before 1914, however, industrialisation in countries such as Italy and Russia, if it brought about no narrowing of the gap, at least meant that it was no longer widening, although this was not true for countries like Spain and Romania and the backward regions of the Austro-Hungarian Empire. North-western Europe was clearly closing the gap with Britain, and some countries, Sweden in particular, had established rates of growth higher than those in most other parts of the world, although this had not given them real incomes significantly above those of their neighbours by 1914; the crucial factor was, of course, the starting point of growth.

The absence of information with regard to income distribution is particularly unfortunate because the historical evidence presented here and in our earlier work strongly suggests that in explaining European economic development much more emphasis should be given to the role of demand. The role of inventiveness and of the heroic entrepreneur, for example, much emphasised by others, was of little importance compared to the development of the market. Within countries the pattern of industrial activity and the size and range of output of individual industries was mostly determined by the nature of the different domestic markets. Over Europe as a whole there were wide differences in the amount of spendable income, in its pattern of distribution and in the pattern of consumption and these differences were the result of that complex set of historical and economic influences which we have tried to analyse. We do not wish to minimise the role of raw material discoveries nor of differences in factor endowment in determining the extent and timing of development in European economies. On the contrary, the historical evidence suggests that the haphazard national distribution of geological and geographical advantages caused by the arbitrary nature of most European frontiers was very important and that in certain circumstances development was retarded because the lack of a particular raw material or combination of resources could not be overcome. However, the evidence suggests that differences in demand were more important in determining the nature and the complex pattern of European economic development than differences in supply.

For a small country like Belgium, deprived successively of free access to the French and then the Dutch markets, the creation of new market opportunities was crucial to any further progress. In the east, in Russia and Romania for example, the extreme maldistribution of income prevented any rapid expansion of the mass consumer goods industries, restricted their technological achievement, and either inhibited development altogether or forced development to come through the expansion of capital goods industries as a result of government help and foreign investment. Even in countries with higher income levels technological innovation was often delayed through the absence of a market large enough to justify it. We argued in our earlier work that it was the delay in railway construction

Table 90   *Shares of different sectors in national products*[1]

	Agriculture	Manufactures	Services
Austria-Hungary (1911–13)	49	38	13
Hungary (1911–13)	57	26·5	16·5
Belgium (1910)	8·9	45·9	45·2
Denmark (1910)	30		70
France (1908–10)	35	37	28
Germany (1910–13)	23·4	44·6	32
Italy (1913)	37	26	39
Netherlands (1913)	16·3	26·7	57
Norway (1910)	24	26	50
Sweden (1906–10)	25	33	42
United Kingdom (1907)	7	43	50

[1] All figures are for gross national product except those for Germany and the United Kingdom which refer to net national product

Source: F. Fellner, 'Das Volkseinkommen Österreichs und Ungarns', in *Statistischen Monatschrift*, vol. 21, 1917; C. Carbonelle, 'Recherches sur l'évolution de la production en Belgique de 1900 à 1957', in *Cahiers économiques de Bruxelles*, vol. 1, 1959; W. G. Hoffmann, *Das Wachstum der deutschen Wirtschaft seit der Mitte des 19. Jahrhunderts* (Berlin, 1965); G. Fuà, *Formazione, distribuzione e impiego del reddito dal 1861; sintesi statistica*, Istituto nazionale per lo studio della congiuntura (Rome, 1972); L. Jörberg, *The Industrial Revolution in Scandinavia 1850–1914* (London, 1969); S. Kuznets, 'The Industrial Distribution of National Product and Labor Force', in *Economic Development and Cultural Change*, vol. V, 1957, appendix 2; P. Deane and W. A. Cole, *British Economic Growth, 1688–1959* (Cambridge, 1962).

rather than the relative cost of raw materials or the lack of dynamic entre-preneurship which meant that the puddling and coke smelting processes did not dominate iron technology in France until 1850[1] and this book presents similar examples from other industries. It is to be hoped that future research will apply itself to the key question of who bought what over this period.

The patterns of production that produced these incomes are shown in Table 90. The share of agriculture varied from 9 per cent in Belgium to 37

:nt in Italy, 49 per cent in Austria-Hungary and certainly higher levels
still in Russia and the Balkans.[2] It is striking that Denmark, the classic
example of a specialist food exporter, derived only 30 per cent of her
income from that sector, so rapid was the growth of industry and services
for home consumption. Belgium had the highest share from manufacturing, followed by Germany, Austria-Hungary, France and Sweden. At the
other extreme the shares of industry in Bulgaria and Romania have been
estimated at around 15 per cent. Labour productivity in agriculture was
everywhere below that in industry; Kuznets's calculations put that in
service occupations somewhat surprisingly above the average. Total
income therefore depended partly upon productivity in each sector and
also upon the distribution of labour between these sectors. It would appear
from their respective censuses of production that in 1914 industrial
productivity in Sweden was as high as it was in British industry. But Britain
had a much higher proportion of her labour force in industry than did
Sweden and consequently her overall per capita income was higher.
In general, countries were poor because productivity in all sectors was low
but also because they had the bulk of their workforces concentrated in the
sector of lowest productivity, agriculture.

FACTORS IN DEVELOPMENT

This book and its predecessor have essentially represented a search for the
factors behind these variations. We have deliberately used no single model
of analysis because it was obvious to us that the variety of experience was
so vast that to attempt to place the process of European development
within a single framework would involve an unacceptable distortion and
simplification of historical reality. Nevertheless, it is incumbent upon us to
assess these experiences according to particular types of analysis. One
approach to this would be to examine the input of factors of production.
It may be, for example, that differences in growth rates can be explained
by differences in the resources devoted to capital investment. The figures
are unreliable and hard to come by but it is known that whereas from 1900
to 1914 Britain devoted 14 per cent of its gross national product to capital
formation, over a slightly longer period Germany devoted 24 per cent. In
addition Britain used over 5 per cent for investment overseas whereas
nearly all German capital was employed at home. Although total national
income in Britain would benefit from this overseas investment, one would
expect domestic product in Germany to grow much faster as a result of the
higher level of home investment; this was in fact the case. But in Denmark,
where growth was as fast as in Germany, from 1890 to 1909 gross domestic

capital formation was only 13·5 per cent of gross domestic product and much the same was true of Sweden.

The evidence, therefore, does not suggest close correlations between rates of growth and levels of capital formation between countries. It is generally true, however, that within any one country increases in the proportion of resources devoted to capital formation tended to be correlated with increases in growth rates. This is particularly noticeable in developed countries like Germany and France but also in the less developed like Italy in the years after 1896. The variations between countries arose from the fact that some industries and technologies required more capital to achieve a given rise of output than did others, so that much depended on the peculiarities of the mixture of industries present as well as on the distribution of output between sectors. Also, different combinations of labour and capital could be used, depending upon the relative prices of capital and labour. There were also great differences in the uses that might be made of capital. A high level of investment in housing or in education did not produce conspicuous returns in the form of physical output, at least in the short run. The early stages of development required heavy investment in transport and in other public utilities but better transport reduced the investment required for holding stocks. Developments in agriculture frequently needed less capital for any rise of output than in industry. All these factors influenced the capital:output ratio. Big capital using innovations like hydro-electric plants increased the ratio but many other industrial innovations were capital saving and so brought it down. The effects of capital investment therefore depended on the structure of an economy at any time. Nevertheless, investment in any one country had to rise to achieve more rapid growth and we have seen in many countries how important was the efficiency of the capital market in channelling funds within sectors and from sector to sector within an economy as well as from country to country. In the more advanced countries the stock exchange played a vital role in bringing opportunities to the notice of the professional investor. At the other extreme there were the Raiffeisen-type banks originating in Germany but found in many peasant communities to enable them to make better communal use of their savings; for this Raiffeisen himself must surely be accounted one of the unsung heroes of nineteenth-century development.[3] The work of investment banks in international promotions of great complexity has also been stressed.

As for the second factor, labour, the growth of population in almost every country brought a striking rise in potential supply even allowing for those who emigrated. In Chapter 2 of our earlier book and in our studies of southern and eastern Europe we have shown how disastrously this could affect an agricultural society where there were no means of finding alternative occupations for these extra workers. But potentially it offered a great spur to development. Where the marginal productivity of a worker in agriculture was lower than in industry a move would bring a rise in total output; indeed, in the most overcrowded regions his productivity in agriculture was at best nil since output on the farm would not suffer if he went away. Because of the easy supply position labour would be prepared to work for very low wages in industry. This, in turn, would lead to high profits for industrialists, a high level of reinvestment and further increases in productivity. So runs the argument put forward by Lewis and others on economic development with unlimited supplies of labour.[4] Studies of European development since 1945 continue to stress the importance to industrial growth of ready supplies of cheap labour through shifts between sectors and from country to country and there is every reason to believe they were equally significant before 1914. The impact varied of course. In Belgium cheap labour came from the unwillingness of peasants to emigrate and from the facilities provided for cheap travel from the farm to the factory. In Germany cheap labour moved from the east to Berlin and the Ruhr, to be replaced on the farm by even cheaper migratory labour from Poland. Even in France, where it is sometimes argued that the effect was minimised by the great attractions of rural life, migration to the towns was substantial in periods when industry was expanding. This was by no means the whole story; there were shortages of particular types of labour and certain remote regions like the Ukraine might suffer from a shortage in an economy which otherwise had a surplus of labour, but it was none-theless the predominant situation, particularly in an era when trade unions were by and large ineffective.

The input of land was an important aspect of growth, for great efforts were made to increase its supply by drainage and other forms of reclamation. But in many areas of the east land was very sparsely populated and for much of the century the crisis pending because of the rise in population was forestalled by taking up this spare land. At the end of the century in a country like Serbia the problem of rural poverty was less serious than the low level of technology would suggest because the pressure on land supplies was still not intolerable and emigration was non-existent. Much depended on the technology employed when the new land was taken up. In the eighteenth century the expansion to the south in Russia saw merely a shifting of existing patterns of cultivation and this was true also in the next century of the extension of arable farming in Wallachia. But the exploitation of the southern steppe lands of Russia and the great Hungarian plain in the nineteenth century was brought about by using western tech-nology with consequently much higher increases in productivity. The exploitation of indigenous mineral resources was a major element of industrialisation and in this regard parts of Europe were well favoured. New regions were still being opened up and in the last decades before 1914, for example, two huge areas of iron ore deposits in Sweden and southern Russia were being fully exploited for the first time. But already such was the pace of growth and such the demands of technology that a main feature of the European economy during that period was the development of sources of supply from outside Europe in the same way as supplies for the major textile industries had been widened earlier in the century. In particular, as the internal combustion engine transformed demand for oil after 1900, it became apparent that western Europe would become almost wholly dependent on supplies from outside the area. For basic foodstuffs, however, continental Europe continued to rely mainly upon its own resources.

This leaves us with the factor generally classed as technological progress, which embraces such elements as economies of scale, improvements in the quality of labour through education, as well as advances in technological knowledge itself. It also includes transfers of labour from low-productivity occupations, such as farming and self-employed trades, to those with higher productivity, which we know to be a basic feature of nineteenth-century experience. Some highly speculative calculations which appear to give technological progress by this wide definition a major explanatory role in development have led some historians to attach great importance to one component in particular, education. It is doubtful, however, if this argument can be completely sustained. We have good reason to believe that education made an important contribution in Germany and Denmark, in the first instance by encouraging technological innovation and in the second by producing a peasantry educated enough to appreciate the advantages of co-operation. But we must also remember that Britain began the industrialisation process on the basis of an extremely modest educational system and that despite being the only western country without compulsory education before 1914 Belgium was no laggard in the growth race either. It may be that modern technology makes great calls upon education and that this kind of technology was growing in importance by 1900 but it is by no means clear that the need was so great over the century as a whole.

All these elements were interrelated, none more so than investment and technological progress. Most new technologies in the nineteenth century required more capital per unit of output than now although since that time the bias towards capital saving innovation has become very pronounced. The relative prices of capital and labour influenced the nature of technological change and its rate of adoption in different countries. An educated workforce was more important for high technology processes than for mass production of textiles or simple machinery; machines were substitutes for a lack of skilled labour. Which were the more crucial variables for growth varied from circumstance to circumstance. There were, too, buffers in the process; experience suggests, for example, that if industrialisation was proceeding in circumstances of capital shortage, it was possible to economise on social investment and allow overcrowding and slum conditions in the expanding towns to worsen. In the long run, as Russian experience showed, this could have devastating political consequences. It is significant that many employers in Germany and Austria in particular made considerable efforts to ameliorate such conditions in the vicinity of their works in the hope of staving off worker discontent and reducing labour turnover.

MODELS OF DEVELOPMENT

The major difficulty confronting economic historians has been to establish a regular sequence by which these mechanisms of development can be systematised. Given the complexity of historical experience it is not surprising that such models as have been produced fail to accord with many aspects of what actually happened in Europe. Nevertheless, the best are thought-provoking and undoubtedly heighten our understanding of what happened, at least in a general way. The most famous is certainly that of Marx which related the structure of human society to the development of different modes of production. Reduced to a very simplified form it saw the fundamental pattern of human history as the movement of society from a pre-capitalist agrarian servile state to a 'capitalist' system based on industrial rather than agricultural production, to a crisis of capitalism arising from a falling rate of profit, and the eventual overthrow of capitalism and the emergence of a classless society no longer dependent on the economic exploitation of one social group by another.

The development of what Marx calls 'capitalist production' has as its central aspect the introduction of a new mode of production whose characteristic is a high level of capital investment in technological innovation. The impediments to the full emancipation of the human being which had existed in pre-capitalist societies were replaced, in his view, by a new servitude to the process of production by machines based on the accumulation of capital and its reproduction. Capitalist production, however, was but a stage on the road to full emancipation in a classless society and it was this view of historical change which gave to Marx's economics a dynamic quality setting out a path of economic and historical development for all societies.

Marx's concept of the process of the original accumulation of capital by which the reproduction and reinvestment of the 'surplus value' from the production process ultimately leads to the stage of 'capitalist production' did not exclude the development of capitalist relationships in agriculture comparable to those in industry. Nevertheless the transition to capitalist production and the process of economic development appears in his work as fundamentally a process in which industrial capital is reproduced and as the reinvestment in industrial production of a fraction of the 'surplus value' which emerges from a previous act of production. To that extent Marx was explaining the evolution of capitalist production in terms of the most visibly impressive economic changes in the world around him. The increase in human productivity which technological innovation in manufacturing in the nineteenth century brought about was the central problem to be comprehended and explained for nineteenth-century man. But Marx's work, by the scope and force of its explanations, strengthened the tendency, already emerging before he wrote, to narrow the interpretation of the process of economic development to a search for the origins and consequences of changes in industrial production. What emerges as most representative of the stage of capitalist production in his work is a secular improvement in technology and, in theory, a progressively increasing rate of accumulation of capital, although in practice the latter was a much more complicated question.

The 'primitive' accumulation of capital in the pre-capitalist stage of the economy has, of course, to take place in an agricultural framework. But to lump together for mental convenience the varied and complex agrarian European society of the eighteenth century under one 'pre-capitalist' label is unsatisfactory. And although Marx, when discussing 'primitive' accumulation, does partly avoid this weakness the tendency of his whole work is, nevertheless, to establish a clear break between 'pre-capitalist' and 'capitalist' society. The change in the productive basis of society from agriculture to industry was certainly so central an event in human history and had implications so far-reaching as to merit its place in Marx's analysis. The term 'industrial revolution' ultimately is derived from and justified by the delineation by Marx of the tremendous social consequences of this change. It would be an extremely narrow view of the process of industrialisation which denied that it was finally dependent on drastic adjustments in the life of the individual and sweeping changes in the distribution of political power in society.

We have frequently used the term 'industrial revolution' to describe this change in the mode of production because the implications of industrialisation where it took place rapidly did amount to a revolution in human existence. But the historical evidence suggests that the term is of only limited value in analysing the process of economic development throughout Europe because, firstly, it describes only a part of that process and, secondly, it is more applicable to some societies than others. The growth of capital investment and technological innovation was not necessarily expressed in rapid industrialisation and there was no clear divide between pre-capitalist agrarian society and capitalist industrial society. The development of certain countries, Germany and Italy for example, did embody a rapid and relatively uninterrupted transformation of which the principal aspect could fairly be described as the sudden investment of large amounts of capital in new productive processes. Here change was so rapid as to seem even in retrospect to be an almost complete break with a previous stage of society. But this was by no means a universal pattern. Marx's theory does leave room for a variety of development patterns, but does not appear to have envisaged them.

As for the subsequent stages of Marx's model, in the period before 1914, only in Russia were there any real indications of a 'crisis' of capitalism and of its overthrow, and subsequent experience has done nothing to change the impression that Marx's model has had particular and not general application. Indeed, before 1914 the most serious crises arose in the less developed countries, and from the failure of development and incomes to proceed as quickly and successfully as in the more advanced countries.

Nevertheless, the concept that a falling rate of profit would eventually bring the end of capitalist production is worth pursuing a little further since it has wider implications. Lenin's somewhat modified argument, which conformed more to apparent historical fact, was that the rate of profit would have fallen under capitalism but for the emergence of cartels keeping profits artificially high by restricting competition, but for foreign investment, and but for growing control over large areas of the undeveloped world by the developed economies. In the previous chapter we suggested that this was too simplified an approach to imperialism but that it was not without some general validity. It cannot be shown that foreign investment was ever more than a minor part of total European investment and therefore it was not a major factor in determining the course of development in advanced economies. But control of foreign raw material supplies and markets through investment, tariff pressures and cartels was in some cases a substitute for technological progress and the easiest response to a squeeze on profits. This does not mean that colonies were vital to save capitalism but that they could be a cheap substitute for investment at home. The greater proportion of German investment that was made at home may have resulted from the fact that no other choice was ever seriously considered by German business and resulted in a more intensive level of technological progress than might otherwise have been the case. German experience, however, does not entirely bear out the idea that cartels were a defensive substitute for technological progress and a basic weakness of Lenin's approach was his inability to appreciate the extent to which such progress, fostered by German cartels, was able to maintain the rate of profit and at the same time markedly raise the level of income for the mass of the labour force. Technological progress did this even at times of falling supply of surplus labour or a shortage of materials and without need for recourse to overseas exploitation; the introduction of the Gilchrist–Thomas process is a perfect example of this. In the face of such trends the alternative of colonialism, though undeniably present, was a minor force.

An attempt to set up a more specific stage model which explicitly seeks to counter that of Marx and Lenin, is that of W. W. Rostow in his *Stages of Economic Growth*.[5] He envisages economies moving through a series of six stages of which only the first three need detain us here. The model begins with the traditional society, one where investment covers depreciation and such rises in population as occur but does not provide any increase in average income levels. This is followed by a transitional stage where the pre-conditions for faster growth are established. Investment will be somewhat higher and there may be a small rise in incomes but above all it is a period of adaptation of institutions to the requirements of greater investment and economic change generally and of experimentation with basic technologies. Then comes the take-off itself where the level of investment rises sharply and suddenly, the rate of growth accelerates and though this may in later stages slacken, the higher income levels are maintained and improved.

The theory has been sharply criticised in detail, most of all because Rostow has defined his stages so generally that it is difficult to determine when, and above all why, a country moved from one to the next. It must be clear from this and our previous work that the division between the first two stages creates great problems because of the difficulty of defining a traditional society, and certainly for many countries the idea of a stage of transition before rapid growth sets in can only be meaningful if it is allowed to cover a very long period of time. As regards the concept of a traditional society, the first chapter of our previous work illustrated the great variety of relationships that existed in rural society and the varying degrees of sophistication of both agricultural and industrial technologies and structures found in eighteenth-century Europe.[6] In this respect Rostow's model has the same initial weakness as that of Marx. France in 1700 had a more complex economic structure than most other countries yet it would hardly be reasonable to say that she was poised for the take-off that Rostow describes. The pre-conditions for more rapid growth in the form of adjustment of the economic and social relationships in rural society, for example, had simply not taken place and did not come until the Revolution. Nonetheless, it does not make much sense to think of France as a traditional society and to put Russia, labouring under the iron bonds of serfdom, into the same category; the steps that each would have to make to reach the next stage were infinitely different. Yet French growth in the eighteenth century itself, distinct though it was, consisted for most of the century of expansion along old lines and did not involve that preparation for modernisation that Rostow envisaged. Even less developed societies such as Spain had centres of modern industry in the eighteenth century but for some reason this transitional state led to no further advance. In Russia too Peter the Great forced through significant changes in economic activity even within the framework of serfdom. But there were always limits to what could be achieved by personal magnetism and exploitation; sustained development called for a far greater transformation of the productive structure and so for a reform of society itself. If we are prepared to allow for more elements of growth, as opposed to development, within the limits of a traditional society than Rostow seems to do, then the concept becomes somewhat more meaningful.

This still leaves us to define the actual pre-conditions for development, a problem made the more difficult by the fact that development was often stimulated by the absence of such pre-conditions. The lack of skilled labour, of managerial traditions, of risk capital forced Russia to look for alternatives in the form of foreign investment and capital-intensive technologies. Nevertheless, if by pre-conditions we stress the need, however vaguely conceived, for rural society to abandon its static traditional state and to be put in a condition of change, then Rostow's second stage has real meaning in the context of our own studies. We shall return to this later.

Most interest has been focused upon Rostow's 'take-off' stage with its concept of a sudden rise in the investment ratio and a dramatic increase in per capita output. Some countries can be fitted to such a pattern without doubt: Belgium after 1835 and Germany after 1850 are excellent examples. There is every reason to believe that at these times the investment ratios did rise sharply in those countries; the same was also true of Italy after 1890. In other countries, however, the pattern was one of more gradual development with no such short period of transformation. France is the obvious example for although there was a boom during the 1850s it was more a consummation of previous economic changes than a sudden take-off into another stage of society. The Netherlands, Denmark and Sweden all enjoyed the same relatively steady development of their economies after 1850 and though historians in each have tried to identify a precise period for their own country's industrial revolution, and the years after 1900 offer the only tenable period in all three, the event hardly transformed the whole economy in the way Rostow envisaged. They were already too developed.

It is indeed the basic tenet of our work that processes of development would vary more widely in accordance with national historical backgrounds than with anything else. Countries with different structures, in different geographical circumstances, with different timing of change, were bound to have different patterns of development. It is for this reason above all that we have paid scant regard to the thesis of the so-called *globalité*, or unity, of European development. The fact that natural resources such as coalfields and forests spanned political frontiers gave an international dimension to the growth experience, but the differences were far more important than the similarities. Indeed, it might well be argued that eighteenth-century society was more pan-European than it was in the nineteenth. There were, after all, basic similarities in the life and role of the nobility and the peasant over much of the continent. Industrialisation at varying rates and in a variety of circumstances created more differentiation between countries than had existed before. The present movement towards unity, admirable though it be in most respects, must not be allowed to give the impression that in the nineteenth century there was anything but a minor degree of unity in European economic experience. It is not surprising that some countries should develop quickly on the basis of some striking event such as the building of railways in Belgium or by a complicated coincidence of such events as in Italy. Equally it is not surprising that countries with a longer history of development or a greater emphasis on non-industrial sectors such as Denmark and the Netherlands should advance in a less dramatic fashion. Those that set out on the path of more rapid growth earliest in general went more slowly than those that followed; they were under less competitive pressure, had to create their own technologies and institutions and the less developed world around them offered less buoyant markets. Those coming later borrowed from this experience, jumped whole stages in developmental sequences and at times fashioned new institutions to allow them to do so. Nevertheless, as Rostow rightly pointed out, some events such as the coming of railways and the new steelmaking processes did have dramatic consequences for most parts of western and central Europe. Sometimes, as in Spain, the gains were small and the cost in the form of unbalanced budgets and balance of payments deficits serious, but this was not the usual case. Whether or not there was a take-off in any one country after the manner specified by Rostow, that whole area of Europe was never the same again. Some gained more than others but the effects spread and the overall consequences were striking. In that special sense there was a unity to European development, occurring within a limited area for a limited period of time.

Gerschenkron tried to take account of the variety of historical backgrounds by arguing that the more backward a country was and the greater the institutional and technological gaps, the more determined had to be the effort to modernise and so the greater the break with the existing modes of society.[7] In other words, the more backward a country the less autonomous its development and the greater the discontinuity with the past if progress was to be made. The role of government in fostering investment had to be more positive; investment banks, sometimes with the backing of the state, were required to bring about capital accumulation because the more traditional methods of raising money were either deficient or inadequate for the needs of modern industries. The lack of internal demand arising from a general backwardness in agriculture forced a greater emphasis on government support and on the production of capital as opposed to consumer goods. This emphasis and the need to economise in skilled labour led to the use of large-scale highly capitalised plants which had to be financed by new types of investment institutions.

Britain, with its slow continuous development and negligible government assistance, and Russia with its intense state-aided development from the 1880s onwards form the two extremes in this model. In the context of this model Gerschenkron points also to similarities in Russian and Italian experience but it is here that one can begin to discern weaknesses in the approach. Envisaging Italy as a backward country before 1890, and following the course predicted by his model, Gerschenkron emphasises the role of the German banks in creating similar institutions to perform in Italy the role they had played in Germany. But what was important in Italy was in fact the wide variety of credit institutions available; a long banking tradition, going back unbroken to the seventeenth century at least, played its part alongside the more recently founded merchant banks. And in addition to the spur received from government finance and from foreign banks the adoption of Raiffeisen banking helped development on its way. The superficial resemblance between Russian and Italian experience conceals the reality of uniqueness in each case. There were, too, contrasts in the role of the state and of investment banks in western Europe – between, for example, Belgium where such banks were very important and the Netherlands where for historical reasons a more traditional practice was followed – which have nothing to do with stages of backwardness. The greater role of investment banks in Belgium and Germany compared with France reflected above all the type of industry that was dominant. Heavy industries by and large needed investment banks; consumer goods industries did not. Such banks were found in Sweden, Denmark and Austria too wherever the financing of heavy industry was called for. But although governments played an active role at certain times in countries such as Belgium and Germany, the most frantic efforts outside Russia were made in southern and eastern Europe where the development gap was most serious. Our study of economic development in south-eastern Europe showed that such government efforts could not have induced the necessary development over a long enough period of time without a more balanced stimulation of the agricultural sector than that posited by Gerschenkron's model. The model is excessively general and oversimplified, and can only form the initial stage in an analysis of historical reality. Looking at our own work, what further historical realities should we stress?

SUCCESS AND FAILURE IN DEVELOPMENT

In the first place the role of geography must not be forgotten. If a country was poorly endowed with raw materials its development was seriously hampered. It might, like Switzerland, create speciality industrial exports, but only relatively small populations could be sustained in that way; large regions devoid of useful materials, such as Italy and much of European Russia, were in difficulties for that reason alone. Once development was under way on the basis of local materials then imports could be used as these supplies ran out; this after all was the essence of what happened in Belgium. But the real problem was in starting. Then it must be remembered that the nature of agricultural improvement was such that it benefited most of all the countries of high rainfall and moderate temperatures of western and northern Europe. The new crops and rotations were not easily adopted in hot dry lands. But this was not the only consideration; where capital was available substantial progress could be made in such areas. Machinery was most effectively used for cereal cultivation on the large estates of the east; some of the most efficient farming in Europe was carried on in small areas of the Spanish coast where citrus crops were grown with heavy investment in irrigation. But in general capital was more difficult to come by in the dry lands for a variety of historical reasons, as we have seen in our study of Spain, the Balkans and Russia.

Sustained development everywhere depended upon the effective modification of the institutions of rural society and improvement in agricultural technology and output. This is not to say that any particular pattern of institutional arrangements had to be set up; provided that market opportunities were at hand, many different kinds could produce efficient farming if they produced the conditions for experimentation and investment. Social change could be gradual or brutal; it was necessary but it was not the primary conditioning factor. For that we must look to the country's physical resources and to the immediate economic resources of society. In favourable circumstances agriculture could be a major force for growth in itself. Denmark may seem to be the obvious example but we must remind ourselves that output and productivity in agriculture there did not begin to rise significantly until the 1890s.[8] More remarkable is the fact that calculations of the rate of growth of agricultural output in Hungary from 1867 to 1914 are set at a minimum of 1·8 per cent per annum while in Belgium, not normally renowned for her advances in this sector, total factor productivity in agriculture rose by 50 per cent between 1880 and 1910.[9]

It remains true however that in the more advanced countries agriculture was rarely for long a leading sector even where the stimulus came from external demand. Compared with industry, rises in productivity were limited and urban development quickly took the lead. Yet everywhere successful development required balanced development; there were leading sectors varying from place to place but development was sustained only where the agricultural sector responded sufficiently to provide an adequate level of internal demand for the developing sectors initially to build upon. It also could help the balance of payments at this often crucial period through food exports or limitation of imports. It also had to provide an effective degree of mobility on the part of many elements of rural society, to enable the fuller employment of capital resources, human resources and technology. This meant not only providing labour for other sectors but, more vitally for the laggards, taking the pressure off the land and avoiding the disastrous consequences of subdivision of already meagre holdings. Often this meant emigration too. The tragedy was that the poorest regions seemed unable to release enough of their people in that way. Maybe the peasants could not afford to move; maybe their extreme poverty brought them to a state of resignation that led them to believe that they had to be rescued by others rather than by their own efforts. In this sense the saving role of the Russian commune and the Italian *mafia* had much in common. The poorest agricultural regions thought differently because they were the poorest. The problem was to make the transition to the ways of the more wealthy, to the belief that a man could do more than trust to help from others; he could improve his lot by his own efforts.

In following this line of argument we are reverting to an older historical tradition which placed great weight upon the so-called 'agricultural revolution', and it is a weakness of the work of Rostow that he pays scant attention to this aspect of development. There is also a basic conflict here with the view of Gerschenkron who in general held that there were substitutes for almost every path of development. We have ourselves stressed the uniqueness of developmental experiences and of the variety of paths that rural society could take but we would maintain the overriding importance and necessity of basic change in rural life. Of course, in this context an agricultural revolution is not simply a matter of output and technique but the effective spread of a feeling that it was possible to raise output and incomes, that it was safe and desirable to do so and that obstacles to such aspirations would have to be removed. It was the weight of these historical forces and the need for fundamental modification in rural relationships that explained why it was that a Europe so anxious to copy the eighteenth-century industrial revolution in Britain was so much more hesitant about emulating its agricultural revolution.

By stressing the role of agricultural change we are not arguing that this was the main, or even the initial, cause of development. The interaction between industrial and agricultural change in western Europe was so close that to attempt to find the starting point is foolish. But the contrast between regions, sometimes within the same country, where this interaction was working and those where it was not could be stark and the consequences appalling. Bohemia and Upper and Lower Austria were regions with the employment structure typical of developed economies. Their populations were growing at only a moderate rate and farming was commercially based. The early development of textile industries there had formed the basis for subsequent industrial expansion and of a market for local foodstuffs. The estates were successful commercial enterprises, engaging in beet refining and brewing. Yet close to them lay Galicia and Bukovina who with their rapidly rising populations, primitive farming techniques, limited range of crops and intense subdivision of holdings were making scarcely any progress. There was no industry, little transport, widespread illiteracy, possibly the lowest standard of living in all Europe and, worst of all, no hope.

Reference to balanced growth does not mean that sectors advanced at the same pace, nor indeed that the agricultural sector might not eventually fall markedly behind the others but simply that at the stage of transition to modern development, the rural sector had to be an active one. For example, in a relatively highly developed country such as Norway, largely as a result of foreign trade influences in the eighteenth and early nineteenth centuries, there were active growth sectors such as fishing, timber, shipping and shipbuilding but their isolated development left the agricultural sector still in a very underdeveloped state and little boost was given to internal industrial expansion. After a burst of growth between 1850 and 1880 the shipping and shipbuilding industries entered a long period of stagnation and their demand for labour fell sharply. The growing population in the coastal areas had no alternative but to return to farms which could not possibly support them, or remain unemployed, or – and this was the option many chose – to emigrate.[10] The absence of balanced growth left the economy very vulnerable when any major sector faltered.

Exactly why countries failed to find an effective path of development is not clear. The evidence indicates that the simple pressure of industrial development was never of itself enough to force significant change upon agrarian society. De Witte's industrial drive after 1890 was in that sense doomed to failure as he himself finally realised when he turned his interest towards reform of the village system. The suggestion that resources for developmental investment arising from increased peasant productivity could, if necessary, be obtained through a fall in peasant incomes is not borne out by European experience. The drive by Stolypin to force a massive change in the traditional ways of Russian agriculture so soon after the de Witte experiment is eloquent testimony on this point. In the eighteenth century the differences between agricultural societies were not just those of technology and farm organisation but involved whole social systems, the relationship between lord and peasant, between both and the state, systems and distribution of land ownership, burdens of taxation, markets and credit. Where deficiencies in these relationships stood in the way of development, they could not be resolved in the short run by anything other than positive government action and naturally this varied in its nature and consequences with the force of economic and political pressures at the time.

The peasant emerged in a favourable economic situation in France, western Germany, Denmark and Austria as a result of quite different circumstances. Success in peasant agriculture in those countries came partly as a result of legislative action to establish land rights, partly as a function of weather conditions, urban markets and crops that suited the scale of peasant farming, and partly as a result of the efforts made to provide the farmer with sufficient credit either in the manner first established in Germany by Raiffeisen or by the more formal co-operatives set up in Denmark. The French peasant has been accused of conservatism but this was in the nature of most peasants: after all, the output of French agriculture was rising at 1·5 per cent per annum in the first part of the nineteenth century which was idyllic compared with less fortunate regions. To be raising output steadily and basking in the deeper pleasures of an old way of life was living indeed. Whether French peasant agriculture was well structured to meet the demands of the more rapid rates of change in industrial technology seen in the developed parts of Europe after 1870 is another matter but the basic pre-conditions for development had been satisfied.

Commercial grain cultivation developed successfully in East Prussia, southern Russia and on the Hungarian plain. This was a result of investment in machinery and in the land itself, of favourable price trends and effective access to the major markets. Even in Romania the existence of opportunities for the export of grain meant that the quality of ploughs, for instance, was clearly better than in the other Balkan lands. Elsewhere the problem of achieving agricultural development was not resolved at all. On the big estates of Spain and Romania the standard of cultivation remained low and the maldistribution of landholding severe. In Austrian Galicia and Spanish Galicia were very small farms, largely subsistence holdings, reduced by constant subdivision. In southern Italy the estates were farmed under a form of sharecropping that discouraged all initiative and resulted in low yields and general impoverishment of people and land.

Yet in its social context sharecropping was hard to displace; the cropper preferred it to wage labour and the owner was spared the bother of supervision. This lassitude was both cause and effect of the absence of technological progress.

Yet countries committed to development sought to resolve their problems outside the rural sector – not surprisingly for the problems there were daunting. However, the strategy did not succeed. Railways helped most the medium-sized farms near the centres of urban population that least required it; the same tended to result from improvements in the supply of credit. Neither in Spain nor the Balkans were the railways the force for development they were elsewhere and in fact they probably involved a significant misallocation of resources. On their own they could not bring about any basic change upon an unreformed agrarian society. The idea that new technologies quickly devastated old patterns of living is one of the myths of nineteenth-century history. They hastened change only if society was ready to be changed; otherwise it was a long, slow business. Short of capital, short of skills, lacking in knowledge, with poor markets, often in a disadvantageous position with regard to the supply of raw materials, now facing the competition of countries with half a century or more of experience of modern industrial development behind them, the chances of fostering industries were not high. Without that the prospects for a rural population usually growing faster than elsewhere were grim indeed. The belated but successful industrial revolution in Italy came in the northern regions, in an area with industrial traditions, able to benefit from the new technology of hydro-electric power, and where agriculture was less backward and markets more accessible. It nonetheless remains a surprising event and left Italy like Austria a land of stark contrasts.

In part, the problem was that politicians and intellectuals in the less developed economies, looking for solutions, took as their models interpretations of the history of countries which had developed earlier. The models were misconstrued because such rapid change was difficult for contemporaries fully to comprehend and explain. And, equally dangerous, such models were rarely good guides as to what was economically possible for those starting later. The way in which Russian intellectuals interpreted the rapid changes in western Europe in the first half of the nineteenth century prepared the ground for the favourable reception which was accorded by a wide variety of intellectual groups to *Das Kapital* when it was eventually translated into Russian, even though Marx himself knew very little about Russian conditions. Even more striking was the way in which liberal bourgeois groups all over the continent saw Britain and post-revolutionary France as models of economic and political organisation to be copied by their own societies if development was to be achieved. Either Britain, with its limited democracy, its constitutional safeguards and free trade, or France where the individual legal and constitutional 'rights' of the citizen remained unscathed whatever the government, was seen as the epitome of a society where arrangements were particularly conducive to modernisation and development. The uniqueness of national historical experience usually meant that following what was construed as the 'French' model of economic development, and in some cases the 'British' model, was wholly inappropriate elsewhere.

This is well seen in Spain and Italy where the initiation of the French model by the liberal movements failed to set free the same dynamic forces for development. Much of Spanish and Italian society, still primarily agrarian in its productive base, remained unaffected by these changes. Much more positive stimuli were needed there than the secularisation and rationalisation of political society and the modernisation of the land law. Because the motivation in choosing a past model as exemplar was industrialisation and because of the difficulty of coming to terms with the rapid development of technology, industrialisation was seen as the equivalent of development and the role agriculture had played in the initial stages of development and growth in the richer countries was seldom understood. In a country like Romania, for example, the agricultural sector was seen only as the background sector in industrialisation, although more than 80 per cent of the population depended on it for their incomes. The touchstone of policy was to make the agricultural sector serve the primary goal of producing the rapidest possible rate of growth of industrial output; the sector was never in the early stages thought of as having in itself the potential for growth of the other sectors. The model first chosen was again that of France, necessitating the removal of those historical accretions which prevented the full commercialisation of agriculture. As the inapplicability of this to Romanian conditions became apparent the model changed to that of Russia where the failure of the de Witte system had produced the same realisation. But copying Stolypin's agricultural reforms in Romania was no more appropriate; Romania had far less modern industry than Russia and had the Romanian government persisted in following their new model the choice for a large part of the rural population would have been starvation or emigration. The more instructive experience for Balkan countries might have been that of Hungary where agriculture made so sustained and important a contribution to growth, but at the time no one seems to have been aware of what had happened in Hungary. History was all-pervasive in influencing countries in the choices they made. Even had it been correctly interpreted it may have been of only marginal value, however inescapable its realities. But then, as now, its correct interpretation was hard to differentiate from natural hopes and prejudices, and its capacity to mislead and to encourage the formulation of oversimplified models was great.

THE PROCESS OF INDUSTRIALISATION

As for industrialisation itself, there is no doubt that the growth of rural industry in parts of Europe in the eighteenth century, with its concentration points of still largely domestic industry requiring only modest investment, was extremely important in creating reservoirs of skilled labour and of entrepreneurship from which further growth could, though not always did, take place. In some of these centres there seems to have been a link with agriculture in that interregional competition forced farmers in less fertile areas to develop these rural industries as a substitute form of activity. Here and there early industrialisation involved import substitution to some degree, for Belgian iron in western Germany, for Swedish iron in France, for British textiles in a number of European countries during the Napoleonic period, but such substitution was much more important for the late industrialisers, Russia and Italy. Rarely, even in small countries, was industrial growth based initially upon exports, Swiss textiles being an important exception, although such countries soon came to depend upon them. Much more important at the start were home markets, expanding for a variety of reasons. Populations were growing; incomes might be rising as a result of increased agricultural productivity or better terms of trade for food producers; markets could be expanded by elimination of artificial barriers or by transport improvements; finally the new technologies created their own demand through the reductions in costs and prices that they achieved. There were all manner of associated factors influencing the pace of growth – institutions for credit supply, commercial policies, the extent of technical education – quite apart from the broader questions of labour and capital that we have already discussed. There seems little evidence to support the view that differences in the quality of entrepreneurship had much effect upon rates of growth in the early developing countries of Europe. It is not clear that the social standing of business, for example, was higher in England or Germany than it was in France; the persistence of the family firm was a feature not of particular countries but of particular industries. In those parts of Europe where the social environment was different, where experience of commercial standards and practices was limited, where gaps in knowledge were more serious, then the difficulties were sufficient to require the state to take action to provide substitute forms of entrepreneurship. In western and central Europe this was not the case. Whether experience of industrialisation brought an ossification of managerial attitudes is another matter more relevant to an understanding of British industrial history than that of any part of the continent of Europe before 1914.

Once development of the 'western' kind was under way there was a decided tendency for it to become cumulative. Industrialisation itself involved the creation of new or of extended industrial centres. This in itself created a massive demand for building materials of all kinds and the cities began to develop a growth impetus of their own through the emergence of local industries to satisfy the needs of local incomes. Public utilities called for the development of transport machinery and electrical machinery industries as well as raising the demand for steel. The greater number of large towns in Germany than in France reflected a higher rate of industrial growth but also helped to perpetuate that difference. Urbanisation also stimulated more intensive farming in the vicinity; the raising of animals produced more manure and higher yields. Unhappily the growth of towns in the backward countries due to the flight from the land had no such cumulative effect simply because it was based on poverty and desperation; indeed, the whole self-reinforcing process of industrialisation through demand and technological linkages made the penalty of backwardness more severe in the second half of the century than in the first and the gap between successful and unsuccessful widened. The argument that relative resource endowment was an important matter in shaping the pattern of industrial development has already been applied to the emergence of rural industries in the eighteenth century in areas with a comparative disadvantage in farming. But unfortunately the process did not work like this for the poorest. Spain, for example, though agriculturally backward, did not have the means to develop her resources of iron ore and pyrites. Their exploitation came through foreign companies, creating enclaves of activity that hardly rubbed off on the rest of the economy at all.

Cumulative growth of industry came through technology itself. Textile producers begat machinery makers and they in turn machine tool makers. Stocks of skills, knowledge and research eventually consolidated these advantages. From being cumulative internally it developed into being cumulative externally both within and without Europe. Within Europe it came through the spread of industrialisation not only to Russia and Italy but to smaller economies like Sweden and the Netherlands too. To some degree this meant an intensification of competition but this was easily offset by the growth of incomes that ensued. Outside Europe the effects were felt through the growing search for raw materials.

Nothing is so remarkable in the economic history of Europe before the First World War as the great acceleration of growth that occurred nearly everywhere after the mid-1890s. In part it owed something to the effects on world money supplies of the new gold discoveries, in part to the better terms of trade for primary producers so that the gains from the continued improvements in industrial technology were more widely spread. External factors such as the growth of demand outside Europe together with the pressure to imitate the successful industrialisation of others, pressure of a military as well as an economic nature, combined finally to override those internal factors which were hindering development in all but the most backward parts of Europe. The breakthrough came in Hungary as well as in Russia and Italy; the smaller countries like Denmark and the Netherlands industrialised more rapidly; industry in France expanded again as rapidly as in the mid-century; in Sweden as well as in Germany net emigration ceased. Certain innovations – most of all the Gilchrist–Thomas process and the developing use of electric power – played their part too, and all were driven on by the expansionary force of the arms race.

However, the pattern of industrialisation was always uneven. Inequalities of growth rates between countries were matched by those between regions of the same country. It may be that the gains won in the form of scale economies through industrial concentration in the bigger countries were paid for partly by sacrificing the less favoured regions. It is possible that had the number of smaller independent countries been greater, there would have been greater efforts to spread growth more evenly. As it was, in Spain, Italy and Hungary governments tended to capitalise on what successes they had and pay no attention to the failures. The problems of southern Italy may be better known than most but they were in no way unique; the regional problem of our own time is different in that it also involves the running down of formerly successful industrial areas but in its essence it is not a new problem and the difficulty of finding a solution, sometimes for areas that appear to have no comparative advantage in anything, is not new either.

The historical evidence presented here and in our earlier work suggests that there has been much too close an identification in European history between industrialisation, modernisation and economic development. At the heart of this misconception lies the idea of the 'industrial revolution', that the fundamental process of economic and social change in modern history is related to a cataclysmic change in the mode of industrial production. The greatness of Marx comes from the way in which he was able to elaborate the profound consequences of this change and in so doing develop a powerful analytical tool for explaining the process of development on a wide but unified historical, political and economic front. But subsequent model builders have been unable to escape entirely from this view of economic development even when they have been mainly concerned to refute Marx's conclusions. We would not claim that the lessons of history are any more appropriate to underdeveloped economies now than the lessons of French economic development in the nineteenth century were to Romania; they are no doubt equally misleading. But we would argue that the historical evidence on the economic development of continental Europe shows that successful economic development was in the initial stages, sometimes for longer, almost always balanced development.

So great was the impact of industrialisation and technology on nineteenth-century thought that it tended to obliterate this vital underlying truth and to capture the attention of statesmen and scholars to an excessive degree. Modernising statesmen in the underdeveloped countries, Cavour in Italy, de Witte in Russia and Xenopol in Romania, all unquestioningly accepted the identification of industrialisation with modernisation and economic development. Each of these cases showed that if little of value for development was to be learned from a correct interpretation of history only disaster resulted from its positive misinterpretation.

It was certainly important in the first stages of development that the process of modernisation should take place as much in the agricultural as in the industrial sector, indeed sometimes more important. By balanced development, however, we do not mean that the sectors of the economy advanced at similar speeds. There are isolated examples where the agricultural sector played a leading part in development for a surprisingly long time, as in Hungary or Sweden. But the industrial sector, once development was under way, in most cases soon developed the capacity to generate modernisation and development by itself. Nevertheless in the vital initial stages the real forces of modernisation and development could in some cases be far removed from the technological innovations which were fundamental to the industrial revolution. The role of the service sector in nineteenth-century economies remains relatively unexplored and it may be that in this context in certain economies, such as the Netherlands, it would be worth exploring. To formulate better models of the economic development of continental Europe much more research is now necessary on levels of demand and patterns of income distribution and consumption over the whole continent. We hope that our work has gone some way to change a view of economic history which, although often only vaguely expressed, is potent; that it leaves for the future what is still of value in the older models and interpretations, and that the weight of historical evidence which it presents will form the first necessary stage in a more accurate and historically sophisticated model of European economic development.

Our work has been concerned with development. A country might enjoy simply economic growth for a while but there were limits to what could be achieved along traditional lines. The essence of nineteenth-century economic history in Europe was change in all its aspects. But people do not necessarily like change and this brings us back to our introductory remarks: we have not tried to say anything about welfare. We cannot say if people enjoyed themselves more, if Europe was a 'better' place. For one obvious and terrible reason it was not, since the technology and wealth created were now to be employed in the appalling butchery of the First World War, surpassing anything previously experienced in the amount of human misery it created. On the other hand it is hard not to feel that millions enjoyed being raised from the humiliation and suffering of a subsistence livelihood, and who is to say that the factory was worse than the unending toil of the land? For some the rewards certainly approached those enjoyed by only the very privileged few of earlier centuries. But the new way of life allowed more people to survive, and it is of course impossible to estimate whether the level of happiness of those at the line of extreme poverty improved or not. Society used very little of its wealth to help the sufferers; emigration was the lot of many and for each person who saw it as an opportunity there was another to whom it was an intense tragedy. As for the quality of life we are reminded of the story told by that illustrious scholar R. H. Tawney. He approached a French peasant, haranguing him with ideas of abandoning strip cultivation, growing new crops, using new techniques and so forth; an hour's conversation left him convinced that the traditional mode of peasant farming was the only one consistent with the dignity of man.

NOTES

1 A. S. Milward and S. B. Saul, *The Economic Development of Continental Europe 1780–1870* (London, 1973), p. 198–9.
2 The high figures for Austria-Hungary may reflect in part the very low level of service activity; the estimate is, however, an early one and the service sector is likely to be understated.
3 See above, p. 58.
4 W. A. Lewis, 'Economic Development with Unlimited Supplies of Labour', in *Manchester School of Economic and Social Studies*, vol. 22, 1954.
5 W. W. Rostow, *Stages of Economic Growth* (Cambridge, 1960).
6 A. S. Milward and S. B. Saul, op. cit., ch. 1, pp. 26ff.
7 A. Gerschenkron, *Economic Backwardness in Historical Perspective* (Cambridge, Mass., 1962), ch. 1.
8 A. S. Milward and S. B. Saul, op. cit., pp. 510–11.
9 See above, pp. 292 and 152.
10 A. S. Milward and S. B. Saul, op. cit., pp. 522–7.

Appendix

Table 91 *Population of the major European cities (000s)*

City	Year	Population	City	Year	Population
Paris	(1911)	2,888	Kiev	(1909)	469
Berlin	(1910)	2,071	Turin	(1911)	428
Vienna	(1910)	2,031	Rotterdam	(1909)	418
St Petersburg			Frankfurt am Main	(1910)	415
(Leningrad)	(1910)	1,908	Lodz	(1909)	394
Moscow	(1909)	1,481	Düsseldorf	(1910)	359
Hamburg	(1910)	931	Lisbon	(1900)	356
Budapest	(1910)	880	Stockholm	(1912)	347
Warsaw	(1909)	781	Palermo	(1911)	342
Naples	(1911)	723	Nuremberg	(1910)	333
Milan	(1911)	599	Riga	(1908)	318
Madrid	(1910)	598	Charlottenberg	(1910)	306
Munich	(1910)	596	Antwerp	(1910)	302
Leipzig	(1910)	590	Hanover	(1910)	302
Barcelona	(1910)	587	Bucharest	(1911)	295
Amsterdam	(1909)	568	Essen	(1910)	295
Copenhagen			Chemnitz		
(inc. Fredericksburg)	(1912)	559	(Karl Marx Stadt)	(1910)	288
Marseilles	(1911)	551	Stuttgart	(1910)	286
Dresden	(1910)	548	Magdeburg	(1910)	280
Rome	(1911)	539	Genoa	(1911)	272
Lyons	(1911)	524	The Hague	(1909)	270
Cologne	(1910)	517	Bordeaux	(1911)	262
Breslau (Wroclaw)	(1910)	512	Oslo	(1912)	247
Odessa	(1908)	479	Bremen	(1910)	247

Source: National statistical handbooks.

Table 92   *Value of foreign trade per capita in European countries in gold francs, 1911*

	Imports	Exports
Netherlands	1185·4	971·6
Belgium	607·4	482·2
Switzerland	480·1	334·9
United Kingdom	416·4	341·0[1]
Denmark	313·8	270·5
Norway	272·3	173·0
France	205·8	155·1
Germany	186·4	156·1
Sweden	173·5	167·0
Italy	97·7	63·2
Romania	78·2	95·6
Greece	66·1	53·6
Austria-Hungary	67·8	50·6
Spain	49·9	49·0
Bulgaria	45·9	42·6
Serbia	39·5	40·2
Russia	18·9	26·0

[1] Direct exports and re-exports

Source: National trade statistics.

Country	Total length of track (km)	Territory per km of track (sq. km)	Track per 10,000 inhabitants (km)[1]	Freight per inhabitant (000 tons)	Number of passenger journeys per inhabitant
Austria-Hungary	44,820	13·54	9·06	2·96	5·60
Belgium	4,679	6·30	6·30	10·89	26·80
Bulgaria	1,934	49·98	4·46	0·53	0·81
Denmark	3,691	10·37	13·39	2·66	10·95
France	40,635	13·20	10·37	3·09	12·60
Germany	61,978	8·72	9·55	9·50	25·30
Greece	1,573	41·74	5·98	0·28	3·46
Italy	18,394	15·69	5·31	1·29	3·80
Netherlands	3,190	10·34	5·45	2·63	7·66
Norway	3,085	105·44	12·90	2·42	5·98
Portugal[2]	2,868	31·16	4·81	0·81[3]	2·50[3]
Romania	3,479	37·66	3·43	1·30	1·58
Russia[4]	68,027	324·17	4·23	1·47	1·32
Finland	3,421	109·21	11·62	1·52	5·10
Serbia	949	51·21	3·26	0·26[5]	0·34[5]
Spain	14,783	34·14	7·42	1·46	2·52
Sweden	13,942	32·32	25·25	6·89	10·92
Switzerland	4,534	9·13	12·08	4·84	31·00
United Kingdom	32,223	9·70	7·13	11·62	28·60

[1] The population is taken in each case in 1911 or 1910 except for Greece (1907), Netherlands (1909) and Romania (1912)
[2] The population figures but not the figures for area of Portugal include Madeira and the Azores, where there were no railways
[3] 1910   [4] Excluding Finland   [5] 1906

Source: G. Cioriceanu, *La Roumanie économique et ses rapports avec l'étranger de 1860 à 1915* (Paris, 1928); F. Hertz, *Die Produktionsgrundlagen der österreichischen Industrie vor und nach dem Krieg* (Vienna, 1917); B. Mitchell, *European Historical Statistics, 1750–1970* (London, 1975); K. Popov, *Stopanska Bulgariya* (Sofia, 1920).

Table 94 *National territory per km of navigable waterway in certain countries, 1913 (sq. km)*

Netherlands	7
Belgium	14
United Kingdom	33
Germany	35
France	39
Sweden	66
European Russia[1]	88
Italy	97
Hungary	105
Austria	106

[1] Excluding Finland

Source: F. Hertz, *Die Produktionsgrundlagen der österreichischen Industrie vor und nach dem Krieg* (Vienna, 1917), p. 58.

Table 95 *Number of mail items per inhabitant in European countries, 1911*

United Kingdom	131·2
Switzerland[1]	122·8
Belgium	114·2
France[1]	96·5
Netherlands	95·3
Germany[1]	92·3
Austria[1]	66·8
Denmark	63·1
Sweden[1]	46·7
Norway	45·6
Hungary	44·1
Italy[1]	42·2
Romania	23·1
Serbia	22·3
Spain	18·9
Russia (1909)	12·1
Greece (1910)	11·7
Bulgaria[2]	3·8

[1] Excludes newspapers
[2] Letters only

Source: B. Mitchell, *European Historical Statistics, 1750–1970* (London, 1975).

Table 96 *Number of tele-
phones per 1,000 inhabitants
in certain countries, 1 Jan-
uary 1914*

Denmark	45
Sweden	41
Norway	34
Switzerland	25
Germany	21
United Kingdom	17
Netherlands	14
Finland	12
Belgium	9
France	8
Austria	6
Hungary	4
Italy	3
Romania	3
Russia	2

Source: *Archiv für Post und
Telegraphie*, vol. I, 1916, Beib-
latt zum Amtsblatt des Reichs-
postamtes, Berlin.

Index

Abbreviations: (B)–bank. (Co)–company. (Pr)–province. (R)–river. (W)–works